PROBATION AND PAROLE

PROBATION

AND

PAROLE

Selected Readings

Edited by

ROBERT M. CARTER
LESLIE T. WILKINS

JOHN WILEY & SONS, INC.

New York · London · Sydney · Toronto

Library of Congress Catalogue Card Number: 79-94918

SBN 471   13853   3

Printed in the United States of America

To
JOSEPH D. LOHMAN
friend and colleague

Foreword

This anthology on probation and parole is designed to fill what heretofore has been a significant gap in the literature of corrections. In this volume, the editors have provided materials of sufficient scope to meet the needs of the campus community for a general, all-purpose text on probation and parole, as well as of the correctional practitioner and administrator in reviewing the important literature of the field. The anthology also could clearly have a role in the development and conduct of training programs within correctional agencies. For the nonprofessional, interested citizen, the anthology provides a portrait of probation and parole, relating to both theory and practice.

Probation and parole are two increasingly necessary forms of community corrections. Their complexity and scope — historically, traditionally, operationally, and legally — are illuminated by this broad range of readings. The contributors of these theoretical, empirical, and descriptive materials are administrators, practitioners, scholars, and researchers from both within and without the field of corrections, and this wide cross-section assures an overview of sometime divergent perspectives of probation and parole.

Although the anthology portrays the background of probation and parole as well as the current level of achievement, it serves a particular need in pointing to the requirements of the future. The increasingly complex challenge of crime and, accordingly, to corrections demands insight and knowledge about past and present, so that the future may be more meaningfully utilized in achieving some measure of control over crime through corrections.

G. Albert Wahl
Chief United States
Probation and Parole Officer
Northern District of California
San Francisco (Retired)

Preface

The purpose of this anthology on probation and parole is to provide both student and practitioner with convenient access to some of the most significant literature in the field. By a compilation in one volume of the important contributions of administrators, practioners, researchers, and scholars, the reader will be able to appreciate more fully the heritage and tradition of probation and parole and the scope and current status of these noninstitutional treatments of offenders. The needs and directions for future efforts — that which remains be done — will be more apparent from this volume, which presents past and present levels of knowledge and operations.

The anthology is divided into six topical sections: probation, parole, supervision, legal aspects, research and prediction, and personnel. The basis for this organization insures a systematic overview of the two segments of corrections that are becoming increasingly important — both in terms of absolute numbers and percentages, in the total administration of justice in the United States.

Space limitations have imposed a distinct handicap, since many worthwhile materials have reluctantly been placed aside. Our desire to provide general coverage of probation and parole and to avoid a purely academic or "how-to-do-it" operational text required decisions concerning inclusion and exclusion: we accept full responsibility for our selections and omissions.

We must emphatically add that inclusion or exclusion of particular materials cannot be used to support the concept that what has been, or is being, done in probation and parole is the best that might be done. Indeed, we hope that this anthology is a stimulus to those concerned with these phases of corrections to improve the systems of probation and parole by review of the current status of knowledge and level of operations. Those who are concerned may be better able to exercise their critical abilities to facilitate and expedite development where it is needed.

We express our deep gratitude to the authors and publishers of the selections in this volume for their kind permission to reprint material. It is clear that the current state of the art in probation and parole results, in large measure, from these contributors.

Robert M. Carter

Leslie T. Wilkins

Berkeley, California, 1969

Contents

PROBATION AND PAROLE

PROBATION

This section begins with United Nations materials describing the legal origins of probation and the development of probation in the United States. Following this historical background, the standards for probation established by the American Correctional Association and the recent evaluation of probation in the United States by the Task Force on Corrections operating under the President's Commission on Law Enforcement and Administration of Justice are presented. Articles by Professor Lewis Diana and retired Federal Prison Director Sanford Bates complement these materials by providing insight into the dynamics of the probation process.

Attention is next focused on preparation of the presentence report—one of the primary tasks of the probation officer. The model for presentence reports presented is that used in the federal court system. This model indicates the nature and scope of these documents, and additional commentary is provided by correctional administrator Paul W. Keve. These presentence materials are then related to operational presentence practices in the federal system by Professor David H. Gronewold, based on a survey conducted at the Federal Probation Training Center at Chicago. The issue of confidentiality of presentence reports is discussed by United States Probation Officer Jacob B. Barnett and Professor Gronewold.

The decision-making process and the presentence report are examined by presentation of four articles dealing with this phenomenon. Clinical psychologist Seymour Z. Gross examines probation officer conceptions of the usefulness of parts of the presentence report, while Yona Cohn, Director of Probation

Services in Jerusalem, examines the criteria for probation officer recommend-ations to the juvenile court. An article by one of the editors reports on the basis for presentence recommendations by federal probation officers, utilizing the recently developed decision-game technique. Finally, the editors provide the results of a study describing some of the latent aspects of the presentence report process and their impact upon sentencing.

Two articles relating to sentencing follow. The complexities and difficulties of sentencing are described by United States Judge Irving R. Kaufman, and Chief United States Probation Officer C. Alexander Rheiner examines the period of probation.

1

The Legal Origins of Probation

UNITED NATIONS

The origin, development and fate of specific methods for the treatment of offenders can be properly understood only against the wider background of contemporary cultural, social and economic forces. In so far as crime is defined as socially undesirable behavior subject to legal sanctions, the primary and constant object of criminal policy is the elimination or reduction of crime. The use or avoidance of specific methods, however, has varied very widely in both time and space, and these variations have tended to correspond with variations in social and political structure, in levels of knowledge, and in cultural values.[1]

Probation is an essentially modern method for the treatment of offenders and as such, it is rooted in the broader social and cultural trends of the modern

SOURCE. *Probation and Related Measures*, United Nations, Department of Social Affairs, New York (Sales No.: 1951. IV. 2), E/CN/.5/230, 1951, pp. 15–26.
[1]*Cf.* Thorsten Sellin, "Foreword." to George Rusche and Otto Kirchheimer *Punishment and Social Structure* (1939), p. vi: "Fundamentally . . . the aim of all punishment is the protection of those social values which the dominant social group of a State regard as good for 'society'. . . . The means to secure the protection of 'society' have varied greatly because the law-enforcing powers of different societies have chosen those means which they believed to be at a given time most likely to secure obedience to their law. These beliefs are in turn dependent on tradition, the level of knowledge, and the nature of social economic institutions and conditions. The sanguinary punishment and tortures of old are no evidence of bloodthirstiness or sadism on the part of those who used them. They rather testify to the fact that those who designed them could conceive of no better, that is, more efficient, way of securing protection for the social values which they treasured. The character of punishments, then, is inextricably associated with and dependent on the cultural values of the State that employs them."

era. In the history of criminal policy, the development of probation and related measures constitutes an integral part of the more general movement away from the traditional punitive and repressive approach, and towards the substitution of humanitarian and utilitarian considerations for considerations of general deterrence and retribution. This modern trend coincides with attempts to prevent crime by the improvement of social conditions and by the development of social services. It is characterized, furthermore, by the recognition of the social rehabilitation of the individual offender as a main object of criminal policy, and the rational selection and development of effective means to this end.

The origin of probation was not the result of a deliberate creative, legislative or judicial act, but rather the result of gradual growth, and almost unconscious modification of existing legal practices.

THE ORIGINS OF PROBATION AND ENGLISH COMMON LAW

Several attempts have been made to trace back the legal origins of probation to mediaeval and early modern European law. The precedents found in this period of legal history, however, generally relate to the suspension of punishment subject to good behavior rather than to probation as such, that is, a *combination* of the conditional suspension of punishment and the personal supervision of the released offender during a trial period. There can be little doubt that there has not been any continuous process of historical development linking early Continental instances of the use of the conditional suspension of punishment with contemporary probation. Probation as it is known today has been derived from the practical extension of the English common law, and an analysis of the legal origins of probation must therefore be principally concerned with England and America.

In England and the United States of America probation developed out of various methods for the conditional suspension of punishment. Generally speaking, the court practices in question were inaugurated, or adopted from previously existing practices, as attempts to avoid the mechanical application of the harsh and cruel precepts of a rigorous, repressive criminal law. Among these Anglo-American judicial expedients which have been mentioned as direct precursors of probation, are the so-called benefit of clergy, the judicial reprieve, the release of an offender on his own recognizance, provisional release on bail, the provisional "filing" of a case, and other legal devices for the suspension of either the imposition or the execution of sentence. With a view to a full understanding of the legal origins of probation, it is necessary to review briefly the nature of these practices.

The Benefit of Clergy

The so-called benefit of clergy was a special plea of devious origin by virtue of which certain categories of offenders could, after conviction, but before judgment, claim exemption from, or mitigation of, punishment. In practice it was primarily a device to avoid capital punishment. The importance of this plea in the criminal proceedings of the eighteenth and early nineteenth century is beyond any doubt: "According to the common practice in England of working out modern improvements through antiquated forms, this exemption was made the means of modifying the severity of the criminal law." It is, however, extremely doubtful whether this device had any direct influence on the later development of the suspension of sentence or of any other immediate precursor of probation.

The Judicial Reprieve

The judicial reprieve was a temporary suspension by the court of either the imposition or the execution of a sentence. It was used for specific purposes such as to permit a convicted person to apply for a pardon, or under circumstances such as where the judge was not satisfied with the verdict or where the evidence was suspicious. Although this measure involved only a temporary stay of imposition or execution of sentence, it did lead, in some cases, to an abandonment of prosecution. It does not appear, however, that in England this device "was ever extended to embrace what is now termed an indefinite suspension of sentence, particularly in cases which presented no peculiar reasons, arising out of the lack of or limitations on procedure, for withholding execution of sentence." On the other hand, "there is, no doubt, more than a modicum of good reason in tracing the later pretensions of American courts to a power of indefinite suspension of sentence back to this early practice of reprieve in English courts."

The Recognizance

The recognizance is a legal device deeply embedded in English law. It originated as a measure of preventive justice, and as such it "consists in obliging those persons, whom there is a probable ground to suspect of future misbehavior, to stipulate with and to give full assurance to the public, that such offence as is apprehended shall not happen. . . . " This "assurance to the public" is given by entering into a recognizance or bond (with or without sureties) creating a debt to the State which becomes enforceable, however, only when the specified conditions are not observed. The recognizance is entered into for a specified period of time.

At an early date the use of the principle of the recognizance (or binding-over) was also extended to actual offenders arraigned before the criminal courts. The device came to be used both to ensure the appearance of an offender before the court at a future date when called upon, and as a disposition (or part thereof) in the case of convicted offenders. With the passing of time, the recognizance came to be used almost exclusively with reference to criminal proceedings rather than as a measure of preventive justice. It should be noted, however, that the recognizance, when used in connection with persons arraigned before criminal courts, does not lose its character as a measure of preventive justice but is actually designed to ensure the future law behavior of the offender or, as Blackstone said, "must be understood rather as a caution against the repetition of the offence, than [as] any immediate pain or punishment."

For centuries the courts of England on occasion bound over and released minor offenders on their own recognizance, *with or without sureties*. Similarly, instances of this practice can be found in the records of the American colonies. During the first half of the nineteenth century this device was adopted with increasing frequency particularly in the case of youthful and petty offenders, the imprisonment of whom did not appear to be warranted. The practice seems to have been common in New England (particularly Massachusetts) at the time, and was to be found also in other jurisdictions of the United States of America.

The device of binding-over was used extensively and imaginatively by Judge Peter Oxenbridge Thacher during his term of office (1823–1843) in the Municipal Court of Boston, and the practices developed by him were of particular significance in the later development of probation in Massachusetts. The earliest recorded case in this connection is the case of *Commonwealth* v. *Chase* (1830). In Judge Thacher's opinion we find in this case a clear statement of the nature of the practice of binding-over as employed by him:

"The indictment against Jerusha Chase was found at the January term of this court, 1830. She pleaded guilty to the same, and sentence would have been pronounced at that time, but upon the application of her friends, and with the consent of the attorney of the commonwealth, she was permitted, upon her recognizance for her appearance in this court whenever she should be called for, to go at large. It has sometimes been practised in this court, in cases of peculiar interest, and in the hope that the party would avoid the commission of any offense afterwards, to discharge him on a recognizance of this description. The effect is, that no sentence will ever be pronounced against him, if he shall behave himself well afterwards, and avoid any further violation of the law. . . . "

In 1836, the State of Massachusetts, as part of a general revision of its statutory law, gave legislative recognition to the practice of release upon recognizance, *with sureties*, at any stage of the proceedings, in so far as it applied to petty offenders in the lower courts. In the report of the commissioners charged with the revision of the statutory law of the State, the commissioners formulated the theoretical basis of this alteration in the law relating to the punishment of petty offenders, as follows:

"This alteration consists in the discretionary power proposed to be given to the courts and magistrates, before whom this class of offenders may be brought, to discharge them, if they have any friends who will give satisfactory security for their future good behavior, for a reasonable time. When such sureties can be obtained, it can hardly fail to operate as a powerful check upon the conduct of the party, who is thus put upon his good behavior. And if his character and habits are such that no one will consent to be sponsor for him, it must forcibly impress on his mind the value of a good character, while it deprives him of all ground of just complaint of the severity of the law, or the magistrate."

It is significant to compare this formulation of the theory underlying the use of release on recognizance, with a British formulation of the second half of the nineteenth century. In a book published in 1877, Edward William Cox, Recorder of Portsmouth, specifically described the release of offenders on their own recognizance, with sureties, as a "substitute for punishment," and he noted that, while the conduct of the released offenders was proper, no further action was taken. In particular, he was strongly motivated by the desire to avoid the demoralizing and contaminating influence of short terms of imprisonment, especially in the case of first and juvenile offenders. As for the *rationale* of the use of the recognizances, with sureties, he says, "The suspension only of the judgment, the knowledge that if he [the offender] offends he may yet be punished—the hold which his bail thus has upon him, to a great extent guarantee that if there is in him an inclination to redeem himself he will return to a life of honesty."

Provisional Release on Bail

It has been noted in the preceding paragraphs that the device of releasing an offender on his own recognizance (binding-over) may be used *with or without sureties*. Conversely, the device of sureties (or bail) may be employed either with or without simultaneously binding over the defendant on his own recognizance. The significance of the device of sureties, when combined with the recognizance, as a precursor of probation, has already been discussed; it remains to be pointed out, however, that both in England and in the United States of America the device of bail as such (that is, when not used in conjunction with the recognizance) has similarly been of major historical significance in the evolution of probation, namely, as a device for the provisional suspension of punishment in relation to rudimentary probation practices.

Binding-Over, Bail and the Origins of Probation

It has been noted above, that the recognizance is essentially a preventive rather than a punitive measure of dealing with actual or potential offenders. In the early nineteenth century the increased use of this device was motivated, no doubt, to a considerable extent by considerations of mercy and in this respect the device was one of the measures employed to reduce the hardships involved in the mechanical application of a rigorous criminal law. The rehabilitative object of the measure—i.e., the prevention of crime by the restoration of the offender as a law-abiding member of society—was, however, always present. Nevertheless, during this era the device came to be applied with an increasing realization of its rehabilitative potentialities, and came to be accompanied by increasingly effective safeguards and aids in the form of the personal supervision of, and assistance to, the released offender during the trial period. It should further be noted that the recognizance has always contained the germs of supervision—it involves the conditional suspension of punishment, and some vigilance is required to ascertain whether the conditions concerned are being complied with.

It is clear that the provisional release of offenders in the charge of sureties similarly contained the germs of probationary supervision (irrespective of whether this device was combined with the recognizance or not). In view of their financial interest in the conduct of the provisionally released offender, sureties are bound to try to ensure the good behavior of the offender through personal supervision, assistance or influence. The deliberate use, by the courts, of the salutory influence of sureties on offenders released conditionally, either on their own recognizance or on bail, indeed seems to have been in a very real sense the first, rudimentary stage in the development of probation.

The Provisional "Filing" of Cases

The practice of provisionally "filing" a case seems to have been peculiar to Massachusetts. This device consisted of the suspension of the imposition of sentence when, "after verdict of guilty in a criminal case . . . the Court is satisfied that, by reason of extenuating circumstances, or of the pendency of a question of law in a like case before a higher court, or other sufficient reason, public justice does not require an immediate sentence. . . ." The use of this procedure was subject to the consent of the defendant and of the prosecuting attorney, and the suspension was made subject to such conditions as the court in its discretion might impose. The order that a case be laid on file was not equivalent to a final judgment, but left it within the power of the court to take action on the case at any time, upon motion of either party.

CONCLUSION: THE SUSPENSION OF SENTENCE AT COMMON LAW

By way of summary, it may be noted that there existed, during the nineteenth century and earlier, several legal devices which enabled the English and the American courts to suspend either the imposition of sentence (recognizance to keep the peace or to be of good behavior and to appear for judgment when called upon, provisional release on bail, the provisional "filing of a case," and the judicial reprieve) or the execution of sentence (also the judicial reprieve). That these devices existed, and allowed *at least* for the *temporary* suspension of sentence for *specific purposes*, is beyond any doubt. The question whether the English and American courts possess, at common law, an inherent power to suspend sentence *indefinitely* is, however, more problematic.

In analyzing the question of an inherent judical power to suspend sentence *indefinitely*, it is necessary to distinguish clearly between the use of the special devices of the recognizance and bail, on the one hand, and other devices used for the provisional suspension of punishment, on the other hand. Prior to statutory provisions to this effect, the courts both in England and in the United States of America *did*, in fact, engage in the suspension of the imposition of sentence when releasing offenders on their own recognizances, and took no further action with regard to the infliction of punishment if the condition of good behavior was complied with. Similarly, this procedure was followed, prior to statutory authorization, in at least two of the other countries of the British Commonwealth, viz., New Zealand and Canada. Both in England and in certain jurisdictions of the United States of America (notably Massachusetts), the conditional suspension of the imposition of sentence, with the ultimate release of the offender from all punishment in case of good behavior, was practised (without statutory authorization) also in relation to the provisional release of offenders on bail.

For all practical purposes it may be said that—beyond the relatively circumscribed practice of suspending the imposition of a sentence by means of releasing an offender on a recognizance and/or bail—the English courts *did not* assume the existence of an inherent common law power to suspend sentence indefinitely. In the United States of America, however, a variety of practices developed, with a tendency to extend the suspension of sentence beyond the employment of the recognizance and/or bail. In particular, this involved the suspension of the imposition or of the execution of sentence on the basis of the common law precedent of the judicial reprieve. With the increasing use of the conditional suspension of punishment, with or without some sort of probationary supervision, courts in different jurisdictions adopted contradictory points of view on the question of the existence, at common law, of an inherent judicial power of indefinite suspension of sentence. While some held that the courts had such a power, others rejected this view arguing either that the conditions justifying the recognition of such a power in England did not obtain in the United States, or that the indefinite suspension of sentence by the court constituted an encroachment on the executive prerogative of pardon and reprieve, and thus infringes upon the doctrine of the separation of powers.

The United States Supreme Court finally expressed itself on the issue in question in the so-called *Killits case*. In his opinion in this case, the late Chief Justice White decided that English common law did not give the Federal courts the power to suspend sentence indefinitely:

"It is true that, owing to the want of power in common law courts to grant new trials and to the absence of a right to review convictions in a higher court, it is we think, to be conceded: (*a*) that both suspensions of sentence and suspensions of the enforcement of sentence, temporary in character, were often resorted to on grounds of error or miscarriage of justice which under our system would be corrected either by new trials or by the exercise of the power to review; (*b*) that not infrequently, where the suspension either of the imposition of a sentence or of its execution was made for the purpose of enabling a pardon to be sought or bestowed, by a failure to further proceed in the criminal cause in the future, although no pardon had been sought or obtained, the punishment fixed by law was escaped. But neither of these conditions serves to convert the mere exercise of a judicial discretion to temporarily suspend for the accomplishment of a purpose contemplated by law into the existence of an arbitrary judicial power to permanently refuse to enforce the law."

With reference to the decision in the Killits case, the *Attorney General's Survey* concludes as follows:

"For practical purposes it may be said that this decision served to explode the erroneous belief that had grown up in some States. . . . It may be concluded, therefore, that there is no historical warrant in the English common law for the claim that American courts have an inherent power to suspend sentence indefinitely. Where this power has been asserted, it has been based on a misconception of English authorities or recognized because it tempered the criminal law with mercy and had grown as a local practice."

It should be noted that Court's decision in the Killits case did not seek to invalidate the practice of releasing offenders on their own recognizances but referred to "the fact that common law courts possessed the power by recognizances to secure good behavior, that is, to enforce the law. . . ." This fact did not, however, afford support for "the proposition that those courts possessed the arbitrary discretion to permanently decline to enforce the law."

From the point of view of the development of probation as a distinct method for the treatment of offenders, the extent to which the judicial devices in which it had its historical origins, were, in fact, extra-legal and not warranted by the English common law, is of small significance. The important point is that these devices developed, and could in fact only develop, in a system of common law jurisdiction which is flexible enough to allow for the gradual adjustment of existing practices to new needs and new objectives. In England this process of adjustment was more conservative and it is probable that the courts stayed within their common law powers; in any case, the legality of the devices used for the conditional suspension of punishment, in relation to early pre-statutory probation practices, was never challenged in England, in Canada or in New Zealand. In the United States of America, the courts over-stepped their common law powers, and the resulting diversity and confusion of principles and authorities necessitated the authoritative revision of the legal bases of the practices that have developed. Nevertheless, the definitive explosion of the doctrine of an inherent judicial power to suspend sentence indefinitely came when probation was already a well established part of the administration of criminal justice, and when public opinion had already been fully prepared for this new method for the treatment of offenders. Consequently, the final rejection by the Supreme Court of the doctrine of a common law judicial power of indefinite suspension of sentence actually served as a stimulus for the enactment of statutes expressly authorizing the suspension of sentence and probation.

2

The Origin of Probation in the United States

UNITED NATIONS

The state of Massachusetts shares with England the honor of having given the probation system to the world. During the first half of the nineteenth century, Massachusetts judges sought diligently and in a variety of ways to render the administration of justice more humane, and a favorable judicial climate was thus established for the development of rudimentary "probation" practices.

The first bold step taken beyond the initial rudimentary probation practices (consisting of release on recognizances with sureties) was taken in Boston in 1841. On a day in August of that year a local cobbler, John Augustus, attended the police court in that city, and decided to stand bail for a man charged with being a common drunkard. The court permitted this, and the defendant was ordered to appear for sentence in three weeks, at which time the defendant was brought back showing convincing signs of reform. Instead of the usual penalty—imprisonment in the House of Correction—the judge imposed a nominal fine of one cent and ordered the defendant to pay costs.

Encouraged by his first experience, Augustus proceeded to stand bail for more offenders, and to undertake the task of supervising and guiding their behavior during the period pending judgment. All the early cases handled by him were adult males charged with common drunkenness, but he gradually extended the scope of his activities to include women (at first also common drunkards) and children, and ultimately persons charged with a wide variety of offences. He also extended his activity to include work in the municipal court.

SOURCE. *Probation and Related Measures*, United Nations, Department of Social Affairs, New York (Sales No.: 1951. IV. 2), E/CN/.5/230, 1951, pp. 29–42.

Subsequently Augustus continued his labors for eighteen years until his death in 1859. During this period he "bailed on probation" almost 2,000 persons and achieved a very high proportion of successes.

During this period of his activities in the courts of Boston, John Augustus developed several of the features that later became characteristic of the probation system.

As regards the selection of probationers, he confined his efforts "mainly to those who were indicted for their first offence, and whose hearts were not wholly depraved, but gave promise of better things. . . ." He did not assume the responsibility for an offender "merely at the solicitation of the unfortunate, or without due investigation into the merits of their cases and a scrupulous examination into the history and character of each individual." "Great care was observed . . . to ascertain whether the prisoners were promising subjects for probation, and to this end it was necessary to take into consideration the previous character of the person, his age and the influences by which he would in future be likely to be surrounded, and although these points were rigidly adhered to, still they were the circumstances which usually determined my action."

When Augustus undertook the responsibility for offenders, he agreed to "note their general conduct," and to "see that they were sent to school or supplied with some honest employment." In addition, he very often provided, or arranged for, accommodation.

He agreed also to make an impartial report to the court, whenever required to. In addition he maintained a careful register of all cases handled.

After the death of John Augustus, his work was continued by Rufus R. Cook, Chaplain to the county gaol and representative of the Boston Children's Aid Society, and other less well-know pioneer "probation officers" whose work was largely voluntary. These men "seem to have carried out the essential features of probation—investigation of defendant before release, the regular reports and home visits. . . . However, their work was of the 'rescue' sort. . . . It is evident that the investigations were necessarily meagre, that probation periods were very short (only a few weeks at the start), and that records, plans of treatment and close supervision were not much in evidence."

By a law of 1869, the State of Massachusetts provided for the appointment of a state agent of the Board of State Charities to investigate cases of children tried before the courts, to attend such trials and to receive children for placement if the court so ordered. The state agents appointed under this new measure (with the assistance of voluntary organizations) exercised supervision over the behavior of deliquent children placed on probation under the existing common law practice.

Probation came to be regulated by statute for the first time in 1878, when Massachusetts passed a law providing for the appointment of a paid probation officer for the courts of criminal jurisdiction in the city of Boston. It is of no mean significance that this pioneer statute on probation specifically contrasts probation with punishment by directing that "such persons as may reasonably be expected to be reformed without punishment" should be selected to be put on probation. Of equal significance is the fact that the statute does not restrict the application of probation to any particular class of offenders (first offenders, young offenders, etc.) or to any particular class of offences, but postulates the likelihood of the individual offender's being reformed without punishment, as the only criterion for the selection of offenders to be released on probation.

The Massachusetts statute of 1878 was designed to deal with the appointment and duties of a probation officer rather than with the legal issues involved in probation. It provided for the annual appointment, by the Mayor of Boston, of a "suitable person" either from the ranks of the police force of the city or "from the citizens at large." The incumbent of the position was to be "under the general control" of the chief of police of the city.

The statute prescribed the duties of the probation officer as including court attendance, the investigation of the cases of persons charged with or convicted of crimes or misdemeanors, the making of recommendations to the courts with regard to the advisability of using probation, the submission of periodical reports to the chief of police, visiting probationers, and the rendering of "such assistance and encouragement [to probationers] as will tend to prevent their again offending."

The statute further gave to the probation officer the power to re-arrest a probationer, without further warrant but with the approval of the chief of police; in such a case the court might "proceed to sentence or make such other disposition of the case as may be authorized by law."

In accordance with the provisions of the statute of 1878, the Mayor of Boston appointed Captain E. H. Savage, formerly Chief of Police, as first statutory probation officer. Generally speaking, the previously existing common law practice of probation remained unaltered, the only significant innovation being the official nature of the new arrangements for the exercise of probationary supervision. The practice of probation under this new arrangement is described as follows, in contemporary records:

"[The probation officer] obtains information from the police and in other ways regarding those who have been arrested, and when their cases are called for trial, he takes on probation by authority of the courts those who may reasonably be expected to reform without punishment.

"The term of probation ranges from three months to one year, under such conditions as seen best suited to the case. The officer becomes bondsman in a certain sum for the faithful performance of these conditions and for the prisoner's appearance at court from time to time until the case is finally disposed of. The time of continuance for appearance usually ranges from six to twelve weeks."

The correctional authorities in Massachusetts soon showed that they were aware of the importance of the new arrangements provided for by the statute of 1878. In their annual report published in 1880, the Prison Commissioners made reference to the "very important experiment" that was being tried in the city of Boston, and recommended that legislative provision be made for the extension of the system to other cities.

By a statute of 1880 the right to appoint probation officers was extended to all cities and towns in Massachusetts. In contrast with the statute of 1878 relating to Boston, the statute of 1880 was merely permissive and only a few towns or cities in the state exercised the option of appointing probation officers. Probation was established on a state-wide basis in Massachusetts in 1891, when an act was passed transferring the power of appointment of probation officers from the municipal authorities to the courts, and making such appointment mandatory instead of permissive. Each police district and each municipal court was required to appoint a probation officer, and the probation system was thereby firmly established throughout the lower courts of the state. It was extended to the superior courts by an act of 1898 which authorized the latter to appoint their own probation officers.

It should be noted that the Massachusetts statutes of 1878 to 1898 were designed to supplement, not supplant, the existing common law system of probation. The essential legal features of the common law system—the suspension of the imposition of sentence, "bailing on probation," and the return of the probationer to the court, to be discharged or disposed of otherwise, at the end of the probation period—were taken for granted. The statutes in question dealt primarily with the appointment, remuneration, control and duties of probation officers, and thus enabled the courts to use probation more freely and more effectively. In fact, the introduction of statutory provisions in relation to probation should be seen as an integral part of a continuous process of growth and development, applying both to the probation system in Massachusetts as such and to its acceptance by public opinion. Only this circumstance made it possible for the first probation statute in the world to be passed practically without public discussion or controversy.

3

Standards for Adult Probation

AMERICAN CORRECTIONAL ASSOCIATION

Probation may be defined as a sentence, as an organization, or as a process. As a sentence, probation represents a judicial disposition which establishes the defendant's legal status under which his freedom in the community is continued, subject to supervision by a probation organization and subject to conditions imposed by the court. As an organization, probation is a service agency designed to assist the court and to execute certain services in the administration of criminal justice. As a process, probation involves the presentence investigation for the court and the supervision of persons in the community.

To be effective as a sentence, as an organization, or as a process, probation requires standards. The standards which follow will help to insure a program capable of achieving the goals of probation, the protection of society, and the redirection and successful adjustment of the individual in the community.

1. *Legal Framework*. Legal provision gives discretionary authority to the court to use probation following conviction of a defendant for any offense when it is in the best interest of the offender and not in conflict with the interest of society.

2. *Organizational Structure*. Progressive administrative organization includes centralized state responsibility for uniform standards of personnel practices, services to the court, staff supervision and training, and services to the probationers and the public.

SOURCE. *Manual of Correctional Standards*, American Correctional Association, Washington, D.C., 1966, pp. 98–99. Library of Congress Catalogue Number: 66–17761, Copyright, 1966, by the American Correctional Association.

3. *Personnel.* Administrative professional and clerical personnel are provided with high standards and character, thoroughly trained, adequately compensated, and in sufficient numbers to perform their necessary responsibilities.

4. *Selection of Clientele.* Selection of defendants is essential to the success and effectiveness of probation. Through the presentence investigation, the court can judiciously select those individuals to be placed on probation where it is in the best interest of the defendant and society.

5. *Social and Psychological Practice in Probation.* The principles, skills, and knowledge used in sociology, psychology, criminology, and generic social work are applicable in the probation process.

6. *Workload Standards.* A workload of 50 units, computed on a rating of one work unit for each probationer supervised, and 5 work units for each presentence investigation completed and written in a given month is recommended as the maximum for a probation officer.

7. *Supervision of Staff.* Professionally competent personnel having the responsibility for and the authority over the work of others is required. Trained staff should have responsibility for development and training of personnel.

8. *Statistics and Research.* Probation statistics are vital to a sound correctional system. Each state should have a central correctional statistical system where data is collected, analyzed, and published.

9. *Community Relations.* Probation personnel should be concerned with social and law enforcement agencies and resources for the dual purpose of community planning and interpretation to the public of the purposes, functions, and needs of probation.

10. *Ancillary Services.* Within the probation organization, additional services related to the work of the court, such as medical and psychiatric service, may be incorporated for purpose of administration and co-ordination.

4

Probation

PRESIDENTS' COMMISSION ON LAW ENFORCEMENT AND ADMINISTRATION OF JUSTICE

Slightly more than half of the offenders sentenced to correctional treatment in 1965 were placed on probation—supervision in the community subject to the authority of the court. Table 1 sets forth data from the National Survey of Corrections and the Federal corrections system on the number of persons under probation on an average day in 1965 and the number in institutions or on parole. Also shown are estimates of what these populations are likely to be in 1975. As the table indicates, probation is the correctional treatment used for most offenders today and is likely to be used increasingly in the future.[1]

The estimates for probation shown in the above table project a growth in the number of adults on probation almost $2\frac{1}{2}$ times greater than the growth in institutional and parole populations. The projected growth in juvenile probation is also substantial. As chapter 4 will show, there are rapidly developing very promising intensive community supervision and residential programs, which could further shift the number of juveniles destined for institutions to community-based treatment. Thus, the projections for juvenile probation might actually be low.

SOURCE. *Task Force Report: Corrections*, The President's Commission on Law Enforcement and Administration of Justice, Washington, D.C., U.S. Government Printing Office, 1967, pp. 27–37.

[1] These projections are drawn from the special study completed by R. Christensen, of the Commission's Task Force on Science and Technology. The projections, together with the 1965 data supplied by the National Survey of Corrections and special tabulations provided by the Federal Bureau of Prisons and the Administrative Office of the U.S. Courts, indicate the following: The number of adults in jails and prisons and on parole in 1965 was 475,042; for 1975 it is projected as 560,000. There were 459,140 adults on probation in 1965; for 1975 the number is projected as 693,000. The population of juvenile training schools and parole programs in 1965 was 123,256; for 1975 it is projected as 210,000. The number of juveniles on probation in 1965 was 224,948, and for 1975 the number is projected as 378,000.

Table 1   *Number of Offenders on Probation, and on Parole or in Institutions, 1965;*
Projections for 1975

Location of Offender	1965		1975	
	Number	Percent	Number	Percent
Probation	684,088	53	1,071,000	58
Parole or institution	598,298	47	770,000	42
Total	1,282,386	100	1,841,000	100

SOURCES. 1965 data from National Survey of Corrections and special tabulations provided by the Federal Bureau of Prisons and the Administrative Office of the U.S. Courts; 1975 projections by R. Christensen, of the Commission's Task Force on Science and Technology.

The best data available indicate that probation offers one of the most significant prospects for effective programs in corrections. It is also clear that at least two components are needed to make it operate well. The first is a system that facilitates effective decision-making as to who should receive probation; the second is the existence of good community programs to which offenders can be assigned. Probation services now available in most jurisdictions fall far short of meeting either of these needs.

PRESENT SERVICES AND NEEDS

Current probation practices have their origin in the quasi-probationary measures of an earlier day. The beginnings of probation are usually traced to Boston, where in 1841 a bootmaker bailed a number of defendants in the lower court on a volunteer basis. In 1897, Missouri passed legislation that made it possible to suspend execution of sentence for young and for petty offenders. This statute did not make provision for the supervision of probationers. However, Vermont established such a plan on a county basis in 1898, and Rhode Island established a State-administered system in 1899.[2]

After the turn of the century, the spread of probation was accelerated by the juvenile court movement. Thirty-seven States and the District of Columbia had a children's court act by 1910. Forty of them had also introduced probation for juveniles. By 1925, probation for juveniles was available in every State, but this did not happen in the case of adult probation until 1956.

Within States, probation coverage is still often spotty. Services for juveniles, for example, are available in every county in only 31 States. In one State, a National Survey staff observer noted, only two counties have probation services. A child placed on probation in the other counties is presumed

²Paul W. Tappan, "Crime, Justice, and Correction" (New York: McGraw-Hill Book Co., 1960), pp. 546–549.

to be adjusting satisfactorily until he is brought back to court with a new charge.

Table 2 shows the number of delinquents and adult felons on probation at the end of 1965 and the annual costs of these services. It is quickly apparent in terms of the number of persons served and of total operating costs that the juvenile system has relatively greater resources than the adult. Cost comparisons, however, require qualification. The juvenile total includes the cost of many foster homes and some private and public institutional costs.

Table 2 *Number of Felons and Juveniles on Probation, 1965, and Annual Costs of Services for Each Group*

Type of Probation	Number on Probation	Annual Costs
Felony	257,755	$37,937,808
Juvenile	224,948	75,019,441
Total	482,703	112,957,249

SOURCES. National Survey of Corrections and special tabulations provided by the Federal Bureau of Prisons and the Administrative Office of the U.S. Courts.

Furthermore, juvenile probation in some jurisdictions has a substantial responsibility for orphaned or other non-delinquent dependent children.

Probation in the United States is administered by hundreds of independent agencies operating under a different law in each State and under widely varying philosophies, often within the same State. They serve juvenile, misdemeanant, and felony offenders. In one city, a single State or local agency might be responsible for handling all three kinds of probation cases; in another, three separate agencies may be operating, each responsible for a different type of probationer. All of these probation programs must contend with similar issues.

ADVANTAGES OF PROBATION

There are many offenders for whom incarceration is the appropriate sanction—either because of their dangerousness or the seriousness of their offense, or both. But in the vast majority of cases where such a sanction is not obviously essential, there has been growing disenchantment with relying heavily on institutions to achieve correctional goals. The growing emphasis on community treatment is supported by several kinds of considerations.

The correctional strategy that presently seems to hold the greatest promise, based on social science theory and limited research, is that of reintegrating the offender into the community. A key element in this strategy is to deal with problems in their social context, which means in the interaction of the offender and the community. It also means avoiding as much as possible the isolating and labelling effects of commitment to an institution. There is little doubt that the goals of reintegration are furthered much more readily by working with an offender in the community than by incarcerating him.

These justifications seem to be borne out by the record of probation services themselves. Probation services have been characteristically poorly staffed and often poorly administered. Despite that, the success of those placed on probation, as measured by not having probation revoked, has been surprisingly high. One summary analysis of outcomes observed in 11 probation studies indicates a success rate of from 60 to 90 percent.[3] A survey of probation effectiveness in such States as Massachusetts and New York and a variety of foreign countries provides similar results with a success rate at about 75 percent.[4] An exhaustive study was undertaken in California when 11,638 adult probationers granted probation during the period 1956–1958 were followed up after 7 years. Of this group, almost 72 percent were successful in terms of not having their probation revoked.[5]

These findings were not obtained under controlled conditions, nor were they supported by data that distinguished among the types of offenders who succeeded or the types of services that were rendered. Nevertheless, all of the success rates are relatively high. They are the product of a variety of kinds of probation administered at different times and places. Even when interpreted skeptically, they are powerful evidence that a substantial number of persons can be placed on probation and have a relatively high rate of success.

Two controlled experiments, one in Utah and one in California, in which the relative effectiveness of institutionalization and community supervision under special conditions with small caseloads and specifically designed treatment programs, were directly tested with randomly selected groups. In both instances the special community treatment was clearly superior in terms of reducing recidivism.

Perhaps the best known effort to determine the extent to which probation services could be used was a demonstration project conducted in Saginaw, Mich., over a 3-year period.[6] Here, trained probation officers with relatively low caseloads were assigned to an adult criminal court that had used probation a little more than the 50 percent average for the State. With full services available, including complete social histories for the use of the

[3] Ralph W. England, Jr., "What is Responsible for Satisfactory Probation and Post-Probation Outcome?" *Journal of Criminal Law, Criminology, and Police Science*, 47: 667–676 (March–April 1957).

[4] Max Grünhüt, "Penal Reform" (New York: The Clarendon Press, 1948), pp. 60–82.

[5] George F. Davis, "A Study of Adult Probation Violation Rates by Means of the Cohort Approach," *Journal of Criminal Law, Criminology, and Police Science*, 55:70–85 (March 1964).

[6] "The Saginaw Probation Demonstration Project," Michigan Crime and Delinquency Council of the National Council on Crime and Delinquency (New York: The Council, 1963).

court at the time of sentencing, judges imposed prison sentences for only about 20 percent of all of the defendants who appeared before them. There is some evidence that the revocation rate for those granted probation was lower than in the prior 3-year period. Although these findings require more rigorous testing, they lend weight to the view that a high percentage of offenders can be supervised in the community and succeed.

Offenders can be kept under probation supervision at much less cost than in institutions. The National Survey found, for example, that the average State spends about $3,400 a year (excluding capital costs) to keep a youth in a State training school, while it costs only about one-tenth that amount to keep him on probation.

Objections might be raised as to the validity of such comparisons, since expenditures for probation services are now much too meager. However, with the 1-to-10 cost ratios prevailing, probation expenditures can clearly be increased several fold and still remain less expensive than institutional programs. This is especially true when construction costs, which now run up to and beyond $20,000 per bed in a correctional institution, are included. The differential becomes even greater if the cost of welfare assistance for the families of the incarcerated and the loss in taxable income are considered.

PROBATION SUPERVISION

There is an extremely wide variation among States in both the laws permitting probation and the way in which probation is practiced. Probation agencies range from those that depend on the ingenuity of a single probation officer to large multidivisional programs offering clinical, diagnostic, detention, foster care, and local institutional programs.

Badly undermanned in general by staff who are too often undertrained and almost always poorly paid, probation agencies only occasionally mount the type of imaginative programs that fulfill their potential for rehabilitation. The extent to which probation is used varies widely from jurisdiction to jurisdiction, paralleling to a large extent the adequacy of staffing ratios.

The Standard Caseload

The administrative problem that has probably plagued probation officials most has been the achievement of a manageable workload for probation officers. Whenever probation programs are subject to criticism, the oversized caseload is usually identified as the obstacle to successful operation. Efforts to reduce caseloads have been the source of a continuing struggle between probation administrators and local and State budget authorities. Some apparently simple but quite important issues are involved.

Over the past decade, a number of efforts have been made to improve the effectiveness of probation and parole supervision by simply reducing the size of an officer's caseloads. Caseloads have been reduced under experimental conditions from 75 to 30 and to 15.[7] It appears from these studies that the simple expedient of reducing caseloads will not of itself assure a reduction in recidivism. Those experiments with reduced caseloads have shown that to reduce recidivism requires classification of offenders with differential treatment for each class.[8]

The concept of an "average caseload" is administratively convenient when calculating broad estimates of the resources necessary to effect some improvement in staffing ratios. However, this useful idea usually becomes translated into the "standard caseload" that each officer should carry. Differences in individual probationers' needs require different amounts of time and energy from a probation officer. The typical probation caseload is usually a random mixture of cases requiring varying amounts of service and surveillance but usually treated as if all the cases were much the same. Clearly, the value of differential treatment requires that probation manpower ratios vary directly with the kind and amount of services to be performed.

Further work is needed to specify with greater accuracy the levels of service required for various kinds of cases. But enough experience is already available to implement a broad, if somewhat rough, system of differential treatment such as is already being used in various forms by a number of agencies.

Planning for Differential Treatment

Differing caseload sizes are only one aspect of the need for differential treatment adapted to the type and circumstances of the offender. Another major requirement for using a differential treatment system is an adequate case analysis and planning procedure. Probably no deficiency is more universally apparent in current programs than the nearly complete lack of careful planning by probation officers, their supervisors, and clinical program consultants, including the active participation of offenders themselves. A common observation of probation officers who have moved from routine to intensive experimental programs is that, for the first time, they are provided an opportunity to develop systematically a plan that is carefully tailored for the offender.

[7]California Department of Corrections, Division of Adult Parole, "Special Intensive Parole Unit, 15-Man Caseload Study" (Sacramento: The Department, November 1956) and "Special Intensive Parole Unit, 30-Man Caseload Study" (Sacramento: The Department, December 1958). See also Bertram M. Johnson, "An Analysis of Predictions of Parole Performance and of Judgments of Supervision in the Parole Research Project," California Youth Authority Research Report No. 32 (Sacramento: The Authority, December 1962).

[8]See Stuart Adams, "Effectiveness of Interview Therapy With Older Youth Authority Wards, An Interim Evaluation of the PICO Project", Research Report No. 20 (Sacramento: California Youth Authority, January 1961); Joan Havel and Elaine Sulka, "Special Intensive Parole Unit, Phase 3" (Sacramento: California Youth Authority, March 1962); Walter Burkhart and Arthur Sathmary, "Narcotic Treatment Control Project, Phases 1 and 2," California Department of Corrections, Division of Research, Publication No. 19 (Sacramento: The Department, May 1963); M. Q. Warren et al., "Community Treatment Project, 5th Progress Report," California Youth Authority, Division of Research (Sacramento: The Authority, August 1966).

Such planning must determine the kind and intensity of supervision needed by the probationer. For some, assignment to relatively high caseloads for nominal supervision may well be indicated.[9] Other probationers will require assignment to specialized caseloads with varying intensity and kinds of supervision. Programs may range from assistance in dealing with important social agencies such as schools, to group counseling or family counseling. Alcoholics, addicts, and those with mental or physical problems may require special treatment.

In planning, the ability to place an offender in the community where he is most likely to succeed is an important factor. Of significant assistance in providing this capacity has been the Interstate Compact for the Supervision of Probationers and Parolees. Under the leadership of the Council of State Governments, this program has developed to the point where today thousands of probationers and parolees are able to return and be supervised by agencies in their home States, after being adjudicated criminal or delinquent elsewhere. All States are members of the compact for adults. Several have yet to ratify a similar compact for juveniles, and this failure creates a needless gap in services.

Another important part of probation planning is determination of the period during which various kinds of probation supervision are required. Studies of both probation and parole outcome reveal consistently that most difficulties with offenders occur within the first 1 or 2 years under supervision. For those who avoid difficulty through this period, the probability is exceedingly good that they will no longer be involved in criminal activity. Some offenders require extended periods of probation; for them, reduced supervision may be feasible during the latter portion of their probation terms. However, for the vast majority of offenders, inflexible and lengthy probation terms result in unnecessary restraints and costs.

Manpower Needs

More manpower is needed for probation services than is now available. Data as to exact size of the manpower gap based on careful experimentation with differential treatment must await further studies. However, sufficient data are available now to give a fair approximation of the numbers of officers needed.

Using as a desirable caseload average for juveniles and adult felons the level of 35 an approximate picture of the need for probation officers can be gained. Table 3 shows the size of caseloads in which probationers are currently supervised. With fewer than 4 percent of the probation officers in the Nation

[9]Joseph D. Lohman, Albert Wahl, and Robert M. Carter, "The Ideal Supervison Caseload: A Preliminary Evaluation," The San Francisco Project Research Report No. 9 (Berkeley: University of California School of Criminology, February 1966). For a study of differential caseload levels, see "California Department of Corrections Parole Work Unit Program, Report Submitted to Joint Legislative Budget Committee" (Sacramento: The Department, December 1966).

Table 3   *Percentage Distribution of Probationers, by Size of Caseload in Which Supervised, 1965*

Caseload Size	Juvenile Probation	Felony Probation
	(Percent)	(Percent)
Under 40	3.7	0.8
41–60	19.7	5.0
61–80	49.2	14.1
81–100	16.7	13.1
Over 100	10.7	67.0

SOURCE. National Survey of Corrections.

carrying caseloads of 40 or less, it is obvious that the gap between optimal and actual levels of staffing is great.

In 1965 there were 6,336 juvenile probation officers and 2,940 probation officers supervising offenders convicted of felonies.[10] These officers are responsible for both presentence investigations and supervision. Providing enough officers to conduct needed presentence investigations and also reduce average caseloads to 1 officer for each 35 offenders would immediately require an additional 5,300 officers and supervisors for juveniles and 8,500 for felons.

PROBATION AND REINTEGRATION

Probation was introduced initially as a humanitarian measure. The early pioneers simply wished to keep first offenders and minor recidivists from undergoing the corrupting effects of jail. They were volunteers—ministers and others—whose philosophy was that the offender was a deprived, perhaps uneducated person who needed help in adjusting to his environment.

During and after World War I, however, a marked change occurred in this orientation. As probation services continued to expand, there was increasing demand for professionally educated people, especially trained social workers, to serve as probation officers. The training of social workers, in turn, was profoundly influenced by the introduction of psychiatric, expecially psychoanalytic, theory, and was primarily concerned with the individual and his emotional problems and deficiencies.

The emphasis was on seeing the offender as a disturbed person for whom some degree of psychotherapy was indicated. The professional probation caseworker, therefore, came to be valued for his ability to offer such individually oriented therapy.

More recent theories of reintegration are now influencing the training of probation officers and place greater emphasis on developing the offender's effective participation in the major social institutions of the school, business,

[10]Estimate derived from the National Survey of Corrections and data supplied by the Federal Bureau of Prisons and the Administrative Office of the U.S. Courts.

and the church, among others, which offer access to a successful, nondelinquent career. Experience with programs that have attempted rehabilitation in isolation from these institutions indicates that generally such efforts have only a marginal bearing on an offender's success or failure.[11]

This point of view does not deny the importance of increasing individual capacity, but it does make clear that correctional techniques are nearsighted when they fail to take into account and make needed changes in an offender's social and cultural milieu. Successful adjustment on his part will often require some kind of personal reformation, but it will also usually require conditions within the community that will encourage his reintegration into nondelinquent activities and institutions.

This type of approach has several implications. One of these is the location of probation offices. Characteristically, most are now located in a county courthouse or in a juvenile hall. Probationers are expected to report to these places for counseling and then are visited occasionally in their homes or on their jobs. The kind of approach discussed here would indicate that many probation offices should be relocated, particularly into the centers of high crime and delinquency and close to the community resources that are needed for an effective program.

For those offenders who need minimum supervision, probation officers need to have immediate access to channels to which these persons can be diverted. For others, probation officers need to be close to and interacting with major social influences in the offenders' lives. Centers situated in areas of caseload density, for example, could provide an opportunity for frequent, possibly daily participation of probationers in organized programs calculated to contribute to their socialization.

Neighborhood-based probation services could well be housed with other community services such as welfare, employment, and health agencies. Already some experimentation in this direction indicates that probation services can be brought more directly into the social as well as the psychological life of the probationer.

The reintegration procedures through which the offender is geared into the school or the job are not clearly defined or established. The problems are much easier to describe than the solutions. However, an approach can be defined and some specific correctional strategies discussed for dealing with the major social institutions—the family, the school, and employment.

The Family

Few would challenge the all-important role of the family as the universal social institution that nurtures, protects, and shapes the individual from infancy

[11]See H. G. Meyer, E. F. Borgatta, and W. C. Jones, "The Girls at Vocational High" (New York: Russell Sage Foundation, 1965), pp. 180, 205–217; and Evelyn S. Guttman, "Effects of Psychiatric Treatment on Boys at Two Training Schools." Research Report No. 36 (Sacramento: California Youth Authority, 1963).

to independence. The dysfunctional, inadequate, or broken family emerges as a principal source of delinquency. Particularly in the case of the preadolescent or early adolescent delinquent the effort to strengthen the family function is of prime importance.

Two major approaches shape the methods of family therapy. One is the use of the family as a field for corrective intervention on behalf of one or more of its members. Personality difficulties of these members are addressed with the family as the milieu from which the individuals emerge, but the focus is on the individual rather than the family as a whole.

The other approach sees the whole family as the target for treatment. This is the essentially reintegrative type of family therapy. Its objectives are the rehabilitation of the entire family as a healthy functioning unit. There is heavy concentration on instilling healthy child-rearing practices in cases where the children are young, on developing in adolescents the ability to cope with their present situation and those in which they may eventually find themselves, and on making complementary the dual roles of husband-and-wife and father-and-mother. An effort is made to strengthen family ties generally, and to help the family (including the delinquent or pre-delinquent) become effective in the community.

The Youth Development Project, conducted at a psychiatric outpatient clinic connected with the University of Texas Medical Branch, involves a team of therapists who engage in an intensive diagnostic-treatment effort lasting 2 or 3 days, during which the entire family of a delinquent are patients at the clinic. Described as multiple impact therapy, the treatment seeks to give insight and direction to the family that is motivated to seek help with its problems. Probation officers participate in these programs and later maintain contacts with the family in an effort to encourage and renew the self-reformation effort. The technique is particularly appropriate to those sparsely populated regions where treatment resources are scarce.

Other forms of family therapy have been used with the families of delinquents in large cities, often from lower socio-economic groups. Nathaniel Ackerman, of New York City, a pioneer in family therapy, has worked with families of delinquents using an approach which combines analysis, group therapy, and family education. Virginia Satir, of a group in Palo Alto, Calif., which has developed "conjoint family therapy," has coached a variety of workers in correctional institutions and community-based programs in methods of family therapy.

At Wyltwick School for delinquent boys in New York, an experiment has been carried on for some time with families of delinquents from slum areas. At first, the family is interviewed together, using joint therapists. Then the parents talk with one therapist and the children with another. Often in these second sessions "the lid comes off" and the parents and children express their true feelings about each other and what is wrong with the family situation. Delinquent acts may be revealed as rooted in complete misunderstanding by the children or the parents. Reassembled once more, the family may be able to clear up some of these misunderstandings and jointly find a way to deal with the roots of delinquency.

The experiment is now being evaluated. Charles H. King, superintendent of the school, believes that the vast majority of families of delinquents can profit from family therapy, although some families will gain more from it than others and retain their gains better.

The School

Among social institutions, the school clearly is second only to the family in its universal impact. It encompasses all youth, including those most prone to law violation. Chapter 3 of the Commission's General Report examines the operation of the school, particularly the slum school, in relation to delinquency. The inability of poorly financed, overcrowded, and inadequately staffed schools to meet the needs of delinquency-prone populations is described in some detail. The linkage between a child's failure in school and his involvement in delinquency is clearly drawn.

The inability or disinclination of many school systems to cope with the problems of the potential delinquent is intensified where the identified offender is concerned. Once the delinquent label has been officially affixed, all the problems of the marginal youth become more acute; the school's anticipation of trouble tends to be realized, and the level of tolerance of deviant behavior is lowered. Behavioral difficulty and failure to achieve in school frequently lead to truancy, then to dropping out or to expulsion. Once the delinquent youth's ties with the schools are severed, the probability of further delinquency is substantially increased.

The general problems of education for disadvantaged youth have great relevance to corrections, but the solutions obviously lie well beyond the capacity of correctional agencies to undertake. Large-scale programs, now underway, stimulated by Federal legislation in 1965, attempt to create substantial educational opportunities for the disadvantaged. Identified delinquents will benefit directly from these programs. Educational programs for delinquents in institutions are being assisted by Federal grants from the Office of Education.

Educational programs for offenders in the community are of several kinds. The first group is directed toward increasing the competence of offenders to participate more effectively in school programs through special classes for the educationally retarded and the use of programed learning techniques. The availability of funds for probation officers to purchase such services when needed would be particularly useful here.

Other programs directed toward offenders include those which simultaneously affect their motivations, behavior, and education skills. A particularly interesting attempt in this direction is the Collegefield project carried on in conjunction with the Newark State Teachers College, New Jersey. Delinquents assigned by a juvenile court participate in group counseling sessions for half of the day and then are taught by teachers experienced in the public school system. In this setting, youngsters are enabled not only to upgrade their academic skills but also to learn the kind of behavior required to participate in school. Moreover, the group experience increases motivation as peers define success in school as important to status in the group. When youths complete this program, they are moved into regular classroom situations.

Another major category of programs for offenders are those which direct their effort toward the school system itself. Some juvenile courts, for example, make a probation officer responsible for encouraging a specific school to develop intensive programs to attract and hold youths with deficiencies and to develop a greater tolerance on the part of administrators and teachers toward them.

A program which focuses on the school and the offender at the same time is carried out as part of the California Community Treatment project. Experienced and certificated tutors assist marginal students to meet the demands of the educational system. In addition to educational coaching, the tutor counsels the youth concerning his personal behavior in school. He invests considerable time in communication with school counselors and other officials in order to interpret the youngster's needs and problems, to secure development of specialized, low-stress school programs—in short, to increasing the tolerance level of the school system. Program supervisors credit this special program with maintaining a substantially larger proportion of the delinquent population in school and with assuring some educational achievement for the youth who has been suspended or expelled.

Employment

The kind of job a person holds determines, to a large extent, the kind of life he leads. This is true not merely because work and income are directly related, but also because employment is a major factor in an individual's position in the eyes of others and indeed of himself. Work is therefore directly related to the goals of corrections. Glaser concludes in his extensive study, "The Effectiveness of a Prison and Parole System," that "unemployment may be among the principal causal factors in recidivism of adult male offenders."[12] It is difficult for probationers, and often to a greater extent for parolees, to find jobs. They are frequently poor, uneducated, and members of a minority group. They may have personal disabilities—behavior disorders, mental retardation, poor physical health, overwhelming family problems. And they have in any case the stigma of a criminal record to overcome.

A recent study of Federal releasees shows that, during the first month after release, only about 1 out of every 4 releasees was employed at least 80 percent of the time, and 3 out of 10 were unable to secure jobs. After 3 months, only

[12] Daniel Glaser, "The Effectiveness of a Prison and Parole System" (Indianapolis: Bobbs-Merrill, 1964), p. 329.

about 4 out of 10 had worked at least 80 percent of the time, and nearly 2 out of 10 still had not been able to find work of any kind.[13]

VOCATIONAL TRAINING AND PLACEMENT PROGRAMS. The problem can be alleviated somewhat by improving the employment skills of offenders and by having more job-placement programs in correctional agencies. Offenders typically lack information about the local labor market as a whole, especially if they have not had very much work experience. Several Federal antipoverty agencies have established programs specifically aimed at improving employment opportunities for offenders and have included offenders in other programs. The Department of Labor has initiated several special projects for offenders, including a parole employment evaluation center in New York City under the auspices of the New York Division of Parole that provides intensive and continuing vocational counseling services and makes special provision for bonding when indicated.

The 1965 amendments to the Vocational Rehabilitation Act also opened significant vocational opportunities to offenders. By previous definition, the handicapped were persons with physical and mental conditions which created obstacles to employment. The amendments revised this definition in such a way as to cover offenders by interpreting physical and mental to include behavioral disorders characterized by deviant social behavior or impaired ability to carry out normal relationships with family and community which may result from vocational, educational, cultural, social, and environmental factors. A number of research and demonstration programs in correctional institutions and community programs have been funded under these provisions. The most far-reaching of the demonstration programs was inaugurated in November 1965 to serve Federal offenders. This is a series of eight projects in which State vocational rehabilitation agencies provide intensive service to offenders at Federal probation offices and correctional institutions.[14] Programs such as this offer distinct promise for the future and merit active support.

The offender, like any other citizen, may take advantage of the placement service offered by the local public employment service. In some States, the U.S. Employment Service has undertaken special cooperative arrangements with correctional agencies. Some employment offices report a significant number of referrals and placements of offenders; others achieve minimal results. One significant factor appears to be whether there is an especially interested placement officer who is willing to devote extra time, provide some special counseling, and persist even though initial referral or placement of an individual offender does not effect permanent employment. The other important ingredient is the close support of probation or parole staffs in seeing that offenders keep their appointments and follow through when referrals are made.

[13]Ibid., p. 328.
[14]Richard A. Grant, "Vocational Rehabilitation Involvement in the Field of Corrections" (paper presented at the Midwest Institute on Correctional Manpower and Training, Topeka, Kans., Mar. 28, 1966).

In most states, parole and probation officers must help find employment for offenders. Many experience severe difficulty in discharging this task. Some correctional personnel, however, have exhibited special interest and skill in the employment field and have found work for a significant portion of their caseloads. Their performance indicates that, with the appropriate commitment of correctional manpower and training, the unemployment problem of offenders could be better controlled. In larger probation and parole agencies, special staff could profitably be provided for job placement.

RESPONSE OF THE COMMUNITY.   A survey conducted in 1966 by the Minnesota Division of Adult Corrections gives an idea of employer policies on hiring offenders. Among 983 firms, it found that almost 40 percent indicated at least a general reluctance to hire offenders for any position. Another 28 percent would hire them for specific jobs only. Perhaps these attitudes toward offenders are similar to those expressed by the average citizen. In any case, they represent a substantial barrier to employment and a challenge to correctional agencies. Where negative attitudes have existed, agencies have shown that they can be diminished by good communication between correctional personnel and employers. It is clearly the responsibility of all correctional agencies to seek out that kind of communication as a basis for more specific efforts.

Some unions have been hostile toward providing opportunities for offenders, and others have been indifferent to requests for assistance. However, where union and correction officials have attempted to discuss the problem of the employment of offenders and work toward solutions, the results have been gratifying. In Connecticut, New York, Ohio, and Washington unions have been found sympathetic to the employment of offenders, and some have taken positive steps to help. For example, at the Federal penitentiary in Danbury, Conn., the International Ladies' Garment Workers Union has established a program to train sewing machine repairmen on machines furnished by several local companies and provides a card to graduates of the program which helps them to find employment on release.

Business has also set up training programs at Danbury. The Dictograph Corporation trains microsoldering technicians in the penitentiary and employs them when they are in work-release or parole status. In several prisons IBM trains key punch operators, programers, and systems analysts, hiring some itself and referring others to jobs elsewhere.

Training programs offered either directly by unions or by employers with union approval have been a useful method of developing positive relationships between corrections and employment. The creation of trade advisory boards and other liaison groups has also helped to improve the employment climate.

RESTRICTIVE POLICIES AND PROCEDURES.   General attitudes toward offenders have in some cases been formalized into policies that do not allow for special circumstances and require specific changes in laws or rules. Among these are bonding and licensing. Bonding against theft by employees is common practice in larger retail and service businesses, usually through blanket bonds covering all employees.

Both employer and offender often assume that all bonding automatically excludes individuals with criminal records, and some employers probably use bonding requirements as an excuse to turn away applicants with records. In some cases, bonding requirements do automatically bar offenders, and in others offenders have difficulty in satisfying the bonding company of their reliability. Letters received from 12 correctional administrators in answer to the Commission's inquiries agreed that bonding is a problem for the offender, particularly in clerical, sales, and commercial occupations.

Some experimental programs to overcome bonding problems are now underway. The Labor Department has funded a bonding demonstration project under the Manpower Development and Training Act that will contract with a bonding company to provide bonds for 1,700 individuals in New York, Washington, Chicago, Los Angeles, and other cities. Programs similar to these are also being funded by the Department of Health, Education, and Welfare. An interesting variation is offender participation in the development and operation of such programs. In one project, persons bonded will become members of a corporation, Trustworthy, Inc., and will participate in recruiting and screening prospective candidates for bonding. Efforts of this type need extensive expansion and support, and individual employers and insurers must be encouraged to eliminate flat restrictions on bonding for offenders.

The same need for elimination of blanket or irrational restrictions on offenders exists with respect to regulatory and licensing laws relating to employment and other activities. In the employment field, a survey by Spector in 1950 for the Council of State Governments found that most States regulate entry to over 75 different occupations, ranging from law and medicine to barbering and undertaking.[15] Conviction may well be relevant in some cases to the protection of the public through such regulation. It is relevant to the offense they have committed to revoke the license of a lawyer convicted of embezzling the funds of clients or a teamster convicted of vehicular homicide. But it is hard to see why, on the other hand, a man convicted of larceny should not be permitted to cut hair or run a restaurant.

Nonetheless, licensing laws and authorities usually do not confine restrictions to situations in which there is a rational connection between an offense and the practice of an occupation. Licenses are in many cases primarily revenue measures or else products of pressure by unions or trade associations to limit access to an occupation. In other instances they may indeed serve the purpose of protecting the public through the establishment of standards of competency and honesty, but they may rely on excessively broad prohibitions to do so. Licensing authorities may interpret a general requirement such as "good moral character" as a flat proscription against all offenders. A general overhaul of all State and local licensing and employment regulations to eliminate such

[15] Sidney Spector and William Frederick, "A Study of State Legislation Licensing the Practice of Professions" (Chicago: Council of State Governments, 1952), pp. 1–8.

irrational barriers would do much to help in the reintegration of offenders as useful citizens.

GOVERNMENT AGENCIES. Local and Federal Government agencies have traditionally barred offenders from employment. In doing so, they have raised serious questions about their commitment to the rehabilitative efforts of other public agencies and have set a conspicuously poor example for private employers.

Recently, the Federal Government has significantly modified its position. The Civil Service Commission, on August 15, 1966, announced a new Federal employment policy regarding the hiring of former offenders. The Commission and the employing agencies will accept applications from persons who have records of criminal convictions and will consider for employment those adjudged to be good risks.

A number of State governments have made outstanding gains in employing offenders. Local governments are reexamining their policies. In January 1966, the city of New York ended its 50-year-old policy of automatically rejecting persons as employees who had been convicted of crimes and began to hire such persons, including parolees. The new standard is based on individual evaluation of the applicant. According to the city, its experience has been very good.

While these are encouraging steps, much more needs to be done. Every level of government should revise its policies to provide the offender a reasonable opportunity for appropriate employment.

RESTRICTIONS AND CONDITIONS ON PROBATION

The use of probation is influenced importantly by requirements imposed by statute or sentencing courts. The basic structure of sentencing laws is discussed in Chapter 5 of the Commission's General Report and the report of the Task Force on Administration of Criminal Justice. The most important types of legal restrictions and conditions on probation use are touched on here.

Statutory Restrictions

The use of probation in juvenile cases is rarely restricted by statute. Whatever restraints courts may labor under in this area are usually only the result of custom or the pressure of community feeling about certain offenses. This is not the case in probation for adults.

Only 15 States have no statutory restrictions on who may be granted probation in felony cases. In the remaining 35 States, probation is limited by such factors as type of offense, prior convictions, or whether the defendant was armed at the time of offense. The type of offense is the most commonly used device for restricting probation; offenders guilty of rape and murder are the most widely excluded from probation consideration. Beyond these two there is little consistency between States.

The report of the Task Force on Administration of Justice advocates the general reduction of the various outright prohibitions and restrictions on probation and, in their stead, the provision of statutory standards to guide courts in using their discretion in decision-making. The sense of this approach is that probation legislation cannot take into account all possible extenuating circumstances surrounding the commission of an offense or the circumstances of particular offenders.

The key to differential treatment of various offenders lies in the ability of decision-makers, in this case the sentencing judge, to base their decision on a full appraisal of the offender, his personal and social characteristics, and the available types of programs which are best suited to those characteristics. Inflexible restrictions based on narrow criteria defeat the goals of differential treatment by restricting the options from which a judge may choose.

Probation Conditions

This is another area where patterns typically vary between juvenile and adult systems. A number of juvenile courts follow the common adult practice of spelling out probation conditions in detail and of routinely imposing a standard set when granting probation. A more usual practice in juvenile courts is simply to require the cooperation of the probationer with the probation officer. In effect this leaves the imposition of restrictions to the discretion of the probation officer responsible for the supervision of the case.

Delegating rulemaking power to a probation officer invites possible abuse of that discretion. Additionally, a number of correctional officials will argue that a difficult role conflict is created when the probation officer is given the task of being simultaneously rulemaker, enforcer, and helper. If a violation of a rule can serve as the basis for a revocation of probation, it needs to be clearly defined to the probationer. Best practice would require that such rules and conditions imposed be carefully reviewed by the court.

Differential treatment requires that rules be tailored to the needs of the case and of the individual offender. The procedure followed in a number of courts is to have the probation officer who submits a presentence report make recommendations about the conditions which seem indicated in a specific case. They therefore can be discussed with the prospective probationer and his counsel as well as the probation officer. Such a procedure is superior on several counts and could well be emulated by all courts.

Other issues related to probation and parole conditions are discussed in connection with parole. Two points, however, are peculiar to probation. The first of these is the practice in some courts of routinely imposing a jail term as a "condition" to probation prior to the start of the probation period. The argument usually advanced for this practice is that it gives the offender a taste of incarceration that tends to deter him from further criminal activities.

Correctional personnel have generally sought to discourage commitments to jail as a condition of probation, questioning whether it in fact operates as a deterrent and pointing out that a jail term may complicate reintegration by causing an offender to lose his job and otherwise disrupting his community ties.

The question of the deterrent effect of such a condition requires research and experimentation that has yet to be undertaken. It seems clear, however, that the indiscriminate use of incarceration in a class of cases that presumably includes many offenders not likely to repeat their acts and amenable to other corrective methods is unwise. Whether or not to use short-term detention as a deterrent should be carefully determined in each individual instance, and until more knowledge is available as to its effectiveness in accomplishing these purposes it should be used extremely sparingly.

Financial reimbursement to victims is another condition used quite frequently in probation. It is not uncommon for a large probation agency to supervise the collection of millions of dollars in restitution for crime victims each year. Restitution can serve a very constructive purpose and of course it represents practical help for the victim. The central problem is to make certain that the rate of such payments is related to the ability of the offender to pay so that it does not prevent an offender from successfully reestablishing himself in the community, or so that it does not automatically destine him for a jail term for failure to meet the conditions of probation. An installment plan is a partial remedy for the problem. In many cases only partial restitution may be possible. Perhaps the best approach is for the probation officer to include in his presentence report an analysis of the financial situation of the defendant, an estimate of a full amount of restitution for the victim, and a recommended plan for payment.

ADMINISTRATION AND ORGANIZATION

Let us emphasize the need to develop organizational coherence in corrections. Nowhere is this more needed than in probation services. In the main, as shown in Table 4, adult probation services are State functions while juvenile probation services are local functions, though there are within these generalizations a very wide variety of administrative patterns.

In 32 States, juvenile courts administer probation services. Elsewhere, juvenile services are operated by State correctional agencies in five States, by the State welfare department in seven, and by other State or local agencies in the remainder. In 30 States, adult probation is combined with parole services. In the others such services are administered by a separate State board or agency or are under local jurisdiction. This diversity is largely the result of historical accident. Since juvenile probation services were developed in juvenile courts, they were administered locally. Services for adults, in the majority of States, were grafted onto existing state-wide parole supervision services.

There are two major questions in regard to organization and administration. The first is the desirability of direct administration of local probation services

Table 4   *Administration of Juvenile and Adult Probation, by Type of Agency, 50 States and Puerto Rico, 1965*

Type of Agency	Number of Jurisdictions	
	Juvenile	Adult
State:		
Corrections	5	12
Other agencies	11	25
Local:		
Courts	32	13
Other agencies	3	1
Total	51	51

SOURCE. National Survey of Corrections,

by a judge, and the second is the relative merits of State and local administration.

Local Administration of Probation by Courts

Some city and county probation systems are administered directly by a judge and others by relatively independent probation agencies. When probation is administered immediately by a judge, there frequently exists the kind of shared knowledge of function and communication about program content that is found nowhere else in the correctional apparatus. The judge in these jurisdictions is probably as well informed about correctional alternatives as any decision-maker in corrections. This is particularly true of the juvenile system. Moreover some juvenile court judges have, by virtue of their position, succeeded in developing considerable attention and official support for juvenile probation services. This has also happened to a much lesser extent in adult services.

In most major cities, however, the probation department is a complex organization requiring continuous and intensive administrative attention by professional, full-time managers. This is particularly true of local juvenile probation departments, which often operate detention homes, psychiatric clinics, and foster homes, as well as carrying out supervision functions. To manage so widely dispersed an operation requires specialized expertise and close control which are almost impossible for a judge whose career investment is not in administration. Moreover, organizational effectiveness and continuity of policy are apt to be seriously impaired in an agency subject to detailed administrative direction by both a judge and a chief probation officer.

Various procedures have been adopted by city and county probation agencies to give greater autonomy to probation staffs. One of the most common is to provide that a chief probation officer is hired by a committee of judges and is responsible to them in broad policy matters. Detailed administration is left in his hands. Other systems involve the use of citizen groups or city or county officials in the appointment of probation staffs.

A consideration frequently voiced against shifting probation services away from direct judicial administration is that a judge may more fully trust the information and services provided by staff under his immediate control. However, probation administrators in city, county, and State jurisdictions where probation services are provided to the courts by independent agencies contend that this is not a significant problem. They point out that, in many localities and States where such systems exist, close and very satisfactory working relationships develop between sentencing judges and probation staffs.

State vs. Local Administration

The second major organizational issue is that of State as against local administration. Table 4 showed that in the juvenile field 16 States have centralized State administration for probation services, while in the adult field 37 States are so organized. Other States continue to locate probation departments at the county level. In this group are 9 of the most densely populated States.

A number of reasons are advanced for probation being a local function. First, local programs can typically develop better support from local citizenry and agencies. Once the offender is adjudged criminal or delinquent, and turned over to a State agency, there is a tendency to withdraw local services. Agencies at the same jurisdictional level tend to be united by a variety of administrative and traditional ties that do not extend to other levels. Employees of local jurisdictions usually have greater identification and ties with their communities, hence greater access to local resources.

Secondly, smaller operations tend to be more flexible and less bound by bureaucratic rigidity. Given aggressive leadership and community support, they may indeed outstrip the larger, more cumbersome State service. Finally, combining all local probation services in several large States, such as New York, Illinois, or California, could result in very large State operations. It would place a tremendous burden on administration. If it were weak, ineffectual, or politically determined, serious damage could result. While all of these risks prevail at lower levels of government—indeed they probably occur more frequently—the impact of any single poor leader is less widely spread.

On the other hand, State administration has some clear advantages. First there exists a greater probability that the same level of services will be extended to all areas and all clients. Uniform and equitable policies will be applied in recommendations for institutional and out-of-home placement. Wide variations in policy are manifest where administration is local. Some economies in detention and diagnostic-services are possible if they are operated regionally rather than locally.

Another major advantage in the State's operation of probation services is the possibility of combining them with parole services and also better coordinating them with institution programs. Presently 30 of the 50 States combine felony probation and parole services for adults while 13 do so wholly or in part for juveniles.

The advantages of such combined services are several. A single agency is able to offer a continuity of service. Thus, the youngster placed on probation who fails and is sent to a training school can be handled by the same community agency when later released on parole. Information about the youth is readily available to the agency and important contacts with families and other significant persons can be maintained and further developed.

Combined services provide economies in the distribution of services. A single officer in a sparsely populated area of a State can service both probation and parole cases in the area. Similarly, the officer in an urban area can mobilize community resources in a given area of a city for both types of cases.

Additionally, there is a tendency for a local agency to "solve" a problem case, or one that requires a substantial investment of services or money, by commitment to the State institution. This would be minimized if a single agency operated both programs.

The greatest resistance to combining probation and parole services generally stem from the fact that this inevitably means that probation services would become part of a State system and move away from local control. The opposite alternative—parole supervision services being administered by a series of local agencies—is clearly undesirable. Virtually every correctional authority contends that parole services must be centrally administered and coordinated with the institutional system, particularly in view of the increasing need to coordinate such services with various institutional and part-way programs.

A final argument for State administration of probation services is the historical fact that State agencies have generally been in the forefront of developing innovative programs, demonstration projects, and correctional research. Extensive research and demonstration are almost nonexistent at the local level.

State Responsibilities to Local Programs

Even without State administration, various State services can nonetheless be used to bolster local programs significantly. As in the case of intake and detention services, a central agency concerned with probation administration is needed at the State level. It could provide centralized statewide statistics on such matters as probation recommendations and adjudicative dispositions; frequency of use of jails and State institutions; the number of successful completions and revocations of probation; and the use of residential centers and homes.

Information on outcomes of various treatment efforts needs to be maintained at a central information center. Such a center could also provide assistance in the design and operation of demonstration and research projects at the local level and provide data-processing capability that only the larger operations can develop. Through these devices all jurisdictions could be assisted in program experimentation and innovation.

A most important service for the State agency is the provision of assistance to local services in staff training and recruitment. The State agency could do much to bring together the academic community and the world of practice. The "career day" program, where social science faculty and students are invited to observe correctional programs and participate in discussions with practitioners, is an example.

Training is another area in which vigorous State agency efforts might develop not only the knowledge and talent of local staff but some uniform levels of program adequacy and policy consistency as well. Traveling teams, local or regional institutes, seminars based at universities and colleges, training conferences for administrators and supervisors are all media that can be used by a State agency to assure statewide dissemination of current correctional theory and practice concepts.

Standard setting is commonly considered an appropriate State agency function. Normally, this would consist of establishing some objective norms for staff qualifications, possibly for staff salary level, and some outlines of the kind of information to be contained in various reports. Standards of treatment or practice are more difficult to define, although some norms concerning fair procedures could be developed with reasonable clarity. Standard setting should be done jointly by State agencies and local agencies, both public and private. Statewide consultation services are vital to the implementation of those standards.

Perhaps the most effective way of improving local services is by direct State subsidy for all or part of the cost of local probation services. Such subsidies now are used quite effectively in many States. Some of the most effective State subsidies include salaries; cost of local camps, institutions, foster homes, group homes, and halfway house operations; and cost of special clinical, diagnostic, and consultation services. Logic would dictate that the State subsidy be invested in a manner calculated to effect the greatest improvement for the tax dollars spent. That is, it should not be simply a device for transferring a portion of a local correctional budget upward to the State level, but rather should depend upon measurable improvement and performance.

A variant of the subsidy is the provision of specific services by the State agency. Noninstitutional placements in State-operated group homes and residential centers, clinical diagnosis, and consultation are examples.

Probation services under optimal conditions would be administered at the State level. If they are located there, they require sound financial support and backing. If they are to continue to be administered at the local level, it is clear that staff training and program content can be assured only if the State government provides undergirding services and vigorous leadership in making sure that local programs are effective.

5

What Is Probation?

LEWIS DIANA

SUMMARY OF HISTORICAL DEVELOPMENT OF PROBATION

Some authorities trace the roots of probation to the middle ages when such devices as the benefit of clergy and the law of sanctuary made it possible either to avoid or at least to postpone punishment.[1] It is more likely that there was not any continuous linear development of probation, although one can point to various forerunners such as the judicial reprieve, by which the court suspended the imposition or execution of a sentence, and the practice of releasing an offender on his own recognizance. Consequently, probation was probably more directly an outgrowth of the different methods in England and America for suspending sentence.

Under the common law the courts of England had for many years bound over petty offenders to sureties or released them on their own recognizance even without sureties.[2] Such practices were also common in some of the American colonies, especially Massachusetts, which in 1836 recognized by law the releasing of minor offenders with sureties. In 1869 this same state also authorized the placement, after investigation, of youthful offenders in private homes under the supervision of an agent of the state.

Credit for the first use of the term probation goes to John Augustus, a Boston shoemaker, who apparently became interested in befriending violators

SOURCE. *Journal of Criminal Law, Criminology and Police Science*, **51**, July-August 1960, pp. 189–204. Copyright © 1960, by the Northwestern University School of Law, Reprinted by special permission. (Editorial Adaptations.)

[1]Halpern, "Probation," *Encyclopedia of Criminology* 388 (Philosophical Library, New York, 1949).

[2]United Nations, Department of Social Affairs, *Probation and Related Measures* 16 (1951).

of the law, bailed many of them out of jail, and provided them with sympathetic supervision. This was as early as 1841. It was not until 1878, however, that the first probation law was passed, Massachusetts again taking the lead. In that year the mayor of Boston was given the power to appoint probation officers, and only two years later, in 1880, the law was extended to apply to other communities within the state. Then in 1891 Massachusetts passed a second law, which required the extension of probation to the criminal courts. By 1900, though, only five states—Massachusetts, Missouri, Rhode Island, New Jersey, and Vermont—recognized probation legally.[3] By 1933 all states except Wyoming had juvenile probation laws, and all but thirteen states had adult probation laws. This latter group had been cut to five states by 1950: Mississippi, Nevada, New Mexico, Oklahoma, and South Dakota.[4]

The variety of legislation governing probation in the United States may have stemmed (1) from the Supreme Court's denial in the *Killits* case that there existed any inherent judicial power to suspend sentence or any other process in the administration of the criminal code and (2) from the different points of view which developed concerning the practice of probation. The result, in the United States at any rate, has been to give to the courts a fairly wide discretion in the use of probation.

It remains to be said that with the creation of the Cook County Juvenile Court in 1899, probation as a principle and as a practice received great momentum. Great hopes have since been pinned upon it.

DEFINITIONS OF PROBATION

Probation as a Legal Disposition Only

One point of view sees probation simply as a suspension of sentence by the court. Since sentence is not imposed, the offender remains in the community until the length of the sentence has expired, unless, of course, in the meantime he has engaged in any conduct that would warrant carrying out the sentence. This system leaves everything to the probationer and makes of probation a simple policing procedure. Therefore, it implies two things to the probationer: another chance, and the threat of punishment should he fail to improve his behavior.

In point of time this view has been expressed by authors, mostly with a legal background, writing in the first decade of the twentieth century. I have found no references to it after 1908 when Judge McKenzie Cleland put it this way: probation is a plan "of suspending over offenders the maximum sentence permitted by law" and of allowing them "to determine by their subsequent

---

[3]Barnes and Teeters, *New Horizons in Criminology* 760 (2d ed., Prentice-Hall, New York, 1955).

[4] *Ibid*.

conduct whether they should lose or retain their liberty . . . with the full knowledge that further delinquency meant . . . severe punishment."[5]

Probation as a Measure of Leniency

In a review of the literature I found but one author who took this approach to probation.[6] However, it probably best represents the general lay point of view, as well as that of most probationers. This fact presents a basic problem to professional personnel, who view probation as a form of treatment. Many offenders, however, especially among juveniles, feel their acts are unfortunate slips, and while possibly inexplicable, they are, in the final analysis, choices between right and wrong, choices which the offenders feel capable of controlling. Consequently, in their own minds they are not sick persons or necessarily even the products of undesirable environments and so certainly in no need of treatment.

Probation as a Punitive Measure

This again represents a view which has found little acceptance in the literature, especially during the last fifty years. I discovered only one writer who made punishment the *dominant* note in his theory of probation. According to Almy, probation must be presented to the probationer as a form of punishment, one which permits him to escape commitment and its stigma but one which also makes other demands. If these demands are not met, then the probationer can expect to receive the same type of punishment as other offenders.[7] The assumption underlying such a view is that it is the certainty of punishment which deters.

Probation as an Administrative Process

It is likely that the earlier ideas of reform and rehabilitation attached to probation came about as a reaction to the various abuses associated with the imprisonment of children. As a result, a great deal of sentiment was tied to the concept of probation in its beginnings. This sentiment, together with the goal of reform or rehabilitation, formed the nucleus of the conception of probation as an administrative process. Essentially what probation consists of under this conception is the execution of concrete measures aimed at helping the offender stay out of further trouble. The ultimate goal of complete rehabilitation in this approach, however, was something which was more hoped for than worked for. In this respect it is a fairly negative approach consisting mainly of things done for the offender in the *hope* that they will *somehow* deter him from a further career in crime. Thus, arranging for medical treatment, making appointments

[5]Cleland, "New Gospel in Criminology; Municipal Court of Chicago," 31 *McClure's* 358–362 (June 1908).

[6]Smith, A. C., "Does Probation Aid or Prevent Crime?," 125 *Annals* 242 (1926).

[7]Almy, "Probation as Punishment," 24 *Survey* 657 (1910).

for the administration of tests, effecting school transfers, seeking employment for the offender, checking on his activities, and so on constitute the major content of probation under this viewpoint.

Slightly more than thirty percent of the authors writing in this field have· seen the administrative process as the major framework of probation.[8] Most of these, however, date from 1902 to 1920. Since 1935, only two writers have espoused this concept. This fact may indicate the close identification of the correctional field with social work, which was largely administrative in the earlier years. Later, changing concepts and techniques in social work quickly found their way into child welfare and juvenile court probation services. The newer approaches represented by casework and its psychoanalytic foundations have not found unanimous approval, however.

Thus, Dr. Philipp Parsons of the Department of Sociology, University of Oregon, has stated:

"In the rehabilitation field . . . research and administration become the all important factors. Research consists in getting the facts of a given situation, and administration consists in devising programs adapted to the facts and in carrying out these programs by whatever techniques the conditions may make practical. . . .

". . . changing conditions, economic, political, and social, have shifted the major emphasis in remedial work from individuals and families to groups and conditions. Training for remedial work, therefore, must be built upon a base of research, organization, and administration rather than upon the case work which was the foundation of social work training in the past generation.

". . . rehabilitating convicted persons in connection with a scientific system of penology . . . is primarily an administrative job and also primarily a job for men."[9]

The process of probation which follows an administrative pattern is illustrated in an article by Jessie Keys. Writing in *World's Work* in 1909, Miss Keys stated that the search for ultimate causes is not the least important work of the juvenile court. These causes were usually felt to be parental neglect or parental vice or both. To illustrate she cited the case of a boy who had a mania for stealing pocket knives:

"His father and paternal grandfather had been master mechanics. After his father died his mother led an irregular life and neglected the boy. His hereditary instincts came to the surface. Since his mother refused to help him gratify his desire for mechanics, he undertook to gratify it in any way he could."[10]

Unlike modern casework, no attempt was made during the boy's probation to help him "verbalize" and express his feelings and so come to a personal solution based on the untapped resources of his deeper personality. Instead: "We went to his mother and she awoke to her responsibility. We talked to the

[8] All of the available literature since 1900 has been reviewed.

[9] Parsons, P. A., "Qualifying Workers for the Correctional Field," *Yearbook, Nat'l Probation and Parole Ass'n* 66–86 (1938).

[10] Keys, "Cases of the Children's Court," 18 *World's Work* 11612 (1909).

boy firmly and found him willing to work. Finally, we found a position for him."[11]

The probation process not only included finding work for the boy but also included telling the mother how to keep her house clean and giving her other directives. It literally forced the boy into a certain mold, by the use of pressure, and sometimes intimidation, to do what he was told was right. Thus the probation officer attempted to produce what was not ordinarily a part of the boy's pattern of behavior.

In 1910 Maude E. Miner, Secretary of the New York Probation Association, reported that probation for the convicted girl consisted of a process of character building through discipline and correction. These were applied by obtaining employment for the girl, visiting her home, getting the cooperation of her parents, providing needed medical care, and bringing her into contact with beneficial influences such as churches and clubs.[12]

In 1911 the Illinois law on adult probation provided that certain categories of first offenders could be placed on probation. The court was obliged to impose certain conditions designed both to protect the community and to give the probationers some "sensible practical aid." These conditions included paying court costs, supplying bond, supporting dependents, and making regular reports to the probation officer.[13] Obviously, under such circumstances probation could be little else than administrative.

From a figure well known in corrections, C. L. Chute:

"The probation officer must investigate all offenders and must keep himself informed concerning their conduct and condition. He must report on each case at least once every month to the court and must use all suitable methods not inconsistent with the conditions imposed by the court, to aid persons on probation and to bring about improvement in their conduct and condition."[14]

Or:

"The probation officer helps a man to get and keep a job, finds him wholesome amusement, looks after his leisure hours and generally backs him up to playing a man's part in the world much as the special war agencies kept up the morale of the army."[15]

The supposed therapeutic effects of administrative techniques are illustrated in an article by Platt:

"Get a boy into a good club, give him duties and see what happens—interest, pride, loyalty, ambition, cooperation, social teamwork, social sense, all will probably soon follow."[16]

[11] *Ibid.*
[12] Miner, "Probation Work for Women," 36 *Annals* 27 (1910).
[13] "New Illinois Law on Adult Probation," 26 *Survey* 18 (1911).
[14] Chute, "Probation a Federal Need," 43 *Survey* 775 (1920).
[15] "Emptying the Jails: Probation System in New York City," 100 *The Independent* 40 (1919).
[16] Platt, "Does Punishment Pay?," 55 *Survey* 605–607 (1926).

In 1919 no less an authority than the sub-committee of the National Conference of Social Work summed up this point of view by reporting that the office of the probation officer is administrative. It may have its authority beyond the court but accountability to the court is, in the final analysis, the foundation of probation service.[17]

Probation as Social Casework Treatment

Reinemann has defined probation as follows:

"Legally, in the case of an adult offender, probation is the suspension of sentence during a period of freedom, on condition of good behavior. In the case of a delinquent child, the juvenile court uses probation as a form of *case disposition* which allows the child to live at liberty in his own home or in the custody of a suitable person, be it a relative, a friend of the family, or a foster home, under supervision of an agent of the court and upon such conditions as the court determines. *Socially, probation is a form of treatment* administered by probation officers on a case work basis."[18] (Emphasis added.)

The dichotomy between adult and juvenile probation seemingly is disappearing. In any event definitions of probation as a legal disposition are rarely found in current literature. On the contrary, the bulk of the literature—between eighty-five and ninety percent of it since 1940—views probation as some form of treatment, more often than not as casework treatment.

Casework and its foster parent, psychiatry, have had extensive influence in the juvenile court movement. This influence is illustrated by the broad scope of many of our juvenile court laws, by the shunting aside, in the rising tide of a clinical ideology, of legal precedents in favor of loose and informal procedures, by the indeterminate sentence, by the emphasis on the total situation of an offender, by the absorption with emotional problems, and by the prevailing adherence to a psychoanalytic theory of causation.

The point of view which identifies probation with casework treatment is difficult to analyze. It cannot be presented as a consistent or well-defined approach and appears, rather, to represent an attitude or state of mind in lieu of a technique or substantive theory. In any event the literature presenting probation as casework treatment generally defines probation as the *application* of casework principles and techniques in dealing with the offender. But what is casework?

Taber describes it this way:

"Case work . . . may be defined as a process of attempting to understand the needs, impulses and actions of an individual and of helping him to recognize these in a way that is satisfying to himself and yet in accord with the demands of social living.
". . . treatment cannot be forced upon another person. . . . To help another person

---

[17] Parsons, H. C., "Probation and Parole; Report of the Sub-Committee," *Nat'l Conference of Social Work* 113 (1919).
[18] Reinemann, "Probation and the Juvenile Delinquent," 261 *Annals* 109 (1949).

we must accept him as he is with an honest respect for his capacity as well as regard for his need to solve his own problem with whatever help the worker can give him. The case worker is concerned with assisting the individual to realize his own capacities to the fullest extent, as well as to orient him to the resources existing within his environment which will provide a satisfying outlet. In short, change to be effective depends upon the individual's willingness to help himself. . . . He must be assisted in finding his own way at his own pace. . . .

"Every phase of behavior has a different meaning for each individual, and treatment if it is to be effective must be differentiated according to the individual's need. . . . There are no formulas which we can readily apply . . . but we can sharply define in a warm but objective manner the alternatives which confront a delinquent in order that he may redirect his behavior if he has the strength and will to do so."[19]

Most concepts of casework also include assumptions concerning the nature and causes of delinquent behavior:

"Delinquent behavior and other forms of conflict are generally compensating substitutes for experiences and impulses which the individual fears to recognize and dares not express. The tension resulting creates frustration and fear. Whether or not the release takes the form of a criminal act is purely fortuitous and is dependent upon the attitudes and tensions operating at the time. . . .

"If we accept the fact that the probation officer's work concerns itself with helping the man under supervision to bring to conscious expression his underlying emotional conflicts and thus rid those deep-seated unknown drives of their tension and potency, and if we recognize that the probationer's moral decisions must be his own, not the probation officer's, then is the generic problem of interpretation with which the probation officer is faced any different from that which must be met by the case worker?"[20]

Miss Genevieve Gabower, formerly Director of Social Work in the Juvenile Court, Washington, D.C., refers to casework in this way:

"The worker sees a need for giving service in the case of a child where either the solicitude or the indifference of the parents, or a combination of extremes of the two operates as a barrier to his growth and development. He can be of service by developing and maintaining a relationship of continuing interest and acceptance and thus assisting in establishing stability. Case work . . . through this kind of relationship . . . may operate as a medium through which the youth can find that he has ability to conform to community standards."[21]

In other words, from Miss Gabower's point of view, the relationship which by some is described *as* casework is here presented only as an instrument of casework. But what casework is, is still not explained.

One thing is certain, however: the casework point of view represents a

[19]Taber, "The Value of Casework to the Probationer," *Yearbook, Nat'l Probation and Parole Ass'n* 167–179 (1940).

[20]Reeves, "Administrative Procedures and Case Work Services," *Yearbook, Nat'l Probation and Parole Ass'n* 180–192 (1940).

[21]Gabower, "Motivating the Delinquent to Accept Treatment," *Yearbook, Nat'l Probation and Parole Ass'n* 207–219 (1940).

shift in emphasis from the social conditions of behavior to individual behavior itself, especially such behavior as can be approached from the standpoint of the "dynamics" of psychoanalytic mechanisms. The shift has been from a social to a clinical frame of reference. Crime and delinquency are acts containing social implications, but it is chiefly the individual personality which interests the caseworker. Thus, Miss Louise McGuire, also one-time Director of Social Work in the Juvenile Court, Washington, D.C., states: "Back of the overt acts are the motives. These latter are our concern and the basis of case work treatment."[22]

Miss McGuire's article represents an attempt to delineate casework into three phases: (1) social inquiry into the total situation of the client; (2) social diagnosis, that is, inquiry into the relationships and attitudes of the client; and (3) social casework treatment. In this last phase there are three objectives: (1) to induce right notions of conduct (responsible behavior) in the client; (2) to induce motives which will assure loyalty to good norms of conduct; and (3) to develop the client's latent abilities.

To achieve these objectives casework treatment is divided into two sections: mechanistic devices and deep therapy. The former consist in the utilization of the resources of community agencies. The latter, deep therapy, refers to the process of changing the attitudes of the probationer, giving him insight through interpretation.[23]

This essentially clinical approach is supported by most other writers outside the academic disciplines of criminology and sociology. Hagerty, for example, has said, "We offer as our major premise that solution of the crime problem involves chiefly the study and personality treatment of the individual offender."[24] He goes on to define casework as an aid in the restoration of self-support and self-respect in the "client."

More recently Hyman S. Lippman, Director of the Amherst H. Wilder Child Guidance Clinic, St. Paul, Minnesota, has declared that casework on the part of the probation officer is the essential ingredient in his "treatment" of delinquency.[25] While not defining casework, Lippman does specify *relationship* as the major contribution of a probation officer and the interview as his main tool. The unconscious conflicts of the neurotic delinquent of course, "are deeply imbedded, and can *only* be brought to light by the psychiatrist trained in psychoanalytic techniques."[26] (Emphasis added.)

David Crystal, Executive Director, Jewish Social Service Bureau, Rochester, N.Y., sees probation as a treatment process of the entire family. But the process

---

[22]McGuire, "Essentials of Case Work with Delinquents," *Yearbook, Nat'l Probation and Parole Ass'n* (1935).

[23]*Ibid.*

[24]Hagerty, "The Delinquent as a Case Problem," *Yearbook, Nat'l Probation and Parole Ass'n* (1935).

[25]Lippman, "The Role of the Probation Officer in the Treatment of Delinquency in Children," 12 *Federal Probation* 36 (1948).

[26]*Id.* at 37.

is curiously enough still described in clinical terms as the focus of casework is:

1. How does the probation officer help the probationer accept the conditions of his current reality?
2. How does and can the family relate to the probationer in terms of the new experience?

(*a*) Can they express honestly their feelings of guilt, of anticipated reprisal, of uncertainty about the impact this will have on their future lives?

(*b*) Will they require special help from a worker other than the probation officer, in a different kind of agency in the community? Can they now or later accept the need for help?

(*c*) Is the total responsibility for change to be lodged exclusively on the offender, or can the family see change as a reaction not to one but multiple causes and that they too are part of the change, externally and internally, by their physical presence and concrete offering of shelter and food and job and by the attitude with which these visible and tangible things about the family are given?[27]

Henry J. Palmieri, Director of Social Services of the Juvenile Court of the District of Columbia, declares probation is a casework service and a method of treatment which "is no longer an ideal" but "a reality."[28] However, he defines neither casework nor treatment but assumes their identity with probation.

Glover outlines four basic principles of treatment without, however, specifying how they are effected: (1) treatment based on consent of the offender; (2) treatment planned for the individual; (3) treatment planned around the offender's own situation; and (4) treatment planned to redirect the offender's emotions.[29]

The strong clinical orientation of casework seeking to induce proper motives, to aid in the achievement of insight and self-respect, and to change attitudes of the offender may be worthwhile and desirable. But the aims and the orientation do not define the process of casework. *How* is insight produced? *How* are interpretations given? *How* are attitudes changed? *How* is relationship established? The answers to these questions are rarely mentioned in the literature, and casework continues to be defined in broad and general terms as, for example, "an art in which knowledge of the science of human relations and skill in relationship are used to mobilize capacities in the individual and resources in the community appropriate for better adjustment between the client and all or any part of his total environment."[30]

One of the most recent and well-known texts defines casework as follows: "Social casework is a process used by certain human welfare agencies to help

[27]Crystal, "Family Casework in Probation," 13 *Federal Probation* 47–53 (1949).

[28]Palmieri, "Probation Is Treatment," 13 *Federal Probation* 20 (1949).

[29]Glover, "Probation: The Art of Introducing the Probationer to a Better Way of Life," 15 *Federal Probation* 8 (1951).

[30]Bowers, "The Nature and Definition of Social Casework: Part III," 30 *J. Soc. Casework* 417 (1949).

individuals to cope more effectively with their problems in social functioning."[31]

The elements, then, which are said to comprise the principles of casework invariably stamp it as a clinical process for the most part. It is often stated, for example, that casework implies that the probation officer has a respect for individual differences and that he should have not only a natural desire to serve others but also an understanding of the processes that develop personalities. The probation officer *accepts* and the client then may show "movement" because for the first time he is seen able to talk freely and naturally to another person about himself and how he feels. The worker understands and conveys that understanding to the "client," thereby relieving the "client's" anxieties and stimulating a more constructive outlook.

Biestek explains a casework relationship on the basis of seven needs of the client. "The caseworker is *sensitive* to, *understands*, and appropriately *responds* to these needs" and "the client is somehow *aware* of the caseworker's sensitivity, understanding, and response."[32] The seven needs of the client embody corresponding principles:[33]

The need of the client	*The name of the principle*
1. To be treated as an individual.	1. Individualization.
2. To express feelings.	2. Purposeful expression of feelings.
3. To get sympathetic response to problems.	3. Controlled emotional involvement.
4. To be recognized as a person of worth.	4. Acceptance.
5. Not to be judged.	5. Nonjudgmental attitude.
6. To make his own choices and decisions.	6. Client self-determination.
7. To keep secrets about self.	7. Confidentiality.

Casework thus attempts to formalize, standardize, and professionalize the display and exercise of warmth, sympathy, respect, and understanding, all of which are considered to be basic elements in therapeutic treatment of the individual. In probation, also, any punitive quality in the process has been removed, and the goal has become not merely the elimination of the probationer's anti-social conduct but, whenever possible, the improvement of his personality and the achievement of a more nearly perfect total adjustment. What probation is, therefore, must include the means by which those goals are realized. This casework usually does by simply stating casework *as* the means or process. There have been attempts at clarification, but the field defies synthesis.

Miss Witmer has pointed out that:

"... social work is a very specific system of organized activities based on a body of values and technical rules which are becoming increasingly well-formulated ... it

---

[31] Perlman, *Social Casework, A Problem-Solving Process* (Chicago, University of Chicago Press, 1957).

[32] Biestek, *The Casework Relationship* 17 (Chicago, Loyola University Press, 1957).

[33] Reproduced from Biestek, *op. cit. supra* note 32, at 17.

has a definite function to perform. It is not a vague, indeterminate method of doing good or promoting welfare, or even of helping people out of trouble, indistinguishable from psychiatry at one end and uplift work at the other. . . .

". . . social case work centers around helping individuals with the difficulties they encounter in a particular group relationship. . . ."[34]

Miss Witmer also suggests that while probation presently involves the use of casework, it is mainly executive and diagnostic, centering on changes in the environment of the offender. Such casework "lacks the sharpness of focus and precision of method which perception of specific function has given to case work in other fields."[35] But in my experience, at least, this "sharpness of focus and precision of method" of casework in other fields is more an attribute of casework in the literature than of casework in the field. What is specific and precise in any other agency is not mentioned. It appears that it is the field or area of operation of these other agencies that is more or less precise and not necessarily their techniques.

Miss Witmer denies the similarity of casework and psychiatry or therapy but nevertheless states its aims in therapeutic terms: "Modern case work works with the client rather than on his behalf" since the sources of difficulty are supposedly known only to the "client."[36] However, the caseworker assumes the existence of underlying or unconscious conflicts and so is practically committed to a psychotherapeutic point of view. Where this is denied, superficial distinctions are usually drawn between casework and therapy, such as the fact that in therapy it is the "client" himself who seeks the therapist, or that in therapy one delves more deeply into the unconscious and there is a more intense emotional involvement of "client" and therapist. There is convincing evidence, however, that points to the emergence of casework, and certainly of psychiatric social work, as another therapeutic profession.

In conclusion, probation as casework concentrates not so much on crime and delinquency as on criminals and delinquents, and not so much on criminals and delinquents as on criminals and delinquents with emotional problems. In general, as Sutherland has pointed out,[37] casework in probation follows psychiatric conceptions in that insight by the probationer into the reasons for his behavior is the chief goal of treatment. A person with such insight is felt to be unlikely to repeat his delinquent activities. The primary method consists of intensive interviews through which the probation officer not only comes to understand the probationer but the probationer, to understand himself. An identification with the probation officer then helps the offender emulate his behavior until finally the point is reached where the probationer becomes

---

[34]Witmer, "Social Case Work in the Field of Juvenile Probation," *Yearbook, Nat'l Probation and Parole Ass'n* 153–166 (1941).

[35]*Ibid.*

[36]*Ibid.*

[37]Sutherland, *Principles of Criminology*, 399–400 (Philadelphia, J. B. Lippincott Co., 4th ed., 1947).

independent of this identification and can carry on normal and socially acceptable behavior on his own.

Probation as a Combination of Casework and Administration

This point of view regarding probation does not, as it might suggest, constitute a catch-all for those approaches which do not fit the categories discussed thus far. From this standpoint probation is represented both by casework functions and by administrative or executive procedures. Where casework is paramount, administrative functions are supplementary. Where administrative duties are indicated as the primary plan of approach, casework skills and techniques, however defined, must be utilized in the performance of those duties. In other words, some cases may be felt to require intensive interviews more than anything else. But in the course of most cases there are, practically without exception, other things to be done as well: arranging a transfer of schools, scheduling medical and other appointments, and so on. Other cases may be felt to call for mainly administrative functions, such as those just mentioned, plus limited and superficial contacts with the probationers. But in performing those functions and in making those contacts, a casework approach must be applied. In this respect the utilization of casework techniques is usually manifested in the attitude taken toward the probationer.

Murphy illustrates this school of thought:

"Probation officers have another task, that of controlling, guiding and rehabilitating probationers. Here they are called upon to make accurate personality diagnoses and plan comprehensively to improve the probationers' environment and economic life, to adjust delicate family problems, find employment, provide for necessary medical treatment and health assistance, determine recreational needs and social needs, stimulate spiritual and moral improvement. ... Patterns of behavior can be changed only when attitudes, loyalties and group relationships can be altered or recreated."[38]

In summary, then, this point of view sees probation as the simultaneous application of casework and administrative functions, but in specific cases it is more one than the other. Whichever is paramount in any particular case, the other is complementary. About twenty percent of the literature reviewed supports this approach to probation.

WHAT IS PROBATION?

With the exception of the first three categories (legal, punitive, merciful), all views emphasize the treatment aspects of probation. In the literature

---

[38] Murphy, "Training For and On the Job," *Yearbook, Nat'l Probation and Parole Ass'n* 93–108 (1938).

reviewed only five percent of the writers thought of probation wholly as a legal disposition or as a measure of either punishment or leniency. In fact, in the literature of the past thirty years such views receive no mention at all. Therefore, notions of probation as either casework or administration, or a combination of the two, are prominent. These leading approaches overlap considerably so that their differentiation consists almost solely in their respective points of emphasis. Thus, all three would agree that probation is a legal disposition and that probation is not to be thought of as mere leniency or as mere punishment; but in the first instance, it is viewed as basically casework treatment; in the second, administrative supervision; and in the third, both of these. Each, however, contains elements of the other. So in all cases probation is seen as a social as well as a legal process, as a method of supervision and guidance in which all available community resources are used, and as a process which should aim at the total adjustment of the offender. The casework approach overshadows the rest by far, so that in phrasing a composite definition derived from the literature it should receive its obvious prominence.

As culled from the professional literature, then, probation may be thought of as the application of modern, scientific casework to specially selected offenders[39] who are placed by the courts under the personal supervision of a probation officer, sometimes under conditional suspension of punishment, and given treatment aimed at their complete and permanent social rehabilitation.

Probation in Reality

What is depicted in the literature does not often represent a very real or accurate representation of what exists in reality. The result of abject worship at the holy shrine of psychoanalysis has not been the development of scientifically validated techniques for the treatment of offenders on probation.[40] In fact, few probation officers, either in the literature or in the field, give a clear and specific description of what they mean by treatment, casework or otherwise. Probation officers, whether trained in schools of social work or not, frequently express the opinion that just about anything that is done in the way of investigation of cases, bringing into play any of the skills one may have acquired in training or by his experiences, comes under the heading of casework treatment. This would include any service, advice, counseling, or surveillance.

Undoubtedly part of the difficulty lies in the fact that the field of social work seems to have no well-defined and consistent theory which it can call its

[39]It is standard practice to accept for probation only those offenders whose cases have been investigated and found to meet the requirements of favorable prognosis set up by the individual courts. Therefore, offenders placed on probation may be thought of as specially selected.

[40]See Cressey, "The Nature and Effectiveness of Correctional Techniques," 23 *Law & Contemp. Prob.* 754–771 (1958).

own. Casework can mean anything from "working with an offender" to helping a "client" to "grow" or to achieve insight, helping him to help himself, a form of therapy, or a "method which recognizes the individual's inner capacity as to the key to his adjustment, and the necessity of his participating in the process of rehabilitation."[41]

How these things are accomplished, however, is rarely specified except in terms of an *administrative* process. So the probation officer will be told, ideally, that he must have a plan of treatment, that his attitude toward the offender must be non-punitive, and that he will try to "win the confidence" of the probationer and overcome the resistance of parents, or of husband or wife, as the case may be. The constructive kind of relationship that the probation officer thus aims for apparently is to be gained through frequent and periodic contacts at the office of the probation officer or at the offender's home or even school, in the case of a juvenile. In addition, the probation officer will be acquainted with most, if not all, of the resources of the community and will hold frequent conferences with the offender's employer, school principal, teacher, or school social worker and refer the offender to any one of a number of other agencies which might help him on his road to readjustment.

It is interesting, then, to compare such a description of probation as case-work treatment with what probation officers actually do. At the Juvenile Court of Allegheny County in Pittsburgh, Pennsylvania, it was found that more than half the probation officers did active work with only thirty to forty percent of their caseload. Even if telephone conversations and correspondence with an offender, members of his family, and others are counted as contacts, sixty-four percent of the staff had fewer than six contacts with a child over a period of one year.[42] As a matter of fact more than half the probation officers considered that the most important part of their work consisted of their contacts with a child and others during the investigation period prior to the hearing.

Half of the probation officers reported they did no planning on *any* of their cases, one-fourth indicated that they approached from five to ten percent of their caseload with a plan in mind, and the remaining fourth said this was true in forty to fifty percent of their cases. Thirty-five percent of the probation staff felt that many of the children under their supervision at any one time could probably get along *without any* probation service at all, and ninety-five percent felt that some of the children under their supervision could adjust without it.

It is fairly certain that most probation, however it may be conceived in the literature or in the field, still amounts to little more than administrative supervision. But in order to compare the views of the professional personnel represented in the literature with the views of those whose work actually determines what is probation, I asked twenty of the most experienced probation

[41] Taber, *op. cit. supra* note 19.

[42] All the figures and information in this section were obtained from the Juvenile Court, Pittsburgh, Pa., in 1951, when the author was a probation officer of the court.

officers from eight courts, including officers both trained and not trained in schools of social work, to write me their answers to the following questions:

1. How would you define probation? Generally speaking, of what does it consist in practice?
2. Is casework an essential part of probation? If so, how would you define casework?
3. What are the aims of probation?
4. What do you believe probation *should* be ideally?

The following are the verbatim replies to question (1) which I received:

1. Probation is a kind of status the child obtains as a result of the court hearing.
2. Probation is a suspended sentence to begin with, as a basis for providing supervision. In practice it is a continuation of a suspended case, to see if the child does all right. There is no intention of doing anything, though most probation officers won't admit it. Probation is putting a threat over the head of a child. Authority puts weight back of probation. You can see this with our success with neglected and delinquent cases which other agencies have given up. We're the policemen back of the agencies.
3. What it simmers down to is police work. There is no planning, but giving supervision to prevent violations or repetition of delinquent behavior.
4. Probation is an instrument of the court. The child is under the jurisdiction of the court. There are certain areas in which he is expected to function in a certain way. This consists of periodic reports made by the youngster or his family to the probation officer, or the probation officer's contacts with the family and the child, or any collateral contacts, the purpose of the contacts being to determine the child's ability to adjust in the community and to offer additional assistance in a supportive way to help the child adjust.
5. Probation is to help instill in a boy enough confidence in himself to make an adjustment in society, with the knowledge that he can always call on the probation officer for information and advice when needed.
6. Probation consists of the contacts which a probation officer has with a boy after the court hearing. It is also supervision to see how the boy adjusts in the home and the community. Through probation we try to select what boys have to abide by and to explain to them the negative and the positive sides of a situation, explaining limitations and the need to face them.
7. Probation means that the court feels that whatever a child has done he can adjust at home under the supervision of his parents. We look the parents and the home over and decide whether they can handle the supervision. The probation officer merely gives support to that supervision, like a doctor who prescribes. He isn't going to go to your home and make you take the medicine, but if he feels the patient needs to go to the hospital, he goes.
8. Probation is comparable to commitment; that is, it is handled through a court order. But it is not leniency. Probation can be as severe as commitment. Probation is not only law but also a mutual relationship in which we are trying to get children to accept limits.
9. Probation is a period of time during which a child is expected to realize he has made a mistake and that he must be careful to avoid repetition while he is on probation. This realization may or may not be with the help of the probation officer.
10. Probation is using the material brought out by investigation, the causes as

well as the effects of antisocial or asocial behavior on the part of delinquents brought to the court. It is taking that and trying to determine from it the particular mores or standards that have been operating in the growing period of the delinquent and trying to arrive at standards or mores which will fit that child and his family and be satisfactory to society, and using all these in a plan thought best in terms of adjustment.

Probation is not something which comes after the court hearing. When a child becomes known to us, he is thought of as being on probation. There is no reason to wait for the hearing. We try to work with a child as soon as we get him. Finally, probation can only be successful if the basic family make-up is considered. What caused a child to be delinquent must be changed.

11. Primarily we are a court of rehabilitation when it comes to the delinquent. When we put a child on probation we are saying to him, "You have run afoul of the rules of society and this is the court's offer to you to try to prove you can live in society without continuing that type of behavior. It is not only probation on the part of the child but also on the part of the parents, because adult behavior often lies behind a child's behavior. The child has to show he no longer needs supervision other than his own family.

12. Probation has a Latin derivation and means the act or process of giving a chance or trial. It is comparable to repairing damage done to an automobile. You repair it and give it another trial rather than let it run in its poor condition.

13. Probation is the period after a child has been brought to the court's attention as a result of a behavior problem. During this period there is an opportunity to see whether, with the help of the worker, his attitudes and activities can be reorganized so that he can make a better adjustment and conduct himself in a more acceptable manner.

It is a two-way thing. It is not just a period. The child must have someone interested in him, to guide him. Interviews with him may be of a general nature or be related to his specific behavior.

14. Probation is working with a child and his family on the problems presented at the court hearing. For the worker it is almost the role of confidant and adviser.

15. Probation is a helping service to a person with a problem. The problem itself may be adjusted or the person is helped to make an adjustment to the problem. Probation is also a means of keeping in touch with a person in order to prevent further difficulty.

16. Probation has its legal aspects. But it is also helping a child adjust to society and its requirements, which is the chief aim of probation. It should be a constructive experience.

17. Probation is helping a child fit into the school, home and community, fitting him into their standards.

18. In practice probation consists in meeting emergencies as they arise instead of routine treatment, which time doesn't allow.

19. When a child comes to the court and a problem is presented, you are not putting him on probation for punishment but to find causes and remedies. Probation means not only working with a child but also considering all the surrounding factors.

20. Probation is helping the individual to adjust. You utilize your own skills and the community resources within the scope and functions of the agency.

Only one of the above statements mentions the idea that punishment is even an aspect of probation, and the concept of leniency is omitted by all twenty probation officers, though it is implied by some. Four offer a partly legal definition, while none specifically presents the view that probation is essentially either an administrative process or a combination of administrative and casework. Partly this may be attributed to the fact that most personnel in the field probably do not express themselves in the same way as do professional authors who are not primarily workers but administrators and teachers. In this respect perhaps the most significant thing of all is the fact that, although certain cliches appear, *in not one definition is casework itself mentioned.* Yet in reply to the second question, "Is casework an essential part of probation?", fourteen probation officers gave an unqualified *yes.* Five of the others felt casework was essential to probation but limited time precluded its use. Only one answered *no.*

Definitions of casework itself were even more general and vague than the definitions of probation. The explanation which was offered most contained such phrases as "helping people to help themselves," "helping a person make an adjustment," "changing a person's attitudes," "establishing a mutual relationship," "working with a person," and "the ability to work with people." Sixteen of the twenty responses fell into such a classification. Two probation officers felt probation *is* casework and that the definition of casework is about the same as the definition of probation. The remaining two expressed the opinion that almost anything that is done in the way of investigation of cases can be thought of as casework.

Obviously there is no consensus or standardization of opinion concerning probation among these twenty experienced workers, nor have they any clear conception of what casework is. I suspect such a situation is general.

When the aims of probation were considered, half the probation officers said the "total adjustment" of the offender was the chief goal. Five believed "complete rehabilitation" was the end pursued, and four thought that adjustment with respect to the particular problem presented was the purpose of probation. Only one officer stated that supervision alone was the real aim of probation. If the two terms "total adjustment" and "complete rehabilitation" are considered synonymous for all practical purposes, then fifteen of the twenty probation officers concurred on this, the highest goal of probation.

With respect to what probation *should* be, thirteen probation officers felt probation should consist of casework treatment. The remaining seven believed casework is not a general process and therefore should be applied only to those cases which indicate a need for that type of treatment. (Yet in answer to the second question all but one believed casework *is* essential to probation.)

It may well be that few correctional personnel are really aware of whatever techniques they use, and it is very highly probable that only a small percentage of the total are qualified caseworkers. It is also highly probable, and certainly seems to be the case from this writer's experience, that the image that many probation officers have of themselves is a picture of a warm and understanding though objective person, a kind of watered-down or embryonic clinician. In any event the influence of a clinical, casework ideology, along with its confused and contradictory elements, has been pervasive. Convention papers, the literature and supervisors are filled with this ideology, so that it is constantly before the probation officer. It is no more than could be expected, then, if the probation officer feels that whatever he does and however he does it, it *is* treatment.

CONCLUSION

A review of the literature reveals the predominance of the view that probation is a process of casework treatment, and this point of view seems to be shared by probation personnel in the field. However, casework is usually described in general, vague and nebulous language characterized by an abundance of cliches and a lack of clarity and specificity.

Seen from an operational point of view probation appears to be quite different from its ideal, casework conceptions. Probation varies from rare instances of intensive individual treatment, however defined, to simply noncommitment.

Actually, then, probation may be defined as a legal disposition which allows the offender his usual freedom during a period in which he is expected to refrain from unlawful behavior. Operationally, probation is primarily a process of verifying the behavior of an offender (1) through periodic reports of the offender and members of his family to the probation officer and (2) by the incidence or absence of adverse reports from the police and other agencies. Secondarily, probation is a process of guiding and directing the behavior of an offender by means of intensive interviewing utilizing ill-defined casework techniques.

Finally, it can be said that probation in practice is a gesture toward conformity to the school of thought which combines administrative and casework procedures. For the most part, however, probation remains an administrative function with the statement Healy and Bronner made thirty-four years ago still quite accurate: "probation is a term that gives no clue to what is done by way of treatment."[43]

---

[43]Healy and Bronner, *Delinquents and Criminals, Their Making and Unmaking*, 82 (New York, The Macmillan Co., 1926).

6

When Is Probation
Not Probation?

SANFORD BATES

The Courtroom was crowded with spectators, reporters, school students, and athletes, and the judge of the criminal court was holding what he called a "parole court." The defendant, a high school student, had been found guilty of a morals charge. A public hearing was being held to decide what should be done with him—whether he should receive a term in a jail or reformatory, or whether he should be placed on probation (referred to in this particular midwestern state as parole!). The defendant was a very tall young man and had been a valuable member of the school basketball team. The coach had appeared and had spoken earnestly in the hope that the young defendant could be placed on probation and thus save the team from the loss of an outstanding player. Other students spoke in the defendant's behalf. In arriving at its decision the court took note of those present and their views as to whether probation should be granted. They were overwhelmingly in favor of probation. The judge remarked in an aside that he considered the offense a very serious one and felt the defendant should receive a sentence to confinement but what could he do against the almost unanimous feeling of those present? And so probation was ordered.

What is wrong in this picture?

In the criminal court in another midwestern state a young boy had been placed on probation for indulging in narcotics. A condition of probation was

SOURCE. *Federal Probation*, XXIV, December 1960, pp. 13–20.

that he was to give up the habit. During probation the boy's father and mother came to the probation officer and informed him in confidence that their son had gone back to narcotics. They felt he ought to be taken into custody. The probation officer presented these facts to the court, but the judge declined to accept the recommendation of the probation officer, ordered the probation officer to produce the father and mother in court, put them under oath, and required them to testify before him in open court what they knew about the case.

What was wrong in this case?

A young woman social worker who had received a degree from a school of social work had accepted a position of probation officer in a large city court in the midwest. She attempted to keep in touch with her cases through correspondence, and by inviting them to come to her office if they had difficulties. If they did not come after receiving the first postal card she would send them another. When asked why she did not go to the homes and business places of her "clients" she replied that this would be embarrassing to the clients, that they could be more relaxed if they came to her quiet, clean, pleasant office. Most of her "cases" lived in humble dwellings and would be embarrassed or ashamed, she asserted, if she went to their homes.

Is there anything wrong with this attitude?

These and other problems were encountered in a recent survey conducted in 1955 and 1956 by the American Bar Association in selected western and midwestern states and financed by the Ford Foundation. The project consisted of an on-the-spot inquiry into criminal justice, including a study of court procedures, prosecution, sentencing practices, probation and parole, and police practices. Certain pilot states were selected. Situations were disclosed that even the stoutest advocates of probation would regard as disconcerting. The investigators were dismayed at the degree to which probation in actual operation had departed from the high ideals and standards which have characterized the probation movement. What was true in these states is probably true in many others. Unless those responsible for a sound and humanitarian application of probation are cognizant of these defects and take steps to remedy them, probation may become an obstacle to effective law enforcement. From time to time superficial studies have been made of the administration and effectiveness of probation and optimistic conclusions have been reached. Quite often these studies are made by those directly concerned with the development of probation and are constrained to believe that if probation is a good thing, the more probation one can have, the better. True, these studies have usually pointed out there were not enough probation officers, that their caseloads were too high and that they were not adequately trained to be counselors. But it was not until the American Bar Association survey that some of the basic difficulties in the administration of probation have been disclosed. Before commenting on the various practices and problems encountered in the states studied by the Survey it would be well to look back briefly into the history of the probation movement and the underlying philosophy of probation.

HISTORY AND PHILOSOPHY OF PROBATION

Probation started in my home state of Massachusetts back in 1841 when a bootmaker by the name of John Augustus induced the judges of the Boston police court to place certain petty offenders in his charge rather than in jail. The system in Massachusetts[1] developed into one of the best in the country under the guidance of Herbert C. Parsons and a central committee of judges who had steadfastly maintained high ideals in the practice of probation. Perhaps more than any other state in the country, Massachusetts has utilized probation and has kept down the institution population without any apparent increase in the crime rate.

Many contend that the introduction of the practice of placing minor offenders on probation marked the greatest single advance in humanitarian penology in this country. With the growth of population and the increase in the business of our criminal courts, it became evident that all of the convicted offenders could not be sent to jail or prison. To merely fine them—in many instances where there are indigent defendants—was tantamount to sending them to jail on a pretext. On the other hand, there were many cases, minor in nature, where the defendant had made an unfortunate slip, where he could not be found "not guilty" and it was not in the interest of good law enforcement to discharge him entirely. The idea of a suspended sentence was utilized by the courts in such cases but it was soon recognized that without followup procedure whereby the defendant so entrusted could be held accountable for his failure to stay out of trouble, that a suspended sentence was merely equivalent to discharge or a finding of not guilty.

Many courts were quick to see that the adoption of a system of such extramural discipline provided them with a third alternative—a plan under which an offender would be found guilty, admonished by the court, placed in the care of a competent probation officer with limitations on the defendant's conduct, and an obligation to support himself and his dependents. Such a plan met both the humanitarian demands of the situation and also offered the public a certain amount of protection. In fact, probation with the requirement to regulate one's conduct and to work steadily was considered by many defendants as a more onerous disposition than a short spell of idleness in a county jail. And so, this seemingly merciful disposition of minor and first offenders appealed particularly to the public and the demand for the increased use of probation grew rapidly.

Most administrators of penal and correctional institutions soon came to realize the damaging results to personalities from long confinement in prisons and have urged the utilization of both probation and parole as alternatives to prison wherever there is a reasonable probability of rehabilitation and society would not be exposed to undue risk or damage.

After more than 40 years of experience in the correctional field I am

[1]Massachusetts Acts, 1878, Chap. 198: An Act relative to placing on probation persons accused or convicted of crimes and misdemeanors in the county of Suffolk.

thoroughly convinced that, despite the sometimes faulty administration of probation in many jurisdictions, it has proved to be an indispensable element in our law-enforcement machinery.

Health is a good thing, and there are no limitations to better health. Education is an essential to democratic government and there are no bounds to the wisdom of extending educational opportunities to all of our people. Water is a good thing and, in fact, life would be impossible without a sufficient supply. Water out of control leads to disaster. Electricity, when understood and controlled and applied properly, constitutes a great boon to more comfortable living, but can become a destructive force. Probation, likewise, must be intelligently, discreetly, and discriminatingly applied or it may become merely a new name for leniency. The quality of probation is even more important than the scope of its application.

For a conscientious judge to utilize probation wisely, two essential elements must be present: First he must have at his command at the time of sentence of the defendant complete, accurate, reliable, and confidential information on which to base his decision. For a judge to merely guess whether the defendant should receive a sentence to confinement or be given a chance to prove his worth under probation supervision is almost as futile as to expect a physician to diagnose a case by mere observation. We shall come back to the importance and place of the presentence study and report later.

In the second place, if the judge is to do more than merely discharge the defendant, place his case on file, or give him a suspended sentence, he must have the personnel facilities that can make probation something more than keeping records, collecting fines and restitution, or admonitions by the judge. Only skilled and competent persons can effectively serve both as guidance counselors and law-enforcement officers. In a very recent issue of the *Journal of Criminal Law, Criminology, and Police Science* Thorsten Sellin[2] makes the point that the name "probation" should be reserved for that type of counseling and guidance which is assumed to be present but which is often entirely absent. If probation were only a means of enforcing a condition or collecting a fine, Sellin infers, it could be operated by a clerk or a cash register much less expensively than to require college graduates.

DISCLOSURES OF THE BAR ASSOCIATION SURVEY

Probation is not a process which once imposed by the court operates automatically. Probation demands intelligent, courageous, and far-seeing skill and oversight by specially trained and experienced personnel. Probation should be used only in carefully selected cases. It should not be used where supervision is superficial and unintelligent. Even the most enthusiastic advocate of probation will admit this.

The American Bar Association survey reveals that probation is improperly

[2]March-April 1959, p. 553.

administered in many jurisdictions, and that its application is not in accordance with the basic principles underlying the selection and supervision of persons in the free community. In many instances probation is used as a device for the control of the probationer which has little or no association with the basic function of probation—the protection of society through the rehabilitation of the offender. Following are some of the problems in administration, questionable probation practices, and limitations observed in the survey.

1. PROBATION IS GRANTED WITHOUT SUFFICIENT KNOWLEDGE OF THE DEFENDANT AND HIS BACKGROUND. In one city in a large trial court, more than half of the defendants placed on probation did not have the benefit of a formal presentence report. In the case referred to at the opening of this article, there had been no skillful, thorough study of the young man whose future was at stake. As a matter of fact, there were no probation officers in that court, perhaps because the court knew that probation, as practiced there would not meet acceptable standards. The judge even declined to call it probation, but referred to it habitually as "bench parole!"

No physician would undertake to prescribe treatment for a sick man unless he had a full report of his ailment and condition. In like manner a judge should not pass judgment on a defendant without a presentence report even though he may be skeptical of the ability of social workers or probation officers to give him competent advice and counsel. And if he does not have the staff to render this service, he should see to it that the legislature or the county authorities provide it for him.

Instances of miscarriage of justice as to guilt or innocence are few. During the course of the trial rules of evidence must be respected. Neither hearsay nor prejudiced statements are permitted. The single objective during the course of the trial is to determine whether the defendant committed the act with which he is charged.

But there may be numerous instances of miscarriage of justice in the nature of the sentence imposed. Should the defendant be sentenced to confinement? Should it be a long sentence or a short sentence? Should the place of incarceration be a place of "infamous punishment" or in a jail or house of correction? Or should the defendant be placed on probation from the point of view of both the defendant's reformability and the protection of the public? All of these considerations depend on information which is not admissible in the trial. The sentencing function of the court is perhaps the most difficult function he has to perform. Thus the judge must rely on a comprehensive, objective, informative presentence investigation report which will throw light on the prospect of the defendant being rehabilitated under probation supervision.

2. PRESENTENCE REPORTS LACK OBJECTIVITY. It is not uncommon in some courts to find an absence of presentence reports. In some instances, however, the investigators found that presentence reports were definitely slanted to help confirm a hasty decision which the court might have rendered in considering probation and, in a few cases, out of deference to an aggressive lawyer employed by the defendant. It goes without saying that if the court is to place

reliance upon a presentence report it must be totally objective and contain the uncontrolled and impartial facts in the case.

3. PRESENTENCE REPORTS NOT TREATED AS CONFIDENTIAL INFORMATION. Obviously, a presentence investigation report takes into account the community aspects and personal and family background of the defendant. It goes far beyond the facts which relate to the offense and the question of guilt. Information regarding the character, personality, and habits of the defendant as well as statements from his friends, neighbors, and employers, often are not the subject of forensic discussion and should be treated in strict confidence. These facts, nevertheless, are of vital importance in the treatment program, either in prison or while on probation. One state, at least, contrary to the generally accepted requirement of confidentiality in presentence reports, provides that the counsel for the defendant shall have the right to see the report. In one of the states studied by the American Bar Foundation Survey, the judge reserves the right to quote certain portions of the presentence report in open court.

If the confidential information in the presentence report is open to challenge and dispute by the convicted defendant and his counsel, what effect will it have on the decision rendered by the court? Will the probation officer, thereafter, be able to obtain pertinent information if informants know they are to be challenged in court and subjected to reprisals? On the other hand, should not the defendant have an opportunity to challenge or refute any statements in the report which may be damaging to him and deprive him of his liberty? Whether he goes to prison or remains in the free community under probation supervision is of special concern to him. What is the relative importance of giving the defendant, on the one hand, the right to challenge or dispute statements in the presentence report and allowing the judge, on the other hand, to render a disposition that is fair not only to the defendant and his family, but also to the community at large? For some in the field of probation this is a moot question. To what extent should the confidentiality of the presentence investigation report be respected?

4. DETERMINATION OF SENTENCE SOMETIMES MADE A PUBLIC SPECTACLE. The problem of whether probation should be granted in the full glare of publicity or in private with just those few present who are concerned with the case, is one of increasing significance. In some of the courts studied the entire discussion about the case and the possible sentence is held in the judge's chambers and the announcement of the disposition is made in the courtroom. In the case cited at the beginning of this article the judge sought by vote the expressions of all those present in the courtroom to assist him in determining whether the man should go to prison or on "parole" (probation). It is a shocking experience to those who believe that the grant or denial of probation is one which requires specialized knowledge and information and to see that probation is being granted or denied in accordance with a vote in the courtroom of persons who usually constitute those who are friendly to the defendant.

5. IMPROPER USE OF PROBATION.   In two of the states studied probation was being utilized for other purposes than to protect society and to rehabilitate the offender. In these courts probation was used to clear the court docket, to induce the defendant to plead guilty, or to alleviate the crowded conditions in the prisons.

A hopeless congestion had developed in the criminal courts of one of the large counties. A special judge was given the task of clearing it up. He did so by the simple expedient of placing practically every defendant on probation. Since there were no probation counselors in that state and no adequate record of how persons fare on probation, no one knows to what extent clearing of the dockets in this wholesale fashion effected crime in the county in question.

In many instances in the two states the prosecuting attorney, or even the court, would let the defense attorney gather the impression that if his client pleaded guilty there would be a grant of probation. In a few cases observed by the Survey investigators, the judge participated in a conference with the prosecutor, the defense attorney, and possibly the probation officer if there was one. There may well have been a reasonable doubt as to the guilt of the defendant, but under pressure from the court and perhaps the prodding of his own counsel, and also because he did not want to run the risk of a conviction even though he felt he was innocent, the defendant would plead guilty. Then the district attorney would recommend probation and the court would so order. Thus, the trial of one more case was avoided and the heavy trial docket was reduced by one, even though there was no presentence investigation to support the grant or denial of probation or to help the court decide whether the defendant was a likely prospect for probation. Here, also, no conclusive study has been made as to what effect this practice may have on the future conduct of cases disposed of in this manner or the community's attitude toward law enforcement.

In some cases the judge in his consideration of whether a defendant should be placed on probation, was heard to remark that while the court might be in doubt as to the wisdom of such a move, the state prisons were greatly over-crowded and that this fact weighed heavily in favor of probation.

6. PROBATION USED AS A DEVICE TO COLLECT MONEY.   Probation was ordered in many instances to secure the payment of fines and restitution with little or no thought given to the need for guidance and assistance. If the probationer payed the amounts ordered for alimony, fine or restitution, he was in good standing and no question was asked as to how he got his money or how his relationships with his family and his employer were progressing. In numerous cases in which the Survey investigator listened in, a probationer would be called in, taken before the court and asked: "Why didn't you pay the money" or "When can you do better?" One might argue that the man who conscientiously meets his obligations is on the road to rehabilitation. Either because of tremendous caseloads or the inability of the probation officer to render effective guidance, the objective of probation seemed to be "pay the

money—or else." As Professor Sellin says, it is naïve to employ college graduates as collecting agents.

7. Cost of Probation Charged to the Defendant.   In one large trial court it is the practice to tax the defendant for the cost of probation! He gets out of it fairly easily in one jurisdiction where he merely pays a $3 initiation fee for membership in the A.O.P.—Anxious Order of Probationers! And the chances are he will never be bothered by anyone after that. In another court he must pay his share of the cost of the probation system. This is determined by dividing the total cost of probation the previous year by the anticipated number of cases during the current year. This figures out to about $50, so in many instances the first and only obligation of the probationers in that court is that they pay his share of $50. Often he has not the $50, especially if he had a lawyer. So he is accepted for probation with the strict injunction that he had better pay up.

To provide for collecting from probationers the cost of probation, a statute was enacted granting the court the authority to include the costs of probation in the costs of court. Here, again, there appeared many times to be little or no interest on the part of the probation office as to where the money came from. So anxious was the state to collect the money, the court would prolong the period of probation—in some instances even beyond the legal statutory limit of probation—to give the probationer a chance to earn, beg, or borrow, the money to keep the slate clean!

Taxing the probationer for the costs of probation is a convenient device for the court. The judges have been heard to tell the public that probation was a great invention and then give some highly improbable statistics as to the number of persons who have been rehabilitated. They would then climax their support of probation with the remark: "The best of it all is that it doesn't cost the county a penny because the probationers are taxed for the cost."

Consider the plight of a probationer who is made to pay the costs of probation, perhaps even to the neglect of his family and other obligations. He pays for the guidance and help which probation should offer, but he does not get it!

8. Probation Officer Plays a Dwindling Role.   The role of the probation officer as a trained, intelligent, industrious, and responsible officer of the court and our system of criminal justice has been minimized in some of the jurisdictions studied by the Survey. Traditionally the probation officer maintained a role comparable in some respects, to that of the warden of the institution to which the probationer might have been committed. In the courts in question the probation officer at one time had been given a chance to present his presentence investigation report to the court and discuss the case with the judge. If probation were granted the defendant was literally placed in charge of the probation officer who had authority similar to that of the head of an institution. The probationer was under the authority and control of the probation officer.

In one large court the probation officer himself rarely discussed his cases with the court. In the event of a serious violation he made his report to a supervisor but was greatly hampered because of the realization that he would be cross-examined on his report and that his authority over the probationer would be challenged or even denied by the court itself. Unless the probation officer can act as a man of decision and authority, as well as understanding, his supervision efforts will be minimized or even jeopardized. A number of probation officers seen by the Survey's investigators expressed the feeling that the authority they once possessed as officers of the court had dwindled and that they were reluctant to use their authority lest they be overruled by the court. Whether the trend today is to extend and amplify the rights and privileges of the accused under our Constitution is not the entire question. What concerns some of us is whether probation in some jurisdictions is losing its character as a law-enforcement activity and whether it is essential that each time where there is a violation of probation, another forensic battle is called for—a second, or third, or fourth court hearing with counsel—and that someday even a jury may be panelled.

9. SUPERVISION IS NEGLECTED.   As previously stated, the two elements of effective probation are careful selection through the use of reliable and complete presentence investigation reports followed by intelligent, understanding, and authoritative supervision. Without the latter, probation is nothing more than leniency—an entry "case filed" or "suspended sentence" would suffice.

The extent to which effective and intelligent supervision is being employed in the states studied by the Survey is disappointing. In one state, for example, an effective probation system was being developed under the State Department of Welfare, but there was a clash between the permissive school and the authoritative school of supervision. In another state there was practically no supervision. In one large court rarely was a presentence investigation made. It was this court where the court crier or the bailiff merely enrolled the probationer in the A.O.P. "club," took his $3, and wished him luck.

In one county a juvenile court probation officer, with more than 140 cases under supervision, said that his supervision consisted largely of waiting to see if any of his wards got arrested. He would then locate them and find out what they did. In one case, he was gone 3 weeks and left his caseload with the deputy sheriff while he was away!

In many instances heavy caseloads, court pressures, office inquiries left but little time for supervision and practically none for guidance counseling. The more practical members of the staff made occasional rounds, said hello to the probationer's family, asked how the probationer was, and told him not to forget to pay his costs! This lack of professional service and relationships— one of the basic elements in probation—together with the loss of authority and status on the part of the probation officer, will have a detrimental effect on probation.

10. TENDENCY TO OVERLOOK LAW-ENFORCEMENT ROLE OF THE PROBATION OFFICER.   Probation and parole authorities throughout the country have looked rather hopefully toward the professionally-trained social worker to undertake the rough and tumble work of probation and parole supervision. In one state a master's degree in social work is required, but the quick answer is

that it has not worked. A graduate of a school of social work does not like this kind of occupation and the result is that a more "practical" man does not see eye to eye with the social worker and the social worker does not appreciate his point of view. The social worker's approach is that "permissiveness" is the order of the day and that authority should be submerged. The social worker seeks to modify or improve the conduct of the client and the conditions surrounding him, through his personality. He respects the dignity of that personality and does not attempt to threaten nor lead him, but to show him the wisdom and advantage of seeking to improve himself and the situations surrounding him. How successful this approach has been in work with those who transgress the law has yet to be determined. This approach certainly is in accord with our American concept of democracy. No matter how unfortunate a person may be or how deeply involved he is in a delinquent pattern, we all hope he has within him the capacity to improve. But we must keep in mind that probation is not only social work but also a part of the community's law-enforcement efforts. A probation officer may thoroughly understand the principles underlying social work, but he also must remember that he is a law-enforcement officer and on occasion this authority must be invoked.

Take the case of the young woman social worker referred to earlier. She felt she could "identify" better with the client in her office. There may be something to that, but the practical probation officer would feel that it was highly significant that he must not only identify with the probationer, but also with his home, his community, and his associates, and that if he is going to do an effective job in diverting a probationer from a criminal career, to keep him from bad associates and a bad environment, he will have to get as close as he possibly can to both the probationer and his milieu.

Another example was noted, although in this instance it was a parolee rather than a probationer. The parolee was arrested for having a revolver in his car and was held in custody by the police. The parole officer argued with the police that he had set up a good relationship with his parolee, that he was sure that he was not intending to use the revolver for any criminal purpose, that he had a collection of firearms—antiques, so to speak—and therefore urged that the parolee be released and restored to parole supervision. The police were a bit obdurate and called the parole officer's attention to the fact that the parolee not only had a gun in the car, but also a box of bullets, and that they both were hidden where they could not be readily discovered. This example poses the question to what extent is a friendly and intelligent social worker able to convince himself that this was an unimportant breach of parole regulations. To what extent can the confiscation of the gun and the bullets be regarded as the prevention of another crime, and the disciplining of the parolee in the interest of good law enforcement?

I do not mean to imply that these two view points are irreconcilable. Undoubtedly the social worker will learn much from the person not trained in casework skills, and the latter, in turn, may develop respect for persons who have casework training.

A number of articles have been published in recent years on casework in an authoritarian setting. Professor Donald R. Cressey[3] has tried to point out the distinct character of correctional work, suggesting that it has a professional tinge of its own and that one does not achieve professional status in correctional work merely by being a professionally-trained caseworker. Dale G. Hardman has written two challenging articles on the importance of authority in correctional work.[4]

The extent to which the somewhat conflicting points of view of the social worker and the correctional worker effect the law-enforcement responsibilities of probation is still conjectural.

11. INADEQUATE STATISTICS. The American Bar Foundation's Survey reaffirms the impression of previous investigators that the lack of reliable and comparable statistics in the field of probation and parole is appalling. How can one expect to improve or test or evaluate probation without authentic, adequate statistics? On the basis of unreliable statistics we have been making predictions and hopeful assertions as to the value and wisdom of probation. Not more than a handful of states—Massachusetts, Wisconsin, California, and New York—have made any real attempt to collect and interpret probation data. In most states a defendant may appear before a court on Monday and the court would not know he had been in court in another county on the previous Friday.

In one of the states studied the public had frequently been reassured by the statement that only 3 percent of all probationers had failed on probation. A more careful study disclosed that in many cases failures were not classified as such, and that only those probationers who had been brought back to court and adjudged as violators were counted as failures. Those not counted as failures were absconders, those who had turned up in another court, and those who had been discharged with a "without improvement" entry on the docket. The American Bar Foundation's investigators found that the failure rate was closer to 33 percent when all categories were included in the computation.

I have urged the National Probation and Parole Association, now the National Council on Crime and Delinquency, to do what the National Association of Chiefs of Police did in 1931 when they prepared and promulgated uniform and comparable statistical data, and that they also develop definitions as to what constitutes success, failure, and improvement. Such definitions have never been established. Only when this is done can we determine whether probation is properly administered and the extent to which probationers make successful adjustments during probation and after the completion of probation.

[3]"Professional Correctional Work and Professional Work in Correction," *NPPA Journal* January 1959, p. 1.
[4]"Authority in Casework—A Bread-and-Butter Theory," *NPPA Journal*, July 1959, p. 249, and "The Constructive Use of Authority," *Crime and Delinquency*, July 1960, p. 245.

WHEN DOES ANOTHER CHANCE BECOME NEGLECT?

As we uncover the problems and questionable practices relating to probation and parole we are faced with the question as to what extent probationers and parolees should be given a second, even a third chance, and to what extent such considerations are, in the long run, inconsistent with law enforcement and protection of the public. There are many instances where a juvenile delinquent headed for a criminal career, after one or more chances, has been helped to become a law-abiding citizen. But how much positive knowledge do we have as to when another chance—call it "leniency" if you will—becomes neglect and at what point the incipient offender, as a result, continues in a criminal pattern. Probation, and to a greater extent parole, have had an uphill fight to be accepted as integral parts of our system of criminal justice. The fact that they have been so recognized is all to the good and reflects the desires of a humanitarian civilization that its citizens be rehabilitated wherever possible. But some of the attitudes and practices to which I have referred, such as an increasing emphasis on the rights and privileges of the individual offender, a second trial, claim of counsel, forensic proof of his dereliction, seem to be on the increase. Somewhere, somehow a thorough, searching study should be made to determine whether the increasing tendency toward leniency has any relation to the upward trend of crime and delinquency in the United States. In all likelihood an impartial survey would disclose more valid explanations for the increase of crime in our country than that which suggests that the increase in crime is the result of "another chance" based on an intelligent and systematic selection of persons for probation.

I wish to make it clear that nothing in this article is to be construed as an attack on the basic principles of probation. The fact that we have no room in our jails and prisons for all convicted persons may have a bearing, but there is a more basic reason—that is, that a prison with its abnormal environment should still be regarded as a last resort and that only those persons for whom all other rehabilitative efforts have failed should be sent there. Alternatives to imprisonment such as fines, restitution, suspended sentences, probation, labor camps, requittal of service, and temporary sentences comparable to "day-parole" under Wisconsin's Huber Act should be considered. The thesis of this article is that the humanitarian efforts which characterize probation are too essential a part of our system of criminal justice to be stigmatized and injured by its hasty, unwise, and improvident application. There are still too many critics who cling to the belief that swift and sure punishment is the only cure for crime. Our communities should therefore make all the more certain that probation retains its original and primary function of rehabilitation and authoritarian control.

7

The Presentence Investigation Report

ADMINISTRATIVE OFFICE, UNITED STATES COURTS

ITS FUNCTIONS AND OBJECTIVES

The presentence investigation report is a basic working document in judicial and correctional administration. It performs five functions: (1) to aid the court in determining the appropriate sentence, (2) to assist Bureau of Prisons institutions in their classification and treatment programs and also in their release planning, (3) to furnish the Board of Parole with information pertinent to its consideration of parole, (4) to aid the probation officer in his rehabilitative efforts during probation and parole supervision,[1] and (5) to serve as a source of pertinent information for systematic research.

The primary objective of the presentence report is to focus light on the character and personality of the defendant, to offer insight into his problems and needs, to help understand the world in which he lives, to learn about his relationships with people, and to discover those salient factors that underlie his specific offense and his conduct in general. It is not the purpose of the report to demonstrate the guilt or the innocence of the defendant.

Authorities in the judicial and correctional fields assert that a presentence investigation should be made in every case. With the aid of a presentence report

SOURCE. *The Presentence Investigation Report*, Division of Probation, Administrative Office of the United States Courts, Washington, D.C., U.S. Government Printing Office, pp. 1–21. (Editorial Adaptations.)

[1] The Federal probation officer also supervises persons released from Federal correctional institutions and the U.S. Disciplinary Barracks.

the court may avoid committing a defendant to an institution who merits probation instead, or may avoid granting probation when confinement is appropriate.

Probation cannot succeed unless care is exercised in selecting those who are to receive its benefits. The presentence report is an essential aid in this selective process.

The probation officer has the important task of gathering information about the defendant; evaluating, assimilating, and interpreting the data; and presenting them in a logically organized, readable, objective report. Each defendant should be investigated without any preconception or prejudgment on the probation officer's part as to the outcome of the defendant's case.

The probation officer must be completely objective and impartial in conducting the investigation and in writing the presentence report. He not only reports the tangible facts in the case, but also such subjective elements as the defendant's attitudes, feelings, and emotional reactions. He presents them so as to give to the court an accurate, unbiased, and complete picture of the defendant and his prospects for becoming a law-abiding, responsible citizen. Every effort must be made to check the accuracy of information which is likely to be damaging to the defendant or to have a definite bearing on the welfare of the family and the safety of the community.

OUTLINE, CONTENTS, AND FORMAT OF THE REPORT

IDENTIFYING INFORMATION

The following identifying information is requested on Probation Form No. 2, the first page of all presentence reports.

DATE. Give the date the presentence report is typed.

NAME. Enter the name of the defendant as shown on the court record. Also insert the true name, if different, and any aliases.

ADDRESS. Give the present home address.

LEGAL RESIDENCE. Give the legal residence (county and State) if different from the present home address. Otherwise insert "Same."

AGE AND DATE OF BIRTH. Give the age on last birthday and the date of birth. Use the symbol "ver." when verified by an official source.

SEX.

RACE. Race is determined by ancestry; e.g., white, Negro, American Indian, etc. It should not be confused with national origin.

CITIZENSHIP. Give name of country. Citizenship refers to the country of which the defendant is a subject or citizen.

EDUCATION. Give highest grade achieved.

MARITAL STATUS. Single, married, widow, widower, divorced, legally separated, common law.

DEPENDENTS. List those entirely dependent on the defendant for support; e.g., "Three (wife and two children)."

PROBATION FORM **2**
FEB 65

UNITED STATES DISTRICT COURT

Eastern District of Michigan

PRESENTENCE REPORT

NAME   John Jones

ADDRESS   1234 Beach Street
                 Detroit, Michigan 48201

LEGAL RESIDENCE   Same

AGE 38   DATE OF BIRTH   8–25–26
                                          (ver.)

SEX Male   RACE White

CITIZENSHIP   United States

EDUCATION   High School

MARITAL STATUS   Married

DEPENDENTS   Four (wife and three
                        children)

SOC. SEC. NO.   000–11–2222

FBI NO.   678910

DATE   October 14, 1964

DOCKET NO.   56971

OFFENSE   Possession of
                 Distilled Spirits
                 26 U.S.C. 5686(b)

PENALTY $5,000 or 1 year,
                 or both

PLEA   Guilty, 2–14–64

VERDICT

CUSTODY   Personal Bond

ASST. U.S. ATTY.   James E. Carver

DEFENSE COUNSEL

Thomas Flanigan
781 Cadillac Tower
(Court Appointed)

DETAINERS OR CHARGES PENDING: None

CODEFENDANTS *(Disposition)*   Case of Robert Allen pending

DISPOSITION

DATE

SENTENCING JUDGE

SOCIAL SECURITY NO.
FBI NO.
DOCKET NO.
OFFENSE.   Give a brief statement, including statutory citation; e.g., "Theft of Mail (18 U.S.C. 1708)."
PENALTY.   Insert statutory penalty for the specific offense. This should be

obtained from the U.S. attorney in each instance. The probation officer should not attempt to state the penalty on the basis of his knowledge.

PLEA.   Nature and date.

VERDICT.   Date.

CUSTODY.   Give status (summons, personal or surety bond, recognizance, jail) and period in jail.

ASSISTANT U.S. ATTORNEY.   Give name of the assistant U.S. attorney handling the case.

DEFENSE COUNSEL.   Give name and address. When appointed by court, this should be indicated.

DETAINERS OR CHARGES PENDING.   Give the name and address of the office issuing the detainer or preferring the charge. Also give the dates action was taken.

CODEFENDANTS.   Enter the names of codefendants, if any, and status of their respective cases. If there are no codefendants, insert "None."

The following information, below the double rule on form 2, is inserted after the final disposition of the case:

DISPOSITION.   Sentence imposed by the court.

DATE.   Date of sentence.

SENTENCING JUDGE.

Presentence Report Outline

The presentence report outline adopted by the Judicial Conference Committee on the Administration of the Probation System on February 11, 1965, consists of the following marginal headings and the respective subheadings:

OFFENSE

        Official version
        Statement of codefendants
        Statement of witnesses, complainants, and victims

DEFENDANTS VERSION OF OFFENSE

PRIOR RECORD

FAMILY HISTORY

        Defendant
        Parents and siblings

MARITAL HISTORY

HOME AND NEIGHBORHOOD

EDUCATION

RELIGION

INTERESTS AND LEISURE-TIME ACTIVITIES

HEALTH

        Physical
        Mental and emotional

EMPLOYMENT

MILITARY SERVICE

FINANCIAL CONDITION
      Assets
      Financial obligations
EVALUATIVE SUMMARY
RECOMMENDATION

In each presentence report the probation officer should follow the title and exact sequence of these headings.

The suggested contents for the marginal headings are given starting on this page. The items listed under *Essential Data* are those which should appear in *all* presentence reports. Those listed under *Optional Data* will appear in many reports, depending on their significance in the particular case. Each probation officer will determine which of the optional data are essential for the respective defendants under study and how each is to be treated.

In writing the report the probation officer need not follow the sequence of the *essential* and *optional* items. This may prove awkward, hinder readability, disrupt the trend of thought, and obstruct the logical development of the subject matter in question. He will have to shape the general content of the report according to the requirements of each case.

Offense

OFFICIAL VERSION
    Essential Data:
        Nature and date of plea or verdict.
        Brief summary of indictment or information, including number of counts, period covered, and nature, date(s), and place(s) of offense.
        Extent of property or monetary loss.
        Extent of defendant's profit from crime.
        Aggravating and extenuating circumstances.
        Nature and status of other pending charges.
        Days held in jail.
        Reasons for inability to divert (juvenile cases).
    Optional Data:
        Date and place of arrest.
        Circumstances leading to arrest.
        Statement of arresting officers.
        Attitude of defendant toward arresting officers.
        Degree of cooperation.
        Where detained prior to trial or sentence.
        Amount of bond.
        Extent to which offense follows patterns of previous offenses.
        Relation of offense to organized crime or racket.
        Amount of loss recovered.
        Has full or partial restitution been made.
        Other violations involved in addition to those charged.

STATEMENT OF CODEFENDANTS

Essential Data:
  Extent of their participation in offense.
  Present status of their case.

Optional Data:
  Attitude toward offense.
  Attitude toward defendant.
  Their statement of defendant's participation in offense.
  Relative culpability of defendant in relation to codefendants and coconspirators.
Statement of Witnesses, Complainants, and Victims (Optional.)

Defendant's Version of Offense

Essential Data:
  Summary of account of offense and arrest as given by defendant if different
    from official version.
  Discrepancies between defendant's version and official version.
  Extent to which defendant admits guilt.
  Defendant's attitude toward offense (e.g., remorseful, rationalizes, minimizes,
    experiences anxiety, etc.).
  Defendant's explanation of why he became involved in the offense.
  Extent to which offense was impulsive or premeditated.
  Environmental and situational factors contributing to offense, including
    stressing situations, experiences, or relationships.
Optional Data:
  Defendant's feelings from time of offense until his arrest.
  Defendant's reactions after arrest (e.g., defiant, relieved, indifferent, etc.).
  Defendant's attitude toward the probation officer and his degree of cooperation.
  Defendant's attitudes toward prior convictions and commitments if they con-
    tribute to an understanding of the present offense.

Prior Record

Essential Data:
  Clearance with FBI, social service exchange and police departments and sheriffs'
    offices in respective localities where defendant lived.
  Juvenile court history.
  List of previous convictions (date, place, offense, and disposition).
  List of arrests subsequent to present offense (date, place, offense, and dis-
    position).
  Military arrests and courts martial (date, place, offense, and disposition) not
    covered in *Military Service*.
  Institutional history (dates, report of adjustment, present release status, etc.).
  Previous probation and parole history (dates, adjustment, outcome).
  Detainers presently lodged against defendant.
Optional Data:
  Defendant's explanation why he was involved in previous offenses.
  Codefendants in previous offenses.

Family History

DEFENDANT

Essential Data:

Date, place of birth, race.

Early developmental influences (physical and emotional) that may have a significant bearing on defendant's present personality and behavior.

Attitudes of the father and the mother toward the defendant in his formative years, including discipline, affection, rejection, etc.

By whom was defendant reared, if other than his parents.

Age left home; reasons for leaving; history of truancy from home.

Relationship of defendant with parents and siblings, including attitudes toward one another.

Extent of family solidarity (family cohesiveness).

Relatives with whom defendant is especially close.

Optional Data:

Naturalization status (country of birth and place and date of entry into United States).

Order of birth among siblings.

PARENTS AND SIBLINGS

Essential Data:

(All information optional.)

Optional Data:

Parents (name, age, address, citizenship, naturalization status, education, marital status, health, religion, economic status, general reputation). If deceased, also give age at death and cause.

Siblings (same as parents, above).

History of emotional disorders, diseases, and criminal behavior in the family.

Attitude of parents and siblings toward defendant's offense.

Marital History

Essential Data:

Present marriage, including common law (date, place, name and age of spouse at time of marriage).

Attitude of defendant toward spouse and children and their's toward him.

Home atmosphere.

Previous marriage(s) (date, place, name of previous spouse, and outcome; if divorced, give reasons).

Children, including those from previous marriage(s) (name, age, school, custody, support).

Optional Data:

Significant elements in spouse's background.

History of courtship and reason for marriage.

Problems in the marriage (religion, sex, economics, etc.).

Attitude of spouse (and older children) toward offense.

Attitude of defendant and spouse toward divorce, separation, remarriage.

Contacts with domestic relations court.

Juvenile court record of children.

Social agencies interested in family.

Divorce data (including grounds, court, date of final decree, special conditions, and to whom granted).

Home and Neighborhood

Essential Data:

Description of home (owned or rented, type, size, occupants, adequacy, and general living conditions).

Type of neighborhood, including any desirable or undesirable influences in the community.

Attitude of defendant and family toward home and neighborhood.

Optional Data:

Date moved to present residence and number of different residences in past 10 years.

How long has defendant lived in present type of neighborhood.

What race, nationality, and culture predominate.

Prior home and neighborhood experiences which have had a substantial influence on the defendant's behavior.

Education

Essential Data:

Highest grade achieved.

Age left school and reason for leaving.

Results of psychological tests (IQ, aptitude, achievement, etc.), specify test and date.

Optional Data:

Last school attended (dates, name, address).

Previous schools attended covering 5-year period (dates, name, address).

School adjustment as evidenced by conduct, scholastic standing, truancy, leadership, reliability, courtesy, likes and dislikes, special abilities and disabilities, grades repeated, and relationships with pupils and teachers.

Business and trade training (type, school, dates).

Defendant's attitude toward further education and training.

Ability to read and write English.

Religion

Essential Data:

Religious affiliation and frequency of church attendance.

Optional Data:

Church membership (name, address, pastor).

Member of what church organizations.

What has religious experience meant to defendant in the past and at present.

What are defendant's moral values.
What is the pastor's impression of the defendant.

Interests and Leisure-Time Activities

Essential Data:
>   Defendant's interests and leisure-time activities (including sports, hobbies, creative work, organizations, reading).
>   What are his talents and accomplishments.

Optional Data:
>   Who are his associates; what is their reputation.
>   Extent to which he engages in activities alone.
>   Extent to which he includes his family.
>   Extent to which his leisure-time pursuits reflect maturity.

Health

PHYSICAL

Essential Data:
>   Identifying information (height, weight, complexion, eyes, hair, scars, tattoos, posture, physical proportions, tone of voice, manner of speech).
>   Defendant's general physical condition and health problems based on defendant's estimate of his health, medical reports, probation officer's observations.
>   Use of narcotics, barbiturates, marihuana.
>   Social implications of defendant's physical health (home, community, employment, associations).

Optional Data:
>   History of serious diseases, including venereal disease, tuberculosis, diabetes (nature, date, effects).
>   History of major surgery and serious injuries (nature, date, effects).
>   Hospital treatment (hospital, dates, nature, outcome).
>   Last medical examination (date, place, pertinent findings).
>   Current medical treatment (prescribed medicine and dosage).
>   Use of alcohol.
>   Allergies (especially penicillin).

MENTAL AND EMOTIONAL

Essential Data:
>   Probation officer's assessment of defendant's operating level of intelligence as demonstrated in social and occupational functions.
>   Personality characteristics as given by family members and as observed by probation officer.
>   Attitude of defendant about himself and how he feels others feel about him (parents, siblings, spouse, children, associates).
>   Social adjustment in general.
>   Social implications of mental and emotional health (home, community, employment, associations).

Optional Data:

IQ (support with test scores).

Findings of psychological and psychiatric examinations (tests, date, by whom given).

Emotional instability as evidenced by fears, hostilities, obsessions, compulsions, depressions, peculiar ideas, dislikes, sex deviation (include any history of psychiatric treatment).

Defendant's awareness of emotional problems and what he has done about them.

Employment

Essential Data:

Employment history for past 10 years (dates, nature of work, earnings, reasons for leaving).

Employer's evaluation of defendant (immediate supervisor, where possible), including attendance, capabilities, reliability, adjustment, honesty, reputation, personality, attitude toward work, and relationships with coworkers and supervisors.

Occupational skills, interests, and ambitions.

Optional Data:

If unemployable, explain.

Means of subsistence during unemployment, including relief and unemployment compensation.

Military Service

Essential Data:

Branch of service, serial number, and dates of each period of military service.

Highest grade or rank achieved and grade or rank at separation.

Type and date of discharge(s).

Attitude toward military experience.

Optional Data:

Inducted or enlisted.

Special training received.

Foreign service, combat experience, decorations and citations.

Disciplinary action not covered in *Prior Record.*

Veteran's claim number.

Selective Service status (local board, classification, registration number).

Financial Condition

ASSETS

Essential Data:

Statement of financial assets.

General standard of living.

Optional Data:

Net worth statement.

Property (type, location, value, equity).

Insurance (type, amount, company).
Checking and savings account (bank, amount).
Stocks and bonds (type, value).
Personal property (car, furniture, appliances).
Income from pensions, rentals, boarders.
Family income.
Available resources through relatives and friends.

FINANCIAL OBLIGATIONS

Essential Data:
Statement of financial obligations.
Optional Data:
Current obligations, including balance due and monthly payment (home mortgage, rent, utilities, medical, personal property, home repairs, charge accounts, loans, fines, restitution).
Money management and existing financial delinquencies.
Credit rating.

Evaluative Summary

Essential Data:
Highlights of body of the report.
Analysis of factors contributing to present offense and prior convictions (motivations and circumstances).
Defendant's attitude toward offense.
Evaluation of the defendant's personality, problems and needs, and potential for growth.
Optional Data:
Reputation in the community.

COMMENT. Writing the evaluative summary is perhaps the most difficult and painstaking task in the entire presentence report. It has a significant bearing on the future course of the defendant's life. It is here that the probation officer calls into play his analytical ability, his diagnostic skills, and his understanding of human behavior. It is here that he brings into focus the kind of person before the court, the basic factors that brought him into trouble, and what special helps the defendant needs to resolve his difficulties.

The opening paragraph of the evaluative summary should give a concise restatement of the pertinent highlights in the body of the report. There should follow in separate paragraphs those factors which contributed in some measure to the defendant's difficulty and also an evaluation of his personality.

Recommendation

Essential Data:
Recommendation.
Basis for recommendation.

Optional Data:
> Suggested plan, including role of parents, spouse, pastor, further education, future employment.
> Sentencing alternatives.

COMMENT.   Some judges ask for the probation officer's recommendation regarding probation or commitment. Where recommendations are requested, they should be a part of the presentence report. If the judge does not wish to have the recommendations included as a part of the report, they may be given on a separate sheet which may be detached if the presentence report is later sent to an institution.

If it is recommended that the defendant be placed on probation, the proposed plans for residence, employment, education, and medical and psychiatric treatment, if pertinent, should be given. The part to be played in the social adjustment of the defendant by the parental and immediate family, the pastor, close friends, and others in the community should also be shown. If commitment is recommended, the probation officer should indicate what special problems and needs should receive the attention of the institutional staff.

Where the judge asks for sentencing alternatives, they may be included in this part of the report.

8

The Professional Character of the Presentence Report

PAUL W. KEVE

No single instrument in our hands so neatly typifies the modern correctional philosophy as does the presentence report. Its only reason for being is to depict the intimate dynamics of one particular individual offender and to enable the court to dispose of his case with a tailor-made plan that is corrective in intent, whereas without such knowledge the disposition can only be punitive.

This is an idealistic thought, of course. Admittedly, our presentence reports cannot always be so penetrating in their understanding, nor can ideal corrective plans and devices always be found and used by the court. Nevertheless, the potential is there, and if the field of corrections is going to move swiftly on to an enlightened, consistent methodology of professional level diagnosis, leading to individualized treatment, then everyone of us can make a major contribution to that progress by striving for the highest level of quality in his diagnostic reports.

It is understandable that we have not gone as far as we can in assuming the professional character and status that the job potentially holds for us. We are, after all, a new profession and the other professions that surround us and share our general field of interests are ancient by comparison. The most venerable one of them is the closest to us, for we work under the immediate direction of the legal profession, specifically the judiciary. Perhaps it is inevitable that we should feel a modicum of inferiority.

We also tend to be quite deferential to other professions that we ourselves have called upon to help us—medicine, psychology, and psychiatry. It is far too common that probation officers reach for status by borrowing prestige from

SOURCE. *Federal Probation*, XXVI, June 1962, pp. 51–56. (Editorial Adaptations.)

these other professions rather than by perfecting their own. Our work will, of course, properly borrow from other disciplines but we must be appropriate in what we borrow and must integrate the borrowed elements into a social work discipline of our own.

Here are a few signs and symptoms of the inappropriate borrowing from other fields:

1. There is the probation officer who borrows the accoutrements of the constabulary; confusing his profession with the police function, as seen in his use of a police-type badge; the carrying of handcuffs, blackjack or gun; the use of a police radio in his car; the overemphasis given in his presentence reports to detailed accounts of the defendant's offense.

2. The legalistic probation officer whose presentence reports are replete with legalistic language and whose supervision of probationers finds contentment in the upholding of law for the sake of upholding law, whether or not inward improvement of the probationer is accomplished.

3. The probation officer who belongs to the world of investigators. He is an investigator in a special, narrow sense, and his reports take the safe procedure of presenting facts, facts, facts, with impressive thoroughness but with no illumination as to their meaning.

4. The probation officer who obtains reports from psychologists and psychiatrists or other clinicians, but attaches these to, or copies these verbatim into his presentence report without integrating their message with the "facts" he has uncovered in his own investigation.

And perhaps you can think of other examples. It should be apparent that we need not look far to see that there is some confusion as to the professional pose that we should properly assume.

PRESENTENCE REPORTS REVEAL OUR PROFESSIONAL STATURE

The perfection of the presentence investigation and report is not the only way that we can develop our professional stature, but there is good reason for starting there. There is no intent here to neglect the business of treatment—the other half and the more important half of our responsibility. But we need not worry. The treatment process does not lack for skilled advocates. So here we will just talk about the diagnostic process through use of the presentence report, which not only serves to diagnose the client, but also serves incidentally to define our profession for many people. This has some importance for us since in our work we are not exposed to general public scrutiny as much as other professions are. A lawyer, for instance, has a public arena in his courtroom-handling of a case. The work of doctors is well known, despite the privacy of the doctor-patient relationship, for doctors, in contrast to us, do not work with a limited segment of the population, but with practically everyone, and their work is constantly reviewed by patients who love to tell about their operations.

But what does the world see of us and our work with a probationer or parolee. The treatment process that we carry out is a private process, largely known to two people—the probationer and ourselves. When we report to the judge at the end of the probation period we may give him a resumé of the probationer's progress, but we do not really give him a detailed report of the subtle, persistent, patient, imaginative, technical methodology which we used in fostering his progress. We may have done a brilliant job, using specialized, skilled, professional techniques, but no one else knows it except our supervisor, and he is not a person who has to be sold on this profession.

However, the diagnostic process through its product, the presentence report, provides a window to our profession that can help to gain understanding and respect. Through it the judge not only will learn about the defendant, but may learn about the profession of correctional social work. Our report goes to others, too: other social agencies, correctional institutional personnel, etc., and through it they gain their impression of us and our profession. Also, in the course of making our investigation, we meet and talk with a sizeable variety of people in the community, and in the way we handle ourselves in these contacts we can do much to create a good image of our profession for these persons.

While the primary purpose of the report is to diagnose the defendant, it can also serve these incidental and sometimes unexpected uses that can be much to our advantage. It is hard for us always to remember this, and it is easy for us to be unimpressed with the need for producing a good quality report every time. One probation officer commented glumly that it was hard to feel motivated to produce a high-quality report knowing that the judge would read it hurriedly or not at all, and would probably turn directly to the recommendation and let it go at that. This is discouraging, of course, but we cannot afford to assume that poor reception of our reports justifies poor reports. We are not in a position to complain about judges not reading our reports unless we have done our utmost to make them well worth reading.

But what does it mean specifically when we say that the probation officer should assume a status of professional expertness in his own right, and that this should be clearly evidenced in his presentence report?

For one thing, it becomes evident in how he uses clinical services. Many probation officers have little or no access to medical, psychological, or psychiatric services in their work, but many do have such service at hand and more will have as time goes on. Our professional self-concept and skill will reveal itself to some extent in how we use these clinical resources. Do we refer the defendant to a psychologist, for instance, so that the psychologist can tell us what is wrong with him? Or do we follow the better idea of asking the psychologist's help in making our own determination of what is wrong with this defendant? There is a difference!

The unskilled person finds himself investigating a defendant, we will say, whose behavior seems peculiarly illogical, and so he asks the psychologist or the psychiatrist to study him. The officer may make a referral without furnishing any case data which would help the clinician to know what problem needs to be studied and what clinical tools would be best to use. Afterward he takes the clinician's written report and attaches it to his presentence report with no attempt to integrate the two. There have even been such presentations that went to the judge with differing viewpoints of the case problem and solution. This is hardly the sort of presentation that would be helpful to the judge.

The more skillful officer refers the case for a thoughtful, purposeful reason, and gives the clinician background data on the case and an explanation of the gaps that need to be filled in. The clinician's report, then, is used, not as a separate and independent report, but is incorporated into the presentence report as one of the ingredients that contribute to the final, total diagnostic product.

THE PROBATION OFFICER'S RESPONSIBILITY

It is significant to note in this connection the administrative arrangement that is usually maintained between probation officers and clinical personnel when they are both employed in an agency. In a clear majority of agencies that have clinical services, the probation officer is in what we call a "line" position, and the psychiatrist, psychologist, doctor, dentist, nurse, if there are such, are in "staff" positions. We, the probation officers, are in the administrative line, and so we have specific responsibility for the conduct of our cases. The clinician, however, being in a "staff" or consultative position, is without direct responsibility for case conduct. This means that he is not in a position to dictate as to what we should do with a case. The case responsibility is clearly left to us. This is important to both of us, for it leaves the clinician free to advise us in the most uninhibited way as to whatever he sees as clinically needed, even though it may be unrealistic in terms of what the administrative problems are. We need this kind of unhindered, freely conceived professional opinion and advice from him to give us the most complete picture possible of the case problem and solution.

But then *we* have the case responsibility and you abdicate that responsibility if you turn it over to the psychologist or the psychiatrist for the final job of diagnosing and recommending. Diagnosis is sound only when it springs from a study of all facets of the client's life. Remember that the clinician ordinarily sees only the defendant himself, and only in the office or jail setting. He is only filling in gaps in the information we are assembling. We are the ones who visit the home, the neighborhood, the school, the shop. We are the ones who get to study first-hand the defendant's environment and his intimate personal relationships. We are the ones, too, who will have to work with him if he is put on probation. If we convey some of our case knowledge to the psychiatrist or psychologist when we refer the case you get more useful results from the work of these specialists. Even then, however, the presentence report we produce should not be a disjointed series of reports from a probation officer, psychologist, psychiatrist, or others. While it may very properly report on the diagnostic opinion of others such as these, the overall effect of the report should be to present *our* opinion, for we are the only person in the case who occupies a line position of professional status and we have also been the only person who has looked at all parts of the picture.

Whether or not we have clinical services available to supplement our own appraisal of a case, we can sharpen our powers of observation and adjust the focus of our case scrutiny to get a surprising amount of diagnostic information without other professional help. When we visit the defendant's home, what are we looking for? Family vital statistics? Or do we look for family feeling tone and relationships? The difference between these two concepts can be disarmingly simple and at the same time crucially important. It is quite all right to ask for family statistics if they are seen as clues instead of being gathered as primary data.

LOOK AT THE STORY BEHIND THE FACTS

Here is an illustration from an actual experience to show further what is meant by the focus with which we approach the investigation. No family statistics are learned at all in this instance but their absence is no loss. Actually, this was not an investigation situation, but the observation process involved here was essentially the same, nevertheless.

The setting was a PTA meeting in a rural school which happened to be quite remote from any town or store. The school had to offset the lack of near-by merchants by maintaining its own small canteen open briefly each day to enable pupils to buy school supplies or to spend their allowance for candy, pop, or ice cream. During the business session of this PTA meeting one mother rose to point out the severe problem being caused by the canteen. The other parents were obviously perplexed and unaware of any such problem. With persistent questioning they drew out from this mother her reason for concern. The story that slowly developed was that this woman had a 13-year-old daughter in the school and was deeply worried over the girl's recent tendency to steal bits of money when she had the opportunity. The mother seemed mildly surprised that the other parents did not see at once that the canteen was to blame. Her reasoning was that her daughter, with less money (supposedly) to spend than the other children had, was envious of their spending at the canteen and so was stealing in order to have money enough to compete at the candy counter. Mamma's idea was that the canteen was an evil that should be eliminated and then the stealing would stop.

This was all there was to it; just this mother's hesitant and very minimal explanation of a problem as she saw it. Not really enough on which to base a diagnosis of the daughter's problem—yet let us see how far we might venture even with just this tiny glimpse of the family. If *you* had been there too you could have learned much through your eyes as well as through your ears, so we must fill out the visual picture too.

This mother was a woman who dressed plainly and severely. Her dress was drab and devoid of any stylish feature or ornamentation. Her hair was put up in a bun that suggested no thought of trying to be attractive, but only showed a concern with what was economical of effort. She wore no makeup and her prim, tight-set lips gave no hint of knowing how to smile. Everything about her suggested only modesty, conservatism, economy, dryness of personality, and lack of imagination.

These are the things that can be reported factually of what there was to hear and see. With the experience that we have had in working with families, we could quickly fill in some other probable details. A reasonable guess was that this was a family in which the parents were cold, precise, and rigid people. To the outside world they no doubt were seen mainly as god-fearing, industrious, honest, no-nonsense people. They were people who probably rose in the morning to do the chores and filled each day exclusively with activity altogether concerned with the farming, marketing, dishwashing, mending, cleaning, etc. Enjoyment of these, or other activities for the sake of family enjoyment, was probably unknown in this family. Family jokes, picnics, vacation trips were perhaps absent and there was no ability to do things together for the sake of just enjoying each other and expressing for each other their love and affection. Here, then, was a daughter hungry for love and the warm, emotional stimulation that is every child's birthright; but these were denied her and so she was seeking vicarious satisfaction by taking things.

A further ray of light was shed during the discussion when other parents asked this mother just how much allowance the daughter was given, and the answer perplexed them further, for it turned out that this girl's allowance was not less, but was more than any of the other parents were furnishing! Here was further suggestion of the rejecting parent who assuages his conscience by giving *things* when he is unable to give *love*.

This account has been much more diagnostic of this family than we would have any professional right to be on the basis of just sitting in a PTA meeting and listening to and watching the performance of one member of a family. Of course, we cannot become so unprofessional as to write presentence reports on the basis of such superficial contact. But the point can be legitimately made that an experienced probation officer who listens with both of his ears, and watches with both of his eyes, can spot the signs and symbols of underlying problems. In this sort of case, he would quickly see these likely or possible dynamics of the problem and then would probe further to see if his initial impressions are correct. The diagnosis ventured here in respect to this family is too much conjecture to be professional; but in an investigation situation we would make it professional by thoroughly checking out our tentative impressions. We would then finally present to the court a truly diagnostic document instead of a dry recital of facts by themselves.

FACTS ARE ONLY THE BEGINNING

If we do not reach for this evaluative sort of writing we produce the sort of report we might see if we were to hire probation officers who were qualified by previous experience in a bureau of vital statistics. Certainly vital statistics clerks could write a report that would be thoroughly factual, with every family member carefully accounted for and every name, place, birthdate, confirmation date, marriage date, divorce date, remarriage date, and death date accurately listed. We would be told exactly how many days our delinquent was tardy and how many days absent from school; what jobs he had and the dates he started and stopped on each and what the weekly earnings were. But would we have real flesh and blood people?

We are not just vital statistics workers. We are not just people who go around asking questions and putting down the answers. We are people who are first to investigate and find facts, but then if we are to merit the respect, the prestige, and hopefully the pay of professional experts, we must be willing to leave the safe haven of just reporting facts; we must be willing to stick our necks out and analyze our facts and tell the court what they mean.

Actually, it is quite seldom that any probation officer writes the dry, sterile, "vital statistics" type of report, but it is also seldom that we can find the report that takes full advantage of the chance to be diagnostic. More typical is the investigation that uncovers and reports on significant bits of information that have diagnostic value, but then the report does not relate them to each other clearly and does not develop the diagnostic message that is latent in them. Consider, for instance, this example which comes from a brief report on a girl named Betty who was in juvenile court for absenting. Here is an intriguing glimpse of home life:

> Betty says her mother has beat her on different occasions—once with a shoe and once with a stick. The mother denies this. She says she used a strap. The mother admits she called Betty a "whore," but she said Betty called her "an old bag."

Now actually this is a priceless bit of data that gives a highly useful glimpse of the problem in this case. This is *people* instead of just facts or statistics. As far as it goes, it is excellent; but having been tossed the ball, the probation officer does not carry it anywhere in this report. The report contains no other qualitative items about the family or its problems. This bit of narrative should not have been treated as end-result information, but rather as a sort of Geiger counter to indicate where further digging would be profitable. Through it we begin to see what the problem is; but if later we are going to do an effective treatment job with this family, we need to know how this mother-daughter conflict got started and what continuing conditions seem to be fanning the flames. We need to have a notion of how accessible the mother is to casework help.

Let us look at one more example. This one comes from a prehearing report on a 17-year-old girl who was in court for incorrigibility and attempted suicide. These excerpts from the section on the family show the officer's sensitivity to the nuances of family life. Though it has almost none of the facts of family chronology it has what is truly important—the glimpses of personalities and interrelationships that help us to know what makes this girl a problem.

They (the parents) knew each other off and on through their growing-up years and were married in 1942. Soon after their marriage they came here for job opportunities. Peg was born two years later. Both parents have been working consistently at the M—— Co., doing factory work, and for this reason Peg has been left quite a bit to her own resources.... The mother feels that Peg has always been an obedient child who never complained and was very accepting of family plans and goals. However, she comments that it was difficult for Peg to make friends and until just recently she had very few friends.... On the surface the family seems to be a fairly well integrated unit. The father seems to show much more insight and interest in his daughter's activities—at least he seems more sincere and concerned than the mother. The mother speaks much more about her own activities and her job. This and her bright, vivid, stylish clothing suggests that perhaps she is a little too involved with her own goals and not as much the loving mother that Peg has needed.... It is interesting to note that Peg's suicide attempt coincided with a heart attack of her father for which he had been hospitalized for some period of time. During this period of time the mother was out of the home night after night, visiting the father in the hospital.

The above excerpts comprise only a small part of the report but it can easily be seen that the complete report, written with this sensitivity to the feelings behind the facts, would be a truly effective diagnostic account.

The novelists have a knack of telling us in highly readable ways about family dynamics, and they often show much more skill than we do in revealing with a few words some highly lucid descriptions of personality development. Consider, for instance, a few sentences from a novel, *Work of Art*, written by Sinclair Lewis. In this passage, two brothers, Ora and Myron, are speaking of their early life and how it shaped them.

"My father," said Ora, "was a sloppy, lazy, booze-hoisting old bum, and my mother didn't know much besides cooking, and she was too busy to give me much attention, and the kids I knew were a bunch of foul-mouthed loafers that used to hang around the hoboes up near the water tank, and I never had a chance to get any formal schooling, and I got thrown on my own as just a brat. So naturally I've become a sort of vagabond that can't be bored by thinking about his 'debts' to a lot of little shop-keeping lice, and I suppose I'm inclined to be lazy, and not too scrupulous about the dames and the liquor. But my early rearing did have one swell result. Brought up so unconventionally, I'll always be an Anti-Puritan. I'll never deny the joys of the flesh and the sanctity of Beauty."

"And my father," said Myron, "was pretty easy-going and always did like drinking and swapping stories with the Boys, and my mother was hard-driven taking care of us, and I heard a lot of filth from the hoboes up near the water tank. Maybe just sort of as a reaction I've become almost too much of a crank about paying debts, and fussing over my work, and being scared of liquor and women. But my rearing did have one swell result. Just by way of contrast, it made me a good, sound, old-fashioned New England Puritan."

This is not to argue that we should write our reports like novels; yet passages like these, sparingly written but richly communicative, suggest to us that the writing techniques we have been using have often been sterile and dry, whereas they need to be just as revealing of personality as is the writing of any novelist.

9

Presentence Investigation Practices in the Federal Probation System

DAVID H. GRONEWOLD

A study of presentence practices in the federal courts has recently been completed by the Federal Probation Training Center with support from the Federal Probation Officers Association and approval by the Probation Division of the Administrative Office of the United States Courts.[1] The impetus for the study developed primarily because of questions raised by probation officers attending the training school sessions devoted to discussions of presentence investigation practices. Officers frequently commented that while the purpose the presentence investigation appeared to be the same in all districts, the methods of obtaining information about the defendant and presenting it to the court varied. The interest of the probation service as a whole in examining variations and similarities in practice was a further incentive for embarking on the project.

The problem was to seek, in some detail, answers from the probation officers of the judicial districts which would provide a basis for tabulating similarities and differences existing in the methods of conducting and preparing the presentence investigation. A questionnaire was devised based on a study of

Source. *Federal Probation*, XXII, September 1958, pp. 27–32.
[1] This article is a summary of the highlights of a report, *Presentence Investigation Practices in the Federal Courts*, (1957) prepared jointly by Jacob B. Barnett, federal probation officer at Chicago: Wayne Keyser, assistant director of the Federal Probation Training Center at Chicago: and David H. Gronewold of the University of Washington school of social work.

the official worksheets and a number of presentence investigation reports. The questionnaire was submitted to the chief probation officer of each district and to each independent unit. The response from the field was 100 percent. Ninety-nine questionnaires were distributed, and 97 were completed. The only two returned incomplete were from chief probation officers who felt they could not fill out the questionnaires because their appointments were too recent for them to have a thorough knowledge of practices in their respective districts.

Since practices vary and exceptions arise in some situations, the questionnaire was prefaced by the following statement: "The answer to each of these questions should reflect the general practice in your district."

COLLECTION OF DATA FOR THE REPORT

WORKSHEETS AND QUESTIONNAIRES.   United States probation officers, responsible primarily to their respective courts, have developed a uniformity of practice due in large measure to the leadership of the Administrative Office of the United States Courts. The monograph on the presentence investigation,[2] the United States Probation Officers Manual, and the official worksheets have tended to raise standards of practice. The worksheet (Form 1) is a guide in the exploration of the defendant's history. It is helpful in guiding the interview process. Its use assures examination into all areas of the defendant's life.

The tabulated results of the questionnaires indicate the popularity of the official worksheet and its wide use. It is used exclusively in 80 offices. In nine offices, a specially designed worksheet or questionnaire, essentially the same as Form 1, is preferred. Three offices do not use the worksheet.

SOURCES OF SOCIAL DATA

THE INTERVIEW.   The value of interviewing as a tool is highlighted by the practice in all offices of using the defendant as the prime source for social information about himself, and in all but one office the practice of using the relatives of the defendant as a source for family history. Good working relationships between the probation staff and law-enforcement personnel are shown since 94 offices regularly receive family data from law-enforcement agencies in addition to information received from the family and the defendant.

SOCIAL SERVICE EXCHANGE.   Additional sources of data are opened up through the use of the social service exchange, central index, or other confidential clearances. The social service exchange often furnishes avenues of information regarding defendants known to social agencies. It brings federal probation offices into the larger family of community agencies and, in doing so, facilitates better communication and cooperation with other agencies. In more than one-third of the offices (33) the exchange is available and used; in

[2] Richard A. Chappell and Victor H. Evjen, *The Presentence Investigation Report*, Washington, D.C., Pub. No. 101, 1943.

slightly over one-fourth of the offices (25), although available, it is not used; in thirty-six (36) offices, the social service exchange is not available. Three offices did not respond to this question.

MEDICAL, PSYCHOLOGICAL, AND PSYCHIATRIC INFORMATION. The progress made in the physical and social sciences has contributed significantly to the understanding of man and his behavior. The facts supplied by medical practitioners and psychiatrists regarding the physical and psychological makeup of the defendant are often very helpful in the sentencing process. Access to such facts is of the utmost importance.

Veterans Administration hospitals and clinics are located throughout the country and provide an excellent source of medical information on offenders who have been eligible for veterans services. Seventy-four of the federal probation offices reported they have access to information from Veterans Administration records.

Many jails give routine medical examinations to prisoners. Requests for medical reports from the jail are made in 40 probation offices.

Federal probation officers obtain formal medical, psychological, and psychiatric reports from a wide variety of sources such as private practitioners, hospitals, or clinics, and three-fourths of the offices (73) report they usually make it a practice to obtain such reports. However, in many cases, previous examinations have not been made or are not accessible to the probation offices.

In some cases a current evaluation of the defendant's mental or emotional state is indicated. Eighty-one offices, or 84 percent of the probation offices, use Veterans Administration hospitals and clinics, publicly employed psychiatric facilities, or the United States Public Health Service. Fourteen offices report that no public psychiatric services are available. It is surprising that six of the offices not having public psychiatric services available are located in metropolitan areas with populations of over 200,000.

Availability of psychiatric services does not in any sense mean that officers have a resource for every case needing this type of service since intake policies of these medical and psychiatric services dictate the selection of cases for diagnosis and treatment. The questionnaire did not attempt to find out what private facilities are available. An area for further study might be the overall availability of medical, psychological, and psychiatric services to federal probation officers, with a view toward the discovery and fuller use of existing services.

In all, an examination of the sources of information generally used by probation officers reveals a many-sided approach to the problem of obtaining an individual, yet objective, view of the life history of the defendant.

VERIFICATION OF SOCIAL DATA

Verification of data secured from the defendant is a significant and essential part of the presentence investigation process. The probation officer has the responsibility of making a recommendation to the court which is of utmost consequence to the defendant and to the community. Even if he does not make an outright recommendation, the way in which he evaluates the defendant influences the court in its decision. Since the probation officer's recommendation or evaluation is based on the data in the report, the facts must be correct.

Certain social relationships such as marriage, divorce, and child support are verified, as a general practice, in 75 percent of the offices, although positive responses were sometimes qualified by statements such as "when indicated," or "as needed." A wide variation in practice is noted in verification of school records. Some offices routinely verify records of all defendants, some verify records of juveniles and young adults, and in other offices the decision to verify depends on whether the nature of the school record has significance in the individual case. All except four offices, however, indicate some practice of verifying school records. Military records are verified in almost all offices.

Since employment history is considered one of the most reliable indexes for the prediction of success or failure on probation or parole, federal offices routinely verify both past (in 83 offices) and present (in 89 offices) employment, although policy varies from that of verifying employment in every case to verification on a selective basis. The most common methods of verification are personal telephone contacts, verification letters, and pay stubs. The use of the pay stub method in the case of present employment is quite generally used.

COLLECTION OF DATA ON DELINQUENT OR CRIMINAL HISTORY

The sources of data regarding the current offense are the United States attorney's offices, law-enforcement agencies, the defendant himself, and the indictment. Ninety-three of the 97 reporting offices receive information about the current offense from the United States attorney's office. Nearly all of the reporting offices also indicate excellent cooperation and a close working relationship with the federal investigating agencies; federal probation officers make maximum use of the data available in their offices.

Seventy-three offices summarize the indictment as a part of the presentence report, although they do not copy it; 13 both copy and summarize it; 9 copy the indictment but do not summarize; and only 2 neither copy nor summarize the indictment. The requirements of the court generally determine the method of handling indictments in the presentence investigation report.

The splendid working relationship between federal probation officers and juvenile court personnel is shown by the fact that information from the juvenile court is available to 92 of the 97 reporting offices. The problem of how to classify juvenile arrests in the presentence report is handled in several ways. About one half of the offices place information regarding the defendant's juvenile court record under "prior record"; about one-fourth classify it either as a subheading under prior record, or as a separate category such as "juvenile record"; and about one-fifth of the offices include the information under "family history," especially in cases where the data deal with dependency rather than delinquency.

A controversial question is the fingerprinting of juveniles, a practice not in favor with juvenile courts. In the federal system, juveniles are generally fingerprinted as a matter of routine by the United States marshal, although 14 offices report that juveniles are not fingerprinted until after a court finding.

Among the many sources listed by probation officers as valuable for obtaining information about prior arrests and convictions—e.g., local police, FBI fingerprint record, court records, state and county probation and parole offices, sheriff's office, United States marshal, United States attorney, county attorney, state's attorney—one of the most generally used is the defendant himself. While the other sources are essential for corroboration and verification, and show the close cooperation between the parole officer and community law-enforcement agencies, it is the defendant who can best tell about himself, and who can often interpret an unintelligible arrest or fingerprint report, since arrests are often abbreviated or are reported by statute number. Through the discussion of arrests with the defendant, the probation officer can get the defendant thinking about his behavior in relation to the prior record.

In setting down the prior record, over one-third of the offices give only the arrest date, offense, name of the sentencing judge, and disposition. One-fourth of the offices also summarize each arrest and conviction. In about one-third of the offices, the practice varies. In some the material is merely recorded, and in others each arrest and conviction is summarized.

INTERDISTRICT COLLABORATION IN PREPARING THE REPORT

There is some difference of opinion in regard to the interdistrict responsibilities for the presentence report. While each of the federal probation offices is primarily under the direction of and responsible to its respective district court, the work of each office within this framework is coordinated and standardized by the Probation Division of the Administrative Office of the United States Courts, and probation officers from different districts work in close cooperation with each other in investigation and supervision. The volume of interdistrict work is larger than is generally known. In a metropolitan area such as Chicago, for instance, approximately one-fourth of all presentence investigations completed are for other federal district courts.

Which office ought to have the responsibility for the final assembly and preparation of the complete presentence report, when the offense has been committed in another district than that in which defendant and his family live, is an unsettled question. Whereas 50 probation offices consider the responsibility should rest with the jurisdiction where the offender is sentenced, 37 believe the jurisdiction of the defendant's domicile should be responsible for completion of the report. Several districts feel responsibility for compiling a complete presentence report should depend on the availability of the defendant for personal interview, and a number of districts report that when a complete presentence report is received from other districts, it frequently is advisable to attach a supplemental statement for the court's information on investigative findings within the district. What method of dividing the responsibility would be most feasible deserves further study.

SUMMARIZATION AND ANALYSIS OF DATA

Many facets of the defendant's life and behavior are set forth and evaluated in the body of the presentence report. Does the report include a final summary highlighting its contents? To what conclusions do the facts about the defendant lead? Does the summary include a recommendation as to disposition, or an evaluation as to the suitability of the defendant for probation? Is the plan of treatment an integral part of the report? Does the federal probation officer rely wholly on the written document as an avenue of communication with the judge or does he discuss the report with the judge in chambers prior to sentencing?

The concluding statements of the presentence report are of significance since they condense and highlight the significant data in the body of the report. Some summaries are a condensation of the facts of the report; others include inferences and interpretation which may or may not lead to a recommendation. Often the use of a summary is determined by the attitude of the court: some judges want facts and interpretation of facts with recommendations; others prefer presentation of the data with as little interpretation as possible.

SUMMARY IN THE PRESENTENCE REPORT.   Most offices (90) conclude their presentence reports with a final summary. Of the seven who do not include a final summary, three discuss their reports with the judge before sentencing.

RECOMMENDATIONS IN THE PRESENTENCE REPORT.   On the basis of his findings does the probation officer make a recommendation to the judge regarding disposition and evaluate the defendant's potentialities as a good, fair, or poor risk for probation, or does he conclude the report without a recommendation or evaluation? The general practice of federal probation officers is to give the judge some indication as to the suitability of the defendant for probation. A majority (57) of the offices generally make a recommendation for disposition. Of the 36 not making a recommendation for disposition, 24, or one-fourth, evaluate the defendant's potentialities as a probation risk, and 10 offices neither recommend the disposition nor evaluate the defendant's potentialities.

PLAN OF TREATMENT.   The report is a guide for sentencing, and provides a framework for constructive probation supervision. The question, "Do United States probation officers include a plan of treatment in the presentence report?" is related to this latter function. In over two-thirds of the federal probation offices, a treatment plan is included, or sometimes included. Unfortunately the term "plan of treatment" was not defined and the responses in the questionnaire might have been made from different frames of reference.

For instance, some offices may have recorded negative responses because treatment connotes to them "intensive therapy." If "plan of treatment" had been defined and made synonymous with "probation plan" the responses might have been quite different.

CONFERENCE WITH JUDGES. Do federal probation officers have access to their judges, and do they discuss with judges the contents of the presentence report? Does oral communication supplement and reinforce the written report? In over one-half of the offices (53) the presentence report is discussed with the judge in his chambers prior to sentencing, and in nine additional offices the report is sometimes discussed with the judge. Twenty-four offices report that the presentence report is not discussed with the judge in chambers prior to sentencing.

CONFIDENTIALITY OF THE PRESENTENCE REPORT

A prominent federal judge has stated that adherence to the principle of confidentiality in the use of the presentence report has made it possible to attain a better picture of the defendant. Because of this confidentiality, the report has attained a quality which makes it far more reliable and penetrating and thus a better instrument for sentencing and for the treatment of the offender.[3]

To the question, "Prior to sentencing is your presentence report available to the judge only?" the answers show a general trend to treat the presentence report as confidential. The presentence report is available to the *judge only* in 65 districts. In 30 districts it is available to *other* interested parties and in all but 2 of these 30 districts, the United States attorney receives a copy of the presentence report. In 11 districts, the defense counsel has access to the presentence report. In only 3 districts do federal investigative agencies see a copy of the report.

The confidentiality of the report can be violated by the reading of its contents in open court or by filing it with the clerk of the court, for in filing the report it becomes a part of the public record. In 84 districts the report *is not* read in open court; in 12 districts, the report *is read* in court. Of the 12 offices where the report is read, 9 qualified their answers indicating the following: "the highlights of the presentence report are read in open court," "sometimes to our embarrassment the court reads portions of the presentence report in open court to emphasize a point it is making but in the majority of cases the contents of the report are not disclosed in open court." Other qualifying comments indicated that the report is sometimes partially read but that not all of the presentence report is read in open court. In only 7 of the probation offices are presentence reports filed with the clerk of the court.

---

[3] Judge Carroll C. Hincks, "In Opposition to Rule 34 (c) (2) Proposed Federal Rules," *Federal Probation*, October–December 1944, pp. 3–9.

TIME ALLOWED FOR PREPARING THE REPORT

Time is an important consideration in the preparation of the presentence report. The social investigation, or the fact finding phase, is time consuming; interviews with defendants and collateral contacts, perusal of social documents, conferences with social and community agencies, verification of specific aspects of the defendant's history such as military service and out of town employment—steps in the presentence process—require considerable time. In addition, the collected data are assembled and summarized and brought together into a coherent document which affords for the court insight into the behavior of the defendant.

Federal probation officers begin the presentence at different stages in the process of prosecution, and the policy regarding the initiation of the presentence varies from court to court. Forty-five offices do not begin the investigation until after conviction or a plea of guilty. The 30 who begin earlier do not place the report in the hands of the judge until after conviction or plea.[4] They report that the investigation is begun after there is an indication from the defendant or his attorney that he intends to plead guilty. Several make the point that the investigation is not begun until the defendant understands the procedure and is fully informed of his rights.

The time allowed for preparing presentence reports varies considerably. In over half the offices (55), an unspecified time is indicated for bond and jail cases, and in 69 jurisdictions, an unspecified time is allowed for the preparation of reports on juvenile cases. In those courts in which a specific time is set, most officers have more than 14 days to prepare their presentence reports. In 6 offices, 14 or less days are given for the preparation of jail cases, and in 12 offices, 14 or less days are given for the preparation of juvenile cases.

Not only is there variation in the practice of courts as to the time allowed, but there is also considerable variation of opinion of the federal probation officers as to the time needed. Some believe investigations can be completed in 10 days; others would like from 10 to 20 days. About one-fourth of the officers indicate they need from 3 weeks to over a month. Most offices agree that jail and juvenile cases should be expedited. About three-fourths of the offices report they are satisfied with the time allotted by judges for the preparation of presentence reports.

Situations regarding the availability of information vary greatly. Such factors as length of court term, size of community, geography, and mobility of population affect the matter of optimum time. The quality and completeness of a presentence report may likewise be related to the amount of time available.

---

[4]"... The report shall not be submitted to the court or its contents disclosed to anyone unless the defendant has pleaded guilty or has been found guilty." Rule 32 (c), *Federal Rules of Criminal Procedure*, U.S. Government Printing Office, Washington, 1946.

CONCLUSION

The supposition that a common practice in the preparation of presentence reports is emerging throughout the federal probation system is borne out by the results of this study. The activities characterizing this practice in the majority of the reporting offices can be described as follows:

The federal probation officer utilizes a wide variety of sources for the collection of social, legal, and medical data for the purpose of providing the court with a complete account of the defendant's personal history, personal characteristics, and his involvement in the offense. To do so, he secures the cooperation of the defendant, relatives, employers, and law-enforcement and juvenile court personnel. He works closely with federal law-enforcement agencies, particularly with the United States attorneys in gathering facts pertaining to the defendant. He achieves a sense of his own expertness, and is willing either to make recommendations as to disposition of the defendant, or to evaluate the defendant's suitability for probation. That he is able to do so indicates the confidence the court has in his professional judgment. He does not rely solely on the written report as a medium of communication but prior to disposition often confers with the judge regarding the defendant.

He is aware of the significance of the court disposition to the defendant and to the community. He attempts to present as objective a report as possible through verification of the pertinent facts. He sees the presentence investigation both as an aid to sentencing and as a diagnostic tool which includes a suggested plan of treatment.

The results of the study show that the federal probation officer is objective in his handling of the defendant and approaches him with dignity and consideration. He (the defendant) is one of the major sources of information for the data in the presentence report.

In a majority of courts the presentence is considered a confidential document.

The federal probation officer makes a special effort to expedite those cases where a juvenile is involved, or when the defendant is lodged in jail.

The legal and other basic rights of the defendant are safeguarded.

This brief sketch of the reported practices of federal probation officers should not be construed to signify that all officers prepare presentence reports in the manner described. These are the reported practices in the majority of probation offices. The study as a whole indicates that substantial progress has been made in the standardization of practice in the direction of an expert, professionalized service.

10

Confidentiality of the Presentence Report

JACOB B. BARNETT AND DAVID H. GRONEWOLD

Social objectives are now more or less incorporated in the correctional apparatus, and the traditional legal-custodial, punishing nature of the correctional process is shifting towards the rehabilitative goal. The changes in corrections in the past were of an empirical nature. New corrective facilities and processes were added, not in an orderly fashion, but an innovation here, a new facility there—the adding of new laws, new devices, and the introduction of professionals. Changes which were originally discreet, random, and in no way systematic began to be of a more systematic and planned nature under the influence of the professionals. The social scientist, the bar association, and correctional practitioners and their organizations have been studying the total correctional process; and the correctional facilities have been highly organized into centralized structures.

THE PRESENTENCE AND THE CORRECTIONAL PROCESS

Basic to the functioning of the correctional apparatus is the conviction that comprehensive knowledge in breadth and depth of each client is essential. One of the results of this assumption is the large amount of social and psychological data amassed on each individual and the use of this data for varied purposes. A new psychology of casework took root during the thirties in the process of acquiring social and psychological information. The interview situation with the client became focal. The chief source of information about any

SOURCE. *Federal Probation*, XXVI, March 1962, pp. 26–30.

individual is the individual himself. The interview situation provides a great deal of information and understanding about the motivations, capacities, and attitudes of a client. Skill in creating a relationship with a person in a social predicament provides the means of involving the client in bringing out the information through which he is understood. The interview has become one of the chief sources of the diagnostic treatment process.

Implicit in the greater reliance of the probation officer on the defendant himself is the trust created between the two. The offender, because he feels he is understood, and because he perceives that the officer has a helping role, usually talks more freely and reveals more of himself. The assumption is that the information given will be used in a responsible fashion.

In addition to information from the defendant the officer uses the more traditional ways of obtaining information. He makes an investigation of previous arrests and convictions; he interviews members of the family; he secures facts about past and current employment; he consults health records; he obtains information from schools; and as a member of the social work community, he makes use of information from social welfare agencies. His ability to secure information is dependent on the understanding that this information will be used responsibly.

The masses of data acquired from the offender and from collateral sources are of varied quality. Some of the data are factual, and verified by the informant either orally or in writing. Some of the data given as fact are unverified or even unverifiable. Some of the information is from public records and is information of common knowledge, available to anyone. Other material is given confidentially, and with the specification that the informant is not to be revealed. Some of the information is secured from records which are confidential. In addition, from this data, the officer makes certain inferences, certain evaluations. If the report is to be helpful, it must be diagnostic and evaluative. All information which seems pertinent is organized into the document known as the presentence report.

USES OF THE PRESENTENCE REPORT

The use of the presentence report has expanded from its original purpose of supplying pertinent information to the judge to assist him in arriving at a disposition. In the beginning, the probation officer often gave the judge orally the information secured in his investigation. If the report was submitted in writing, it probably was written by the probation officer himself as his own stenographer. Confidentiality of the report depended upon the discretion of the judge and the probation officer.

As the function of the probation office expanded from a one-man operation to an agency including administrative, supervisory, and clerical personnel, the presentence report became part of an agency file which was known to a larger number of people. The protection of the contents of the report was no longer only a matter of the discretion of the probation officer, but became a function of the agency. If the original worker was not available, or had resigned, the new worker found the information in the presentence report very useful in identifying the case, and in outlining problems which he might find. More and more records began to be basic material for the supervisory function of the probation officer. As the concept of supervision took a more significant focus in the probation function, probation officers began to see the presentence investigative process as providing a report which could serve as a basic tool in the supervision of the probationer, as well as a document prepared for the judge for sentencing purposes.

As the probation agency began to be seen not as a separate, isolated correctional entity, but as representing one phase of a more comprehensive correctional system, and as many probation agencies were given parole functions, the presentence report began to be seen as providing valuable data for parole and institutional personnel. Copies of presentence reports were sent automatically to the institution to which the offender was committed.

In addition, the probation task, whether in investigation, or supervision, entailed close communication and cooperation with law-enforcement agencies, with social welfare, and with health personnel. Reciprocal relationships were created: the acquiring of information meant the willingness to give information. What was originally a small circle of people with an interest in the data of the presentence document has been enlarged, necessitating safeguards to ensure the privacy of the confidential material in the report, such as specific regulations governing the transmission of information.

The growing conviction that research is a desirable and necessary activity of correctional agencies has opened up correctional files to the social scientist. The prevalent emphasis on inservice training and the use of material in case records for the teaching of casework in social work schools has further expanded the circle of people who have access to case records. The disguising of individual identity in the use of case records is taken for granted.

The rationale for the wider use of the presentence report in the ways mentioned is quite obvious. The correctional process is not only a one to one relationship, but embraces a large number of people besides probation officers. The presentence report is written for the judge, and is used by both the probation office and the prison personnel. Written communication makes the use of clerical personnel necessary. Research and teaching are basic requirements if practice is to be improved. Social welfare and law enforcement personnel who are engaged in working with offenders have a legitimate interest in certain data from the presentence report that does not need to be protected by the principle of confidentiality.

THE PRINCIPLE OF CONFIDENTIALITY

The principle of confidentiality has been a guiding one for professional people—doctors, lawyers, clergymen, and social workers—who in their practice have close relationships with the people they serve. People with problems must often reveal personal details about themselves and their situation. Essentially, the confidentiality concept is that the professional person can be trusted to use whatever information is secured in a responsible way. In the federal system, the probation officer uses the information to carry out his administrative and helping function. By law he must provide social information for the court, and by the same law he is committed to a helping function. Basic to the assumption of the helping function is a positive orientation toward people, a conviction that offenders are human beings worthy of respect, and that they have potentiality for change. Information secured from them in the interview situation is to be used to carry the probation task. The probation officer knows that treatment relationship can only be effected if trust and confidence can be engendered. Trust and confidence depend in a large measure on the way the officer demonstrates his essential integrity.

He can do this by communicating in the very beginning the nature of the presentence process, his expectations of the offender as a participant, and the expectations that the offender may have of him. He cannot guarantee that information given will not be seen by other people. However, if he is guided by a professional ethic, and if he works for an agency which is committed to the safeguarding of case records, he can assure the defendant of the protections which are available.

The principle of confidentiality should govern the behavior of the professional person in his relationships with his clients and with all other people who supply him data for his presentence report. Because of his status and role as a probation officer, he has access to a great deal of information from members of the offender's family, employers, law-enforcement personnel, social welfare and health agencies. Much of the information is given willingly and without restriction as to the use, but other information is given with the understanding that the source of the information is not to be divulged. Medical information is sometimes given only with the consent of the patient. Medical and welfare personnel are governed by their professional ethic, and would be loath to release data if that data were used irresponsibly. Collaboration and cooperation is only possible if professional confidence exists between collaborators. Emphasis on the use of information received in confidence is that it be used for the welfare of the client or patient. The first canon of the social work code is, "I regard as my primary obligation the welfare of the individual or group served." The principle of confidentiality should permeate activities of workers in all their professional contacts.

DUAL ROLE OF THE PROBATION OFFICER

A confusion regarding the principle of confidentiality as it applies to the field of corrections arises from the dual role of the probation officer. On the one hand he has an administrative role as an officer of the court to conduct an objective investigation. The presentence report enables the judge to make a disposition based on knowledge of the social and personal facts pertaining to the offender. As an investigator, the probation officer includes all the evidence which is pertinent and comes to a recommendation either for or against probation. Information given by the offender, or by collaterals, may lead to a recommendation for commitment or for probation. In a sense, the offender participates and reveals himself to his own salvation or peril.

The probation officer is selected for his job because he is interested in the welfare of people. As the federal probation officer's ethical code suggests, he appreciates the "inherent worth of the individual," respects the "inalienable rights of people." He believes in probation as an alternative to incarceration. He has, or develops, skills in working with people, in establishing a relationship, and in entering into the perceptual life of his probationers. Through these skills he is able to develop basic trust in many of them and through his relationship effects more stable functioning, and often change in their behavior.

Because of the dual role of the probation officer, the defendant may have mixed feelings. Can I have confidence in this person who in his capacity as a probation officer has the power to enable me to live in the community, or to place me behind bars? He appears to be interested in me as an individual, but is it safe to trust anyone in authority?

If the probation officer is honest with the defendant as to the nature of his role, if he discusses frankly both the positive and negative items which will be incorporated in the report, and if he prepares the defendant for the type of recommendation which will be submitted, the confusion is likely to be dispelled. A consistent and basic honesty in the probation officer-defendant relationship can establish confidence.

Proponents of the view that the report ought to be given to the defense attorney and to the offender, argue that the withholding of the report is a denial of basic human rights. They contend that men often are sentenced on incomplete and inaccurate data, and on inferences that are not justified. On the other hand, there is a strong opinion that much of the confidential material in the report could not be included if the report were available to the defendant and his attorney. Experts attending the Brussels United Nations Seminar on the medico-psychological and social examination of delinquents held that certain information is relevant only to treatment and should not be given to the scrutiny of the principals.

Dr. Tappan indicates that the Model Penal Code contains the proposal "That the court should advise the defendant or his counsel of the factual contents and the conclusions of the presentence investigation and should afford him fair opportunity, if he so requests, to controvert them. This would require neither the delivery of the report itself nor revelation of the sources of confidential information. This appears to be a fair and workable compromise of a difficult problem in which conflicting interests must be balanced."

¹Paul W. Tappan, *Crime, Justice and Correction.* New York: McGraw-Hill Book Co., Inc., 1960, pp. 558–9.

This alternative to the two extreme views is a compromise which might on the one hand make it possible for the officer to include in the report material which has a bearing on treatment, but which ought not to be disclosed, and on the other hand make sure that the offender and the defense counsel have knowledge of the factual content and conclusions on which the sentence is based.

Psychiatrists, judges, social workers, and attorneys have been vociferous in their arguments for or against the disclosure of the presentence report. But little is known how offenders themselves have reacted to the use of the presentence report. This certainly should be an area for research.

WHAT HAS THE DEFENDANT A RIGHT TO EXPECT?

Specifically, what expectations should a defendant have in reference to the use of the presentence report? The probation officer should be able to assure him that the report is not in public domain, that it or its contents are not to be given to the press, and that his relatives will not see it. He cannot be assured that the judge will not comment on specific items contained in the report.

The defendant also should be informed that the report is essentially a document for the court and correctional agencies. His relatives should be able to be assured that what they give in confidence will not be revealed to the defendant. Confidential reports from medical and social agencies should not be revealed in open court. It has never been a practice among physicians to give their charts to their patients, or for personnel officers to throw open their files to their employees. It is neither practical nor wise to give to the patient the evaluative and technical findings of the psychiatrist, and it might be harmful to the therapeutic effort. The presentence report is a document used both for determination of disposition, and as a guide to the rehabilitative effort. It is one thing to let the offender know what positive and what negative items are in the report, but another to show him the report. The report is not written for the client, but written for the judge and for rehabilitative personnel.

With the momentous growth of industrial, military, welfare, and governmental agencies in our society, more and more records are being kept. Psychological tests are given in every area of life; evaluative statements are filed about students, employees, and welfare clients. A vast amount of personal and social data is accumulated on individuals in every sphere of human activity. Facts are collected for specific purposes—educational, personnel management, determinations such as sentencing, and social-psychological treatment. Not only is information collected, but evaluations and inferences are drawn from the informational data. Protection of the individual from the misuse and abuse of material becomes an ethical issue.

The purpose of information collected on offenders is the good of society and the welfare of the person served. What protection is there to prevent the use of information for negative or destructive purposes; from it being used only to control, and not to treat; to punish, not to help; to label and stigmatize rather than to individualize for treatment purposes? In the effort to obtain worthy ends, in the collaboration of agencies to attain treatment objectives, the right of the individual to privacy may be endangered. When many people are engaged in treatment, much sacrifice may be made of the intimate, personal, and private in a person's life. Moreover, records may emphasize the static and negative findings, and create attitudes which reinforce negative concepts of self. Records may actually be used to perpetuate deviancy rather than promote individual change. The power of the written word is great. In the long run, the only guarantee for responsible use of information is a service which is governed by professional attitudes, and personnel who subscribe to basic ethical values and are able to translate these values into day by day behavior.

PROFESSIONAL ETHICS OF THE PROBATION OFFICER

Although differences of opinion are held as to the appropriate training of the probation officer, the influence of social work practice has been influential in probation and parole. The professional ethics of the social worker is applicable to probation work. The canons of the code of ethics adopted by the National Association of Social Workers in October 1960 especially relate to the principle of confidentiality:

> I respect the privacy of the people I serve.
> I use in a responsible manner information gained in professional relationships.

These canons are of course very general, but they denote expected attitudes, and the expected behavior of the professional person.

The Federal Probation Officers Association, in its code of ethics, specifies the following guidelines:

> I will strive to be objective.
> I will respect the inalienable rights of all persons.
> I will appreciate the inherent worth of the individual.
> I will hold inviolate those confidences which can be reposed in me.

Certainly both organizations state worthy objectives and subscribe to high standards of attitudes and behavior for the professional worker. The big problem is to translate ethical codes into ethical behavior in specific situations.

For example, if an offender gives information which is of an intimate nature and has no particular bearing on the case, is the probation officer to incorporate that information into the presentence report which is a protected but not a secret document? If something is very personal, and has a bearing on the case, does the officer communicate to the judge that this is an intimate matter, and in no instance should be revealed in open court? Or, to cite another instance, suppose pertinent but confidential material is included in the presentence report, and the case then goes on to an institution where the records are not protected. Is the institution informed that the record should be kept in a separate file?

Are the records of a probation office truly protected? Are there agency rules governing the use of the presentence report and case records in the transmission of information to other agencies? If a person comes in who has a legitimate right to seek information, is the case record itself given to him, or does the probation officer find out what he wants to know and then select from the record what is pertinent, keeping the record in his own possession? Is confidentiality as a principle adhered to in day-to-day operations?

Professional attitudes and agency policies translated into behaviors which protect the confidential records are not all that is necessary to guarantee responsible use of records. Since the correctional process is a collaborative one, and since many people are drawn into the rehabilitative effort, the safeguarding of confidential material is a matter which requires attention outside of agency walls. Judges, as members of a profession which has recognized the confidential nature of professional relationships and that certain information should be kept secret, would welcome discussions with probation officers as to what material ought not to be brought out in open court. The treatment staff of prisons are also governed by the ethics of their calling, and cognizant of the governing principle of confidentiality. Since presentence reports are used by judges, prison workers, and probation and parole officers, the problem of making operational the general principle is a common one. The court and the probation officer, as source and distributor of the presentence, has the joint responsibility for working toward the protection of the report where ever it may be sent.

In the literature of corrections, the principle of confidentiality is seen as an important, a basic value, and as an operational guideline. But no extensive study has been made, and little is known as to the actual practice of probation offices in reference to the confidentiality principle. An interesting subject for research would be the attitudes of judges and chief probation officers toward this matter, the policies of agencies to safeguard information, and the day to day practices in the use of presentence data.

11

The Prehearing Juvenile Report: Probation Officers' Conceptions

SEYMOUR Z. GROSS

The main function of the prehearing report in juvenile court proceedings is to present the sociocultural and psychodynamic factors which influenced the juvenile's alleged delinquent behavior. The prehearing report is supposed to give an objective, integrated, and perceptive evaluation so that the court can arrive at an individualized and rehabilitative disposition. Authorities generally agree on the necessity and importance of the prehearing report in juvenile court proceedings without seeking any objective verification of its predictive validity.[1]

Some social scientists have expressed the belief that, in determining dis-

SOURCE. *Journal of Research in Crime and Delinquency*, **4**, July 1967, pp. 212–217. Reprinted with the permission of the National Council on Crime and Delinquency.

[1]George Everson, "The Standard of Children's Court Work," *Journal of Criminal Law and Criminology*, May 1918, pp. 105–113; Herbert H. Lou, *Juvenile Courts in the United States* (Chapel Hill: University of North Carolina Press, 1927); Paul L. Schroeder, "Minimum Standards for Social Investigation," *Proceedings of the American Prison Association*, 1932, pp. 99–110; Richard M. Eddy, "The Investigation for the Court," *Federal Probation*, August–October 1940, pp. 26–29; Ben S. Meeker, "Analysis of a Presentence Report," *Federal Probation*, March 1950, pp. 41–46; Ben S. Meeker, "Probation and Parole Officers at Work," *NPPA Journal*, April 1957, pp. 99–106; Harold Povill, "The Investigation Process," *Focus*, January 1951, pp. 75–79; Paul W. Keve, *The Probation Officer Investigates* (Minneapolis: University of Minnesota Press, 1960); Paul W. Keve, "The Message in Mr. Piyo's Dream," *Federal Probation,* December 1961, pp. 11–15; Paul W. Keve, "The Presentence Report," *Creative Thinking in Corrections*, Minnesota Corrections Association, Minneapolis, 1961 (mimeo.), pp. 1–11.

position, intuition and experience should be used cautiously.[2] This position was summarized by Shannon:

"It is here [juvenile court] that we may attempt to determine something about the factors that influence the decision to define a juvenile as a serious delinquent or the decision to deal with a juvenile in one manner rather than another. How important, for example, is family status as contrasted with economic status in influencing a judge's decision?"[3]

REVIEW OF PREVIOUS RESEARCH

In published literature of criminology, law, and probation, only one object-ive study focuses exclusively on the prehearing report; however, presentence and prehearing reports have been evaluated in connection with other research subjects. In an extensive examination of juvenile courts in New York City, Eddy found that "a small but significant group of judges ignores completely, or almost completely, the costly and time-consuming probation investigation."[4] Rumney and Murphy conducted a ten-year followup study of one thousand consecutive cases, including 137 juveniles, placed on probation in 1937. Their findings seriously challenged the utility of the prehearing report for persons placed on probation:

"Our studies failed to disclose any significant difference with respect to out-come as between those who were released on probation following investigation by a probation officer and those who were released on probation by the court without pre-liminary investigation."[5]

Lottier attempted to determine which kinds of data have predictive signi-ficance.[6] In his study, twenty-eight clinical judges ranked twenty-five social-psychological variables for predictive significance. After eliminating the less experienced raters, he found that twenty ranked as most predictive the category labeled "criminality, present and past arrests, and sentences," followed in importance by "work record, economic adjustment"; "family background,

[2]William Healy, "Study of the Case Preliminary to Treatment," *Journal of Criminal Law and Criminology*, May 1922, pp. 74–81; Elio D. Monachesi, "Can We Predict Probation Outcomes?" *Federal Probation*, August 1939, pp. 15–18; Elio D. Monachesi, "Predicting Prob-ation Success," *Probation*, June 1939, pp. 70–74; Stanley D. Porteus, "Setting the Sights for Delinquency Research," *Federal Probation*, June 1953, pp. 43–47; Daniel Glaser and Richard F. Hangren, "Predicting the Adjustment of Federal Probationers," *NPPA Journal*, July 1958, pp. 258–267.

[3]Lyle W. Shannon, "The Problem of Competence to Help," *Federal Probation*, March 1961, pp. 32–39.

[4]Alfred J. Kahn, *A Court for Children: A Study of the New York City Children's Court* (New York: Columbia University Press, 1953).

[5]Jay Rumney and John A. Murphy, *Probation and Social Adjustment* (New Brunswick: Rutgers University Press, 1952).

[6]Stuart Lottier, "Predicting Criminal Behavior," *Federal Probation*, October–December 1943, pp. 8–12.

parents and siblings"; and "habits, recreation, drinking." Glaser and Hangren used an actuarial approach to combine statements made by the probation officer in presentence reports expressed in subjective but fairly specific classifications.[7] They found higher predictive efficiency using these statements in contrast to objective items such as work record, residence stability, and age at first arrest. This author knows of only one study which deals objectively with the prehearing report. This recent study by Cohn attempted to determine the criteria by which a probation officer recommended four types of disposition: probation, institutionalization, psychiatric examination, and discharge.[8] The results were not reported in terms of statistical significance, although trends were discussed. The findings indicate that differential behavior and status were the determinants of each of the four types of disposition recommended by the probation officer. For example, juveniles who were more cooperative with the probation officer had a better chance to be placed on probation; the less cooperative child was recommended for institutionalization.

PRESENT STUDY

The comparative lack of objective studies of presentence and prehearing reports suggests a need for further investigation. The present study was to determine how the probation officer handling juvenile offenders conceived the importance of the various sections of the report in terms of usefulness for appropriate or accurate recommendation of disposition. The officers were asked to rank the various sections of the prehearing report. A rank of *one* indicated the data *most* useful in making disposition recommendations; a rank of *ten* indicated the data *least* useful. The ranking task was then repeated to determine how they thought the court would react to the data.

The sample comprised seventy Minnesota probation officers handling juvenile offenders.[9] The seventy officers represented 85.3 percent of the officers who returned questionnaires sufficiently complete to be tabulated. This relatively large response to a mail questionnaire indicates this report covers a representative sample of Minnesota probation officers handling juvenile offenders.

RESULTS

The probation officers ranked as *most* important (1) the child's attitude toward the offense, (2) family data, and (3) previous delinquency problems. The three sections the officers felt the court would consider *most* important

[7]Glaser and Hangren, *supra* note 2.

[8]Yona Cohn, "Criteria for the Probation Officer's Recommendation to the Juvenile Court Judge," *Crime and Delinquency*, July 1963, pp. 262–275.

[9]For a detailed report of the biographical characteristics of the officers, see Seymour Z. Gross, "Biographical Characteristics of Minnesota Probation Officers Who Deal with Juvenile Offenders," *Crime and Delinquency*, April 1966, pp. 109–116.

were (1) present offense data, (2) previous delinquency problems, and (3) the child's attitude toward the offense. In both rankings, the probation officers considered the *least* important sections to be the data on interests, activities, and religion. The largest gap between the officers' personal evaluations and their apperception of the court's view was in regard to "present offense data." The officers perceived the court would consider this section the *most* important, while they ranked it *fourth*. Table 1 presents the results.

Table 1   *Median Ranks of Probation Officers' Personal Rankings of Prehearing Report Sections and Their Apperception of the Court's View*

Report Sections	Officer's Personal Ranking	Apperception of Court's Ranking
Child's attitude toward the offense	2.33	3.02
Family data	3.28	4.70
Previous delinquency problems	3.36	2.50
Present offense data	4.00	1.96
Interview impression	4.43	5.90
School data	5.77	5.96
Psychological test data	6.03	6.06
Psychiatric examination data	6.57	6.07
Interests and activities data	9.00	9.38
Religious data	9.42	9.20

The Spearman Rank-Order correlation, used to determine the extent of agreement between each officer's personal ranking and his anticipation of the court's reaction, reveals that fifty-one officers (72.8 percent) obtained significant agreement ($p < .05$) between their two rankings. (At the 0.05 level of statistical significance a correlation coefficient of 0.564 is required.) The remaining nineteen officers did not exhibit statistically significant Rank-Order correlation between their two rankings; in fact, five of these officers had negative correlation coefficients. This suggests that these nineteen officers represent an interesting subgroup of persons who, since they evidently disagreed significantly with the court, apparently were dissatisfied with their job or with certain aspects of it.[10]

The differentiating descriptive characteristics of the subgroup of nineteen officers (Group I) are summarized to compare with the fifty-one officers (Group II) who agreed with the court. Compared with Group II, the officers in Group I averaged two years older (mean age 33.9, standard deviation 5.9), had higher formal education with master's degrees (43.5 percent of the total group of seventy), more frequently worked exclusively with juveniles (72 percent), indicated a greater number of professional journals subscribed to and read, and placed greater importance on the results of psychological tests and psychiatric examination for recommendations for disposition. When asked

[10]Professor Robert D. Wirt suggested this interpretation.

how much they liked their work, all Group I officers responded in the "strongly like it" and "like it" categories. In a similar questionnaire item, they answered with a 95 percent median value concerning their agreement with the court on specific dispositions of dismissal, probation, commitment, and continuance. If the answers of officers in Group I to direct questions about job satisfaction and agreement with the court were very similar to the majority of the officers, in what way did they disagree in the task of ranking their personal choices and their apperception of the court's opinion?

Table 2 reveals three highly significant differences between Groups I and II (p < .001). Group I did not give as much importance to the relatively objective data usually contained in the categories of "previous delinquency problems" and "present offense" data. They also considered psychological test data more important than the majority of the officers. Group I officers also indicated that "family data," "interview impression," "psychiatric examination data," and "interests and activities" data were more important for disposition than Group II officers held them to be.

Table 3 shows one statistically significant difference between Group I and Group II: Group I officers thought that the court gave greater importance to psychological test data than did the officers in Group II. The trends in the comparison in Table 3 were not as clear as for the officer's own perceptions. The groups were essentially in agreement concerning the court's use of the information in the prehearing report, although personal weighting of the various sections of the prehearing report demonstrated significant subgroup differences among the two groups of probation officers.

DISCUSSION

The subgroup of Minnesota probation officers who disagreed with the way that the court generally was believed to view the prehearing report sections appeared to be oriented toward a psychodynamic or broader social casework approach than the majority of the officers. They placed more importance on report sections dealing with the less precise area of personality and family relationships and had considerably less faith in the use of relatively objective data, such as the description of present and previous delinquencies. In their apperception of the court's view of the prehearing report, however, they agreed essentially with the majority of the officers.

The biographical characteristics which differentiated Group I from the majority (Group II) now appear consistent with the way that they use the prehearing report. The officers in Group I had more graduate degrees and read a greater number of professional journals. The Group I officers identified primarily with the broader field of social casework rather than with the probation officer role.[11] Analysis of the majority of the officers (Group II) indicate

---

[11] Walter C. Reckless, "Training Probation and Parole Personnel," *Focus*, January 1948 pp. 44–48.

Table 2 *Median Ranks of Two Groups of Probation Officers in Personal Ranking of Prehearing Report Sections*

Report Sections	Group I N = 19	Group II N = 51	p
Child's attitude toward the offense	2.66	2.19	n.s.
Family data	2.33	3.58	n.s.
Previous delinquency problems	6.00	3.07	.001
Present offense data	6.75	3.00	.001
Interview impression	3.75	4.60	n.s.
School data	5.13	5.78	n.s.
Psychological test data	4.38	6.20	.001
Psychiatric examination data	5.33	6.82	n.s.
Interests and activities data	8.56	8.98	n.s.
Religious data	9.55	9.16	n.s.

NOTE. The level of statistical significance was obtained by the Median Test.

that their professional identification was primarily that of a probation officer. Their primary concern was community protection; service of the offender was secondary. Since Group II included almost three-fourths of the total number of officers, it may be that Group I officers feel frustrated in dealing with the court as well as with a majority of their fellow officers. It would be interesting to know how active, if at all, the Group I officers are in trying to promote stronger social casework orientation. Whatever the merits of their disagreement with the court and fellow workers, the officers in Group I may present a problem in terms of supervision and communication.

Table 3 *Median Ranks of Two Goups of Probation Officers' Apperception of the Court's Opinion of Prehearing Report Sections*

Report Sections	Group I N = 19	Group II N = 51	p
Child's attitude toward the offense	3.42	2.71	n.s.
Family data	4.33	4.75	n.s.
Previous delinquency problems	2.08	2.71	n.s.
Present offense data	2.00	1.94	n.s.
Interview impression	7.13	5.42	n.s.
School data	6.00	5.85	n.s.
Psychological test data	5.20	6.61	.05
Psychiatric examination data	5.00	6.65	n.s.
Interests and activities data	9.29	9.19	n.s.
Religious data	9.29	9.19	n.s.

NOTE. The level of statistical significance was obtained by the Median Test.

SUMMARY

Seventy probation officers in Minnesota who deal with juvenile offenders ranked sections of the prehearing report on the basis of their own conception of the relative importance of the various sections of the report. They repeated the ranking in terms of how they anticipated the court would view the prehearing report. The three sections ranked in order of importance for the officers' own perceptions were (1) the child's attitude toward the offense, (2) family data, and (3) previous delinquent problems. The three sections the officers felt the court would view as most important were (1) present offense data, (2) previous delinquency problems, and (3) the child's attitude toward the offense. A subgroup of nineteen officers who had higher formal education, subscribed to and read more professional journals, and, in general, appeared to have a broader social casework orientation gave significantly less importance to the more objective types of data. However, there was little disagreement between the subgroup and the majority of officers in their apperception of the court's view. This difference in orientation between social casework and probation may create communication and supervision problems.

12
Criteria for the Probation Officer's Recommendations to the Juvenile Court Judge

YONA COHN

The purpose of this study is to analyze the underlying criteria used by the probation officers of the Bronx (New York) Children's Court in recommending dispositions to the judge at the end of their presentence investigation reports. In other probation settings where the officer's basic assumptions about the delinquent child, the court's philosophy about the role of the probation officer, the officer's professional background, and the community's attitude toward juvenile delinquency may vary, the criteria will, of course, differ from the ones we shall present.

Although a probation officer's recommendation is common practice in the juvenile court, it is not always a formal part of the presentence investigation report. Williamson refers to the formal recommendation in her statement that "the report may or may not contain a recommendation. Some judges desire recommendations; others do not permit them, or else do not request them."[1]

Much has been written about the causes of delinquency, but whether these writings focus on the delinquency itself, on the individual juvenile, his social background, or on any combination of the three, a suitable disposition is required. For example, as far back as 1922, John W. Houston

SOURCE. *Crime and Delinquency*, **9**, July 1963, pp. 262–275. Reprinted with the permission of the National Council on Crime and Delinquency.
[1] Margaretta A. Williamson, *The Social Worker in the Prevention and Treatment of Delinquency* (New York: Columbia University Press, 1935).

considered it inappropriate to give probation treatment to juveniles who had committed serious delinquent acts.[2] Other authors investigated the child's previous convictions, his intelligence, personality make-up, and seriousness of emotional pathology as elements to be considered in recommending probation. Dressler conducted special research on the "probation risk" presented by the "lone wolf" as compared with the gang member.[3] Many, such as Flexner and Baldwin[4] and Teeters and Reinemann,[5] stressed family cohesiveness; while early prediction tables like Monachesi's emphasized interaction of the various social, psychological, and legal criteria as a means of foretelling the successful outcome of a probation period. One of Monachesi's findings was that "no single factor may be important in determining probation behavior" and that "outcome of probation depends upon the accumulative effect of all pre-probation factors."[6]

THE STUDY

Our study analyzes the broad background information presented by the probation officer in his presentence investigation report, with concentration on the four major recommendations he may make: probation, institutionalization, psychiatric examination, or discharge. As a means of obtaining a picture of some general trends, we shall try to isolate the criteria on which his investigation and recommendations are based.

For our study, we examined, in chronological order, 175 presentence investigation reports presented to the judge of the Bronx Children's Court from January 1, 1952 to about the middle of that year. Of these 175, 50 recommended probation, 50 recommended institutionalization, 50 recommended psychiatric examination, and 25 recommended discharge. (This last group was limited to 25 because relatively fewer such recommendations are made to the court. In the tables that follow, these 25 cases were multiplied by two to make comparison with the other groups more convenient.) In addition to the 175 cases selected, another 500 cases were reviewed—about one-third of the yearly total. The following factors were tabulated for each case:

1. sex
2. age
3. religion

[2]John W. Houston, "The Right Selection of Probation Cases," *Journal of Criminal Law and Criminology*, Feb. 1922, p. 577.

[3]David Dressler, *Probation and Parole* (New York: Columbia University Press, 1951).

[4]Bernard Flexner and Roger N. Baldwin, *Juvenile Courts and Probation* (New York: Century Co., 1914), p. 73.

[5]Negley K. Teeters and John Otto Reinemann, *The Challenge of Delinquency* (New York: Prentice-Hall, 1950).

[6]Elio D. Monachesi, *Prediction Factors in Probation* (Minneapolis: The Sociological Press, 1932), p. 110. The Gluecks also stress a multidimensional interpretation. Sheldon and Eleanor Gleuck, *Unraveling Juvenile Delinquency* (New York: Commonwealth Fund, 1950), p. 281.

4. race
5. type of delinquent act
6. seriousness of delinquent act
7. child's role in delinquent act
8. number of previous prosecuted offenses.
9. number of previous unprosecuted offenses
10. number of parents or guardians
11. economic situation
12. type of neighborhood
13. father's personality
14. mother's personality
15. degree of marital stability of parents
16. mother's relationship with child
17. father's relationship with child
18. church attendance
19. school/job attendance
20. school/job conduct
21. school/job performance
22. personality difficulties (including physical handicaps)
23. child's relationship with father
24. child's relationship with mother
25. child's relationship with sibling
26. child's relationship with peers
27. child's relationship with neighbors
28. child's group affiliation
29. child's cooperation with probation officer
30. parent's cooperation with probation officer

The statistical results for cases in each recommendation group were then tabulated and compared with the results for the other groups.

Let us examine the major tables—the distributions for sex, race, and personality of the child and the type and seriousness of his delinquent act—so that we may compare the characteristics of each recommendation group with the others in order to determine the criteria used by the probation officers in selecting these groups.

Table 1 *Distribution According to Sex*

	Male	Female	Total
Probation	47	3	50
Institutionalization	29	21	50
Psychiatric			
examination	41	9	50
Discharge	48	2	50
Total	165	35	200

DISTRIBUTION ACCORDING TO SEX

Table 1 shows a large number of girls recommended for institutionalization and a small number of girls recommended for discharge and probation. While girls made up only one-sixth of the total, they constituted nearly half the group recommended to an institution; restated as a proportion, this means that three times as many girls as boys were recommended for institutionalization.

For 30 out of 35 girls, the probation officer recommended psychiatric examination (diagnosis) or institutional treatment. Cross-tabulation of data for the 21 girls recommended to an institution reveals that most of them had committed delinquent acts against sexual taboos—acts which were generally considered decisive factors in arriving at the recommendation they received.

DISTRIBUTION ACCORDING TO RACE

The racial distribution of the total group of 200 was three white children to one Negro child (Table 2). Of these, fewer Negroes were recommended for psychiatric examination or discharge than for institutionalization. The number of Negro children who were recommended for institutional commitment was cross-tabulated with the kind and seriousness of delinquent act committed, the number of parents or guardians in the home, the mother's relationship with the child, the child's school attendance and personality difficulties, and parental cooperation with the probation officer. The only significant correlation found from this cross-tabulation referred only to the type and seriousness of the delinquent acts committed, which, for these Negro children, were primarily acts against sexual taboos.

The eleven unrecorded cases refer mainly to Puerto Rican children whose race the probation officer could not identify.

PERSONALITY AS A CRITERION

The following classifications of the child's personality were inferred from examination of a number of investigation reports: "No Difficulties," "Disturbed Behavior," "Neurotic Symptoms," "Undiagnosed Symptoms," and "Psychotic Symptoms."

A child was classified under the "No Difficulties" heading under the following three conditions: (1) when the probation officer merely said so, (2) when the officer indicated that the child's behavior problems were not attributed to any emotional disturbance, and (3) when the officer discussed a rehabilitation plan, implying that the child had no personality difficulties.

A child was classified as having "Disturbed Behavior" when the probation officer stated it in his report or when he expressed agreement with the school report's description of disturbed behavior. This classification was also used when the rehabilitation plan set forth by the probation officer seemed to suggest

Table 2 *Racial Distribution*

	White	Negro	No Record	Total
Probation	36	13	1	50
Institutionalization	25	20	5	50
Pyschiatric examination	37	8	5	50
Discharge	44	6	—	50
Total	142	47	11	200

the presence of disturbed behavior. The probation officer's report never contained a clinical description of a child's behavior disorder.

The classification "Neurotic Symptoms" was listed in those instances where the probation officer was quoting from the psychiatric examination report.

"Undiagnosed Symptoms" were reported when the probation officer did not expressly state that the child evidenced neurotic symptoms but merely implied that certain undiagnosed personality difficulties existed. The following descriptions were illustrative of this group: "an occasionally enuretic, nervous, high-strung youngster"; "[has] fear of school boys, unexpressed hostility to mother, [is] not facing responsibility, depressed"; "sullen, uncooperative, unreliable, uncommunicative, [has] temper tantrums, [is] enuretic"; "a quiet child, thumbsucker . . . mixed up, could use psychiatric help"; "a nervous bed-wetting hoodlum"; "the girl seems dazed, sad, hysterical, giggles constantly."

A child was classified as "Psychotic" when a psychiatric diagnosis of psychosis was quoted by the officer.

Personality criteria were recorded by probation officers in slightly more than two-thirds of 200 cases (see Table 3). The high number of unrecorded descriptions of personality for the group recommended to an institution may indicate either the officer's indifference or his hesitation in attaching diagnostic labels to the child when recommending referral to an institution.

Table 3 *The Personality of the Child*

	No Difficulties	Disturbed Behavior	Neurotic Symptoms	Undiagnosed Symptoms	Psychotic Symptoms	No Record	Total
Probation	25	5	1	5	—	14	50
Institutionalization	8	5	5	11	1	20	50
Psychiatric examination	2	10	7	16	1	14	50
Discharge	32	—	1	1	—	16	50
Total	67	20	14	33	2	64	200

The discharge group showed a clear picture of "No Difficulties." In the probation group, two-thirds of those recorded were also classed under this heading; only one was described as showing neurotic symptoms, and none as showing psychotic symptoms. Probation was recommended, however, not only in cases having no difficulties, but also in cases with disturbed behavior or undiagnosed symptoms.

This picture is reversed in the group recommended to an institution, where only one-fourth of the recorded cases were classified under "No Difficulties" and one-third under "Undiagnosed Symptoms." The *same* number of cases with disturbed behavior appeared in the group recommended for institutionalization as well as in the group recommended to probation; but *more* cases with neurotic symptoms were recommended for institutionalization than for probation. The proportional difference is striking: of the 36 recorded cases recommended to probation, only one was diagnosed under "Neurotic Symptoms"; but of the 30 recorded cases recommended for institutionalization, five were so diagnosed.

The "Psychiatric Examination" group contained the highest number of children with undiagnosed symptoms and only two children with no difficulties. But even this particular group shows a smaller number of recorded judgments than the probation and discharge groups. Half of the "Disturbed Behavior" cases, half of the "Neurotic Symptoms" cases, half of the "Undiagnosed Symptoms," and one of the two "Psychotic Symptoms" cases were recommended for psychiatric examination, thus leading to the conclusion that the probation officer recommended psychiatric examination on general grounds— the presence of some sort of personality problem—rather than on the presence of a specific sort of personality problem. He tended to throw all difficult personality cases into the psychiatrist's lap instead of examining each case individually.

From the tabulation it is evident that personality difficulties were important criteria in the probation officer's recommendations; yet the relatively high number of cases in which no personality assessment had been recorded indicates some lack of perceptiveness on the probation officer's part.

THE DELINQUENT ACT AS A CRITERION

Delinquent acts were classified according to whether they were committed against life or property, against sexual taboos, and against parents (Table 4). Delinquent acts against parents usually were reflected in petitions made by parents or guardians against "ungovernable" children—children (especially girls) accused of such acts as running away from home, stealing from home, or destroying furniture. Often, cases of truancy were included in this group (the accusation being that the child was refusing his parents' *legal* demand to go to school).

Type of delinquent act committed was a significant factor in the probation officer's recommendation. Among the three types of acts designated, those

Table 4   *Kind of Delinquent Act*

	Against Life or Property	Against Sexual Taboos	Against Parents	Total
Probation	44	0	6	50
Institutionalization	17	6	27	50
Psychiatric examination	30	7	13	50
Discharge	42	2	6	50
Total	133	15	52	200

against life or property constituted 88 percent of the recommendations to probation and 84 percent of the recommendations for discharge. Sexual delinquencies, which constituted a very small number in all groups, were completely absent from the group recommended for probation.

Delinquent acts against parents are usually referred to the court by the parents. The conflict in the home, evidenced by both the child's delinquent act and his parents' referral, seemed to lead the probation officer to the decision that removal of the child to an institution would be the best solution to the problem. In these "Delinquency against Parents" cases, the officer recommended a psychiatric examination only half as often, and probation or discharge only one-quarter as often, as he did institutionalization. The recommendations for probation and discharge show many similarities on this table. Although the "Institutionalization" and the "Psychiatric Examination" groups are similar in their high number of sexual delinquencies, they are dissimilar in their distribution of delinquent acts against parents and against life or property. Only one-eighth of all children committing delinquencies against life or property were recommended for institutionalization, but one-half of those committing delinquent acts against parents were so recommended.

SERIOUSNESS OF DELINQUENT ACT

The following acts against life or property were regarded as serious delinquencies: a robbery with an assault which resulted in the victim's death, a serious stabbing in a gang fight, sodomy, possession of loaded firearms, an attack on a girl that caused a fracture of her skull, an armed robbery, an auto theft, a forcible rape. Serious delinquent acts against parents included suicide attempts and severe damage of the home; illegitimate births constituted a serious violation of sexual taboos (among girls), when the babies' whereabouts were unknown.

Moderate delinquency included burglary with forced entry into a building; purse-snatching; participation, in a minor role, in a group car theft; minor thefts; assembling for a gang fight; forced entry into a school and theft of valuables there; forgery. Girls' delinquencies against their parents involved staying away from home a few nights.

Mild delinquency included kicking a boy during a fight and attempts at thefts. Delinquency against parents in this category included some truancy cases and cases of coming home late in the evening (see Table 5).

The seriousness of the delinquent act appears to have been of only secondary significance to the probation officer in making his recommendation. The officer who may have hesitated in putting on probation a child who committed a serious delinquent act often did not hesitate at all in recommending a discharge or a psychiatric examination.

Table 5   *Seriousness of the Delinquent Act*

	Serious	Moderate	Mild	Total
Probation	5	35	10	50
Institutionalization	9	39	2	50
Psychiatric examination	14	34	2	50
Discharge	10	26	14	50
Total	38	134	28	200

THE CHILD'S FAMILY RELATIONS

Most mothers of children recommended for probation and psychiatric examination had treated them with "some rejection," as recorded by the probation officers. In the discharge group, the majority of mothers were classified as evidencing "no rejection" of the child, while those children recommended to an institution suffered from "severe rejection" by their mothers.

A similar pattern can be discerned in the less frequently recorded relationship of father and child. (While the maternal relationship was recorded in 157 of the 200 cases, the paternal relationship was recorded in only 96 instances.)

Children in each of the four recommendation groups showed distinctively different types of relationships with their parents. The children recommended to an institution usually had tense relations with both parents; the children recommended for discharge usually had good relations with both; and those recommended for probation or psychiatric examination had fair relations with them. But despite the rather distinctive differences in those cases where such information was recorded, a high number of presentence investigation reports completely omitted this information. Of the 200 reports studied, 86 did not include information on the child's relationship with his mother, and 116 did not include information on his relationship with his father.

A similar trend can be observed when one studies the factor of marital stability of the parents, which was recorded in only about half the 200 presentence reports (104 cases). The highest number of stable marital relations was recorded for parents of the discharge group, the next highest for parents of the groups recommended to probation and psychiatric examination (the figures for both of which were only slightly less than those for the first group), and the lowest number for parents of those in the institution group.

The large number of unrecorded cases—three-quarters of the 200—indicates that the probation officers did not consider the personality of the parents an important factor in arriving at a recommendation for the child. Hence, no pattern could be traced because of the limitations of the sample.

Economic level affected the officers' recommendations in much the same manner as did the familial relationships; high economic level appeared most often among those in the discharge group, least often among those in the institution group.

All data about a child's family background should be significant in determining one or another recommendation. The probation officers in our study, however, were not completely aware of this and so they only partially investigated the family background of the children, frequently omitting some vital information. As noted above, the child's personality difficulties were also frequently ignored in the investigation report.

DESCRIPTION OF EACH GROUP

Children Recommended for Probation

What kinds of children were most likely to be recommended for probation? Rarely were they girls. Girls who appeared before the court usually had committed delinquent acts against their parents or against sexual taboos—acts which the probation officer generally considered products of social background and personality make-up beyond the range of effective probation treatment. Indeed, sexual delinquents were *never* recommended to probation. Racial or religious affiliation was not considered a factor in recommending, or not recommending, probation. The child most often recommended to probation was the one with no personality difficulties; a child with behavior difficulties or undiagnosed symptoms was only rarely recommended. Children suffering from a physical handicap were practically never in this group. Age, gang membership, and delinquent neighborhood made no difference to the probation officer. Where parents were more cooperative with him, probation was recommended slightly more often. Economic status was not considered significant.

The child recommended to probation had both his original parents in more instances than did the child recommended for institutionalization; but marital stability was no more frequent among parents of those in the probation group than among parents of those in the other groups.

The child's school attendance, his conduct at school, and his achievements there neither qualified nor disqualified him for a recommendation to probation. Even church attendance, although it was more frequent in this group than among the institution group, was not a significant criterion for the probation officer. Neither the child's group affiliation nor his good or bad relationship with siblings, neighbors, relatives, and even his mother was significant. (The child's relationship with his peers went practically unrecorded, although more followers than leaders, more "group" delinquents than "lone wolf" delinquents were recommended for probation.) With regard to his mother's relationship with him, he did not differ from the children in the other groups. Interestingly, though, his father less frequently treated him with "severe rejection" than did the fathers of those in the psychiatric examination and institution groups. The parents' personalities, however, were not considered important criteria to the probation officer—and were seldom recorded.

Few children who had committed serious delinquent acts were recommended for probation; to the probation officer, commission of an act against the parents evidenced a family background and personality structure too disturbed to warrant probation. Thus, delinquents who had committed acts against life or property were more often recommended to probation.

Number of previous convictions was not an important criterion, but the group recommended to probation differed significantly from the others in that a larger number had previously committed delinquent acts that had not been prosecuted. If the child cooperated with the probation officer during the presentence investigation, he had a slight edge in his chances of being recommended to probation; this was also true of his parents' cooperation with the officer.

Children Recommended for Institutionalization

Age was not considered significant in the officer's recommendations for institutionalization. As to religious affiliation, the child recommended for commitment was less likely to be Catholic than either Protestant or Jewish. He was slightly less cooperative than the child recommended for probation, and relatively more often handicapped than those in the other groups—but mental deficiency was not a significant criterion.

With respect to personality difficulties, he differed markedly from the other groups and usually had undiagnosed personality problems. A smaller number of those recommended for commitment had behavior difficulties or neurotic symptoms; few were rated as having no difficulties.

The child's family structure revealed factors important enough to influence the probation officer's recommendation. The child had only one original parent in more instances than did those in the other groups. (The number of children with one or both parents who were substitutes was not deemed an important criterion.) His economic status was the lowest of those in the four groups, but the others were just as frequently found in a delinquent neighborhood as he.

Most mothers, but slightly fewer fathers, of these children had severely rejected them, and their relationship with both parents was usually bad. The parents' marital relations were very unstable, although the symptoms characteristic of an unstable personality were found slightly less often among the mothers than among the fathers. The parents were not cooperative with the probation officer. Curiously, the sibling relationship of children in this group was not exceptionally bad.

In other social areas, the child recommended to commitment presented a less clear-cut picture. Although his attendance at church and school was the most sporadic of the four groups, he did not differ in his behavior or achievements at school. His group affiliations were not in any way distinctive, and his relationship with his peers, neighbors, or relatives was too infrequently recorded to show any trend in the probation officer's process of selection.

As to his delinquent acts: those against sexual taboos or against parents more frequently resulted in the child's being recommended to an institution than to any other disposition—a fact which explains the disproportionately high number of girls recommended for institutionalization, even when their social background was better than that of boys committing the same kind of delinquent act.

While the seriousness of the delinquent act was not significant, very few "mild" cases were recommended to an institution. The fact that most children in this group had committed their delinquent acts alone is consistent with the two kinds of delinquencies (i.e., against parents and against sexual taboos) most frequently found in this group. To the probation officers, previous convictions had some significance for this recommendation group, but previous *unprosecuted* delinquent acts had none. The same applied to gang membership. In spite of the high number of Negroes in this group, the kind of delinquent act, rather than a child's race, was what brought him into the institution.

Children Recommended for Psychiatric Examination

What makes the probation officer deem his investigation insufficient in determining a child's difficulties or the proper treatment to be used so that he decides to recommend a psychiatric examination? According to the reports the officers filled out, the answers cannot be found in the child's family background. With respect to family structure and to the economic situation and marital stability of the parents, *all* children recommended for psychiatric examination resembled those recommended for probation. A slightly greater number of families of children in this group, however, lived in a delinquent neighborhood, but no significant differences were reported in the familial relationship—mother to child, child to mother, father to child, child to father. There was a very slight tendency for the father to have an unstable personality, but nothing of note was reported about the mother's personality or the child's relationship with his siblings. Parental cooperation with the probation officer was slightly better in the probation group. Thus, those children recommended for psychiatric examination have family backgrounds very similar to that of the probation group.

With respect to this group's ability to socialize—and this refers to their church and school attendance, school conduct and performance, their relationship with neighbors, relatives, and other groups—no significant trends distinguished the child in the psychiatric examination group from the child in the probation group. Peer-group relationships were unrecorded in so many cases that no conclusion about them could be made. Neither age nor religious affiliation was deemed of any significance.

What *did* distinguish the child in this group from those in the others was his personality structure, which showed a major and marked difference. Here, he had every manner of severe personality disorder. But the probation officer, it is interesting to note, did not attempt to distinguish between various kinds of difficulties. Instead, he recommended to psychiatric examination an equally high number of children with neurotic or undiagnosed symptoms, disturbed behavior, and psychotic symptoms, and did not presume to diagnose certain kinds of disturbances himself. The fact that a disturbance existed was sufficient evidence for him to recommend a psychiatric examination.

Children in this group also differed significantly in their cooperativeness with the probation officer—a difference that was especially outstanding when compared with the probation group, which these children resembled for the most part. When no working relationship was established, the probation officer would ask for a psychiatric examination in hopes that this would make for a better relationship.

The relatively large number of girls recommended for examination (large when compared with those recommended to probation or discharge) could not be analyzed further because the number studied (only nine) was in such small proportion to the total. The fact that girls committed acts against sexual taboos or against parents was enough, apparently, to lead the probation officer to assume that psychiatric help was needed.

The eight Negro children in this group, although as thoroughly investigated did not show as many personality difficulties as the white children, despite the striking similarities in many other areas—a feature which served to emphasize the importance of the child's relationship with the probation officer (rather than any extrapersonal or social factors) in selection for examination.

As to the importance of the delinquent act, previous conviction or previously committed, unprosecuted delinquent acts were obviously not significant criteria for psychiatric examination. Gang membership was, however, as was the fact that a serious act had been committed. Leadership in a group committing delinquent acts against property also had some significance for the probation officer making this recommendation. The large number of "lone wolf" delinquents corresponded to the high number of sex delinquencies and delinquencies against parents characteristic of this group, for whom the probation officer recorded a greater number of combined personality disorders. But there is no evidence that the *kind* of delinquent act alone determined the recommendation for psychiatric examination.

Children Recommended for Discharge

Contrary to what might be expected, children were not recommended for discharge because of the mildness of their delinquent acts. However, this group did show fewer unprosecuted previously committed delinquent acts and slightly fewer previous convictions. In kind of delinquency committed, this group resembled the probation group in that their delinquencies were usually against life or property; very few were against parents or sexual taboos. But this group differed in its delinquency pattern—fewer children involved in group delinquency against life or property were recommended for discharge than were those involved in solo delinquent acts. Gang membership, however, was not any different in this group than in the others.

Slightly more indicative criteria for the discharge group were those pertaining to the child himself. Neither sex nor age of these children differed meaningfully from the sex and age of those recommended for other dispositions; but fewer Protestant and fewer Negro children were recommended for discharge than expected, considering their proportion to the total. In the incidence of physical handicaps, children in the discharge group resembled those of the other groups, although no child with a mental deficiency was recommended for discharge. Outstanding in all these cases was the fact that, by and large, the probation officer did not record any personality difficulties; the discharge group included a great number of children whom he rated "stable." These children were also more cooperative than the others.

The children's family background and superior social adjustment are the major areas which distinguish this recommendation group from the others. Most of the children had both their original parents, who were of good economic status and who had a good relationship with their child. Their marital relations were more stable than those of the parents in the other groups; and, although the father was more stable than those in the other groups, the mother did not differ. Both, however, were conspicuously cooperative with the probation officer. The child's relationship to his siblings was not too different from that of the children in the other groups (an observation seldom recorded for any group, however). These children lived in slightly less delinquent neighborhoods, attended church more frequently, and were comparatively outstanding in school attendance, conduct, and achievement. They did not differ in their spontaneous association with other children. Their relationships with neighbors, relatives, and peers were too rarely recorded to be interpreted.

CONCLUSIONS

Certain salient features emerge from analysis of the criteria for each recommendation. Seriousness of the delinquent act had only secondary significance to the probation officer in making his recommendation; of primary significance were the child's personality, his family background, and his general social adjustment. But the number of items omitted from the presentence investigation report indicates that the probation officer was unaware of the importance of the criteria he was actually using. Items most often recorded were objective in nature: identification of the child (by age, sex, religion, race), the delinquent act (kind, seriousness, role, previous conviction), the family composition and economic situation, and church and school attendance. Omitted were the more subjective, broader criteria: the various personal relationships in the family, the personalities of the parents and, especially, of the child. (The psychiatric examination group, with its highest number of children with personality difficulties, did not show more pathogenic relationships, so that no connection can be made between a child's disturbance and his pathogenic family.) This stress on reporting only the more objective data was extended to school adjustment as well—a child's attendance was much more completely recorded than were his conduct and actual achievement.

Obviously, these objective data can be more quickly and accurately recorded; but on analysis a number of these heavily recorded criteria proved to be quite useless to the probation officer in his choosing among the four kinds of recommendations. Modern casework practice considers the other kind of criteria—often obscured or lost in the records—more important to understanding the social and emotional pathology of the child and his family and crucial to his successful supervision and rehabilitation. Data on the child's personality and family situation, no matter how meagerly recorded, proved their own worth when they were actually used by the officer in distinguishing among the four groups.

More detailed records on the child's social adjustment outside the family would also be helpful. His relationship with his peers is especially important for our cases, since most of these children are in their adolescence—a period of life when peer groups have an important function in the youngster's maturation. The dynamic relationships between parent and child, child and sibling, carry over into the child-peer relationships as well. Therefore, information about the specific character of this relationship is important not only as a diagnostic tool but also as a means by which the probation officer can help effect the youngster's social rehabilitation.

The results of this study show not only a lack of application of these important criteria, but also the use of certain rather inconsequential criteria (sex, age, race, etc.) rather than consideration of the individual child. The high number of Negro children who committed delinquent acts against parents and sexual taboos and were recommended to institutions and the low number of girls who committed the same types of acts and were recommended to probation exemplify this trend.

As to the specific recommendation groups, the following can be said:

PROBATION. Recommendation to probation, as shown in our research sample of 200, was based on rather nebulous and limited criteria. The overwhelming majority of the cases recommended to probation did not have the personality difficulties which would require the personal and social rehabilitation that probation offers. A shift in criteria—reducing the number of cases with no personality difficulties who are recommended to probation and increasing the number of children with behavior disturbances and undiagnosed or neurotic symptoms—would bring more disturbed, but still curable, children to probation and would change the kind of delinquency "needed" to become a member of this group. Children committing sexual delinquencies or delinquencies against their parents could then receive the benefits of casework treatment. Membership in an unstable family would not necessarily mean a child's removal from home and community to an institution, but would allow instead for his inclusion in the probation caseload. This latter disposition would be especially appropriate since probation is an individual treatment situation, built on the relationship between the probation officer, the child, and the child's family. Many of those cases now recommended for probation showed adjustment difficulties that a well-conducted group program would help solve if the child were prepared by the probation officer to participate in it.

INSTITUTION. Institutional treatment is a group experience within a relatively controlled setting, but a child's need for such a group experience should be evaluated before he is sent to an institution.

PSYCHIATRIC EXAMINATION. If the family and the broader social background of the child were investigated in more detail, the group recommended for psychiatric examination would be more carefully selected by type and severity of personality difficulty and would include more children with severe pathology, with neurosis, and with undiagnosed symptoms. There would be no change in the use of the delinquent act as a criterion for recommending an examination.

DISCHARGE. The criteria used in deciding on this recommendation are fully justified; disregard of the delinquent act is, it should be stressed, a constructive approach. The probation officer should concentrate on the juvenile delinquent's general social maladjustment rather than on its particular expression.

The proposed change in selecting children for probation would mean that a number of cases now recommended for probation would become candidates for discharge. But this shift of cases would not affect the criteria now used for this recommendation.

13

The Presentence Report and
the Decision-Making Process

ROBERT M. CARTER

The decision-making process is perhaps the most important—and least understood—single dimension of the correctional system. The decisions made by probation officers, parole officers, institutional officials, paroling authorities, administrators, and others not only determine the specific course of action for a given offender, but also have long-range implications for the direction of the correctional process.

A great variety of decisions are made in every phase of the correctional system. For example, at the judiciary level a decision is made whether to release a defendant on bail or on his own recognizance. If the former, a decision must be made on the amount of bail. The prosecuting agency must resolve the number and types of charges to be brought against a defendant. The probation officer, in writing a presentence report, must make a recommendation for disposition. At the institutional level, further decisions select the facility and program for the inmate. The paroling authority must determine whether to grant parole, the duration of the parole, and any special provisions for this conditional liberty. When supervising in the field, probation and parole officers must elect a course of action which includes the location and time of contacts with the offender and other persons, purpose of the contacts, amount of time to be devoted to specific cases, and so on.

Such decision-making should be related to the currently accepted generalizations about crime and the correctional process. If decisions have no explicit

SOURCE. *Journal of Research in Crime and Delinquency,* **4**, July 1967, pp. 203–211. Reprinted with the permission of the National Council on Crime and Delinquency. Copyright, 1967, National Council on Crime and Delinquency.

basis, they not only tend to be sporadic, confusing, and even disruptive, but may be antithetic to an agency's stated objectives. Wilkins has given us an exhaustive examination of the action-theory relationship.[1]

This study explores the decision-making process at the probation officer level and focuses on the presentence report and the data utilized in recommendations for probation or imprisonment. Certain demographic characteristics of the offender population—prior record, current offense, and data relating to stability—are important in determining the recommendation.[2] However, the order in which probation officers seek such information and the point in their information-gathering activity when decisions are made regarding the recommendation have not been determined. The following questions need clarification and are explored below:

1. At the presentence level, what is the order in which probation officers gather information?

2. At what point in the collection of data is a decision made relating to the recommendation?

3. Once a decision has been made, may any additional data received change that decision?

4. Do officers develop a style for collecting information and making decisions? How consistent is this style from case to case?

THE RESEARCH METHOD

The method utilized in investigating these questions about the decision-making process is a modification of the "decision-game" developed by Wilkins.[3] Five cases, all previously referred for presentence reports, were selected from the files of the United States Probation Office, Northern District of California. The cases were subjected to content analysis and the materials then classified under twenty-four subject headings. The terms of classification were those commonly used in the Probation Office. Each item of information was then reproduced on a file card with a title printed on the lower edge describing the nature of the information on the card. The cards were then arranged and placed in a binder so only the lower edge showing the classification title was visible and all twenty-four titles were visible at the same time. The content of any card could be identified by the title and could be read by turning the card. Each card was numbered for reference purposes.

---

[1] Leslie T. Wilkins, *Social Deviance: Social Policy, Action, and Research* (Englewood Cliffs, N.J.: Prentice-Hall, 1965).

[2] Joseph D. Lohman, Albert Wahl, and Robert M. Carter, "Presentence Report Recommendations and Demographic Data," *The San Francisco Project, A Study of Federal Probation and Parole*, Research Report No. 5, February 1966, School of Criminology, University of California.

[3] Wilkins, *op. cit. supra* note 1, pp. 294–304.

The twenty-four cards contained the following categories of information:

Offense (description)
Plea
Confinement Status (custody or community)
Status of Legal Representation (appointed or retained attorney)
Defendant's Statement concerning Offense
Age
Place of Birth
Race
Education
Religion
Employment History
Marital Status
Residence Data
Military History
Psychological/Psychiatric Data
Drug Usage Data
Alcoholic Involvement History
Homosexuality
Prior Criminal Record
Family History
Leisure-Time Activities and Interests
Medical History
Attitude of Defendant
Family Criminality

The U.S. Probation Officers participating in this "decision-game" were asked to utilize the information on the cards in making a recommendation as to disposition of the case. The data contained most of the information which had been available to the probation officers who had made the original recommendation in these five cases. This meant the probation officer could conduct his presentence investigation and make a recommendation by direct reference to the cards rather than going into the field to collect information.

The participants were allowed to "gather" information or "conduct" the presentence investigation any way they desired; that is, they could first determine the defendant's age by turning the "age" card or the nature of the offense by turning the "offense" card. After the probation officer selected each card, he was asked whether he could make a recommendation as to disposition and, if so, the nature of his recommendation. If unable to make a decision, the probation officer was asked to select another card (gather more information), then another, until he could make a recommendation.

The order in which the cards were chosen and the recommendation decided upon were recorded on separate sheets. Once the officer made a recommendation for a case, he was asked to select not less than three additional cards to ascertain the "correctness" of his decision. He could change his recommendation at any time. However, following any change, he was again asked to select not less than three additional cards. The officers were requested to make their recommendations using as little information as possible, yet at the same time be sure their decisions were "correct." In short, the officers were able to select as much information as they needed to make a recommendation in which they were confident.

Fourteen United States Probation Officers in the Northern District of California participated in this "decision-game," resulting in seventy recommendations. One decision was excluded because a probation officer recognized the case as one for which he had written the presentence report. Thus, sixty-nine decisions were available for review.

FACTORS IN DECISION-MAKING

In this study the decision-making process consisted of three primary components: gathering information preparatory to making a decision; arriving at the decision or the selection of alternatives; and, finally, gathering additional information to confirm, modify, or reject the original decision.

A frequency distribution of the total number of cards selected, both those used in the information-gathering phase (before the decision) as well as those used to confirm, modify, or reject the decision, appears in Table 1.

The data may be rearranged to provide a frequency distribution of the cards selected before the decision was made (Table 2).

A frequency distribution of the first three choices of the cards selected before the decision (Table 3) shows more clearly the value and importance of certain types of information.

Table 1 presents the frequency distribution of the total number of cards selected and reveals that information-gathering, -confirming, -modifying, and -rejecting are accomplished with relatively small amounts of information. The average number of cards selected for the sixty-nine decisions was 7.8 per case. This included the three cards required to confirm, modify, or reject the decision. Two types of information were selected in each case: offense description and prior record. Six other cards were selected in more than half the cases: psychological and psychiatric data, the defendant's statement, the defendant's attitude, employment history, family history, and age. Fourteen cards either were not selected at all or were selected in less than a fourth of the cases.

Table 2 deals only with the cards selected or information gathered before the decision and indicates that one card or item of information—the current offense—was selected in *all* cases. The prior criminal record card was selected in about four-fifths of the cases (81.2 percent). The card containing psychological and psychiatric data was the only other card selected in more than half the cases (52.2 percent). The average number of cards selected prior to making a decision was 4.7. Seventeen cards either were not selected at all

Table 1 *Frequency Distribution of Card-Items Selected By Probation Officers for Presentence Recommendations in Sixty-Nine Cases*

Item on Information Card	Number of Times Card Was Selected	% of Times Card Was Selected
Offense	69	100.0
Prior Record	69	100.0
Psychological/Psychiatric	55	79.7
Defendant's Statement	48	69.6
Defendant's Attitude	43	62.3
Employment History	42	60.9
Age	37	53.6
Family History	36	52.2
Marital Status	29	42.0
Medical History	20	29.0
Education	15	21.7
Military History	12	17.4
Alcoholic Involvement	11	15.9
Homosexuality	11	15.9
Drug Usage	9	13.0
Interests and Activities	9	13.0
Family Criminality	8	11.6
Plea	5	7.2
Confinement Status	5	7.2
Residence Data	3	4.3
Religion	3	4.3
Legal Representation	0	0.0
Place of Birth	0	0.0
Race	0	0.0

or were selected in less than a fourth of the cases. Some recommendations were made with the information on a single card. The most information required by any one officer to make a decision necessitated selection of thirteen cards.

Tables 1, 2, and 3 clearly indicate that the information gathered during the presentence investigation is of varying importance in making a recommendation. The tables further indicate the "essential" quality of some information, most notably data relating to the offender's current and past criminal behavior. Other information, such as data relating to the defendant's attitude, statement of the offense, psychological and psychiatric evaluations, age, employment history, and family background, is of moderate importance. The balance of the information collected is seemingly of minor significance in making a decision.

A fourth frequency distribution (Table 4) presents data on the cards selected after making the decision, the information gathered to confirm, modify, or reject the original decision.

Table 2 *Frequency Distribution of Card-Items Selected before Presentence Decision in Sixty-Nine Cases*

Item on Information Card	Number of Times Card Was Selected	% of Times Card Was Selected
Offense	69	100.0
Prior Record	56	81.2
Psychological/Pyschiatric	36	52.2
Defendant's Statement	31	44.9
Age	24	34.8
Family History	23	33.3
Defendant's Attitude	19	27.5
Employment History	16	23.2
Marital Status	11	15.9
Military History	8	11.6
Homosexuality	5	7.2
Alcoholic Involvement	5	7.2
Drug Usage	5	7.2
Plea	5	7.2
Medical History	5	7.2
Education	4	5.8
Confinement Status	1	1.4
Residence Data	1	1.4
Family Criminality	1	1.4
Interests and Activities	1	1.4
Legal Representation	0	0.0
Place of Birth	0	0.0
Race	0	0.0
Religion	0	0.0

VARIATION AND RECOMMENDATIONS

Because of the limited number of decisions examined, it is difficult to evaluate the full significance of Table 4, particularly as it relates to the data of the previous tables. The general impression provided by the data is that certain kinds of information are used uniformly to arrive at the point of decision, while other types of information are used generally to "confirm, modify, or reject" the decision. Additional data are needed before further analysis of this phase can be made.

Are presentence decisions changed upon the receipt of additional information? The current data indicate that the probation officer is not likely to change his original conclusion, limited as his information may be at that point. Of the sixty-nine initial decisions, sixty-five (94.2 percent) remained unchanged upon the receipt of additional information. Only one was reversed (changing a prison recommendation to a probation recommendation) and three were modified (from recommendations for confinement to recom-

Table 3 *Frequency Distribution of the First Three Card Items[a] Selected before Presentence Decision in Sixty-Nine Cases*

Item on Information Card	Number of Times Card Was Selected	% of Times Card Was Selected
Offense	67	97.1
Prior Record	47	68.1
Defendant's Statement	22	31.9
Family History	18	26.1
Psychological/Psychiatric	15	21.7
Plea	5	7.2
Defendant's Attitude	2	2.9
Alcoholic Involvement	2	2.9
Employment History	1	1.4
Marital Status	1	1.4

[a]Some decisions were reached with information from less than three cards. In this case only the cards selected before the decision are included in this table.

mendations for observation and study under appropriate federal statutes).

A brief examination of the "decision-making" of the probation officers indicates that each officer develops his own style. Four of the fourteen officers followed identical patterns of card selection for each of the five cases; the remainder were quite consistent in their choices of information in each of the five cases, although some minor variations were apparent. None of the officers selected information at random; instead they followed a common basic pattern that was still somehow unique to the individual. For example, one officer never utilized employment information in making a decision but always used that information to confirm his decision. Another officer always studied the type of plea entered by the defendant prior to making his decision, yet no other officer selected that card at any time, either before or after the decision.

The final recommendations made by the officers in these cases showed considerable divergence. In Case 1, all fourteen officers ultimately recommended probation, although the number of cards selected prior to making the decision ranged from two to five. In Case 2, eight officers recommended imprisonment; one, a "split sentence" (jail followed by probation); one, probation; and four that the defendant be committed for a period of observation and study. The number of cards selected in reaching these recommendations was three to eleven. In Case 3, all fourteen officers recommended imprisonment and the number of cards selected was one to thirteen. In Case 4, five officers recommended imprisonment; two, probation; four, a "split sentence"; and two, county-jail commitment. The number of cards was two to ten. In Case 5, seven officers recommended probation; three, probation with psychiatric treatment as a condition; three, commitment for observation and study; and one, imprisonment. The number of cards selected was four to twelve.

Table 4 *Frequency Distribution of Card-Items Selected Following Presentence Decision in Sixty-Nine Cases*

Item on Information Card	Number of Times Card Was Selected	% of Times Card Was Selected
Employment History	26	37.7
Defendant's Attitude	24	34.8
Psychological/Psychiatric	19	27.5
Marital Status	18	26.1
Defendant's Statement	17	24.6
Medical History	15	21.7
Family History	13	18.8
Prior Record	13	18.8
Age	13	18.8
Education	11	15.9
Interests and Activities	8	11.6
Family Criminality	7	10.1
Alcoholic Involvement	6	8.7
Homosexuality	6	8.7
Drug Usage	4	5.8
Confinement Status	4	5.8
Military History	4	5.8
Religion	3	4.3
Residence	2	2.9
Offense	0	0.0
Plea	0	0.0
Legal Representation	0	0.0
Place of Birth	0	0.0
Race	0	0.0

Cases 1 and 3, where the probation officers agreed on the recommendation, were selected by the writer as cases likely to result in consistent recommendations; one for probation; the other for imprisonment. The three other cases, which resulted in considerable divergence of recommendations, were chosen as cases where clear and uniform recommendations were not likely to emerge. However, all five were chosen as typical of those coming to the attention of the U.S. Probation Officer.

The variation observed in the recommendations made by the probation officers in the five cases takes on increased significance when we consider the final dispostion of cases in the district court. Agreement between recommendation of officers and dispositions in court has been shown to be 96 percent for recommendations of probation and 88 percent for recommendations of imprisonment.[4]

While the divergence in recommendations may appear distressing, there is

[4] Robert M. Carter, "It Is Respectfully Recommended . . .", *Federal Probation*, June 1966, pp. 38–42.

a countervailing force in the operational situation; namely, the development of more uniform recommendations through the informal process of discussing cases in the office, at coffee breaks, at lunch, and so forth, and the formal process of case conferences between the officers and supervisory personnel. In addition, if the chief probation officer disagrees with the recommendation of a probation officer, he may append his own recommendation to the present-ence report. Inasmuch as all presentence reports and recommendations are reviewed by the chief probation officer, the tendency toward uniformity is reinforced and formalized. However, these processes are still relatively inexplicit and unofficial aspects in the decision-making process.

IMPLICATIONS

This inquiry into decision-making by probation officers, and, more speci-fically, decision-making as it relates to the presentence report recommendation, utilized the "decision-game" device developed by Wilkins. In general terms, this has been found to be a satisfactory instrument for simulating the present-ence report investigation, although there are obvious limitations to any sub-stitute for analysis of an actual investigation. The "decision-game" technique appears to have far greater application for correctional research than has been utilized to date.

The data suggest probation officers make decisions relating to presentence report recommendations with relatively small amounts of information. The current study reflects an average of 4.7 items of information utilized prior to the decision, and a range of one to thirteen items employed in making the decision. The receipt of additional information after the recommendation has little effect upon the recommendation, although the additional data may result in some modification in a few cases.

The probation officers, as a group, employ similar methods and techniques in their information gathering activities before making a decision. Even though these officers develop a specific and unique method or style, the individual variations are not significant. Attempts to isolate and identify these differences according to the personal characteristics (academic background, years of experience, etc.) of the probation officers were unsuccessful. Further study may establish significant relationships between method of decision-making and the background of the individual officer.

Since most of the data collected in the presentence report investigation is not employed in the development of a recommendation, further research may uncover what information is required and used to make decisions elsewhere in the correctional process. The data not employed in effecting the presentence report recommendation may be of some significance in decision-making by institution and paroling authorities or by the district courts, although such usage appears limited in application as well as relevance.

Although the "research" decisions of probation officers for three of the five cases manifested substantial differences, a greater uniformity actually exists by virtue of both formal and informal processes within the Probation Office. These informal processes and their influence in effecting uniformity also warrant further investigation.

Previous research has identified demographic characteristics which differentiated between offenders recommended for probation and for imprisonment.[5] The data most significant for this differentiation (prior criminality, current offense, and stability factors) are the items of information the probation officers most often collect early in the presentence investigation and use for presentence report recommendations.

This finding raises several questions: How much presentence investigation time is utilized to gather information of very minor significance in making a recommendation? More positively, how long does it take (or how much effort is required) to gather the "essential" information, information on the current offense, prior record, and so on? Do probation officers, after "deciding" on a recommendation early in the presentence investigation, seek further information which justifies the decision, rather than information which might lead to modification or rejection of that recommendation?

Although the current inquiry into decision-making is limited in scope, it clearly indicates the need for additional research into the decision-making process and its relationship to the total correctional process.

[5] Lohman, Wahl, and Carter, *supra* note 2.

14

Some Factors in Sentencing Policy

ROBERT M. CARTER AND LESLIE T. WILKINS

The probation officer as a member of the court staff has two major functions to fulfill. The first is to conduct an investigation of an offender which culminates in a presentence or probation report. This report is frequently accompanied by a recommendation to the court as to the selection of an appropriate sentence. The second function is to provide supervision for offenders placed on probation or some other form of conditional liberty. Despite the recent focus of correctional interest and attention, and a considerable volume of literature, the terms and conditions of these functions remain relatively vague. It is proposed to examine here a segment of one of these, namely the presentence report recommendation and its relationship to the court disposition. Our purpose is not so much to provide data, but to make explicit some questions about presentence report recommendations and their relation to court dispositions.

Even though corrections is a relatively new field in the United States, some of its components have already become so institutionalized that they form a cornerstone for the development of a correctional folklore or mythology. In essence, it appears that the increasing problem of crime and delinquency is being addressed by the application of principles and practices which have not been substantially modified, or even questioned, since their inception. Yet,

SOURCE. *Journal of Criminal Law, Criminology and Police Science*, **58**, No 4, 1967, pp. 503–514. Reprinted with special permission from the *Journal of Criminal Law, Criminology and Police Science*. Copyright © by the Northwestern School of Law, Volume **58**, No. 4.

the correctional systems must change if for no other reason than that of the increasing number of offenders processed. Tradition would have it that the changes be in the direction of increased probation and parole staff, prison personnel, new institutions, and related services. If these be the sole nature of the changes—more of what already exists—there will be a reliance upon a view of the past without a realistic vision of the future.

CASE LOAD SIZE

The fifty-unit workload as the standard for probation and parole supervision is an example of one of the myths. Where did this number come from? On what empirical data is it based? Is it an appropriate limitation of case load size? If it is not appropriate, what should be the workload for corrections? A search of the literature dates the fifty-unit concept back to at least 1922, when Charles L. Chute, then President of the National Probation Association, observed: "To this end fifty cases is as many as any probation officer ought to carry."[1] The fifty-unit concept found its way in the prestigious academic literature when Sutherland[2] in 1934, and Tannenbaum[3] in 1938, suggested that fifty cases "is generally regarded as the maximum number" and "the best practice would limit the caseload of a probation officer to fifty cases." The concept of fifty entered the professional literature when the American Prison Association in 1946 indicated that a probation officer "should not have more than fifty cases under continuous supervision."[4] An almost identical statement appears in the 1954 revision of the Manual of Correctional Standards.[5] Not until 1966, (while still suggesting a fifty-unit workload) did the American Correctional Association indicate that "where methods of classification for case loads have been developed through research, varying standards of workloads may prevail."[6]

The institutionalization of the fifty-unit concept is now firmly entrenched. Budgets for operating agencies, testimony before legislative bodies, standards of practice, and projections for future operational needs all center about this number. There is no evidence of any empirical justification for fifty, nor for that matter, any other number.

The following discussion relates mainly to the federal probation system, and we are indebted to the Administrative Office of the United States Courts for furnishing pertinent data. Information has also been drawn from the San Francisco Project, a study of the federal probation system, supported by the

---

[1]Chute, *Probation and Suspended Sentence*, 12 J. CRIM. L. & C. 562 (1922).
[2]Sutherland, *Principles of Criminology*, 359, (1934).
[3]Tannenbaum, *Crime and the Community*, 462, (1938).
[4]*Manual of Suggested Standards for a State Correctional System* (Am. Pris. Assn.) 13 (1946).
[5]*Manual of Correctional Standards* (Am. Corr. Assn.) 43 (1954).
[6]*Ibid.* 109 (1966).

National Institute of Mental Health.[7] It should be noted that these data cover different populations over different periods of time, and are not to be seen as interesting in themselves, but as throwing light on the presentence report recommendation and court disposition.

RECOMMENDATIONS AND DISPOSITIONS

The Relationship

The presentence report is a document basic to the functioning of both judicial and correctional administrations. The contents of the report, including the recommendation, assist the court in making a judgment consistent with its dual responsibilities to society and the defendant. Within the federal system the report aids the institutions within the Bureau of Prisons in determining classification and treatment programs and also in planning for subsequent release. The report provides information to the Board of Parole, furnishing information believed to be pertinent to its deliberations. Furthermore, the report contributes to the probation officer's rehabilitative efforts while an offender is under his supervision.[8]

In February, 1965, with the publication of a 39 page monograph entitled *The Presentence Investigation Report*, a standard outline and format was adopted for the preparation of presentence reports in the federal courts.[9] The final paragraph headings of the report are "Evaluative Summary" and "Recommendation". The importance of these paragraphs is recognized by the American Correctional Association which includes among its standards for the preparation of presentence reports a "recommendation for or against probation, or for other disposition according to court policy."[10]

The fact that there is a substantial number of sentencing alternatives available to federal judges also means that an equal number of possible recommendations may be considered by the probation officer. The selection ranges, of course, from probation with or without a fine or restitution, and/or a jail sentence, and imprisonment under various statutes which determine parole eligibility, to other dispositions which include commitment for observation and study and continuances for community observation.

Because of this variety of available disposals, the relationship between a recommendation and a disposition may be more simply considered from one of two directions. The first method would be to contrast recommendations for probation made by probation officers with actual court dispositions result-

---

[7] See Lohman, Wahl & Carter, *A Non-Technical Description of the San Francisco Project*, The San Francisco Project Series (April 1965).

[8] The federal probation officer supervises persons released on parole or mandatory release from federal correctional institutions or the United States Disciplinary Barracks.

[9] *The Presentence Investigation Report* (Adm. Off. U.S. Cts.) (1965).

[10] *Manual of Correctional Standards* (Am. Corr. Assn.) 521 (2d ed. 1959).

ing in probation. The second would be from an opposite direction, viewing recommendations against probation (or for imprisonment) with actual court dispositions for probation.

Data developed during the San Francisco Project contrast recommendations and dispositions for 500 consecutive cases processed through the United States District Court in the Northern District of California between September 1964 and August 1965.[11] These data indicate that:

". . . there is a close relationship between the recommendation of probation and the actual granting of probation. Probation was recommended in 227 cases and was granted in 212 of those cases. If the 7 cases of 'observation and study' are not included, probation was granted, when recommended, 212 of the 220 cases or in 96 percent of the cases. In only 2 of the 227 cases was there a substantial difference between the probation officer's recommendation and the court's disposition of the cases. In these instances, prison sentences were ordered where probation had been recommended.[12]

These data closely parallel the California data. The percentages of probation officer recommendations for probation followed by California Superior Courts, for the years cited, are shown in Table 1.

Table 1 *Percentage of Probation Officer Recommendations for Probation Followed by California Superior Courts (%)*

1959	95.6
1960	96.4
1961	96.0
1962	96.5
1963	97.2
1964	97.3
1965	96.7

SOURCE. State of California, Department of Justice. *Delinquency and Probation in California*, 1964, p. 168; and *Crime and Delinquency in California*, 1965, pp. 98–99.

Data on the federal system, arranged by the ten judicial circuits, indicate the relationship, shown in Table 2, between probation officer recommendations for probation and such dispositions in court for Fiscal Year 1964.

The patterns in these first two tables exhibit almost total agreement between a probation officer's recommendation for probation and an actual disposition of probation. However, this trend appears less stable when viewed from the opposite perspective—the relationship between recommendations against probation (or for imprisonment) and court dispositions of probation. California data reveal, in Table 3, the percentages of "against probation" recommendations and probation dispositions in court.

It is noteworthy that California authorities indicate the "superior court

[11]Carter, *It is Respectfully Recommended* . . . , 30 Fed. Prob. 2 (1966).
[12]*Ibid*. 41.

Table 2   *Percentage of Probation Officer Recommendations for Probation Followed by Ten Judicial Circuits, Fiscal Year 1964(%)*

First Circuit	99.4
Second Circuit	96.0
Third Circuit	93.2
Fourth Circuit	93.3
Fifth Circuit	95.2
Sixth Circuit	93.9
Seventh Circuit	89.9
Eighth Circuit	95.0
Ninth Circuit	93.5
Tenth Circuit	97.8
Overall	94.1

SOURCE. Data furnished by the Administrative Office of the United States Courts.

judges are more lenient than probation officers as to who should be granted probation."[13] This pattern has already been observed by one of the authors,[14] and by others,[15] in respect to the federal probation officer. Further confirmation of this pattern is found throughout the federal system as indicated by a review, in Table 4, of "against probation" recommendations and probation dispositions according to the ten judicial circuits for Fiscal Year 1964.

As already indicated, the probation officer has a wide latitude in his choice of a recommendation. Table 5 presents data on the specific recommendations of probation officers in the Northern District of California between September

Table 3   *Percentage of Probation Officer Recommendations Against Probation not Followed by California Superior Courts (%)*

1959	13.5
1960	12.8
1961	14.8
1962	17.4
1963	21.6
1964	21.1
1965	19.9

SOURCE. State of California, Department of Justice, *Delinquency and Probation in California*, 1964, p. 168, and *Crime and Delinquency in California*, 1965, pp. 98–99.

[13] *Delinquency and Probation in California, 1964* (Calif. Dept. of Justice) 166 (1964)
[14] Carter, *supra* note 11.
[15] Lohman, Wahl & Carter, *San Francisco Project* series (Report No. 2) 8 (Berkeley: June 1965)

Table 4 *Percentage of Probation Officer Recommendations Against Probation Not Followed by Ten Judical Circuits, Fisical Year 1964 (%)*

First Circuit	7.3
Second Circuit	9.5
Third Circuit	27.4
Fourth Circuit	31.8
Fifth Circuit	11.5
Sixth Circuit	19.3
Seventh Circuit	15.9
Eight Circuit	16.5
Ninth Circuit	23.3
Tenth Circuit	9.2
Overall	19.7

SOURCE. Data furnished by the Administrative Office of the United States Courts.

Table 5 *Probation Officers' Recommendations as to Sentence Northern District of California, September 1964 to February 1967*

Recommendation	Total	Percent of Total
All Cases	1,232	100.0
No recommendation	67	5.4
Mandatory sentence (Under certain narcotic law violations)	45	3.6
Probation	601	48.9
Regular	(284)	(23.1)
With Fine and/or Restitution	(197)	(16.0)
Split Sentence (Imprisonment up to Six Months Followed by Probation)	(49)	(4.0)
Under Youth Corrections Act	(71)	(5.8)
Fine only	38	3.1
Jail only	35	2.8
Imprisonment	334	27.1
Parole Eligibility After 1/3 Sentence	(234)	(19.0)
Parole Eligibility At Any Time	(64)	(5.2)
Under Youth Corrections Act	(36)	(2.9)
Observation and study	51	4.2
Adult	(39)	(3.2)
Youth	(12)	(1.0)
Continuance for 90 days observation	16	1.3
Deferred prosecution	3	.2
Commitment under federal juvenile delinquency act	2	.2
Other recommendations	40	3.3

SOURCE. Unpublished San Francisco Project data.

1964 and February 1967, and shows the wide variety of possible recommendations.

Table 6 presents overall data on the relationship between recommendations and dispositions of 1,232 cases processed through the District Court in Northern California. The reader will note that of 601 cases recommended for probation, 15 were ordered imprisoned; of 334 cases recommended for imprisonment, 31 were placed on probation.

These data seem to support certain generalizations about the nature of the relationship between probation officer recommendations and court dispositions. We have seen that there is a very strong relationship between recommendations *for probation* and court dispositions of probation, an average agreement of about ninety-five percent. It has also been observed that the strength of the relationship diminishes slightly when recommendations *against probation* (or for imprisonment) are contrasted with court dispositions of probation. Thus, it may be concluded that where disagreements exist between recommendations and dispositions, they occur when the officer recommends imprisonment. In a sense, if this relationship measures "punitiveness" then it may be concluded that the probation officer is more punitive than the judge.

OUTCOME OF SUPERVISION ACCORDING TO THE RECOMMENDATION

Very limited data are available on the outcome of supervision, i.e., the violation rate, according to recommendations of probation officers. The 1964 cohort study of Davis[16] examined the violation status of 11,638 adult defendants granted probation in California Superior Courts between 1956 and 1958. Davis showed that 27.1 percent of the defendants recommended for and placed on probation were "revoked," while 36.7 percent of the defendants placed on probation against the recommendation of the probation officer were revoked. Davis concluded that the "difference in revocation rates was very significant and indicates that the two groups were not alike in their tendency to recidivism."

It is questionable that this single explanation for the ten percent differential in revocation rates occurs simply because of differences in the two groups. There are two other possible explanations for this. One explanation may be that subtle differences exist in the supervision provided by a probation officer who may feel "resentful" in having an individual placed on probation against his recommendation. The second possibility is that the defendant's attitude toward a probation officer who recommended that he be imprisoned instead of placed on probation may affect the outcome of supervision. While there are no measures of these two negative factors, it is possible that they account for

[16] Davis, *A Study of Adult Probation Violation Rates by Means of the Cohort Approach*, 55 J. CRIM. L., C. & P. S. 70 (1964).

Table 6 *Probation Officers' Recommendation and Subsequent Court Dispositions Northern District of California, September 1964 to February 1967*

Recommendation	Total	Disposition								
		Mandatory	Probation	Fine Only	Jail Only	Imprisonment	Observation and Study	Continuances	Deferred Prosecution	Other
All Cases	1,232	45	671	30	27	337	73	18	2	29
No Recommendation	67	—	44	2	2	14	1	—	—	4
Mandatory	45	45	—	—	—	—	—	—	—	—
Probation	601	—	551	5	3	15	17	2	—	8
Fine Only	38	—	14	22	—	1	—	—	—	1
Jail Only	35	—	5	1	19	8	2	—	—	—
Imprisonment	334	—	31	—	2	281	13	5	—	2
Observation and Study	51	—	3	—	—	9	38	1	—	—
Continuances	16	—	6	—	—	—	—	10	—	—
Deferred Prosecution	3	—	—	—	—	—	—	—	2	1
Federal Juvenile Delinquency Act	2	—	1	—	—	—	—	—	—	1
Other	40	—	16	—	1	9	2	—	—	12

SOURCE. Unpublished San Francisco Project data.

a large portion of the observed differential. There are other interesting studies which support the hypothesis of self-fulfilling prophecies.

Another way of viewing Davis' data is to emphasize that 63.3 percent of those who received an unfavorable probation recommendation but were placed on probation completed their probation without revocation. Thus, to deny probation to all those with negative recommendations from probation officers would suggest that approximately two out of every three defendants with such recommendations would be denied the opportunity to complete probation successfully. Davis inquired as to the number of defendants who, denied probation on unfavorable recommendations, would have succeeded on probation if given the opportunity. There are, at this time, no data to answer this question.[17]

Other data are available from the Administrative Office of the United States Courts which indicate that despite considerable variation in the use of probation, the overall violation rates, or the rates broken down by "major," "minor," or "technical" are almost identical. Table 7 of the Administrative Office report is reproduced here to show probation violation rates for 1965, according to the actual percentage of persons placed on probation by the 88 U.S. District Courts, arranged by quartiles.

The data in Table 7 reveal that approximately 19 percent of those placed under probation supervision violate the terms of this conditional liberty, regardless of the percentage of the offender population on probation.

FACTORS AFFECTING THE AGREEMENT BETWEEN RECOMMENDATIONS AND DISPOSITIONS

Reverting to the possible explanations for the high degree of agreement between probation officer recommendations and court dispositions, it is possible that four factors, operating independently, but more probably simultaneously, account for this relationship:

1. The court, having such high regard for the professional qualities and competence of its probation staff, "follows" the probation recommendation—a recommendation made by the person (probation officer) who best knows the defendant by reason of the presentence investigation;
2. There are many offenders who are "obviously" probation or prison cases;
3. Probation officers write their reports and make recommendations anticipating the recommendation the court desires to receive. (In this situation, the probation officer is quite accurately "second-guessing" the court disposition);
4. Probation officers in making their recommendations place great emphasis on the same factors as does the court in selecting a sentencing alternative.

Data from the San Francisco Project confirm the fact that probation officers

---

[17]Wilkins, *A Small Comparative Study of the Results of Probation*, 8 *British J. Crimino.* 20 (1958).

Table 7 (*Table A 18 of the Administrative Office of the U.S. Courts covering 88 United States District Courts*) *Comparison of the Use of Probation in District Courts, by Type of Violation, Fiscal Year 1965 (Excludes violators of immigration laws, wagering tax laws and violators of Federal regulatory acts*)

Item	88 District Courts	Quartile Groups of Courts			
		First 22 District Courts	Second 22 District Courts	Third 22 District Courts	Fourth 22 District Courts
Average					
Actual percent placed on probation	49.0	65.9	53.8	47.2	36.9
Total removed	11,259	2,263	2,759	3,678	2,559
No violations	9,157	1,843	2,267	2,973	2,074
Violated probation	2,102	420	492	705	485
Technical violation	344	78	85	106	75
Minor violation	577	111	120	216	130
Major violation	1,181	231	287	383	280
Percent					
Violated Probation	18.7	18.5	17.8	19.2	18.9
Technical violation	3.1	3.4	3.1	2.9	2.9
Minor violation	5.1	4.9	4.3	5.9	5.1
Major violation	10.5	10.2	10.4	10.4	10.9

Source. Administrative Office of the United States Courts, *Persons Under the Supervision of the Federal Probation System.* (Washington, D.C.: 1965), p. 33.

and judges apply approximately equal significance to similar factors.[18] Examination of 500 probation officer recommendations according to the major categories of recommendations for probation and recommendations for imprisonment (or against probation), produced data on the legal and demographic characteristics of the offender population which had an important effect upon the recommendation selected. In general terms, the proportion of recommendations for probation increased with the number of years of education, average monthly income, higher occupational levels, residence, marital and employment stability, participation in church activities, and a good military record. Recommendations for imprisonment (or against probation) increased proportionately when offenders exhibited such characteristics as homosexuality, alcoholic involvement, the use of weapons or violence in the commission of the offense, the existence of family criminality, and drug usage. Age (in the range examined) did not significantly distinguish between the two recommendations, and racial and religious affiliation differences were absent. The female, however, was more likely to be recommended for probation than the male offender.

Certain offense categories (e.g. embezzlement, theft from interstate shipments or theft of government property, and false statement) usually produced recommendations for probation, while other offense categories (e.g. bank robbery, the interstate transportation of stolen motor vehicles [Dyer Act], and National Defense law violation) usually resulted in recommendations for imprisonment. Offenders who entered a plea of guilty, retained their own attorneys, or who were released to the community on bail, bond, or personal recognizance while the presentence investigation was being conducted, had significantly greater chances of being recommended for probation. It is recognized, of course, that a recommendation for or against probation is generally based upon some combination of characteristics—some obvious, others subtle—rather than upon any single characteristic or piece of information.

It is apparent that not all factors are of equal significance in determining the probation officer's recommendation. Accordingly, statistical computations produced a general ranking of the significance or importance of various factors.[19]

A further examination of the 500 cases was made, reviewing the selection of the sentencing alternative by the court. Again, statistical computations were completed and a second rank order of the significant or important factors was produced.

These two sets of data—one relating to the recommendation, the other to the disposition—are summarized in Table 8. The rankings were based on probability and contingency coefficient values. A correlation was computed and a significant value of .90 was obtained. These data indicate that there is considerable agreement between probation officers and judges as to the significance

[18]See Lohman, Wahl & Carter, *San Francisco Project* series (Reports 4 and 5) (Berkeley: December 1965, February 1966).

[19]*Id.*

Table 8 *Rank of Demographic Factors Utilized by Probation Officers for Recommendations and District Court Judges for Sentencing Alternatives, According to Probability and Contingency Coefficient Values (500 Federal Offenders, Northern District of California September 1964 to August 1965)*

Demographic Factors	Probation Officers' Ranking	District Court Judge's Ranking
Prior Record	1	3
Confinement Status	2	2
Number of Arrests	3	4
Offense	4	1
Longest Employment	5	5
Occupation	6	8
Number of Months Employed	7	6
Income	8	10
Longest Residence	9	7
Military History	10	9
Number of Residence Changes	11	17
Distance to Offense	12	14
Number of Aliases	13	24
Marital Status	14	11
Legal Representation	15	13
Weapons and Violence	16	15
Family Criminality	17	21
Plea	18	18
Education	19	12
Church Attendance	20	16
Narcotics Usage	21	23
Sex	22	19
Alcoholic Involvement	23	25
Crime Partners	24	20
Homosexuality	25	26
Race	26	28
Age	27	22
Religion	28	27

SOURCE. Joseph D. Lohman, Albert Wahl and Robert M. Carter. *San Francisco Project* series, Report 5, (Berkeley: February 1966), p. 68.
Spearman's p = .90

of certain factors and characteristics for decisions relating to probation or imprisonment recommendations and dispositions.

Another possible explanation of the close agreement between recommendations and dispositions is certainly that some cases are clearly probation or imprisonment cases. However, there are no "hard" data to identify which cases are "clearly" probation or prison cases. An actual, but extreme example of an "imprisonment case" is the bank robber who, armed with an automatic pistol and with an accomplice waiting in a stolen automobile, robbed a bank of $35,000, pistol-whipped a teller, and in the flight from the scene, engaged in a gun battle with pursuing police. It is doubted that probation officers or judges would be inclined to see probation as a suitable disposition for such a case, regardless of any other factors involved. An example of the "probation case" is the young married offender, who, unemployed prior to the Christmas season, made a false statement to the Post Office for employment, concealing a prior misdemeanor arrest. In general terms, this type of offender would normally be seen as a suitable candidate for probation.

From observation and conversations with judges and probation officers during the past years, it appears that judges do indeed have a high regard for their probation staff and value their professional judgment as to the disposition of a case. It is suspected that this is especially true in the federal system in which probation officers are appointed by the court and serve at its pleasure. This esteem for probation officers and their services by the court may also contribute to the high agreement between recommendations and dispositions, even though there are no statistical data to support this.

The fourth potential explanation for the close agreement between recommendations and dispositions—probation officers anticipating the recomendation the court desires—is now to be discussed.

VARIATION AMONG PROBATION OFFICERS AND PROBATION OFFICES

Disparities in sentencing have been of considerable interest in recent years and attempts to reduce these frequently observed differentials have normally been focused on judges. For example, sentencing institutes for judges have been developed at the federal and state level, as well as training programs for newly appointed or elected judges. That attention should be directed toward judges—for they impose the sentences—is certainly normal and, on the surface, a logical approach to resolving disparities. However, this pattern ignores one of the facts of community life—in this case the judicial community and its social system—that many persons play a part in the functioning of the community. Included in the judicial community are probation officers, prosecutors, defense attorneys, perhaps to a lesser extent the law enforcement agencies, and other judges on the same bench.

It seems to have been generally assumed that the judges are solely responsible for the disparities and that the remainder of the judicial community plays only a minor role which remains constant, neither supporting nor contributing to the disparities. Although we do not have complete data upon which a judicial "community-effect" can be shown to be a basis for disparities, there are data available which demonstrate the supporting role of at least one member, namely the probation officer.

If we assume that probation officers are "constant" and that judges are "variable", we would expect to find significant differences in the relationship between officer recommendations and court dispositions as we move toward extremes in the use of probation or imprisonment. We would not, in the federal system for example, expect to find the more than 94 percent agreement between recommendations and dispositions spread uniformly throughout the system, for some courts use probation frequently, others infrequently. In Fiscal Year 1965, individual federal courts had a range of probation usage in excess of fifty percent, with one court using probation for 23.8 percent of its cases, another for 75.7 percent of its cases. The percentage of defendants on probation in Fiscal Year 1965 by the ten judicial circuits is shown in Table 9.

Thus, on a circuit-wide basis, there is a high of 63.8 percent in the usage of probation ranging to a low of 43.7 percent, an overall spread of twenty percent, and as noted above, the variation is even more marked among individual courts. Six of the eighty-eight district courts used probation in excess of seventy percent for their defendants; twelve courts used probation for less than forty percent of their defendants.

Despite the variation among courts, individually or circuit wide, the relationship between probation officer recommendations and court dispositions is generally quite constant, whether there is high, moderate, or low usage of probation. This may be seen more precisely in Table 10 which provides data for Fiscal Year 1964 on sixteen selected federal courts: the five with the highest usage of probation, the five with the lowest use of probation, and the six courts which were within one percent of the national average for use of probation.

It will be seen, for example, that in District *A*, probation was recommended for approximately three of each four defendants (147–55); in District *H*, the recommendations are about equal (152–149), while in District *N*, probation is

Table 9 *Percentage Use of Probation in Ten Federal Judicial Circuits (%)*

First Circuit	53.0
Second Circuit	45.2
Third Circuit	63.8
Fourth Circuit	60.8
Fifth Circuit	44.8
Sixth Circuit	44.3
Seventh Circuit	44.4
Eighth Circuit	49.9
Ninth Circuit	49.0
Tenth Circuit	43.7
Overall	49.0

SOURCE. Administrative Office of the United States Courts. *Persons Under the Supervision of the Federal Probation System, Fiscal Year 1965*, pp. 103–105.

Table 10 *Use of Probation and Recommendations for and Against Probation by Selected United States District Courts Fiscal Year 1964*

	Percentage Use of Probation	Recommended for Probation			Recommended Against Probation			Recommendations Given by Probation Officers: Percent of Total Cases
		Number of Defendants	Number Granted Probation	Percentage Granted Probation	Number of Defendants	Number Granted Probation	Percentage Granted Probation	
A	78.3	147	143	97.3	55	20	36.4	73.2
B	71.4	144	137	95.1	90	31	34.4	88.0
C	70.7	27	26	96.3	7	0	—	82.9
D	70.4	20	19	95.0	11	2	18.2	43.7
E	70.2	125	125	100.0	28	1	3.6	77.3
F	50.8	106	100	94.3	112	17	15.2	89.3
G	50.0	16	16	100.0	17	1	5.9	82.5
H	50.0	152	145	95.4	149	19	12.8	80.9
I	50.0	14	13	92.9	9	0	—	60.5
J	49.7	12	12	100.0	36	6	16.7	15.4
K	49.6	29	28	96.6	36	0	—	47.4
L	36.8	28	28	100.0	19	0	—	13.6
M	36.5	61	61	100.0	117	14	12.0	73.0
N	35.6	158	148	93.7	310	21	6.8	87.8
O	28.5	92	82	89.1	74	25	33.8	35.1
P	26.3	44	38	86.4	174	24	13.8	90.8
Total for all District courts	50.2	6868	6463	94.1	7691	1518	19.7	63.1

SOURCE. Data furnished by the Administrative Office of the United States Courts.

recommended for about one defendant in three (148–310). However, the "agreement" rate between probation recommendations and dispositions in District *A* is 97.3 percent, in District *H*, 95.4 percent, and in District *N*, 93.7 percent.

These data indicate clearly that the recommendation-disposition relationship does not vary greatly from court to court, and that disparities in sentencing are supported, at least in terms of recommendations, by the probation officer member of the judicial "influence group". To be sure, there may be differences in the Districts which justify high or low use of probation, but thus far these have not been demonstrated. These data raise some interesting and important questions regarding the utility of sentencing institutes for judges, by themselves, as the solution to disparities, and suggest that probation officers, and perhaps prosecuting and defense attorneys, be included in such institutes.

The data in Table 10 have indicated that there is considerable variation in officer recommendations for or against probation in different Districts, but that rate of agreement between recommendations and dispositions is relatively constant between Districts. Accordingly, we would expect to find a common frame of mind, or "influence group set", among officers in a single District which leads to the agreement in that District, regardless of the frequency of probation or imprisonment dispositions. Thus, where probation is used frequently, we would expect the officers in that court to be sympathetic to such usage and we would anticipate that little variation would exist among officers. If this is the case, we would not expect to find much significant variation among probation officers in a single District. We would not expect to find large differences among colleagues appointed by the same court, operating in a similar fashion as regards court and office policies and directives, appointed under uniform standards, paid identical salaries, and theoretically sharing similar views of the correctional process.

Let us return to our data on the 1,232 recommendations made by the probation officers in the Northern District of California as shown in Table 5. By restricting ourselves to a probation-imprisonment dichotomy, we observe that probation was recommended 64.3 percent of the time (601 of 935 cases) and that imprisonment was recommended 35.7 percent (334 of 935 cases). The recommendations of 19 probation officers in Northern California for probation or imprisonment are presented in Table 11. (Officers who made less than 15 recommendations are excluded.)

The percentage of recommendations for probation is almost 50 percent— from a low of 40.0 to a high of 88.9 percent. Three officers recommended probation for less than 50 percent of their cases; three officers between 50 and 60 percent, six between 60 and 70 percent, five between 70 and 80 percent, and two in excess of 80 percent.

While this individual variation may be attributed, in part, to the geographic basis for assignment of cases or to other administrative reasons, it is statistically significant and suggests that probation officers, even in the same District do not view the correctional process from identical perspectives.

Table 11   *Individual Probation Officer Recommendations for Probation and Imprisonment Northern District of California, September 1964 to February 1967*

Probation Officer	Number of Recommendations	Number of Probation Recommendations	Number of Prison Recommendations	Percentage of Probation Recommendations
1	55	40	15	72.7
2	39	25	14	64.1
3	46	21	25	45.7
4	57	35	22	61.4
5	16	14	2	87.5
6	20	13	7	65.0
7	55	22	33	40.0
8	38	22	16	57.9
9	22	17	5	77.3
10	58	46	12	79.3
11	59	32	27	54.2
12	57	35	22	61.4
13	54	42	12	77.8
14	36	17	19	47.2
15	56	34	22	60.7
16	46	31	15	67.4
17	60	43	17	71.7
18	18	16	2	88.9
19	42	24	18	57.1

SOURCE. Unpublished San Francisco Project data.

What accounts for this variation among officers? In part, administrative and geographic considerations may be an explanation. There may be differences in probation-suitability among persons from metropolitan areas, (e.g., San Francisco-Oakland) and less developed or rural areas such as the northern coast or central valleys of California. But it is equally possible that these variations are due to personal characteristics, including academic training, age, and vocational background. Some general, but not conclusive observations can be made based on the probation officers in Northern California. For example, probation officers with graduate training or graduate degrees in social work or social welfare recommended probation for 56.3 percent of their cases; officers with graduate work or graduate degrees in criminology in 69.6 percent of their cases, and officers with graduate work or graduate degrees in sociology in 67.7 percent of their cases. Officers with the longest service recommended probation for 54.0 percent of their cases, while the "newer" officers recommended probation for 68.4 percent. Three hypotheses are suggested by these and other data:

1. Some of the variation in probation officer recommendations is a product of the individual background of the officer and includes vocational experience and academic training.
2. The differences or variations tend to diminish with the period of employment; that is, officers with different backgrounds are far more dissimilar upon entering the probation service than after exposure to the agency.
3. With an increase in the period of service (i.e., more experience) there is a decrease in recommendations for probation. This may represent a more "realistic" or less "optimistic" view of the benefits of probation treatment for a greater number of offenders, than was the view held by the officer earlier in his professional career.

"SECOND-GUESSING" OR "FOLLOWING"

There is, in our search for variation, the possibility that the probation officer attempts to second-guess the court by making recommendations which are anticipated to be those desired by the court. If this were the case, one measure of this factor would be that different judges receive different rates or percentages of probation or imprisonment recommendations. Thus, properly "second-guessing" a punitive judge would require a larger proportion of imprisonment recommendations; second-guessing a "lenient" judge would require more probation recommendations. Returning to the data on the 1,232 cases in the Northern District of California, and again restricting ourselves to a probation-imprisonment dichotomy, we find some, but not significant variation in the percentage of probation recommendations to individual judges. These data are in Table 12. Since none of these judges has a reputation of being punitive or lenient, we can only surmise that in this District, there is little if any second-guessing.

A review of Table 12 will also indicate that individual judges are equally receptive to recommendations for probation; the relationship between recommendations for probation and such dispositions being 97.2 percent over-all and constant between judges.

It appears that judges "follow" probation officer recommendations; there is no other ready explanation of the individual officer variation in probation recommendations and the high overall relationship between recommendations and dispositions. This also tends to confirm the observation that probation officers contribute to the problems of disparities in sentencing. From these data, all four previously suggested explanations of the close agreement between recommendation and disposition (probation officers and judges giving approximately equal weight to similar factors, the "following" of recommendations by the court, the presence of "obvious" probation or imprisonment cases, and some "second-guessing") appear appropriate.

Table 12 Recommendations for and Against Probation According to United States District Court Judges Northern District of California September 1964 to February 1967

Judge	Number of Cases Disposed of in Court	Number of Recommendations for Probation	Number of Recommendations Against Probation	Percentage of Cases Recommended for Probation	Number of Cases Granted Probation	Number of Cases Denied Probation	Percentage Agreement Between Probation Recommendations and Dispositions
Total	831	527	304	63.4	512	278	97.2
1	64	40	24	62.5	38	23	95.0
2	58	30	28	51.7	29	23	96.7
3	160	103	57	64.4	99	53	96.1
4	156	114	42	73.1	111	38	97.4
5	88	57	31	64.8	57	30	100.0
6	100	58	42	58.0	56	36	96.6
7	60	39	21	65.0	38	18	97.4
8	73	46	27	63.0	44	26	95.7
9	72	40	32	55.6	40	31	100.0

SOURCE: Unpublished San Francisco Project data.

SUMMARY

In this paper, some of the dangers of continued reliance on tradition and the development of a body of correctional folklore have been pointed out. It has been determined that the relationship between recommendations for and dispositions of probation are high and that the relationship diminishes when viewed from the recommendations against and the subsequent grant of probation perspective. Limited data on the outcome of supervision by recommendation and by percentage use of probation are provided. We have inquired into the reasons for the close agreement between recommendation and disposition and suggest that four factors, in varying degrees, account for it. We have observed that the overall relationship between recommendation and disposition does not vary from District Court to District Court, but rather remains relatively constant, regardless of the percentage use of probation. We suggest that disparities in sentencing are supported by the probation officer and it appears that these differences, in part, are a reflection of the officer's individual academic training and experience. Length of service brings about a trend toward conformity with colleagues and the development of a more conservative perspective toward the use of probation.

There are other segments of the presentence report process to which questions should be addressed. These include operational and administrative considerations, the decision-making processes of probation officers, and an examination of the nature and impact of the social system of correctional agencies. Within the operational considerations would be inquiries as to the role of subprofessionals in presentence investigations, the rearrangement of the standard presentence format to provide a developmental sketch instead of the current segmented report, a determination as to the appropriateness of "confidential" presentence reports, the collection of presentence data in a fashion which allows computer analysis, and the separation of the investigation and supervision functions. Although some examination has been made of the decision-making process,[20] we need additional information about the sequence of data collection, the relative importance of certain kinds of data, and the eventual use of the data for decision-making within the correctional system. We find almost a complete void in knowledge on the social systems of correctional agencies, although available data indicate that the system itself has a profound influence on job behavior, beliefs, values, and the definition and achievement of correctional goals. Indeed, we know more about the social systems of the offenders with whom we deal than about the systems of the agencies which provide correctional services.

There are vast gaps in our knowledge about the entire correctional process, but these gaps may be closed by imaginative, innovative, and creative research and operational designs and programs. This requires a willingness to subject our current traditional, correctional models to scrutiny and a willingness to set aside those features, cherished though they may be, which are inefficient and ineffective.

[20]*Id.*

15

Sentencing: The Judge's Problem

IRVING R. KAUFMAN

If the hundreds of American judges who sit on criminal cases were polled as to what was the most trying facet of their jobs, the vast majority would almost certainly answer "Sentencing." In no other judicial function is the judge more alone; no other act of his carries greater potentialities for good or evil than the determination of how society will treat its transgressors.

In 1957, the average sentence for auto theft in the federal courts of eastern Oklahoma was 36 months, while in New Hampshire the average commitment for the same crime was less than a year. It is difficult to discern why the forging of a check should be twice as serious in the middle district of North Carolina as in the eastern district of that same state, but this is just what a breakdown of the average sentences for that year would seem to indicate. In 1958, the average prison sentence meted out in the federal courts ranged from 9 months in Vermont to 58 months in southern Iowa. Of course, examination of the facts in the individual cases may reveal reasons which justify the differences. But, on the surface, the disparity in different sentences for the same offense seems unfair.

The fact that this problem is neither new nor limited to one system of courts is borne out by a study made several years ago of the sentences imposed in more than 7,000 criminal cases by six judges sitting in a state court. One judge imposed prison terms in 57.7 percent of his cases. Another judge com-

SOURCE. *The Atlantic Monthly*, **205**, 1, 1960, pp. 40–46. Copyright, 1959 by The Atlantic Monthly Company, Rumford Press, Concord, N.H.

mitted only 34 percent of the prisoners before him. One judge granted probation in 32.4 percent of his cases; another in only 19.5 percent.

A few years ago, two youths were arrested while trying to break into a gas station in a small Southern town. A third boy made his escape in the car in which the three had been driving. The two arrested youths readily admitted that they had stolen the car from a small city in upstate New York. They had intended to return it after a half hour's joy ride, but once in command of the vehicle, had decided to drive it to Florida. Halfway to their destination, their money exausted, they had been about to ransack the gas station for money and food when a policeman observed them.

In the meantime, the alarm had been spread for the third boy and the car. He burglarized several gas stations along the highway but was finally arrested after having driven less than 150 miles. However, his attempt to escape had put him in a different state. Thus, a few weeks later the boys came before different judges, charged with automobile theft. They were all 15 or 16 years old, they had similar backgrounds, and their records showed no previous convictions. Basically, they all had committed similar crimes, but their sentences did not reflect this fact.

The youth who had escaped and committed additional offenses before his arrest was eventually placed on probation with no prison term. His two companions were each sentenced to 3 years' imprisonment. When two able and conscientious judges reach such startling disparate results in cases with striking similarity, it is plain that our sentencing procedures need to be reexamined.

CHANGING CONCEPT OF PUNISHMENT

Our theory and practice in the area of sentencing have undergone a gradual but dramatic metamorphosis through the years. Primitive man believed that a crime created an imbalance which could be rectified only by punishing the wrongdoer. Thus, sentencing was intially vengeance-oriented. Gradually, emphasis began to be placed on the deterrent value of a sentence upon future wrongdoing.

Though deterrence is still an important consideration, increased emphasis on the possibility of reforming the offender—of returning him to the community a useful citizen—bars the harsh penalties once imposed and brings into play a new set of sentencing criteria. Today, each offender is viewed as a unique individual, and the sentencing judge seeks to know why he has committed the crime and what are the chances of repetition of the offense. The judge's prime objective is not to punish but to treat.

This emphasis on treatment of the individual has created a host of new problems. In seeking to arrive at the best treatment for individual prisoners, judges must weigh an imposing array of factors. I believe that the primary aim of every sentence is the prevention of future crime. Little can be done to correct past damage, and a sentence will achieve its objective to the extent that it upholds general respect for the law, discourages those tempted to commit similar crimes, and leads to the rehabilitation of the offender, so that he will not run afoul of the law again. Where the offender is so hardened that rehabilitation is plainly impossible, the sentence may be designed to segregate the offender from society so that he will be unable to do any future harm. The balancing of these interacting, and often mutually antagonistic, factors requires more than a good heart and a sense of fair play on the judge's part, although these are certainly prerequisites. It requires the judge to know as much as he can about the prisoner before him. He should know the probable effects of sentences upon those who might commit similar crimes and how the prisoner is likely to react to imprisonment or probation. Because evaluation of these various factors may differ from judge to judge, the same offense will be treated differently by different judges.

The task of improving our sentencing techniques is so important to the nation's moral health that it deserves far more careful attention than it now receives from the bar and the general public. Some of those at the bar and many civic-minded individuals who usually lead even the judges in the fight for legal reform approach this subject with apathy or with erroneous preconceptions. For example, I have observed the sentiment shared by many that, after a judge has sentenced several hundred defendants, the whole process becomes one of callous routine. I have heard this feeling expressed even by attorneys who should know better.

In 1958, an experienced lawyer rose to urge me to reduce by 5 years the sentence I had imposed on a particularly vicious narcotics offender. The prisoner was one of the most dangerous and unregenerate men ever to come before me, and his attorney was hard pressed to find plausible arguments in his behalf. Finally, after I had pointed out that everything in the prisoner's long and sordid record demanded long commitment, the lawyer turned to me and said, "But, your Honor, 5 years is a long time."

Of course, every judge is aware that 5 years in a penitentiary is a long time. He well knows that in many cases a prison term not only withers the life of the prisoner but spreads like a stain in an ever-widening circle, blighting the lives of innocent members of the family. Every judge is painfully aware of what 5 years without a father may mean to a prisoner's son. But society must be protected, crime must be deterred, dangerous offenders must be segregated, and prisoners must be reformed. Someone must decide what sentence will best effectuate these objectives. In the federal courts this task falls to the judge, but the problems of the sentencer would be the same no matter what his title.

In our federal court in New York, a single judge may pass sentence on 10 or more defendants in a day. Often, sentencing occupies a large portion of the court day. A lawyer who grows verbose arguing a motion may be prodded by the court, but I have never heard of an attorney being hurried when asking mercy for his client. Respect for the dignity of the individual demands that the attorney be heard fully.

The fair resolution of the forces pulling for severity or leniency is a judge's most important and difficult task. It is an easy thing for a judge to acquire a reputation as a stern, or a humane, jurist by the way he responds to the ever-present forces urging excessive leniency on the one hand and unnecessary severity on the other. But resisting the pressures has its own reward—the satisfaction of being able to say to oneself, "I have never consciously rendered an unjust decision." The day a judge is unable to make that statement should be his last day on the bench.

DETERMINING THE SENTENCE

Congress and the state legislatures make the basic policy decisions in regard to sentencing, through the setting of maximum, and occasionally minimum, sentences. The judge must take this legislative guide and apply it to the particular circumstances of the case before him. He must work within the legislative formula, even if he does not agree with it. Often the special circumstances of the case will demand the most severe penalties set by the statute. At other times, society's aims can be accomplished with a fine or a suspended sentence. This was the situation in the case of an elderly lawyer who, through weakness or stupidity, had become implicated in an embezzlement scheme. This elderly man had known no profession but the law, and even there a serious physical defect had restricted his activities to those of researcher and brief writer. He had neither relatives nor close friends and was entirely dependent upon the income from his legal work. His conviction itself meant automatic disbarment. From that moment, any lawyer who employed this man would be breaking the law. This prisoner was hardly a dangerous criminal to be segregated for society's protection, and the shock of his conviction had already chastened him more than any other punishment that might be imposed. In view of the circumstances, society could gain nothing from this man's imprisonment. He received a suspended sentence and was placed on probation.

However, in many cases, a judge's duty to consider the protection of society means that he must visit unhappiness upon people who did not act out of vicious motives and whom he would like to help, were he free to do so.

This would be true in a case, for example, where the prisoner is a food producer who, though honest enough, is completely inefficient. The record shows that on several previous occasions he has been fined for maintaining filthy premises from which unsanitary foodstuffs were shipped in interstate commerce, and, this time, the report, with its reference to dead rats in the flour bins, reads like one of the more vivid chapters of *The Jungle*. Repeated warnings have proved ineffective, and between warnings dangerously unsanitary products have been shipped. It is clear from the presentence report that further admonitions would be useless and that even a prison term would not change this man's nature. In such a case, the judge might take advantage of the flexibility of modern procedures and place the prisoner on probation, on condition that he completely divorce himself from the bakery business.

The sentence would probably mean the end of a business built up by hard work over many years, but the court's duty to the public might compel such a result.

Often the object of the sentencing judge is to place the prisoner in a position where he can do no further harm. This is the one theory of punishment upon which all schools of thought agree. There are some criminals who simply cannot be permitted to remain at large. However, segregation, while it may prevent certain crimes, will not prevent criminals, and the permanent isolation of all offenders is as economically unfeasible as it is ethically unthinkable.

I do not believe that we live in a den of potential thieves and cutthroats, held in check only by the terror of punishment. I have seen too many examples of the honesty and decency of the American people to believe that. On the other hand, it seems clear that, in many situations, crime has been discouraged by the knowledge that offenders will be treated severely. In 1956, the federal narcotics laws were stiffened to provide for a sentence of from 5 to 20 years for a first offender and from 10 to 40 years for a subsequent offender. A startling decrease in the number of newly reported drug addicts followed. For example, it is reported that in New York state the number dropped from 4,138 in 1956 to 2,836 in the first 11 months of 1958. Other states showed similar decreases. There are other examples of successful deterrence. And yet the wisdom of a rigid high minimum sentence, fixed by statute, with no discretion left to the sentencing judge, has been questioned by many.

Like most judges, I accept deterrence as one basic purpose of any sensible sentencing program. The need to discourage future crime often forces a judge to ignore his own sympathy for the prisoner. Let us consider the case of an illegal immigrant brought before a federal judge. The prisoner tells a truly heart-rending story. A native of an impoverished section of Europe, he had been unable to support his six children and in desperation had smuggled himself into this country aboard a freighter. Once here, he worked hard and sent most of his earnings to his family. The judge might seriously consider merely suspending sentence and ordering the prisoner's deportation. Surely this is no bad man. But the prisoner's record shows that this type of treatment has been tried unsuccessfully several times in the past. The man has simply stowed away on the next United-States-bound ship. It is clear in such cases that, if we continue to be lenient, it will become known that a man with a touching story has nothing to lose by illegally entering the United States again and again. Judges would be encouraging the violation of the very laws they were sworn to uphold. In this situation a judge might well find it his unpleasant duty to impose at least a short prison sentence on that offender as a deterrent to others.

In determining what sentence would be the best from the point of view of deterrence, neither the judge nor the legislature has any real scientific guide. I believe that more severe treatment may be warranted in the areas of narcotic violations and crimes endangering the national security. However, it does not follow from the general theory of deterrence that lawlessness can be completely eliminated simply by increasing the severity of sentences. Sooner or later, a point of diminishing returns is reached. For example, I doubt that there are many potential bank robbers not deterred by the present 25-year maximum sentence who would be restrained by a 40- or 60-year maximum sentence. Furthermore, sentences so high as to be out of proportion to the crimes committed have historically had an effect opposite from the one intended.

Occasionally a legislature, instead of strengthening the law-enforcement agencies which provide the surest deterrence of crime, will attempt a cutrate anticrime campaign by the simple process of increasing the minimum sentences for a particular offense. If this minimum is so high that the public believes it manifestly unjust, the law may well be nullified by juries refusing to convict, even in the face of incontrovertible evidence. Those laws often become dead letters, and the legislature, by attempting to provide too much protection, succeeds in providing none.

The fact that about 65 percent of those admitted to our prisons are recidivists indicates that in many cases even those actually subjected to the theoretically deterring punishment are not discouraged. If we are to reach our idea of the perfect sentencing policy, we must determine in a scientific manner the validity of the deterrence theory in various areas. We must answer such questions as: At what point does punishment stop chastening and begin embittering? What type of criminal activity attracts the type of men who will be deterred by threats? How much deterrence do we gain by an absolutely rigid, and hence predictable, sentence? How much does rigidity cost us in other fields?

The cost of deterring crime by long periods of imprisonment is frightfully high. Long prison terms mean large and costly institutions, and the human havoc thus created must sooner or later be paid for by all of us. Now, if it appears that in certain types of cases little is to be gained by deterrence-oriented sentences, the judges and legislatures might concentrate upon the reformation of the prisoner, with the view toward assuring that we shall never again have to foot the bill for this man while he is in custody, or repair what he breaks while he is at liberty.

The situation is somewhat complicated by the fact that segregation, deterrence, and reformation are not the only factors to be considered in sentencing. The judge and the legislature must also give weight to the impact the sentence will have upon society at large. I realize that the theory that a crime creates an imbalance rectifiable only by punishment is a much deprecated one, but it is a view held by a large segment of the population and must be recognized as a factor in the sentencing process. In speaking of retribution, I most emphatically do not mean that a sentence should be based upon a judge's personal indignation or upon vengeance. Men should not be condemned to prison for terms varying with the state of the court's digestion, nor should the judge permit himself to be influenced by public hysteria.

But the general attitude of the public toward a particular type of crime is a different matter, and it must be taken into consideration if respect for the law is to be upheld. If people are continually shocked by sentences they regard as too lenient or by the granting of probation and parole without selectivity, they begin to believe that the criminal law has failed them and that there is a cleavage between their moral code and the law. The inevitable result is a decrease in public confidence in and reliance on the law.

THE PRESENTENCE INVESTIGATION

Within the last few years, cooperation among judges, lawmakers, and experts working in the rapidly developing behavioral sciences has given judges a series of extremely effective devices for determining how best to treat prisoners. Probably the most widely used of these is the presentence report.

In our court, these reports are prepared by the probation officers. These men go into the field and interview the prisoner, his family, his neighbors, friends, and employers. The voluminous data collected are then carefully analyzed and put into the form most useful to the busy judge. In 1958, investigations were made of 89 percent of the convicted criminal defendants in the federal courts of the United States.

The judge is able to study these presentence reports at home or in chambers and again on the bench. By the time the prisoner stands before him, the judge has a good picture of his background and of the forces and circumstances that led the prisoner from early childhood to his present predicament. The report enables the judge to arrive at reasoned answers to troublesome questions.

On the basis of this information, he can tailor the sentence to fit the situation at hand, confident that he is aware of most of the facts. There are occasions when the presentence report fails to give the whole story because the defendant has been uncooperative in giving information concerning his past or has been deceitful. Other tools have recently become available to the federal judges in such cases.

Early in 1959, one of these new devices proved extremely useful. The case involved a young stowaway. As a first offender guilty of a minor crime, the prisoner would ordinarily have received a suspended sentence or a very light sentence if warranted. But the case troubled the judge. Although the prisoner had been pronounced sane after a preliminary psychiatric examination, the presentence report indicated bizarre behavior patterns. Furthermore, the information he had given concerning his identity and background did not check out. In fact, the authorities knew almost nothing about the prisoner.

A few months earlier, the judge would have had no practical choice but to base the sentence on the information at hand, inadequate as it was. But Congress recently enacted a statute designed to cope with just this dilemma.

Under the new law, the court was able to commit the stowaway to a federal prison for further study before finally determining the length of the sentence. There he was given a long series of tests and examinations. His activity was observed for weeks, and skilled interviewers began gradually to piece together the scraps of information the prisoner inevitably revealed. Five months later, the picture was complete, and the sentencing judge received a full report. This young man, who might have been handled as an ordinary petty offender, was in fact an escapee from a state mental hospital, where he had been diagnosed as a schizophrenic. Had the new sentencing statute not been available, he would have been released, to the great detriment of society and himself. Thanks to the new law, he has been transferred to a state hospital where he will receive the care he requires and will be unable to harm others.

Inquiry into the mental and emotional state of a prisoner does not often require the expensive procedure followed in the case of the young stowaway. Most such investigations can and should be handled locally by personnel attached to the court, and for this reason some of our more forward-looking states have provided their courts with psychiatric clinics. In 1958, the clinic attached to the court of special sessions in New York City made diagnostic examinations of 700 new cases and provided consultation and instruction for a staff of approximately 70 probation officers. The dividends from these activities far exceeded the clinic's annual cost of $72,830.

It is unfortunate that budgetary limitations often deny our courts not only adequate psychiatric consultation but even the staffs needed to prepare the essential presentence reports. Such economy is shortsighted. The premature release of a single dangerous criminal often costs the community far more than the yearly budget of the probation department or psychiatric clinic that could have uncovered the peril in time.

PLACE OF PROBATION IN CRIMINAL JUSTICE

Newly developed diagnostic methods may indicate that the prisoner's chances for reformation are excellent and that this can safely be accomplished outside prison, through probation. Unselective use of probation is a positive danger to society. It is corrosive of the principles of deterrence and segregation and of the court's efforts to uphold public respect for the law. But, when intelligently employed, probation, under an efficient probation department, promises immense savings in human resources and in public funds.

Let us take the case of an embezzler who a judge believes worthy of probation. The man is immediately assigned to a probation officer. The convicted embezzler will visit the officer at stated periods to report on his progress. He will also receive unannounced visits from the probation officer. With the officer's help, he learns to make his adjustment in the same environment that will face him when supervision ends. If this same man had been committed to prison, he would first have had to adjust to the institutional environment, where he would have borne little responsibility. Upon his release, he would have had to make a second and perilous adjustment to normal life. Probation, selectively used, avoids this sudden decompression.

This type of supervision, which has proved so useful in the administration of justice, costs the taxpayers approximately $150 per year per offender, about one tenth the cost of keeping a man in prison for the same period. There are other and greater savings to be derived from this. During the entire parole and probation period, the contrite offender is a productive citizen, contributing his skills to the general welfare, paying taxes, and supporting his family, which probably would have been thrown on the relief rolls had he been imprisoned for an extended period. What may be more important, the family is kept together, and a more normal environment provided for the probationer's children.

It is difficult to measure statistically the success of probation. Since probationers are by definition the most promising of our convicted offenders, it is only to be expected that their rate of recidivism would be considerably lower than the average.

In the federal courts, approximately 40 percent of all guilty defendants are placed on probation. In our court in New York, more than 90 percent of these offenders conclude their term of probation successfully. The credit for this high rate of success belongs largely to our probation department, a dedicated group of approximately 17 officers who have a deep devotion to duty and are motivated by one objective—an interest in the man who finds himself in an unfortunate position and in his rehabilitation.

Even where the reports and the nature of the crime indicate that commitment is necessary, the judge must still consider the prisoner's capacity for reformation. Occasionally a prisoner's only hope is a period of forced confinement that will isolate him from his former associates and force him to take stock of his situation. Often this forced stocktaking is an extremely effective form of treatment. Only incarceration can bring home to some criminals that society actively disapproves of their conduct and has the power to stop them should their crimes be repeated. Surely there are recidivists who return to federal prisons time and time again, despite the efforts made in the prison to rehabilitate them. But we must also remember that there are many prisoners who have been taught a lesson by their incarceration and have returned to the community better citizens.

Perhaps our greatest advances have been made in the handling of young offenders. Prisoners 16 to 23 years of age present a special problem. Generally they are more responsive to intelligent treatment than older prisoners, but prognosis is extremely difficult, and sometimes coddling of the youthful offender who has shown traits of hard-bitten criminality may do injury to both the offender and society. A judge cannot predict how an 18-year-old will react to 4 or 5 years in an institution. Enlightened federal and state statutes meet this problem by providing for special treatment for young prisoners. The statutes also permit sentences under which the maximum, but not the minimum, is set by the judge or by law. The offender is then transferred to a specialized institution and can be released under supervision at any time before the expiration of the maximum sentence when he has shown himself ready to reenter society.

I believe we can take real encouragement from our progress in the area of reformation. True, much remains to be done. We must learn to discover more about the prisoner as an individual and much more about the effects of certain types of treatment. Yet a start has been made.

NATURE OF THE SENTENCING PROBLEM

The nature of the sentencing problem and its causes are easily stated, but arriving at a solution is difficult. Many suggestions have been put forth over the years, but most of these suffer from fatal flaws.

Rigid, legislatively-set minimum sentences in all cases are no answer. They would negate the years of progress we have made in tailoring the punishment to fit the particular situation before the court. It has also been suggested that the sensitivity of judges to particular offenses might be avoided by allowing the juries to set sentences. I believe that such a system, far from being helpful, contains some serious dangers. A few states do give juries sentencing power in certain cases. In these jurisdictions, the courts are often faced with an insoluble dilemma. If they follow the universal practice in criminal cases and withhold from the jury any evidence of the defendant's past misdeeds, the jury will have little information on which to base its sentence. If, on the other hand, they permit the jury to hear about the defendant's prior vicious acts, they run the very real risk that convictions will be based on a determination that the defendant is a bad man, and therefore is probably guilty of the instant offense. Special postverdict sentencing hearings before the jury are probably too cumbersome to be used generally and for all offenses.

Some states have taken the sentencing function partly or entirely away from the judge and have given it to a body whose sole function is sentencing. Under some of these plans, the judge must sentence the prisoner to the maximum sentence provided by statute. In other states, he sets the maximum he considers just. But there his power ends. In effect, the prisoner has received an indeterminate sentence. The offenders are then studied by prison authorities and questioned by boards or authorities, often comprised of experts in the fields most concerned with sentencing. They may include men with experience as prosecutors, policemen, and probation officers. The responsibility for determining the length of imprisonment really rests with the boards. This system has the advantage of enabling sentencing to be deferred until the prisoner can be observed and studied.

However, a sentencing judge can achieve the same ends, in cases that seem to warrant it, by deferring sentence until a thorough study is made of the prisoner. Furthermore, where there are large numbers of prisoners to be sentenced or where this function must be performed in widely scattered localities, a sentencing authority must divide itself into subboards. As a result there may be little, if any, gain in uniformity.

I believe that the sentencing responsibility should remain where it has traditionally rested—with the judge. Of all public officials, he is the best insulated from public and political pressures. Certainly the judge is not an expert sociologist or criminologist, but he need not be. He is an expert in making difficult decisions on the basis of the best information available, and this is exactly what is called for in sentencing.

The fact that I do not believe that the disparity problem can be solved by removing sentencing authority from judges does not mean that I despair of an ultimate solution. In fact, Congress has taken a great step in that direction by authorizing institutes and joint councils on sentencing problems. A pilot institute on sentencing on a national basis, attended by federal judges from various parts of the country, was held at the University of Colorado at Boulder in July 1959. Out of this, it is hoped that guides for the agendas for regional meetings will be formulated. I expect that a considerable amount of disparity will be eliminated by the mere exchange of views as to which factors should be considered and how heavily they should be weighed. The mistakes and successes of one judge in developing sentencing techniques will be available to other judges.

The safeguards provided during trial are a tribute to our sense of fair play. If a ruling of the trial judge violates any of these procedural safeguards, the defendant may appeal and perhaps secure a reversal of his conviction. However, it should be noted that, once a verdict of guilty has been pronounced, there are few further checks on the trial judge's determinations. Were a judge to impose a sentence completely disproportionate to the crime committed, the higher courts might be unable to prevent the injustice so long as the sentence was within the statutory maximum. For this reason, some judges have advocated appellate review of sentencing.

This system has been tried with varying degrees of success in a number of our states and in England. Under one proposed system, the sentencing judge would be required to write or dictate a memorandum explaining the factors he considered in passing sentence. In most cases, the memorandums would be brief and would require little extra work. Only in the case of dispositions differing greatly from the average would the judge go into great detail. A prisoner who believed himself aggrieved by a sentence would have the right to appeal to a court constituted for this purpose. This sentencing court would be made up of trial and appellate judges selected for short periods on a rotating basis. Under other proposals, sentences would be reviewed by the regular appellate courts.

If the reviewing court believed a sentence incorrect, it would vacate it and impose a new sentence, either more or less severe than the original. The possibility that the sentence might be increased would prevent a flood of frivolous appeals and keep the work of this new court within manageable limits. The system is no panacea. It would not eliminate sentences that are so lenient as to make a mockery of the law under which the prisoner was convicted, and the judgment of the sentencing judge would probably be overridden only in the clearest cases.

The reviewing court would be required to write an opinion setting forth the factors which led it to revise a sentence. These would be published, and in time a body of opinions would develop, outlining—albeit roughly—the elements which should and should not be taken into account, and would also give some idea of the weight to be given each. It would be a flexible standard, but a standard nevertheless.

Appellate review would, of course, involve far-reaching changes and could raise numerous problems of its own, including possible constitutional objections to the increasing of sentences, and I do not favor it, therefore, at this time. We must first try to utilize the weapons available to combat disparity.

As I have tried to show, the defects in our sentencing systems are potentially responsive to a rational approach. We must re-examine in the light of modern scientific knowledge some of our sentencing axioms. We must foster greater co-operation between judges, law-enforcement officials, and the other disciplines that have so much to offer in our quest for the correct sentence. Finally, we must attack the disparity problem realistically and achieve a greater interchange of sentencing information among judges. I firmly believe that, once the importance of the sentencing problem is perceived by the public, we will have set our feet firmly on the road to our goal: the imposition, in every case, of the sentence that promises society the maximum protection and the offender the best possible chance to live a useful and productive life.

16

The Period of Probation

C. ALEXANDER RHEINER

The value of probation supervision has been achieved when the immediate problems of the probationer have been resolved, when any special conditions of probation have been met, and when a reasonable degree of stability and responsibility has been achieved by the probationer.

The Federal Probation Act provides that the period of probation or any extension thereof may not exceed 5 years. The Attorney General's Survey of Release Procedures (1939) states in part, that:

"Reformation or rehabilitation may be achieved within a relatively short period, generally 2 years, and if the desired results have not been attained within that period, there is reason to doubt that they may ever be realized. It must also be recalled that a relatively rapid turnover of cases is necessary in order that already over-burdened personnel may be ready to receive the constant stream of new probationers. Continuing cases under supervision for more than two or three years increases the caseload and may jeopardize the probation program as a whole."

Excessively long periods of probation appear to have little value. By far the most violations occur within the first year of probation. Thus we have in action a law of diminishing returns with little to show for the time spent in maintaining supervision for more than 2 or perhaps 3 years.

Probation terms vary according to the statutes in the different municipalities, states, and the Federal Government. In some jurisdictions the term of probation is limited to the term of imprisonment provided by law. This can render probation almost useless in minor infractions punishable in municipal courts by sentences limited to a few months. Other laws permit probation

SOURCE. *Federal Probation*, XXVI, September 1962, pp. 33–36.

periods of 10 or 20 years, or the imposition of consecutive terms of probation on different indictments, or on different counts of the same indictment.

WHAT IS PROBATION LIKE?

To fully understand what the length of the period of probation should be we have to know what probation is like, what we are trying to do on probation, what we are trying to accomplish, and how long it ordinarily will take to achieve what we are trying to accomplish. We therefore must ask ourselves the following questions:

Is probation freedom? Probation rules limit the freedom of the individual and this limitation is nonetheless real even though the probation officer may be most kind, considerate, and helpful in his efforts to rehabilitate the offender. Probation is an ever present threat to a person's freedom. A prison term can, and often does, result from either new violations of the law or from infractions of probation rules. Because of this, we accept the 5-year limitation as a reasonable restriction upon the powers of the court in applying probation.

Is probation punishment? Probation is generally not regarded as punishment, although it may be punishment to some. If probation were to be considered a form of punishment, it would seem reasonable to propose that the term of probation might be at least as long as the term of imprisonment provided by the statutes which often permit sentences of 10 years or more. On the other hand, if probation were considered a period of mere surveillance and detection, the probation officer's work might well be turned over to the police.

Probation is not freedom as we know it nor is it punishment. Some would say it is social work in an authoritarian setting performed by persons trained in the social work field. Others do not regard it as social work but still consider it as a counseling relationship and will refer probationers to social work agencies, both public and private, for special guidance and help which they are especially equipped to render. Probation is certainly unique and to some extent it defies description in terms of other well-known helping agencies whose functions seem to be much more clearly defined.

One need only glance at the printed "conditions of probation" which must be accepted and signed by every federal probationer to appreciate that probation is not freedom. I quote only a few of them: "Do not leave or remain away from the city or town where you reside without permission of the probation officer"; "Notify your probation officer at once if you intend to change your address"; and "Follow the probation officer's instructions and advice. The Probation Law gives him authority to instruct and advise you regarding your recreational and social activities." Certainly this is not freedom as we generally speak of it.

Lest the impression be given that probationers are restricted beyond what appears to be reasonable, I should add that the conditions of probation are general in nature. They were prepared so as to meet the needs of many persons and many contingencies. Some conditions are waived by probation officers and regarded as unnecessary or inapplicable in certain cases and situations. It would be impossible to maintain any kind of enforceable supervision without clearly stating some specific rules. Many of them are much less restrictive and of a more general nature than those cited.

Whether probation turns out to be freedom, restriction, punishment, surveillance, or a counseling relationship depends in a large measure on the attitude and philosophy of the probation officer and the court. And the extent to which probation may be restriction of freedom depends on the probationer. Although probation is not freedom, it need not be and should not be punitive in the sense of being something less harsh than imprisonment. It might be described as a combination of discipline and rehabilitation.

FOR SOME THE PROBATION PERIOD CAN BE REDUCED

We refer to a person on probation as being "under supervision." The term supervision is generally defined: "to oversee" or to "inspect with authority." But probation work is much more than overseeing someone or looking after him with authority. It is a way of helping probationers become better citizens, to accept responsibility, to lead useful lives, and to not slip back into committing unlawful acts. Each meeting of the probation officer should produce some kind of a change for the better in the thinking and behavior of the probationer. Their coming together, therefore, must be something more basic than talking about the weather. Each time they are together the probation officer tries to learn something about the probationer and to influence for the good his goals, desires, and general welfare.

When the probation officer has reached the point where he has done all he can for the probationer and there is reason to believe the probationer will receive no further benefit from probation, the probationer should be discharged from probation. In other words, why keep him on probation for 3 years when he has accomplished as much as he can at the close of 2 years? And why continue a probationer on probation when he has proved himself, is doing well on his job, has a good family relationship, and is accepted in the community? He has reached a saturation point beyond which the relatively restrictive measures of probation could do more harm than good.

In many instances the court cannot tell at the time of sentence whether a probationer will need a year of probation, or 2 years, or more. Under the Federal Probation Statutes the court can reduce the period of probation at any time or extend it to a maximum of 5 years. In other words, the law provides for flexibility in the actual period of probation served.

Certainly no court and no probation officer should feel justified in continuing a person on probation for a longer period than is necessary. To do so would be to defeat the very purpose of probation.

REDUCTION OF PROBATION PERIOD IN DESERVING CASES CAN LOWER THE CASELOAD

To continue persons on probation for extended periods and especially beyond the point where they no longer need the guidance and help of the probation officer, is to needlessly swell caseloads to the point that the probation officer cannot render services to those who require a maximum of attention. Caseloads in most probation offices are too large. They can be reduced and must be reduced if any real impact is to be made by the probation officer on the lives of those under his supervision.

There are two ways of reducing caseloads to workable proportions. The first is through discharge from probation by court order when the maximum benefits to the probationer have been derived. The second is by increasing probation staff. These are listed in order of importance. In the interest of economy there should be no increase in staff until other systematic means of reducing caseloads have been tried.

I do not wish to imply that persons requiring help or a longer period of probation supervision should be discharged early. On the contrary, I should be quite as ready to agree that probation periods should be extended if the need exists.

In the District of New Jersey we use still another method to keep caseloads at a minimum. We group certain offenses in the category of "commercial offenses." These include Interstate Commerce Commission violations, wage and hour violations, and certain food and drug violations. I.C.C. violations often consist of operating trucks over routes on which the offender has no authority to operate. Wage and hour violations consist of failure to pay time and a half to employees for all in excess of 40 hours per week, and food and drug violations may involve selling certain drugs without a prescription or the production of food items without maintaining proper standards of sanitation. Not one of the three types of cases cited is responsive to the generally accepted rehabilitative efforts of a probation officer. For the most part these offenses fall into the category of "business" or "commercial" offenses. Violators may require a type of surveillance or policing which the probation officer is not trained to render. Because of this fact and also in the interest of keeping caseloads at a minimum, we in our District ask the arresting agency to provide whatever supervision they feel is necessary during the probation term. The case is marked inactive in our records but is reinstated to active status if a violation occurs which requires a return before the court on a probation violation charge.

INCENTIVE IN EARLY DISCHARGES

The Conditions of Probation (Probation Form No. 7) used throughout the Federal court system reads in part: "The Court may at any time revoke probation for cause, modify the conditions of probation, and reduce or extend the period of probation." The Probation Act provides that "the period of probation, together with any extension thereof, shall not exceed 5 years."

All of us have asked the court at one time or another to revoke probation for cause. Most of us have asked that the period of probation be extended for one reason or another. But from the statistics I have seen, either we seldom recommend an early discharge from probation or our courts are reluctant to reduce the period of probation. Yet the practice of granting an early discharge creates an added incentive for probationers to comply with the law and with the conditions of probation. I have yet to meet the probationer who wants to be on probation or who has asked that his probation term be extended.

In the District of New Jersey each probationer whose term exceeds 1 year, is told at the time he signs the Conditions of Probation that his case will be reviewed when one-half of the probation term has been reached, and that if his adjustment has been good and his conduct warrants it, he will be recommended to the court for discharge from probation. Thus a goal is set and a reward for good conduct is provided. The positive aspect of rewarding good conduct is given greater stress than the negative approach of threatening a probationer with imprisonment for violating probation rules.

When a probationer is required to pay a fine or to make restitution he is aided in planning payment in such amounts as will result in full payment within one-half of the term of probation in order to become eligible for consideration for early termination. It might seem that we penalize those who are unable to make payment within one-half of the full probation term. In practice we find that those who do not pay within the half-time period are not usually those who cannot pay, but rather those persons who have never taken their financial or other responsibilities seriously. These are the very ones who need some special incentive. We do not hesitate to recommend an early discharge for a person who is on relief or is ill and unable to work, provided his conduct in other respects warrants an early discharge. In such an instance the fine balance becomes an unpaid judgment or if restitution has been ordered, such an order is vacated as a condition of the probation.

The imposition of shorter terms of probation would also reduce caseloads, but several disadvantages to this practice are obvious. The incentive provided by rewarding good conduct through an early discharge is lost. It is difficult to determine in advance the period of time necessary to effect a degree of rehabilitation. It would be possible to increase the probation terms in some instances but this results in a form of punishment for failure rather than a reward for success.

Some persons whose probation has been terminated will get into further trouble. But this is just as true of those who are kept on probation for the full term. Those considered worthy of early discharge appear less likely to violate the law in the future than those who do not merit such consideration. The fact that a relatively small proportion of those discharged may violate the law would seem little reason to continue every case on probation for the entire probation term. Nor would their continuation give any assurance that some of them would not violate anyway. It does mean that such violators are not likely to be returned before the court for sentence on the original charge. But if the violation is anything more than a minor infraction of the law, they will most likely be sentenced by some court for the new offense.

PERIODIC REVIEW OF PROBATION TERMS

What is the court's policy concerning the granting of early discharge from probation? Is there a firm policy dealing with early discharge? How do policies become established and do we review them from time to time to determine their usefulness and validity as of the present?

In 1953 the District Court in New Jersey gave instructions that in every case in which the term of probation exceeds 1 year, a review will be made after one-half of the probation term had been completed, and a recommendation made to the court whether probation should be terminated or continued. This practice was recently extended to include a written review of every probation case on an annual basis. These reviews are submitted to the judge who imposed the original sentence. The reviews need not be lengthy but the important effect is that the probation officer must take the time to review every case. If no provision is made for any other periodic review of cases under supervision, this practice assures that no case can go for more than a year without consideration. In New Jersey during the past 8 years an average of 88 persons was granted an early discharge from probation each year. This is equivalent to discharging the entire caseload of one probation officer every year.

It would be possible for the courts to impose lengthy probation terms which, when reduced, would be about the equivalent of full probation terms imposed elsewhere. The average probation term imposed in the District of New Jersey during 1960 was 3.6 years. The average probation term imposed in 383 cases supervised on transfer from other districts during the same period was 3 years. Those granted an early discharge by the New Jersey District Court served an average of 2.2 years on probation, or almost a third less time than those supervised on transfer. In 1960 and 1961 more of our probationers were discharged by court order than by expiration of the probation term.

CONCLUSION

In summarizing, it is my belief that probation caseloads can, in many instances, be cut by one-fourth to one-third by reducing periods of probation, allowing more intensive supervision in those cases requiring special guidance and help. Then there is the added incentive toward improvement in conduct, as well as the accelerated payment of fines and restitutions, if a reduction of the period of probation were the practice of the court. And finally, it is my firm conviction that there is a point in the period of probation after which most probationers will no longer benefit from continued probation supervision. Beyond this saturation point he may merely "go through the motions" and in some instances may even be hampered in his efforts to be a self-respecting, law-abiding citizen.

PAROLE

Inasmuch as this anthology is concerned with probation and parole, some important and relevant materials concerning institutional practices and problems have reluctantly been omitted.

This section starts with American Correctional Association material on the four procedures by which a prisoner may be released from a correctional institution and describes the essential elements of an adequate parole system, ranging from flexibility in sentencing and parole laws through public understanding. The Task Force on Corrections provides detailed data on parole and aftercare in the United States.

Professor Paul T. Takagi reports on the relationships between inmate, correctional agency, and parole officer in insuring the "success" of prerelease procedures. An article by sociologist Paul A. Thomas is the first of three which deal with decision-making in parole. Professor Thomas establishes the interaction of both formal and informal systems as the basis for decisions regarding those persons to be selected for or denied parole. Researchers Don M. Gottfredson and Kelley B. Ballard, Jr. explore differences in decisions about parole by decision-makers. Parole violators are examined by researcher James Robison and Professor Takagi who report that parole outcome measures, such as recidivism rates, are to some extent governed by administrative influence, supervisory practices, office orientations, and parole agent background and experience.

The section closes with a feasibility study on uniform parole reports by researchers Gottfredson and Ballard and Professor Vincent O'Leary. The study, in addition to creating a model for uniform parole statistics, demonstrates that a viable data collection system and procedures for feedback to participating agencies are feasible and can provide a firm basis for meaningful analyses of parole experience.

17
Parole and Other Release Procedures

AMERICAN CORRECTIONAL ASSOCIATION

PROCEDURES FOR RELEASE

There are four procedures by which a prisoner may be released from a correctional institution: (1) parole, (2) conditional pardon, (3) mandatory (conditional) release, (4) discharge.

Release procedures either complement and enhance or impede the best efforts of the correctional system. They, therefore, should be examined carefully by each state in terms of which offers the greatest potential return on the huge investment every state has made in law enforcement, in jails, in the offices of county and prosecuting attorneys, in courts, in probation services and in correctional institutions. The state's entire system for the administration of justice, if properly directed toward the protection of society, is also directed toward the ultimate correction and rehabilitation of the offender from the time he is arrested and charged with a crime. To release prisoners who are not ready for release, or to release without supervision those who no longer need the security of the institution, but who do need guidance and controls while re-establishing themselves, places the safety of the community in jeopardy and prevents the correctional system from carrying out its responsibility. To hold in confinement those who were long before ready to assume their place in free

SOURCE. *Manual of Correctional Standards,* American Correctional Association, Washington, D.C., 1966, pp. 113–116. Library of Congress Catalogue Number: 66–17761, Copyright, 1966 by the American Correctional Association.

society can be dangerously destructive to the offender and needlessly expensive to the community. Therefore, society has a real stake in knowing how prisoners are released, and in seeing that they are released in the safest and most profitable manner.

—— *Parole* is a procedure by which prisoners are selected for release and a service by which they are provided with necessary controls, assistance, and guidance as they serve the remainder of their sentences within the free community. Leaders in the correctional field agree that although a few persons do not require after-care supervision, *most* persons released from a correctional institution should be released under some form of supervision. The prisoner does not have a right to parole, but for his good and the good of the community, *almost* all should be given the opportunity of a period of supervision after leaving the regimentation and confines of the institution. Any parole system which does not include a process of careful selection of those to be released at the optimum time for their release, in addition to the necessary degree of supervision after release, is not a sound parole system. To fulfill its dual purpose of protecting society and continuing the rehabilitation hopefully started before leaving the institution, parole must contain several essential elements.

—— *Mandatory release* is a form of release sometimes referred to as *conditional release*. The term "mandatory release" was proposed by the National Conference on Parole in 1956 to avoid confusion with parole which, itself, is a form of conditional release. This form of release, as the name implies, is mandatory, by statute, when the accumulated time received for good behavior and for extra institutional credits is deducted from the sentence. The parole officials do not participate in a selection process in this form of release. In fact, the prisoner may have been denied parole on one or more occasions. Mandatory release does, however, enable the parole staff to provide supervision for a period of time as though the offender were on parole. Such a released prisoner is subject to the regulations and controls of parole as if he were on parole. He is also subject to revocation and return to the institution for violation of those regulations.

Crediting of good behavior, work credits, and other extra credits are means of providing incentives and control by institution officials. Early release, on the basis of such credits, makes possible some supervision by parole officials over those who were tractable or who made special efforts while confined. It is not a valid method of determining the proper time for release, but it does offer some control and guidance in the community for those who would not otherwise obtain it under parole procedures. To be effective, the same standards of supervision as that given to parolees must apply to such prisoners.

—— *Conditional pardon* is a form of executive clemency granting release on the condition that specified rules of behavior are complied with. It may or may not involve the processes of selection before pardon or supervision after release. It is an action taken by the Chief Executive or other official. This form of release, except where the need is clearly indicated, should not be used to negate the decisions of the parole board.

Discharge from prison provides neither selection nor supervision in the community as do parole and mandatory release. Discharge is permanent and unconditional. It occurs when the maximum term of imprisonment has expired, when deductions for good behavior or other institutional credits require complete discharge rather than mandatory release, or when an act of clemency commutes the sentence "to the time served," or unconditionally pardons the prisoner. Executive pardon or commutation serves a useful purpose where innocence has been established, where there has been a miscarriage of justice, or where other factors indicate a need for discharge prior to the time when a parole board possesses legal jurisdiction to grant parole (such as where an indeterminate-sentence law is not operating or when certain classes of prisoners are barred from parole by law). In many cases of pardon or commutation, however, the prisoner needs supervision after return to the community. It would be better, in such instances, for parole or mandatory release, which ever is appropriate, to take place.

ESSENTIAL ELEMENTS OF AN ADEQUATE PAROLE SYSTEM

Parole is the best form of release from correctional institutions; but to be completely effective, it must contain the following elements:

1. *Flexibility in the Sentencing and Parole Laws.* There must be sufficient flexibility in the laws governing sentences and parole to permit the parole of an offender at the time when his release under supervision is in the best interests of society.

2. *A Qualified Parole Board.* The parole board must be composed of members qualified by character, intelligence, training, and experience to weigh the complex problems of human behavior involved in parole decisions, and have the knowledge, patience, and integrity required to render wise and just decisions.

3. *A Qualified Parole Staff.* It is essential that the parole services be composed of persons selected in accordance with high standards of ability, character, training and experience, and appointed on a career-service basis. It is necessary that the administrative structure provide an adequate number of administrative and supervisory personnel, field and institutional parole officers, employment, training, research and other specialists, and stenographic and clerical staff, to perform the work of the parole system.

4. *Freedom from Political or Improper Influences.* Complete freedom from improper control or influence, political or otherwise.

5. *Parole Assigned to a Workable Position in the Governmental Administrative Structure.* An administrative structure within the framework of the government as a whole which makes it possible for the parole system, without sacrifice of proper independence, to function in complete co-ordination with other departments and services, notably probation services, correctional institutions, and departments of health, mental hygiene, welfare, and public safety.

6. *Proper Parole Procedure.* A parole procedure which makes provision for orienting the prisoner toward parole, preparation for the parole board of all data pertinent to the case, a parole hearing based upon careful study of such data, formulation, and investigation of a satisfactory parole plan, release under adequate supervision, and return to the institution of those who are unable to readjust satisfactorily under supervision. For young offenders, especially, a facility to house prisoners temporarily after release from a correctional institution (such as a half-way house) in cases where the releasee has no suitable home or other residence available, or who needs assistance in making a gradual adjustment to more complete freedom from the restrictions of close confinement.

7. *Pre-release Preparation within the Institution Program.* Operation within the institution of a program which aims at utilizing the period of confinement for preparing the inmate physically, vocationally, mentally and spiritually for his return to society, and puts forth intensive effort, at the close of the term, toward effecting his release under optimum conditions as far as he, his dependents, and the community are concerned.

8. *Parole Research.* A system of gathering, presenting, and interpreting data concerning the practical operations of the parole system and the effectiveness of the system. Such a system should be kept up-to-date and be used as a guide for the evaluation of the operations and decisions of the parole board.

9. *A Proper Public Attitude toward the Parolee.* A proper public attitude toward the parolee so that he may be accorded fair and helpful treatment in his efforts to make good, especially in matters of employment and social integration.

18
Parole and Aftercare

THE PRESIDENT'S COMMISSION ON LAW ENFORCEMENT
AND ADMINISTRATION OF JUSTICE

The test of the success of institutional corrections programs comes when offenders are released to the community. Whatever rehabilitation they have received, whatever deterrent effect their experience with incarceration has had, must upon release withstand the difficulties of readjustment to life in society and reintegration into employment, family, school, and the rest of community life. This is the time when most of the problems from which offenders were temporarily removed must be faced again and new problems arising from their status as ex-offenders must be confronted.

Many offenders are released outright into the community upon completion of their sentences, but a growing number—now more than 60 percent of adult felons for the Nation as a whole—are released on parole prior to the expiration of the maximum term of their sentences. Parole supervision, which in general resembles probation in methods and purposes, is the basic way—and one of the oldest—of trying to continue in the community the correctional program begun in the institution and help offenders make the difficult adjustment to release without jeopardy to the community. Furloughs, halfway houses, and similar programs are important supplements to effective parole programs, as are prerelease guidance and other social services discussed later in this chapter.

Parole is generally granted by an administrative board or agency on the basis of such factors as an offender's prior history, his readiness for release, and

SOURCE. *Task Force Report: Corrections* The President's Commission on Law Enforcement and Administration of Justice, Washington, D.C., U.S. Government Printing Office, 1967, pp. 60–71.

his need for supervision and assistance in the community prior to the expiration of his sentence. The Federal system and those of a few States have a mandatory supervision procedure for offenders not released on parole. Under such a procedure, when an inmate is released for good behavior before serving his maximum term, he is supervised in the community for a period equivalent to his "good time credit."

Table 1 shows the average number of offenders under parole supervision in 1965 and the yearly cost of operations. Data include the small number of

STATE	TOTAL RELEASES	PERCENT
NEW HAMPSHIRE	122	
WASHINGTON	1,005	
KANSAS	1,154	
UTAH	344	
OHIO	4,460	
WISCONSIN	2,203	
HAWAII	137	
CALIFORNIA	8,724	
MICHIGAN	4,586	
NEW YORK	7,186	
PENNSYLVANIA	2,752	
COLORADO	1,739	
CONNECTICUT	1,079	
NEW JERSEY	2,717	
MAINE	708	
DIST. OF COL.	836	
VERMONT	286	
INDIANA	1,852	
WEST VIRGINIA	686	
MINNESOTA	952	
ILLINOIS	3,681	
ARKANSAS	1,121	
UNITED STATES	**91,533**	
MASSACHUSETTS	1,386	
GEORGIA	3,342	
ARIZONA	850	
NORTH DAKOTA	162	
MONTANA	462	
IOWA	1,023	
KENTUCKY	1,734	
IDAHO	308	
LOUISIANA	2,129	
TEXAS	6,115	
RHODE ISLAND	138	
NEW MEXICO	620	
SOUTH DAKOTA	426	
DELAWARE	138	
ALABAMA	2,813	
TENNESSEE	1,466	
NORTH CAROLINA	2,937	
FLORIDA	2,949	
MISSISSIPPI	926	
VIRGINIA	1,959	
OREGON	969	
MISSOURI	2,064	
MARYLAND	3,864	
NEVADA	210	
NEBRASKA	896	
OKLAHOMA	1,803	
WYOMING	209	
SOUTH CAROLINA	1,305	

Figure 1 Inmates released on parole as percentage of all persons released from state prisons, 1964.

Table 1   *Average Number of Persons on Parole from State and Federal Correctional Institutions, 1965, by Type of Institution from Which Released, and Annual Costs of Supervision*

Type of Institution	Number on Parole[a]	Annual Costs of Supervision
Prisons	112,142	$35,314,047
Training schools	60,483	18,593,975
Total	172,625	53,908,022

[a]Includes a small number of persons released under mandatory supervision.

SOURCE. National Survey of Corrections and special tabulations provided by the Federal Bureau of Prisons and the Administrative Office of the U.S. Courts.

offenders released under mandatory supervision but do not include the very limited number of persons on parole from misdemeanant institutions.

History and Present Extent of Parole.

Parole has had a long history. Its early traces appeared in the United States in the 19th century. The first official recognition came in 1876 at New York's Elmira Reformatory. Parole for juveniles, sometimes referred to as "aftercare," can be traced back to the houses of refuge for children established in the latter half of the 19th century. Juvenile parole developed for many years as part of the general child welfare field, but recently, while still retaining a close involvement with child welfare programs, has assumed a more distinct status.

The growth of parole services has been continuous, though uneven, the adult field expanding more rapidly than the juvenile. There remain, however, significant gaps in its use. The one of probably most general importance is its infrequent use for misdemeanants sentenced to jail. The National Survey of Correction found that most misdemeanants are released from local institutions and jails without parole. Information available from a sample of 212 local jails indicates that 131 of them (62 percent) have no parole procedure; in the 81 jails that nominally have parole, only 8 percent of the inmates are released through this procedure. Thus, 92 percent are simply turned loose at the expiration of their sentence.

In the juvenile field, the administrative fragmentation of parole programs makes it difficult to develop precise statistical data on the extent to which parole is used as a method of release. The National Survey found that, although most youngsters are released under parole status from training schools, supervision programs for them often are inadequate.

More exact data can be obtained about the use of parole for adult offenders released from prisons. Figure 1, adapted from the National Prisoner Statistics of the Federal Bureau of Prisons, discloses sharp variations in the extent of parole use among individual States, from one in which only 9 percent of prisoners were released on parole to others where virtually all were. These reflect in large part differences in sentencing practices as well as parole policies.

Theory and Purpose

While parole has on occasion been attacked as "leniency," it is basically a means of public protection, or at least has a potential to serve this purpose if properly used. Actually prisoners serve as much time in confinement in jurisdictions where parole is widely used as in those where it is not. No consistent or significant relationship exists between the proportion of prisoners who are released on parole in a State and the average time served for felonies before release. The most recent tabulation of median time served for felonies before first release, which was made in 1960, showed that the five States with the longest median time served were Hawaii, Pennsylvania, Illinois, New York, and Indiana. The percentages released by parole in these States in the same year were 99, 89, 47, 87, and 88 respectively. The five States with the shortest median time served for felonies before first release were New Hampshire, Maine, South Dakota, Montana, and Vermont, with percentages of release by parole of 98, 92, 49, 90, and 5 respectively.[1]

Arguments couched in terms of "leniency" deflect attention from a more important problem. The fact is that large numbers of offenders do return to the community from confinement each year. The task is to improve parole programs so that they may contribute to the reintegration of these offenders. The best current estimates indicate that, among adult offenders, 35 to 45 percent of those released on parole are subsequently returned to prison.[2] The large majority of this group are returned for violations of parole regulations; only about one-third of those returned have been convicted of new felonies. Violation rates are higher for juveniles. However, because additional kinds of violations are applicable to them, such as truancy and incorrigibility, precise comparison with adult rates is difficult.

Ideally, the parole process should begin when an offender is first received in an institution. Information should be gathered on his entire background, and skilled staff should plan an institutional program of training and treatment. A continuous evaluation should be made of the offender's progress on the program. At the same time, trained staff should be working in the community with the offender's family and employer to develop a release plan.

Information about the offender, his progress in the institution, and community readiness to receive him would, under such ideal conditions, be brought together periodically and analyzed by expert staff for presentation

[1]U.S. Department of Justice, Federal Bureau of Prisons, "National Prisoner Statistics: Characteristics of State Prisoners, 1960" (Washington: The Bureau, n.d.), table R. 1. p. 67.

[2]Daniel Glaser and Vincent O'Leary, "Personal Characteristics and Parole Outcome," National Parole Institutes. Office of Juvenile Delinquency and Youth Development, U.S. Department of Health, Education, and Welfare (Washington: U.S. Government Printing Office, 1966).

to a releasing authority whose members were qualified by training and experience. After thoughtful review, including a hearing with the offender present, the releasing authority would decide when and where to release him. On release, he would be under the supervision of a trained parole officer able to work closely with him and the community institutions around him. If there were a violation of parole, a careful investigation would be made and the reasons behind the violation evaluated. A report would be submitted to the releasing authority which, on the basis of careful review of all the evidence and a hearing with the offender, would decide whether to revoke his parole.

Unfortunately, there are wide discrepancies between this description of what parole purports to be and the actual situation in most jurisdictions. One purpose of this chapter is to explore the nature and implication of those discrepancies.

LEGAL FRAMEWORK

The legal framework within which parole decisions are made varies widely from one jurisdiction to another. The general structure of sentencing laws is discussed in Chapter 5 of the Commissions's General Report and in the volume on the administration of justice, and it will not be detailed here.

Parole for Adults

Basically, the parole decision for adult offenders may depend on statutes enacted by the legislature, on the sentence imposed by the court, or on the determination of correctional authorities or an independent parole board. For certain offenses some statutes require that various amounts of time must be served before parole can be considered, or they prohibit parole entirely. The basic trouble with such restrictions is that they allow no consideration of individual circumstances. Consistently, correctional authorities have found that they interfere with effective decision-making; at times they cause unnecessary confinement; and at times they result in substantial inequities.

If minimum sentences are to be imposed, clearly the law needs to provide that they can be neither excessively long nor set so close to the maximum as to make discretion in granting parole illusory. In a few States, indeterminate sentencing is authorized, permitting consideration for parole at any time, without service of a minimum term. "Good time" or other credits earned by conduct during imprisonment may reduce the time that must be served in some jurisdictions prior to eligibility for parole.

Under any such variant, eligibility for parole does not, of course, mean that parole will in all cases be granted. In some, offenders may be released outright at the end of their term. The requirement of mandatory supervision in force in the Federal system and several States is one attempt to deal with this problem. In general, mandatory supervision laws require that any prisoner released prior to the expiration of his term by reason of having earned good time or other credits during imprisonment, must be released to a parole officer subject to parole supervision and conditions. Since virtually all prisoners earn good time credits, which may amount to a substantial fraction of their term of sentence, such a provision insures supervision for a period on release unless it is explicitly waived by a parole authority as being unnecessary. The limitation of mandatory supervision to the period of good time credit is one means of insuring that supervision does not become a mere extension of sentence, but obviously it is a rule-of-thumb standard that may bear no relation to the need for supervision.

Parole for Juveniles

With respect to juveniles, a number of legal issues are involved in commitment and subsequent release. Those which most directly affect parole practice are restrictions as to when a juvenile can be released. Of these the most important are: (1) stipulated periods of time a youth is required to stay in a training school; and (2) the requirement of approval from a committing judge before release can be authorized.

The National Survey found that three States stipulate by law a minimum period of confinement before parole can be considered for a youngster. One State has a 12-month minimum, another 18 months, and a third varying minimums. In many other States, minimum terms are established by administrative action. Such requirements ignore the facts of the individual case and can require unnecessary and damaging stays in institutions. While the usefulness of minimum sentences is debated extensively in the adult field, no authoritative body advocates their use for juveniles.

More widespread, and in some respects more difficult to change, is the procedure found in nine States, under which committing judges must become officially involved before juveniles can be released on parole. The problem with this approach is that a judge must be aware of a child's behavior in an institution after commitment by the court as well as current factors in the community situation. Since it is difficult at best to provide both kinds of information to a judge, he is apt to have to act on the basis of incomplete knowledge. Furthermore, such control by the court unnecessarily complicates programing for youngsters while they are in institutions. Judicial control over release has been eliminated by the vast majority of States and should be eliminated in the remainder.

THE DECISIONAL PROCESS

In the main, releasing authorities must depend on others for information about persons being considered for release. The size and quality of the staff who compile and analyze this information is therefore crucial. They must be able to develop and assemble vital information and present it in such a way as to establish its relevance to the decision.

Far too typically, overworked institutional caseworkers must attempt to gather information on a prisoner from brief interviews with him, meager institutional records, and letters to community officials. This information is often fitted into a highly stereotyped format. Frequently, the sameness of reporting style and jargon makes it very difficult for board members to understand the individual aspects of a given case and assess them wisely. This can lead to decisions which are arbitrary and unfair as well as undesirable from a correctional standpoint.

A significant increase in the number of institutional caseworkers responsible for compiling and analyzing information and great improvement in the quality of their work are required. The ratio recommended by the U.S. Children's Bureau for this kind of staff for young offenders in juvenile training schools is 1 to 30. The National Survey shows that it was 1 to 53 in 1965. For adults prisons, the American Correctional Association recommends a ratio of 1 to 150. This appears to be quite minimal when compared to juvenile standards, but it would be a great improvement over the actual 1965 ratio of 1 to 253.

Not only must caseworkers be of sufficient number and quality, but they must also have access to channels of essential information. Close coordination is needed with parole field staff to obtain information about the offender's background, attitudes of his parents, conditions in the community, and the availability of a job. Other vital channels exist within the institution itself. Caseworkers often have far less contact with offenders than do group supervisors, vocational teachers, and others. These individuals are valuable sources of information and should be consulted in preparing reports. Methods need to be devised to use them more fully.

Another type of staff in acutely short supply is clinical personnel. Psychiatrists and psychologists are badly needed for better assessment of cases such as those involving sex offenders and various types of violent offenders. Their skills are important, for example, in helping to decide whether a violent crime was an expression of persistent emotional disturbance likely to be manifested in further violence.

The National Survey showed that in the juvenile field there were the equivalent of only 46 full-time psychiatrists serving 220 juvenile institutions across the United States. More than half of these were in 5 states; one State had 10 of the 46. Not only were these psychiatrists responsible for diagnostic work, but most were carrying treatment responsibilites as well.

Use of Statistical Aids

The data presented to releasing authorities are of many kinds. Assuming that the information is accurate, parole officials must still face the problem of evaluating its meaning. One method, by far the most common, is for the decision-maker to depend basically on his own judgment of the circumstances in an individual case.

Another way of approaching a parole decision is through the use of statistical analyses of the performance of offenders paroled in past years to determine the violation rates for various classifications. Violation rates are related to age, offense, education, work history, prior record, and other factors. The categories are then combined to produce a "probability-of-violation score" for an offender according to his characteristics.

A series of efforts have been made in recent years to develop such procedures.[3] Experiments have also been undertaken to compare the case method and the statistical method. Psychiatrists, psychologists, sociologists, and prison officials have been asked to classify large numbers of cases on the basis of probable success on parole. When statistical prediction methods have been applied to the same group of cases, they have proved better able to determine the probabilities of parole violation for groups of inmates.[4]

Despite the utility of statistical techniques and the potential for increased usefulness with the advance of computer technology, no serious authority has proposed the substitution of the statistical for the case method. Factors unassociated with risk must be considered. Moreover, any individual case may present considerations which are too detailed for statistical analysis or which must be weighed from the standpoint of fairness.[5] Nonetheless, statistical analysis is useful as a general means for educating parole authorities in the significance of various factors in assessment of cases, as a way of evaluating the effectiveness of various treatment alternatives upon parole, and as a check for individual case dispositions. Much further work is needed to develop statistical analysis, particularly to predict the likelihood of violent crimes, as opposed to other offenses, and as a means for determining the optimum time for release.

National Reporting System

Closely related to the development of such research within each parole agency is the need for a national system of sharing parole statistics. At present, it is very difficult to assess the significance of different rates of revocation, since gross figures do not permit any comparisons among programs in different jurisdictions.

Some data are now available from pilot attempts to develop a national

[3]See Norman Johnson, Leonard Savitz, and Marvin E. Wolfgang, "The Sociology of Punishment and Correction" (New York: John Wiley and Sons, 1962), pp. 249–309.

[4]Don Gottfredson, "Comparing and Combining Subjective and Objective Parole Predictions," California Department of Corrections Research Newsletter, 3: 11–17 (Sept.–Dec. 1961). See also Hermann Mannheim and Leslie T. Wilkins, "Prediction Methods in Relation to Borstal Training" (London: Her Majesty's Stationery Office, 1955).

[5]Norman S. Hayner, "Why Do Parole Boards Lag in the Use of Prediction Scores?" Pacific Sociological Review, 1: 73–78 (Fall 1958).

parole reporting system that would permit comparisons. Under a grant awarded by the National Institute of Mental Health to the National Parole Institutes[6] in 1966, 30 States were experimenting with the development of common definitions and methods for reporting. Only as such definitions are developed can meaningful comparisons be made. And only when these comparisons are made can answers be found to such questions as these: How do the results of parole compare from one agency to another? What are the results of different parole programs for different kinds of offenders? What is the result of releasing certain kinds of offenders earlier or later?

Parole Hearings

Releasing authorities can also achieve more rational decision-making by improving their hearing procedures. Improvements must promote both fairness and regularity, as well as effective correctional treatment. In several States there are no hearings at all for adult offenders; decisions are made by parole authorities solely on the basis of written reports. In juvenile programs, hearings are even less common, with reliance again on written reports and also on staff conferences at which the offender may not be present.

Procedures for parole hearings are extremely diverse. In many States, especially those with numerous institutions, the parole board is divided into subcommittees, each of which conducts hearings. In some States, one or more board members conduct hearings and report back to the rest of the board. In still other States, boards conduct all hearings *en banc.*

Policies with regard to hearings on revocation of parole are even more varied. About half the States grant hearings as a matter of "grace," rather than regarding them as a normal function of the parole board. Again, some States have no hearings at all on revocation questions. Often, when hearings are held, they occur some time after a parolee's freedom has been terminated and he has been returned to prison.

Authorities on parole procedures regard well-conducted hearings as vital to effective decision-making, in terms of expanding the information available to the board as well as for their effect on offenders. Hearings commonly give parole boards an opportunity to identify important points on which information is needed in making their decision. For example, a board may well find from interviewing an inmate that he has several contacts in the community not mentioned in any official report, which later investigation by staff may reveal to have considerable bearing on the place to which he might subsequently be paroled.

The other aim of a hearing is to create conditions which enhance the treatment goals for an inmate. This does not mean that the hearing should take

---

[6]The National Parole Institutes are cosponsored by the Interstate Compact Administrators Association for the Council of State Governments, the U.S. Board of Parole, the Association of Paroling Authorities, and the National Council on Crime and Delinquency.

on the character of a counseling session. The simple opportunity of being given what he perceives to be a fair hearing can be important in creating those conditions. Board members also can often influence the behavior of inmates by encouraging their participation in institutional programs and other self-improvement efforts or by frankly discussing with them, at appropriate times, the probable consequences of failure to participate in programs or of misconduct.

Well-conducted hearings further the trend for parole boards to increase the involvement of inmates in the decisions which affect them and to confront them more directly with the information upon which a decision is being made. Earlier concepts concerning the treatment of offenders placed most emphasis upon the need to resolve their emotional problems. A more recent refinement of this view stresses the need for the offenders to be helped to confront and deal with "here and now" issues as a means of strengthening their problem-solving abilities.

An illustration of the trend toward "confrontation" is the way in which inmates are notified of parole decisions. Typically, parole decisions have been to tell inmates if parole was granted or denied. They have had little opportunity to discover the reasons for the decisions and discuss them with parole board members. An increasing number of parole boards have adopted the practice of calling inmates back after a hearing to discuss the decision on their cases. Institution staff and board members in these States—for example, Minnesota and Iowa—report it to be an improvement over prior methods.

Board members are most helpful when they demonstrate a genuine interest in the welfare of an inmate, an ability to withstand manipulation or deception, and a willingness to discuss candidly with an inmate the realities of his case. It is important, however, that board members avoid trying to use the hearing for extensive problem-solving with inmates or as a substitute for work which should be done by staff.

ORGANIZATION OF PAROLE AUTHORITIES

The administrative organization of parole authorities is another factor that aids or impedes decision-making. Again, there are wide variations in practice among jurisdictions and also a historical separation between the juvenile and adult fields that persists to this day.

Existing Patterns of Organization

In the adult field, every State has an identifiable and separate parole authority, although in four States the power of these authorities is limited to recommending a disposition to the Governor. A sense of the growth of parole in this country can be obtained by a review of the Wickersham Report of 1931 which indicated that 20 States had no parole boards at all. By 1939, the Attorney General's Survey of Release Procedures indicated there were still 16 States in which the Governor was the paroling authority.

In 41 States today the parole board is an independent agency; in 7 States, it is a unit within a larger department of the State; and in 2 States, it is the same body that regulates correctional institutions. In no jurisdiction in the adult field is the final power to grant or deny parole given to the staff directly involved in the operation of a correctional institution.

The situation in the juvenile field is quite different. The great majority of releasing decisions directly involve the staff of training schools. This is the case in 34 of the 50 States and Puerto Rico. In the other 17 jurisdictions, boards and agencies are used that, to varying degrees, are independent of the training school itself. Table 2 illustrates the variety of releasing authorities used in those 17 States.

Independence and Integration

The two dominant patterns of the juvenile and adult fields—the juvenile centering parole decision-making primarily in the institutions and the adult centering it in autonomous groups—symbolize two points of view about parole decision-making. The basic argument for placing release decisions in the hands of institutional staff is that they are most intimately familiar with the offender and are responsible for developing programs for him; thus they are most sensitive to the optimum time for release. It is also argued that autonomous boards tend to be unconcerned or insensitive about the problems of institutional programs and the aims of their staffs, that their tendency to be preoccupied with issues apart from the rehabilitative aspects of an individual's treatment

Table 2 *Types of Parole Authorities for Juveniles, Other than Training School Staffs, 17 States, 1965*

Paroling Authority	Number of Jurisdictions
Youth authorities	4
Training school board	3
Institutions board	2
Department of Corrections	2
Department of Public Welfare	2
Parole board	2
Board of control	1
Ex-officio board	1

SOURCE. National Survey of Corrections.

leads them to make inappropriate case decisions. Such autonomous groups are often viewed by institutional personnel as unnecessarily complicating decision-making and infringing on the "professional judgment" of competent staff.

Division of labor between institutional staff and autonomous releasing authorities is complicated by the growing use of partial release programs, for work, study or the like. The result may be anomalous as when, for example, an institution decides that an inmate should be allowed to go into the community on a work-release basis and he does well there, but a parole board subsequently decides that he should not be paroled. This can occur because a parole board usually takes into consideration various factors which are less emphasized by institutional officials, such as the disposition of co-defendants' cases or his probable behavior in an environment other than the town adjoining the institution, where leisure time will be much less structured.

A major argument against giving the parole decision power to institutional staff is that they tend to place undue emphasis upon the adjustment of offenders to institutional life. There is a temptation to set release policies to fit the needs of the institution, to control population size and even as a means for getting rid of problem cases even though longer control may be desirable. The opposite, but equally unfortunate, temptation is to use unwarranted extensions of confinement as penalties for petty rule violations. Finally, decision-making by institutional staff lends itself to such informal procedures and is so lacking in visibility as to raise questions concerning its capability to maintain fairness or even the appearance of fairness.

There have been a number of attempts to devise organizational means for promoting closer coordination between the staffs of institutional programs and releasing authorities. At one extreme is the integration of the releasing authority within a centralized correctional agency, with the parole board appointed by that agency. Wisconsin and Michigan have had such a system for some years, and Ohio has recently adopted a variant of it for its adult system.

Another way of promoting integration between releasing authorities and correctional systems can be found in the youth authority structures in Illinois, Massachusetts, Ohio, California, and Minnesota. Here the power of release is given to the board that has general control over the entire correctional system, both in institutions and in the community. No serious efforts in recent years have been made to extend such patterns to the adult area.

A third method, used in Alaska, Tennessee, and Maine, is to have the director of corrections serve as chairman of the paroling authority, with the members appointed by the Governor. This system may produce better coordination, but the director of corrections usually has so many other responsibilities that he cannot adequately carry parole board duties. To meet this problem, Minnesota has the parole board chairman appointed by and serving at the pleasure of the director of corrections, with other members appointed by the Governor. Other States have used coordinating committees, on which parole board members sit with institutional officials, or they housed both agencies in the same State department, giving each a great deal of autonomy.

In juvenile parole, where only a few totally independent parole boards exist and there have been no significant efforts to establish more, the main issue is whether there should be a central correctional authority with release power, or whether this decision should rest entirely with the institutions. The view of most leading juvenile authorities is that there should be a decision-making body within a central correctional agency of the State that controls all releases to the community and returns to institutions. Institutional recommendations and opinions should, in their view, weigh heavily, but final decisions should rest with the central body.

The principal advantages cited for this system are that it would meet the need in large multi-institution programs for maintenance of consistency in policies among institutions or among field offices which make revocation decisions and would minimize policy conflicts that can arise between releasing authorities and institutions. Properly developed, it also could provide procedural safeguards against capricious or irresponsible decisions.

Such an independent decision-making group within a parent agency seems to be the most effective solution to the problem of coordination within juvenile agencies. It is the one to which the juvenile field is apparently moving and is the alternative to which the adult field also seems to be heading.

Parole Board Personnel

Sound organizational structure is important, but it cannot substitute for qualified personnel. Increasing the competence of parole decision-makers clearly deserves high priority for the development of effective correctional programs.

In the juvenile field, staff responsible for the paroling functions are in most States persons drawn from central juvenile agencies or juvenile institutions. Thus, the quality of parole personnel is generally related to the level of training and experience required of staffs in the juvenile programs of specific jurisdictions. Improving personnel quality for juvenile parole decision-making can be undertaken generally in a straightforward way.

For boards dealing with adult offenders the problem is more complicated. For example, the National Survey revealed that in four States, in 1965, membership on the parole board was automatically given to those who held certain public offices. In one of these States, the board consisted of the Governor, the Secretary of State, the State Auditor, the State Treasurer, and the Superintendent of Public Instruction. Clearly, such ex-officio parole board members have neither the time nor the kind of training needed to participate effectively in correctional decision-making. Correctional authorities have uniformly advocated the elimination of ex-officio members from parole boards.

A more pervasive problem in the adult field is the part-time parole board. At present, 25 States have such part-time boards; 23 States have full-time boards; and 3 jurisdictions have a combination of the two. Part-time parole boards are usually found in smaller States; of the 21 jurisdictions with the smallest population, 19 have part-time parole boards. Among the 10 largest States, only Illinois has a part-time parole board.

Usually the part-time member can give only a limited amount of time to the job and almost inevitably part-time parole board members also have business or professional concerns outside the parole field which demand their attention and energy. Even a relatively small correctional system requires a considerable investment in time and energy if careful study and frequent review are to be given to all parole cases and if prompt and considered action is to be taken in parole revocation. It would appear that a full-time releasing authority should be the objective of every jurisdiction. Even in smaller correctional systems there is enough work generally to occupy the full-time attention of board members. An alternative to the complete replacement of the part-time parole board members in States with very small populations is to supplement them with parole examiners, a concept discussed in more detail in a subsequent section.

Appointment of Board Members

One of the most critical issues in obtaining qualified parole board members is the method of their appointment. Table 3 shows the methods by which adult parole board members were appointed in 1965. As indicated there, parole board members in 39 States were appointed by Governors.

In many jurisdictions, highly competent individuals have been appointed to parole boards and some have gained experience through service for many years. But in 1965 parole board members in 44 jurisdictions in the United States were serving terms of 6 years or less. It is not unusual to have new parole board members appointed whenever there is a change in a State administration. On some occasions, this system has resulted in the appointment

Table 3 *Method of Appointment to Adult Parole Boards, 50 States and Puerto Rico, 1965*

Appointing Officer or Agency	Number of Jurisdictions
Governor	39
State officials	4
Corrections agency	4
Ex-officio	4

SOURCE. National Survey of Corrections.

of board members largely on the basis of political affiliations without regard to qualification for making parole decisions.

To avoid this situation, Michigan and Wisconsin have adopted a "merit system" for appointment of parole board members. Appointees are required to have a college degree in one of the behavioral sciences and also experience in correctional work. Some have previously held important positions in correctional institutions or in field supervision.

Other steps can be taken to help insure the appointment of parole board members with requisite education and training. Maine, California, and New Jersey outline some qualification requirements in their laws. Florida requires that appointees pass an examination in penology and criminal justice, administered by experts in these fields. The system of making appointments from a list of candidates nominated by committees of qualified persons, as used in the appointment of judges in some jurisdictions, could be adapted to the parole setting.

Qualifications and Training of Members

The nature of the decisions to be made in parole requires persons who have broad academic backgrounds, especially in the behavioral sciences, and who are aware of how parole operates within the context of a total correctional process. It is vital that board members know the kinds of individuals with whom they are dealing and the many institutional and community variables relating to their decisions. The rise of statistical aids to decision-making and increased responsibilities to meet due process requirements make it even more essential that board members be sufficiently well trained to make discriminating judgments about such matters.

The number of persons with the requisite skills is presently quite limited. Training programs designed especially for parole board members are badly needed. An effort in this direction was the National Parole Institute's training programs. Supported by a grant from the Office of Juvenile Delinquency between 1962 and 1965, the institutes provided a series of week-long intensive training programs for parole decision-makers and developed useful publications and guides. Programs of this type need to be expanded and maintained on a regular basis.

Use of Professional Examiners

Another device to aid in improving parole decision-making is the use of professional parole examiners to conduct hearings and interviews for the parole board, which delegates to them the power to make certain kinds of decisions within the policies fixed by the board. Under this system, a parole board can concern itself with broad policy questions, directly pass on a limited number of specific cases, and act as an appellate body on the decisions of its examiners.

California now has examiners in both its adult and youth authorities. The U.S. Board of Parole has recently appointed an examiner. The decision-making responsibility given to these persons varies according to the system. Experience thus far indicates that the use of such officers could be greatly expanded.

The major argument for this approach is that it permits the development of a corps of professional examiners who have the background and skills necessary to perform the complex tasks involved. At the same time, it frees the parole board to carry out functions that should not be delegated. Another argument for this system is that professional examiners with tenure, training, and experience in the correctional field would be able to bridge more effectively the gap between parole boards and institutions.

The use of examiners would also reduce the need for constantly increasing the size of parole boards to meet increasing workload. One State now has a parole board of 10 members; in others, 7-member boards are not uncommon. With examiners a parole board would perhaps need no more than five members. As noted, in those States where part-time boards were still retained, the professional hearing examiner would be particularly useful.

One objection to use of examiners is that inmates wish to confront decision-making authorities directly. However, the limited experience to date indicates that this need not be a serious problem if examiners are given prestige and authority.

SUPERVISION OF PAROLEES

Among the principal sorts of limitations on the parole decision-maker are the resources available for community supervision: number of staff, their training and organization, and the community resources at hand for effective programing. Releasing authorities face one sort of question in considering parole for an offender who will be supervised in a small caseload by a trained parole officer working intensively with the offender and community agencies. The questions are very different in considering release to a parole officer who is so overburdened that he can give no more than token supervision.

Some Major Supervision Issues

Originally, parole involved a "ticket of leave" system under which a released prisoner reported regularly to police officials. Emphasis was almost entirely on controlling the offender to make certain that he conformed to the conditions of his release. Increasingly, as parole agencies developed their own staff, the tasks of control were supplemented by efforts to provide assistance to parolees. At first such assistance was direct and tangible in form, such as obtaining housing and money for the parolee. Later, more stress was placed on referral to other agencies and counseling of various kinds. Most recently, as in the case of probation, emphasis has been placed also on use of the parole officer to mediate between offenders and community institutions and to stimulate and organize needed services.

Again as with probation, control and assistance constitute the main themes of parole supervision. In fact, several research projects have been able to classify parole officers on the basis of their relative concern about the two.[7] These differences in emphasis are associated with different behavior on the part of officers.

Experiments indicate that certain offenders perform more successfully with parole officers who use certain styles of supervision than with others.[8] This has led to the development of specialized caseloads in which offenders with designated problems or characteristics are supervised by officers with special aptitude for managing them. In the adult field, 10 States now report the use of caseloads of this kind. The majority are for narcotic offenders; others are for alcoholics, mental defectives, or violent offenders. The State of New York has even developed specialized caseloads for "gifted offenders."

Research is needed to develop two kinds of information: (1) an effective classification system through which to describe the various types of offenders who require different styles of supervision and the types of parole officers who can provide them; and (2) a set of treatment theories and practices which can be applied successfully to the different types of parolees.

The Transition to the Community

The time when an offender re-enters the community presents special problems and needs. Statistical data clearly demonstrate the critical problems of prerelease preparation. Table 4 shows the months on parole completed by those who were declared violators during 1964 in the State of Washington where because of its sentencing system virtually every parolee has a number of years remaining on his sentence when he is paroled. The pattern of violation which is shown is common to all jurisdictions. Violations on parole tend to occur relatively soon after release from an institution, nearly half of them within the first 6 months after offenders are released, and over 60 percent within the first year.

Obviously, prerelease and immediate postrelease programing should receive a very high priority among efforts to strengthen parole services. Theoretically, as noted above, preparation for release—the ultimate goal of

[7]Daniel Glaser, "The Effectiveness of a Prison and Parole System" (Indianapolis: Bobbs-Merrill Co., 1964), pp. 429–442.

[8]Stuart Adams, "Interaction between Individual Interview Therapy and Treatment Amenability in Order Youth Authority Wards," in "Inquiries Concerning Kinds of Treatment for Kinds of Delinquents," Monograph No. 2 (Sacramento: California Board of Corrections, 1961), pp. 27–44.

Table 4 *Months Completed on Parole by Parole Violators, State of Washington, 1964*

Months on Parole	Violators	
	Number	Percent
6 or less	476	43
7–12	208	19
13–18	93	8
Over 18	328	30
Total	1,105	100

SOURCE. "Post-Institutional Behavior of Inmates Released from Washington State Adult Correctional Institutions," Washington Department of Institutions Research Review, 19:56 (April 1965).

correctional institution programs—should begin on the first day of admission. In reality, concern about release, as measured in specific program efforts, usually begins during the last days of confinement.

The Federal system and several States, however, have prerelease classes in penitentiaries. Michigan and Colorado, among others, have separate facilities to which inmates are assigned for a period of time before release. Although such programs are a step forward, they suffer from being located far from the community where the released offender must make his adjustment. Location of prerelease centers in the heart of the community would overcome some of these obstacles, permitting inmates to go into the community, deal with real problems, and return each day to receive some help in coping with their problems. Parole staff would be given invaluable opportunities to observe progress under the actual stresses of community life. Existing half-way house programs in a number of cities provide models for such centers.

The role of the parole officer is also crucial in preparing for the return of an offender. The officer should be in contact with the offender's family prior to release and make arrangements when necessary with schools, mental health services, potential employers, and other community resources. Prerelease visits by parole agents to offenders in institutions are very useful in providing continuity of treatment upon release, although distance makes such visits difficult in some jurisdictions.

Employment as a Condition for Release

Over the years, parole systems have been plagued by large numbers of inmates who have been granted parole but have no jobs to go to on release. Stable and meaningful employment has been consistently stressed by correctional authorities as critical to the successful reintegration of offenders into the community.

Many releasing authorities therefore require the offender to have a job as a condition of release. Thus a number of inmates have been held in prisons pending the development of employment, a situation highly demoralizing to the inmates and their families. Moreover, the inmate who is required to find a job before release may well secure one which is temporary or unattractive as permanent employment.

Several States have adopted modified requirements that provide for release without employment for certain inmates under stipulated conditions. An example is a New York plan called "release on reasonable assurance." Under this procedure, selected parolees can be released without a prearranged job if they have a stable home situation, a marketable employment skill or evidence of clear community interest in helping them to find work.

Research has found that inmates released under these circumstances have no higher violation rates than those who were required to find a job before release.[9] Inmates who are allowed to find jobs after release must, of course, be able to be able to do so quickly and to hold the jobs they find. Success in this depends heavily on the ability of the parole agency and allied community resources to generate employment opportunities.

General Control Concerns

The major frame of reference around which a parole officer exercises control is the rules and conditions established by the paroling authority. Such rules for adults generally forbid unauthorized association with persons having a criminal record and seek to control behavior in such areas as drinking, employment, and mobility. Parolees usually must secure permission to change their residence, to travel to another area, to marry or to buy a car. With juveniles there is much less uniformity, and in some jurisdictions few specific conditions are used.

The strictness with which parole rules are enforced varies greatly from jurisdiction to jurisdiction, depending in part on the training of the parole officer but chiefly on the formal and informal policies of the parole system. Enforcement involves many unofficial understandings. Extremely detailed rules are often overlooked by parole officers, particularly if they have reason to feel confident about a parolee. On the other hand, where conditions are relatively broad, researchers have demonstrated that both officers and parolees understand that certain rules operate although they are never explicitly set out in the parole agreement.[10]

A key problem in both situations is how to enhance a parole officer's ability to use discretion and at the same time provide checks against its abuse. It is important to recognize that parole rules are not an end in themselves. They are

---

[9]John M. Stanton, "Is It Safe to Parole Inmates Without Jobs?" *Crime and Delinquency*, 12: 147–150 (April 1966).

[10]Glaser, "The Effectiveness of a Prison and Parole System," fn. 7 suprà, p. 428.

meant to be tools of supervision that assist an officer to work with an offender to prevent further crime. Overly stringent rules that are strictly and universally enforced are self-defeating. Conditions that are rarely enforced make parole supervision almost meaningless.

Rules of parole seem to be best when they are relatively few, simple, and specifically tailored to the individual case. But no matter how well rules are chosen, the final test lies in how well they are applied and sanctioned. This involves great skill and sensitive judgment on the part of the parole officer. Training, rigorous personnel screening methods, and effective staff supervision are critically needed if that level of skill and judgment is to be developed and maintained.

Specific Law Enforcement Duties

A number of parole laws provide that officers can order a parolee to be taken into confinement, usually pending an investigation about commission of a new offense. Clearly, this is a power that can be badly abused, and on occasion it has been. There have been instances in which parolees have been confined for extended periods of time on alleged parole violations or simply as punishment for misconduct. Consequently the parole officer's power to detain the parolee has been increasingly surrounded with procedural safeguards in many parole systems.

A more general question that has troubled parole authorities, especially those in the adult field, is the method by which essentially law enforcement functions should be carried out when serious violations of parole conditions are suspected. The predominant opinion in the parole field is that supervision staff should not assume the role of police officers. A recent survey of parole board members, for example, showed that only 27 percent of them believed that parole officers should be asked to arrest parole violators and only 13 percent believed that parole officers should be allowed to carry weapons.[11] The task of a parole officer is generally seen as developing close working relationships with police departments rather than performing law enforcement functions directly. But this does not mean that parole officers can neglect responsibility for control and surveillance.

Programs to effect liaison with police departments have been developed in the States of New York and California. There, certain parole officers, designated as investigators, are specially trained and assigned to units responsible for liaison with police departments. They cooperate in police intelligence efforts, and they relieve parole officers of some surveillance responsibilities. Most often they undertake investigations in cases at the request of a parole officer who suspects that a parolee is involved in crimina

[11]"Description of Backgrounds and Some Attitudes of Parole Authority Members of the United States," National Parole Institutes (New York: National Council on Crime and Delinquency, August 1963, mimeo.).

activities. They also initiate inquires on the basis of information from other contacts, often the police.

These efforts to achieve effective police relationships need careful study. Some observers question the practice, contending that it is not an appropriate activity for a parole agency or that it could better be handled by each parole agent in his own district, Advocates of this system contend that it creates much closer cooperation with police agencies, defines the role of the regular parole officer more clearly, and relieves him of tasks for which he has little training.

Staff Needs

The National Survey found that in 1965 there were about 2,100 parole officers and administrative staff responsible for adult parole services in the United States and another 1,400 assigned to parole for juveniles. Table 5 shows the estimated size of caseloads in which parolees were being supervised in 1965.

One fact stands out: There are simply not enough parole officers available to carry out the tasks assigned to them. The Survey shows that adults released on parole are surpervised in caseloads averaging 68. Not only is the parole officer responsible for those 68 cases, but in 30 States he will probably be conducting presentence investigations in probation cases. In virtually all States, he will be investigating release plans and developing future employment for offenders still in prison. It should be noted, too, that over 22 percent of adult parolees were being supervised in caseloads of more than 80 in 1965.

In the juvenile field, a number of States have well-developed aftercare programs, but in many others such services are nonexistent or depend upon extension of help by local probation officers or welfare departments. The average caseload for juveniles is about 64. This average does not include those juveniles released on parole in 10 States where the Survey found it impossible to estimate the adequacy of aftercare services because the parole

Table 5 *Percentage Distribution of Parolees, by Size of Caseload in Which Supervised, 1965*

Caseload Size	Juvenile Parole (Percent)	Adult Parole (Percent)
Under 50	28.2	7.9
51–60	4.7	25.4
61–70	48.8	20.7
71–80	5.7	23.2
Over 80	12.6	22.8

SOURCE. National Survey of Corrections.

cases were so mingled with others such as welfare clients or were handled on such an informal basis that virtually no organized data were available. As in the case of adults, this caseload average does not include the heavy time commitments that juvenile aftercare workers must make to contacting parents and others in the community in preparing for release of juveniles.

As with probation, there is no single caseload standard which can be applied to all parolees. Different cases require different kinds of supervision. Some need intensive contact, while others can be managed in larger caseloads. The most complete data available as to the optimum average caseload was developed from a series of studies made in California during the last decade. Recently the State's adult parole system has sought to determine what an average caseload would be when different types of parolees were matched with appropriate kinds and degrees of supervision. At present, the results from this particular study indicate that caseloads should average around 37, although the average has been dropping the longer the study has run.[12]

The best estimate available from current research seems to be that caseloads should generally average 35 per officer. At that level, some offenders who needed it could be closely supervised in caseloads of 20 or lower, and others could be handled adequately in caseloads as high as 75 or even more. Such a caseload average would permit intensive supervision of those offenders who appear to have a potential for violence, as well as those with special treatment needs. It would enable the officer to have significant face-to-face contacts with offenders and to deal with emerging problems before they led to failure and perhaps to further offenses. With such a reasonable workload, the officer would have time to contact employers, families, schools, and law enforcement agencies as well as the parolees themselves.

Field Staff Administration

In 34 States, the agency that administers the State training schools and camps also provides parole supervision services for juveniles released from those institutions. In the remaining 16 States, these services are provided through a variety of sources. Some of those States provide virtually no services at all. In five States, local probation departments are given responsibility for aftercare programs, though they have no official relationship to the agency administering the training schools. In other States, training schools make special arrangements with local agencies to provide aftercare supervision, sometimes on a case-by-case basis.

Although there is some disagreement, the dominant view among standard setting agencies such as the U.S. Children's Bureau is that parole supervision in the juvenile field should not be the responsibility of an institution but should be administered by an agency with responsibility for both the institution

---

[12]See "California Department of Corrections Parole Work Unit Program, Report Submitted to Joint Legislative Budget Committee" (Sacramento: The Department, Dec. 1966).

and the field staff. There is no significant support for an independent parole board controlling the field staff that serves juvenile offenders.

The existence of independent parole boards in the adult field, however, has meant that controversy has centered on whether parole officers should report to the independent parole board or to a central department of corrections which also operates correctional institutions. The National Survey covering the 50 states and Puerto Rico showed that 31 jurisdictions have field parole staff reporting through an executive to the parole board responsible for the release of offenders. The other 20 jurisdictions have field staff reporting through an excutive to a State department of correction or similar agency.

The arguments for placing parole supervision services under an independent parole board can be summarized as follows:

1. The paroling authority is in the best position to promote parole and gain public acceptance for it. Since it is held responsible for parole failures, it should be responsible for supervision services.
2. Paroling authorities in direct control of administration are in the best position to evaluate the effectiveness of parole services.
3. Supervision by the paroling authority properly divorces the parolee from the correctional institutions.
4. An autonomous paroling authority in charge of its own services can best present its own budget request to the legislature.

Among the arguments for including both parole supervision and institutions in a single department of corrections, with the parole authority having responsibility and authority only for case decisions, are these:

1. The correctional process is a continuum. All staff, institutional and parole, should be under a single administration rather than being divided, with resultant competition for public funds and friction in policies.
2. A consolidated correctional department has the advantage of consistent administration, including staff selection, in-service training, and supervision.
3. Boards are ineffective in performing administrative functions. Their major focus should be on case decisions, not on day-by-day field operations.
4. The growing number of programs part way between institutions and parole can best be handled by a single centralized administration.

Local factors are quite important in deciding on the best course to follow. If the management of a State prison system is stagnant and the parole board is active and effective, obviously parole supervision should stay with the parole board. On the other hand, where there is at least equal capacity and motivation on the part of the parole board and the department of corrections, the value of integrating institutional and field programs seems to be an overriding reason for one responsible administration covering all correctional programs. The trend in recent years has been in this direction.

19

The Role of the Inmate
in the Prerelease Process

PAUL T. TAKAGI

One direction in current research and theory in the sociology of deviance is the notion that organizational outcomes, such as recidivism in correctional organizations, are not entirely an attribute of the client, but represent, in part, the judgments of the worker, who is influenced by the organizational context in which he operates. The semiprofessional worker in organizations designed to provide services for the client has received considerable attention in recent years and, although the studies vary in their foci and in their descriptions of problem areas, there are interesting parallels which cut across what appear to be quite disparate occupational activities: differential nursing services to patients,[1] employment placements by social workers,[2] police arrests of juveniles,[3,4] tracking of high school students by school counselors,[5] and revocation rates of parolees[6] are examples of studies on organizational outputs

SOURCE. Unpublished manuscript prepared at the School of Criminology, University of California, Berkeley, 1968.

[1]Esther L. Brown, "Nursing and Patient Care," in Fred Davis (ed.), *The Nursing Profession,* Wiley, 1966.

[2]Peter M. Blau, *The Dynamics of Bureaucracy*, The University of Chicago Press, 1955.

[3]Irving Piliavin and Scott Briar, "Police Encounters with Juveniles," *The American Journal of Sociology*, **69** (September 1964), 206–214.

[4]Aaron V. Cicourel, *The Social Organization of Juvenile Justice*, Wiley, 1968.

[5]Aaron V. Cicourel and John I. Kitsuse, *The Educational Decision-Makers*, Bobbs-Merrill, 1963.

[6]James Robison and Paul T. Takagi, "The Parole Violator: An Organization Reject," unpublished manuscript prepared at School of Criminology, University of California, Berkeley, 1968.

governed by worker attitudes and training on the one hand, and by the social organization of the work place on the other.

A body of literature which attempts to "explain" the behavior of officials in administrative organizations has been entitled recently as the "societal reaction school."[7] This perspective suggests that officials categorize deviants in order to facilitate the managing and processing of them within an organization. For example:

"The office [agents of social control] was developed to solve a problem in social management. A number of strangers typed as deviants have either gotten caught or have given themselves up to public regulation. The theory of the office supplies the answer to the question of what is to be done with them. The theory specifies the number and kinds of establishments that will process these deviants. . . . Office theory sets down, then, the principles for the management of social deviance."[8]

The concept that officials tend to regulate and order deviants into routine agency terms implies that the deviant is a passive receptor, being sifted and sorted into officially conceived categories. Bordua notes this as being a fundamental assumption in the "labeling" school.[9] There is, however, empirical evidence to indicate that the administration of deviants in accordance with agency concepts and rules may be problematic; that is, the deviant can sometimes influence the desired outcome. Cicourel, for instance, and also Piliavin and Briar, offer some evidence to indicate that juveniles in contact with the police can determine the outcome by displaying the proper attitude.[10,11]

The purpose of the present article is to examine further the role of the deviant or, more precisely, the officials' conception of the role of the deviant, and to determine how these conceptions hamper the bureaucratic routine. Specifically, we examine the actions of workers (parole agents) in a parole agency in a task-specific activity where the administratively defined task objectives have come to be redefined. I suggest that the redefinition of the objectives might be in response to client participation where the individual efforts of the deviant represent one source of pressure on correctional officials.

DATA

The data were obtained in a study of a parole agency during the summer of 1964. Systematic collection of data in the form of field observations, interviews with officials, surveys, and examination of official documents continued

[7]David J. Bordua, "Recent Trends: Deviant Behavior and Social Control," *The Annals*, **369** (January 1967), 149–163.

[8]Earl Rubington and Martin S. Weinberg (eds.), *Deviance: The Interactionist Perspective*, MacMillan, 1968, p. 110.

[9]*Op. cit.*, Bordua.

[10]*Op. cit.*, Cicourel, 1968.

[11]*Op. cit.*, Piliavin and Briar.

until October, 1965. The survey data are based upon 262 of 264 parole agents and 38 first-line supervisors. Only a portion of the data is reported here.

THE PRERELEASE TASK

The paroling process begins when the parole board sets the terms and conditions and the release date of the prison inmate. Following this, the inmate typically establishes his own parole program by indicating his destination and his work and residence plans. A few weeks before the established release date, the preparole plans are sent to the parole agency and a parole agent is assigned to investigate the planned program. If the plans appear to be satisfactory, the agent prepares what is called a Release Program Study, which is an approval of the plans, and the inmate is then released on schedule. In no case is an inmate released from prison without the agent's approval.

The prerelease task of investigating the parole plans of the inmates, and of developing programs in those cases where the inmate's plans are indefinite or unsatisfactory, is one of high priority in the order of things in the parole agency. The parole agency I studied is a state-wide system charged with the responsibility of processing and managing a population of 11,000 parolees. Prescriptions for official actions are to be found in the parole agent manuals and in the administrative bulletins issued by headquarters. The official objectives of the prerelease tasks are specified in policy statements.

"... inmates released on parole should have satisfactory employment to which they can immediately report ... and that they have a place of residence that will approximate their needs." [12]

Policy also states that the case need not be accepted for supervision by the agent if the placement is not in the best interests of the parolee, the agency, or the public. Policy also permits postponement of an approval of the inmate's release until such time as the worker is able to develop a satisfactory employment and residence program. Thus the parole agent has a number of options. He can approve the inmate's release plans, he can reject the case for supervision, or he can postpone the release of the inmate until such time as a satisfactory program can be developed by the agent.

One-half of the inmates scheduled for release are able to establish bona fide jobs and residences either through personal contacts with former employers, friends, or family members; whereas the remainder, because of poor work records, lack of skills, or through long term confinement having lost their contacts in the community, are totally dependent upon the parole agent to develop jobs and places to stay. Among the latter group, some inmates

[12]*Parole Agent Manual*, Division of Paroles, State of California, 1964, Sec. II–01.

establish fictitious sponsors of employment in order to get out of prison on the scheduled date. Hence, for the first group, the parole agent has a relatively easy task, but for the second group, jobs are extremely difficult to arrange especially when the employee is not even available for an interview with the prospective employer.

In actual practice, almost all inmates are released on their scheduled release dates, that is, few cases are rejected for supervision or retained in the prisons beyond their release dates. This finding would indicate that the parole workers are doing a good job in locating employment or in making "arrangements" for employment and residence for the clients. In order to check what the parole agents were actually doing, I examined 2600 prerelease approvals submitted by the workers over a six month period. Only one-half of the cases approved for release were able to report to a job immediately upon release as required by policy. In other words, 1300 parolees did not have a job to report to, as was indicated on the prerelease report prepared by the parole agent. Of those who did report to a job, approximately 450 parolees were still on the jobs some sixty days later.

The findings are extremely interesting because policy is rather liberal in that it permits the parole agent a number of alternatives, and yet it appears as if the agents are providing shoddy services for the clients. To pursue this further, I began interviewing both agents and first line supervisors and discovered that the task objectives had become redefined. Both workers and supervisors agree that the objective in pre-release work is to "get the man out" or "no overdues" and not the objectives of obtaining suitable employment and residence as specified by policy. Responses to questionaire items support the great concern among parole agents concerning "overdue cases." About 81 percent of the agents feel that the supervisor is concerned about "overdue cases," and one-half of the supervisors admit that they are concerned about agents having "overdue cases."

The importance of "getting the man out" is such that 70 percent of the workers and 69 percent of the supervisors feel that some agents are indeed forced to

Table 1 *Concern about Overdue Cases: (The agents were asked, "Is your supervisor concerned about overdue cases?" The supervisors were asked, "Are you concerned about agents having overdue cases?")*

	Agents (%)	Supervisors (%)
Almost always	81.0	50.0
Most of the time	15.0	28.0
Some of the time	3.0	19.0
Almost never	1.0	3.0
	100.0	100.0
	N = 258	N = 38

deviate to "get the man out." Deviations in the performance of the task involve approving a release to a program with a low probability of a job actually materializing.

Table 2 *Deviations to Get the Man Out. (The agents and supervisors were asked, "Do you believe under our present system of prerelease procedures that the agent is sometimes forced to deviate to get the man out?"*

	Agents (%)	Supervisors (%)
Agree strongly	21.0	25.0
Agree moderately	49.0	44.0
Disagree moderately	20.0	15.0
Disagree strongly	10.0	15.0
	100.0	100.0
	N = 259	N = 38

Some one-half of the agents and supervisors agree that they would not let a case become overdue although retaining an inmate in prison beyond his release date is specifically permitted by policy.

Table 3 *Parole Workers Would Not Let Cases Become Overdue. (The agents and supervisors were asked, "If I (an agent) cannot formulate a satisfactory program, I would (he should) let the cases become overdue."*

	Agents (%)	Supervisors (%)
Almost always	8.0	3.0
Most of the time	15.0	6.0
Some of the time	27.0	47.0
Almost never	50.0	44.0
	100.0	100.0
	N = 258	N = 38

Task accomplishment is admittedly difficult, but policy provides for these contingencies, and yet, parole officials find it necessary to limit the number of overdues even engaging in deviations to "get the man out." In my interviews with agents and supervisors, I interviewed one agent with a number of overdue cases, and as the agent explained, his caseload area covered a transient and lower socioeconomic section of the community where the residents were largely unskilled workers. Both headquarters and his supervisor were upset with the agent for having so many overdue cases. Despite pressures upon the agent in the form of reminders, telephone calls from headquarters, and the supervisor's orders to reduce the number of overdues the agent was obstinate in his refusal to release inmates without a "solid" program. The agent told me that he believed that an unemployed parolee can create problems, such as financial dependence, supervision difficulties and even violations; hence, he would not approve an inmate's release without a job to report to. The agent was subsequently "sanctioned" when his request to be reassigned to a "plum" experimental program was denied. The agent said that the reason given him was that he needed to develop greater ability in finding employment for his clients, and since the success of the experimental program depended upon agents with good all-around ability, he would not be suitable.

It is interesting to note in the foregoing situation that the agent mentioned reminders and telephone calls from headquarters and the supervisor's orders to reduce the number of overdues. This would suggest that agents, by approving the release of virtually all inmates, are not simply attempting to shirk their responsibilities, but rather, pressures, emanating from headquarters, "force" the release of inmates either with or without satisfactory programs.

Although I did not interview inmates or parolees in this study, it appears as if one source of pressure upon the parole system is the inmate in prison whose primary motivation is to get out. The inmate, from the moment of entry into prison until he walks out the "front gates," is concerned above all with one thing—to get out of prison. Thus when he becomes overdue, and his discussions with the prison counselor reveal that release can only be activated by the parole agent, the only avenue open to the inmate is to write letters to anyone and everyone. If the inmate has relatives and friends, they can in some instances, apply pressures by visiting the offices of the worker or the supervisor, but this does not account for the pressures emanating from headquarters.

Letters are also directed to the governor of the state, to the heads of organizational units, and to members of the parole board. By this means, the inmate, perhaps knowingly, "short circuits" the system, that is, by not going through channels he is able to activate a fundamental characteristic of correctional bureaucracies—letters of complaints even from a low status prison inmate require attention and an "explanation." Typically, the letters are passed down the organizational hierarchy with instructions: "to take care of the matter." The inmate's letters along with the instructions eventually reach the desk of the agent responsible for processing the case. The letters are received with feelings of resentment because the worker is not only burdened with additional paperwork, but is now required to provide an accounting of his efforts to his supervisor, the supervisor to his superior, and so on back up the hierarchy. Thus the case of the overdue inmate is no longer a routine matter.

One might raise the question why someone in the correctional system does not attempt to explain to those enquiring why some cases are rejected or postponed? One reason seems to be that regardless of the time allocation for task completion, satisfactory programs cannot be obtained in all cases, and the failure, or the refusal, of the agency to take this fundamental fact into account might be related to the performance evaluation structure within the organization. Somehow, accountability, or the criterion for performance evaluation in the prerelease task is the number of overdue cases.

If overdue cases are a measure of performance, what impact does a large number of overdue cases have on the correctional system? Interviews with correctional officials indicate that large numbers of overdues can occur as a result of depressed economic conditions or from a shift in policy toward releasing a larger number of inmates which can overtax the agents' ability to find them employment. Whatever the reason for inmates being overdue, their stays in the prisons create two types of problems. One is the problem of bed space and feeding of inmates which are budget limiting considerations. Budgets for correctional systems are based upon a projected prison population for a given fiscal period, and it is assumed that a specified number of inmates will be released within a specified time period. Population pressures are especially critical, since inputs into the system via court commitments or parole violations cannot be controlled by the prisons. The budget issue is of less concern for the parole agency, which can absorb an increasing parolee population since additional workers may be hired at any time on a formula basis.

The overdue cases are perceived by officials as presenting still another kind of problem. A prison riot is perhaps the major concern of prison officials, where riots are believed to be caused by over-population, idleness or inequities. The concept of equitable justice means that similar offense groups more or less receive approximately the same prison terms, all other things being equal.

"Undoubtedly the major problem confronting the parole board is that of making equitable, realistic and consistent decisions as to length of term and time on parole . . . . To perform these functions well, the board is required to have a clear conception of what constitutes equitable standards of sentence length for offenses of various types and for criminal histories of diverse kinds."[13]

A prison inmate generally knows, on the basis of length of sentence, whether he is going to receive a parole date as he makes his periodic appearances before the parole board although there are always contingencies on receiving a date depending upon such things as disciplinary incidents while in prison, prior felony convictions, or the nature of the commitment offense, for example, extensive publicity during the trial or what officials refer to as an aggravated offense, where multiple legal violations are charged.

But to the extent that the parole date may be predicted on the basis of sentence length, then the operation of the correctional system is perhaps based on the concept of *distributive justice*, where inmates appear before a parole board, and one man is granted a parole and the other man is turned down. Then the man turned down, if his conditions resemble the other that was

---

[13]*Probation, Jails and Parole*, Board of Corrections, State of California, 1957, p. 40.

rewarded, may display anger and frustration.[14] If it is true that sentences are meted out on the principle of distributive justice, then this would imply that officials are indeed governed by potential sources of inmate anger and frustration.

Similarly, the parole date is believed by inmates to be a "right" to be released from prison, and to the extent inmates are retained in prison on an overdue status, this too may create an angry and frustrated body of inmates. There is some evidence to suggest that officials are concerned about soothing the anxieties of the inmates.

"The early receipt of prerelease approvals or progress reports provides the prison staff with information that minimizes and relieves anxieties of inmates."[15]

It appears, then, that one of the reasons for administrative pressures upon the parole agent "to get the man out" is the belief that overdue cases can contribute to a group of restless and dissatisfied inmates, which, in turn, can make the prison a potentially dangerous place. In a sense, the parole agents' prompt approval of the release of inmates on their scheduled release dates lessens not only the inmate's anxieties, but those of the officials as well.

DISCUSSION

The analysis of the prerelease task lends support to Bordua's recent criticisms of the "labeling" theory of evidence. He notes that the "labeling" school assumes ". . . an essentially empty organism or at least one with little or no autonomous capacity to determine conduct."[16] The recent work by Cicourel and the present analysis of the prerelease task provide evidence that the deviant is not entirely a passive participant in the official's attempts to standardize task responsibilities into a bureaucratic routine. Even in the prerelease task where the agent has no direct face-to-face contact with the client, the latter is able to generate considerable leverage in producing a desired outcome.

In the prerelease process, the inmate's primary interest is to be released on his parole date, and at that moment, is probably less concerned about a job and a place to stay while on parole. It would seem then, that given the choice of an overdue status *or* being released to a shoddy program, he would take the latter.

Officials are similarly interested for the inmates to be released on schedule. Officials aid and abet the release process because of (1) myths about the causes of prison riots, (2) the interest to run a quiet administration, and

[14]George C. Homans, *Social Behavior: Its Elementary Forms*, Harcourt, Brace and World, 1961, pp. 72–78.

[15]*Op. cit., Parole Agent Manual*, Sec. II–13.

[16]*Op. cit.*, Bordua, p. 153.

(3) among parole agents, to circumvent task demands which are difficult to meet. Prison riots, for example, occur often enough to be of major concern among correctional officials, but whether riots are indeed caused by over-population, idleness or inequities in justice, remain an unsolved problem. It is, however, probably true that these beliefs do influence administrative decisions to minimize those conditions which are believed to contribute to potentially violent situations.

A related issue is that correctional operations have potentially high visibility, because inmate and parolee cases are news-worthy material—unofficially, this is referred to as a case "blowing-up." Hence, the writing of letters, such as to the governor of the state or to legislative officials, might make visible an aspect of the correctional system which officials may not wish to reveal.

The parole agent is confronted with the difficult task of developing pro-grams, especially jobs, which are not always available. Thus the informal objective of "no overdues" permits the agent considerable relief.

It is therefore the combination of the interests and concerns of the inmate, of high level officials, and of the parole agent, which make the prerelease procedure "work."

20

An Analysis of Parole Selection

PAUL A. THOMAS

Parole selection and release procedures take place within both a *formal* system of rules, regulations, statutes, and norms and an *informal system* of attitudes of parole board members, public sentiment, custom, and values. The interaction of these two systems forms the basis of the parole board's decision on whom to select or release on parole. This paper will attempt to analyze this process by making particular reference to the procedures used by Indiana's first full-time parole board, which has been in operation since July 1, 1961.

THE FORMAL SETTING

The board, appointed by the commissioner of correction with the approval of the governor, consists of three members, of whom no more than two may have the same political affiliation. Ordinarily, each member will be appointed to a four-year term of office; at the beginning, however, one member was appointed to a term of four years, another to three years, and the third to a two-year term. Prior to his appointment, the chairman of the board had been employed for twenty-seven years as deputy warden (Treatment and Classification) at the Indiana State Prison. The second member, a graduate of Harvard,

SOURCE. *Crime and Delinquency*, **9**, April 1963, pp. 173–179. Reprinted with the permission of the National Council on Crime and Delinquency. Copyright, 1963, National Council on Crime and Delinquency.

is a Negro attorney who has practiced law for thirty-three years in Gary and had served on the prison's part-time parole board. The third member, the author, has taught in college for some twenty-eight years and had taken on a number of assignments at the Indiana State Farm.[1] As we shall see later, the backgrounds of parole board members are important elements in the paroling process.[2]

This new, full-time board has sole and final jurisdiction over parole for the Indiana State Prison, the Indiana State Reformatory, and the Indiana Boys School. By statute, it is authorized to release on parole any inmate in the first two institutions (except one under the death sentence) who has served his minimum sentence, and any boy at the School recommended for parole by the Classification Committee there. The board may subpoena witnesses and documents and, since it has all the powers and duties of the Clemency Commission, can recommend to the governor commutations of sentence and, occasionally, remission of fines and of bond forfeitures. The governor alone has the power of pardon.

I am citing these facts to indicate the responsibility and the power that lie *formally* in the board's hands. In addition, of course, the board has significant obligations to the Department of Correction and the state itself, as well as to professional organizations and their principles, such as those stated in 1939 at the National Conference on Parole. Thus, the legislation that created the board also conditions the board's behavior and is an even present part of the formal framework in which it operates.

Let us look at the formal setting in the institution when the board meets. At the prison and at the reformatory, parole hearings are held two months ahead of the earliest possible release date,[3] and about two weeks before that date at the Boys School, to determine whether or not an inmate should be granted parole, be paroled and discharged, be released to a wanting authority, have his case continued, or be denied parole. One month before the hearing, the board members receive copies of inmate classification summaries for the regular applicants, reconsideration cases and other special cases, and parole violators. (The monthly total of these summaries for the three institutions is about 500.) Each man must have been on good behavior for at least a year. Two votes for *or* against an applicant determines the decision. From a sociological viewpoint, some of the most interesting moments of making a decision on selection and release center in the influences board members exert upon each other.[4]

The reader should bear in mind that the board's actions take place within a legal framework—the statutory basis of its authority and the offender's

[1]The author's term of office expired on August 24, 1962.
[2]See L. E. Ohlin, *Selection for Parole* (New York: Russell Sage Foundation, 1951), p. 28
[3]That is, the date on which the inmate has served out his minimum sentence.
[4]To those interested in small group theory and analysis, participation on a parole board is most revealing and rewarding.

designated sentence. For this reason, the institutional parole officer must provide the members with accurate information in the classification summaries.

In addition to the inmate and the board members, the only other person present at the formal hearing is the institutional parole officer, who acts as recording secretary. Other persons may attend only through invitation and qualification and must be identified if the inmate does not already know them.

The formal factors that enter into the process of selecting or rejecting an inmate for parole will be old hat to most readers. As Giardini states:

"The protection of society is paramount and should constitute the basic criterion for release on parole. . . . A man should be kept in prison until the community is ready and willing to receive him and he is ready and willing to return to a law-abiding life. Here we have two basic and inclusive criteria for parole selection . . . [which] can be broken down into a number of factors.[5]

Thus, the board will doubtless consider the nature of the inmate's offense, his criminal record, physical and psychological reports, attitude reports, institutional conduct and time served, the proposed parole plan, the family's attitude, community sentiments, and perhaps a prediction table.

THE INFORMAL SETTING

But these formal considerations are always tied in with the board members' own values, experiences, and beliefs. For example, if a member believes that rehabilitation cannot be effected within a correctional or penal institution,[6] he may give slight attention to formal criteria and reports. That is, he may be convinced that a prison cannot be expected to "reform" a man because of all the cross-purposes at work in the institution. Or, he may argue that reform is too much to expect, especially when all other social institutions seem to have "failed" in the particular case. Thus, the *informal* system is at work with (or against) the formal one.

Many state customs also impinge on the parole board. Take, for instance, the fifteen years a lifer must serve in Indiana before he is eligible for clemency consideration. This regulation has become quite formalized and, as a matter of fact, quite inflexible even though it is not statutory. It has, in effect, become a formal criterion. At one time, this term was ten years, until a former "exalted dragon" in the Ku Klux Klan was charged with and convicted of having done away with his paramour, at which time the Clemency Commission abolished the ten-year rule and extended the period to fifteen years. Thus, public sentiment, public judgment, public attitudes, which all of us must take into account,

---

[5]G. I. Giardini, *The Parole Process* (Springfield, Ill.: Charles C. Thomas, 1959), p. 131.
[6]H. B. Gill, "Correction's Sacred Cows," *NPPA Journal*, July, 1959, pp. 247–248; Giardini, *op. cit.* note 5, p. 131; National Council on Crime and Delinquency, *Parole in Principle and Practice*, 1957, p. 56.

have an impact upon the formal or quasi-formal criteria used by the board or commission. Where would the Indiana Parole Board be if it had tried to "hear" men serving life sentences earlier than the customary fifteen years? So, lifers, who in some observers' estimation need or merit release long before they have served fifteen years, still must comply with the customary rule.

"Time served" was cited above as one of the formal factors the board considers before arriving at a decision. But is it really a *formal* factor? Perhaps, but only as the words signify the inmate's completion of his minimum sentence. Once this minimum has been served, however, and the board can dabble in the question of "sufficient amount of time served"—insofar as this is a criterion of parolability—whose standards is the board using? And what is the basis of these standards? That is, do the board members base their opinion of what constitutes "sufficient time served" on (1) the nature of the offense, (2) the legal sentence, or (3) what they think will rehabilitate the offender? At this point, the formal and informal systems meet head-on. Institutional staff recommendations may clash with the board members' opinions and attitudes. "How long is long enough?" and "Now may be the time" are phrases often heard in their discussions about the potential parolee. Nothing is cut and dried, black or white, about the process of parole selection. It is not concise and exact but rather a guessing game of no mean proportions.

"Our efforts to develop scientific predictive devices have not been very fruitful so far. So the task of selecting prisoners for parole, even under the most favorable conditions, remains largely a practical, common-sense process which becomes more refined and exact with the increasing experience of the operators."[7]

Perhaps we should rely entirely on I.B.M. cards, since certain reports from Illinois and California appear to have shown that such "scientific" predictive instruments serve as well as or possibly better than the personally calculated risks taken by parole boards.

To illustrate further the interaction of the two systems, let us examine the way in which board members' attitudes toward different types of crime may cloud the issue. Suppose the outlook for a particular inmate, convicted of rape, appears very favorable, but one of the board members has a strong bias against anyone guilty of this type of crime. He may partially or wholly ignore institutional staff recommendations that the inmate be released. In view of this conflict of attitudes and standards, the factor of "time to be served" is used against the release of the inmate. Each member of the Indiana Parole Board, for example, has revealed strong prejudice against at least one particular crime – (1) rape, (2) homicide, (3) white-collar crime. In my opinion, the significance of this personal bias must not be understated, for it is something that a conscientious parole board member must be mindful of when he makes his judgment. Is he considering only the inmate and the offense? Or is

[7]Giardini, *op. cit.* note 5, p. 131.

he also considering his own scale of values? What does each of the parole board members see when hearings with a "dangerous" criminal are held?

INFLUENCES ON THE BOARD

But these subjective undertones in the hearing do not end here. If, for instance, one or more of the board members is influenced by the community in which he lives, a crime wave or pessimistic survey of the crime situation may suffice for him to deny a man parole, despite an excellent prognosis from the institutional staff. Thus, we see how important the background, training, experience, and values of the board members are in parole selection.

If paroling an inmate at a certain time will stir up strong protests from the public and the press,[8] then public prejudices also enter into the parole selection process. Although society is not present at parole hearings in Indiana, its voice is heard when the board's action reflects the public mood. For example, irate citizens have on occasion sent letters and newspapers have written editorials about some action taken by the Indiana Parole Board. A community that has experienced a great volume of armed robbery may try to dissuade the parole board from releasing any inmate sentenced for that crime. In such instances, too, the apparent judgment of the community may take precedence over the favourable reports on a potential parolee.

But there is another side to the coin. Sometimes efforts are made to influence the board members by means of political pressure or bribery. If they yield to such pressures, the formal factors fade away in the decision-making process. Furthermore, such efforts may produce in the board member a feeling of resentment and even antagonism, which may carry over into his evaluation of the applicant for parole. Here again formal criteria for parole are made subordinate to other factors that have occurred informally.

In this connection we must not overlook the inmate's attempts to "put the bite" on board members whenever they are present in the institution. In both the prison and the reformatory, for example, parole board members have special quarters, a dining room, and barber facilities. The porter, the waiter, and the barber, therefore, have certain advantages which they may exploit through actions and words to remind the board of their superior qualities and prospects.

Often, we read in the classification summary that a man is a "model" inmate. But is he also a stool pigeon, without whom the staff cannot operate fully? If so, is the Board obliged to render him—or the porter, waiter, or barber, for the matter—the special consideration apparently expected of us by both staff and inmates? The consequences of such "special consideration," in terms of inmate morale and future board action, would be calamitous.

[8]F. L. Bixby, "The Board Member and Parole," *The Welfare Reporter,* July, 1959.

For these reasons, the Indiana Parole Board tries to judge each case on its own merits. To do this, however, it must face certain difficulties. We have heard inmates say, "Both of us did the same thing, but you treat him one way and me another," and we have been confronted with family claims that son, husband, or friend "hasn't had one mark against him in the institution." It is very hard to explain to these persons that "good behavior" in the institution is not the sole, much less an important, criterion of parolability.[9] Everyone is ready and willing to advise the board on the proper amount of time an inmate should serve, but will pay little or no attention to the formal requirements of the case. To repeat, then, parole selection is not a neat, precise, black-or-white process, but a very gray business indeed.

RELEASING THE INMATE

The interaction of the formal and informal settings in the parole selection process may also be observed in the release procedure-especially in the areas of a parolee's job requirement and placement, in which the board must take into account a man's age and health, the nature of the job he should have, and where he should live. Here, the board members' ideas on what is the "proper" job for an inmate, or the proper place for him to live, may clash or coincide with the formal requirements. What is on the members' minds when they think of the neighborhood and the home life to which the parolee will return? What does the board know of the family's interpersonal relationship? Should board members deny parole to a man whose family is "beneath" their standards? Or should they knowingly place him in a situation that is "too good" for him? If we accept as accurate what the parole officer states, will we always agree with him? And if we do not agree, does the ensuing denial of parole reflect our own social class origins, current status, and standard of living? Should parole be denied for these reasons?[10] Although we try to place an inmate in a situation that is splendid by our own scale of values and standard of living, we may be contributing to his poor adjustment if too much is expected of him in a situation to which he has never been accustomed.

In Indiana, the general parole conditions are read to and by the parolee. Board members, who are aware of this, may overemphasize these conditions through the use of special stipulations. A member who may feel strongly about nonsupport can either reinforce or vitiate these and other formal conditions of parole. For example, he may threaten the parolee: "If you miss *one* payment, you will be violating parole and be returned to the institution." Thus, his strong biases regarding family life may make him oblivious to the emotional and economic adjustment the parolee must make. Shouldn't parole boards, who generally stipulate only what a parolee must not do, also stipulate

[9]Giardini, *op. cit.* note 5.
[10]Ibid.

what he *ought* to do "in order to live successfully on the streets"?[11] The negative tone which seems to be prevalent in the release of inmates sometimes can be followed by unplanned and unfortunate consequences.[12]

Among the inmates the Indiana Parole Board interviews each month at the three institutions are parole violators, who, almost without exception, are "set"; i.e., they usually have a definite term added to their original sentence. Because of the violation, a "set" is almost always expected. If the parole violator is returned a very short time after his release, the board tends to give him a stiff additional term. Although not required to do so, the board feels obliged to impress the parole violator and potential parolees with the significance of the parole conditions and of supporting the parole officers in the field. Yet, in our concern with making this impression, do we, or any other boards for that matter, allow the parole violator to make his own adjustment according to his needs?

Similarly, when a man has, by most standards, unqualifiedly violated parole, the board is inclined to impose a heavy assessment so that the factor of "time to be served" looms large again. Is the board, by the heavy term it imposes, merely showing disappointment in and embarrassment over its own action?

Exactly what is on the board's mind in setting an additional term? Is it punishment or is it an attempt to rehabilitate or provide the man with more training? If a board member does not believe that prisons, reformatories, boys' schools, and the like can rehabilitate inmates, what would make him agree to imposing a heavy "set"? Whose expectations is he trying to fulfill when he acts against his own beliefs?

Sometimes friends on the outside or sympathetic institutional staff will "push" for an inmate's parole —a situation that helps fog the entire picture for the board and that may eventuate in the board's decision to parole the man. Suppose the board, having gone through all the processes of parole selection, turns the inmate down because of, say, the nature of the offense, and suppose it continues to deny him for several years. Then, say six years after the initial rejection, the board comes up with some information which qualifies the inmate for parole—despite the fact that the longer the time served, the poorer the chances of succeeding on parole. Or the board may suddenly consider paroling a lifer who has served twenty-five years and has been deemed an unfavorable prospect for parole. What is behind the board's sudden decision to grant parole, even though all formal indices are against the inmate's release? Does the "push," so to speak, come from the personal judgment of a staff member who has formed a friendship with the inmate? From humanitarian sentiments?

[11]Gill, *op. cit.* note 6, p. 247.

[12]For example, when a board will allow for *no* mitigating circumstances whatsoever to the marriage stipulation (which says that a man "may not marry without the parole officer's approval" or "may not marry for one year"), the parolee may be forced to abscond in order to marry, thus violating his parole.

The irony in all this is that the inmate in question may be paroled against his own wishes; he may not want to be out "on the street." Despite the intercession of family and parole officer, the parolee may make no attempt to succeed on parole. Thus, both the formal and informal processes that have led to his parole and release are invalidated and he returns to the place where he feels most secure.

21
Differences in Parole Decisions Associated with Decision-Makers*

DON M. GOTTFREDSON AND KELLEY B. BALLARD, JR.

Are differences in parole decisions associated not only with the character-istics of the offenders themselves (or their crime) but also with the persons responsible for the decisions? One is apt to hear equally vigorous discussions of this question among prison inmates, paroling authorities, and correctional administrators.

Suppose no differences were to be found. Then two arguments might dominate the discussion:

1. The first would support the view that the parole board is impartial; each case is decided on its merits, and personal biases of the decision-makers are excluded. Further, it would support the contention that board members apply a consistent general policy while making individual case decisions. In addition, it demonstrates the need for board decisions rather than individual

SOURCE. *Journal of Research in Crime and Delinquency*, **3**, July 1966, pp. 112–119. Reprinted with the permission of the National Council on Crime and Delinquency.

*This investigation was supported by Public Health Service Grant OM-823 from the National Institute of Mental Health.

Views expressed in this paper are the authors' and do not necessarily reflect the views or endorsement of the Institute for the Study of Crime and Delinquency or the California Youth and Adult Corrections Agency.

judgments, because differences in perception or judgment are resolved in discussion; this is an important safeguard against personal bias.

2. Quite the contrary: if no differences are found among board members, the board, as such, may not be needed at all, at least for individual case decision-making. If all tend to make the same decisions, then one decision-maker will suffice. This line of thinking would support the view that decisions are made in a quite mechanical way, and that the decision, properly based upon careful attention to individual differences, has become an institutionalized, routine procedure missing its originally intended mark.

Those who would support and those who would criticize a paroling authority can deal just as well with the alternative results. If differences were found, the argument might proceed as follows:

1. Differences clearly support the necessity for board rather than individual decisions. This is precisely the justification for group decision making: members bring different sets of experience to the decision, as well as different perceptions of the offender, his needs, society's needs, and the requirements of the prison system. Decisions that are partly clinical and partly judicial will be more valid when based on expertise from a variety of fields of experience; and differing frames of reference can be utilized fully only if the decision is made on the basis of consensus and full use of the individual differences among members. These differences are far from handicapping; instead, they are *required* for sound decisions. Further, if we all agreed, why have a board?

2. Where is the concept of justice when a sentence is determined not exclusively by the offender's misdeeds, his institutional progress, his assets and liabilities, and the probable degree of threat to society, but also by who happens to hear his particular case?

If one is not concerned with rules of logic, similar conclusions that "sound reasonable" may be reached from opposite assumptions, or one may arrive at quite different conclusions from the same assumption. Of course, these positions about the role of a parole board actually cannot be derived from a demonstration that there are or are not differences in decisions associated with personal idiosyncracies of the decision-makers. The validity of these points of view will not be assessed so readily.

When both defensive and critical arguments are eliminated, a good deal of general agreement remains on certain issues:

1. Personal biases of the decision-maker should be excluded from sentencing or paroling decisions.

2. A consistent *general* policy should be applied.

3. Consensual judgments guard against personal bias, permit greater perceptual accuracy in evaluating offenders, aid the implementation of general policy, and best protect the offender and the public.

4. Decisions affecting individuals should be made with due regard for uniquely individual circumstances.

If it is assumed that these principles are sound, we might ask how study of variation in decision outcomes associated with decision-makers can contribute to decisions consistent with these principles. It can do this in two ways. It can provide data to indicate the extent to which general policy is consistently applied; and it can provide feedback to the decision-maker himself so that he may compare his actions with those of others.

Suppose the decisions of one parole board member are at variance with those of his colleagues. Does this imply that his decisions are less sound? That it does *not* is clear when we remember that study of variation in the outcomes of the decision itself does not necessarily include any reference to the *goals* of the decision, although ultimately it should.

Ultimately we ought to be able to link differences in approaches to the decision, when demonstrated, to the goals that the decision-makers wish to achieve; determining whether there is such variation is only a step in this direction. The purposes of this paper are merely to demonstrate that the question may be investigated quite readily if information on board actions is systematically collected and is then summarized in ways which can help to answer the question; and to illustrate the useful role of prediction methods in producing such comparisons.

To answer the question with thoroughness, we need an experiment designed so that different decisions might be compared for the same individuals or at least for individuals who might be regarded as comparable. A research design that would allow this, however, is usually not feasible. We are confronted, then, with misleading comparisons of decisions on dissimilar groups of offenders. It may be, for example, that there were biases associated with the various institutions in which cases were heard, or in the types of calendars to which board members were assigned. Differences which might be attributed to members might actually be due to unknown differences among the offenders. The aim of the study described below was to illustrate the use of prediction methods to allow comparisons of decisions by taking into account the known relevant differences in the offenders whose cases have been heard. This amounts to substituting statistical for experimental controls.

METHOD

In order to control statistically for known relevant differences in the offenders whose cases were heard, we developed and tested two prediction methods. These devices, described further elsewhere,[1] permit the calculation of an expected number of months in prison when the actual sentence will be set

---

[1] D. M. Gottfredson and K. B. Ballard, Jr., "Estimating Prison and Parole Terms under an Indeterminate Sentence Law," Institute for the Study of Crime and Delinquency, Vacaville, Calif., July 1964 (mimeo.).

by a paroling authority under an indeterminate sentence law.[2] The expectation is based only on information available when the man is received in prison. Unlike parole prediction methods which purport to predict parole violations, the methods used here were intended to predict the behavior of the paroling authorities in setting prison terms.

The two devices, shown in Figures 1 and 2, together provide for each individual a score which represents the expected number of months to be served in prison.[3] The two methods were used rather than one because it was found that prediction was improved by development of separate scales for men who

---

A. Add 7.4 for all cases

        A. ....

B. If PV-TFT (Parole Violator to Finish Term), add 36.9

        B. ....

C. Prior prison incarceration:

if	add
One	3.3
Two	6.6
Three	9.9
Four or more	13.2 C. ....

D. Legal offense:

if	add
Forgery or NSF checks	2.0
Grand theft, embezzlement, petty theft with prior, auto theft, attempted grand theft, fraud, receiving stolen property, or burglary 2nd degree	4.0
Robbery 2nd degree or burglary 1st degree	8.0
Robbery 1st degree	10.0
Narcotics (possession or sale)	12.0
Assault	20.0
Homicide	24.0
Rape	26.0
Sex acts with child under 14	42.0 D. ....

E. Add A + B + C + D

        E. ....

F. If PV-WNT (Parole Violator with New Term), subtract 4.0

        F. ....

G. Expected number of months in prison:

    E − F = Expected number of months after minimum eligible parole date   ....

    Add months to minimum eligible parole date   ....

    Total expected number of months in prison   G. ....

Figure 1 Calculation of expected number of months in prison: Form P (prior prison term)

---

[2]It is not assumed that the prediction methods will be valid in other jurisdictions or in the same jurisdiction at another time.

[3]Definitions of items in these scales are given in Gottfredson and Ballard, *supra* note 1.

A. Add 19.2 for all cases   A. ....

B. Offense severity

    <u>if</u>   <u>add</u>

    Minor theft, no evidence of deliberation   0.0

    Normal sex, minor, 15 or over with mutual consent; Walk-
        away (escape without force); Abnormal sex, adults, mu-
        tual consent; Checks (involving little deliberation); Car
        theft, simple; Possess marijuana   2.2

    Accidental death, negligence; Minor theft, planned;
        Attempt crime, no threat; Theft, unplanned; Checks
        (four or more and $60 or more each); Sell marijuana;
        Theft, planned; Burglary, 2nd degree; Possess heavy
        narcotics   4.4

    Burglary, 1st degree; Sell heavy narcotics to support
        habit; Escape with force   6.6

    Abnormal sex, minor (age 15 to 18) with mutual consent;
        Car theft, planned   8.8

    Criminal act, weapon, no injury; Criminal act, involves
        fear; Attempt crime with threat to harm; Violence,
        spur of the moment   13.2

    Sell heavy narcotics for profit; Criminal circumstances
        resulting in bodily harm; Sex act with force or threat;
        Sex act with child, no force or threat   15.4

    Criminal circumstances resulting in death; Violence,
        planned, causing death or bodily harm; Sex act with
        child, with force or threat   19.8

    Any act not covered by above including receiving stolen
        property, abortion, and bigamy   11.0   B. ....

C. If offense does not involve "illegal economic gain," add 2.9   C. ....

D. Add A + B + C   D. ....

E. Number of prior incarcerations:

    <u>if</u>   <u>add</u>

    None   0.0
    One   1.2
    Two   2.4
    Three   3.6
    Four or more   4.8   E. ....

F. If no history of any opiate use, add 7.7   F. ....

G. Add E + F   G. ....

H. Subtract D—G   H. ....

I. Expected number of months in prison:

    Expected number of months after minimum eligible
        parole date   ....

    Add months to minimum eligible parole date   ....

    Total expected number of months in prison   I. ....

Figure 2 Calculation of expected number of months in prison: Form N (no prior prison term).

had previously been in prison and for men who had not. When each scale is used with its appropriate subgroup, the expected prison sentence for each man may be found. The prediction method was based on study of 1,086 men randomly selected each month, over a one year period, from a larger pool of men paroled. It was tested with a validation sample of 1,086 men paroled during the same year. The obtained validity coefficient of .67 (the correlation of expected and actual sentences in the test sample) showed that about 45 percent of the variation in prison terms is associated with the items which are included in the scales.

If these expected prison terms are calculated for each man, then we may take into account several sources of variation in expected and actual sentences:

1. Variation in terms *expected* on the basis of the characteristics of offenders.
2. Variation in *expected* terms associated with members.
3. Variation in *actual* sentences associated with members.
4. Variation in *actual* prison terms significantly associated with members when the expected prison sentences (based on offender characteristics) are taken into account.

RESULTS

The variation in terms set by various paroling authority members was analyzed for 2,053 randomly selected cases in which parole was granted over a one-year period. Only that portion of the total sentence which represents the number of months served in prison after the legal minimum eligible parole date was studied. It is only this part of the prison term which is served, in the jurisdiction studied, at the discretion of the paroling authority.

Average prison terms, after subtraction of this legal constraint upon the decision, are shown (according to board members participating in the decision) in Figure 3 and Table 1.[4] Besides the *actual* averages, the average *expected* values are shown. The expectancies are based on the equations presented in Figures 1 and 2 for estimation of the prison portion of the sentence. That is, the expected number of months to be served in prison after the minimum eligible parole date was calculated for each man, and the averages of these expectancies are shown along with the average sentences actually required.

The column at the extreme right of Table 1 shows the correlation coefficients which describe the relationships of the expected values to the actual sentences, separately for each member. These correlations are fairly high, and they are about the same for each member; they show that about 36 percent to 52 percent of the variation in prison sentences is associated with the offender characteristics taken into account by the prediction methods.

[4]Hearing representatives who participated in the hearing and a parole board member who participated in the decision but not in the interview were not considered.

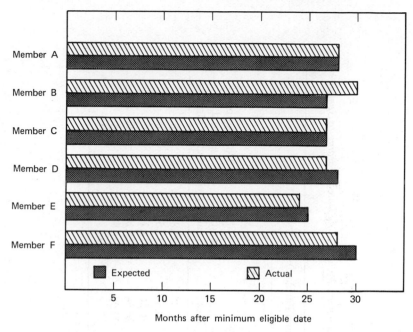

Figure 3 Expected and actual average months served after the minimum eligible parole date, according to sentences set by various board members.

There is variation not only in the prison terms actually set, but also in the terms expected on the basis of characteristics of offenders which are known to be related to the actual sentencing decision outcomes; this is shown in Figure 3. Therefore, a more adequate analysis should test, first, whether the variation in *expected* averages is significantly associated with members (that is, were the offenders different?); second, whether the variation in *actual* averages is significantly associated with members (that is, were the prison terms different?); and third, whether the variation in prison terms is significantly associated with members *when relevant differences in cases heard are taken into account*.

The analyses of variance and covariance[5] completed for these purposes and summarized in Table 2 show the following:

1. Some variation in *expected* terms was associated with members. The groups of offenders seen by members were different; that is, they were not directly comparable.

2. None of the variation in *actual* terms may be attributed to members. The differences among the members may be attributed reasonably to chance.

[5]The analysis of covariance is based on the method of unweighted means, according to the procedures described by K. B. Ballard, Jr., and D. M. Gottfredson, "Analysis of Variance and Co-Variance with Unequal Treatment Groups," Institute for the Study of Crime and Delinquency, Vacaville, Calif., July 1964 (mimeo.).

Table 1 *Expected and Actual Average Months Served After the Minimum Eligible Parole Date According to Sentences Set by Various Board Members*

Member	Number of Men	Months in Prison after Minimum Parole Date				Correlation of Expected and Actual Months
		Expected		Actual		
		Mean	Standard Deviation	Mean	Standard Deviation	
A	227	28.35	16.54	28.35	23.86	.61
B	213	27.31	15.03	29.69	27.55	.65
C	426	26.56	14.87	26.56	24.79	.60
D	442	27.69	16.56	26.58	25.10	.66
E	343	25.06	15.16	24.08	22.86	.69
F	402	30.00	18.02	27.78	24.88	.72

Table 2 *Analysis of Variance and Covariance of Expected and Actual Months Served in Prison after Minimum Eligible Parole Dates, Based on Decisions of Six Board Members (2,053 Men Paroled)*

Analysis of Variance in Expected Terms

Source of Variation	Sums of Squares	Degrees of Freedom	Mean Square	F
Between Members	5,127	5	1,025.40	3.94[a]
Within Members	533,295	2,047	260.53	
Total	538,423	2,052	262.39	

Analysis of Variance in Actual Terms

Source of Variation	Sums of Squares	Degrees of Freedom	Mean Square	F
Between Members	5,266	5	1,053.20	1.71[b]
Within Members	1,255,431	2,047	613.30	
Total	1,260,697	2,052	614.37	

Analysis of Covariance

Source of Variation	Adjusted Sums of Squares	Degrees of Freedom	Mean Square	F
Adjusted Means	3,370	5	674.00	1.93[b]
Within Members	713,993	2,046	348.97	
Total	717,363	2,051	349.76	

[a]Significant at the 1 percent level of confidence.
[b]Not significant at the 1 percent level of confidence.

3. When the differences in groups of offenders considered by different members are taken into account, the variation in prison terms, by members, is not statistically significant.

There is no support for the hypothesis that differences in parole decision outcomes may be partly attributed to the decision-makers rather than to offenders. The analysis shows instead that the paroling authority members tend to make similar sentencing decisions when the different kinds of offenders considered are taken into account in the comparison.

One important limitation to this study is that no separate study was made of any subgroups of the offender population. Interactions between specific types of offenders and decision-makers that may affect the decision outcomes would not be identified when the total group only is studied. Given an orderly record-keeping system for paroling authority decisions, however, similar analyses of any subgroups of offenders could be made quite readily whenever the decision-maker wished this kind of check on his actions compared with others.

As an isolated investigation with one look at the total group of offenders, the study is something of an academic exercise; but, as a method of providing feedback to the decision-maker, it could prove helpful. It illustrates one means by which a board might study its decisions from a variety of vantage points. A similar method could be used, for example, to provide feedback to the paroling authority concerning differences in paroling decisions associated with any offender subgroupings, any treatment classifications, and decisions made at different times under different policies.

22

The Parole Violator as an Organization Reject

JAMES ROBISON AND PAUL T. TAKAGI

INTRODUCTION

Correctional Objectives

Correctional systems, comprising prisons and parole, are given responsibility for protecting society through the control of identified offenders. The means available for control are both external (through confinement and surveillance) and internal (through rehabilitation). Rehabilitation is expected to lessen the likelihood of return to criminal pursuits, and recidivism rates are supposed to measure whether this has been accomplished. One of the stated objectives of a correctional system, and the one to which most attention is usually directed, is to "minimize" recidivism. Parole provides a setting in which a modicum of external control exists and one in which treatment processes may be extended, but it is primarily the testing ground for the entire system.

Any separate program or operation within the correctional system, regardless of its immediate and specific aim, is likely to be initially justified on the basis of its presumed relevance to the lowering of recidivism, and the operation will be evaluated on the basis of its effect on the parole revocation rate. Specific criteria are sometimes developed with reference to particular programs, and the evaluation is made in accordance with these (for example,

SOURCE. Unpublished manuscript prepared at the School of Criminology, University of California, Berkeley, 1968.

measured grade improvement of inmates exposed to academic instruction, postrelease job attainment of those who receive vocational training, or changes in psychological test performances of inmates or parolees in group counseling); but the question which almost always takes precedence is: what percent of offenders in the program violated parole, as compared to the same type offenders who did not receive it? An unequivocal answer is usually unobtainable, because few programs have operated under an adequately controlled research design. In those programs where adequacy has been approached (that is, those controlling for "expected" performance through the employment of randomized assignment, actuarial risk classification, cohort follow-up), statistically significant and positive outcome findings have been rare, and the percent differences disappointingly slight when measured against the expenditures invested to obtain them.[1] It becomes important to examine just what is being measured by the parole revocation criterion.

The Criterion of Effectiveness

Confinement (or reconfinement) is usually viewed as an undesirable but necessary step taken in response to certain damages or dangers suffered by the community. When a recidivism rate rises, persons who accept these rates as a fairly direct index of parolee performances are quick to assume that the rise reflects a deterioration in the quality of offenders passing through the system. Other persons, stressing the indirect quality of the link between offender behavior and official dispositions, assume instead that the rise may reflect merely a change in policy or in the techniques of counting:

"The evaluation of prison programs aimed at changing behavior must ask the question: Do formal parole dispositions reflect only parolee behavior, or are there other sources of variance of parole violation rates, stemming from the parole decision itself?"[2]

There is considerable evidence which indicates that these dispositions are a function of the decision-maker—evidence usually in the form of statistical disparity in decision practice which may not be plausibly attributed to client differences. These sources of variance, once isolated, are more easily subject to control than those stemming from client behavior; consequently, they promise an economical opportunity for dramatic shifts in recidivism rates and reduction in public costs.

[1] Within the California Department of Corrections: the Pilot Intensive Counseling Organization, the Intensive Treatment Project, the Special Intensive Parole Unit, the Increased Correctional Effectiveness Project, the Narcotic Treatment and Control Project, and the Parole Work Unit Program.

[2] Robert Martinson, Gene Kassenbaum and David Ward, "A Critique of Research in Parole," *Federal Probation*, Vol. **28**, No. 3, (September, 1964).

PAROLE OUTCOME IN CALIFORNIA

In California, statewide trends over the period 1960–1965 showed an increasing proportion of unfavorable outcomes for parolees. This resulted primarily from a rise in the number of those who were returned to prison to finish term, particularly those returned on technical violations. Meanwhile, there was an almost constant rate for parole violators returned with a new prison commitment. Thus, the increased violation rate was almost wholly a function of the behavior of decision-makers within the state correctional agency, thereby attesting to the position that the exercise of administrative discretion of the sort involved in the technical return can have a significant impact upon the apparent effects of a program.

The awareness of the possibilities for choice among policy options as well as variability in the interpretation of fixed policies is critical to the understanding of outcome statistics. It follows that since decision-making behavior is of such consequence, recidivism rates and public cost can be reduced (or increased) by changing parole agent behavior (decision criteria) without any expectation that it would mediate change in parolee behavior; or by changing agents (training) for the purpose of mediating parolee behavior change (treatment gain).

Statistics on parole dispositions over a number of years revealed that some parole offices in the state produced lower violation rates than others. With the introduction of a control for differences among offices in terms of their actuarial risk of return to prison for parolees, statistically significant deviations from the actuarially "expected" performance still remained for a number of the offices. Among the empirical findings, in addition to performance differences among offices for the same period, were differences within offices over time[3] and differences among individual agents.[4]

In addition, documentation that the paroling board—the official administrative decision-making body—closely followed the original report recommendation was obtained when Robison determined that nearly 80 percent of the recommendations of parole agents against revocation and over 90 percent of their recommendations for revocation were accepted by the Adult Authority.

PILOT STUDIES

Since it was evident that parolee dispositions (violation rates) were not direct indices of parolee behavior and that these measures were influenced by

[3]Dorothy Jaman and P. Mueller, "Evaluation of Parole Outcome by Parole Districts of Release, 1957–1960 Releases," Research Report No. 21, Measurement Development Section. Research Division, California Department of Corrections, 1965.

[4]J. Robison, "Progress Notes: Toward the Proposed Study of Parole Operations," San Francisco Research Unit, 1965, unpublished.

variables within communities and the correctional agency, pilot studies aimed at some specification of the operant variables in these dispositions were undertaken by Robison, Gaines, and Takagi.

Community Factors

Robison and Gaines[5] rank-ordered parole offices on the basis of the direction and magnitude of difference between expected and observed performances of parolees released to them. Noting that the "unfavorable outcome" criterion was a composite—in that if any of several alternative "most serious dispositions" (that is, jail sentence of 90 or more days, prison return WNC [with new commitment], prison return TFT [to finish term]) was accorded a parolee, the parolee's outcome was classified as unfavorable—the investigators rank-ordered offices on each of the separate outcome components and compared these rankings. Their findings were:

1. A strong inverse relationship (Spearman's rho = $-.754, p < .01$) existed across offices between the incidence of long jail sentences and of prison returns to finish term.
2. Across offices, neither long jail sentences nor prison returns to finish term were significantly related to prison returns with new commitment (rho: long jail versus return WNC = $+.121$; rho return TFT versus return WNC = $-.166$; rho necessary for significance at $p < .05 = .455$, at $p < .01 = .644$, one-tailed tests).
3. A direct and significant relationship was found across parole offices between expected-observed performance differences and the TFT rate; districts with a high observed-versus-expected outcome difference had a higher incidence of prison returns to finish term (rho = $.634, p < .05$). Offices with higher incidences of long jail outcome fared better than those with low in terms of expected-versus-observed differences, but not significantly so (rho = $-.249$).

Robison and Gaines interpreted these findings as suggestive that long jail sentences and technical returns to prison were true alternatives and raised the question "how much discretion exists within the parole district office regarding the choice between these alternatives?" They speculated that the prison return TFT might, in part, be a response to a deficit in available jail facilities within the geographic area covered by a parole office, and constructed a jail capacity index (daily jail population versus total county population) on which parole districts were compared. They found a positive (rho = $.567, p < .05$) relationship between the incidence of long jail sentences accorded parolees and the index of jail capacity for the districts' area of supervision;

---

[5] J. Robison and Helen Gaines, "On the Evaluation of Parole Outcome by District of Release:" Supplement to the Jaman-Mueller Study of 1957–1960 Releases, unpublished.

an inverse (rho $= -.497$, $p < .05$) relationship was found to exist between prison returns TFT and the local county jail capacity.

Robison and Gaines concluded that since parole units which appeared to be doing more poorly than expected in terms of unfavorable disposition were those with a higher utilization of technical prison return, and that since such districts tended to cover geographic areas with a relative deficit in county jail capacity, support was provided for the hypothesis that parole districts' performances as ordinarily evaluated (obtained-versus-expected with B.E. control for parolee risk level) were partially constrained or facilitated by local community factors external to the state correctional agency. Thus, a variable within the community was linked to "unsuccessful" offender outcomes.

Parole Agent and Office Factors

While Robison and Gaines looked beyond the correctional agency for factors connected with violation rates, Takagi looked for variables within the agency. He undertook a pilot study of two parole district offices—one which historically had a low rate of technical parole violation, and another with a high rate.[6] Identical sets of stimuli (nine actual parolee case histories in which behavior had occurred which prompted a consideration of violation) were submitted to the agents in both offices with a request to make recommendations on these cases to either continue the subject on parole or return him to prison. The findings of this study were:

1. A difference in "violation rate" existed between the two offices on the standardized task, and this difference corresponded to their actual histories of performance.

2. No agent among the fourteen in the experiment produced sets of recommendations which agreed, above a level expected by chance, with the actual case recommendations. (Responses ranged from 9 out of 9 "return to prison" recommendations by one agent, to 9 out of 9 "continue on parole" recommendations by another agent.)

3. Questionnaire responses to items about parole practice indicated differing orientations among agents in the two offices, and these orientations tended to be associated with the differences in parole outcome.

The present paper is concerned with the problem of variation in agent recommendations across district offices and regional areas. The study is a replication of Takagi's pilot study expanded to include all the units in a state parole agency.

[6] P. Takagi, B. Granlund, and J. Robison, *Uniformity in Decision-Making*, San Francisco Parole Research Unit, 1964.

PROCEDURE

All members of a state parole agency were the subjects. These included 260 caseload-carrying agents, 38 unit office supervisors, 5 regional administrators, and 15 additional members from regional and headquarters staff, including the chief of the parole agency. Data collection was completed within a six-week period in late 1965.

Two sets of data were collected from the subjects. The first set consisted of responses to a questionnaire with the usual demographic items, career plan items, professional versus administrative conflict items, and an assortment of items on actual parole operations in the areas of prerelease, supervision, and case decision-making. The second set consisted of responses to ten actual parolee case histories already processed by the parole agency and the parole board. The case histories were abstracted and summarized. In each case an emergency (or incident) had occurred and the subjects were requested to make a decision on what they would do if they were handling the cases, that is, recommend "return to prison" or "continue on parole." Thus, data were obtained from subjects who were all members of the same organization, were governed by the same rules and regulations, had the same parole board in mind in arriving at their case recommendations, and responded to a constant set of stimuli (case histories).

For the ten cases selected for the study, about two-thirds of the agents' recommendations were "return to prison" and one-third "continue on parole." Recommendation patterns for individual cases ranged in severity from one case which 90 percent of the agents chose to "continue on parole" to another which 93 percent chose to "return to prison."

The Respondents' Recommendation Distribution

The subjects had been asked to provide a recommendation of either "return to prison" or "continue on parole" for each of the ten cases presented to them. An individual subject could conceivably have decided to "return" as few as zero or as many as ten of the cases. Table 1 presents the distribution of recommendations for all 318 subjects (supervisors and administrators included).

About half the subjects (49 percent) decided to return either six or seven of the cases. The range among the 318 was from one agent who chose to continue all but one case on parole to five agents who chose to return all ten to prison. Subjects who continued the same *number* of cases on parole were not often in agreement about *which* of the cases they would continue. For example, the most frequent number of "continue" recommendations was three cases (seven returns), produced by 88 subjects; these 88 arrived at three "continues" in over twenty different ways, and every one of the ten cases appeared in at least one of these combinations of three.

Variability in the response of different individuals to a common stimulus

Table 1 *Number of Return Recommendations on Ten Cases (N = 318)*
Return Recommendations.

	Zero	One	Two	Three	Four	Five
Number of respondents	0	1	2	7	26	36
Percent of respondents	0.0	0.3	0.6	2.2	8.2	11.3

	Six	Seven	Eight	Nine	Ten	Total
Number of respondents	67	88	53	33	5	318
Percent of respondents	21.1	27.6	16.7	10.4	1.6	100.0

is, of course, to be expected. Nevertheless, it is striking that parole agents, given materials based on and very similar to the originals prepared by parole agents, and called upon to arrive at recommendations from the types of information they routinely use in preparing their own violation reports, vary in their responses to the extent that they do. The actual "legal" decision-makers for the correctional agency—the members of the Adult Authority—rely most heavily upon violation reports of this sort (and the parole agent recommendations accompanying them) in arriving at the final disposition on actual cases. The variability among agents on case recommendations, as documented above, offers some support for an assertion often heard from parolees: "Whether or not you make it on parole all depends on which agent you happen to get."

Position in the Administrative Hierarchy

The respondents were classified by their position in the organization hierarchy, and the percent of total recommendations which were to "continue" was obtained for each class (Table 2).

The lowest status members in the agency hierarchy (Parole Agents I) tended to recommend to continue least often (or conversely, to be most likely to recommend return to prison); at each step up in organizational rank there was an increase in the proportion of recommendations to continue. Given identical case stimuli, caseload-carrying agents (PA I—full caseload; PA II—half caseload) produce an average of 3.27 "continues" (33 percent) for the ten cases, while those in full supervisory or administrative positions average 4.07 (41 percent). In Table 3, respondents are cross-classified on the basis of

Table 2 *Percent Continue Recommendations by Position in the Parole Agency*

Number of Subjects	Position in Agency	Percent "Continue" Recommendations
20	Administrators and HQ staff	45.0
38	Unit supervisors (PA III)	38.4
33	Assistant supervisors (PA II)	34.8
227	Parole agents (PA I)	32.4
318	All subjects	34.2

whether they carry actual caseloads and whether the number of "continue" recommendations they offered was above the median for all subjects.

Thus, for the cases used as stimuli in the present study, a statistically significant difference exists between the recommendations of caseload-carrying agents and those in supervisory or administrative positions, with the former class being more "conservative" in their judgments of appropriate case dispositions.

Geographic Region

At the time these data were collected, the state was divided into five parole regions, with a separate regional administrator for each area. Each region contained from six to ten parole unit offices. The regional administrator was the final level of review within the parole division on violation reports prepared by the parole agent for submission to the parole board, and the administrator or his representative was the person in attendance before the parole board when the case was presented for disposition. The agent's written recommendation was appended to the report, and the agent's unit supervisor, as well as the regional administrator, might add his own written agreement with or dissent from the agent's recommendation.

Table 3 *Comparison of "Continue" Recommendations by Position in the Agency*

Position	"Continue" Recommendations Three or Fewer		"Continue" Recommendations Four or More		Total
Supervisory, administrative	19	(33%)	39	(67%)	58
Line, caseload-carrying	160	(62%)	100	(38%)	260
All subjects	179		139		318

X^2 (1 d.f.) = 14.81, $p < .001$ (two-tailed)

Table 4 *Number of "Continue" Recommendations by Parole Region (Parole Agents and Unit Supervisors)*

Region	Total Subjects	"Continued" above Median	Average "Continued"
III	52	25 (48.1%)	3.52
IV	72	33 (45.8%)	3.68
II	64	29 (45.3%)	3.48
V	63	22 (34.9%)	3.78
I	47	16 (34.0%)	3.13
State	298	125 (41.9%)	3.34

The case recommendation data were examined to determine whether there were differences in recommendation pattern among the five geographic regions (Table 4).

Though regions varied from one in which 34 percent of the subjects recommended that four or more cases be continued to another with 48 percent, the differences among regions were not found to be statistically significant (X^2, 4 d.f., $= 4.03$, $p < .50$, two-tailed).

The Parole Unit Office

A typical parole unit office is staffed by a unit supervisor, an assistant supervisor, and six parole agents. In the data which follow, no distinction has been made between the parole agents and the assistant supervisors, who also carry a partial caseload. Thirty-eight offices were represented in the study. The case recommendations for the two most extreme offices are presented in Table 5.

The average number of cases continued ranged from 1.62 in office X to 4.62 in office O. In office X, where the supervisor continued only one of the ten

Table 5 *Number of "Continue" Recommendations in Two Extreme Unit Offices*[a]

Number of Subjects	Number of Cases "Continued"							
	Zero	One	Two	Three	Four	Five	Six	Seven
5	X							
4	X			O				
3	X			O			O	
2	X		X	O			O	
1	XS	X	XO	O			OS	

[a]X, agent in office X; O, agent in office O; and S, office supervisor.

cases, there were only two agents who continued as many as three; in office O, the supervisor continued six cases, and only one agent there continued as few as three. It has long been generally believed in this agency that the unit supervisor sets the tone of the office. Further attention will be paid to the matter of correspondence between the recommendations of supervisors and their agents at a later point in this report. First, however, the case recommendation data will be examined against the parole agents' career backgrounds in terms of educational specialty and prior work experience.

Parole Agent Background, Education

Over three-fourths of the caseload-carrying parole agents in the study were college graduates, and over 90 percent had at least 90 units of college training. In Table 6, for each group of agents indicating a particular area of study, the number and percent of agents responding with more than the median number of recommendations to continue are shown.

Among those representing the more clearly defined educational specialties, agents who had majored in Social Work (a fairly small group, numbering 18) appear markedly oriented to continuation, with over 70 percent continuing four or more of the sample cases; agents with a background in Criminology seemed slightly return-prone, with less than 30 percent offering as many as four continues. Many of the agents selected more than one alternative on the area of study questions, while some specified a different major from any listed, and a few failed to respond. These subjects (several, other, no response) were removed and the median test was applied for the remaining and more clearly defined academic groups. Statistically, a trend association is demonstrated between educational background and orientation to case decision-making (X^2, 5 d.f., $= 10.80$, $p < .10$, two-tailed).

Table 6   *Broad Area of Study by Number and Percent of Subjects Above Median or "Continue" Recommendations*

Broad Area of Study	Number of Subjects	Number of "Continues" above Median	
Social work	18	13	(72.2%)
Sociology	50	20	(40.0%)
Psychology	51	19	(37.3%)
Criminology	31	9	(29.0%)
Law, other social sciences	30	13	(43.3%)
Education, humanities	21	6	(28.6%)
Several, other, no response	59	20	(33.9%)
Total	260	100	(38.5%)

Table 7   *Prior Work Experience by Number and Percent of Subjects Above Median on "Continue" Recommendations*

Number of Subjects	Prior Work Experience	"Continues" above Median	
39	Social casework, welfare	19	(48.7%)
52	Probation, juvenile hall	23	(44.2%)
28	Law enforcement	9	(32.1%)
34	State corrections: counselor	10	(29.4%)
51	State corrections: officer	14	(27.4%)
56	Other, no response	25	(44.6%)
260	Total	100	(38.5%)

Parole Agent Background, Prior Work Experience

Parole agents were asked what kind of work they had been doing immediately prior to becoming a parole agent, and their responses were classified into the categories shown in Table 7.

Agents who entered parole service from some other position within the state correctional system and those who came from law enforcement jobs (police, deputy sheriff) appear somewhat more conservative in their recommendations than agents from the remaining groups. Former correctional counselors appear no more lenient than former correctional officers. However, when the large "other, no response" category (which contained former businessmen, students, military men, etc.) was removed and the median test was applied, no statistically significant association was demonstrated between prior work experience and case recommendations (X^2, 4 d.f., $= 6.58, p < .20$, two-tailed).

A Parole Agent Value

In carrying out the task of case supervision, the parole agent is regulated, to a large extent, by minimum contact requirements specified by the parole agency. Similarly, the parole agent manual specifies many conditions under which the preparation and submission of a report is required. Nevertheless, the type of recommendation to be made on a violation report (for example, return to prison, continue on parole) is always to be decided on the basis of the agent's professional judgment. These judgments are, of course, tempered by what the agent feels is expected of him. The agents were asked to respond to the question, "If a parole agent wishes to continue working with a case, do you feel he should be permitted to do so even though a 'return' is called for according to policy?" Table 8 presents the relationship between answers to this question and the number of respondents scoring above the median in "continue" responses.

Table 8   *A Parole Agent Value and "Continue" Recommendations*

"Should Agent Be Permitted to Continue when Policy Calls for Return?"	Number of Subjects	"Continues" above Median	
"Agree" or "strongly agree"	120	52	(43.3%)
"Disagree" or "strongly disagree"	134	44	(32.8%)
Total	254[a]	96	

[a]Six subjects failed to reply.

The median test was applied to the data in Table 8, and a weak association was found to exist between agents' beliefs about whether they should be permitted to continue working with cases despite contrary policy, and their performance on the case recommendation task ($X^2 = 2.54, p < .10$, one-tailed). The responses of all agents in each office to the "value" item were averaged to provide an index for comparison against a similarly obtained office index on the case recommendations task. The median test was applied to determine if there was an association between the two measures on an office-by-office basis. The finding was not statistically significant ($X^2 = .95, p < .25$, one-tailed).

Agent Perception of the Unit Supervisor

In actual cases of parolee violations, the unit supervisor has the right to dissent from the recommendations of his parole agents, but is not empowered to alter or overrule their recommendations. However, since the supervisor ordinarily has more experience in the organization than his subordinates have and, since he is also in a position of authority over them in regard to many administrative aspects of parole, it is plausible that parole agents orient themselves toward the unit supervisor in their approach to the professional task of determining appropriate case recommendations.

An item on the study questionnaire addressed to parole agents' perception of their supervisors asked, "Does your supervisor favor recommending continuance or reinstatement of marginal parolees?" Agreement on this item was compared to agreement on the agent "value" item discussed in the previous section. In Table 9, responses of individual agents are compared in terms of their agreement or disagreement (by agent), and unit offices are compared on an index of agreement (by office).

From Table 9, it is evident that responses to the two questionnaire items are not closely associated—whether the comparison is made on the basis of individual agents or of unit offices, nearly half (45%) of the sample is incongruent (that is, agent values right to continue but believes supervisor disfavor

Table 9   *Parole Agent Value and Belief About Unit Supervisor Regarding "Continue"*

	By Agent (Agree-versus-Disagree)		By Office (Above-versus-Below Median Agreement)	
Both in favor	60	(24%)	10	(26%)
Agent in favor	60	(24%)	9	(24%)
Supervisor in favor	53	(21%)	8	(21%)
Neither in favor	81	(31%)	11	(29%)
Total	254 Agents	(100%)	38 Offices	(100%)

"continue" on marginal cases, or vice-versa). In a statistical test, a trend-level association was found on the agent-by-agent data (by agent: X^2, 3 d.f., = 2.39, $p < .10$, one-tailed; by office: X^2, 3 d.f., $p < .40$, one-tailed). This is a rather weak indication that agents' orientations coincide with, or are tempered by, the orientation of the supervisor.

In the previous section, findings indicated a low-level association between agents valuing the right to continue cases despite policy and their performances on the case recommendation task. In the preceding paragraph, the association between this value and agents' beliefs about their supervisors' orientations is also shown to be slight. The data were next examined to determine whether a correspondence existed between agents' beliefs about their supervisors and their own performance on the case recommendation task (Table 10).

The association between parole agents' beliefs about whether their supervisor favors continuation and their own performance on case recommendations is found to be highly significant statistically on the agent-by-agent comparison (X^2, 1 d.f., = 9.43, $p < .005$, one-tailed), as well, as on office-by-office comparison (X^2, 1 d.f., = 3.16, $p < .05$, one-tailed). Thus, while a supervisor's influence over his agents' *value orientation* appeared slight, his influence over their *performance* is quite evident.

The considerable variability found across parole unit offices on the case recommendation task (see section on The Parole Unit Office) warrants the

Table 10   *Agent "Continue" Recommendations and Beliefs About Unit Supervisor*

Agent Belief	Above Median, by Agent			Above Median, by Office		
	Total	Number	Percent	Total	Number	Percent
Supervisor "favors" continue	113	55	48.7	18	12	66.7
Supervisor "disfavors" continue	141	41	29.1	20	6	30.0
Total	254 Agents			38 Offices		

inference that the unit office be considered the most important organizational influence on decision-making. The findings in the present section strongly suggest that the unit supervisor's orientation has a powerful impact on the case recommendations of his subordinates. Whether this impact is associated with informal but direct coercive influence by the supervisor, or is a spontaneous outcome of the parole agents' respect for him, unit offices where agents are above the median in believing that the supervisor favors "continue" are more than twice as likely to be above the median for offices on test cases continued by these subordinates (67 percent vs. 30 percent for the remaining offices). This is an association that could only be produced if there were some consistency in belief among the agents within the separate offices. However, since both measures are based on responses from subordinates, there is no guarantee that the belief about the unit supervisor is valid. As a check, the supervisor's own responses to the case recommendation task were compared for each office against his agents' belief about him. Across the 38 districts, a statistically significant association was found to exist (X^2, 1 d.f., = 4.45, $p < .025$, one-tailed) when the median test was applied.

Agents' and Supervisor's Value, Belief, and Performance

In the preceding section, responses to two questionnaire items—one dealing with parole agents' values about their right to continue cases and another directed at whether they believed their supervisor to be in favor of continuing cases—were each found to have some correspondence with their performance on test case recommendations. It was also noted that the tendency to answer both these items in the same direction (Table 9) was not strong. In Table 11, agents have been classified into three categories on the basis of congruence or disparity between value and belief, and these types examined against the case recommendation responses.

A large difference exists between the two congruent types ("neither favors continue" and "both favor continue") on the case recommendation task; with the type of agents who believe "both favor continue" more than twice as likely to provide an above-median number of "continue" recommendations.

Table 11   *Agent "Continue" Recommendations Versus Value and Belief About Supervisor*

	Number of Cases "Continued"					
	Three or Less		*Four or More*		*Total*	
Neither favors "continue"	59	(73%)	22	(27%)	81	(100%)
One in favor, other against	72	(64%)	41	(36%)	113	(100%)
Both favor "continue"	27	(45%)	33	(55%)	60	(100%)
Total	158		96		254	

Table 12   *"Continue" Recommendations of Supervisors And Their Subordinates*

The Supervisor Continued	The Subordinate "Continued"				Total	
	Three or Less		Four or More			
Three or more cases (N = 25 supervisors)	103	(57%)	77	(43%)	180	(69%)
Three or less cases (N = 13 supervisors)	57	(71%)	23	(29%)	80	(31%)
Total (N = 38 supervisors)	160 Agents	(62%)	100 Agents	(38%)	260	(100%)

Within the disparate type (one in favor, other against), which falls between the others on case recommendation responses, are to be found two subtypes—one with the agent favoring and his supervisor seen as opposed and the other with the supervisor favoring and the agent opposed—32 percent of the former subtype and 42 percent of the latter gave an above-median number of "continue" recommendations. The median test, applied to the data in Table 11, shows the recommendation difference among the three agent types to be statistically significant (X^2, 2 d.f., = 11.54, $p < .005$, one-tailed). The difference between the two disparate subtypes is not significant (X^2, 1 d.f., = .79, $p < .50$, two-tailed).

Given the findings presented earlier—the correspondence of the agent's belief about the unit supervisor with both his own and the supervisor's performance on the case recommendation task—one would, of course, expect there to be a correspondence between agents and supervisory on case recommendations. In Table 12 unit supervisors have been separated into those who made four or more "continue" recommendations on the ten test cases, and those who made three or fewer. The recommendation performance of agents under each of the types of supervisor is presented.

It was noted earlier that the supervisors were generally more likely than were subordinates to continue the test cases. In this study two out of three supervisors gave four or more "continues", compared to two out of five subordinates. Despite this general difference, the data in Table 12 reveal a statistically significant association between supervisor and subordinate performances (X^2, 1 d.f., = 4.03, $p < .025$, one-tailed).

Discussion of Findings on Hypothetical Performance

The situation prepared by the investigators is, of course, an artificial one; responses to questionnaire items and judgments about what one would do with a case based simply on knowledge from a report do not have any necessary bearing on what happens in real life. While the test cases selected appear to cover a wide range on a "continue-likelihood" scale from one which 90 percent of agents say they would retain on parole to one which 93 percent say they would return, there is at this time little knowledge about just how representative the test case parolees are of those to be found in the actual parole population. It seems likely, however, that the ten cases are not typical but are, for the most part, "marginal" types. Probably the majority of actual violators are more "clear-cut", in that parole agents would have less difficulty agreeing with one another about whether "continue" or "return" was the appropriate disposition. The investigators did believe, and some evidence from the pilot study offered support for such a belief, that even though they were working with "artificial" data which might exaggerate real differences, these data correspond to the actual state of affairs. Additional findings relevant to this issue are contained in the next section of this report.

RESULTS: ACTUAL PERFORMANCE

The Outcome Criteria

For the purpose of documenting whether the measures applied in the current investigation bore any relationships to what was actually happening in parolee violation and recidivism, the data were compared with that available on all parolees released from prison to California supervision in 1965—the year in which the "hypothetical" data were collected. Each parolee was followed for one year subsequent to his release from prison, and the most serious disposition which he received during that period was recorded. Since the hypothetical data were collected in late September 1965, this meant that some of the parolees were released ten months prior to, and would be followed two months subsequent to, the time of questionnaire administration, while others would not yet be released for two months and were consequently followed to a point fourteen months after the agents were studied. Most of the parolees were between these extremes and therefore more closely anchored in time to the hypothetical data.

Material was available on 7301 parolees, classified by the parole unit office to which they were released.[7] Two indicators of parole performance at one year were selected for examination. The first indicator, and the one most obviously relevant to the hypothetical data, was return-to-prison-to-finish-term—an administrative disposition within the authority of the parole board which can occur subsequent to a law infraction or technical violation. These prison-returns are to be distinguished from returns-to-prison with new commitment—a court action taken subsequent to a felony conviction occurring during parole. The second indicator selected, favorable parole outcome is accorded to a parolee who, throughout one year subsequent to release, ha had no difficulty or only minor difficulty (for example, suspended jail sentences jail sentence under 90 days, misdemeanor probation).

[7] Dorothy R. Jaman, "Parole Outcome for Six Years of Felon Releases to California Parole," Staff report, CDC Research Division Measurement Unit, October 1967.

Two types of comparison were employed for each of the criteria. The first involved asking the question: How many of the parole offices which are above the median for offices on this criterion (for example, percent of releases with favorable parole outcome at one year exposure) are also above the median on another measure (for example, "continue" recommendation measure obtained from hypothetical data)? The second type asked the question: What percent of the parolees released to offices above the median on a given measure received a particular disposition (for example, technical return to prison) in their first year on parole?

While the two outcome criteria, technical prison return and favorable outcome, are mutually exclusive in regard to any given parolee, there is no necessary inverse relationship between these two measures in terms of parole office performance. One might expect that unit offices with a higher technical return rate would consequently have a lower overall rate of favorable out-comes. It has, however, been argued that an office can, through judiciously invoking a technical return, offset some other unfavorable outcome, thereby nullifying any decrease in (and conceivably increasing) its favorable outcome rate. (See section entitled Pilot Studies: Community Factors, for findings related to this topic.) On the 1965 outcome data, a comparison was made of office performance on these two criteria (median test) and no significant association was found (X^2, 1 d.f., = 2.64, $p < 20$, two-tailed).

Hypothetical Recommendations and Actual Outcome

The parole unit offices were divided into those above and those at or below the median on "continue" recommendations offered by parole agents in the test situation, and two types of determination were then made for these districts from the actual 1965 outcome data: (1) the offices' locations above or below the median on the actual outcome, and (2) the number of parolees in these offices who received the criterion disposition. The findings for the second type of comparison appear in Table 13 for both technical prison return and favorable outcome.

Table 13 *Hypothetical Recommendations and Actual Outcome*

Office Performance on Test Cases	Parole Outcome at One Year, 1965 Releases		
	Number Released	Technical Returns	Favorable Outcomes
Above median continued (18 offices)	3810	525 (13.8%)	2482 (65.1%)
At or below median continued (20 offices)	3491	564 (16.2%)	2181 (62.5%)
Total	7301	1089 (14.9%)	4663 (63.9%)

The more continue-oriented offices, as measured by parole agents' recommendations on ten case stimuli, had a significantly higher proportion of favorable parolee outcome for cases released in the same year (X^2, 1 d.f., = 5.51, $p < .01$, one-tailed), and a significantly lower proportion of parolees returned to prison to finish term (X^2, 1 d.f., = 7.92, $p < .005$, one-tailed). Thus, agent behavior in an artificial test-taking situation is found to be associated with actual recidivism rates, lending support to the hypothesis that formal parole violations are a function of decision-maker judgment as well as an index of parolee performance.

In regard to the magnitude of differences between high and low continue-oriented offices, some points of reference may be helpful. Offices above the median on "continue" recommendations for test cases show a 2.6 percent lower technical return rate and a 2.4 percent higher favorable outcome rate than offices at or below the median. The difference, though statistically significant, appears negligible in size. Had the lower group of offices performed at the same rate as the higher, there would have been 82 fewer technical returns to prison and 92 more favorable outcomes. Another perspective regarding the size of the obtained differences is provided by an answer to the question: Considering only the actual outcome rates, just how great is the difference between the performances of those offices above the median on these rates as compared with offices at or below the median? The answers are 6.4 percent for technical prison returns (12.4% versus 18.8%), and 6.9 percent for favorable outcome (68.1% versus 61.2%). Thus, the differences obtained by classifying offices on the case recommendation task should be viewed against the maximum difference attainable under these conditions (that is, 2.6% obtained versus 6.4% limit for technical return and 2.4% obtained versus 6.9% limit on favorable outcome). One may legitimately wonder whether, since the limiting differences are so small, there is really any point in paying so much attention to performance variation among parole offices. Several considerations are relevant to this question. First, as has been earlier acknowledged, since the majority of decisions about continuing cases on parole or returning them to prison probably pose little uncertainty, variability in case recommendation can be expected to occur only on cases which are more or less marginal. However, the problem of defining marginality has not been solved. Second, the differences in percent have been presented using all outcomes as a base, rather than the criterion outcome (that is, technical return). Thus, suppose that the low-continue offices had performed at the same level as high-continue offices on the technical return rate and returned 82 fewer parolees (482 rather than 564). Viewed against this base, 15 percent of the cases considered were marginal ones who would have been continued rather than returned. Third, a median split provides a conservative index of the differences among offices. For the one year outcomes on 1965 prison releases, individual parole office technical-return rates ranged from 9.3 percent to 28.7 percent, and favorable-outcome rates ranged from 54.5 percent to 73.3 percent.

Agent Value and Belief, and Actual Parole Outcome

In earlier pages of this report, two questionnaire items were described, compared with one another, checked against hypothetical case recommendations, and finally combined to provide three basic types:

1. Agent values "continue" and believes supervisor favors it.
2. Disparity between agent value and belief about supervisor regarding "continue".
3. Agent does not value "continue" or believes supervisor favors it.

For the purpose of testing these questionnaire responses against actual parole performance, the 38 parole offices were cross-classified in the three types with a reliance upon whether the office was above or below the median on each of the two measures. This procedure generated nine type 1 offices, eight type 3 offices, and twenty-one type 2 offices. Within type 2 (the disparate class) there were ten offices of the *agents* favor-supervisor disfavors subtype, and eleven of the reverse subtype. In Table 14, actual parole performance is examined in terms of technical return and favorable outcome rates across the three basic office types.

Statistically significant differences were found to exist among office types on each of the outcome criteria (technical return, X^2, 2 d.f., = 10.4, $p < .005$, one-tailed; favorable outcome, X^2, 2 d.f., = 4.75, $p < .05$, one-tailed). Unit parole offices, classified in terms of whether the agents value and believe their supervisor to favor continuation of cases on parole, provide actual parole outcomes in correspondence with their orientation. Within type 2, the two office subtypes produce identical technical return rates (15.4 percent) while a 64.8 percent favorable outcome rate exists for the supervisor favors-agents disfavor subtype, as compared to 63.1 percent for the reverse subtype.

Table 14　*Actual Parole Performance versus Agent Value and Belief About Supervisor*

Office Type	Parole Outcome at One Year, 1965 Releases				
	Number of Releases	Technical Returns		Favorable Outcomes	
1. Both agents and supervisor favor "continue"	2146	278	(13.0%)	1399	(65.2%)
2. Disparity between agents and supervisor regarding "continue"	3587	553	(15.4%)	2296	(64.0%)
3. Neither agents nor supervisor favor "continue"	1568	258	(16.5%)	968	(61.7%)
Total	7301	1089	(14.9%)	4663	(63.9%)

SUMMARY AND CONCLUSIONS

In 1967, there were 7584 adult male felons admitted to California state prisons. One out of four of these men (1867) were administrative re-admissions—cases returned to prison by the parole board for infractions or faulty adjustment on parole. An additional 11 percent of the admissions (847) were also parole violators, but these were judicial re-admissions—cases returned by the courts on a new felony commitment. With 25 percent of prison intake in the hands of parole board members, it is important to examine the process by which parole revocation occurs.

The revocation decision is, in part, a penalty and, in part, a prediction. One problem is to decide whether the immediate act or the chronic adjustment which precipitated the violation report warrants, in itself, imposing the punishment of further incarceration. The other problem is an attempt to foresee whether, if the man were continued under parole supervision, future incidents of a still more serious nature would be likely to occur. In weighing this risk, limited-term protection can be purchased by reimprisonment, which postpones the opportunity for new violations to occur, but may increase the likelihood of their eventual occurrence by interruption in the process of offender-readjustment to the community. Maintenance of an offender in a prison is over three times as costly as maintaining him on parole ($50/mo. versus $166/mo. for the California Department of Corrections), but the cost to society of new crimes can also be great. Under conditions of potentially great loss and uncertainty about the likelihood of its occurrence, one is tempted toward cautious solutions and conservative decisions. In buying insurance for awhile against a few, it is probable that many parolees who pose no serious threat are also reincarcerated; in the absence of sufficient information, there is a dilemma for decision-makers as to where the balance is to be struck.

The present study has demonstrated marked inconsistencies in judgment among parole agents about the appropriate case disposition to be made after a parolee incident. The decision task with which the agents were presented might be considered artificial and unfair, and designed to promote uncertainty and lack of reliability; however, the task is a good simulation of the real decision task with which the parole board is routinely faced. It is true that the parole board members have more information available at the decision point (i.e., a case history of the subject's past prison experience and earlier social adjustment), but it is unlikely that this older source of information has much separate impact on the decisions, given the fact that a high correspondence exists between those decisions and the parole agent's recommendation on the violation report. It is accepted that uncertainty may have been increased because of the types of case on which judgments were to be made (they may be atypical, and more "marginal" than the everyday distribution of violators) and that the findings consequently exaggerate the level of disagreement that might be routinely expected. *Regardless of the extent to which this is so, findings from that "artificial" situation have been shown to correspond with differences on actual revocation rates produced by the same parole agents—* suggesting that the marginal case is commonly confronted in real practice.

Parole agents appear to be quite susceptible to influence about the type of case recommendation they will make, even though recommendations are to be based on their professional judgment. There are tendencies toward agreement among agents within a given office, but large differences in recommendation patterns between offices. While there is some indication that the agent's personal background (his educational specialty and prior types of job) has a bearing on these judgments, and that his current value orientation is involved, the most definite correlate shown in the present study was the agent's assessment of his supervisor's orientation. Further indication of this willingness (or at least capability) to provide expected parolee performances was yielded by the definite fall in the actual revocation rate subsequent to the present study. That fall is attributable to increased pressure upon agents to recommend continued parole supervision for many types of violator—a pressure originating from headquarters and transmitted through the unit supervisors. Whether these pressures are formally or informally exerted, the response to them can markedly shift the overall *rate* of revocation; it does not necessarily follow that *variability* in judgment of recommendation among parole agents will be reduced. In the two years subsequent to the 1965 study on which this report is based, considerable attention was directed by the agency to the matter of case decisions—reports by agents were subjected to closer scrutiny at each level of review, and training sessions for agents were focused upon case reporting and recommendation. This emphasis might be expected to increase the reliability of judgment. However, when the ten test cases from the 1965 study were readministered in late 1967 and early 1968, variability in the recommendation-pattern was still quite evident.

The average number of cases continued was considerably higher than before—4.87 for new agents who had not been present for the earlier study, and 4.97 for experienced agents undergoing re-test; the average in 1965 had been 3.27. Seventy-one percent of the new agents, and 78 percent of the experienced ones continued four or more of the ten cases, compared to only 38 percent in 1965. Despite this marked shift in the central tendency—or overall "revocation rate"—on these cases, the range of response was still high.

One of the main difficulties facing correctional administrators in their attempts to improve effectiveness of operations has resulted from the failure to systematically record and analyze the material on which decisions at critical choice points are made. Ordinarily, when such efforts are made, the energy is misspent by a concentration of attention on output (the number of dipositions of a given sort by parole board members) with almost no attention devoted to the extent of its correlation with input (parole agent recommendations) or to the substance of that input (reported information characteristics which may have little reliability or actual relevance). Though a substantial proportion of parole agent work time is devoted to the preparation of narrative reports for the parole board, little opportunity is provided for obtaining a cumulative systematic knowledge base, since translation of the narrative form into a code structure which will permit analysis is a laborious and seldom-attempted process.

Correctional experience, then, has been recorded in fragments, separated into case folders, stuffed into filing cabinets, and eventually burned. That is the past. Will the future be different?

23

Uniform Parole Reports: A Feasibility Study*

DON M. GOTTFREDSON, KELLEY B. BALLARD, JR., AND
VINCENT O'LEARY

Two major weaknesses are usually found in crime and delinquency program research and practice—lack of adequate information for program evaluation and, even when information becomes available, failure to ensure the utilization of new knowledge in everyday practice. A unique opportunity for developing procedures which can aid parole administrators in dealing with both these basic issues was given by the exploratory study discussed here. The aim of the study was to determine whether an immediately usable information system might be developed as a joint effort of those administratively responsible for action programs.

There is a need for a comprehensive system of collection, storage, and

SOURCE. *Journal of Research in Crime and Delinquency*, **3**, July 1966, pp. 97–111. Reprinted with the permission of the National Council on Crime and Delinquency. Copyright 1966; National Council on Crime and Delinquency.

*This paper is adapted from the more detailed National Parole Institutes' report with the same title–Gottfredson, Ballard, and O'Leary: *Uniform Parole Reports: A Feasibility Study* (New York: NCCD, December 1965). The NPI program is supported by a grant from the Office of Juvenile Delinquency and Youth Development of the United States Department of Health, Education, and Welfare; administered by the National Council on Crime and Delinquency; and sponsored by the Interstate Compact Administrators Association for the Council of State Governments, the United States Board of Parole, the Association of Paroling Authorities, and the Advisory Council on Parole of the National Council on Crime and Delinquency.

retrieval of information pertinent to crime and delinquency problems. Currently, the major sources of information, each meeting a different portion of the general requirement, are the Federal Bureau of Prisons' *National Prisoner Statistics*, the Federal Bureau of Investigation's *Uniform Crime Reports*, publications of the Bureau of the Census, and publications of the United States Children's Bureau.[1]

Two general approaches to development of an eventual, unified, comprehensive system are open to us. We might attempt the entire task in a global fashion, striving to meet as well as we can the differing demands for information for various sectors of the courts, law enforcement, probation systems, juvenile and correction agencies, and parole systems; but this would be a large, complex task. A more realistic alternative is to develop portions which do not overlap with existing resources but can fit readily into a more general system that will be established later.

The study was limited to parole. While the development proposed as a result of this study can be incorporated later—within a more general and comprehensive system—we believe that this plan for a Uniform Parole Reporting System has significance in its own right, with immediate application.

How can the use of an information system be ensured? What steps can be taken to increase our confidence that the research results will be applied? The answer, we believe, lies in development of the system as a joint enterprise of research workers and agency administrators. If the aims and procedures of the information system are promoted cooperatively, we may expect increased commitment to them from both research workers and administrators. If the system's development can follow a flexible course, responsive to the interests and needs of administrators, greater commitment to an ultimately more useful product may be anticipated. Increased practical application of research results should follow from increased commitment to an information system with recognized relevance to practical issues.

Through its committee on Uniform Parole Procedures, the Advisory Council on Parole of the National Council on Crime and Delinquency reported that "The lack of comparable data from state to state and even within states has been a serious handicap in demonstrating the value of parole to the general public and has handicapped individual systems in evaluating the effectiveness of their own policy and procedures. [This Committee reported that their discussion] . . . clearly points to the need for a demonstration project involving a few . . . states for the purpose of demonstrating procedures for the compilation of comparable data."

As a result of this Committee's recommendation, further exploration of the need and feasibility of such a system was initiated in September 1964 by the National Parole Institutes. Before going into this study in further detail,

---

[1] A related program, dealing with uniform reporting of mental hospital population movement, is the Model Reporting Area program of the Public Health Service.

we will discuss the need for uniform reporting procedures, the potential utility of systematic collection of comparable data for evaluation of parole programs, the contribution this might make to more rational parole decisions, and the aid it might provide to parole administration.

UNIFORM REPORTING

Can uniformly recorded data describing the nation's experience with parole be useful in evaluating the effectiveness of parole programs in reducing crime and delinquency? Can parole programs, differing widely in complex ways, be compared to give needed information concerning the probable effects of various parole treatment methods? Can such a system yield information useful to parole decision-makers and program administrators by providing a more rational basis for either individual parole decisions or development of program innovations?

We lack information on the behavior of parolees. Some agencies do not maintain records systematically and therefore do not have even a crude measure of parole violation rates. Where records are kept and rates are reported, agencies use widely different criteria for "parole violation," various methods of follow-up after parole, and a number of different ways of defining "rate."

We also lack knowledge of offender characteristics *predictive* of later parole behavior. A series of investigations since at least 1928 has led to a number of consistently reported results; but the prediction methods emanating from these investigations have, for the most part, not been validated on samples from populations other than those originally studied. Therefore, these methods cannot be applied with much confidence in their validity in jurisdictions other than the one originally investigated.[2]

Some paroling agencies have research programs within their organizations; a large number do not. Many do not have even an administrative accounting program which can provide a base for evaluation. Thus many paroling agencies make decisions, markedly affecting large numbers of persons, without the simplest kind of basic feedback concerning the consequences of these decisions. A few agencies have periodically conducted studies correlating offender characteristics with later parole behavior, but most agencies have not been able to complete this kind of basic research, and few have been

---

[2]Several excellent summaries of research aimed at prediction of parole behavior are available. See Daniel Glaser, *The Effectiveness of a Prison and Parole System* (New York: Bobbs-Merrill, 1964) and *Gross Personal Characteristics and Parole Outcome* (New York: National Council on Crime and Delinquency, July 1964); T. Grygier, "Treatment Variables in Non-Linear Prediction," paper presented at the joint meeting of the American Society of Criminology and the American Association for the Advancement of Science, Montreal, December 1964; H. Mannheim and L. T. Wilkins, *Prediction Methods in Relation to Borstal Training* (London: Her Majesty's Stationery Office, 1955).

able to keep this information up to date through periodic assessment of its validity. A few items of information—notably age, prior imprisonment, and some offense classifications—have been shown repeatedly in different jurisdictions to be related to parole violation (as variously defined). There is, however, little basis for generalization from these results to offenders in jurisdictions other than those studied.

Prediction studies are not separate and distinct from program evaluation. Prediction methods are the outgrowth of experience with various groups of people, summarized in appropriate statistical form. As such, they provide a way of quantifying expectations. They are needed for application to each person *before* assignment to treatment. When persons are assigned to specific kinds of treatments, we may ask whether the actual outcome is more or less favorable than *expected* from past experience with other similar groups. Since we wish to find treatments that improve the chances of success, we will be pleased if the effectiveness of treatment makes the prediction device invalid.[3]

If the outcome can be predicted *before* and *regardless of* treatment, it is hard to argue that this treatment makes any difference to the specific outcome studied. However, persons assigned a given treatment may "succeed" (or "fail") significantly more often than expected from their risk classifications. If the validity of the prediction device has been established on other groups, the observed differences in outcome must be due to treatment, or to factors associated with treatment, or to both.

Further research, using experimental designs, might then be developed to test theories about the source of the difference. Meanwhile, the administrator can be made aware of the relationship—positive, negative, or none—between the program and the outcomes.

The study of "natural variation" within an agency is one way in which the administrator, by use of some of the tools of statistics, can obtain feedback. It requires that he keep records and keep score, and that he substitute *statistical* methods of control for the lacking *experimental* controls.[4]

A systematic and continuous program for evaluation of parole programs will require information in four areas:

1. Outcomes of parole must be defined in such a way that criteria of "favorable" and "unfavorable" parole performance are meaningful for

---

[3] L. T. Wilkins, "What Is Prediction and Is It Necessary in Evaluating Treatment?" in *Research and Potential Application of Research in Probation, Parole, and Delinquency Prediction* (New York: Citizens Committee for Children, July 1961).

[4] See Don M. Gottfredson. "The Practical Application of Research," *Canadian Journal of Corrections,* October 1963, pp. 212–228; Don M. Gottfredson and R. F. Beverly, "Development and Operational Use of Prediction Methods in Correctional Work," *Proceedings of the Social Statistics Section of the American Statistical Association* (Washington, D.C.: American Statistical Association, 1962); Grygier, *supra* note 2; Mannheim and Wilkins, *op. cit. supra* note 2.

program evaluation and acceptable to leadership of a large number of parole agencies.

2. Program variations must be studied so that programs which are different in specified ways may be compared with respect to outcomes.

3. Different types of offenders need to be studied (and here prediction methods may be particularly helpful), since differing parole outcome rates may be associated with differences in offenders rather than programs.

4. Information is needed on interactions between types of programs and types of offenders which affect program outcomes. Then the apparently most fruitful programs for each type of offender can be identified, further studied, and expanded, while programs that are harmful or not helpful can be eliminated.

CASE HISTORIES

In nearly every paroling agency, decision-makers are provided with fairly extensive case history materials regarding the offender. There is little systematic study, however, linking this information with the parole outcomes. In order to improve, eventually, individual case decisions, systematic feedback should be available as an aid to these decisions. At present, the paroling authorities are guided more by selective experience and subjective judgment than knowledge of the probable consequences of alternative actions.

Confronted with the task of developing new programs, the parole administrator currently fares no better than the parole board member. In the absence of information describing the outcomes obtained with similar programs used elsewhere, he must make his decision on the basis of his own experience, his feelings and those of his staff, or logic alone. Maintenance of adequate records can facilitiate a study of "natural variation" in parole practices. The parole programs of the nation vary markedly in size, in economic resources, in the use of parole—that is, the proportion of all persons released from confinement who receive parole supervision, in the legal constraints imposed on parole decisions,[5] and in methods of parole supervision.

The wide variation in problems, resources, and practices suggests that efforts toward a uniform parole reporting system, intended as an aid to evaluation efforts, are destined to be futile. The complexity, however, may be turned to advantage. If we ask, "What variation in parole behavior outcomes is associated with parole program variation?" the variations can be utilized to provide a "natural experiment." Systematic study of the outcomes of this "natural experiment" can provide information on probable effects of parole treatment alternatives. Paroling authorities and parole administrators will be able to compare the outcomes of their own programs with those of other

---

[5] Don M. Gottfredson, Kelley B. Ballard, Jr., and Vincent O'Leary, *Uniform Parole Reports: A Feasibility Study* (New York: National Council on Crime and Delinquency, December 1965).

agencies. It may often be found that a suggested new program for one agency, perhaps one considered with much anxiety about anticipated consequences, has already been attempted in another agency. If so, what were the results? At present, we usually do not know; or we know only through subjective impressions, most of them quite likely to be biased.

Comparisons of parole outcomes among correctional agencies are not now meaningful or useful because of the differences in the data accounting and reporting procedures associated with differing structures, policies, or interpretations. Though the faulty nature of such comparisons is frequently cited, these comparisons nevertheless *are* made whenever paroling authorities and administrators get together.

An important contribution to development of the system will be the provision of a commonly defined vocabulary. This can mean that research conducted independently by various agencies can—to the extent this common framework is used—be mutually supportive.

For this "natural experiment" an adequate accounting system must be created through collaborative planning by as many parole agencies as possible. Therefore, the feasibility study described here was made as part of a more general plan for orderly development of the system envisioned. Three phases were proposed: (1) a "prepilot" study (the work reported here), (2) a pilot study, and (3) initiation of the fully developed system.

1. The goal of the preliminary study was to determine the major problems and what was feasible. Since reporting for individual persons was required by the evaluative aim of the system, samples rather than populations were studied.[6]

2. The pilot study calls for further development and demonstration of a data collection system, involving an increased number of agencies and an associated series of User Seminars. As the system is developed, results can be made readily available to participants in the User Seminars, and communication can be more certain. This can guard against misinterpretation of results, and it can increase the likelihood that meaningful findings will be used appropriately. A particular concern in the User Seminars will be assistance to agencies in utilizing the system in their own self-study efforts.

3. Initiation of the uniform Parole Reporting System, with voluntary

---

[6]Many parole agencies stated that a shortage of clerical help would preclude an immediate attempt to study total populations of parole violators.

National Prisoner Statistics (Federal Bureau of Prisons), *Uniform Crime Reports* (Federal Bureau of Investigation), and the *Model Reporting Area* program (National Institute of Mental Health) are all based on *summary* statistical reporting. If the system developed is to be more helpful in program evaluation, however, it is necessary to obtain data not only for groups but for individuals. This can permit a greater control, in program comparisons, for selection biases associated with differing programs. With full development of the system, summary reporting of population movement could be generated from the individual reporting base.

participation by agencies responsible for parole of offenders from correctional institutions or for their parole supervision, would follow the pilot study.

All agencies that might participate in the fully developed system were asked to help in planning; all were asked to send a representative to a two-day planning meeting held in Chicago in December 1964. Twenty-five state adult parole agencies, the District of Columbia Board of Parole, the Illinois Youth Commission, the United States Parole Board, and the Administrative Office of the United States Courts were represented. Agencies participating in this meeting were presented with a tentative model, including tentative definitions. The draft of the feasibility study was reviewed, discussed, and revised by the agencies' representatives and the National Parole Institutes' staff.

Participating agencies were then asked to explore the application of the model in their own agencies in order to test its feasibility without disturbing their agency's own systems.

To identify further problems and test the feasibility of the proposed data collection procedures, a limited program of actual data collection was initiated. Eight parole agencies[7] of those at the December meeting were selected for the pretest of the preliminary data collection model. They represented, so far as possible, the major geographic divisions of the United States and the national variation in legal sentencing structures, agency size, resources, and paroling practices.

The remaining agencies were asked to attempt an additional exploration of the feasibility of coding for the proposed system. In response to this request, sixteen agencies[8] applied the coding procedures to representative samples of persons paroled in 1963 and provided suggestions for the revision of coding instructions.

PERSONS SELECTED FOR STUDY

Subjects included in the Prepilot Data Collection Test were selected through use of a table of random numbers from monthly lists of all persons

---

[7] Alabama Board of Pardons and Paroles, Colorado State Department of Parole, Connecticut State Farm and Prison for Women, Connecticut Board of Parole, Iowa Board of Parole, Maryland Department of Parole and Probation, Ohio Pardon and Parole Commission, and Texas Board of Pardons and Paroles.

[8] Alaska Division of Youth and Adult Authority, District of Columbia Board of Parole, Florida Probation and Parole Commission, Georgia Board of Pardons and Paroles, Hawaii Board of Paroles and Pardons, Kentucky Parole Board, Michigan Parole Board, Nebraska Board of Pardons, New Jersey State Parole Board, New York State Board of Parole, Oregon Board of Parole and Probation, Pennsylvania Board of Paroles, South Dakota Board of Pardons and Paroles, United States Board of Parole, Virginia Parole Board, and Wisconsin Division of Corrections.

A detailed analysis of the coding procedures in relation to the agency's own information system was provided by the California Youth and Adult Corrections Agency.

paroled by the eight agencies participating. Those with "detainers" (that is, released to custody in another jurisdiction) were excluded.

OFFENDER ATTRIBUTES AND CHARACTERISTICS

All information studied was extracted from individual case files. Any part of the official agency records was considered admissible for this purpose, but in most agencies the source of preparole information was an admission summary or progress report prepared for the paroling authority, and the arrest record ("rap sheet"). Sources for coding information on parole performance were commonly the parole officer's report, the paroling authority's findings of alleged violation behavior, reports from law enforcement agencies, and the arrest record. Only information contained in official records was used; personal knowledge or judgments about the case were excluded.

The items of information studied and their definitions are given in the more complete report of the study.[9]

The problem of definition of "parole violation" is particularly complicated by differing paroling authority policies and differences in interpretations of widely used terms. A number of parole performance events of interest were excluded from consideration in order to achieve a common framework for participating agencies, but might be included in further development of the system. They included problems of adjustment under parole supervision which involve difficulties short of legal conviction or paroling authority action. Examples are failure to maintain steady employment, excessive use of alcohol, suspected use of drugs, arrests not resulting in convictions, and allegations of offenses not admitted.

Eight categories of parole performance were employed, ranging from "no difficulty" (defined as no major or minor convictions and no actions by the paroling authority other than those specifically excluded) to return to prison because of a new major offense committed during the period of parole supervision under study.[10]

The earliest date of "parole violation" behavior was recorded, along with the number of months under active parole supervision and the date of discharge or death, in order that periods of exposure to "the risk of difficulty" in various jurisdictions would be comparable.

RESULTS OF THE PREPILOT TEST

Information describing 2,012 paroled men and women and their parole performance in the first six months after release was collected monthly from

---

[9]Gottfredson, Ballard, and O'Leary, *op. cit. supra* note 5.

[10]A "minor" conviction refers to a sentence of at least sixty days but less than one year. A "major" conviction refers to a sentence of one year or more.

the eight participating agencies for one year.[11] The eight agencies found the tentative definitions as well as the monthly procedures quite workable. All agencies were prompt in submitting requested information.

This experience, by itself, demonstrates that agreed upon definitions can be used to permit a useful data collection system. Since the major purpose of the Prepilot test was to determine the feasibility of the data collection procedures developed, it is clear that its main purpose was served. Beyond this essential first step, the extent to which valid generalizations may be made from the data thus far collected is limited.

LIMITATIONS OF THE DATA THUS FAR COLLECTED

Since this study was intended primarily to demonstrate the feasibility of the data collection model, only relatively small numbers of cases per agency have become available thus far. Also, the proportions of subjects sampled (from all parolees) have varied among agencies so that workload requirements could be met. Thus the parolees studied may not be adequately representative of all parolees released by the eight agencies.

For the purpose of tables presented below, only one definition of "major difficulty" is considered. It was selected somewhat arbitrarily, to give an illustration of the type of summary which can be produced from the data collection procedures. For this reason, "major difficulty" was defined to include any case classified, during the six-month follow-up period, as "absconder" or "returned to prison because of parole violation."

The six-month follow-up period is relatively short; it cannot be concluded that similar results necessarily will be obtained with a longer study of parole performance.

Persons coding information from case records were given a common vocabulary and a common set of definitions, but to see whether different persons are extracting the information in the same way it is necessary to determine whether they tend to code the *same cases* in the same way. A preliminary reliability study was completed; the results tend to support the reliability of coding, but a more extensive study is needed.

RELIABILITY OF ITEM CODING

Twelve cases were randomly selected from samples of each agency to determine the degree of agreement between NPI staff and the participating agencies' personnel. A lack of agreement may reflect an ambiguity of definitions in coding instructions, a failure by either NPI or agency staff

---

[11]Of the persons selected for study, sixty-one were discharged before six months. See Table 1, note, *infra*.

to be sufficiently careful in coding, or conflicting evidence in the case files.

A further possible source of disagreement was the unfamiliarity of NPI staff with the agencies' record-keeping practices. Abbreviations, the location of information in the records, paroling and parole revocation practices, and the degree of standardization of record keeping all contribute to a considerable variation in the case files.

Despite this shortcoming, agreement was generally quite high. Aside from the items on which no disagreements were found, such as the date of release, sex, or the agency to which the person was paroled, the percentage of agreement (over all items and over all agencies combined) was 89 percent. The extent of agreement for each item of information considered separately ranged from 81 percent to 94 percent, except for one item. (Disagreements in coding "Prior Sentences Other than Prison" occurred about half the time, pointing up a need for improvement in definition.)

When all agencies were combined, agreement on the Parole Performance item was 91 percent. In three agencies there were no disagreements; in one agency there was some disagreement in about one-fourth of the cases examined.

In general, this small reliability study suggests that the definitions used were, for the most part, adequate.

AGENCY DIFFERENCES IN PERFORMANCE

When the data collection system pretest had been in operation for twelve months, data had been collected for 2,012 persons, distributed over the eight agencies involved as shown in Table 1.

The variation among agencies in the parole performance criterion is reflected in Tables 2 and 3. Proportions with no difficulty over the six-month follow-up period ranged from 49 percent to 86 percent.[12] Over all agencies combined, three-fourths of the parolees were reported as having "no difficulty" during the first six months after release.

When parole performance was classified as "favorable" or "unfavorable" in terms of the major difficulty criterion, results shown in Table 3 were obtained.[13] Favorable performance ranged among agencies from 52 percent to 87 percent.

In all agencies combined, 7 percent of the parolees were classified as absconders. Another 7 percent were returned to prison classified as technical violators, with no new convictions. Three percent were returned as technical violators with minor or lesser convictions or in lieu of prosecution for these

---

[12]For definitions of the categories of parole performance studied see Gottfredson, Ballard, and O'Leary, *op. cit. supra* note 5.

[13]With the exception of the one agency dealing entirely with women, females have been excluded (sixty-one persons).

Table 1 *Number of Parolees in Pretest of a Data Collection System, and Per Cent of All Persons Paroled by Eight Agencies, April 1964 through March 1965*

Month of Parole	A	B	C	D	E	F	G	H	Total
April '64	15	41	24	29	31	13	19	18	190
May	10	37	34	25	36	18	18	24	202
June	8	34	29	25	29	26	11	14	176
July	8	42	27	22	31	15	16	19	180
August	12	27	25	24	34	16	22	5	165
September	4	28	20	28	26	14	16	12	148
October	8	35	20	18	26	17	16	20	160
November	9	20	19	25	27	16	17	17	150
December	11	34	21	26	27	23	21	23	186
January '65	3	42	15	24	23	13	16	16	152
February	6	31	12	20	19	19	15	13	135
March	7	34	24	29	10	25	27	12	168
Total	101	405	270	295	319	215	214	193	2,012[a]
Per Cent of All Paroled by Agency	20	10	10	25	25	25	50	100	18

[a] Sixty-one persons who were discharged before six months after release under parole supervision were excluded from study, since they were not exposed to the risk of parole violation for a period of time comparable to the rest. The numbers of persons excluded for this reason are as follows: Agency A, 3: B, 0; C, 11; D, 4; E, 13; F, 6; G, 5; H, 19.

offenses. Five percent were returned either with new major convictions or in lieu of prosecution for major offenses.

One agency reported that a fourth of all subjects were returned to prison as technical violators with no convictions. (The rate for all agencies combined was 7 percent.) This type of prison return, along with absconders, contributes very markedly to this agency's overall "major difficulty" rate, the highest of the eight considered.

OFFENDER DIFFERENCES IN PAROLE PERFORMANCE

A number of comparisons were made to see whether offender attributes are associated with parole performance. Female subjects were excluded, and this is the reason for the smaller total number of subjects (1,704) and for the different overall "favorable" parole performance rate of 79 percent.[14]

[14] Agency "H" deals only with women; the others are responsible for both men and women. For the further study described here, all "H" subjects were excluded along with all women from the remaining agencies.

Table 2 *Parole Performance during a Six-Month Follow-up of Persons Paroled by E*

Agencies Participating in Te

Parole Performance	A No.	%	B No.	%	C No.	%	D No.	
No difficulty	73	74.5	336	83.0	204	78.8	248	8
Continued on parole after minor conviction (s)			5	1.2	1	0.4	2	
Return to prison, no violation			1	0.2	1	0.4	1	
Absconder	9	9.2	29	7.2	10	3.9	10	
Returned to prison as a technical violator with no conviction (s)	13	13.3	21	5.2	15	5.8	8	
Returned to prison as a technical violator with minor or lesser conviction (s) or in lieu of prosecution on minor or lesser offenses			5	1.2	2	0.8	9	
Returned to prison as a technical violator on a "major offense" charge and returned in lieu of prosecution	1	1.0	2	0.5	13	5.0	13	
Convicted and recommitted to prison in same jurisdiction with new major conviction (s)	2	2.0	6	1.5	10	3.9		
Convicted and recommitted to prison in any other jurisdiction with new major conviction (s)					3	1.2		
Total	98	100	405	100	259	100.2	291	

Table 4 indicates that type of admission is associated with parole outcome.[15] The largest proportion of favorable outcomes is found for subjects classified as new court commitments who were sentenced to prison following a revocation of probation. New court commitments are generally more often found among the group with no major difficulty than are parole violators re-released to parole supervision. The men classified as parole violators and returned to correctional institutions without new court commitments were proportionately less often found in the favorable parole outcome group.

[15] For definitions see Gottfredson, Ballard, and O'Leary, *op. cit. supra* note 5.

Agencies April 1964 through March 1965

Data Collection Procedures

E		F		G		H		All Agencies	
No.	%	No.	%	No.	%	No.	%	No.	%
199	65.0	180	86.1	147	70.3	86	49.4	1,473	75.5
1	0.3	1	0.5	3	1.4	2	1.1	15	0.8
				1	0.5	2	1.1	6	0.3
28	9.4	6	2.9	16	7.7	37	21.3	145	7.4
18	5.9	9	4.3	11	5.3	45	25.9	140	7.3
13	4.2	7	3.3	24	11.5			60	3.1
24	7.8	5	2.4			1	0.6	59	3.0
16	5.2	1	0.5	7	3.3	1	0.6	43	2.2
7	2.3							10	0.5
306	100.1	209	100	209	100	174	100	1,951	100

Earlier research has often shown relationships between the offense classification at commitment to prison and later parole violation rates.[16] Offenses usually associated with a higher violation rate involve taking some-one else's property, either by stealth or by deceit. In many jurisdictions, auto theft has been associated with the highest rate of parole violations. Other kinds of stealing, including shoplifting, "carboosting," and burglary, are also associated with a greater likelihood of parole violation after release. In addition forgers (often persons with alcoholic problems) are also found

[16]See Glaser, *op. cit. supra* note 2; and Gottfredson and Beverly, *supra* note 4.

Table 3   *Favorable Parole Performance during a Six-Month Follow-up of Persons Paroled by Eight Agencies, April 1964 through March 1965*

Agency	Parole Performance		Per Cent Favorable	Total Number
	Number Favorable (No Major Difficulty)	Number Unfavorable (Major Difficulty)		
A	73	25	74	98
B	342	63	84	405
C	206	53	80	259
D	251	40	86	291
E	200	106	65	306
F	181	28	87	209
G	151	58	72	209
H	90	84	52	174
Total	1,494	457	77	1,951

Chi square = 125.93 which, with 7 degrees of freedom, is significant at the 1 per cent level of confidence. (This is a test of independence. If "major difficulty" were independent of the agency reporting—that is, if outcomes were not associated with agencies—the results obtained would be expected by chance less than 1 per cent of the time.)

to violate the conditions of parole more often. Offenses often reported as associated with the lowest parole violation rates are crimes against persons, including homicide and rape.

These characteristic results of earlier studies may be compared with those of Table 5. As expected from earlier studies, the "homicide or manslaughter" and "assault" classifications are associated with the highest proportion of favorable parole performance. The offense with the lowest percentage of favorable parole outcome during the six-month follow-up period is "vehicle theft," with 60 percent. Similarly, confirming earlier studies, the offense classification "forgery, fraud, or larceny by check" is the next lowest, with 66 percent in the favorable category.

Past criminal record has been found, in many jurisdictions, to be related to parole performance; but of course this is capable of classification in many different ways.[17] It is true that if an individual's prior criminality is determined only through the record of crimes for which he was convicted, our information may be incomplete; nevertheless, lower parole violation rates have been consistently found for those with no prior criminal record. Parole violation rates also increase with the *number* of prior prison terms.

These earlier results are supported by our own findings, as shown in Table 6.

[17]See Glaser, *Gross Personal Characteristics and Parole Outcome, op. cit. supra* note 2; and Gottfredson and Beverly, *supra* note 4.

Table 4 *Type of Admission and Favorable Parole Performance Based on Six-Month Follow-up of Men Paroled by Seven Agencies, April 1964 through March 1965*

Type of Admission		Parole Performance			
		Number Favorable (No Major Difficulty)	Number Unfavorable (Major Difficulty)	Per Cent Favorable	Total Number
New Court Commitment	{ Not from Probation	988	245	80	1,233
	{ Probation Revoked	195	39	83	234
Parole Violator	{ No New Commitment	80	51	61	131
	{ With New Commitment	78	28	74	106
Total		1,341	363	79	1,704

Chi square = 30.45 which, with 3 degrees of freedom, is significant at the 1 per cent level of confidence.

Table 5   *Offense and Favorable Parole Performance Based on Six-Month Follow-up of Men Paroled by Seven Agencies, April 1964 through March 1965*

| Offense | Parole Performance | | Per Cent Favorable | Total Number |
	Number Favorable (No Major Difficulty)	Number Unfavorable (Major Difficulty)		
Homicide, Manslaughter	108	8	93	116
Robbery	180	37	83	217
Aggravated Assault	82	7	92	89
Burglary	393	120	77	513
Forgery, Fraud, or Larceny by Check	161	81	66	242
Theft or Larceny except Vehicle	149	35	81	184
Vehicle Theft	47	32	60	79
Other Fraud	29	5	85	34
Rape	30	6	81	36
Sex Offenses against Juveniles	34	8	81	42
Other Sex Offenses	13	4	76	17
Violation of Narcotic Drug Laws	42	15	74	57
All Others	73	5	94	78
Total	1,341	363	79	1,704

Chi square = 79.67 which with 12 degrees of freedom, is significant at the 1 per cent level of confidence.

A history of illegal use of drugs, particularly of opiates, has been reported consistently as related to later parole violation; persons with no previous history of narcotics use are found less likely to violate the conditions of their parole.[18] Evidence on the relative risk of persons committed for narcotic *offenses* is inconsistent, but relatively high violation rates are found when a history of *use* of drugs, rather than the legal offense category, is considered. When the 1,704 men studied were classified as to known drug *use* history and the parole performance criterion, men for whom there was no known history of drug use were found in the favorable category in 80 percent of cases. Those

[18]Gottfredson and Beverly, *Supra* note 4.

Table 6 *Number of Prior Commitments to Adult Correctional Institutions (Reformatories or Prisons) and Favorable Parole Performance, Based on Six-Month Follow-up of Men Paroled by Seven Agencies, April 1964 through March 1965*

Number of Prior Prison Commitments	Parole Performance			Total Number
	Number Favorable (No Major Difficulty)	Number Unfavorable (Major Difficulty)	Per Cent Favorable	
0	916	170	84	1,086
1	244	111	69	355
2	111	42	72	153
3	44	24	65	68
4+	26	16	62	42
Total	1,341	363	79	1,704

Chi square = 60.17 which, with 4 degrees of freedom, is significant at the 1 per cent level of confidence.

for whom drug use was known were found in the favorable outcome group only 66 percent of the time.

The age of the offender also has been shown to be related to parole violations.[19] In general, paroled younger offenders have been found to have higher violation rates. This consistently reported result was not supported by the data collected in our Prepilot Study. The differences in parole performance, by age group, could be attributed reasonably to chance.

OFFENDER DIFFERENCES AMONG AGENCIES

Important to later development of the system, if it is to be useful in allowing comparisons of parole performance among agencies, is the question of whether offenders released to parole supervision by the various agencies are comparable. If the persons released tend to be different, particularly in characteristics related to parole violation, these comparisons cannot be made meaningful unless we account for the differences.

Examination of prior prison commitments and offense classifications illustrates the differences which may be found when agencies are compared according to classifications of the offenders they parole. As already indicated, both the prior prison commitment record and the offense classification were found to be related to the parole performance criterion used.

Table 7 shows that the proportion of men with no prior prison commitment record ranged from 52 percent to 73 percent. The statistical test used shows that prior prison commitment records are not independent of paroling agencies; the variation shown in Table 7 may not be attributed reasonably to chance.

Proportions in the various offense classifications also vary among the agencies studied; this may be seen in Table 8. For example, in Agency D, 26 percent of the parolees were committed to prison after conviction for homicide, manslaughter, or assaultive offenses—offenses found associated with relatively high rates of favorable parole outcome; only 2 percent of offenders paroled by Agency A were found in this offense category. The proportion of men in prison for forgery or check convictions ranged from 4 percent in Agency F to 27 percent in Agency A. The differences in offense classification, by agency, cannot be attributed reasonably to chance.

IMPLICATIONS

These results are presented only as suggestions of the types of analyses which might be completed from the continuation of the project. The questions

---

[19] Glaser, *Gross Personal Characteristics and Parole Outcome, op. cit. supra* note 2.

Table 7 *Number of Prior Prison Commitments of Men Paroled by Seven Agencies, April 1964 through March 1965*

Number of Prior Commitments	Paroling Agency														All Agencies	
	A		B		C		D		E		F		G			
	No.	%	No.	%	No.	%	No.	%	No.	%	No.	%	No.	%	No.	%
0	54	57	223	58	180	73	199	72	179	60	143	72	108	52	1,086	64
1	27	28	85	22	39	16	50	18	70	24	38	19	46	22	355	21
2	9	10	42	11	21	8	13	5	27	9	11	6	30	14	153	9
3+	5	5	33	9	7	3	13	5	21	7	6	3	25	12	110	6
Total	95	100	383	100	247	100	275	100	297	100	198	100	209	100	1,704	100

Chi square = 64.41 which, with 18 degrees of freedom, is significant at the 1 per cent level of confidence.

Table 8 *Offense Classifications, Men Paroled by Seven Agencies, April 1964 through March 1965*

Offense	A No.	A %	B No.	B %	C No.	C %	D No.	D %	E No.	E %	F No.	F %	G No.	G %	All Agencies No.	All Agencies %
Homicide, Manslaughter, Assault	2	2	28	7	15	6	70	26	20	7	45	23	25	12	205	12
Robbery	9	10	58	15	22	9	29	10	34	11	41	21	24	11	217	13
Burglary	17	18	123	32	104	42	65	24	99	33	50	25	55	26	513	30
Forgery, Checks	26	27	64	17	37	15	27	10	64	22	8	4	16	8	242	14
Theft or Fraud Other than Checks	33	34	74	19	37	15	61	22	43	14	33	17	16	8	297	17
Other	8	8	36	9	32	13	23	8	37	12	21	11	73	35	230	14
Total	95	100	383	100	247	100	275	100	297	100	198	100	209	100	1,704	100

Chi square = 298.74 which, with 30 degrees of freedom, is significant at the 1 per cent level of confidence.

to be answered, the types of analyses to be conducted, and the format of the reporting system should all be determined jointly by participants in the Uniform Parole Reports System.

The results presented here do not demonstrate differences among agencies in the effectiveness of their programs. They demonstrate, rather, that simple comparisons of violation rates of differing agencies do not necessarily reflect differences in agency programs, since they may be due to differences in the types of offenders placed on parole, and that the types of offenders paroled by the different agencies vary so much that it will be particularly important to take account of this variation in any comparisons. This can be done in a variety of ways. For example, as larger numbers of parolees are studied, we may compare parole performance by specific types of offenders paroled from different agencies.

Though these results must be viewed tentatively, in view of the limitations mentioned above, they show that our efforts ultimately can provide a firm basis for meaningful analyses of parole experience based on uniform reporting from all our diverse parole systems. The main contribution of the eight agencies participating in this test of monthly reporting procedures is the demonstration that the agreed upon procedures are adequate.

Sixteen additional agencies[20] completed a further study, on a total of 880 persons, examining the feasibility of applying the tentative model in their agencies. The different sampling methods they used limited the extent to which we may generalize from the information collected. The main question to be answered, however, was whether the codes and definitions were workable and meaningful. In each case where comments were made, some general indications were given that they were.[21]

SUGGESTIONS FOR FURTHER DEVELOPMENT

The further development of the system should continue as a joint enterprise of administrators responsible for parole agency decisions. What are the administrators' information needs? In what way should the results be summarized and reported in order to be most helpful? The questions to be answered, the types of comparisons to be made, and the methods of reporting should all be determined by a consensus of participants.

A critical part of the planned Pilot Study will be the program of User Seminars already mentioned. These will provide frequent "two-way feedback"—reporting results of the reporting system to agency administrators, and reporting practical needs to all concerned with the system. Further

---

[20] *Supra* note 8.

[21] Further results are given in the National Parole Institutes' report. The data collected for the 880 parolees from these agencies show variation among offenders and agencies consistent with the results of the eight-agency test.

development of Uniform Parole Reports procedures should continue to be responsive to the interests and needs of administrators. Although this requires some flexibility at the start, it should lead to stabilization of a demonstrably useful system by the end of the Pilot Study.

The National Institute of Mental Health has awarded a grant for the three-year Pilot Study as proposed above. This means that the solid steps taken by the participating agencies in this feasibility study can provide a foundation for the eventual reality of a Uniform Parole Reporting System.

III

SUPERVISION

The test of probation and parole is found in the community to which convicted offenders are released under some form of conditional freedom. While supervision by the probation or parole officer is the operational component of probation and parole best known to the general public, and the outcome of supervision is critical in the public eye, accurate evaluation of the effect of supervision remains a very elusive factor for analysis and review.

The materials in this section commence with an article by Professor Charles L. Newman exploring the concepts of treatment in supervision, which is followed by writings of the editors describing some conceptual models of caseloads into which probationers and parolees are normally grouped for supervision by an individual probation or parole officer. Inasmuch as supervision is frequently ill-defined, attention is placed upon practice through a survey of supervision practices in the Federal probation and parole system. This survey, conducted by the Federal Probation Training Center at Chicago and reported upon by Professor David H. Gronewold, provides important data on such relevant factors as intake and interviewing, office and caseload management, relationships with other agencies, and court and parole board policies.

Professor Arthur P. Miles' article on the utility of case records—an important part of the supervision picture—points out that, while extensive records are compiled and maintained by probation and parole agencies, there is rather limited use of these records and a need for revision of recording systems. Professor Robert H. Vasoli, in reviewing the various methods utilized to determine outcome of (probation) supervision, shows clearly the complexities in determining success or failure or other measures of "adjustment," as well as the inherent difficulties experienced in obtaining meaningful data for administration, decision-making, interpretation and research. Professors John P. Reed and Charles E. King, through research on revocation cases in North Carolina, demonstrate that decisions are frequently officer- or social order-oriented rather than offender-oriented. Their article again reveals the difficulty in evaluating the effect or outcome of supervision.

Although supervision may be dealt with in quite specific terms, such as by offender type (the alcoholic, the addict, the violent, the female) or by treatment approach (case work, psychotherapy, group counseling), there is one characteristic or relationship which cuts across all others—the use of authority. In an article by Professor Arthur E. Fink, the importance and significance of the constructive use of authority in the correctional process are examined. Space limitations preclude examination of separate types of supervision for various types of offenders.

The section on supervision closes with the survey report of research administrator Stuart Adams, who reports on findings from various caseload research projects. Dr. Adams' article, as is the case with others in this section, clearly points out the complexities of evaluation of supervision, types of offenders, types of treatments, types of probation and parole officers, and the like. His article also suggests the enormous research problem confronting those who wish to understand the manifest, as well as the latent, aspects of probation and parole supervision.

24

Concepts of Treatment in Probation and Parole Supervision

CHARLES L. NEWMAN

The word "treatment" is probably one of the most overworked words in the correctional lexicon. Whatever its semantic meaning, treatment and the treatment approach have come to suggest several connotations: that "it" replaces an "old system" of dealing with offenders; that trained people can do "it" better than untrained ones; that "it" is more effective than other systems of dealing with offenders; that "it" considers the person, his needs, strengths and limitations, as they differ from other individuals around him. Increasingly within the correctional field, we have come to accept the idea that the treatment approach to the offender is better than any other method. Hopefully we can eventually demonstrate the greater effectiveness of this method over any other "nontreatment" oriented approach.

These are values to which we must subscribe even though the research to date does not substantially support our position. Part of the difficulty rests with the fact that the treatment approach requires of the field not only an ideological acceptance of the philosophy, but also the preparation and existence of a corps of suitably trained persons with the technical know-how, and the actual implementation of treatment practices. Even when so-called intensive treatment programs have been tried, it has frequently been with the use of personnel with

SOURCE. *Federal Probation*, XXV, March 1961, pp. 11–18.

limited professional training, in an atmosphere which is suspicious or even hostile to new approaches.

Within the correctional field we are probably further ahead in an acceptance of the philosophy involving treatment of the offender than we are with adequate staffing, but this would be hard to support in the face of punitive and coercive restriction which is so much a part of the entire correctional cycle: police, courts, probation, institutions, and parole.

Redirection and reeducation of persons who have demonstrated antisocial and illegal behavior are complex matters requiring both time and skill. Involved is the discovery of strengths within the individual offender which can be mobilized for constructive social behavior. Not infrequently, it will involve modifying the social situation in which he finds himself. But so long as we continue to assume, as we seem to do in so many jurisdictions, that probation, parole, and institutional treatment services can be provided by anyone with the proper political affiliation, one head, a good heart, and a meagre appetite for the luxuries of life, then it will be a long time off before we can truly implement the philosophy and goals of the correctional field.

Most correctional institutions make no claim to the provision of more than a custodial program for their inmates. But continuously, in both probation and parole, we claim to provide community treatment. Query: can we, or do we, under the circumstances?

We recognize that the basic purpose of probation and parole is the protection of the community. Any system which runs contrary to that precept cannot be acceptable to society. When an offender has been institutionalized, we are reasonably assured that, for a while at least, he will not be involved in further depredations against the community. But in our wisdom, we have learned to recognize that not all offenders need the physical control which an institution provides. This decision-making process must involve more than sentimentality, sympathy, charity, or a count of prior violations. Rather it demands a meaningful diagnosis and a prognosis that the individual does have sufficient internal strength to return to the community where essentially the same physical, social, and psychological forces are present as were at the time of commission of his criminal act, and to make an adequate adjustment in spite of those factors.

TREATMENT AN INTERRELATED THREE-STAGE PROCESS

In order to assist the individual to adjust to the community, the field correctional worker implements a three-stage treatment process: *investigation*, *diagnosis*, and *treatment supervision*. Contrary to the popular misconception that a given set of preliminaries is necessary before the treatment stage can be implemented, it should be clearly recognized that interaction (and consequently, treatment) occurs from the very first moment of contact. Obviously, if we are to work successfully with a person, we must be able to understand his inner-working.

In the *investigation* stage, we attempt to find out what is and was within him and outside him that made him the person with whom we are dealing. With skillful questioning, he will find himself looking at aspects of his life, so very necessary if he is to gain insight into the nature of his behavior. From this frame of reference it is not too difficult to see the investigation as a very vital part of the treatment process.

In our culture, we place a great deal of emphasis on putting labels on all sorts of things, including behavior. The words "neurotic," "psychopath," "psychotic," "behavior disorder," and many others are used with such ease that we sometimes think we know what they mean. In the diagnostic process, the goal is not to attach a label to the person. Rather, the *diagnosis* is the codification of all that has been learned about the individual, organized in such a way as to provide a means for the establishment of future treatment goals. It becomes immediately obvious that as we learn more about the individual through future contact, the diagnosis will be modified, and the treatment goals raised or lowered as the case may be.

The *treatment supervision* process, as it will be discussed here, entails the elaboration of knowledge about the individual through the process of communication, so that the individual will gain a more realistic appraisal of his own behavior, thereby enhancing his own ability to function more acceptably in the community. The provision of certain material services may also be involved in the treatment process.

INVESTIGATION FOR TREATMENT

In the finding-out process, the most important source to help the officer is the offender himself. He frequently is also a most difficult source. The offender may consider it to his interest and advantage to give a misleading picture. Here is the real test of the correctional officer's skill—the art of understanding and dealing with human nature. The extent to which a person reveals himself is in direct proportion to the degree of confidence (rapport) which the worker has succeeded in developing. Other sources of information lie outside the offender himself and require tact in approach and intelligence in selection. A problem which every worker faces is to obtain, within the limits of time, as many illuminating facts as possible without causing discrimination against the offender. The investigation should give a comprehensive picture of the offender's own world, his personality, his relationship to others, and his immediate environment as seen in relation to himself. We should know something about his likes and dislikes, his hopes and desires, his values and disappointments, his ambitions and plans (or lack of them), his assets and qualities as well as shortcomings. However, we should not let our own cultural biases and values seduce us into giving "feeling content" to the material which the probationer or parolee may not have. But truly knowing what are his feelings in regard to past and present experiences is central to dealing effectively with him in a treatment relationship.

Listing a series of isolated physical and social facts about a person provides only a bare skeletal diagram of that person. So frequently, for example, pre-sentence, classification, or preparole reports will be limited to a cursory state-ment about the family composition, designating the names, ages, and occupations of family members. What do these facts mean? Without elaboration or interpre-tation, such facts are of limited value in arriving at a recommendation or in providing meaningful supervision. What we really need to find out is the type of relationship which has existed between the person and other significant people in his life: natural family, family by marriage, friends, neighbors, coworkers.

We have no hesitation about discouraging continued contact with previous associates. But what about family? Are these relationships always worth main-taining? With knowledge about those interrelationships, it may be most desir-able to encourage the person to stay far away from his family as well as previous associates. Even though our culture strongly supports the notion of enduring marriage, we cannot assume, *a priori*, a positive family relationship exists solely because a man and woman are living together in marriage. Nor can we assume that a person has necessarily been damaged emotionally by the fact of growing up in a broken home. These are things we must find out.

Basically, the point is this: in the treatment relationship, the generalizations about human behavior (to which most of us subscribe) have applied value only to the degree that they fit the circumstances and the personality of the indi-vidual situation. We must know the individual first in order to understand him and to counsel with him.

An interview is a conversation with a purpose. In his role, the correctional worker is not interested in persons in the aggregate, but in the specific indivi-dual. Our goal, through the interview process, is to be able to know the offender's personality in action. We are interested in his immediate environment, the way he reacts to frustrations and opportunities. We want to know his attitudes toward others and himself. From that point, we can assist him to gain a better self-understanding, thereby affecting his ability to function constructively in the community around him.

Whether the interview occurs during the presentence investigation or during the period of supervision, it is important to recognize that both the worker and the offender bring prior life experiences into the interview situa-tion. If the worker has been able to develop insight and self-awareness about his own behavior, there is a likelihood that he will be more tolerant and effec-tive with the persons with whom he is working. This is particularly necessary in the implementation of authority. The mature worker will recognize that it is the situation and not his own need for power, which calls for the use of authority.

TREATMENT BEGINS WITH THE FIRST CONTACT

While it can be true of every session, the first contact between the worker and the offender is of extreme importance. In all probability the person will be experiencing a certain amount of anxiety which, with skillful handling, can be mobilized from the very beginning to achieve the treatment goals. The person should be given the feeling that there is no need to hurry in exploring the many avenues which may develop in the initial interview. If the worker takes time to listen, the probability is that he will hear more than if he devotes the time to talking himself. At the beginning, the offender is making a number of observations about the officer, the office, and comparing his current impressions with his own preconceptions. At the same time, the worker should be making his own observations, such as the person's appearance, the way he enters the office, the way he conducts himself, how he sits down, how he talks, the tone of his speech, and other nonverbal communicative aspects. Whether we are capable of observing it or not, in many instances a *transference* occurs from the individual to the officer from the very beginning. The mature worker will recognize that fact, and interact accordingly.

The content of the first interview, as with all subsequent contacts, will vary with the individual. Part of the time is spent in gathering factual information. However, unless there is reason to believe that information already on file is erroneous, generally there is no need to repeat the operation. Being asked the same questions over and over again can easily give the impression that it does not matter too much what you say since no one pays any attention to the answers. Accurate recording (even though it takes time) is of vital necessity if we hope to do a respectable job of treatment. By recording basic information as well as progress contacts, we are in a better position to see the progress which has been made in the case and alter treatment goals accordingly. Without such information, a shift in caseload requires the new worker to start out from the beginning, which we would agree is a great waste of time and effort.

After the initial interview, the officer is faced with the monumental task of making a fast appraisal, on the basis of a single interview, of the person's ability to reside in the community with only limited external controls. One of the better means of appraisal comes from an understanding of the degree of discomfort which the individual feels in relation to his social or emotional problem. Further, the officer will have to determine what part others may have in the problem, and the extent to which they are affected.

The timing of subsequent interviews must, in large measure, be determined by a variety of factors, including the type and immediacy of the problem, the size of caseload, and the need of the person for support and control. Unfortunately, too much of probation and parole supervision is little more than routine monthly reporting. Admittedly, in some cases, this minimal type of control may be quite adequate. But generally speaking where problems of adjustment to the home and community exist, it is questionable whether any value is derived from infrequent contact. In too many probation and parole offices, moreover, a person is seen only after he has demonstrated some emergent problem situation. To insure the protection of the community, as well as to assist the person in adjustment, probation and parole supervision *must* provide preventive as well as remedial treatment services.

SURVEILLANCE VERSUS COUNSELING

Within the context of the need for sound correctional treatment programs, several elements emerge. First, we must recognize that the community continues to be concerned about the activities of the probationer and the parolee. Whether or not he is involved in further illegal activity, the law violater has demonstrated his capacity to disregard society's rules and regulations. By virtue of his prior behavior, the community is justifiably concerned.

Secondly, we must recognize that it is neither feasible nor desirable to maintain continuous surveillance of the offender's activities. At best, we can sample his behavior at various moments and *hope* that we are able to detect certain indicators which suggest that the person is *more* of a presumptive risk to himself and to the community. Greater protection than this to the community through surveillance is not possible in a democracy. Moreover, surveillance, as opposed to treatment supervision, is essentially a police responsibility. It involves techniques for which the therapy-oriented and trained practitioner in corrections is unprepared to handle with maximum effectiveness. This does not obviate the need for surveillance, but rather places its implementation in the hands of the police, whose responsibility it is in the first place.

It becomes obvious, then, that the correctional worker (whether in the institution or field services) should be in a position to recognize, understand, and deal effectively with subtle as well as obvious shifts in the behavior and personality of the offender. Not infrequently, these shifts can be indicative of problems which the individual is experiencing and for which he is unable to find a solution. I do not mean to suggest that to find a person in a particularly irritable mood during a field visit is cause for revocation. On the other hand, such irritability, persistently detected, may be a clue which directs our attention to the movement of the person into behavior which ultimately may get him into difficulty.

RULES AND TREATMENT

Recalling our intention to protect the community through probation and parole services, we impose a number of controls upon the offender and his behavior. Not uncommonly, the person is instructed to abide by a series of rules and regulations which are universally applied to all offenders within the particular jurisdiction. Many times, the specific rule may not have any particular relationship to the offender and his prior conduct. The imposition of rules and conditions can have a therapeutic value. However, to do so, the rules must have a relationship to the prior behavior pattern of the individual upon whom they are imposed. Moreover, the officer must see these rules as a part of his treatment plan rather than external controls imposed by someone other than himself, and which, reluctantly, he must enforce.

Limit-setting involves specifying what behavior the officer, as the community's representative, will or will not accept from the person under supervision. First, however, the limits must be clear in the officer's own mind. Reluctance or vacillation in the enforcement of rules can easily lead to a situation where the officer will be manipulated by the person under supervision. If limits and rules are consistently applied, the spurious argument that one concession calls for another is easily overcome.

The point should be quite clear: if the boundary limitations or prohibitions are specified for an individual because it is known that he will endanger himself or others if he violates, then the officer has a clear course of action. Failure to be consistent adds only to confusion on the part of the person under supervision. If the violation of a rule does not result in the offender doing harm to himself or others, then the rule is not necessary in his case, and should not be invoked.

THE THERAPEUTIC RELATIONSHIP

One of the first major accomplishments of treatment comes about when the offender becomes aware both intellectually and emotionally that the officer represents not only authority with the power to enforce certain restraints and restrictions, but that he is also able to offer material, social, and psychological adjustmental aids.

Hardly a day passes that the correctional worker does not come upon a situation where a statement made has fallen somewhat short of the truth. Sometimes these statements may be the consequence of faulty recollection, or they may involve outright misrepresentation. The "natural" reaction is to feel irritated. From a treatment focus, however, one would have to ask the question: since the account seems unreasonable, what defenses are being used that prevent a more truthful representation? Then: what purpose do these defenses serve for the individual? Do they contribute to his sense of well-being, or do they provide him with the needed sense of discomfort. The next step in counseling emerges from this knowledge.

I do not mean to suggest that probation and parole officers should attempt to practice psychiatry, or otherwise involve themselves in depth analysis with their caseloads. In correctional work, we should be dealing primarily with conscious level material. Thus we do not get into dreams or use narcotherapy. But there is a wide range of difference between depth therapy and a "go forth and sin no more" approach. Few correctional workers have the skill or training to approach depth therapy with competence, and the moralistic approach does not work too well over the long run.

In the therapeutic, clinical management of the probationer and parolee, crime prevention is incorporated in the treatment process. As was pointed out earlier, probation and parole supervision must go beyond mere surveillance, for recognition of possible future antisocial behavior through an awareness of the individual's deteriorating personal and social relationships are more effective for community protection than periodic barroom visitation.

The officer's awareness of the fact that the person is having a problem in adjustment is seriously handicapped when interviews are held across a counter in a crowded office, and limited to a 2- to 5-minute examination of the previous month's activity report. The "how-are-things going?" probe question is more suited when sufficient time, interest, and understanding are provided than when the response of "okay" or "so-so" is expected.

The correctional worker will lose one of his most important tools if he defines very carefully and structures very rigidly the interrelationship which he will allow between the offender and himself. If the probationer or parolee is not permitted to express anxiety, hostility, or other feelings toward the officer, employer, wife, or even the next-door neighbor, then the interview is forcing a response pattern which does not give an accurate picture of the person's feelings. Nor does it allow for the implementation of counseling techniques which interpret and assist in the resolution of the problem with the person. This is not to suggest that the probation or parole supervision interview should be devoted solely to ventilation. Rather, the officer must be in a position to recognize that, as a social therapist in an authoritative setting, certain types of interrelationships are desirable and necessary. The interaction must be geared to the dynamics of the offender's personality, and not to the exclusive satisfaction of the worker's own ego.

Beyond this, the officer must go into the field, into the family home, the neighborhood, and the job setting. No offender exists in a vacuum, and it is not improbable that adjustmental problems will be related to external as well as internal, intrapsychic factors. Discretion, of course, is both desirable and necessary because we do not want to jeopardize what acceptance the offender may have been able to reestablish for himself in the community. It is essential, however, that we constantly remember that the offender must do his adjusting in the community and not in the probation office exclusively. Adjustment is a great deal more than showing the necessary and expected deference to the wishes of the correctional officer.

A not-uncommon type found in probation or parole offices is one who appears to be unable to function effectively in the working world. Our middle-class morality suggests that work is desirable, and that "good" people want to work. Hence, failure and unemployment are often considered to be related to lack of motivation, laziness, or a configuration of morally-related values. Frequently, we find that these same individuals express a feeling of paralysis in what appears to them to be a hostile world. We can write off these complaints as characteristic of the convict culture, or we can seek more definitive answers for the individual case. In evaluating the situation, there are a number of questions which the officer can explore. When attempting to find out how long a problem has existed, the officer should also evaluate the degree of discomfort which the person feels about it. Are his feelings appropriate to the situation, and are his actions consonant with his stated feelings? Looking to the employment situation, for example, the officer can ask: Is what has been demanded of this person really compatible with his true potentialities? What has been the relationship between the offender and his employer, and to what extent do these external factors impinge upon the stability of the family relationship? Obviously, this is not the sort of information which can be obtained when the only knowledge about employment is taken from the monthly income report.

A person's previous employment record can be a very valuable diagnostic tool if it is evaluated in depth. And from that evaluation, certain treatment goals come to the fore. It is wise to look at the direction of change in position of employment, as well as the frequency. Did the person move from job to job with no appreciable improvement in position or salary? Has he been on the skids? Or, has the direction of change been in terms of upward mobility? Have external factors put demands upon him to move upward socially? If so, why? We can see then that a variety of reasons may account for vocational instability. It is vital that the officer does not try to implant his own moral values on the facts, but rather, that he derives their values from those who are directly affected by them.

In a reported situation, George A. was constantly in and out of work before he got into difficulty with the law. His references were poor, in that they showed him to be quick-tempered, with a "holier than thou" attitude. George had married in his second year of college, and with great struggle managed to graduate shortly before his wife bore them a second child. The wife appeared to be a very passive, yet demanding person. Her demands were always in terms of an improved living situation, which in her own eyes, at least, were realistic demands. George's change of jobs in part reflected her demands. But the job changes also reflected his inability to present himself in a desirable prospective so that he might get a much wanted promotion and increment in salary. Writing checks in nonexistent accounts finally led to his downfall.

Placed on probation, George was able to adjust quite readily in the counseling relationship. A job was found, and the position lasted for almost a year. Then, one day, George came in to report that he had just had an argument with the office manager of the firm where he was employed and that he had quit. The officer asked about the circumstances, but George was sullen and uncommunicative, somewhat daring the officer "to do something about it." Referring to his record, the officer then reviewed some of the glowing comments that George had made about the employer: how kind and considerate he had been, etc., etc. Yes, those things were true, but not that blankety-blank office manager. Then for the next 5 minutes George ventilated about the office manager, and covered most of the transgressions of man and nature. Finally, in a very tired voice, he told the officer that his wife was pregnant again, and that she was putting the pressure on him to get a better job. Had the worker responded with authority at the beginning, he would have lost what eventually developed into a situation where effective counseling could be accomplished.

Only as a person is able to gain insight into the nature of his behavior will he be able to make a satisfactory adjustment within himself. If the behavior seems unreasonable, then the counselor must seek to find out what defenses are preventing a more accurate perception of reality. Importantly, though, the officer must know how vital it is to the probationer's or parolee's sense of equilibrium that he maintain a self-defeating defense pattern. Creation of anxiety in the counseling situation is an important factor in precipitating change, but such a technique must be handled with a great deal of dexterity, and with the knowledge that it will not push the person into undesirable behavior, which may have been his pattern of reaction under earlier circumstances.

The correctional officer must be aware continuously of the concept that man's behavior and thinking are the outgrowths of his life's experiences. But man is not the blind product of social and physical forces around him. From the moment of birth, a relationship is established between the outside world and himself, and for which a reciprocal interrelationship evolves. Mother influences child and child affects mother-husband-other child relationships. The whole confluence on the individual is extremely difficult to evaluate, particularly in the face of the large number of interactions we experience during the course of a lifetime.

THE NEED FOR SECURITY

Although human needs can be stated in an almost endless variety of ways, survival is a deep-rooted impulse of the organism. In order to survive it is necessary to be safe, and any threat to security causes a person to feel either anger or fear. Anxiety is the response to an internal feeling of threat. Whether that threat is directed from physical survival or from psychological and social concomitants, excessive anxiety interferes with physical and mental well-being. Further, when anxiety exists, a person strives to resolve it or defend himself against it. There are specific psychological mechanisms which he may employ as a defense against anxiety-producing situations, and the consequences may take either adjustive or socially disapproved forms.

THE NEED TO EXPRESS NEW FEELING

A person's feelings are mixed when he experiences a mutual incompatible combination of feelings. When feelings are mixed, anxiety arises, and the greater the anxiety, the more the feelings are mixed, and so on. Conflict is almost inevitable when feelings are mixed. Some of the kinds of behavior whose roots lie in conflict are: inconsistency, procrastination, hostility, unreasonableness, seclusiveness, inability to make up one's mind, rigidity. Chiding the person, or shaming him for these and related behaviors serves only to alienate the relationship, and does not get beyond the symptom of the disturbance. When the correctional therapist understands the motivating forces behind such behavior, he is then able to provide the needed help.

One way is to help the person bring out true feelings in the open for an airing, and to help him grasp the idea that double feelings are universal and that there is nothing wrong in having them. This is not to suggest that we condone destructive behavior either inner-directed or vented against the external world. But we do accept the person as an individual and help him to cope with the mixed feelings. In the matter of criminality, offenders probably experience every conceivable degree and every possible combination of positive and negative feelings: from joy of not being institutionalized (as on probation or parole) to bitter resignation and resentment at being tricked by fate.

The correctional worker can sometimes provide a desired treatment effect by listening and feeding back (nondirectively) what has been said with patience and acceptance. At other times, particularly with individuals whose response patterns reflect a primitive level of development, the officer may find it necessary to *teach* how to behave less disturbingly in confronting life situations. Some instances call for support; other situations call for the creation of anxiety to accomplish given treatment ends.

CONCLUSION

Treatment is a sophisticated process involving both time and skill. It is not something which starts after a given set of preliminaries, but rather, gets under way, desirably, with the very first contact. Obviously, there is no one method of treatment with all law-violators, or any other group of individuals who manifest unacceptable behavior. There are certain generic similarities to be found among all people, and the offender is no exception to this rule. But each personality is made up of a number of elements which are blended together in proportions and relationships which are unique to the individual. External changes can be accomplished through a change in the social environment of the individual, but without the vital internal changes in personality, we cannot expect more than a repetition of the previous unsuccessful and unsatisfying behavior. The objective, regardless of the approach, is to create in a person a self-acceptance which did not exist before.

25

Caseloads: Some Conceptual Models

ROBERT M. CARTER AND LESLIE T. WILKINS

There may be some doubt that crime and delinquency are rapidly increasing in the United States. There can, however, be no doubt that crime and delinquency are outgrowing our present capacity to deal effectively with them. This situation will undoubtedly continue as long as the mounting problems of crime and delinquency are addressed by conventional models utilizing the principles and traditions of the past.

In corrections, we try to cope with the problem by taking additional measures, but tend to focus on providing traditional services to the increased numbers of offenders processed through the systems. It seems probable that changes in corrections are likely to have a "more-of-the-same" quality—increased probation and parole staff and prison personnel, more bastille-like institutions, and expanded, but essentially similar programs.

We cannot continue, however, to employ additional personnel indefinitely, build new institutions, or recreate established programs. The trend in corrections has been quite consistent—to create more of what already exists and to depend upon past experience[1] without much attempted innovation. In the main, our current and planned correction procedures are determined neither

SOURCE. Unpublished manuscript prepared at the School of Criminology, University of California, Berkeley, 1968.

[1] For an example of tradition in corrections see Carter, Robert M. and Takagi, Paul T. *"Persistent Problems and Challenges in Correctional Supervision"*, Criminologica, November-December, 1967, **Vol 5**, Number 3.

by imaginative and creative thinking supported by the utilization of available technology nor by other new knowledge in the social and behavioral sciences.

CASELOAD SIZE

The purpose of this paper is to examine the area of caseloads in correctional supervision. A review of recent relevant research points to the futility and frustration engendered by continued "numbers-research," that is, the "proper" ratio of presentence investigations to cases under supervision or "optimal" caseload size. We propose that explicit models for caseload supervision can provide a new perspective for viewing caseload management.

A brief summary of four research studies—three relating to parole in California and one to probation and parole in the Federal system (each, in part "numbers-oriented") provides a background against which the necessity for the construction of caseload models becomes apparent.[2]

BACKGROUND SUMMARY

The Special Intensive Parole Unit (SIPU) studies by the California Department of Corrections began in 1953. Phase I of SIPU, involving 4300 men established experimental caseloads of 15 parolees and control caseloads of 90. The 15-men caseloads were supervised intensively for the first three months following release and were then reassigned to regular 90-man caseloads. A review of the California data did not show significantly better parole adjustment for those in smaller caseloads.

Phase II of SIPU commenced in 1956 and involved some 6200 parolees. The experimental caseloads were increased to 30 and length of stay in these caseloads was increased to six months before reassignment. At the end of Phase II, significant differences in outcome were again absent.

Phase III of SIPU was undertaken in 1957. It had 35- and 72-unit caseloads and involved some 3700 parolees. The first findings of Phase III reflected somewhat better performance of the 35-man caseloads, particularly for certain types of offenders, namely, the medium-risk category. One of the important findings which emerged was that the effect of caseload size was not a simple function of number but of the interaction of several factors, including types of parolees and possibly types of agents.

Phase IV of SIPU, beginning in 1959, had several components, including a study of high-risk category parolees and an agent-parolee interaction study. The latter project made use of a research design which placed agents and

---

[2] For a recent review of caseload research, see S. Adams, "Some Findings From Correctional Caseload Research", *Federal Probation*, December, 1967.

parolees together in patterns which had both logical and empirical justification. Thus, "low-maturity" parolees[3] were matched with external-approach (control orientated) parole agents, and "high-maturity" cases were supervised by internal-approach (casework oriented) agents. Caseload sizes were reduced to 15 and 30 for the experimental group caseloads as compared with 70 for the control group caseloads. Phase IV findings indicated that the only recorded variable which made a difference in parole outcome was the amount of time the agent devoted to supervision. Further, the 15-man caseloads performed no better than the 30-man caseloads.

A 1959 variant of the SIPU studies involved narcotics offenders in the Narcotics Treatment and Control Project (NTCP). Here 30-man caseloads were compared with 70-man caseloads. The results of two initial phases of the project were inconclusive with respect to caseload size. A two-year third phase of the NTCP research involved 15- and 45-man experimental caseloads in tests against 70-man caseloads. No differences were found between 15- and 45-man caseloads, which tends to confirm the findings of Phase IV of SIPU, although the experimental group performed better than the control group in the 70-man caseloads.

In 1965, the California Department of Corrections moved into a parole work unit program based upon estimates of the needs of parolees and the time required for parole officers to provide appropriate services. Here, emphasis was was shifted from *number of cases* to *amount of time* required to meet parolee needs. A three-fold classification system was developed along the traditional lines of maximum, medium, and minimum supervision. Maximum cases were allotted about 5 units of time, medium 3 units, and minimum about 1 unit. Parole officers were to supervise 120 time-units of work, that is, caseloads of about 25 maximum risk cases, 40 medium risk cases, 120 minimum risk cases, or some combination thereof. Some 6000 parolees were involved in the work unit program; 6000 other parolees were supervised in 72-man caseloads. During the first six months of the programs, work unit parolees did no better than conventionally supervised parolees, but in the second six months, the work unit parolees performed better in several categories, some of which may be equated directly with cost-savings.

The San Francisco Project, a study of federal probation and parole, began in 1964 under a National Institute of Mental Health grant to the University of California. Four types of caseloads, with probationers and institution releasees randomly assigned to each, provided varying intensities of supervision ranging from minimum to intensive, and varying caseload sizes from 25 to 100. Preliminary data from this study indicate that the offenders assigned to varying size caseloads have violation rates well within those which would be expected of federal offenders under normal levels of supervision. These data are of particular significance when it is observed that the outcomes of supervision (violation rates) among the four types of caseloads are almost identical despite

[3] *Ibid.*

enormous variation in attention given the cases as measured by the number of contacts by probation and parole officers.

In summary, the various experimentation on caseload size and performance of adult offenders on probation or parole has produced results which are far from encouraging. It appears certain that mere manipulation of caseload size is irrelevant to success or failure under correctional supervision—that is, the "numbers game"—be the number 15, 25, 30, 45, 50, 70, 90 or 100—is not significant in contrast to the nature of the supervision experience, the classification of offenders, officers, and types of treatment, and the social systems of the correctional agency.

THE NEED FOR MODELS AND SIMPLE EXAMPLES

The data which have been presented thus far suggest the need to create, make explicit, and examine various models for correctional supervision. As far as we know, supervision models have not previously been constructed, and the simple examples which will be presented should be taken to represent no more than a stimulation to complex analyses.

The initial problem in our model construction is the portrayal of the offender population. Since there is variation among offenders, whether the characteristic examined is height or weight, education, or prior criminal record, the distribution may be seen as taking the form of a curve. On some characteristics, this curve might be statistically "normal," on other characteristics, it may be skewed to the left or right. For our purposes, let us envision the offender population as comprising a normal curve as shown on Chart 1. The possibility of its shape being skewed left or right is indicated by the broken-line curves labeled "A" and "B."

Since the conventional method of assigning offenders to caseloads is motivated in part by administrative desires to maintain "balanced" caseloads, and as a result case 1 is assigned to officer A, case 2 to officer B, 3 to C, 4 to A, 5 to B, 6 to C, and so on, we find that each officer receives for supervision, offenders who comprise a caseload that is a miniature reproduction of the total

Chart 1   Offender distribution curve.

offender curve, *whatever its real shape*. This conventional model is illustrated in Chart 2.

The conventional model illustrated is not, of course, found in most field operations, for probation and parole agencies normally consider the extent of the geographic area to be covered by their agents. In general terms, caseload sizes are equated with geography: the principle applied is that as the supervision area increases, caseload size decreases. Thus, the probation or parole officer working in a densely populated metropolitan area will have a smaller geographic area and a larger number of cases than his rural or suburban counterpart who has a greater area to cover.

Chart 3 illustrates the conventional supervision model with geographical considerations. It is to be noted that the supervising officers again receive offenders who comprise a miniature reproduction of the total offender curve. It is, of course, possible that significant differences exist—or that separate curves exist—for urban, suburban, and rural offenders.

Another model encountered in probation and parole supervision includes the single-factor specialized caseloads. Based upon a single factor or characteristic, such as sex, age, high violence-potential, or drug use, certain offenders are removed from the general population for placement in specialized caseloads. Thus, female offenders, or drug addicts are grouped into single caseloads for supervision purposes and, on occasion, a distinct treatment or approach is utilized for these caseloads. In the main, however, it appears that

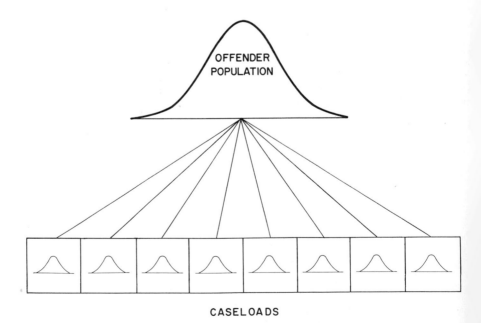

Chart 2   Conventional supervision model.

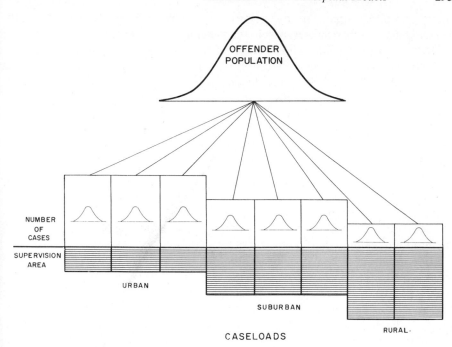

Chart 3   Conventional supervision model with geographic considerations.

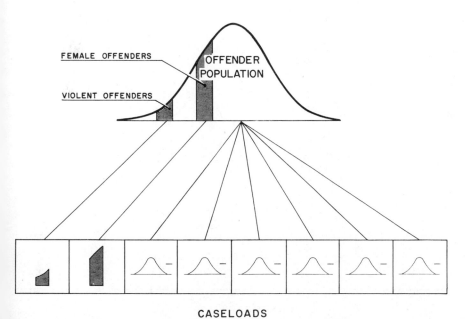

Chart 4   Single-factor specialized caseloads.

there is simply an organization of some caseloads around a single characteristic. The single-factor specialized caseloads are illustrated in Chart 4.

It is important to note, however, that the removal of a group of offenders from the general offender population on the basis of a single factor *does not* actually remove a portion of the curve as illustrated in Chart 4. Rather, there is an isolation of a grouping of offenders, who themselves constitute a separate curve, probably skewed right or left depending upon the characteristic measured. Female offenders, for example, are not a distinct and separate portion of the total offender curve, but rather comprise a cross-section of the total offender curve as portrayed in Chart 5. One of the dilemmas for treatment posed by these single factor classification caseloads is that the caseloads are not made homogeneous simply because all offenders assigned to them share a single characteristic such as sex or history of drug use.

Let us briefly examine the supervision model which serves as the basis for the numbers game. Chart 6 illustrates the arrangement of caseloads for a probation or parole agency providing supervision for 700 offenders. These caseloads are arranged in two different fashions—70 and 100 offenders per caseload. If the conventional method of assigning offenders is utilized so that caseloads are balanced, the only difference between the 70 and 100 offender caseloads is number. Each caseload receives a miniature distribution of the total offender population: there is no classification by treatment needs, types of offenders, types of probation or parole officers, or any other consideration. This may well explain some of the difficulty, indeed futility, of attempting to produce

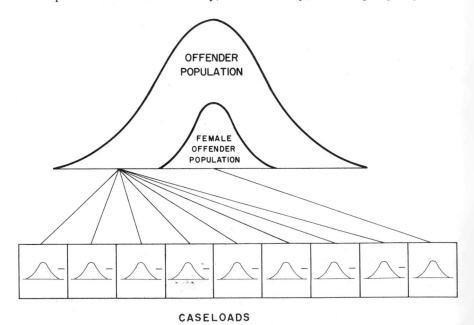

CASELOADS

Chart 5   Single-factor specialized caseloads.

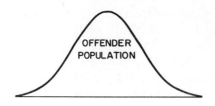

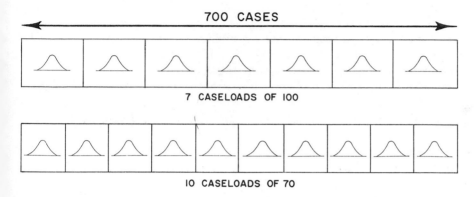

Chart 6 The "number game" supervision model.

changes in the outcome of supervision by mere manipulation of caseload size.

SLIGHTLY COMPLEX MODELS

We have seen the development of multi-factor classification tables for offenders. Often called expectancy or actuarial devices, these tables are created from various combinations of factors and predict, to a greater or lesser extent, success or failure under probation and parole supervision. In a sense, these experience tables attempt to make more explicit the "experienced opinions" of probation and parole officers, administrators, and others charged with decision-making functions in the correctional process. It should be noted that these various tables are geared toward predicting the outcome of supervision—in terms of success or failure and only infrequently for determining the needs of the offenders during the period of supervision.

Chart 7 reflects a model curve for an offender population distributed along a numerical scale from 0 to 100 based upon any combination of factors. In this model, the offenders toward the "0" end of the curve are considered low-success potential, those toward the "100" end, are high-success potential.

This model of the offender population can serve as a basis for the development of caseload management principles, even though it does not concern itself with types of officers or treatments, or considerations of the offender population other than those specifically measured. A multi-factor classification of offenders and their distribution along a normal or some other shaped curve can be meaningfully utilized only if we are willing to move away from what might be called a "horizontal" organization for caseload management, both for the offender distribution and for caseloads. The supervision process may be more meaningful if we constructed and operated from "*vertical*" models and multi-factor classification.

The "vertical" model requires that the offender distribution curve, arranged by some multi-factor classification, and the organization of case-loads, be "turned on end" as shown in Chart 8. Assuming a total offender population of 1000 with 15 probation and parole officers for supervision, this model is based upon the view that not all offenders need equal amounts or intensities of supervision and the need for the creation of varying size caseloads which allow for varying intensities or types of supervision. The high-success potential or low-need offenders are grouped into larger caseloads; the low-success potential or high-need offenders are grouped into smaller caseloads. The high-low need and high-low success potential elements are estimated by the multi-factor classification.

In Chart 8, twenty-five percent of the high-success potential/low-need offenders have been grouped into a large caseload of 250. Ten percent of the low-success potential/high-need offenders have been grouped into small caseloads of 25. The remaining offenders have been grouped into two other size caseloads on the same potential and need criteria. These numbers are for illustrative purposes only; the operational organization of such caseloads would be administratively determined, in part by the number of offenders to be supervised, officers available for supervision, and the type of the offender distribution curve.

We are now in a position to compare the conventional model with a "vertical model," in both instances using a 1000 offender population and 15 probation or parole officers. This is shown in Chart 9.

A number of problems emerge from the suggested "vertical" model of supervision as a replacement for the conventional "horizontal" models. The

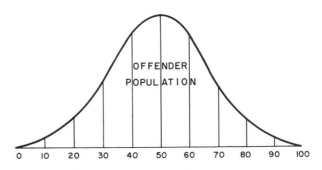

Chart 7   Multifactor classification curve.

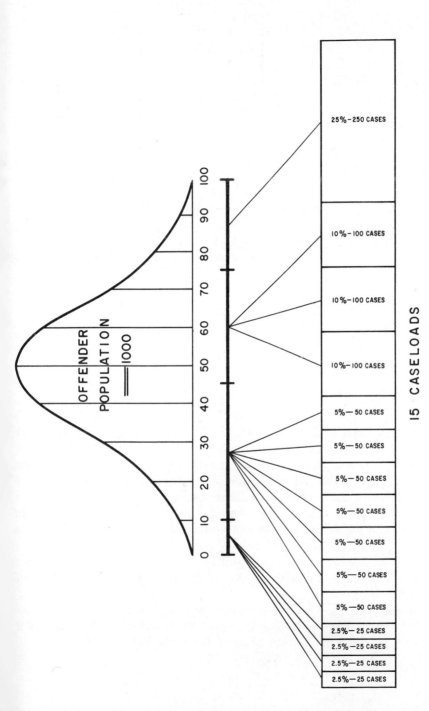

Chart 8 Multifactor classification and vertical caseloads.

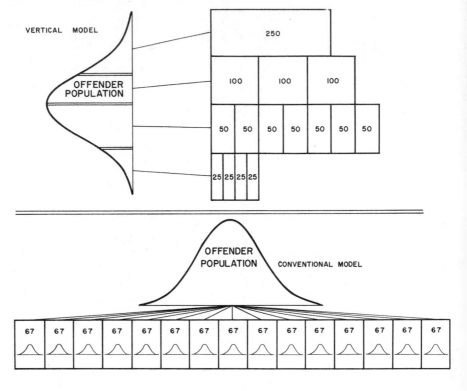

Chart 9   Conventional versus vertical model: 1000 cases—15 officers.

most important relates, of course, to the effectiveness of the suggested model as measured by a number of variables including, but not limited to, outcome of supervision and cost. These variables are directly involved with two basic premises of corrections—the protection of society and the best interests of the offender. We must inquire as to the appropriate maximum and minimum size of caseloads, and to types of probation and parole officers who provide supervision, and there must be concern for the types and nature of the supervision experience. The factors utilized for classification must be examined to determine their appropriateness and perhaps to distinguish classification for the purposes of treatment and classification for the predicted outcome of supervision.

In summary, we have proposed another way of viewing caseload management and probation and parole supervision. Whether the "vertical" model is indeed a better conceptualization of supervision remains to be tested.

26

Supervision Practices in the Federal Probation System*

DAVID H. GRONEWOLD

A survey of supervision practices in the United States probation offices was recently completed by the Federal Probation Training Center at Chicago. A questionnaire on supervision was sent to the 175 offices of the Federal Probation System. Field offices vary in the number of probation officers, from 1 to 22. Eight offices have 10 or more probation officers, and 65 represented in the report are 1-man offices. One hundred sixty-five, or 94 percent, of the questionnaires were returned; the 10 not returned were from branch offices.

A 20-page questionnaire with more than a hundred questions covered a wide range of topics related to intake and interviewing practices, office and caseload management, relationships with other agencies, and court policies. The purpose of the survey was to bring to light predominant supervision practices which have developed over the 33-year span of the Federal Probation System in the hope that the findings would have practical application in the improvement of probation supervision.

SOURCE. *Federal Probation*, XXVIII, September 1964, pp. 19–25
*This article is a summary of the highlights of a report, *A Survey of Supervision Practices of Probation Offices in the United States District Courts* (1964), prepared jointly by Wayne L. Keyser, deputy chief probation officer at Chicago; Harry W. Schloetter, deputy director of training of the Federal Probation Training Center at Chicago; and David H. Gronewold of the University of Washington School of Social Work.

INTAKE AND INTERVIEWING POLICIES

Assignment of Cases

In each of the 165 offices responding to the questionnaire, probation officers conduct presentence investigations and also supervise probationers and parolees. In general, the probation officer is assigned a case on an across-the-board basis, regardless of its special problems and needs. There are some exceptions. In six offices probation officers, on the basis of interest or previous experience, are assigned juvenile or youth offenders. Persons addicted to narcotics are specially assigned in four offices, and those with alcoholic problems in one office. In two offices some cases are assigned to probation officers who speak Spanish. Comments from two offices indicate that female clients are assigned to female officers.

Ideally, the assignment method should consider the special skills and interests of the staff. But economical use of time is perhaps the basic factor for the prevalent assignment of cases according to geographic location. The assignment of an officer to a particular community may also result in closer community relationships and a better use of community services. How to use the time and skills of the probation officer effectively within the framework of an assignment system, and to keep that assignment system both equitable and easy to administer presents a difficult problem.

Continuity of Service

The duties of the probation officer are divided into two broad classifications: (1) presentence investigations and (2) supervision. The investigative phase is primarily a diagnostic process, while the supervision phase has been designated as "treatment." However, the treatment process actually begins during the presentence investigation, when relationships are being formed and the probation officer acquires an understanding of the defendant and his problems. Most officers, through assignment policy, facilitate continuity of service to the offender by assigning the same probation officer from the time of court referral to termination of supervision. Assignment of probationers to the person who conducted the presentence investigation occurs in 95 percent of the offices; of parolees, in 92 percent of the offices.

Precommitment and Postcommitment Counseling

Counseling is a basic tool in supervision. It is especially important at certain critical times. The probationer is seen in almost all the offices immediately after probation is granted.

Precommitment counseling with those offenders committed to institutions is conducted in 78 offices, or almost half of them. The basic purpose of the precommitment interview is to prepare and to lend support to the offender for the new situation with which he is confronted.

Postcommitment counseling with families is done in almost two-thirds of the offices. While the offender is serving his sentence, problems often arise within the family. These many be economic because of the loss of the wage earner, or may be due to stresses resulting from interrupted family relationships.

Prerelease Counseling

Almost one-third of the supervision load of probation officers is composed of offenders who have been released from federal correctional institutions. Communication and collaboration with the Federal Bureau of Prisons is essential if continuity of treatment is to be achieved. For over a decade the Bureau of Prisons has regularly conducted group sessions of inmates about to be released. Probation officers have been invited to speak with inmate groups regarding parole supervision and conditions in the community. The Administrative Office of the United States Courts provides for the transportation of probation officers to Bureau institutions to take part in prerelease counseling sessions. In addition to the services rendered the offender, this program has made it possible for probation officers to obtain more intimate knowledge of the specific programs of the Bureau. Seventy-six offices—almost one half— have participated in prerelease counseling.

Group Counseling

Only one office replied affirmatively to the question asking whether group counseling sessions are held regularly for selected clients. In this office, 60 percent of the staff is engaged in group counseling, with 90 percent of the clients participating. Since many experts hold that group counseling has great potential as a treatment method, much more experimentation is indicated. Certainly, the program underway should be carefully evaluated.

The Initial Interview

The appearance before the court, both at the time of referral for presentence investigation, and for sentencing, is a trying emotional experience for the defendant. It is a time of personal crisis and the role of the probation officer is a significant one. Often he is in court as a reassuring figure and almost always he interviews the defendant immediately after he is placed on probation. One hundred fifty-seven offices (95 percent) reported that the defendant is seen by the probation officer on the day probation is granted.

At the time of being placed on probation, or shortly thereafter, every probationer is furnished with a copy of the order placing him on probation and a written statement of the conditions of probation. Likewise, persons released on parole or mandatory release are furnished written statements of the conditions of their supervision. The conditions of supervision offer a framework which guides both the probationer and the probation officer. Often the first request made by a probationer is for the probation officer to interpret what he can and cannot do. He is anxious to know where he stands. All 165 offices reported that the supervision conditions are interpreted to the probationer by the probation officer.

Associated with the interpretation of conditions is the opportunity given to the probation officer to define his role, to describe his interest in the welfare of the probationer and his intention to act with the probationer's welfare in mind.

Office and Home Visits

Who sets the frequency of office interviews for clients? Responses indicate that officers are generally given considerable professional discretion in the supervision of their cases. Frequency of office interviews is determined by the probation officer in 124 offices (75 percent); by the probation officer together with the chief probation officer in 23 offices (12 percent); and by a supervisory person in 15 offices (9 percent). The replies show a varied pattern of visiting in many offices, and would indicate the differential use of contacts according to the needs of each case. The most common pattern is the monthly contact which has been traditionally associated with the monthly report. Other cases are seen at intervals ranging from once a week to once a year. That 51 offices, or 31 percent of the total, set a weekly pattern for some clients indicates that intensive supervision is given to selected cases in these offices.

Notification of Clients of Home Visits

The probation officer is faced by a dilemma in determining whether he ought to notify his client of an impending visit. On the one hand he is guided by the ethic of respect for the individual and on the other by his obligation to protect society. Moreover, he is limited by certain practical difficulties which he sees inherent in his job.

The replies from 156 offices, or 94 percent, indicated that the client is *not* notified before a home visit is made. Forty-five, or 27 percent of the replies, stated that unexpected home visits reveal the true nature of the home situation without being staged or "dressed up" as might be the case if advance notice were given. Other replies stated that office policy follows practical considerations, such as the inability to maintain a set schedule. A number of offices commented that visits without notification should be interpreted to the client at the initial visit.

Since supervision is individualized and since a treatment plan is developed according to the particular needs of the client, should not the problem of notification be handled differentially? Many persons under supervision are not in need of surveillance and should be afforded the courtesy of advance notification.

OFFICE AND CASELOAD MANAGEMENT

In the Federal Probation System each probation officer has a management responsibility. He is assisted by broad general policy and guidance from his supervisors in his task of making presentence investigations and supervising clients, but much depends upon his resourcefulness, work habits, and skill in allocating time to his many chores. As a general practitioner the probation officer operates at a professional level and does not require detailed instruction on his day to day activities. On the other hand, problems arise in working with clients which are difficult for the most experienced probation officer and as these problems arise, he recognizes that he cannot work alone but must frequently consult with his supervisor in a joint effort to find solutions. Eighty-three of the 90 judicial districts in the federal court system have chief probation officers and only 7 districts (one-man offices) have no chief probation officer. From the standpoint of administrative organization, all but 7 probation officers of 522 have supervisors with whom they can consult.

A handicapping factor, however, is that 45 districts have branch offices, in some cases 200 or 300 miles from the headquarters office where the chief probation officer is stationed. The nature and quality of supervision of branch offices is a possible subject of administrative study. Of the questionnaires returned, several made note of the fact that special conditions operated because they were located in a one-man office.

Probation Officers' Contact With the Office While in the Field

All federal probation officers divide their time between the office and the field. For some, field trips rarely extend beyond a day while others may be away for a week or more. The problems of maintaining communication with the office during these trips differs in relation to the time away from the office, distances traveled, and the personnel remaining in the office while field visits are being made. Of the 165 offices responding, 103 said that contact is made with the office while the probation officer is in the field.

Special Office Hours

Most clients are wage earners and the majority are employed during the day. Unless special office hours are maintained, the clients lose time from work to call at the probation office. When this happens, the value of the interview may be impaired. Eighty-five offices (approximately 52 percent) stated that special hours are scheduled for client interviews. Forty-nine offices reported that evening hours are kept and 26 offices said that Saturday hours are maintained.

Verification of Employment or School Attendance and Adjustment

Supervision of clients implies the responsibility that the probation officer must keep himself informed about their respective situations and circumstances. This is one of the purposes of office and home interviews. Keeping informed means also knowing the job or school situation.

In one hundred fifty-eight of the 165 offices responding, employment verifications are made either routinely or on a selective basis. Sixty-two offices reported routine employment verification. Verification is made by examination of pay stubs, on-the-job visits, by contact with the family, direct contact with the employer, or through community visits.

For persons of school age, 136 offices reported that school attendance is verified routinely, and 22 more verify on a selective basis. Verification is made by examination of report cards, contact with school authorities, and interviews with parents.

Classification of Cases

The classification of cases has two objectives: (1) to assure that the probationer is treated flexibly according to his needs for counseling and (2) as a control of the work of the probation officer which will give maximum time for work with those probationers most in need. All but four of the respondents answered that some type of classification is used. One hundred forty-eight offices reported that probationers are classified informally without reference to a precise formula, while 13 offices reported that probationers are classified formally according to office policy.

An essential step in case management is a plan of supervision for each client. Accordingly, the question was asked: Does the probation officer outline a tentative plan of supervision in the recording of the initial interview? Ninety-three answered affirmatively, 69 in the negative, with 3 giving no answer. The response to this question, however, does not necessarily reflect the extent of recorded plans of supervision by federal probation officers, since many officers include a plan of treatment in the presentence report.

Private Offices for Probation Officers

Responses to the survey indicated that all but 43 probation officers (less than 10 percent) have private offices. Substantial progress has been made since the early days of federal probation, when but few probation officers had a private office. The Federal Probation System promotes the general policy that clients are to have the opportunity of private interviews with their probation officer.

Confidentiality of Supervision Records

The policy is clearly enunciated in the United States Probation Officers Manual that confidential information in probation case records should not be divulged without the approval of the court, and in parole cases without permission of the Board of Parole. People in the helping professions—doctors, lawyers, social workers, probation officers—have been guided by the principle of confidentiality. Their clientele reveal many personal details about themselves and their situation, believing that the professional person can be trusted to use whatever information is secured in a responsible way. The probation task involves communication and close cooperation with law enforcement, social welfare, and health personnel. Reciprocal relationships are established with cooperating agencies, and the acquisition of information means the willingness to give information. The probation officer as a professional person must discriminate between information which can be shared, and what is confidential.

Information is given to federal investigative agencies by 135 offices; to United States attorneys by 124; to social agencies by 115; to local police officials by 92; and to representatives of business firms by 40. The means of sharing information is by letter, telephone, person-to-person discussion, the probation officer reading the file to the agency representative, and by the representative reading the file. No attempt was made through the questionnaire to elicit the kind of information given. It should be noted that in four of the five methods of sharing information, the probation officer has control of what is given. He relinquishes control when the representative of the agency is given the file.

Supervision of Staff

The uses of supervision have been succinctly outlined in *Standards and Guides for Adult Probation:*

"Supervision of staff (as distinguished from supervision of probationers) means assignment of an employee with demonstrated professional competence, training, and experience to work closely with and have authority over a number of other officers. . . . Through supervision the officer is helped to recognize his own prejudices and biases which are reducing his helpfulness to his probationers. In the process he learns how to handle authority so that it will help the probationers and thereby the community. . . . The laws and agency policies within which the probation department operates are interpreted and applied through supervision. . . . Supervision is most imperative for officers whose casework skills are not fully developed and who are not yet qualified to proceed independently. Supervision is necessary also for experienced officers, to help them maintain their skills, continue to improve their performance, and gain new insights."[1]

---

[1] *Standards and Guides for Adult Probation.* New York: National Council on Crime and Delinquency, 1962, pp. 26–27.

Regularly scheduled case conferences are the means through which the objectives of supervision can be accomplished. Only 39 offices hold regularly scheduled conferences between the probation officer and his superiors: 9 are held weekly, 5 semimonthly, 7 monthly, and 14 quarterly. It must be remembered, however, that 65 one-man offices are represented in this survey. An additional 97 offices stated that conferences are held at unspecified intervals on request of either the probation officer or his supervisor.

Staff Development

While the Federal Probation System engages in a national program of inservice training through regional meetings and attendance at the Federal Probation Training Center at Chicago, each of the 90 chief probation officers in the system has a responsibility for encouraging the professional development of each of his probation officers. The chief probation officer is in a position to give continuity to the inservice training sessions held on a national basis. The case supervision conference between probation officer and supervisor is recognized as a primary means of improving the level of professional work. In addition, many agencies engage in staff development meetings held periodically in the office for the purpose of increasing knowledge and improving techniques. Of the offices responding, 70 stated that staff development meetings are held: 14 weekly; 5 semimonthly; 14 monthly; and the other 37 at less frequent intervals.

RELATIONSHIPS WITH OTHER AGENCIES

The federal probation officer makes frequent use of community resources on behalf of persons under his supervision. Referrals are made to social agencies in the community, to health facilities and employment services. Generally he will not make a referral unless the problem can be handled with greater skill and effectiveness by another agency.

Availability of services varies. Public employment services are available to all but two of the offices; alcoholic treatment agencies to four-fifths. Almost two-thirds of the offices have access to family counseling agencies and almost as many to psychiatric facilities. The use of the community resource is determined by the perception the probation officer has of his client's need, his knowledge of what community resources have to offer, and the willingness of the client to use that resource. Other factors are the ability of the agency to respond to the particular referral in terms of the problem, of agency waiting lists, and, in some cases, of the financial status of the person referred.

Replies to the questionnaire show that probation officers generally make frequent use of public employment agencies and, although not as frequent, extensive use of alcoholic treatment agencies. Occasional use is made of family counseling services and of psychiatric clinics. Private employment agencies are available in over half of the offices, but are used infrequently in most of them.

Forty-two offices report that when another agency is simultaneously engaged in counseling a probationer or parolee, major responsibility for supervision may be, at times, placed on that agency. The social agency provides all casework services, and only the official court requirements are then left to the probation officer.

COURT POLICIES AND RELATIONSHIPS

Federal probation officers work under the jurisdiction of their respective district courts. Policies governing the practice of probation, however, are jointly determined by the district courts and the Probation Division of the Administrative Office of the United States Courts. Many of the practices described thus far have related primarily to the officer's work with and on behalf of the person under supervision and to the objective of bringing about improvement in his conduct and condition. The probation task, in addition to its unique rehabilitative features, is also a part of a larger law enforcement function. Many of the activities of the officer are interdisciplinary in nature, and require close collaboration with the court, and at times, with the United States attorney. Some of the supervision practices relate to specific orders of the court such as fines and restitution, early termination of probation, and transfer of jurisdiction. Specific actions result from legal determinations. In many instances, court orders are made after a recommendation by the probation officer.

Some special orders make it possible to individualize treatment, such as the court order for committing a narcotic addict to a United States Public Health Service Hospital as a condition of probation. The court order terminating probation provides an incentive to probationers to make a good adjustment. Collaboration with the United States attorney is necessary in revocation and deferred prosecution matters.

Fines and Restitution

The use of fines and restitution in the different federal courts varies greatly. Replies to the questionnaire show that in many offices a high percentage of probation cases are required to pay either fines or restitution: 58 offices report that over 20 percent pay fines and 78 offices state that over 20 percent pay restitution. Probation offices very often have the responsibility for seeing that fines and restitution are collected: 108 offices have responsibility for fines; 153 for restitution. Thus, collection of monies can become a time-consuming activity.

Early Termination of Probation

One hundred twenty six offices reported that recommendations are made to court for an early termination of probation when it appears that the probationer has received maximum benefit from supervision.

Use of Deferred Prosecution

One hundred thirty six offices stated that juveniles, in some instances, are placed on supervision under the deferred prosecution procedure. Under this plan, prosecution is deferred for carefully selected juveniles who are placed under informal supervision and are not stigmatized by a court record.

Revocation Hearings

In the majority of officers the probation officer collaborates closely with the United States attorney in revocation matters, and sends him a written violation report. Most probation officers are not sworn in to testify on hearings of probation violation: in 36 offices, officers are sworn in; in 117, they are not.

IN SUMMARY

The systematic manner with which the federal probation officer approaches his task is high-lighted by the findings of this survey. Certain methodological procedures are regularly followed by most probation officers. Some of these procedures are related to case diagnosis and evaluation. Presentences are prepared for 86 percent of the cases granted probation. A plan of supervision is recorded in the initial interview in over half of the reporting probation offices, and in many others it is included in the presentence report. Cases are classified as to supervision needs in 161 offices of the 165.

Other procedures regularly followed are related to the initial phase of the probation period. In 95 percent of the offices, the client is interviewed by the probation officer immediately after he is placed on probation. All offices report that probation officers interpret to the client the conditions of probation and parole, and that written conditions are not given or sent to him without interpretation.

Other practices, which do not follow a set pattern, are geared in a large measure to the particular needs of the case within the limits of time available to the probation officer. Patterns of office and home visits vary from case to case, and frequency of contact is determined exclusively by the probation officer in three-quarters of the offices. In 158 of the 165 reporting offices it is a general practice to verify employment, but more offices verify on a selective basis than as a matter of routine. The supposition is that in the majority of cases a probationer who reports that he is employed actually is employed.

When he is not employed, in fact, he tends to seek employment assistance from his probation officer. On the other hand, routine verification of the school attendance of juvenile and youthful offenders is considered important in four-fifths of the offices. Many youth offenders have had a school attendance problem.

The differential use of referrals is another illustration of how practice is related to the needs of the particular case. The findings show a frequent use of the public employment services in almost three-quarters of the probation offices. There is occasional use of family and psychiatric services in almost one-half of those offices in which those services are available. The frequent use of the services of the public employment agency might be related to its availability, and also associated with the perception on the part of the probation officer that employment is paramount in the social adjustment of the probationer.

The recognition by the Federal Probation System of the importance of a sustained relationship between officer and client is shown in the generally accepted policy of making the officer responsible for a case from its inception as a presentence investigation throughout the supervision period to termination. This policy is followed in over 90 percent of the offices.

Practices in some of the offices suggest that counseling is considered especially important at certain critical times. The probationer is seen in almost all of the offices immediately after probation is granted. Precommitment counseling is a practice in almost half the offices. And nearly half of the offices have participated in the prerelease counseling program of the Federal Bureau of Prisons. These practices are based on the assumption that the correctional client has special need of information, and of psychological support at those periods when he is facing new and unknown situations. Postcommitment counseling with families, practiced in almost two-thirds of the offices, suggests that probation officers are aware of the importance of the family to the social functioning of the parolee.

The practices of probation offices in the sharing of information from the case supervision record with other agencies vary considerably. The findings reveal that in many offices the representative of the other agency is given the case record to read for himself. Material cannot remain confidential with such a practice.

Inservice training and staff development at the regional and national level are provided through regional meetings and through regularly scheduled training sessions at the Federal Training Center. Efforts toward staff development at the local level consist of the use of the supervisory conference, and of staff development meetings. Only a relatively small number of offices have incorporated frequent, regularly scheduled conferences as a part of the agency program. The staff development meeting is a training device used in 70 of the offices, but the frequency of meetings varies from those scheduled on a weekly basis to those held semiannually or annually.

Respect for the offender is demonstrated by the provision of privacy in interviewing. Consideration is shown the client through the maintenance of special hours for office visits in some offices, an indication of agency adaptability.

Certain flexibilities have been introduced in probation practice by the use of alternate court procedures. Early termination of probation is used in three-fourths of the offices, a practice which provides an incentive to the probationer and a more effective use of the officer's time.

Extensive use is made of the "deferred prosecution" plan for the juvenile offender, a plan which saves the juvenile from the stigma of a court record. Deferred prosecution was once an innovative practice known as the Brooklyn plan. Many other practices, now widely followed by many offices, such as pre-commitment counseling, prerelease counseling, and special office hours, were originally experiments in a few field offices. Professional organizations and the professional literature, the leadership of the Probation Division of the Administrative Office of the United States Courts, the experimentation of imaginative probation officers—all have contributed to new ways of doing things. Gradually these ways become "customary actions" (which, by the way, is one of the definitions of practice) widely followed throughout the Federal Probation System.

The questionnaire was designed to find out current practice, and did not attempt to uncover new approaches or innovative projects with which field offices might be experimenting. Such a task might be the focus of a future study. The findings of the survey do indicate that the Federal Probation System has incorporated supervision practices which provide the means for the achievement of the objectives of probation. The phenomenal growth of the probation service in terms of the number of field offices, probation officers, and clientele served has been accompanied by a corresponding development and maturation of probation practice.

27

The Utility of Case Records in Probation and Parole

ARTHUR P. MILES

THE PROBLEM

Probation and parole officers compile and maintain extensive case records. These records presumably have the following uses: to provide assurance that statutory and administrative responsibilities have been met, to insure adequate service to clients, to assist in supervision, to function as a guide in case planning, and to provide research data.[1] These uses have been emphasized without factual documentation as to whether they are being met or not.

Inasmuch as the preparation and maintenance of case records are major activities of a probation and parole agency—from the point of view of the amount of professional staff time expended as well as clerical costs—they have recently come under scrutiny. For example, a recent time study of Wisconsin probation and parole officers showed that the largest amount of the officers' time is spent on "recording and related activities.[2]" According to the study,

SOURCE. *Journal of Criminal Law, Criminology, and Police Science*, **56,** No. 3, 1965, pp. 285–293. Copyright 1965, by Northwestern University School of Law. Reprinted by special permission. This article is based on a portion of the research undertaken by the author while employed by the Wisconsin Division of Corrections as a Research Consultant during the summers of 1960–1964.—EDITOR.

[1]Hamilton, Principles of Social Case Recording 8–9 (1946).

[2]Miles, A Time Study of Wisconsin Probation and Parole Agents (1964). Probation and Parole Officers in Wisconsin, and in some other jurisdictions, are officially designated as "Agents." The term "Officer" will be used in this article.

male officers spend 30.9 percent of their time on recording and female officers spend 34.2 percent of their time on this activity. When added to the other "indirect" activities of officers—travel and office work—it was found that officers spent nearly six-tenths of their time on "indirect" activity. In other words, they spend only four-tenths of their time in "direct" services to individuals.

Time studies in other jurisdictions have also shown that a large amount of the officers' time is devoted to recording. A time study of state parole officers in Pennsylvania showed that they devote 24 percent of their time to recording.[3] A time study of county probation officers in Contra Costa County, California, showed that the officers spend 22.2 percent of their time on "office work", primarily recording.[4]

In addition to the time spent by probation and parole officers it is also obvious that a great deal of time of other staff members is devoted to the preparation, maintenance, and handling of case records. In Wisconsin there is one full-time stenographer for every two probation and parole officers. The majority of the stenographer's time is devoted to work on case records. In district offices and in the state office, file clerks are engaged in filing materials in case folders. Numerous administrators, such as District Administrators, Regional Administrators, Parole Board Members, and the Supervisor of Inter-State Placements, spend a great deal of their time reading case records as a basis for decision making.

It became clear in Wisconsin, therefore, that an examination in depth of the system of case recording of probation and parole officers was essential. For one thing, it was deemed necessary to secure factual information about the utilization of the records by the principal users. For another thing, if probation and parole officers were to devote more of their time to direct services with probationers and parolees they had to spend less time on indirect activities. When the indirect activities were analyzed it became apparent that most elements in this category—such as, travel time, for example—could not be cut down. This meant that the only element that seemed to be subject to reduction was recording and related activities. Accordingly, an experimental study was designed to determine whether or not an abbreviated system of recording would accomplish this result.

One of the by-products of the study was a detailed analysis of the use of case records by the principal users. This article is based upon this analysis.

HISTORY OF CASE RECORDING

Case recording began as soon as social agencies were established. The early records were abbreviated chronicles of the practical activities of the

[3]Jacks, A Time Study of Parole Agents 4 (1961).
[4]Davis, An Approach to Performance Budgeting for Probation Services 21–22 (1958).

agency. The records consisted largely of lists of amounts of relief given, or children placed in institutions. Early case records were almost totally devoid of individualized, psychologically-oriented materials.[5] In probation and parole the early records were largely legal in nature—such as police and court records and orders for the revocation of parole. An occasional crisp comment would declare that "subject was taken by officer to the State Reformatory. Received receipt for same."

The invention, and subsequent widespread use, of the typewriter made it possible to expand the scope of case records. Carbon copies of letters, as well as written accounts of home visits, made their appearance in case records. The greatest incentive for more detailed recording, however, was the development of interest in the social sciences, especially the psychological, aspects of the helping process. This was due to the advances of the social sciences, accepted by social work, especially in the immediate post-World War I period.

The interest of social workers in psychiatry resulted in more than an increase in the volume of case records; it brought about a virtual revolution in the quality of social work as well. Social workers ceased to be concerned primarily with a record of their stewardship and became concerned, as well, with the interrelationships of the agency and the worker with the client.

In the late 1920's and early 1930's sociologists became interested in the research potential of social case records. As a result, they gave advice to social workers which resulted in a greater volume of recording. The sociologists pleaded for more objectivity, inclusion of special material relating to social problems, and, in some instances, verbatim recording so the details of the relationship between the social worker and the client could be studied.[6]

The administrative requirements of specialized social agencies also became more pronounced. Child welfare agencies placing children for adoption required proof of the suitability of the physical aspects of the home and the psychological adjustment of prospective adoptive parents. Agencies administering mother's aid and old-age assistance needed legal proof of eligibility. Probation and parole agencies wanted the records to reflect the extent of surveillance. Parole boards demanded social evidence of the proposed plans for the release of inmates. In short, as new public agencies with specific statutory responsibilities developed they had to have extensive documentation of proof of the fulfillment of their obligations.

As previously noted, professional social work, especially as seen in the work of private agencies, was adopting a psychiatric, or more precisely a psychoanalytic, interpretation of human behavior.[7] This too resulted in much more detailed case histories. The early history and development of the client,

[5]Sheffield, The Social Case History 5–18 (1920).

[6]Reddick, *The Relation of Sociology to Social Work*, 8 Family 357 (1928); Burgess, *What Social Records Should Contain to be Useful for Sociological Interpretation*, 6 Social Forces 532–534 (1928); Young, *Should Case Records be Written in the First Person?*, 11 Family 153–154 (1928).

[7]Robinson, A Changing Psychology in Social Case Work (1930).

especially in relationship to his mother and father, became important in diagnosing the case and formulating a plan for treatment.

The development of a more intensive and detailed process of supervision also added to the length of case records. The first "General Secretaries" and "District Secretaries" of the Charity Organization Societies were probably the original casework supervisors. They inducted, trained, and oversaw the work of the "charity visitors." Supervision was the art of teaching new social workers on the job. As the process was institutionalized, the supervisory conference became more significant. In many offices the agency policies required that all dictation had to be recorded and typed before the conference could be held. The supervisors, relying more and more (so they claimed) upon the record for insight regarding the psychological interaction between worker and client, demanded more and more "process" in recording.

The requirements of teachers of social casework have likewise served to inflate case records. The student in field work was expected to prepare careful and detailed notes in long-hand. He was also taught to record, in "process", all that went on between himself, the client, and the community. Records chosen by teachers of social casework for teaching in schools of social work were also expected to show the details of client interaction. Inasmuch as it was considered an honor to have an agency record chosen for teaching, the agency catered to the demands of the teachers.

All of these factors had their influence in probation and parole services. The administrative and statutory responsibilities of probation and parole are self-evident. Although the "psychiatric deluge" was not so pronounced in probation and parole as in other agencies, it was by no means absent. The supervisory process was accepted and expanded in probation and parole agencies. Probation and parole has been less intense in its association with schools of social work, but, especially in recent years, this has been an additional factor. All in all, the same forces were at work for the expansion of the case records in probation and parole as in other agencies.

Within the past ten years, however, there have been numerous questions about the validity of extensive case records in social agencies. In 1954 two Chicago agencies—the Family Service Bureau of the United Charities and the Jewish Family and Community Service—started an analysis of their case records. The following year (1955) they carried on an experimental study with a summarized system of recording. Among other things, the study concluded that the supervisory process is based mainly upon verbal communication. The supervisors, they found, spent only 8 percent of their time reading records. The study also concluded that caseworkers preferred a system of recording that is organized, specific, and explicit.[8]

Brevity in recording had also been recommended for family service agencies

[8]Frings, Kratovil, & Polemis, An Assessment of Social Case Recording: An Experimental Study in Two Family Agencies 76–77 (1958).

by Wilda J. Daily and Virginia P. Hogan in 1958.[9] A similar recommendation
was made for child welfare agencies in 1963.[10]

THE WISCONSIN STUDY

The Wisconsin study of experimental recording was undertaken in three
districts from October 1, 1963 to October 1, 1964.

In Wisconsin the Division of Corrections of the State Department of Public
Welfare has responsibility for the administration of state-wide parole for
juveniles and adults and state-wide probation for adults. This is true, except
in Milwaukee County. There the state has responsibility only for adult and
juvenile parole. The administration of juvenile and adult probation is a responsibility of local courts in Milwaukee County.

The state employs approximately 150 probation and parole officers to carry
out this responsibility. Administratively, the state is divided into 14 districts—
four of these are in Milwaukee, two in Madison, and the remainder in the
rest of the state. Each district is headed by a District Administrator, with
probation and parole officers assigned to areas where they usually maintain
their own offices (except in the large cities where they are located in
the district office). Three districts, presumably representative of various
types of districts were chosen for the study. One of the districts was in
Milwaukee, chosen because it is an all urban district. Another was one
of the Madison districts, chosen because it was an urban-rural district.
The third was the Eau Claire District, chosen because it was more rural in
nature.

Each probation and parole area has a number, which indicates the district,
sex of the officer, and a number for the area. These numbers served as the basis
for the selection of one-half of the officers, by sex, for the control group, and
one-half for the experimental group. Sixteen or 12.3 percent of the total number
of officers were contained in the experimental group. The same number was
contained in the control group. The two groups were chosen by the use of
random numbers.[11] Officers in the experimental groups recorded according to
an abbreviated system, designed for the study. Officers in the control groups
continued to record, as did all other officers in the state except those in the
experimental groups, in the usual manner.

A new "face sheet" was designed for use in the study. This "face sheet"
was four pages in length and was used for probation social studies, presentence
investigations, institutional admission investigations, and sex crimes studies.
It also contained basic identifying information (such as name, date of birth,

[9]Daily & Hogan, *Brief Systems of Recording*, 39 Social Casework 278–282 (1958).
[10]Panor & Peterson, *Current Trends in Case Recording*, 42 Child Welfare 230–234 (1963).
[11]Based upon tables in Wallis & Roberts, Statistics: A New Approach (1956).

height, weight, race, social security number, etc.), offense and court data, the offender's version and the victim's statement of the offense, plea, and sentence. In addition, the "sheet" included social information—marital history, parents, siblings, religious affiliation, education, employment, etc. Finally, it also contained the officer's evaluation and plan for the case.

This "face sheet" included the data of the old "face sheet" and also incorporated data for various types of social studies. It was no longer necessary for officers in the experimental group to fill out a "face sheet" and prepare a special probation social or pre-sentence investigation. The relative brevity of the reports plus the ease in finding pertinent data proved to be popular with judges.

Monthly and semi-annual reports were substituted for all "running records." These reports were one page in length and contained space for financial data, types of contacts the officer had with the offender, and a short space for the officer's comments. This meant that contacts with offenders were not reported in the running record each time they occurred, but only in the summaries.

A special "Violation Report" was designed for the study. On this report the officer reported the type of violation: conviction of another offense, revocation to be requested, charged with another offense, arrested but not charged, rule violation, and violation of an officer's directive. A "Statement of the Violation and Substantiating Details" and a statement of the officer's "Disposition of the Violation" were also required on the form.

A "Case Closing Summary" was also included. This form filled out on all cases closed, required the officer to check the type of case, marital status at the termination of supervision, employment during supervision, use of institutional training, disruptive use of alcohol, school adjustment, cooperation with officer, persons associated with the offender during supervision, dependency obligations, feeling toward others, success of plan, and prognosis when discharged.

These forms took the place of the "running records" that were continued by all officers except those in the experimental study group. Under the system of "running records" only a few special forms—such as a "face sheet" which did not incorporate data for social studies—were used. Every time something happened on the case—a home visit, an office visit, a rule violation, etc.—a chronological entry describing the event was typed into the record with carbon copies sent to district administrators, regional administrators, parole board members, etc. All these lengthy chronological entries were eliminated for those officers in the experimental study group. The information was abbreviated and summarized on the various forms noted above.

Various tests were used to assess the utility of the experimental records. One was a time study of the experimental and control agents. This was to discover whether or not less time was spent in recording by officers in the experimental groups. Interviews, in depth, were conducted by the research staff in an effort to discover the effectiveness of the records to the principal users.

Still another test was one designed to discover the utility of the records to users in the state office.

A complete set of records is maintained in the state office where they are available to various administrative officers. A system was set up whereby the users of experimental records were required to indicate their use. A luminescent tag stating "Experimental File—See Instructions" was placed on the tag of each experimental record. The tag was not only luminescent, but was also very brightly colored (orange). Hence, these records could hardly be missed by users. Securely stapled on the inside of the jacket was an explanatory account of the study, with space for the users to make certain notes. The user was required to give the date of use, his name and title, the purpose for the use of the record, and a "comment on adequacy and utility of record." Under this last heading the user was asked to check whether he found the record to be "very good, good, average, fair, poor, or very poor." Administrative regulations were issued clearly indicating the responsibility of employees to record their usage of the experimental records. Attempts were made to follow up on these instructions. It is the analysis of the use of the experimental records that is the principal basis of this article.

ADMINISTRATIVE USE OF CASE RECORDS IN PROBATION AND PAROLE

It is usually contended that probation and parole agencies have administrative and statutory responsibilities that give unique obligations to probation and parole officers and place special requirements upon probation and parole case records.

An offender who is released from an institution on parole is still serving his sentence. The fact that he is doing so outside the institution does not mean that he is free from controls. Indeed, the parole officer has a special responsibility to see that the offender does not disobey the rules of parole. The parole officer's supervision of the parolee requires documentation. His admonitions to the parolee in regard to drinking, frequenting with bad companions, and keeping late hours needs to be recorded. Continuous disregard of the rules or of an officer's specific directives may be the basis for the subsequent revocation of parole.

A probation and parole officer has certain statutory responsibilities in regard to those whom he is supervising. Wisconsin law, for example, requires that a monthly report must be submitted to the officer by the parolee. There are also definite restrictions placed upon parolees: they may not marry, travel, or change jobs without approval from their probation and parole officers.

Courts often require probationers to pay restitution to a victim as a basis of his probation. In such cases the officer must collect and disburse the restitution payments. This obviously requires recording. The same is true when the court orders the payment of support money by a man who has been found guilty of non-support of his family. Not only does the probation and parole officer require a record, but repeated failures to pay support money or make restitution payments could be a basis for subsequent revocation.

Hence, the probation and parole officer has a basis of reality for his contention that he has unusual statutory and administrative responsibilities whose fulfillment should be recorded in the case record.

Administrative officers who use the records often do so because of their legal responsibilities. For example, members of the Parole Board use records as a basis for determining eligibility for parole. They need to have details about the offense, the inmate's adjustment, and the proposed plan for release. The Supervisor of Inter-State Placements uses the record to determine if a specific case is a suitable risk for supervision in another state. Regional administrators use records to determine whether or not revocation should be requested. Other departments of state government, especially the Governor's Office and the Office of the Attorney General, use records.

The potential administrative uses of records by other administrative offices is very great. Probation and parole officers, who compile the records, know this and often attempt to have information recorded.

USE OF RECORDS IN SUPERVISION

Traditionally, casework supervisors have contended that case records have been one of the principal bases for the supervision of workers. The record shows that the worker is carrying out his responsibilities and it is also a basis for understanding the worker's job performance.

In analyzing the supervisory process in the Wisconsin system of probation and parole we found that the supervisors did not rely primarily upon the records as a basis of supervision. They often said they did, but upon more detailed examination it was found that they did not. The chief means of carrying out the supervisory process was through personal discussion between the supervisors (District Administrators) and the officers. The supervisors used the records primarily to alert themselves to problems and as a record of fulfillment of administrative and statutory responsibilities. For the details of the casework process the supervisors depended, almost entirely, upon personal discussion with the workers.

There are some who might contend that the supervisory process may be unique in probation and parole. In this respect, however, the Wisconsin probation and parole service is similar to the Family Service Bureau of the United Charities and the Jewish Family and Community Service (the Chicago agencies involved in a recording study). They too found that supervisors carried on the process of supervision mainly by personal discussion with workers.[12]

---

[12]Frings, Kratovil, and Polemis, *op. cit. supra* note 8.

It would appear, therefore, that the belief that supervisors are dependent primarily upon the written record for the supervisory process may be one of the unfounded bits of folklore in casework agencies.

USE OF RECORDS BY PROBATION AND PAROLE OFFICERS

One of the principal users of case records in probation and parole are the officers themselves. There are a variety of ways in which probation and parole officers use the records.

First of all, the record serves as a guide to the probation and parole officer as to the facts of case activity. From the record he knows the details of the offense, the social history of the offender, the date of the last home visit, the amount of restitution paid, the work record of the offender, etc. The officer also secures simple, but nonetheless important, identifying information from the record: address of the offender, directions for finding the home (particularly important in a rural area), and address of the place of employment. These are the kinds of information that cannot be stored in the officer's head; they have to be maintained in the record.

Secondly, the record makes it possible to have a fairly smooth transition from one officer to another on a specific case. Unfortunately, there is often a fairly heavy turnover of officers on a specific case. This is due, in part, to the turnover of employees in probation and parole agencies. It is also due to the increases in population with concomitant increases in the numbers of offenders. It is also due to the increased emphasis upon professional quality in corrections. This results in an increase in the number of officers and a decrease in the size of caseloads. All of these factors mean that there is a constant turnover of probation and parole officers. The new officers must have records to inform them about the facts of their cases as developed by their predecessors.

Thirdly, the officer uses the record to organize his thinking about the case and to plan future courses of action. Through reading the record and recording his contacts with the case in the record the officer organizes his thinking and prepares his plans for the case.

Finally, the officer uses the record in the supervision of the offender. For example, an offender has been ordered to pay support money. He fails to make payments for several months. When accosted by the officer he contends that he made a payment during the last month. The officer consults the record and then, once again, informs the offender that the record shows that no support payments have been made for two months.

In our study we found that case records are widely used by the officers themselves. Some of the uses of case records—for supervision of officers, for teaching, and for research—have been over-emphasized. The uses of records by officers themselves, however, have been under-emphasized.

USE OF RECORDS BY OTHER AGENCIES

Formerly caseworkers used to go to other social agencies that had known the client and read the case record. This rarely happens today. It is not because clients are not known to numerous agencies. In fact, there are many "multiple problem" families. Families who have members who are offenders against the law also have members in mental hospitals, members who receive public aid, and members who are patients in psychiatric clinics. Modern social agencies, however, provide specialized services and usually do not duplicate the work of other agencies. Despite the fact that a large volume of services is given to the "hard core" cases, social agencies are not among the principal users of agency records.

Probationers and parolees are invariably experienced in dealing with social workers. They have been known to social workers in schools, juvenile courts, psychiatric clinics, and public assistance agencies. These agencies, as already noted, have special responsibilities and are interested in securing specific information from the probation and parole agency.

In our study we found very little evidence of use of records by representatives of other agencies. This was never mentioned by the probation and parole officers and, therefore, seems to be of negligible significance in the total usage of records.

USE OF RECORDS FOR RESEARCH

Social case records were once assumed to contain much significant research data. In the days of heavy foreign immigration many sociologists used social agency records as a source of information on the assimilation of immigrants. One of the sociological classics of this period—The Polish Peasant[13]—utilized social agency records as a major source of data. In the late 1920's and early 1930's sociologists advised social workers regarding the form and content of case records. Professor Thomas D. Eliot, for example, suggested that case records contain both subjective and objective data. Both types of materials, however, should be clearly identified as an aid to the sociological researcher.[14] Elon H. Moore pleaded for maximum accuracy in case records, also for the benefit of sociological researchers.[15] Pauline Young declared that verbatim recording was desirable in case records, both as aid to the social workers in diagnosis and the sociologist in research.[16]

At the present time, however, the research value of case records is recognized to be less significant than formerly. Case records are still used as a basis

---

[13]Thomas & Znaniecki, The Polish Peasant in Europe and America (1927).

[14]Eliot, *Objectivity and Subjectivity in the Case Record*, 6 Social Forces 539–544 (1928).

[15]Moore, *How Accurate Are Case Records?*, 12 Social Forces 498–507 (1934).

[16]Young, *op. cit. supra* note 6.

for research, but it is now recognized that the research value of the records is quite limited. Generally speaking, the research data in case records is factual information that is not contained in the so-called "running record." In probation and parole cases such information as the offense, age and sex of offender, sentence, etc. are the kinds of data that have research value. Lengthy, verbose recording does not add to the research value of the case records.

This we found to be the case in the Wisconsin probation and parole system. The records are used extensively for research by graduate students from the University of Wisconsin and the University of Wisconsin-Milwaukee. In the main these students are looking for basic factual data in the records and are not searching for details of the "dynamics" of the psychological inter-action between probation and parole officers and offenders.

USE OF RECORDS IN TEACHING

Traditionally, case records have been the chief source of teaching the principles of casework. Case records from social agencies are edited to insure anonymity and are then reproduced for discussion purposes for casework classes in schools of social work. Teachers want a maximum of "process" so that students will have opportunities for detailed discussions of the relationships between the caseworker and the client.

Agencies have also used the case record as a basis for the induction of inexperienced workers to the agency. Beginning workers often record in great detail—sometimes first submitting materials in longhand—so that the supervisor will be able to carry on this educational activity.[17]

The Wisconsin probation and parole system is no exception. Field work units for students from the Schools of Social Work of the University of Wisconsin and the University of Wisconsin-Milwaukee are maintained in Madison and Milwaukee. Beginning workers are also expected to record in somewhat greater detail.

The development of tape recording and its extensive use in education has brought some of the assumed educational values of case records into question. No matter how extensive the recording of "process" the case record does not have the details of a tape recording. Furthermore, the record is probably not as valuable to the learning of the beginning worker as his first-hand observation of an experienced worker.

We found this to be true in our study. Thus there is increased recognition of the limitations of case records as a basis for teaching casework and for the induction of new workers. This is not to imply that case records have no educational values. Rather, the implication is that these are not major factors and should be so considered in the determination of the content and format of case records.

[17]Bristol, Handbook on Social Case Recording (1936).

EXTENT AND ADEQUACY OF RECORDS AS JUDGED BY ADMINISTRATIVE OFFICERS

As previously noted, all experimental folders were tagged with special identification. Between October 1, 1963 and July 1, 1964 all users of the records were required to indicate their use on a special form. On July 1, 1964 an analysis was made of the extent of the use of these records.

On July 1, 1964 there were 928 experimental records. Of these, 856 had no record of use during the period October 1, 1963 to July 1, 1964. Due to errors, 18 of the records had had no "Evaluation Forms" placed in them. The remaining 64 records had been used one or more times. This means that only 6.9 percent of the records had been used according to the listings on the "Evaluation Forms."

The actual usage of records was probably somewhat larger than this. Despite the administrative orders and attempts to supervise the system it is obvious that some who used the records did not record the fact. Some of them may have forgotten the requirement. Others who use records secure large groups of records at one time. Such is the case of persons who use records to secure information regarding potential transfers of inmates from one institution to another. Using a large group of records at one time they may not have time to record their usage. For whatever reason it is obvious that not all of the users recorded their usage.

The central office files are "open." That is, there is easy access to them by all employees and any employee can secure records merely by going to the files and taking them. A "closed" filing system where only one employee could check out records and thereby keep track of individual employee usage could have eliminated this problem.

The actual usage of records is also greater than indicated because of the duplicate copies of records, the usage of which went unrecorded. Members of the Parole Board have their own copies of records. Presumably they read the record of every case they hear and take the records with them to hearings.

We have no way of knowing the extent to which usage was not recorded. As already indicated, however, we know that it occurred in some instances. We know that the total use of records is restricted to a relatively small number of employees. It is doubtful if the total number of users, including Parole Board Members, is double the amount recorded. Even if one arbitrarily declares that 15 percent of the records were actually used, there were still 85 percent of the records that were unused for a period of nine months.

The records, as already noted, were used by a comparatively small number of employees. The Supervisor of Interstate Placements, the two Regional Administrators, the Supervisor of Institutional Classification, and the Supervisor of Education were the principal users.

The users of records in the central office have definite purposes in mind when they read case records. They seldom read a record in its entirety. Rather they are searching, as rapidly as possible, for answers to specific questions. For example, the Supervisor of Classification had a request for the transfer of an inmate from one institution to another. From the record he attempted to secure information about the institutional adjustment of the inmate, the nature of the offense, the inmate's possible release date, and other facts that would assist him in making the decision. The Executive Secretary of the Special Review Board (sex crimes parole board) sought data about the prior adjustment of the inmate when he had been on probation. To give still another example: the Supervisor of Interstate Placements read a record to secure information about an offender who wished to be released under supervision to a neighboring state.

Although the central office staff uses a limited number of records there are several points that should be kept in mind. The first is that the use of the records is crucial in making decisions by certain strategic administrative officers. Regional Administrators make decisions regarding the revocation of parole. In doing so they rely primarily upon the records in the central office. In many cases they also call the probation and parole officer on the telephone to secure the most recent information on the case. Nevertheless, the record is often the sole basis for making a decision. Another point is that although a limited number of cases out of the total number are used for decision-making in the central office no one can tell what cases may be used. As noted above, only about 15 percent of the cases are read by administrative officers. All records, however, have to be prepared on the assumption that they may be included in this 15 percent.

Administrative officers who used the cases in the central office did not demand extensive recording. Actually, they want specific facts and they want them in a hurry. Abbreviated recording is at least as satisfactory to them as chronological recording. Only 10.4 percent of the administrative officers who used the abbreviated records in the experimental group found them to be unsatisfactory. In fact, 21.8 percent of them reported the experimental records to be "very good" and an additional 32.1 percent reported them to be "good." Many of the administrative officers were especially pleased with the abbreviated recording because it enabled them to find specific information faster than they could have found it in the regular records.

It is also interesting to note that administrative officers who used records to aid in decision-making appeared to put a somewhat greater emphasis upon the records when discussing this with members of the research staff than actually was the case in practice. Direct telephone conversations with the officers, as already indicated, appeared to be of greater significance to them in decision-making than one might believe by discussing the problem with them. Despite this fact, it is still true that one of the principal uses of records is for decision-making by administrative officers in the central office.

CONCLUSIONS

A number of conclusions regarding the utility of case records in probation and parole can be drawn from our study in Wisconsin:

1. Case records in probation and parole agencies, if the Wisconsin agency is typical, have limited usage by a relatively small number of persons. The Wisconsin study showed that only 6.9 percent of the experimental records were read by anyone in the central office during a nine-month period. Even if as many as 15 percent of the records were actually used during this period it means that 85 percent of the records were not used.

The records were used by a small number of key administrative officers who were searching for specific factual information. Regional Administrators, the Supervisor of Interstate Placements, the Supervisor of Classification, and the Supervisor of Education were the principal users.

2. The small percentage of records used for administrative purposes are very strategic in this decision-making. The records are often the principal basis for the revocation of parole, the transfer of an inmate from one institution to another, and the granting of permission for a parolee to be supervised in another state. Because of the significance of these decisions the records should contain, in readily accessible form, the factual information essential for action.

3. Probation and parole officers themselves are principal users of case records. They use the records to know what action was taken by their predecessors, for basic identifying facts about cases, and as a plan for treatment. The process of recording is significant to probation and parole officers because it is through this process that they are able to organize their thinking about a case.

4. The case record is not the chief basis for the supervision of probation and parole officers. Supervisors use the record to call their attention to specific facts about a case. The basic tool in supervision, however, is personal discussion between the supervisor and the officer.

5. The value of case records as tools in teaching has been over-emphasized. Despite the fact that case records have been widely used in schools of social work and in in-service training programs it is apparent that other devices—such as tape recording and direct observation of an experienced worker by an inexperienced worker—have more value.

6. Case records have limited value in research. Factual information—such as offense committed, age and sex of offender, sentence, etc.—can be secured from case records. The research potential of records for studies of the psychological and sociological aspects of offenders, however, is limited.

The limited use of case records plus the tremendous amount of staff time devoted to the preparation and maintenance of records indicates that revisions of the recording system are needed. Probation and parole agencies could benefit from detailed analyses of case recording. Such analyses should lead to a streamlining of the records.

28

Some Reflections on Measuring Probation Outcome

ROBERT H. VASOLI

When questions are raised about the price tags on correctional procedures, especially the more expensive ones, a fairly common response is that they entail savings in "human costs" that defy calculation. After all, how can we translate into dollars and cents the amount of money society "saves" when a parolee goes straight, or what it is worth to a family when its head is placed on probation instead of being sentenced to prison? Yet, when the chips are down, justifications for these same correctional procedures are, for good or bad, usually erected upon a quantitative base. Thus one statistical justification which enjoys considerable vogue is the estimate—and it is scarcely anything more—that imprisonment is about 10 times as expensive as probation.

Cost factors, whether calculated in abstract or monetary terms, are but one form of statistical rationale behind probation. No less important are high rates of success and low rates of failure. According to *Persons Under the Supervision of the Federal Probation System* for fiscal 1965, slightly better than 80 percent of all federal probationers who were removed from supervision during the fiscal year 1964 showed no probation violations. Judging from annual reports issued by other jurisdictions, impressively high success rates

SOURCE. *Federal Probation*, XXXI, September 1967, pp. 24–32.

are not peculiar to the federal system. Besides serving to justify probation, violation and success rates are also used to extract appropriations from legislative bodies. Legislatures, as is well known, have traditionally been reluctant to invest in correctional systems and programs. If cost comparisons between imprisonment and probation can be used to show the fiscal soundness of probation, low violation rates can be similarly used to demonstrate its worth as a correctional instrument. In a very real sense, then, the effectiveness of a probation system can stand or fall on its violation rates. These rates, in turn, depend not only on the behavior of probationers but also on how success and failure are defined and measured. Just as average hitters in baseball can be transformed into stars by making a .250 average the mark of excellence, so too can probation failures be made into successes—or failures—by changing the criteria of probation outcome.

"OBJECTIVE" MEASURES OF OUTCOME

Although the frame of reference for the ensuing discussion of probation outcome will be the Federal Probation System, this article is not meant to be a critique of that system. As it happens, I am on more familiar terms with the federal system than with others. All the same, much of what follows has relevance for probation in lesser jurisdictions. This follows from the fact that probation everywhere is marked by certain basic uniformities and from the fact that the administration of justice on the federal level often provides models for state and local probation agencies grappling with similar problems.

Finally, although recent changes in federal statistical procedures might partly nullify comments that follow, the reader is reminded that many nonfederal probation systems have yet to adopt these changes.

Whatever the jurisdiction, probation outcome can be gauged in several ways.

1. *Filing of Petition.* It may be evaluated on the basis of whether the probation officer petitions for revocation. Should the petition be granted, the court may issue a bench warrant for the apprehension of the probationer. Next comes the revocation hearing itself, with the probation officer, the probationer, and the defense counsel present.[1] At hearing's end, the court decides whether to impose or execute the sentence previously suspended, or to allow probation to continue.

2. *Issuance of a Warrant.* A second possible measure of probation outcome

---

[1]An oft-asked question is whether the probationer is entitled to counsel during a revocation hearing. Three years ago the chief judge for the Northern District of Indiana, Robert A. Grant, directed that probationers brought before his court for revocation be represented by counsel if they desire. If the probationer cannot afford a lawyer, the court will appoint one. More recently, on February 13, 1967, the Supreme Court agreed to consider whether a probationer has a constitutional right to counsel during a revocation hearing.

the counterpart of a criterion used in some parole prediction studies,[2] is the issuance or nonissuance of a warrant. Although a petition for revocation and the issuance of a bench warrant usually go hand in hand, they are by no means merely different ways of referring to the same thing. The court, after all, is not constrained to approve the probation officer's recommendation that the probationer be arrested preparatory to the revocation hearing.

3. *Revocation.* Probation success or failure may be determined by whether revocation does, in fact, occur. Neither by heeding a petition for revocation nor by issuing a warrant does the court guarantee that it will decide for revocation. The judge who presides over the hearing might simply admonish the probationer, or warn him, then rule that he be continued on probation. When probation is revoked, it is supposedly an ultimate sign of the offender's inability to benefit from supervision.

4. *Recidivism.* Whether an offender succeeds or fails on probation may be reckoned in terms of recidivism. In order to bring about revocation, recidivism must ordinarily entail the commission of at least one felony or a series of misdemeanors. Although felonious behavior would seem automatically to result in revocation, in practice this is not always the case. The writer, in a study of 814 federal offenders probationed between 1946 and 1960, found that 155 of 622 probationers officially counted as successes had committed at least one felony during their probation terms.[3] Indeed, as Table 1 shows, several probationers committed more than one felony.

How could this be? There were a number of ways it could occur, but typically it happened when a federal probationer was convicted and imprisoned for a state offense. Instead of filing a detainer against him, the district probation officer would often terminate probation, thereby relinquishing jurisdiction over the probationer to the state. The district office, in its monthly statistical report to Washington, seldom indicated why probation had been terminated. Since 1963 this situation has been largely rectified by supplementing district statistical reports with information provided by FBI "flash notices." Accordingly, if a probationer serving a state term has been previously counted a success, the Administrative Office will, upon receipt of the "flash notice," shift him into a violation column. This is a vast improvement over the older method of bookkeeping, though it is still possible, as will be shown later, for serious offenses committed by probationers to go unrecorded in the national violation tally.

A variation on the recidivism theme has been suggested by one noted criminologist, who recommends extending it to include the postprobation period. He maintains that "the decisive test of effectiveness must be the extent to which those who are subjected to probation refrain from committing further

[2]See for example Lloyd E. Ohlin, *Selection for Parole.* New York: Russell Sage Foundation, 1951, pp. 43–45.

[3]Robert H. Vasoli, "The Predictive Value of the Federal Presentence Investigation." unpublished doctoral dissertation, Notre Dame, Indiana, 1964, pp. 126–32.

Table 1   *Felonies Committed during Probation Term by 155 Probationers Officially Counted as Having Completed Probation Successfully*

Offense[a]	Total Times Committed
All Offenses[b]	184
Homicide	1
Rape	2
Robbery	12
Aggravated assault	1
Burglary	31
Larceny-Theft (except auto theft)	33
Auto theft	34
Forgery	16
Embezzlement and fraud	26
Offenses against family and children	12
Narcotics	6
Other	10

[a]Categories adapted from *Uniform Crime Reports.*
[b]Some probationers committed more than one offense.

offenses once the orders have been terminated; for offenders may respond to probation while under supervision, yet lapse again into crime."[4]

5. *Adjustment Criterion.* Probation outcome can be evaluated in terms of "adjustment." Thus, Rumney and Murphy regard probation outcome as "adjustment to a number of basic areas of social life."[5] That being the case, a probationer is considered adjusted if "he has established satisfactory relationships in his domestic and economic affairs and is free from serious physical and mental handicaps."[6]

6. *Combining Criteria.* Finally, it is possible to determine probation outcome by various combinations of the measures listed above.

ASSESSING MEASURES OF OUTCOME

As might be expected, each of the measures has both advantages and disadvantages. The researcher in quest of a statistically reliable index of probation outcome is likely to choose from among the petition for revocation, the warrant, revocation itself, and recidivism. All four measures are readily quantified and all are ostensibly objective, at least in the sense that their pre-

[4]L. Radzinowicz, ed., *The Results of Probation*, Vol. X, English Studies in Criminal Science. London: Macmillan & Co., Ltd., 1958, p. 2.
[5]Jay Rumney and Joseph F. Murphy, *Probation and Social Adjustment.* New Brunswick, N.J.: Rutgers University Press, 1952, p. 12.
[6]*Ibid.*, p. 93.

sence or absence should be apparent to anyone examining a case to ascertain how it turned out. Viewed another way, however, their objective character is not beyond reproach. While they may be objective from a statistician's perspective, they can be highly subjective from the standpoint of probation officers and judges. In other words, behavior that impels one probation officer to seek revocation might be overlooked by another. Similarly, judges vary in their response to petitions for revocation, in their issuance of warrants, and in their acceptance of grounds for revocation.

As previously shown, not even felonious recidivism is a guarantee of revocation. Moreover, although these five criteria are amenable to quantification, in practice their accuracy is a mere approximation of reality. No matter which measure is used, it does not represent the actual number of violations probationers commit. This is due, in part, to the probation officers' discretionary powers which enable them to overlook certain instances of misbehavior, or to handle without setting in motion the machinery leading to revocation, or without reporting the violations to a statistical collections bureau. Discrepancies between the actual and reported number of violations are also due to the sheer inability of probation officers to be cognizant of all the misbehavior committed by probationers. Total awareness presumes total surveillance, something which cannot be achieved even in a maximum security prison.

If probation failure is equated with reversion to crime and probation success with its avoidance, then recidivism is obviously the most appropriate of the so-called objective measures of outcome. The recidivist could be counted a failure even when his criminality does not lead to a petition, a warrant, or revocation. However, this is not as cut and dried as it initially seems, if only because the gravity of recidivism varies from case to case. Also, the petition, the warrant, and revocation may be directly due to recidivism. The situation here is analogous to that of indexes of crime in general. Students of crime rates remind us that "crimes known to the police" is the best available index of the actual volume of crime because it is the one closest to the criminal act. By the same token, recidivism would be superior to the other "objective" indicators of probation failures since it is closest to crimes known to have been committed by probationers. Yet the weakness inherent in a measure based on recidivism alone becomes all too apparent when it is realized that criminality is not the only form of misbehavior by probationers. Probation can be breached by violating conditions of probation other than those which explicitly prohibit lawbreaking. Such breaches of probation, usually called "technical" violations, will be discussed in detail.

ASSESSING "ADJUSTMENT"

The petition, the warrant, revocation, and recidivism may be relatively objective as measures go, but they also share an essentially negative focus.

Since they ordinarily reflect antisocial behavior, some writers oppose their use as principal outcome criteria. It has been suggested that we rely instead on "adjustment," a broader criterion that directs our attention to the more positive aspects of the probationer's response to supervision. Needless to say, this approach dovetails neatly with the current emphasis on rehabilitation. At the same time, the errant ways of some probationers need not be ignored, for if "adjustment" signifies success, then "maladjustment" can denote failure. "Maladjustment," of course, can include any or all of the more objective but negative measures cited above. Thus, the reasoning goes, the "adjustment-maladjustment" scheme is preferable to other measures because they can be subsumed under it and because it takes positive as well as negative behavior into account.

Conceivably, a probationer who occasionally ventures into petty crime but succeeds in mending a shaky marriage and in improving his financial status and work habits might wind up being classified as "adjusted" when a balance is struck between his good and bad points. Indeed, success in this sense need not be restricted to probationers who commit infrequent petty offenses. It is entirely possible that a probationer's behavior is, despite one major relapse into crime, so exemplary in other respects that the probation officer and judge favor continuing his probation. For all that may be said in behalf of these possibilities, their very existence suggests that the "adjustment" criterion is not an unmixed blessing. If considerable wrongdoing can lurk beneath comparatively specific measures like the petition, the warrant, recidivism, and revocation, a measure as broad as "adjustment" is likely to conceal an even greater amount of forbidden activity. Such activity will be masked by the probation officer's judgment that there was enough approved behavior for "adjustment" to have occurred.

Since "adjustment" is as vague as it is comprehensive, it does not lend itself to the kind of quantification and objectivity associated with quality statistical data. To be sure, a tally can be made of probationers labeled "adjusted" or "maladjusted." But in the final analysis both labels depend almost as much on the personal judgments of probation officers as they do on the actual behavior of probationers so designated. Admittedly, subjectivity can distort the other measures as well, though hardly to the same extent as is the case with "adjustment." No doubt there would be some consensus on what "adjustment" and "maladjustment" mean; few probation officers are likely to initiate revocation proceedings with a probationer who has managed to steer clear of major trouble, and few are likely to regard felony recidivists as "adjusted." Beyond this, however, we can only guess as to how well developed consensus among probation officers would be. A probationer who has lived up to the letter but not the spirit of probation might be deemed "maladjusted" by some officers even though no formal action is taken to terminate probation and invoke the sentence previously suspended. In a word, unless the meaning of "adjustment" and "maladjustment" is further clarified, they are doomed to be nebulous catchalls that tell us little about how probation turned out

Another objection to the "adjustment" criterion, at least in the sense of the Rumney-Murphy definition, is that it implies a virtual utopian faith in what probation can do. Presumably the primary end of probation is to make the offender a law-abiding citizen once more but without subjecting him to the alleged evils of imprisonment. To the extent that this is true, it is difficult to see why probation should be saddled with the herculean task of revamping his entire existence. If the probationer succeeds in obeying the law, do we have a right to expect that he should also become, among other things, a model husband, a dependable breadwinner, and a devout church-goer? The establishment of "satisfactory relationships" in the probationer's "domestic and economic affairs," a goal devoutly to be wished, may well be functionally related to newly found or reborn respect for law. But to regard probation as the main instrument for bringing this state of affairs to pass is to attribute to it an omnipotence it surely does not possess. Probation, after all, is only one of a multitude of social forces at work on the offender. And while the skillful probation officer will try to mobilize and exploit as many of these forces as possible for the offender's rehabilitation, this is a far cry from the assumption that probation has the wherewithal to replace, or take precedence over, or even organize, all the other factors working to shape the offender's attitudes, behavior, and destiny.

PROBLEMS WITH POSTPROBATION RECIDIVISM

A similar objection applies to the idea that the crucial test of the efficacy of probation is whether the offender reverts to crime during the post probation period. If after probation ends the ex-probationer refrains from further criminal behavior, it may be said that probation has yielded a highly desirable though not obligatory dividend. It is so much icing on the cake. As many probation officers will attest, frequently it is problem enough to steer the probationer clear of lawbreaking during his probation term, much less after its termination. Furthermore, if something goes awry during the postprobation period, it does not automatically follow that probation is to blame. By the same token, if nothing untoward occurs after probation ends, it is equally illogical to assume that all the credit should go to probation. Once supervision stops, the probationer is likely to be subjected to myriad forces, pressures, and frustrations that are wholly unrelated to the probation term itself. If these new elements, alone or in combination with the old, produce new criminality or law-abiding behavior, it is scarcely logical to assume a simple cause-and-effect relationship between the probation term and whatever might follow it. Probation may or may not be the hero or villain.

Two other difficulties, each on a more practical plane, arise when postprobation recidivism is used to gauge outcome. Keeping abreast of the probationer's behavior, a trying task during the probation term, is that much harder when supervision is halted. Unless probation officers take it upon themselves to devote considerable attention to the activities of former probationers as well as those on their current caseload, a measure incorporating postprobation recidivism is bound to lead to inflated success rates. A second difficulty concerns the length of time the postprobation term must be free of criminality before probation is adjudged successful. Reputable manufacturers rarely if ever offer lifetime warranties on the best of products whose performance is ordinarily simpler and more predictable than that of human beings. Hence this method of measuring probation calls for the establishment of limits on the amount of time the postprobation period must be free of recidivism before probation is deemed successful. Such limits must inevitably be arbitrary, akin to the medical practice of defining postoperative cancer patients as "cured" if no relapse occurs within 5 years.

FEDERAL OUTCOME CRITERIA

Until 1963 the Federal Probation System used revocations to measure probation success and failure. At that time the Administrative Office of the United States Courts began to publish outcome statistics that were broken down into "no violations," "major violations," and "minor violations." The latter embraced (1) "technical" (noncriminal) infractions of the rules of probation, (2) convictions and sentences leading to incarceration of less than 90 days, and (3) new offenses that resulted in a probation term of less than a year.

A "major" violation, in contrast, referred to arrest and detention on a felony charge, conviction and incarceration for 90 days or more, and absconding with felony charges outstanding.[7] Beginning in 1965, these outcome categories were further refined by separating "technical" violations from "minor" ones. Thus violations are now classified as either "major," "minor" or "technical."[8]

Criminal statistics are like the weather—nearly everyone complains about their sorry state but seldom does anything to improve them. The Federal Probation System is a notable exception to this rule, for it has on several occasions revised its statistical procedures in the hope that the changes would produce more meaningful and useful outcome data. Perhaps even more commendable has been its readiness to modify the basis for calculating violation rates, for such revisions can make the system look bad by creating an apparent rise in the proportion of failures. Prior to 1963, when violations were synonymous with revocations, the latter were typically based on felonious recidivism. The violation rate was primarily a reflection of what are now called "major violations." The changes installed in 1963, when "minor" (including "technical") as well

[7]*Annual Report of the Director of the Administrative Office of the United States Courts*, 1964 footnote 3, p. 178.

[8]Administrative Office of the United States Courts, *Persons Under the Supervision of the Federal Probation System, Fiscal Year 1965*, p. 20.

as "major violations" were tallied, meant risking a "paper" increase in the aggregate violation rate.

Another important modification in the offing, reported in *Persons Under the Supervision of the Federal Probation System* for fiscal 1965, is a plan to compute outcome rates for annual cohorts of probationers. Outcome rates will then be based on the calendar or fiscal year in which offenders were placed on probation rather than on the calendar or fiscal year in which their probation terminated. Under present procedure the violation rate for any given fiscal year is something of a misnomer. Since this rate is obtained by dividing the total number of removals during a year into the total number of violations for that same year, the year when these offenders were placed on probation is not taken into account. The rate for fiscal 1963, for example, encompasses offenders placed on probation from the end of fiscal 1958 to the outset of fiscal 1963. It is conceivable that those placed on probation during 1960 contributed more than their share to the 1963 violation rate. But such a fluctuation would be "lost" in the current method of calculating violation rates. The cohort method, on the other hand, will provide more accurate violation rates for any given year as well as more relevant data for plotting outcome trends over longer periods of time.

The federal system's three-fold breakdown of violations does not really represent a radical departure from the various measures of outcome discussed above. The petition for revocation and the issuance of a warrant may be sought because of what have now been termed "major," "minor," or "technical" violations. As regards recidivism, relatively mild instances of it are subsumed under "minor violations," while relatively serious recidivism is embraced by "major violations." Lastly, all three types of violations can be utilized as indicators of varying degrees of "maladjustment," and the absence of violations as a sign of "adjustment."

SOME RECOMMENDATIONS

However high the calibre of federal probation statistics, room for improvement still remains. The "major-minor-technical" classification, while superior to its predecessors, reveals little about the ultimate outcome of probation. We may know that a certain percentage of terminated cases were tallied as major violations, but there is no way to determine from the data now published how many violators were continued on probation and how many ended up in prison. It is like knowing all the details of a game except the final score.

Second, it would be instructive if the outcome data indicated the frequency of violation per offender. As matters stand, the probationer who commits one felony and the probationer who commits five both appear in the outcome statistics as "major" violations. The same thing happens with "minor" and "technical" violations. Lumping cases into categories is practically inevitable when making statistical compilations, but in this instance it masks two important concerns: (1) the total number of known violations committed by all probationers who went off supervision during the year, and (2) the number of violations per offender. It might even be desirable to have the outcome data show how often "major" violations are accompanied by "minor" and "technical" ones. Further, if these data were cross-tabulated with revocations, we would have a much clearer idea of the amount and types of misbehavior the courts will tolerate before deciding to revoke probation.

These two recommendations involve data already available. Undoubtedly the Division of Procedural Studies and Statistics has on hand masses of outcome data which, because of time, space and staff limitations, do not appear in the annual reports. Further, to print all the data would be self-defeating; the average reader would be smothered by tables and numbers. All the same, these facets of outcome would be valuable supplements to what is now published.

ABSCONDERS AND ABSCONDING

Third, the practice of counting absconding a "major" violation only when it is accompanied by a felony charge raises serious questions. Suspension of sentence occurred under common law long before John Augustus volunteered to advise and act as surety for the first misdemeanant placed in his care. In other words, probation since Augustus has consisted of two irreducible elements: suspension of sentence *and* supervision. Although in many jurisdictions the supervisory aspect of probation is frequently perfunctory, it is nevertheless an absolute prerequisite if probation is to function as it is supposed to function. Since absconding entails cessation of supervision, it is manifestly one of the more serious forms of probation violation. So strongly does it run against the grain of probation that it should always be a "major" violation, irrespective of the conditions which may or may not accompany it. Perhaps the reluctance to class all absconders as "major" violators is an outgrowth of the lack of agreement on precisely what absconding means. Supposedly, it refers to clandestine and unwarranted departure from supervision. But in practice there are no universally accepted norms that define how long and under what circumstances a probationer must be absent before he is declared an absconder.

At bottom, absconding means pretty much what the individual probation officer judges it to mean. It may refer to breaking off supervision by flight from the jurisdiction, flight within the jurisdiction, disruption of supervision for 3 months, for 12 months, or even to failure to file a succession of monthly reports by a probationer who has no willful intent to evade supervision. Despite the absence of firm guidelines, it still remains difficult to understand why instances of absconding not involving a felony should be defined as merely "technical" violations.

"HIDDEN" VIOLATIONS

Fifth, reporting procedures in the district probation offices could be tightened so that the annual outcome statistics will include violations now "buried" in the files. As noted, FBI "flash notices" have been used since 1963 to augment the monthly statistical reports sent to Washington by the district probation offices. This drew the net more securely around violations that previously went uncounted in the annual outcome figures. But the "flash notice," of course, presumes that the probationer-recidivist has been arrested, fingerprinted, and that the prints have been forwarded to the FBI. Needless to say, this does not always happen, if only because some law enforcement agencies do not submit fingerprint data to the FBI. Apart from this, the "flash notice" deals almost exclusively with criminal activity; that is, "major" and "minor" violations. One "technical" violation, absconding, may show up on the notice, but by and large other "technical" violations appear only in an implicit way. Thus, if a probationer under the supervision of the Northern District of Illinois is apprehended in Santa Fe for auto theft, it may be deduced that he has committed the "technical" violation of leaving the district. By and large, however, the "flash notice" reveals very little about "technical" violations.

The "hidden" violations referred to here do not include breaches of probation which never come to the attention of persons in a position to report them. Criminal and "technical" infractions not known to the police or the probation officer always will remain beyond the pale of outcome statistics. Instead, our concern is with violations that are recorded in the probation files but which, for one reason or another, never make their way to Washington. Careful study of 814 cases on file in one district turned up many such violations. In this district, it might be added, "flash notices" were requested as a matter of routine, which made it possible to check violations appearing thereon against the rest of the probationer's file.

Not unexpectedly, criminal breaches of probation are more likely to be reported than noncriminal infractions, and serious criminality is more likely to be reported than lesser crimes. All the same, close inspection of the files revealed unreported violations that were "major" as well as "minor" and "technical." Nor did these violations reach Washington via the "flash notice."

"Technical" violations are the nether world of probation outcome statistics. Unless they are responsible for revocation, or unless they accompany a "major" or "minor" violation that results in revocation, "technical" violations rarely come to the attention of the probation system's statisticians. Their unexplored character is compounded by the fact that "technical" violations alone seldom lead to revocation. Among the 814 probationers were 192 revocations, but only about 10 percent of the revocations were brought about by "technical" violations only. Most of these cases involved absconding.

No evidence of any violation could be found in the records of 252 of 622 probationers who, according to the official statistics, successfully completed their probation terms. The files for the remaining 370 official successes contained the recorded but unreported "technical" violations which are listed by type and frequency in Table 2.

At first glance, these violations appear to be mere peccadilloes. What, after all, is so terrible about a late or neglected monthly report or the failure to keep an appointment with the probation officer? Is this not much ado about nothing? Such questions might be effective rhetoric, but they unfortunately brush aside a genuine issue in the keeping of probation statistics. For there are times when one man's peccadillo is another's cause for revocation. Seemingly trivial infractions like "curfew violation" or "association with another probationer" have been the only grounds offered for revocation. In the same vein, granting that delinquent monthly reports are ordinarily harmless, inadvertent slips, in some instances three or four consecutive "slips" turn out to be, at least retrospectively, all the evidence needed to show that a probationer absconded.

There are no clearly discernible patterns that point to when "technical" violations lead to revocation and when they do not. Indeed, as was already indicated, not even absconding follows any set pattern. Some probationers were deemed absconders after a 3-month break in supervision, but one probationer who was AWOL for 22 months and another missing for 33 were never officially regarded as having absconded. If there is any semblance of a pattern with respect to "technical" violations, it might be a slight tendency for probation officers to be somewhat less tolerant of "technical" violations of younger offenders.

These findings barely scratch the surface of the problems presented by "technical" violations. There is a crying need for further exploration into the incidence of "technical" violations, their relation to criminal infractions,

Table 2 *"Technical" Violations Committed during Probation Term by 370 Probationers Officially Counted as Having Completed Probation Successfully*

Type of Violation	Total Times Committed
All violations[a]	1453
Delinquent monthly report[b]	954
Missed appointment with USPO	322
Left jurisdiction without permission	87
Moved without permission	67
Falsified monthly report	9
Associated with forbidden person (e.g., parolees)	11
Curfew violation	3

[a] Most of the probationers had more than one violation.
[b] Report late or never submitted.

and the types of responses they elicit from judges and probation officers. "Technical" violations, to a greater extent than the other kinds, point up the sizable discretionary powers at the disposal of the court and its probation staff. The court's discretion comes into play in its readiness to accept or reject certain violations as sufficient grounds for revocation. But "technical" violations, in contrast with "minor" and "major" ones, generate additional discretion inasmuch as it is the court's prerogative to establish special conditions of probation over and beyond the rules that apply to all probationers. These special norms can direct or forbid virtually anything under the sun, from insisting that the probationer write weekly letters to his probation officer to prohibiting the probationer from drinking.

Certain discretionary powers which inhere in the probation officer's role are also in a very real sense judicial. It is he who decides whether a violation will be reported, winked at, dealt with by a warning, or made part of a revocation petition. The writer knows of one jurisdiction, for example, where the probation officers were exceedingly reluctant to report any violations, including the most serious ones, because they felt the judge was disposed to overkill in his handling of violations. The judge in question had publicly avowed to revoke probation and impose the maximum sentence if a probationer so much as ran a red light. Sentences meted out in the cases immediately following this utterance proved that the threat had substance. Needless to say, violations kept from the judge were also withheld from statistical tallies of probation failures. At all events, we know next to nothing substantive about decision-making on the part of judges and probation officers in the whole revocation process. We do know, however, that even in the federal system violation rates vary from one district to another. These variations are mainly due to differences in supervision and in the selection of offenders for probation. Regrettably, we can but speculate on precisely how these and other pertinent variables are intertwined.

CONCLUSION

What, if anything, emerges from all this? Perhaps the most obvious conclusion is that probation success and failure are very difficult things to define and measure. This stark admission helps to explain why none of the existing measures of probation is entirely satisfactory. At worst, they exaggerate the rate of success and understate the rate of failure; at best, they afford close approximations of what we wish to know. In view of their imperfections, why bother with them at all?

They are worth bothering with because we must have some reasonably systematic way of determining whether probation is doing what it is supposed to do. Assessing the results of probation even by means of crude yardsticks is vastly better than relying on impressions, guesses, and intuition. Yet for all the optimism of behavioral science, it appears that most measurements of human behavior are destined to be mere estimates, some more exact than others. But at least we can be unrelenting in our efforts to diminish the margin of error that springs from limitations that inhere in our measuring devices and in our subject matter.

It would be rather futile to try to select any one measure of probation outcome as the best way to reckon success and failure. Far more preferable would be the use of several measures, either presented side by side or incorporated into a composite measure of some kind. Publication of outcome rates based on a variety of measures would facilitate more balanced analysis than is now possible. It could show at a glance, among other things, how often a petition leads to a warrant, how often the warrant results in revocation, how often recidivism is the basis for these procedures, the proportions of "major," "minor," and "technical" violations found in other measures, the incidence of absconding, and how often these measures are associated with "adjustment" and "maladjustment." Development of a composite index based on several measures would allow the assignment of different weights to each of the index's components. Then, by means of a scoring system of some sort, it would be possible to determine degrees of success and failure with greater precision than is now afforded by the "major-minor-technical" violation scheme.[9]

Of the measures discussed above, "adjustment" is, in our present state of knowledge, probably the least satisfactory. It is much easier to determine when a petition has been drawn up, a warrant issued, when a violation has been committed, when revocation has occurred, and even when a probationer has recidivated than it is to decide whether he is "adjusted" or "maladjusted." But this is not to advocate abandonment of attempts to work out an effective way to reckon probation in terms of "adjustment." However, if this approach to outcome is to have real utility, the concept "adjustment" must be greatly refined and clarified. This might be done by formulating more objective indices of "adjustment," such as "steady employment," "regular restitution payments," and so on. Indeed, a list of indexes might also include so-called negative measures like recidivism. Degree of adjustment could be calculated by assigning numerical values to positive and negative indexes, then using these values to arrive at an overall "adjustment" score. Similarly, some thought might profitably be given to the formulation of an adjustment scale along the lines of instruments which have been developed in efforts to measure such phenomena as "authoritarianism" and "dogmatism." In this connection, it is interesting to note that during the early 1930's the then budding Federal

---

[9]Professor Marvin E. Wolfgang proposes the use of "seriousness scores" to obviate much of the difficulty in making valid comparisons of the criminal statistics of different countries, or of different jurisdictions within a given country. Although the "major-minor-technical" plan is in effect a crude scale indicating gravity of violation, application of the concept of "seriousness scores" to probation might provide more discriminating measures of outcome along the success-failure continuum. See Marvin E. Wolfgang, "International Criminal Statistics: A Proposal," *Journal of Criminal Law, Criminology and Police Science*, 58, 1967, pp. 65–69.

Probation System experimented with a scale designed to assist probation officers in rating their charges for degree of adjustment. For reasons now obsure, the scale fell into disuse. Perhaps the time is ripe for resurrecting the ideal of devising a more sophisticated instrument for measuring "adjustment."

Rates of success and failure are to a probation system what strikeouts and runs allowed are to a pitcher. Even though they may not tell us as definitively whether a system has attained star status, they can provide vital information on how a system is performing. It almost goes without saying that the more realistic and accurate these rates are, the greater will be our confidence in the validity of our judgments on a system's effectiveness. Equally important, outcome rates provide us with invaluable clues to whether the courts are selecting the "right" offenders for probation. For all their imperfections, then, measures of outcome can still perform crucial functions in any attempt to make quantitative judgements on the efficacy of any probation system.

29

Factors in the Decision-Making of North Carolina Probation Officers

JOHN P. REED AND CHARLES E. KING

Decision-making has been the concern of a number of a recent publications.[1] The treatment accorded it has usually been in terms of levels, processes, and factors which have ranged from group size, pressures, and leadership to psychological and ethical values. Whatever the treatment, however, the focus has generally been on relatively high-status performers and law-abiding behavior.

This paper is concerned with decision-making factors. Unlike other publications, the following discussion makes use of written cases and focuses on the probation officer and his choice of decisional alternatives. Factors operative in the decisions of law enforcement officers are generally of an unknown quality. Except for studies of judicial decision-making, the literature in this area consists of inspirational messages, bread-and-butter complaints of low wages and heavy caseloads, and polemics for upgrading the service.[2]

SOURCE. *Journal of Research in Crime and Delinquency*, **3**, July 1966, pp. 120–128. Reprinted with the permission of the National Council on Crime and Delinquency.

[1]Glendon Schubert, ed., *Judicial Decision-Making* (Glencoe, Ill.: Free Press, 1963); Paul Wasserman and Fred S. Silander, *Decision-Making, An Annotated Bibliography* (Ithaca, N.Y.: Graduate School of Business and Public Administration, Cornell University, 1958).

[2]Don C. Gibbons, *Changing the Lawbreaker* (Englewood Cliffs. N. J.: Prentice-Hall, 1965) pp. 220–21.

DESIGN AND POPULATION

The questionnaire we devised and administered to North Carolina probation officers consisted of eight cases randomly selected from the files of the North Carolina Probation Department, a cover sheet, and the Eysenck-Nagel "Survey of Opinion."[3] Each case selected was digested, condensed, and presented in the same manner. The format included a fact situation, background characteristics of the probationer, his current violation, decisional summaries, and a multiple choice question which confronted the probation officer with decisional alternatives for each of four different case situations—(1) when the officer alone knew of the violation; (2) when a reliable party told him of the violation; (3) when the police were holding probationer for the violation; and (4) when the judge asked the officer for a recommendation in the hearing of the violation. In each case situation the probation officer was to select the decisional alternative that best represented what he would do—given the facts, background characteristics of the probationer, and the probation violation in question. Decisional alternatives and case situations were followed by a question which asked the officer to explain briefly why he had chosen a particular alternative in each situation.

STRATEGIES AND RESPONSE

The questionnaire was administered to 108 field officers in May and June of 1965, during their annual in-service training program at the Institute of Government in Chapel Hill, N.C. All materials were presented *de novo*; there was no mention that all cases were rewritten revocations from the files of the probation department. Under these circumstances an atmosphere was created for a first-hand study of decision-making, with confidentiality of information promised to those who participated.

FACTORS AND DECISIONS

One of the assumptions we made in developing the questionnaire was that certain factors were more significant than others in the probation officers' decisions and rationalizations about decisions. These factors were sex, race, college major, role played, age-crime type preferred, average monthly caseload, revocations, previous employment, organizational memberships, residence, and liberalism-conservatism. It was thought that these "background characteristics" would differentiate officer decisions and rationalizations sufficiently

---

[3]Stuart C. Nagel, "Off-the-Bench Judicial Attitudes," *Judicial Decision-Making*, Schubert, *supra* note 1, pp. 29–53.

to contribute to a growing body of "revelation research" in the law enforcement field.

For the sake of convenience in treating the data, categorizations and protocols were adopted. Among these were classifications of officer choices of action as "unofficial" (U), "official" (O), and "revocation" (R). "Unofficial" meant that the officer would handle the violation himself rather than go through official agencies or channels. Where official channels or agencies were resorted to, the choice of action was categorized as "official" or "revocation." Decisions were then cross-tabulated with characteristics of the case and the case situation in order to facilitate presentation and interpretation of the data.

Officer rationalizations for choice of action were similarly handled (Table 1). These "reasons why" were classified as being oriented toward the probationer (P), the probation officer (PO), or the social order (SO). The first of these meant that the alternative chosen was rationalized as being in the best interest of the probationer. Rationalizations that were officer-oriented reflected the officer's inability to cope with or do anything more for the probationer, or the need for more information on which to base a decision. Rationalizations oriented toward the social order were likely to stress the probationer's criminal behavior or his behavior in violating probation and its effects on others.

Applying Lambda measures to cross-tabulated data, however, failed to reveal consistent relationships. In cross-tabulations by the case, roles[4] and scores[5] produced the highest values, and number of organizational memberships the fewest. Concentrations of values appeared in Cases 2, 3, 5, and 6. In each there had been, before the violation which causes the revocation, a number of minor infractions by the probationer and warnings by the officer. Three of the four (Cases 2, 3, 6) involved sixteen-year-old males with good family backgrounds but with previous records of assault or automotive offenses. One (Case 5) was a 32-year-old male with an improper license plates offense. Three were white; one of the youngsters was a Negro. All four revoking violations occurred publicly or involved arrest or custody by police before the probation officer was aware of what had happened. Of the revoking violations, three were automotive and the fourth was a curfew violation.

This cluster of characteristics was not as much in evidence in Cases 1, 4, 7, and 8. For one thing, the probationers were generally older (eighteen, twenty-three, twenty-nine, forty-two) and two (Cases 7 and 8) had bad reputations. For another, the pattern of minor infractions, warnings, and public or official involvement because of the violation was not uniformly present. In Case 1 (driving recklessly and without a license) and Case 4 (absconding) there were no prior infractions or warnings. Infractions appeared in Case 7 but

---

[4] Roles which the officer could select include big brother, big sister, friend, policeman, manager, stranger, and Good Samaritan. Most officers selected big brother or sister, friend, and manager roles; some selected multiple roles or had no role preferences.

[5] The median score for officers who answered the Eysenck-Nagel "Survey of Opinion" was 113. All above were treated as liberal; all at 113 and below, as conservative.

Table 1 *Choice of Action and Rational Supports by Case and Characteristics of North Carolina Probation Officers (Lambda Measures)*

Characteristics	Case 1		Case 2		Case 3		Case 4		Case 5		Case 6		Case 7		Case 8	
	CA	RS	CA	RS	CA	RS	CA	RS	CA	RS	CA	RS	CA	RS	CA	RS
College Major		.07		.03	.05	.08	.05		.01	.11	.09	.03			.01	
Roles You Play		.02	.10	.01	.12	.11			.06	.10	.04	.10				
Sex			.02		.08	.07	.05			.02	.05	.03				
Age-Crime type		.03		.02	.02	.15			.02	.08	.09	.10	.07		.02	.07
Race			.02	.04	.03	.05				.01	.03	.02		.04		
Average monthly caseload					.01	.01	.04		.08		.08					
Scores		.18		.22	.04	.12	.13	.18	.04	.20	.02	.18		.17	.01	.13
Revocations	.02			.11	.12	.09	.01		.05	.09	.07	.06	.03		.05	
Memberships					.01	.03				.05	.05	.08				
Previous employment				.03	.03	.13				.10	.05	.06				.05

they occurred too close to the revoking violation (breaking, entering, and larceny) for warnings. In Case 8 (nonsupport) police were not involved; the probationer had asked for and was given additional time to catch up on his support payments, and, when he failed to make the payments, the officer was confronted with a multiple support violation.

Rational support (RS) values were generally more numerous and higher than values for choice of action (CA). Whether these variations in values were due to subjective bias in classifying reasons or simply differential responses is a moot question. If differential responses are implied, then even official handling and revocation may be rationalized contrary to reasonable expectations (i.e., for the probationer's benefit rather than for society's).

Relationships of choice of action and rational supports to the same factors were generally limited. Some exceptions were found in Cases 3 and 4, where "roles" and "scores," respectively, produced meaningful associations. In Case 3, "roles" produced associations of .12 (CA) and .11 (RS) with "big brother and sister" roles strongly in favor of "unofficial" action for "officer-oriented" reasons. Other roles preferred "official" action or "revocation" with "multiple" roles for "probationer-oriented" reasons and the remainder for reasons that were oriented either toward the officer or toward the social order. In Case 4 similar disharmonies were produced. "Scores" yielded values of .13 and .18, with "liberals" for "unofficial" and "conservatives" for "official" actions. The rationalizations for the action, however, were mainly "officer-oriented" for the "liberals" and about evenly divided between "officer" and "social order" for the "conservatives."

Part of the explanation for the general lack of high values, relatedness of the same factors to choice of action and rational supports, and the inconsistency of decisions and reasons would seem to lie with the cases themselves. Purpose rather than randomness in the selection of cases from probation files might have enabled one to differentiate decisions and reasons on the basis of the characteristics that were used.[6] As it turned out, the cases were not too dissimilar and the outcomes were rather limited in character. Apart from the cases, the geographical area has a conservative subculture. The conservativeness of the subculture is manifest in the liberalism scores of the officers and the rationalizations for the decisions they made. Officer scores ranged from 74 to 141, with a median of 113, for 108 officers who filled out the Eysenck-Nagel "Survey of Opinion."[7] If anything, the scores understate the conservatism of the officer because, unknown at the time, some of the ideas and areas of investigation were covered in in-service training sessions with the officers the year before the questionnaire was administered. Rationalizations, on the other hand, were predominantly social order- or officer-oriented. In only ten of 248

---

[6]Two immediate possibilities for better differentiation are graded violations and further refinement of the revoking pattern of minor infractions, warning, and public or police involvement of the last or revoking violation.

[7]Nagel's median was 109 on a scale that ranged from 41 to 195.

instances did 50 percent or more of the officers rationalize decisions in terms of probationers.

SITUATIONS AND DECISIONS

Another basic assumption was that, according to the situation, officer decisions and rationalizations would vary. Each case, consequently, was broken down into four case situations which replicated the source and origin of officer knowledge about probation violations. In brief, the situations were "you knew," "party told you," "police were holding," and "judge asked." Under this breakdown the officers made decisions and rationalizations in situations much as probation file materials suggested they did on the job. The results of these decisions and rationalizations in situations are presented as Lambda measures in Table 2.

Examination of the table indicates that meaningful associations were slightly greater than double those found in Table 1. In order of their effectiveness, scores, age-crime type preferences,[8] race, college major,[9] caseload,[10] and roles produced the greatest number as well as the highest values, while memberships again produced the fewest. Of the case situations, "you knew" and "judge asked" were the most volatile, with the latter alone accounting for twenty-one of forty-six associations of consequence. Case volatility in Table 2, however, was dissimilar from that in Table 1. In Table 2, Cases 3, 4, 5, 7, and 8 were the most fruitful, while the remainder were relatively weak in generating meaningful associations. In volatile cases, most of the meaningful associations were decisional rather than rationalizational.

Decisions and situations deserve some additional attention because, despite the generally mild nature of the cases, the values indicate that officers make decisions in situations that vary according to their background characteristics. In instances where values were produced the variations were in rather discernible directions. Liberals, no and multiple age-crime type preferences, big brother and sister roles, Negroes, and social science majors were more likely to be for "unofficial" action and against "revocation" than their officer counterparts. If one pursues the differences situationally, the variations

---

[8] The age-crime types from which the officers were to select those they preferred to supervise were the following: no preference, youthful property offender, adult property offender, youthful sex offender, adult sex offender, youthful alcoholic, adult alcoholic, youthful motor vehicle offender, adult motor vehicle offender, and multiple age-crime types. Only four, however, were usable because of the pronounced avoidance of sex, alcohol, and motor vehicle types.

[9] Social science, education, and business administration comprised the usable college major categories.

[10] Average monthly caseload gave mixed results. Sometimes the "minimum" and sometimes the "moderate" and "maximum" loads diverted from "revocation" or "official" action. The explanation would seem to lie in the departmental practice of assigning lighter loads to newer officers.

Table 2 *Choice of Action and Rational Supports by Case, Situation, and Characteristics of North Carolina Probation Officers (Lambda Measures)*

	You Knew		Party Told You		Police Were Holding		Judge Asked	
	UOR[a]	PPOSO[b]	UOR	PPOSO	UOR	PPOSO	UOR	PPOSO
Case 1								
College Major	.04							.09
Roles you play								
Sex	.03							
Age-Crime	.11							.15
Race	.05						.40	
Average monthly cases	.03						.04	
Scores	.08							.10
Memberships	.05							
Revocations	.08							
Case 2								
College Major					.08			
Roles you play	.14		.08		.20			
Sex					.05			
Age-Crime	.11	.02			.09			.02
Race								
Average monthly cases	.02				.02	.03		
Scores					.02	.06		.02
Memberships								
Revocations					.05			
Case 3								
College Major	.11	.04			.05			.08
Roles you play	.16		.11					
Sex	.07	.04						.10
Age-Crime	.09	.19						.18
Race							−.25	.05
Average monthly cases	.09			.04	.06			.05
Scores	.11							.10
Memberships	.07							
Revocations	.04							.06
Case 4								
College Major	.22		.11					.11
Roles you play								
Sex	.08							
Age-Crime								.02
Race							.27	
Average monthly cases	.10		.16	.04				.02
Scores	.34		.28			.40		.07
Memberships	.07							
Revocations	.05		.04					

[a]Choice of action as Unofficial, Official, or Revocation.

[b]Rationalization for choice of action classified as oriented toward the Probationer, the Probation Officer, or the Social Order.

Table 2 *(Continued)   Choice of Action and Rational Supports by Case, Situation, and Characteristics of North Carolina Probation Officers (Lambda Measures)*

	You Knew		Party Told You		Police Were Holding		Judge Asked	
	UOR[a]	PPOSO[b]	UOR	PPOSO	UOR	PPOSO	UOR	PPOSO
Case 5								
College Major		.08				.05		
Roles you play	.04				.09			
Sex								.05
Age-Crime	.02						.16	.10
Race		.07					−.46	.02
Average monthly cases	.11				.13	.04		
Scores		.02				.10		.02
Memberships								
Revocations	.06							
Case 6								
College Major	.02						.04	
Roles you play	.05							
Sex	.05							.02
Age-Crime								
Race		.07					.29	.04
Average monthly cases	.07				.12			
Scores								.18
Memberships	.03	.09						
Revocations				.08				.02
Case 7								
College Major			.03		.10	.04		
Roles you play					.11			
Sex								
Age-Crime								
Race	.02		.14		.03		−.62	
Average monthly cases	.07		.02		.16	.09		
Scores			.02		.09	.03		
Memberships								
Revocations					.01		.13	.02
Case 8								
College Major								.13
Roles you play								
Sex		.02						
Age-Crime		.16						.18
Race							−.63	.03
Average monthly cases							.03	.05
Scores							.17	.11
Memberships								.01
Revocations								.09

become even more pronounced. Moving from private and semiprivate involvement of the violations to police and court involvement gives rise not only to more values but to values of greater intensity. In other words, with these cases and characteristics the officers are best differentiated at points of maximum exposure to official agencies and process.

RESIDENCY, SCORES, AND DECISIONS

Perhaps the best results were achieved by combining selected factors with decisions and supports. Application of Q measures to residency[11] and scores illustrates this approach, which produced meaningful associations in all cases and situations. With some exceptions, the patterns and interpretations noted in Tables 1 and 2 are applicable to Tables 3 and 4. The exceptions in Table 3 are to be found in Cases 1, 4, and 8, and relate to the explicitness of the revoking patterns or to extenuating circumstances. In Case 1 (reckless driving and without a license) and Case 4 (absconding), public or police involvement in the last or revoking violation occurred but prior infractions and warnings were absent. These three cases dealt with minority (1), affliction (4),[12] or an essentially noncriminal violation (8).

In Tables 3 and 4, residency had the effect of further differentiating the conservative and liberal elements in the officer population. "Rurals" were consistently less for "unofficial" action than "urbans" and markedly so if they had conservative scores. Urban liberals, on the other hand, exceeded all other combinations in being for "unofficial" action and expectedly against "revocation" in instances involving the revoking pattern, extenuating circumstances, and points of exposure to official agencies or processes.

Other combinations—roles and scores; and residency, scores, and rational supports—also proved effective. The latter, like decisional outcome, suggests a continuum, with conservative rurals at one end and urban liberals at the other. Rationalizations of the conservative rurals were predominantly "social order-" or "officer-oriented," in contrast with urban liberals, who were "probationer-oriented." Roles and scores provided meaningful associations when role categories were rotated against each other and conservative and liberal scores.

SUMMARY AND CONCLUSIONS

Despite case and officer homogeneity, some rather pronounced differences were encountered in decisions and rationalizations in written cases by a group

---

[11] Residency categories of rural and urban were based on the cover sheet question of "place of longest residence" which it was thought better reflected the molding milieu of officer attitudes and values than place of birth.

[12] In Case 4 probationer was retarded.

Table 3 *Association of Residency, Scores, Choice of Action, and Rational Supports (Q Measures)*

RURS[a]	Choice of Action			Rational Supports		
	U	O	R	P	PO	SO
Case 1	.17	.23	1.00	.43	—	.54
Case 2	—	—	.27	.21	—	—
Case 3	.22	.27	.22	.13	.39	.22
Case 4	.14	—	1.00	.47	—	.31
Case 5	—	.48	.15	.14	—	.23
Case 6	.13	.33	.14	.60	.32	.30
Case 7	.22	—	.28	—	.55	.36
Case 8	.45	.35	—	.22	.49	.31

[a]Rural-urban residence and scores.

of 108 North Carolina probation officers. Both decisions and rationalizations, however, tended to vary by the case and the case situations devised for the study. In Cases 2, 3, 5, and 6, existence of a revoking pattern generated some of the more meaningful associations between roles played in supervision, scores, and decisions and rationalizations by the probation officers. Big brother and sister roles preferred "unofficial" action for "probationer-" or "officer-oriented" reasons to "official" action or "revocation" by friends and managers who gave "social order-" or "officer-oriented" reasons for their decisions. As determined by scores (based on the Eysenck-Nagel "Survey of Opinion"), liberals and conservatives were similarly split for much the same reasons. In case situations, police or court involvement with the violation produced more

Table 4 *Association of Residency, Scores, and Decisions by Case and Situation (Q Measures)*

RURS	You Knew			Party Told You			Police Were Holding			Judge Asked		
	U	O	R	U	O	R	U	O	R	U	O	R
Case 1	.13	.47	—	—	.75	—	—	.50	—	.18	—	—
Case 2	—	.12	.34	—	.33	.30	.18	.11	.42	—	.23	.15
Case 3	.18	.17	.12	.40	.78	.36	—	.25	.24	.11	.56	.20
Case 4	.18	—	—	—	—	—	.28	.10	—	.21	.17	—
Case 5	.22	—	.11	.16	.77	—	.15	.61	.14	.58	.23	.43
Case 6	.22	.19	—	.21	.26	.33	—	.80	—	—	—	.16
Case 7	.55	—	.26	.15	—	.29	—	—	.31	—	—	.25
Case 8	.74	—	.33	.49	—	—	.32	.23	.23	.84	.74	.17

and higher values than private or semiprivate involvement. Situational values were primarily decisional and were obtained, for the most part, in cases where the revoking pattern was found. The exceptions occurred in instances of extenuating circumstances of minority, affliction, or technical violation of probation.

All of this suggests that exposure—disruption of private or semiprivate supervisory practice by intervening public, police, or court involvement in the case—may well be the key to differentiating the officer population. Social science majors, liberals, no and multiple age-crime type preferences, Negroes, and big brother and sister roles are more likely to be in favor of nonrevoking types of action than officers with other characteristics.

Of all the factors used, the officer's place of longest residence and scores produced the best results. Q measures of this combination of factors indicated a continuum of decisions and rationalizations with the rural conservative at one end and the urban liberal at the other.

30

Authority in the Correctional Process

ARTHUR E. FINK

As one starting point in a discussion of authority in relation to the correctional services it may be useful for us to consider the all-pervasive place of authority throughout our lives. Certainly, if we reflect upon it a bit we can recall how early we begin to become aware of authority in its many manifestations. We may encounter this early in our family situations, especially in relation to our parents—the limitations that are imposed and our struggles against what we are obliged to do and the prohibitions about what not to do. These rules may not make very much sense to us, nor are we overly enthusiastic about respecting them, but little by little and each of us in our own way make some kind of working accommodation to them. We have met authority and we will never be without it as long as we live.

AUTHORITY IN THE SCHOOL AND COMMUNITY

Then our little world of the family opens to a larger world of the school and the community and we experience authority as it is expressed by other persons and imposed by other rules. Certainly the teacher and the principal, with all of their professed willingness to help us, seem to resemble our parents and to have a liberal assortment of prohibitions, commands, and regulations with which some of us begin to have trouble. Sometimes, some students have so much

SOURCE. *Federal Probation*, XXV, September 1961, pp. 34–40.

trouble that it seems necessary for school officials to take restraining action or, in aggravated situations, to disassociate such youngsters from the school system. Regardless of what action the school takes, all students have experienced its authority and some have come into uncomfortable conflict with it.

COMING TO TERMS WITH AUTHORITY

In the larger community, of which the school is only one part, the adolescent—we will assume for the purposes of our discussion he, or she, is that far along—meets many more rules, limits, injunctions, indeed laws. Here, again, there will be varying adaptations to these demands, and not unrelated to the degree of success achieved in earlier encounters with authority. In some instances these earlier difficulties may be so unresolved that action may have to be taken by an agency known as the juvenile court. The man, or woman, who presides over this court, insists he wants to help and this sounds just like what some other people have said; in fact, the judge is painfully reminiscent of those other authority figures—parents, teacher, principal—and he seems to have even stricter rules than they did.

With all due respect to parents, teachers, and principals, it may be observed that perhaps for the first time the youngster has had to come to grips with authority, that literally and actually he is face to face with authority as he and the judge look at each other. In all likelihood the judge knows something about him already, for another person who looks familiar and who is in the same room, has prepared some material which, too, sounds familiar. One of the large tasks of the judge will be to set in motion the process by which this youngster can begin to get help in coming to terms with authority, as he, the judge, acts on behalf of and as an agent of the community and as he, at the same time, acts for the welfare of the boy. Nor are these purposes contradictory; rather they are integral aspects of the very service for which the court was created and for which it continues to exist.

Let us assume the judge, having examined the material the probation officer has prepared and making his own analysis of the youngster and the difficulties he is having, decides to place the boy on probation. Here, again, the boy faces authority—authority of the community, of the court, of the judge, and now the authority of the probation officer. Like the judge, the probation officer has a service: Primarily serving the community but also so serving the offender as to conduce to his welfare. As he begins to work with the boy the probation officer may encounter considerable resistance. This may take the form of silence or mumbled and unintelligible replies; or resentment and sullenness; or a blaming of his troubles on other people; or an aggressive hostility expressed against the court, the judge, and the probation officer. The disciplined probation officer will recognize and understand these various manifestations, seeing them as some of the many ways in which human beings in trouble try to keep from having to face their own part in their difficulties. The probation officer who not only represents authority, but *is* authority, must get past this shielding front, and must help the boy to begin to take hold of what he can do about himself.

Not infrequently as the boy begins to open up and to permit communication between himself and the probation officer he may press for a relaxing of the authority which the probation officer is exercising. To some people it may seem to make good sense to ease up on the use of authority—after all this boy has had a hard time at home and at school, other people have been too strict with him, and besides that he is only a boy as yet. To other people it may seem very important to bear down on this boy; to let him feel the full force of society, and to teach him a lesson this early. The competent probation officer may see it differently. As he gets to know the boy he becomes aware that while there has been authority in the family and in the school the boy has managed, by one means or another, to avoid coming to terms with it. Perhaps there has been too much strictness, or not enough, or a too erratic use of it. The probation officer's job will be to take this boy as he is, where he now is, and to help him with the reality of the struggle he is now having with authority.

This help which the probation officer offers the boy around authority is ineffective when presented in lecture form. It takes on meaning when it is handled with respect to specific items, such as the conditions of probation. For an apparently simple example I will quote from an actual record.

"For the time being, he would be obliged to observe a 10 p.m. curfew and attend school daily. Carl balked at this. He was 16 and didn't want to go to school. We talked about this, Carl complaining that he wanted to work and I pointed out that I wondered if he would really be satisfied with that and wondering, too, if he could really be self-supporting. The factor most impressive to Carl, however, was learning that although at 16 he had a legal right to stop school, in the eyes of the law he was still a minor and could not leave home without his parents' permission. . . . Carl looked most unhappy and fumed for awhile. I suggested he think about that seriously and commented we could talk about these things at his next interview. The remainder of the time was spent preparing Carl for his Mental Hygiene Clinic examination. Carl did not like the idea at all. . . . I explained why we felt a psychiatric examination was important and made arrangements for a later interview with him. He left the office in a very disgruntled frame of mind.

Carl came in on time for his next appointment. I was greatly encouraged by this interview because for the first time Carl was really able to talk back, almost to the point of arguing. True, everything he put out was negative and hostile, but it does show he can be reached. He even shed a few tears which he didn't try too hard to hide this time. We talked in spurts for well over an hour and Carl did not appear ready to bolt as on previous occasions.

He was angry about his Mental Hygiene Clinic examination because I thought he was 'crazy.' As we struggled with this and finally cleared it up we got to talking about 'trust.' Carl did not even trust his mother, why trust the court?"

There are a number of comments that can be made about these fragments of interviews with Carl that bear on our discussion of authority. For one, authority can be dealt with most effectively, especially with an adolescent who heretofore has not come to terms with it, in small bits. To tackle authority in all of its manifold aspects and in its totality would be overwhelming for Carl—indeed would be meaningless. To relate it to such tangible requirements as school and a curfew provides him with something he can handle, or can refuse to handle. He can then know what he is doing and can be held to his part in it by his probation officer.

TAKING ON RESPONSIBILITY

This leads to another aspect of authority—namely, the responsibility which the individual carries in relation to it. The imposition of authority from above or from the outside is not effective of itself alone. It is only as the individual who encounters authority takes some responsibility for what that authority means to him or does to him that any beneficent action follows. As long as Carl can keep himself untouched—really untouched inside of himself—by any authority so long can he continue to resist the demands of society and go his own way. However, when authority impacts upon him in small, but not unmeaningful, areas of his living, then he must come face to face with it and carry the responsibility for dealing with it negatively or positively. If he deals with it negatively he can still keep it outside of himself and respond to it destructively; if positively, he begins to internalize it and lets it begin to operate constructively in his life.

THE STRUGGLE WITH LIMITS

Another aspect of authority relates to the struggle that all of us, including the offender, have around limits. We push against limits and yet we would be terrified without them. They are essential to growth, to change, and to all aspects of living. Many years ago Kenneth Pray remarked about the need for such limits.

"These limitations are not only ineradicable facts of life to which ... we are bound to adjust ... they are, in fact, the very bases upon which we discover our own capacities, for we must have something to struggle against in order to find ourselves, to achieve selfhood with all its satisfactions. Without these limits we are lost in a tidal wave of surging impulses, none of which is better or more satisfying than any other."

It is the probation officer's job to understand this and to work with the delinquent in his struggle with limits for by so doing he, the probation officer is enabled to offer the constructive possibilities of authority.

NECESSITY FOR CHANGE FROM WITHIN

Let us assume that Carl and his probation officer are working together satisfactorily and let us take up with Bill who has made such little use of probation that the judge has felt obliged to revoke probation and place Bill in a training school. The judge has no illusions about the training school, he will not expect miracles, but he does hope the more controlled setting of the training school will provide Bill with the opportunity to settle down a bit, to take a look at himself, and with the help of a trained worker to take steps toward bringing about some change within himself. Bill may not have learned yet to live within limits; nor to have come to terms with authority; and he has probably managed to hold off any genuine change within himself. He may resent the rules of the institution and may start out breaking as many of them as he can. He may defy authority as it is embodied in the person of the superintendent and members of the staff. These are all matters with which he and his worker will need to do something about.

At the one extreme the response of the institution may be to bring the full force of its total power to bear upon Bill and to flatten or crush him. The other extreme would be based upon feeling sorry for Bill and all his misfortunes and to cushion the impact of the institution upon him. It is here suggested that neither of these extreme measures is likely to prove useful. In the one instance Bill's unresolved struggle with authority may be sharpened and intensified still further. In the other—the easing up—it would be a disservice to Bill because it would be relieving him of his own share of responsibility for the situation in which he finds himself. There is a useful service somewhere in between the two.

Bill needs to feel the power and the authority of the institution as something that can be used helpfully in relation to his problems. As mentioned earlier this is not gotten over to Bill via the lecture method, but around specific situations as they arise and as Bill handles them and as he can talk things over with his worker. In this process undoubtedly Bill will make mistakes, but with the help of the worker he can learn from those mistakes. If he is overprotected he does not have the opportunity to test himself against the reality in which he is and hence can gain no benefit from the experiences. Throughout all of this—this mean between two extremes—it is essential that change shall come about in Bill. This is something that Bill must do and be responsible for; it is not something that another person, not even the worker, can do for him.

AUTHORITY AND THE MAN IN PRISON

As we did with Carl let us do with Bill—let us move on to another kind of situation in which we can examine authority in relation to the correctional process. Let us assume we are dealing with an adult offender who has been on probation, whose probation has been revoked, and who is now in prison.

Many of the foregoing remarks also apply to the man in prison. Perhaps they apply in greater degree by reason of not having been worked out earlier in life: The struggle with limits; coming to terms with authority; taking on responsibility for one's self; and the necessity for genuine change.

One of the hardest jobs the prisoner has is to get himself *into* prison. To the layman this must sound like double-talk; of course the man has gotten himself in. However, a closer examination of these words—or perhaps more strictly speaking what is behind the words—reveals there is such a thing as being in prison physically and another thing which is being in prison psychologically. In the latter sense this means facing what it is that has gotten him there; not merely the act or acts for which he was tried, convicted, and sentenced but essentially the kind of person he is that has gotten him to this pass. From the start it will be the worker's job to help the inmate face all of that. Many, if not most prisoners, may feel that they have been sent to prison unjustly. It is not uncommon for the inmate to insist it was someone else who committed the offense; or that the other person got off with a light sentence; or if he was the only one involved that he wasn't given a fair trial; or that he drew a "bum rap." There are an infinite number of ways of denying one's involvement of being in prison, and it is frequently in this kind of situation that the worker must start. His first job may be to help the prisoner to face the real fact that he is in prison, that he has gotten himself there. This will be necessary before the worker can help the prisoner get something out of the prison experience, and ultimately to be ready to get himself out of prison, able to stand on his own feet, and taking responsibility for himself.

Some prisoners may express their disinclination to face being in prison by open defiance of the prison's rules. This aggressive behavior may be a way of a prisoner denying he is in prison. True, he knows his body is behind walls and in a cell, but he is unwilling to face his real self in his predicament. A competent worker recognizes what is going on within the prisoner, recognizes as an employee of the prison that rules must be obeyed, and sees the prisoner's responses as offering an opportunity to look at himself, to struggle with limits, to come to terms with authority, and to bring about some change within himself.

Another prisoner may, right from the beginning, bend all his efforts to getting out by legal recourse. Again, the skillful worker will see this as a way of not facing being in prison. Here, the worker's efforts will be directed to helping the prisoner to express, largely by words and feelings, his responsibility for himself and his part in being where he is. It will not be until the prisoner can be helped to get past this point that he can begin to use what prison has to offer and really prepare himself for release.

Another way of getting out is by escape, and understandable to the layman as this desire may be it still has meaning to the prison worker as a refusal to face one's self and the situation one has brought about. Nor do prisoners customarily discuss their intentions with staff workers, but on at least one occasion this happened. After bringing this to the attention of the appropriate prison official the worker recorded his account of the experience. A portion of this is excerpted here for the purpose of illustrating some of the points of our discussion.

"I asked him how he was feeling now about being here and about wanting to be out on the 'street.' Was he still thinking about escaping? He did not look at me; instead he stared at his hands, looking very dejected. He said he still thinks about it; he cannot help but think about it. Every night he thinks about his family and how much he feels his place is with them. The agonizing slowness of time makes him want to scream sometimes at night. He would feel better if he could do this, but he is afraid they will send him to state hospital if he does. He feels his life is being wasted in here. His rightful place is with his wife and child. He thinks about getting out a lot. I told him I knew that getting out was important to him, and I wanted to see him get out, but not by means of escape. I wondered if he knew what escaping would mean to his wife. What would she think about it? He said he has never really asked her directly, but he knows she would disapprove. He told me he thinks he is going to try to be with her for their anniversary. I wondered if he were successful in getting out, how long did he think he could stay out. He knows what he would face when he came back (if he came back alive), then how about the next anniversary, and the next one, and the next one, and the ones after that. How long could he expect his wife to wait for him if he received additional time?"

Despite having access to a hacksaw this prisoner did not escape nor try to escape; the prison officials took the situation in hand and nothing happened. The important consideration for us here was that a worker could help the prisoner to face something of himself; could help him to take some responsibility for himself; could help him in his struggle with authority; could help him to be "in" prison so that he, the prisoner, could in time really get himself "into" prison, and then to begin working toward bringing about the kind of change within himself that would enable him to move toward getting himself out of prison. The getting "out" here means only getting his body out, but within that body, or person, enough inner change happening so that he could take responsibility for himself, and for what he thinks and does so to keep him as a self-respecting and useful citizen—useful to himself and to other people too. Incidentally, this particular prisoner did serve out his minimum term, had his difficulties in prison, but was deemed ready for parole supervision and was eventually released. He may not have been a new man at the time of his discharge, but he was certainly a changed man because he had used the prison experience to do something different about himself than had been true previously.

Another way that a prisoner may have of not facing himself and his situation is to want to escape from it by way of self-annihilation. The worker records, later, the following incident with the same prisoner.

"Another long silence followed and then he remarked that if he were man enough, or had courage enough, he would take his own life. I inquired if he really felt it took a man to do that. He nodded. I said that if he really wanted to solve all of *his* troubles, that would be the easy way to go about it. It did not take courage."

It is to be hoped that these several excerpts will give substance to the points about helping the offender in struggle with authority. Obviously, this is not done by the lecture method nor by telling the prisoner what he ought to do. He knows what he ought to do. The help consists of working understandingly with the prisoner, enabling him to get certain things out of his system, and confronting him with his own share of responsibility for what he is and what he does. It consists in helping him to make the decisions about himself. He has to make them; another person, no matter how gifted, cannot make them for him.

What has just been said about the man in prison is just as true of the woman in prison. Here in North Carolina we have become familiar with some of the constructive possibilities of working with women offenders after they are committed to Women's Prison. Each year students from the School of Social Work have carried on their field work training under the supervision of a qualified staff at Women's Prison. All of the points that have just been discussed, about the offender, are very real in the working experience of these students—the struggle with limits; the coming to terms with authority; the necessity for inner change; and the taking on of responsibility for one's self. Not infrequently it is around this last point that students have the hardest time. As they work with women prisoners they become increasingly aware of the tendency on the part of the prisoner to put the blame on someone else or something else. One of the hardest jobs the student has (assuming she has learned it to the same degree within herself) is to help the prisoner to admit to herself the share she has in her own difficulties. It is quite understandable that the student may have genuine feeling for the predicament the prisoner is in, especially if there are children in the home outside. However, the student learns, and usually the hard way, that it is no service to the prisoner to get caught up in her—the prisoner's—difficulties and to overlook the necessity to help her face her own responsibility. It is only as the prisoner can be helped to come to this—to really get herself into prison—that she can begin to use the opportunity prison offers and thus move step by step toward ultimately getting herself out of prison.

AUTHORITY AND THE MAN ON PAROLE

Now let us look at the last of the situations in which as professional workers in the correctional field we are engaged, namely parole. Again, we will have to make some assumptions. The man who is on parole has encountered authority in its many forms from his early life onward. More recently he has been in prison, and the judgment has been made that he is ready to leave the institution and to make a go of it on parole. No more than any other person can he avoid the demands that will be made upon him as he tries to live and work in a kind of modified liberty. Indeed, by reason of all that he has gone through— the behavior that got him to a court and then to prison, and the person that he is—he may have a more difficult time working out his salvation than other persons.

The parolee finds that even though he is out of prison there are rules to go by. Many of these seem restricting and even though he may have learned something from the prison experience these restrictions may prove irksome if not at times downright frustrating. As with all of us the struggle goes on interminably—the struggle between the inner and the outer. The rules are explicit—about working, supporting one's dependents, the kind of company one keeps, the limitations on travel, etc. Does one conform to these requirements only as they are insisted upon by the parole officer with all of the force of the law which he embodies; or does the parolee act upon the basis of some change within himself that has been going on for sometime? I am willing to suggest that it may make a great deal of difference as to how the parole officer goes about his job with the parolee.

The way the parole officer works will depend to a great extent upon his convictions about people—his respect for them as human beings, with all of their shortcomings; his appreciation of the uniqueness of each person with whom he is working; his belief in the capacity of people to change; and his conviction that true change must come from within. As he works on these premises he can approach each of his parolees as individuals who have difficulties of a serious nature and who need help in getting themselves straightened out—and that he has the skill to help. He, too, must believe in the rules, and must realize that his helping is within the bounds set by the rules.

Suppose we take a simple, and not unusual situation which is taken from the actual record.

"Much of Jim's troubles come from his not having found himself and in not being sure of what he wants. This was particularly true about his job. He was also aware that he needed to find companionship and affection. He remarked, 'I guess I want what I have never had.' He seemed to see the point when I said most of his trouble was in his own attitude toward people, his unwillingness to trust himself and others enough to give them friendship. We talked of ways of solving the problem constructively and of his other choice of escaping from his troubles as he had before into vagabondage and crime."

An examination of this excerpt reflects a willingness on the part of the parole officer to talk things over with his parolee. There was a back and forth quality about this intercommunication. The parole officer was giving Jim the chance to talk over some of his difficulties and enabling Jim by what he was saying and doing to come to decisions about himself. He was quite willing to have Jim engage himself in his own problems and to hazard some of his—Jim's—own solutions.

Several months later Jim brings Marie to his conference, and his parole officer records some of the interview as follows:

"Jim then reminded me that he had mentioned Marie to me as the girl with whom he was going and added that her mother objected strenuously to him. Marie smiled and nodded agreement. It quickly became apparent that they were in love and Jim said they hoped to be married. However, the chances for it did not look so good because of her mother's opposition and Marie was only 19. I said it must seem pretty tough if they were fond of each other, and wanted marriage but found the way blocked. What did they propose to do? Jim said they would have to wait until Marie was 21 unless her mother changed her mind. He added, 'Of course, we could always go over the state line.' I asked him what he thought of this last remark as a solution. Jim replied it would be a risk since he was on parole. I agreed, saying I too thought it would be a great risk. He might get away with it but if he didn't he would have a lot of time ahead of him."

Here, again, the parole officer could involve Jim in his own thinking and consequences. It might appear to many people—uninformed people—that the simplest thing would be to impress upon Jim what he could do and what he could not do. This we all know as the ordering and forbidding technique, but we also have doubts about the lasting effect of decisions made along that line in contrast to the value of decisions made by the individual in a self-responsible way. This requires of the individual—Jim—that he face up with himself, that he recognize the limits within which he has to operate, that he be fully aware of the authority that surrounds him, and that he make his own decision upon the basis of change that has taken place within him—and that he carry responsibility for the decision he has made. These are the identical points that have been stressed throughout these pages—and are as applicable to the man on parole as to any of the other persons about whom these remarks have been made.

CONCLUSION

In conclusion I refer again to Kenneth Pray. It will be recalled that earlier I quoted some of his remarks about limitations. Written in the middle 1940's the wisdom in them is as firm today as yesterday. Referring to freedom Mr. Pray insisted it was a relative term when he said:

"There is no absolute freedom anywhere in this world and there ought not to be. None of us has absolute individual freedom; none of us believes in it; none of us would know what to do with it if we had it. Some structure of authority, defining and enforcing the necessary limits upon individual personal responsibility and conduct, as a condition of social cooperation, is an indispensable basis of any kind of life in any society. Such authority is essential in the prison; it is essential in the outside community.

"... Within these essential limits of social cooperation, freedom for every individual to make his own choices and judgments, to take responsibility for his own life, is not only an invaluable right of personality, it is an inevitable and immutable fact of life. Every individual will ultimately take and use that freedom whether we like it or not. That is to say, in the last analysis every individual will behave as he himself wants to behave, for his own reason, to attain his own ends. ... We may of course, while he is within our immediate influence, get him to behave outwardly the way we want him to behave—sometimes under practically physical compulsion; for a somewhat longer time, perhaps, through fear of painful consequences of acting otherwise; for a still longer time, probably, through hope of ultimate reward such as an earlier release from confinement. But when he leaves our sphere of power—and all prisoners will ultimately do so—he will act as he himself, deep down inside, wants to act.''

Several times it was remarked that the method of lecture or admonition was not especially effective in helping the offender to deal with himself or the difficulty he is in. Yet for many people it seems so natural to tell others what they ought to do or not to do, and then to assume that others will do what they are told simply because they are told. And when it comes to working with the offender who has not yet come to terms with authority it seems to make even more sense to tell him what to do or even to direct his life for him. I am moved to observe that such an approach if not downright harmful is of limited usefulness or of no use at all, because it is based upon a misleading notion of human behavior. The worker in the correctional field is likely to be far more effective if he can engage the offender in the process of doing something about himself. Basic to this process is the quality of the relationship between the helper and the helped whereby the one enables the other to express ideas and feelings and even actions—and to which the helper responds in such a way as to increase the opportunity for the offender to take an additional responsibility for himself.

Thus as we bring to a close our discussion of authority in the correctional process it is essential that we be convinced of its usefulness; indeed of its indispensability. We need to value it—as much for the worker in corrections as for the person being helped. But we need to see, also, the other aspects as they are related to the use of authority, namely, the use of limits, self-responsibility, and inner change. By our understanding of these and our skillful use of them we thereby offer to the offender the opportunity to realize more fully his own capacity as a human being to live satisfyingly and constructively.

31

Some Findings from Correctional Caseload Research

STUART ADAMS

If correctional research in California during the past 15 years has had an overriding objective, it has been to discover whether caseload size influences correctional outcome. This research has been strongly supported from a number of directions. Correctional administrators, treatment staff, and professional association leaders have long maintained that if caseloads are reduced corrections will become more effective. This consensus has crystallized in published standards that call for caseload sizes much smaller than current averages.

There have been other research interests in corrections, of course. We have seen much work on the development of prediction methods, the assessment of old programs and new program ideas, the creation of diagnostic typologies, cohort followups, and other kinds of studies. The heavy emphasis, however, has fallen on studies of the effects of reducing caseload size.

Thus far we have had SIPU (Special Intensive Parole Unit) in the California Department of Corrections, TOPS (Test of Probation Services) in the Los Angeles County Probation Department, the Reduced Caseload Project in the California Youth Authority, and the San Francisco Project conducted in the federal probation office at San Francisco.

SOURCE. *Federal Probation*, XXXI, December 1967, pp. 48–57.

In addition to these massive studies, which have focused primarily on caseload size, there have been other projects in which small caseloads have been featured. Some have grown out of the larger, numbers-oriented investigations. Others have arisen from special enterprises in which intensive supervision seemed necessary to achieve the desired correctional objectives and caseload size was reduced accordingly. Included here are such projects as the Community Treatment Project (CYA), the Intensive Supervision Caseload Project (LA), the Willowbrook-Harbor Intensive Supervision Project (LA), the Parole Work Unit Program (CDC), the Community Delinquency Control Project (CYA), and the Workload Determination Project (LA).

Hopefully, the past 15 years of hard and costly research effort in four major correctional organizations in California have brought significant information and meaningful changes to caseload practice and theory. What, actually, have been the outcomes of this research?

THE MAJOR PROJECTS

It will be useful, as a beginning, to summarize the various projects of relevance here. The following review takes the studies in chronological order by agency. Table 1 recapitulates the essential points of the review.

SIPU PROJECTS. *SIPU* I ran from July 1953 to December 1955 in the California Division of Adult Paroles.[1] It set up caseloads of 15 men in experimental status against the regular 90 men in control status. The experiment involved 4,300 men released from Department of Corrections institutions. The 15-man caseloads were supervised intensively for the first 3 months after release—presumably the most vulnerable months for failure. After this the parolees were reassigned to the regular 90-man caseloads.

Initially, in SIPU I, there were reports of superior performance by the experimentals, particularly those of some offense types. Under subsequent reviews of the data, the evidence for superiority failed to hold up.

SIPU II ran from January 1956 to December 1957 and involved about 6,200 men.[2] The experimental caseloads were increased to 30 parolees and the lenght of stay in the reduced caseloads before reassignment was raised to 6 months.

At the end of this phase of the project, no significant differences were evident between the performances of experimentals and the regulars. It was concluded at this point that intensive supervision may have been ineffective because the agent-parolee relationship had been interrupted and that perhaps 1 year of intensive supervision would avert the difficulty.

[1]Division of Adult Parole, Adult Authority, *Special Intensive Parole Unit, Phase I: Fifteen-Man Caseload Study*, November 1956.

[2]Division of Adult Parole, Adult Authority, *Special Intensive Parole Unit, Phase II: Thirty-Man Caseload Study*, December 1958.

SIPU III began in July 1957 with 35-man caseloads versus regular caseloads, which had been reduced to 72 by administrative negotiation.[3] A total of 3,700 parolees was involved in this phase of the project. Intensive supervision ran for 1 year.

The initial findings of this phase were that the men in the 35-man caseloads performed significantly better than those released to regular caseloads. This was true at both 12 and 24 months after release. It was also found that reduced caseloads showed the best results with medium-risk parolees rather than with the best or the poorest risks. These findings supported the impression that the effect of caseload size was not a simple function of numbers but the consequence of various kinds of interactions.

SIPU IV was undertaken in 1959 to explore some of these complexities.[4] One part of this phase was a study of the interaction between parolee and parole agent types. Another was a "high base expectancy study." There were several others, but the one perhaps the most noteworthy focused on agent-parolee interaction. This put together agents and parolees in patterns that had both logical and empirical justification. Low-maturity parolees were matched with "external-approach" agents and high-maturity parolees with "internal-approach" agents. Caseload sizes were reduced to 30 for some experimentals and 15 for others; the controls were managed in 72-man caseloads.

The major findings for SIPU IV were reported in 1964—5 years after the start of the Phase IV projects. It was concluded that the only variable that made a real difference in parole outcome was the amount of time the parole agent had to devote to supervision. Interaction between agent and parolee characteristics did not appear related to outcome in this phase. Furthermore, the 15-man caseloads performed no better than the 30-man caseloads. The Phase IV report asserted, however, that inability to show results in this stage of the project may have been due in large part to lack of precision in the study designs and to lack of adequate knowledge of the parole process.

NTCP I AND II.   One offshoot of the SIPU studies involved narcotic offenders in the Department of Corrections. With the establishment of the Narcotic Treatment Control Project (NTCP) in 1959, 30-man caseloads of former addicts and 70-man caseloads to which some former addicts were assigned provided the data. Phases I and II of the NTCP project were inconclusive with respect to caseload size.[5]

NTCP III.   The third phase of this project was designed in 1962 and terminated in 1964. It made use of 15-man and 45-man experimental caseloads in tests against the conventional 70-man caseloads. It also placed some of

[3]Joan Havel and Elaine Sulka, *Special Intensive Parole Unit, Phase III*, Research Report No. 3, California Department of Corrections, March 1962.

[4]Joan Havel, *Special Intensive Parole Unit, Phase IV: The Parole Outcome Study*, Research Report No. 13, California Department of Corrections, September 1965.

[5]Department of Corrections, *Annual Research Review*, December 1962, pp. 77–78.

the experimentals in an NTCU prerelease center for a brief period of treatment prior to parole.

The major finding from Phase III was that the experimentals as a whole performed significantly better than the controls, but no difference was apparent between the 15-man and 45-man caseloads. Also, the men released from the NTCU treatment center performed significantly worse on parole than men released directly from prison.[6]

PAROLE WORK UNIT PROGRAM. In 1965, building on findings from SIPU III and IV, the Department of Corrections moved into a Parole Work Unit Program. This was an attempt to introduce new concepts into caseload management. Increased emphasis was to be given to (1) supervision of each parolee in accordance with a careful appraisal of his service needs, and (2) allowing agents sufficient time to accomplish the tasks required of them. In comparison with the caseload designs under SIPU, attention now shifted away from *numbers of cases* to *time required to meet the special needs of the men* in the caseload.

An integral part of the new program was a classification system that focused on parolee service requirements. Three classes of parole supervision were conceptualized: (1) Special—for "difficult" cases; (2) Regular—for "average" parolees; and (3) Conditional—for parolees requiring minimal supervision.

It had been established by now that a certain irreducible minimum of agent time had to be reserved for general field and office duties, leaving the rest for direct supervision of parolees. The "rest" was defined as a workload of 120 units. A "special" parolee was regarded as requiring about 5 units of time, a "regular" as requiring 3 units, and a "conditional" about 1 unit. A full caseload would thus contain about 25 specials, or 40 regulars, or 120 conditionals, or some combination of the three.

The Legislature in 1965 provided about $1 million to man the Work Unit program with approximately 100 new agent positions. This permitted application of the new concept to about 6,000 parolees, who comprised about one-half the total parole caseload of the Department of Corrections. The Work Unit caseloads varied in size but averaged 36 parolees. The other 6,000 parolees were carried in the conventional 72-man caseloads.

In the first 6 months of the program, Work Unit parolees performed no better than conventional parolees, the Department reported.[7] In the second 6 months, however, it was reported that Work Unit parolees outperformed the conventional parolees in several categories. They had difficulties of lesser seriousness on parole, fewer new felony convictions, and more time in the community under active supervision in opiate, high-risk, and low-risk

---

[6] Alfred N. Himelson and Blanche C. Margulies, *Narcotic Treatment Control Program, Phase III*, Department of Corrections, September 1965.

[7] California Department of Corrections, *Parole Work Unit Program: An Evaluative Report*, December 1966.

non-aggressive groups. The average base expectancy scores for the Work Unit and conventional parolees were essentially the same, signifying comparable populations in the experimental and regular caseloads.

Not only significant reductions in returns to prison were reported for the Work Unit program. There were also savings in new correctional costs incurred by parolees in the program—enough to offset additional expenditures on the program. It was estimated that the Work Unit concept could be extended to all Department of Corrections parolees, with costs fully covered by savings in new community and institutional correctional services, as a result of the improved behavior of the parolees.

TOPS PROJECT.   The TOPS Project of the Los Angeles County Probation Department was simplicity itself in comparison with SIPU.[8] It consisted of only one Phase, which began in 1957 and continued until 1959. It was carried out with Rosenberg Foundation support and some additional funding by Los Angeles County.

The project dealt with juveniles only. For purposes of the experiment, caseloads were reduced from the conventional 75 supervision cases and 8 investigations per month to 50 supervision cases and 6 investigations per month. In preparation for the experiment, deputy probation officers received special training in casework dynamics, caseload management, and recording techniques.

The results showed the new procedures to be more effective than the old. Several objective measures were used to ascertain effects, and in almost every area of client performance and management behavior, the reduced caseloads showed themselves superior. There was a reduction in average length of detention at time of admission, reduction in the time a case remained active, reduction in unnecessary court hearings, and greater use of informal services by the experimentals.

One of these results alone—reduction in average time detained at admission—if applied to the approximately 20,000 annual admissions to detention facilities in the department, was estimated to be nearly enough to pay for reduced juvenile caseloads across the entire department.

One of the results of the TOPS experiment was County approval of a new way of computing yardsticks, based on credits for informal as well as formal cases, that brought an appreciable reduction in caseload sizes for juveniles.

INTENSIVE SUPERVISION CASELOADS.   The next significant study of caseload reduction in the Los Angeles County Probation Department came in 1963, about 4 years after the close of the TOPS Project. This was the Intensive Supervision Caseload Project.[9] It arose because "hard-to-place" girls were overcrowding Juvenile Hall, and the question was raised as to the econo-

---

[8]Los Angeles County Probation Department, *The Effectiveness of Reduced Caseloads for Juvenile Probation Officers*, 1959.

[9]Stuart Adams and Calvin C. Hopkinson, *Evaluation of the Intensive Supervision Caseload Project*, Los Angeles County Probation Department, Research Report No. 12, May 1964.

mic feasibility of managing these girls in the community in caseloads of 15 rather than in the conventional placement caseloads of 50. This idea had been suggested by the California Youth Authority's success with its caseloads of 12 in the Community Treatment Project, referred to later in this paper.

Four ISC caseloads were set up under specially selected officers, and a matched group of controls was identified in regular caseloads to provide a basis for comparison. The project showed that ISC cases stayed out of detention longer, were sent back to Juvenile Hall less frequently, stayed there for shorter periods of time when sent back, and were sent to the Youth Authority less frequently. When these various actions and services were costed out, the average monthly expenditure on the experimentals was found to be $185, and on the controls, $240.

The success of the 15-girl caseloads led to an expansion of the program to 12 caseloads, including both boy and girl groups. The year after, the number of ISC caseloads was to be increased again to 24, but County fiscal problems have delayed the second stage of the expansion.

WORKLOAD DETERMINATION PROJECT. In October 1964 the Probation Department received a recommendation from a management consultant firm (which had been retained by the County to study the Department) that a more rational procedure for establishing workloads be adopted.[10] This recommendation, which arose out of the consultant firm's study of the new Parole Work Unit Program of the Department of Corrections, sought to displace the "equal numbers" concept as the basis for caseload formation. The result was the Workload Determination Project (WDP).

The primary objective of WDP was to determine the most appropriate size of workload for a deputy probation officer. There were other objectives, such as (1) improvement of caseload planning procedures and caseload management, and (2) increasing the effectiveness of the unit supervisor in work planning and management. However, the central theme in the new approach was the substitution of time allocation for case counting as the key to caseload management.

During an exploratory period there emerged a frame of reference for planning probation services under the new concepts. First, 25 percent of a deputy probation officer's time was defined as unassigned. Second, 15 percent of his time should be reserved for demand services. Third, 60 percent of his time should be planned for specific case services.

Three kinds of service objectives were defined, each relating to a different type of client:

(1) Rehabilitation, requiring 1 to 16 units of time;
(2) Control, requiring 1 to 12 units of time;
(3) Minimal service, requiring 0 to 2 units of time.

[10]Cresap, McCormick, and Paget, *Management Survey: The Los Angeles County Probation Department*, April 1965.

Under this classification scheme, which is primarily time-oriented, the numerical caseload for a deputy probation officer could range from a low of 16 maximum rehabilitation cases to a high of 384 minimal service cases that required only demand services.

During an 11-month period ending in late 1966, the caseload size in the juvenile WDP units stabilized at about 50 cases per officer. Nonproject cases in the same locations averaged about 62 per officer.[11]

The juvenile cases at 11 months were showing evidence of superior casework and improved cost-effectiveness relationships. There were greater numbers of early dismissals, fewer court appearances on active cases, lower average duration of detention, and fewer new arrests. Preliminary cost estimates suggest that the cost of the additional staffing is more than met through savings to the County in lowered expenditures for arrests, court hearings, detention, and probation services.

For adult cases, the WDP caseloads settled down at about 90 cases per officer. This was in contrast with the average of 210 cases in the non-WDP caseloads in the same areas. The 11-month followup of the adult cases suggested that the WDP units were providing more effective supervision. Probationers were reporting more regularly, making support payments more regularly, and requiring less time before discharge from probation. The project officers were also returning probationers to court more promptly when violations occurred. The net effect of all these differences on cost-related factors implied that the WDP procedures carried an appreciable potential for cost reductions in the management of adult cases.

W HISP.   One further experience with small caseloads in the Los Angeles County Probation Department is worth noting. In March 1965 the Department, with Office of Economic Opportunity assistance, undertook the Willowbrook-Harbor Intensive Supervision Project.[12] This dealt with boys ordered to forestry-camp placement by the juvenile courts. The WHISP Project randomized a small number of boys from one geographical area into experimentals, who went into 16-boy community treatment caseloads, and controls, who went into the forestry camps as the court ordered. The design and procedures had been worked out beforehand with the courts.

By mid-1966, the first major report on this project indicated that 84 percent of the experimentals were still functioning satisfactorily in the community. The remaining 16 percent had been sent on to the County forestry camps or to the California Youth Authority institutions. Average monthly costs for the

    [11]Los Angeles County Probation Department, *Juvenile Comparative Data: Workload Determination Project*, WDP 66–4, August 1966: also, *Adult Comparative Data, Workload Determination Project*, WDP 66–3, August 1966.
    [12]Los Angeles County Probation Department, *The Willowbrook-Harbor Intensive Supervision Project: A Proposal*, November 1964.

management of the experimentals were estimated at $115; for the controls, $326.[13]

This appears to be a suggestion, based on 20 experimental cases, that under intensive supervision in the community most of the boys who are ordinarily placed in forestry camps can be managed in the community at about one-third the forestry camp cost, and with a success rate equal to or better than the camp success rate.

REDUCED CASELOAD PROJECT. The California Youth Authority became involved in a reduced caseload project in 1959—6 years after the Department of Corrections and 2 years after the Los Angeles County Probation Department. Ten caseloads of 36 wards each were set up against five control caseloads of 72 boys each. Both sets of caseloads covered a common geographic area—Alameda County, in the San Francisco Bay Area. The populations of the caseloads were built up by long, carefully controlled processes of randomization.

The project ran until September 1961, when it was discontinued because of apparent lack of results. In the initial months of the project there was statistical evidence of superiority in the performance of the experimentals, but this later disappeared. The final conclusion was that there seemed to be some value in reduced caseloads if they brought an actual increase in frequency of agent-parolee contact.[14]

COMMUNITY TREATMENT PROJECT. In 1961 the Youth Authority shifted its attention to a different form of project—one in which caseloads of 8 (later 12) juveniles were to be formed in a test of community v. institutional treatment. The basic procedures began with identification, among boys and girls who had been sent to the Youth Authority by the juvenile courts, of individuals who could be accepted as eligible for immediate return from the reception center to these small community treatment caseloads. The eligibles were then randomized into community treatment and institutional treatment cases. The experimentals received intensive individual and group therapies; the controls went on through the institutions in traditional manner.[15]

Phase I of the Community Treatment Project was perhaps less a test of the efficacy of small caseloads than of the general concept of intensive supervision in the community as a substitute for conventional institutional experience. The test was elaborated by including the device of classification by an interpersonal maturity typology—the so-called "I-levels"—in an effort to discover whether community treatment might be more effective for some types of juveniles than for others. In Phase II of the project, which has been made

[13]Eugene G. Feistman, *Comparative Analysis of the Willowbrook-Harbor Intensive Supervision Program*, Los Angeles County Probation Department, Research Report No. 28, June 1966.

[14]Bertram M. Johnson, *Parole Research Project: Evaluation of Reduced Caseloads*, California Youth Authority, Research Report No. 27, January 1962.

[15]Marguerite Q. Grant and Martin Warren, *An Evaluation of Community Treatment for Delinquents*: CTP Research Report No. 1, California Youth Authority, August 1962.

possible by a second grant from the National Institute of Mental Health and additional legislative support, the test has been further elaborated by widening the range of treatment options in the community.[16]

Two findings of general interest came from Phase I of the project. First, the great majority of boys and girls ordinarily committed to the Youth Authority appear readily manageable in the community under intensive treatment. Second, this manner of treatment is much less expensive than management in training schools which is followed by the usual kind of aftercare. With reference to numbers, 75 percent of the boys and 90 percent of the girls committed to the Youth Authority have been deemed eligible for retention in the community for intensive treatment. In the matter of costs, present estimates are that treatment in the community comes to about one-half to two-thirds of the cost of conventional institutional and parole management.[17]

COMMUNITY DELINQUENCY CONTROL PROJECT.—One early consequence of the success of the Community Treatment Project was the establishment of the Community Delinquency Control Project. This Youth Authority project provided for the bypassing of institutions and the placing of cases directly on intensive parole in special units with 15-boy caseloads. The units receive referrals from the reception center and expose them to a year of experience in group counseling, individual counseling, remedial education, group-home placement, and other treatments. At the end of the year, wards are transferred to regular caseloads for less intensive supervision until discharged from parole.[18]

By 1966 these two programs—Community Treatment and Community Delinquency Control—were handling about 600 juveniles, which is more than the capacity of a Youth Authority institution. It is estimated that this means a saving of $7 million to $8 million in construction funds, plus the difference in costs between community and institutional maintenance.[19] Using current estimates of $3,000 versus $4,500 per ward year, the maintenance saving on 600 wards approximates $900,000 per year.

In these two projects, the California Youth Authority has established that caseloads of 12 to 15 are operationally feasible, bring reduced rates of recidivism, and are economically advantageous. They are more effective in resocialization of youngsters, and they promise to obsolete much of the physical plant that planners once thought to be necessary in the remote future of the Youth Authority. Since it takes time to implement such complex programs as the Community Treatment Project, inroads on traditional practice and plant may be slow. Nevertheless, it is easy to see why many knowledgeable persons con-

[16]Marguerite Q. Warren and Theodore B. Palmer, *Community Treatment Project: Fourth Progress Report*, California Youth Authority, October 1965.

[17]Heman G. Stark, "Alternatives to Institutionalization," *Crime and Delinquency*, April 1967, pp. 323–329.

[18]*Ibid.*

[19]President's Commission on Law Enforcement and Administration of Justice. *The Challenge of Crime in a Free Society*, 1967, p. 170.

sider this project one of the most significant developments in the recent history of juvenile corrections.[20]

THE SAN FRANCISCO PROJECT.   The San Francisco Project, a study of federal probation and parole, began in September 1964. Funding came primarily from the National Institute of Mental Health. The project was designed to examine the relative effectiveness of minimum, regular, ideal, and intensive caseloads. The *minimum* caseload, nominally the largest in size, called for reporting by mail and service upon demand. The *regular* caseload contained 85 persons—100 units of workload, counting investigations. The *ideal* caseload was a 50-unit workload, as recommended by the American Correctional Association. The *intensive* caseload was a 25-unit workload—one-half that recommended by the ACA.[21]

New probationers were assigned randomly to these various caseloads. At the end of 2 years, performance of the minimum cases was not significantly different from that of the regulars. The regular and ideal caseloads showed violation rates of 22 and 24 percent, respectively. The intensive caseloads had a violation rate of 38 percent. This inflated rate contained a high proportion of technical violations, presumably a consequence of the higher amount of supervision provided. If technical violations were excluded from the analysis, there were no significant differences in violation rates between minimum, regular, ideal, and intensive caseloads.[22]

The most recent report on the San Francisco Project concludes that random assignment of offenders to caseloads that vary in intensity of supervision is not followed by the variation in outcome that might be anticipated. The report suggests that improvement in outcome will perhaps be a function of types of treatment, types of officers, and types of offenders.[23]

The report identifies four factors as critical for the classification of offenders: age, prior record, current offense, and psychological stability. It proposes four types of caseloads for an effectively functioning probation and parole service: *minimum*, with 350 offenders per caseload; *normal*, with 65; *ideal*, with 40; and *intensive*, with 20. Assignment to one of the four types would be determined by the offender's profile with respect to the age-offense-record-stability variables. In general, the more difficult the profile or pattern presented by the offender, the smaller the caseload size to which he would be assigned.

The following table (page 375) is a very concise summary of the foregoing projects.

[20] *Wall Street Journal*, December 28, 1966, p. 1.

[21] Joseph D. Lohman, Albert Wahl, and Robert M. Carter, *The San Francisco Project: The Minimum Supervision Caseload*, Research Report No, 8. September 1966.

[22] Joseph D. Lohman, Albert Wahl, Robert M. Carter, and Shirley P. Lewis, *The San Francisco Project: The Intensive Supervision Caseload*, Research Report No. 11, March 1967.

[23] Joseph D. Lohman, Albert Wahl, Robert M. Carter, and Leslie T. Wilkins, *The San Francisco Project: Classification Criteria for Establishing Caseload Models*, Research Report No. 12, The University of California, May 1967.

DISCUSSION

It is perhaps premature to attempt a definitive summing up of the results of the foregoing projects. Nevertheless, there should be much value in trying to define some of the major consequences of the research and to state some of the most plausible implications for the future.

Most readily evident are several operational consequences. As a result of the favorable findings in SIPU III and SIPU IV, the Department of Corrections was authorized staff increases that reduced caseloads to an average of 36 parolees across one-half of the Department's 12,000 parolee population. As a result of TOPS, the Los Angeles County Probation Department was permitted substantial modification of its juvenile caseload yardstick. As a result of the Intensive Supervision Caseload Project, the Probation Department has won budgetary support for caseloads of 15 "hard-to-place" boys and girls. And as a result of WHISP, the Probation Department appears to have accepted the use of intensive supervision in the community as an alternative to forestry-camp placement.

Probably the most impressive operational consequence is in the Youth Authority. As a result of the Community Treatment Project, caseloads of 12 and 15 have won firm departmental and legislative support, and treatment in the community as an alternative to institutionalization is now fully accepted. The fact that about 10 percent of institutional commitments have been returned immediately to the community for intensive supervision is important, but this appears to be only a beginning. If we accept the findings of the Community Treatment Project that the vast majority of youthful offenders ordinarily placed in California training schools are suitable candidates for intensive treatment in the community, the implications for state-level juvenile corrections not only in California but also nationwide are far-reaching.

In addition to operational consequences, the research on caseloads has had its effect on legislation. The Community Treatment Project and the Delinquency Control Project were instrumental in the formulation and adoption of the California Probation Subsidy Act of 1965. The Act proposed that State subvention be used to strengthen community correctional processes, particularly noninstitutional kinds, for both adults and juveniles. Preliminary estimates suggest that the Act has had remarkable effects, holding in the community many offenders who would ordinarily have gone to the Youth Authority or to the Department of Corrections. From these estimates it has been predicted that 1,800 offenders will stay in the community under intensive treatment rather than be sent to state prisons or training schools in 1967. For a subsidy outlay of $7 million, the State appears likely to save a much larger amount.[24]

There also have been consequences for probation procedure. New ideas in caseload design and management and in unit supervision have begun to

[24]*NCCD News*, March-April 1967, p. 5–6.

Table 1 *California Correctional Caseload Studies*

Department and Project	Dates	Remarks	Results[a]
California Department of Corrections			
SIPU I	15 vs. 90 cases	1953–1955	Experimentals transferred to regular caseloads after 90 days	ns
SIPU II	30 vs. 90	1955–1957	Experimentals transferred to regular caseloads after 180 days	ns
SIPU III	35 vs. 72	1957–1959	Experimentals transferred to regular caseloads after one year	+ + +
SIPU IVa	15 vs. 72	1959–1963	(No difference in results between 15- and 30-man caseloads)	+ + +
SIPU IVb	30 vs. 72			+ + +
NTCP I	30 vs. 70	1959–1961	Experimental project for narcotic cases	ns
NTCP II	30 vs. 70	1959–1961	Higher degree of control than in NTCP 1	ns
NTCP IIIa	15 vs. 70	1962–1964	(No difference in results between 15- and 45-man caseloads)	+ + +
NTCP IIIb	45 vs. 70			+ + +
PWUP I	36 vs. 72	1965–1966	First 6 months were transitional	ns
PWUP II	36 vs. 72	1966–		+ + +
Los Angeles County Probation Department			
TOPS	74 vs. 107 units	1957–1959	Juveniles: reduced caseloads versus regular field services	+ + +
ISC	15 vs. 50 cases	1963–1964	Juveniles: intensive versus regular placement caseloads	+ + +
WHISP	16 vs. 65	1964–1965	Juveniles: intensive community treatment vs regular camp	+ + +
WDP-Juv	50 vs. 62	1964–	Juveniles: WDP versus regular field services	+ + +
WDP-Adult	90 vs. 210	1964–	Adults: WDP versus regular field services	+ + +
California Youth Authority			
RCP	36 vs. 72 cases	1959–1961	Reduced caseloads versus regular parole services	ns
CTP	12 vs. 72	1961–	Intensive community vs. traditional institution & parole	+ + +
CDCP	15 vs. 72	1964–	Intensive parole vs. regular institution and parole	+ + +
Federal Probation and Parole			
SFPa	? vs. 100 units	1964–	Minimum versus regular caseloads	ns
SFPb	50 vs. 100	1964–	Ideal (ACA Standard) versus regular	ns
SFPc	25 vs. 100	1964–	Intensive versus regular	ns

[a]ns indicates no significant difference in performance between experimentals and controls;
+ + + indicates statistically significant difference in criterion behaviors or evidence of cost benefits.

proliferate. Also conspicuously evident are new procedures for the classification of offenders as a basis for assignment to supervision or to treatment. The Youth Authority moved decisively into this area by experimenting with the I-level typology for caseload and treatment assignment. The Department of Corrections followed with its "special," "regular," and "conditional" parolee types, and the Los Angeles County Probation Department came after with its "rehabilitative," "control," and "minimal service" types. In the two latter agencies, classification was accomplished by relatively gross judgments. The San Francisco Project with its four critical factors and its 54 profiles now proposes to make the classification process more systematic and objective.

The caseload studies of the past 15 years contain much of interest when viewed primarily as research enterprises. One is struck, first of all, by the apparent fruitlessness of most of the first-phase projects. Despite preliminary indications of superior performance of the experimentals in the early months of the CDC and CYA studies, these indications eventually vanished. The San Francisco Project now finds itself reporting the same nonsignificant performance differentials.

The TOPS Project proved an exception in the first-phase studies. It showed superiority for the small caseloads for reasons that are not yet clear although worthy of speculation. At least two points come to mind. First, TOPS started as something more than small caseloads against large. There was perception of a need to employ effectively the anticipated disposable time, so caseworkers were given orientation in case management and in the dynamics of case behavior. Second, the TOPS project dealt with youngsters who had not yet left the community. It was concerned with relatively amenable material in a situation better endowed with treatment resources than the world of the adult prisoner or the juvenile who has reached the state training school.

Still viewing these projects as research enterprises, it is impressive how quickly results began to emerge when emphasis turned away from sheer numbers to treatment concepts: community versus institutional treatment, group and family therapy versus conventional probation supervision, and assignment to treatment by offender type. This aspect of caseload research gives point to one of the frequently voiced criticisms of the early research: *We have reduced the caseloads, but we haven't told the parole agents what to do with the extra time.* In that kind of procedural vacuum, there arose the possibility that the agent would use the free time to increase the number of technical violations. From several of the study reports, it is evident that this possibility frequently became reality.

A point of interest now arises as to whether the sharpening focus on offender types will be equally as productive as the recent focus on treatment content and format. The use of an offender typology proved disappointing in SIPU IV, and possibly also in the first phase of the Community Treatment Project. However, there remains a vast field for exploration in offender types, and the San Francisco Project, the Work Unit Program, and the Workload Determination Project may have set some useful new directions.

Another aspect of the foregoing studies that deserves comment is the success of the ultrasmall caseload with juveniles but its apparent failure with adults. The Youth Authority and the Los Angeles County Probation Department found caseloads of 12 and 15 to be economically and behaviorally advantageous, with juveniles. At the same time, the Department of Corrections and the San Francisco Project discovered that performance in 15- and 25-man caseloads was no better than in those twice as large. Does this mean that small caseloads are inherently advantageous for juveniles but not for adults? Or does it merely mean that thus far our design of small caseload programs for adults has been too uninformed, our management too ineffective, our measurement too imprecise?

As a final point of interest, one is impressed by the fact that all the reduced caseload projects of the Los Angeles County Probation Department have shown small caseloads to be more effective. All have shown the experimentals to have significantly lower failure rates or to produce cost reductions sufficient to justify the heavier staffing.

Why this total success for the Probation Department in contrast with the initial difficulties for the three other agencies? Is it that probation departments deal with intrinsically more promising material? Is probation staff better trained or more dedicated? Do probation departments have better command of treatment resources at the community level? Is the community an inherently better setting for treatment?

If, in fact, probation departments are at an advantage in the correctional process, this has important long-term implications. Corrections might conceivably be about to retrace the steps of mental health, which for a long time moved maladaptive people out of the community into large "warehouses," and is now in the process of returning treatment to the community.

Whether this will occur in corrections will depend ultimately on where corrections proves more effective, assuming that social effectiveness continues as a value in American society. The ability of probation to show more consistent gains through the reduction of caseloads is interesting evidence. More to the point, perhaps, is a recent study within a cost-effectiveness framework of a continuum of correctional treatments.[25] These range from individual psychotherapy within a prison to informal group work with delinquent gangs. The data from the study suggest that the earlier in the continuum one makes an expenditure on well-designed treatment, the greater the economic return on the treatment. They also seem to imply that the earlier in the career of an offender a unit of treatment effort is applied, the greater the return on the effort.

Two interpretations of the foregoing data might reasonably be made at this point. First, it would be logical to expect that probation would be the

[25] Stuart Adams, "A Cost-Effectiveness Comparison of Correctional Treatments." Paper presented at the Seventeenth Annual Meeting of the Society for the Study of Social Problems, San Francisco, August 1967.

correctional activity best able to make an effective showing with a procedure such as reduced caseloads. Second, one of the most promising areas for the expansion of effort in the wide spectrum of corrections is the area of community treatment, particularly the area now defined as probation.

CONCLUSION

This review of correctional caseload research in California has disclosed a number of significant informational and operational breakthroughs. Some of the findings, especially in the earlier or first-phase studies, were disappointing and perplexing. Nevertheless, it is easy to conclude that more has been learned than is generally recognized. It also appears likely that much additional will be learned, since there is much unfinished business in the area of caseload research.

Some general concepts that have emerged from the past years of research will undoubtedly serve as guides in future years. It will continue to be important to attempt to classify offenders in ways that are relevant to treatment content and form. There will continue to be concern for the appropriate kind of treatment for particular types of clients. There will be concern about the qualifications and characteristics of treatment staff and the possibility of interaction between therapist type and offender type. Some interest will be centered on appropriate duration and intensity of treatment. Finally, there will be much attention to the locus of treatment, with increasing focus on the possibility that probation and other open-community procedures will play far more important roles in the total correctional process.

It seems reasonable to assume that for a long time to come the crucial research in corrections will continue to be that which focuses on the treatment workload. This seems to be the heart of corrections—the defining situation for the continuing interaction between the agent or therapist and the client. It is an endless field of inquiry, in part because of the variety of factors involved, and in part because of the complexity of the interaction among these factors. But it is unquestionably a valuable field of inquiry, and progress in corrections will depend largely on how rapidly this field is mastered.

LEGAL ASPECTS

The editors feel it essential to present some of the legal aspects of probation and parole. While we all are familiar with recent court decisions and rulings which have significantly affected law enforcement, there is less awareness of an emergent development of a body of law governing the conduct of probation and parole. Much of our administration and operation is dependent upon a correctional rather than legal tradition; in view of the likelihood that future court action will make quite explicit the terms and conditions of probation and parole, an examination of current status here seems appropriate.

This section begins with an article by Sol Rubin, the legal counsel for the National Council on Crime and Delinquency, who examines probation and due process of law. Political Science Professor Heinz R. Hink's article from the *University of Chicago Law Review* examines constitutional standards of protection applicable to probation. The "Conditions of Probation" utilized by the United States District Courts are presented, followed by an analysis of probation conditions by attorneys Judah Best and Paul I. Birzon. Chief United States Probation Officer Eugene C. DiCerbo deals with the difficult question of when probation should be revoked.

A similar series of selections concerning parole begins with a note and comment from the *New York University Law Review* by Michael Gottesman and Lewis J. Hecker on the legal foundations of parole. Nat R. Arluke, Chief of the New Jersey Bureau of Parole provides a current summary of parole rules in the United States. The "Certificate of Parole" utilized by the United States Board of Parole is presented for review. Attorney Ronald B. Sklar's review of law and practice in probation and parole revocation hearings completes the legal aspects of conditions and revocation of parole.

United States Judge Alexander Holtzoff reviews the power of search and seizure on the part of probation and parole officers—a specific example of increased judicial interest in the conduct of probation and parole operations in the field. Finally, Attorney Ralph C. Brendes provides an overview of the interstate probation and parole compact.

32

Probation and Due Process of Law*

SOL RUBIN

In 1941 the Illinois Supreme Court said: "Any person indicted stands before the bar of justice clothed with a presumption of innocence, and, as such, is tenderly regarded by the law. Every safeguard is thrown about him. . . . After a plea of guilty . . . instead of being clothed with a presumption of innocence they are naked criminals, hoping for mercy but entitled to justice."[1] I doubt that such a statement would be made today. The fact is that after conviction there are a number of safeguards, not only around the defendant but also against error by the court. These things are better understood today, partly because of new decisions and statutes. The safeguards fall into two categories, procedural due process and substantive due process.

PROCEDURAL DUE PROCESS OF LAW

Procedural due process of law in probation refers (1) to those procedural elements in the presentence investigation which are requisite to a valid proceeding and (2) to the rules governing probation status and supervision.

SOURCE. *Crime and Delinquency*, **11**, January 1965, pp. 30–38. Reprinted with the permission of the National Council on Crime and Delinquency. Copyright 1965, National Council on Crime and Delinquency.

*Adapted from a speech presented at the Annual Conference of the Probation Association of New Jersey, March 21, 1962.
[1] People v. Riley, 376 Ill. 364, 368, 33 N.E. 2d 872, 875, *cert. denied*, 313 U.S. 586 (1941).

Presentence Investigation

One of the due process elements is the statutory requirement, in nine states and in the federal courts, that a presentence investigation be made before sentence is pronounced. A sentence passed without the investigation would be invalid. It has been so held;[2] and it would seem to follow from the cases litigated under statutes by which the investigation is *not* mandatory. In these cases it is held that the judge's refusal to order the investigation is not a violation of due process or an abuse of discretion.[3] However, the results would undoubtedly be different under the mandatory statute, which makes it clear that a sentence shall not be pronounced without the investigation.

This is an interesting development. I do not interpret it as merely strengthening probation. Many statutes formerly said, and some still do, that a defendant could not be *placed on probation* without a presentence investigation. However, he could—and still can—be *committed* without one. In its origin, then, the presentence investigation was related to probation, but the ordering of the investigation in relation to *all* sentencing constituted a real jump in jurisprudence, so altering the sentencing process that the presentence investigation became an essential part of it. That is why we no longer talk about a "probation investigation" as we used to; it is a *presentence* investigation.

A second element of due process in connection with the presentence investigation is its development (both in jurisdictions where it is mandatory and in those where it is not) as something more than the mere authorization of an officer of the court to supply the court with information. Some of the statutes require certain qualities in the report. For example, some declare that the report shall be "accurate," or "fair," or "made promptly." These are not merely administrative admonitions; they are requirements that underlie the very validity of a sentence imposed. In an Illinois case the state supreme court reversed a commitment on a plea of guilty where the defendant sought to withdraw the plea because of the quality of the probation officer's report. The court sent the matter back for a new arraignment because, in its words, "It cannot be said in this condition of the record that the report of the probation officer was either of that accurate or prompt character which the statute requires."[4]

In a Pennsylvania case this happened: The presentence report was incorrect in what it said about the defendant's past conduct and the extent of his participation in the crime to which he had pleaded guilty. In Pennsylvania the defendant does not have a right to see the report, so that the man was

---

[2]State v. Culver, 23 N.J. 495, 129 A.2d 715, *cert. denied*, 354 U.S. 255, 77 Sup. Ct. 1387 (1932).

[3]People v. Roveano, 130 Cal. App. 222, 19 P.2d 506 (1933); People v. Bailey, 328 Ill. App. 584, 66 N.E.2d 477 (Ill. 1946); People v. Sudduth, 14 Ill. 2d 605, 153 N.E.2d 557 (1958).

[4]People v. Adams, 379 Ill. 323, 40 N.E.2d 730 (1942). See also Klingstein v. United States, 217 F.2d 711 (1954).

committed before he discovered the misinformation in it. He was held to be entitled to a writ of habeas corpus. The appellate court said:

"If unknown to this prisoner or his counsel he was sentenced on assumptions concerning his past criminal activity which were untrue or upon misinformation as to other facts, 'such a result [in the language of *Townsend v. Burke*, 334 U.S. 736, 68 Sup. Ct. 1252], whether caused by carelessness or design, is inconsistent with due process of law.'"[5]

Not just the quality of the report is involved in this case. Here, and in other cases and statutes, the content of the report is involved also.

Investigations commonly report on the defendant's prior criminal record. One interesting statutory development is found in Massachusetts, where a statute provides that records of arrest eventuating in a not guilty verdict may not be included in the report. In the absence of a statute, the cases are not in agreement.[6]

A few decisions mention other content and indicate what would be deemed irrelevant or prejudicial, but sometimes without considering the error sufficient for reversal. In a California case, for example, the appellate court declared that the probation officer had gone "far afield" (1) in obtaining from a state board an estimate of the amount of property stolen but not indicating the source of his data, (2) in informing the judge that employers in the oil industry were watching the case with interest and that "the attitude of the general public and more particularly of the oil industry should be considered," and (3) in taking these things into account in his recommendation against probation by making "an apparent effort to influence the court by argument, which is not to be approved." However, it affirmed the commitment, declaring:

"We must reject the contention the court was influenced by the improper statements and arguments in the reports. While the matter was being discussed, the court expressed criticism of the report in these particulars and we think it is reasonable to suppose that the recommendation against probation was weakened in the mind of the court, by some of the faulty reasoning upon which it was based."

---

[5]*Ex parte* Hoopsick, 172 Pa. Super. Ct. 12, 91 A.2d 241 (1952). To the same effect, Commonwealth v. Cater, 396 Pa. 172, 152 A.2d 259 (1959) (reversing murder convictions).

[6]"Counsel might not have changed the sentence, but he could have taken steps to see that the conviction and sentence were not predicated on misinformation or misreading of court records, a requirement of fair play which absence of counsel withheld from this prisoner." (The errors in this case were the defendant's prior record and admission of arrests for charges that had been dismissed or of which the defendant had been found not guilty.) Townsend v. Burke, 334 U.S. 736 (1947), discussed in "Due Process and Legislative Standards in Sentencing," 101 *U. Pa. L. Rev.* 257, 265 (1952). On previous charges admissible, see People v. Escobar, 264 P.2d 571 (Calif. 1953); Taylor v. United States, 179 F.2d 690 (1950). On reversal for misuse of police records, see State v. Pohlabel, 61 N.J. Super. 242, 160 A.2d 647 (1960). The Connecticut Sentence Review Division does not take into account arrest records and nolle contenderes in reviewing sentences; see "Appellate Review of Primary Sentencing Decisions: A Connecticut Case Study," 69 *Yale L.J.* 1453, 1457 n.73 (1960).

The court also said:

"In other respects the reports were fair. They spoke highly of the appellant's past record and . . . closed with the statement that the officer did not believe that appellant, if granted probation, would commit any further offense."[7]

The probation officer's recommendation is part of the report and must conform to the requirements of fairness. In a New Jersey case the probation officer's recommendation of the maximum sentence was held to be "of doubtful propriety." On this and other grounds the court reversed, and ordered a new presentence investigation.[8]

Although the observations regarding the report's "fairness," "promptness." etc., and some of the developments regarding its content are derived in part from the statutes, these statutes evidently express propositions of such elementary fairness that they would seem to be inherent requirements in *any* investigation, even one made under a statute that said nothing about the quality or content of the report; and several courts have said as much. If a court relies on a report for guidance in forming the sentence, the report must satisfy the elementary attributes required of any information the court might use, if the sentence is to be valid. If the contents of the report do not have these attributes, the court must either disregard such parts or obtain other information.

Finally there is the controversial question of whether a defendant has a right to see the presentence investigation report. I have argued that it is good casework for defendants to have this right;[9] most administrators argue that for various reasons it is inadvisable for the defendant to see it. Whether he has the right to see it as a matter of law (aside from statute)—that is, whether seeing the report is a matter of such elementary fairness (i.e., due process) that any proceeding in which the right is denied would be void—has not yet been ruled on by the U.S. Supreme Court, although state courts have upheld denial of access.[10]

Williams v. New York[11] has received a certain fame in connection with the issue of use of the presentence investigation. But the view that it deals with, let alone disposes of, this issue is erroneous. The issue in the Williams case was not the defendant's access to the report. That matter was never raised.[12]

---

[7]People v. Fenton, 141 Cal. App. 2d 357, 296 P.2d 829 (1956).

[8]State v. Pohlabel, *supra* note 6.

[9]Rubin, *Crime and Juvenile Delinquency: A Rational Approach to Penal Problems* ch. 13 (1961).

[10]United States v. Schwenke, 221 F. 2d 356 (1955); State v. Moore, 49 Del. 29, 108 A. 2d 675 (1954); State v. Benes, 16 N.J. 389, 108 A.2d 846 (1954); Smith v. United States, 223 F.2d 750 (1955).

[11]Williams v. New York, 337 U.S. 241 (1949).

[12]See Williams v. Oklahoma, 358 U.S. 576, 3 L. Ed. 2d 516 (1959), *rehearing denied*, 359 U.S. 956, 3 L. Ed. 2d 763 (1958). The court had ruled that the defendant had no right to cross-examine the informants.

Rather the issue was confrontation of informants and their cross-examination.[13] The U.S. Supreme Court has not passed on the question of access. Considering some of the comments of the court in the *Williams* case and the court's record on due process, the defendant's right of access to information in the hands of the police and the prosecutor, and the general test of fairness, I believe that, if the issue arose there, the U.S. Supreme Court would be likely to hold that the defendant does have a right of inspection. In a case in Canada (where the defendant has the right to see the report) the court made the following statement:

"I would be loath to believe the Supreme Court of the United States intended to hold that while a trial judge has a wide latitude as to information he may ask for and receive in a presentence report without being hedged about by the procedural formalities of strict proof of the facts alleged therein he may read this material in the privacy of his own chambers and then take his place on the bench and allowing such material to influence him against the prisoner, sentence that prisoner thereon without disclosing a word of what has been placed before him by an official acting pursuant to the provisions of a statute." [14]

In some of the cases that have been reversed as a matter of law because of inaccuracy or unfairness in the presentence investigation report, the defendant and the appellate court came to know about the report almost accidentally. If the defendant has the right to have an appellate court pass on the validity of his sentence and, in so doing, consider the presentence investigation on which the sentence was based, how can this process operate intelligently unless the defendant knows enough about the report to challenge it where necessary and unless the court has the report in front of it? The fact is that some appellate courts *have* called for the reports.[15] Certainly if the defendant can raise issues about the report, he has a right to examine it to see whether it is legally adequate in his case.

Probation Status and Supervision

If the defendant is placed on probation he is subject to the supervision of the court and probation service, which, in turn, are also subject to certain legal requirements—the defendant's consent to probation, the limiting rules of

---

[13] The statements made by the judges as to Williams' background "were not challenged by appellant or his counsel, nor was the judge asked to disregard . . . or discredit any of them by cross-examination or otherwise." (The implication was that if the defendant *were* to raise these challenges, his right to do so might be upheld.)

[14] Rex v. Benson, 3 West. Weekly R. (n.s.) 29 (1951) (Ct. App. B.C.).

[15] People v. Adams, Klingstein v. United States, *supra* note 4; also Commonwealth v. Cater, *supra* note 5; People v. Guiden, 172 N.Y.S.2d 640 (1958). By statute, the Review Division of the Superior Court in Connecticut may call for the report—Conn. Gen. Stat. § 51–196. See "Appellate Review of Primary Sentencing Decisions," *op. cit. supra* note 6. *Contra*, Hurt v. Commonwealth, 333 S.W.2d 951 (Ky. 1960).

law governing the validity of the conditions of probation, the procedures of supervision and revocation, and the administration of the probation service.

CONSENT.   A defendant has a right to refuse probation.[16] At first blush the right to prefer imprisonment to freedom does not seem like much of a "right." But in some situations the right may well have practical significance. A man may be offered probation for two or three years—or a short term in prison; he may choose the latter. In a jurisdiction that attaches a term in jail as a condition of probation, probation is *not* an offer of freedom.

A defendant may refuse probation where the conditions would, in his opinion, be too onerous.[17] Accordingly, the better practice—and it is required under some statutes—is for the court to obtain consent to probation and to the conditions of probation.[18]

CONDITIONS.   Does requiring the conditions to be subject to the defendant's consent produce sufficient control over the nature of the conditions? Because of the defendant's status, consent is, except in rare cases, automatic. However, the law itself exercises some controls. Some cases state that a condition of probation may not require behavior which would be illegal, immoral, or impossible.[19] A court may not impose, through a condition of probation, a punishment not otherwise authorized. For example, it may not impose an unwarranted fine[20] or suspend a driver's license for longer than authorized by the Motor Vehicle law.[21] The pecuniary conditions, such as restitutions, may not be unreasonable or unrelated to the crime or other responsibility of the probationer.[22] Probation conditions specifying religious behavior probably could be questioned.[23] The legal rule enunciated in *Logan v. People* sounds like good casework to me:

"Since the purpose of probation is educational and reconstructive rather than primarily punitive or oppressive, the program of probation should envisage only such terms and conditions as are clearly and specifically spelled out in the statutes, and

---

[16]Lee v. Superior Court, 8 A.C.A. 801, 201 P.2d 882 (1949); Marks v. Wentworth, 199 Mass. 44 (1908); *In re Osslo*, 334 P. 2d 1 (Calif. 1958); State v. Cole, 241 N.C. 576, 86 S.E.2d 203 (1955). *Contra*, Cooper v. United States, 91 F.2d 195 (1937).

[17]People v. Caruso, 345 P.2d 282 (Calif. 1959).

[18]Required by statute, D.C. Code § 24–102; S.D. Code § 34.3708–2; Vt. Public Laws § 8878 (1933); 2 *United States Attorney General, Survey of Release Procedures* 254 (1939).

[19]State v. Harris, 116 Kans. 387, 226 Pac. 715 (1924).

[20]People v. Labarbera, 201 P.2d 584 (1949).

[21]People v. Williams, 144 C.A.2d 144, 30 P.2d 734 (1956).

[22]Karrell v. United States, 181 F.2d 981 (1950); People v. Funk, 193 N.Y. 202, 117 Misc. 778 (1921). See State v. Scherr, 9 Wis. 2d 418, 101 N.W.2d 77 (1960). An order for restitution for injuries to the person was held improper where the crime was leaving the scene of an accident— People v. Becker, 349 Mich. 476, 84 N.W. 2d 833 (1957); State v. Barnett, 110 Vt. 221, 3 A.2d 521 (1939).

[23]Jones v. Commonwealth, 38 S.E.2d 444 (1946), declared unconstitutional a juvenile court order requiring regular attendance at Sunday School and church: "No civil authority has the right to require anyone to accept or reject any religious belief or to contribute any support thereto.'

such other conditions as fit the probationer by education and rehabilitation to take his place in society."[24]

When we examine the rulings pertaining to conditions of probation, we see that the courts protect the probation status, consistently with one of the guiding principles of American law, the protection of individual liberty. Since the courts are leaning in the direction of narrowing the conditions of probation that may be imposed, I would suggest as a proper general rule that the authorized conditions should be only those necessary for protection of the public or rehabilitation of the defendant, and not peripherally those devised to induce the defendant to behave like a gentleman, or even like a good husband, father, or worker.

SUPERVISION. Does supervision include the right to intervene in the offender's life in such matters as control of his finances? It would not seem so except insofar as a condition spells out a monetary obligation by the offender, whether by restitution, fine, or support—and even then, a probationer has rights of privacy. How far does the officer's right of visitation extend? Does it include the right to search the residence of the offender? Probably not (unless the officer has a search warrant). I know of few cases which deal with these points, but probation practice does present these questions.

REVOCATION. The cases and many statutes clearly hold that a probationer is entitled to a hearing on notice of a charge of violation. Some reasonable quantum of evidence must be submitted to sustain a revocation.

SUBSTANTIVE DUE PROCESS OF LAW

The procedural requirements have given rise—perhaps unintentionally—to substantive rights. For example, as a matter of procedure, probation may not be revoked unless a violation is alleged, notice is given, a hearing held, and so on. All this implies a corresponding *right*. A probationer has the right to remain on probation until satisfactory proof is submitted and a finding made that he has violated a condition of probation. When probation is said to be a matter of grace, what is being referred to is the sentencing stage, *not* the status of a man on probation. His continuance on probation is a matter of right, not grace. Probation cannot be terminated by judicial fiat. Practically every statute upholds this proposition, and the courts almost uniformly adhere to it.

In a Maryland case a few years ago the state supreme court reversed a revocation for a very petty offense, saying:

"To hold that merely because a man attaches a poster to an unoccupied building he thereby ceases to be law-abiding and must be locked up for three months is, on its face, somewhat shocking. . . . A [probationer] is not expected or required at once to achieve

[24]Logan v. People, 332 P.2d 897 (1958).

perfection. If his conduct is that of the ordinary well-behaved person with no more lapses than all people have, with no serious offenses charged against him, and with no indication that he intends in the future to pursue the course which led to his original conviction, the courts and probation officers should not seek for unusual and irrelevant grounds upon which to deprive him of his freedom.[25]

One can infer from this the suggestion that no condition of probation is an absolute and that a violation must be of sufficient seriousness to return a man to prison.

Presentence Investigation and Substantive Due Process

We seem to be more aware of procedural and substantive rights pertaining to probation status and supervision than of the substantive rights that have developed in connection with the presentence investigation. Many judges—most, for all I know—believe that the sentence they choose to impose is within their absolute discretion, provided it is authorized by statute. Their discretion has, in fact, been modified by the effect of the probation statutes.

Some courts have expressed the belief that denial of probation may not be arbitrary, may not be in contradiction to the presentence report.[26] In a recent California case the defendant had waited in a car while her companion killed a man in a store holdup. She pleaded guilty and was sentenced to life imprisonment, with the judge indicating in advance of the sentence hearing that he would not consider probation. The state supreme court reversed on the grounds that the California statute requires that consideration be given to the presentence investigation and to the desirability of probation in the light of the presentence investigation report. The court held that a judge may not commit a defendant, even on a murder charge, without considering probation as a possible disposition.[27]

A federal court has held that sentences against co-defendants must be consistent, considering their backgrounds—a holding that, in effect, required the trial court to grant probation.[28]

Cases like these may promise some very important developments. In all the centuries of sentencing defendants, the courts and the constitutional conventions and the legislatures have not developed working criteria to guide judges in sentencing. That is why the range of sentences for similar offenses committed by defendants not very much different from one another is ridiculously broad. Even under the best statutes some judges use probation in 5 per-

[25]Swan v. State, 90 A.2d 690 (1952).

[26]People v. Cooper, 123 Cal. App. 2d 353, 266 P.2d 566 (1954); State v. Ivan, 33 N.J. 197 162 A.2d 851 (1960); People v. Silver, 10 App. Div. 2d 274, 199 N.Y.S.2d 254 (1960); People v Walker, 5 Cal. Rptr. 283 (1960); State v. Pohlabel, *supra* note 6. *Contra*, People v. Stover, 31 Ill. 191, 148 N.E. 67 (1925).

[27]People v. Wade, 1 Cal. Rptr. 683, 348 P.2d 116 (1959).

[28]United States v. Wiley, 278 F.2d 500 (1960).

cent of their cases; others, in the same jurisdiction, use it in 70 percent. Some commit defendants for long maximum terms; others, in the same situation, suspend sentence.

No criteria have been developed to control this chaotic exercise of discretion. Yet the California case mentioned above says that *every* offender must be assessed for his *suitability for probation*. It may be a great step from that decision to a practical rule by which probation will actually be a defendant's right, under the proper circumstances—a right, not a matter of utter "grace" by the court. If that leap seems great and impossible, we ought to bear in mind that in several cases in New York the Appellate Division of the Supreme Court has ordered probation where the trial judge had committed a defendant. (New York is one of the fairly large number of jurisdictions in which a defendant may appeal from the sentence.)

Another of the few criteria supportive of probation is the holding that a court may not reject probation or increase a sentence because of the jury's action,[29] or because the defendant had put the state to the trouble of a jury trial by pleading not guilty.[30]

Finally, the sentencing judge should be required to place on record the reasons for the sentence. The Arizona supreme court recently reviewed the commitment of a defendant convicted of manslaughter in the second degree. His previous record was immaculate. The issue raised on review was the denial of probation. Holding that denial was not an abuse of discretion, the court said:

"Nor can we agree that because other judges have suspended sentence and granted probation in cases where the prisoner at the bar was apparently less worthy of mitigation of punishment than was the defendant in the instant case, that this amounts to a denial of the constitutional rights of due process or equal protection of the laws."

(The court added—though it was no consolation to the defendant: "We do agree with counsel that there is room for improvement in the rationalization of the standards of sentencing."[31])

This decision is very unsatisfactory. I do not suggest that identity of treatment can or should be sought; with all of the differences in human beings, that is impossible. But—especially in view of the other criteria for discretion discussed above—the sentencing judge has an obligation to explain his sentence in terms of either equality or individualization. The matter is not too different from the problem of equality in law enforcement, on which a considerable volume of law has been written. Although the writers do not all take the same stand, there are numerous cases to the effect that a conviction based on

[29]State v. Mitchell, 77 Idaho 115, 289 P.2d 315 (1955); United States v. Wiley, 267 F.2d 455 (1959). The jury had been charged on involuntary manslaughter as well as reckless driving. It brought a verdict of manslaughter. Despite the defendant's clear record and good reputation, the judge refused to consider probation because the jury had convicted on the more serious charge.

[30]People v. Guiden, *supra* note 15.

[31]State v. Douglas, 87 Ariz. 182, 349 P.2d 622 (1960).

discriminatory law enforcement is invalid.[32] It seems to me that nondiscrimination in sentencing is just as mandatory.

In Pennsylvania the supreme court reversed two death sentences because the sentencing judge had failed to individualize, and it sustained a third, saying:

"The court erred in stating that 'all three [defendants] went to Cater's house to procure the gun before the holdup.' The fact is that there is no evidence in the record to support this statement against either Cater or Rivers. Similarly, the court was mistaken in its belief that as to Cater and Rivers the motive for the crime was 'the discharge of aggressive hatred.'"[33]

It is not difficult to see that the presentence investigation is the basic soil for the kind of individualization this supreme court calls for.

In New Jersey the judge is required to state the reason for his sentence. In many of the cases that have made law in sentencing, the judges who were reversed had put on the record their reason for the sentence—and the reason turned out to be wrong. If the judges had said nothing, in many cases the ground of appeal would have been undetected and the legal fiction would operate that the mute judge was most wise. The law assumes (where the judge does not demonstrate the contrary) that his mental process is consistent with law. The New Jersey rule corrects this.

We have a long way to go to develop working criteria in sentencing, but there are some straws, and it is clear that the development of probation and the presentence investigation have played and will continue to play a big part in it.

---

[32]Comment, "The Right to Nondiscriminatory Enforcement of State Penal Laws," 61 *Colum. L. Rev.* 1103 (1961).

[33]*Commonwealth v. Cater, supra* note 5.

33

The Application of Constitutional Standards of Protection to Probation*

HEINZ R. HINK

In searching for legal standards for the protection of persons convicted of a criminal offense three procedural stages following conviction have to be considered: sentence, probation, and parole.[1] Until recently students of public law, political scientists and lawyers alike, have neglected these aspects of criminal procedure. Responsibility for the conceptual exploration of these areas has been assumed by criminologists and persons interested in penal reform. The traditional concern of the public law profession for the protection of

SOURCE. *The University of Chicago Law Review,* **29**, 1962, pp. 483–497. Copyright 1962, by the University of Chicago.

*This article is based on ideas originally set forth in a paper delivered at the annual meeting of the Western Political Science Association, Berkeley, California, April 1960. The author wishes to express his gratitude to his co-panelist, Professor Ned V. Joy, of San Diego State College, for a stimulating interchange of ideas.

[1]*Sentence* means the pronouncement by the court of the penalty to be imposed on the defendant. *Probation* is the release of a convicted defendant by the trial court, ordinarily without imprisonment, but subject to certain conditions imposed by the court. *Parole* is release granted to the prisoner by an administrative act after he has served a portion of his sentence. See Orfield, Criminal Procedure from Arrest to Appeal 535 (1947); Wood & Waite, Crime and its Treatment 630 (1941); Weber, *Explorations in the Similarities, Differences and Conflicts Between Probation, Parole and Institutions,* 48, J. Crim. L., C. & P.S. 580 (1958).

individual rights has expressed itself in vigorous attention to the constitutional safeguards of a person *accused* of a crime. Committed to the Bill of Rights, the due process and equal protection clauses of the fourteenth amendment, and corresponding provisions in state constitutions, students of public law have closely followed—and at times have stimulated—judicial interpretation of such constitutional rights as freedom from arbitrary arrest, from unlawful search and seizure, from excessive bail; the right to proper notice and to a fair and impartial trial, to trial by jury, to the assistance of counsel;[2] and the constitutional protection against *ex post facto* laws, cruel and unusual punishment, and double jeopardy.

But public lawyers have given little attention to the legal protection of an individual once he has been *convicted* of the crime for which the law secured him every possible procedural safeguard while he stood accused. Several reasons may be offered in explanation of this failure, but perhaps the most important one may be found in the absence of *specific* constitutional provisions for the protection of procedural rights in a criminal case once the defendant has exhausted all appellate remedies. With the exception of prohibiting cruel and unusual punishment, the United States Constitution and the constitutions of most states do not contain specific provisions designed to safeguard the rights of a convicted defendant whose case has become res judicata.

The primary concern of the public law profession is with constitutional controversies, and the legal forum for the decision of these issues traditionally has been the United States Supreme Court. Consequently, lawyers and political scientists have approached public law from an operational vantage point in intellectual proximity to the Supreme Court. Concern with lower courts has been mainly to the extent to which their decisions have been the basis of Supreme Court review. The important legal issues involved in parole and probation show the limitations attached to this position. The wide range of trial court discretion in matters of sentence, probation, and parole has found appellate courts highly unwilling to establish definite criteria for the use of trial judges. The highest tribunals in most states and the federal Supreme Court have been reluctant to discuss these aspects of criminal procedure in constitutional language. But from this it does not follow that there are no constitutional problems connected with probation. It merely requires that students of public law should leave their traditional vantage point and follow more closely the jurisprudence of lower state and federal tribunals in areas of constitutional significance. Public lawyers may find that the work of these courts offers research opportunities that in the past have largely been ignored.

[2]The continuing concern of the Supreme Court of the United States with due process again was evidenced in one of the first cases decided this Term. In Hamilton v. Alabama, 368 U.S. 5: (1961), the Court held that arraignment was so critical a stage of Alabama criminal procedure that the defendant was entitled to counsel at arraignment. The defendant's conviction was reversed even though no prejudice was shown to have resulted to him from the denial of counsel

I

For two reasons, probation should receive attention in terms of constitutional standards of protection. First, for the same reason by which the law insists on the rigorous observance of constitutional standards in the treatment of a person accused of a crime, it should be concerned with the adequate procedural protection of the same individual once he stands properly convicted. A recent decision of the Michigan Supreme Court clearly defines this obligation: "We reject, instanter, any thought that the defendant, because a convicted criminal, stands before us with any degree of vulnerability, that he is shorn of any of his constitutional rights. These guarantees, in truth, meet their real challenge when sought to be employed by the wicked. The upright and the righteous need them not."[3] One may disagree with the author of the opinion that "the upright and the righteous" do not need the protection of constitutional guarantees, but in any case the point is well taken that the strength of a constitutional system lies in the protection it affords those who have trespassed.

In the problem at hand, a second consideration reinforces and illustrates the validity of the first. From the point of view of the substantive protection of an individual, the traditional distinction between the rights of the accused and the rights of the convicted defendant is unrealistic and injures the professed objectives of our modern system of criminal justice. Under the influence of the classical school of criminology the nineteenth century has seen the statutory enactment of more humane and reasonable standards of punishment. We have made the punishment fit the crime. But we have done more than that. Following the positivist school in their belief that deterrence and retribution are not enough, but that reform and social rehabilitation should play a vital part among the functions of criminal law, we have also made punishment suitable to the defendant. Flexibility in the type as well as in the amount of punishment is the motto of modern criminology; the indeterminate sentence, probation, and parole are its products.

It is not suggested here to argue against the usefulness or desirability of these advances over the chain gang and penal colonies. It is suggested, however, that the advantages of a flexible system of punishment allocation may be lost, unless flexibility is brought into line with procedural standards cognizant of the fact that the defendant is as much interested in the actual punishment he will receive as he is in the safeguards protecting his innocence. Criminal procedure should clearly realize that the defendant's interest is not limited to the right of having every possible opportunity of contesting the charge brought against him. The real interest of a guilty defendant extends to the nature of the punishment society inflicts upon him. One of the purposes of flexibility in punishment is to permit the rehabilitation of the criminal, especially the first offender. For this we pay a heavy price, in that we have lost in modern criminal law the certainty characteristic of the common law. But we also will endanger the

---

[3] People v. Becker, 349 Mich. 476, 487, 84 N.W.2d 833, 839 (1957).

success of flexibility and lose both certainty and social rehabilitation if we withhold from the convicted offender that degree of predictability which only adequate standards of procedural protection reasonably can secure.

Against this it may be argued that an insistence on rigid forms of procedural protection could defeat the whole probation program. Judges may be discouraged from granting probation if the probation process should be subjected to highly technical rules. There is much validity to such an argument, and this paper is not intended to advocate that *all* standards applied at criminal trials be extended to probation. The real question is to what extent procedures can be employed that will permit probationers a greater degree of safeguards without defeating the purposes of the probation system. Similar questions could be asked, of course, with regard to the indeterminate sentence and parole, though the following remarks will be limited to probation.

The problem of probation standards arises mainly in two areas: (1) the conditions which may be imposed upon granting probation; and (2) the procedure which may be employed in revoking or modifying a probation order. The first areas raises questions of procedural and substantive protection, the second one is primarily concerned with procedural standards.

II

The power of the trial court to grant probation is inherent or statutory.[4] In neither case does the grant of probation constitute an infringement on the executive power to pardon.[5] The granting of probation is entirely within the discretion of the trial court. It is "an act of grace and clemency to be granted in a proper case, and a person is not entitled to it as a matter of right."[6] Probation is the power of the sentencing court, "when satisfied that the end of justice and the best interests of the public as well as the defendant will be served thereby,"[7] to release the defendant.

The importance of probation as a modern corrective device can be seen

[4]The first probation statute was enacted in Massachusetts in 1878. *Mass. Acts* ch. 198 (1878). For the history of probation and the earlier common law expedients of benefit of clergy, judicial reprieve and recognizance, see *U.N. Dep't of Social Affairs, Probation and Related Matters* 15–50 (1951). For a discussion of the inherent or statutory nature of probation see *Justice Dep't Att'. Gen Survey of Release Procedures*, vol. II (1939); 15 Am. Jur. *Criminal Law* § 494 (1938); *Puttkammer, Administration of Criminal Law* 218 (1953); Orfield, *op, cit. supra* note 1, at 582; *Wood & Waite, op. cit. supra* note 1, at 631. For a discussion of specific state probation statutes see Aultman, *Probation and Parole Act of 1956*, 29 *Miss L. J.* 76 (1957); Taylor, *Probation and th Suspended Sentence in Texas*, 34 *Texas L. Rev.* 104 (1955).

[5]Riggs v. United States, 14 F.2d 5 (4th Cir. 1926).

[6]*Ex parte* Trombley, 31 Cal.2d 801, 811, 193 P.2d 734, 741 (1948). *Accord*, Burns v. Unite States, 287 U.S. 216, 220 (1932): "Probation is thus conferred as a privilege and cannot be demande as a right."

[7]18 U.S.C. § 3651 (1958). Release is ordinarily accomplished without imprisonment. *But se Cal. Pen. Code* § 1203 (1958), which permits as a condition of probation that the probationer b required to serve a part of his sentence.

from its increasing utilization by the courts. For most states up-to-date statistics are difficult to obtain and, in fact, in many states only very fragmentary records are kept of the state-wide use of probation. However, the following figures should suffice to prove the point. In California in 1955, 6,734 persons convicted, or 44.2 percent of those sentenced, were placed on probation. For 1956 the corresponding figures are 7,348 or 43.5 percent; and for 1957, 9,014 or 45.9 percent.[8] In federal courts, during the year ending June 30, 1959, a total of 10,726 (19.7 percent) adult offenders were given suspended sentences and placed on probation, of a total of 27,033 criminal defendants convicted and sentenced. During the same period 653 (48.1 percent) of a total of 1,356 juvenile defendants convicted and sentenced were granted suspended sentence and probation.[9] During the year ending June 30, 1960, 10,391 (38.9 percent) adult offenders of a total of 26,728 sentenced and convicted in federal courts were placed on probation, and 690 (48.3 percent) of the total of 1,428 convicted and sentenced juvenile offenders were granted the same privelege.[10] In the Superior Court of Maricopa County, Arizona, 538 of a total of 1,058 adults convicted and sentenced between July 1, 1960 and June 30, 1961 remained free on probation, or slightly more than 50 percent.[11] These statistics speak for themselves. They indicate the need to attend to the legal problems surrounding probation, which so far have received surprisingly little attention.[12]

Probation, in the strict sense of the term, requires some degree of supervision by a probation officer, though in some cases the defendant simply may be released from custody with only the restriction that he does not violate the law again while his sentence is suspended. Courts may grant suspension of sentence either by imposing sentence and suspending the execution thereof, or by suspending the imposition of sentence. As long as a probationer fulfills the conditions imposed by the court the result of either method is the same, *i.e.*, the release of the defendant;[13] but in case of revocation of probation

---

[8]*Cal. Bureau of Criminal Statistics, Crime in California* 80 (1957).

[9]*1959 Ann. Rep. Administrative Office of the United States Courts* 236–238 (1960).

[10]*1960 Ann. Rep. Administrative Office of the United States Courts* 304–309 (1961). There are now more than 26,000 persons under the supervision of United States probation officers. *Id.* at 310–315. In England and Wales, of 116,000 persons found guilty by the courts in 1956, 28,000 were placed on probation (16,000 out of 39,000 young offenders; 12,000 out of 77,000 adult offenders). See *Report of the Cambridge Department of Criminal Science, The Results of Probation* ii (1958). Figures for England and Wales from 1948–1955 are also given. *Id.* at 110.

[11]Adult Probation Dep't Ann. Rep. Superior Court of Maricopa County (1960–1961) on file in Adult Probation Department, Maricopa County Courthouse, Phoenix, Arizona.

[12]Two recent discussions represent notable exceptions to this lack of attention: Note, *Legal Aspects of Probation Revocation*, 59 Colum. L. Rev. 311 (1959); and Comment, *Probationer's Right to Appeal; Appellant's Right to Probation*, 28 U. Chi. L. Rev. 751 (1961).

[13]15 Am. Jur. *Criminal Law* § 479: "The courts use the phrase 'suspending sentence as meaning both delay in the giving of sentence and also staying the execution of a sentence imposed." Korematsu v. United States, 319 U.S. 432, 435 (1943): "The difference to the probationer between imposition of sentence followed by probation . . . and suspension of the imposition of sentence . . . is one of trifling degree."

the consequences attached to each method may be substantially different.[14]

Since probation is an act of grace, judges have considerable latitude as to the substantive content of conditions they may wish to impose. Probation statutes usually give the trial judge broad discretion. According to the Federal Probation Act the judge may impose "such terms and conditions as the court deems best."[15] The California Penal Code provides that conditions of probation must be "reasonable."[16] To determine the meaning of such legislative language is difficult, though attempts in this direction have been made.[17] These attempts have not always been successful. For example, a California District Court of Appeals has found it a reasonable condition of probation that the syphilitic defendant, convicted of statutory rape, submit to a vasectomy.[18] It is difficult to see where such sterilization, though it would prevent the procreation of syphilitic descendants, would suppress a future recurrence of the anti-social urges for which the defendant was convicted. On the whole it appears that the cases interpreting "reasonable" have not added much content to probation standards.

An interesting problem is raised where the court requires the probationer to leave the state and not to return for the period of probation. In a 1930 Prohibition case the Michigan Supreme Court has held such a condition invalid on the grounds that the practice of a state to "dump" its criminals on other states would invite retaliation and was in violation of the fundamental equality of states. The condition was rescinded on the ground that it was against accepted public policy.[19] A California court, in a case involving a similar condition, refused to rule on the trial court's power by holding that the defendant had indicated her refusal to accept probation.[20]

Another group of cases discusses the power of the sentencing judge to make payment of a sum of money by the defendant to a third party a condition of probation.[21] In this type of case appellate courts may look for a standard of

---

[14]The distinction between imposition of sentence followed by probation and suspension of the imposition of sentence also is of no practical significance in the area of probationer's right to appeal. See Comment, *Probationer's Right to Appeal; Appellant's Right to Probation*, 28 *U. Chi. L. Rev.* 751, 757 (1961). However, the distinction is not always artificial. It can be of considerable significance upon revocation of probation. See Part IV *infra*.

[15]18 U.S.C. § 3651 (1958). Similarly, *Ariz. Rev. Stat. Ann.* §. 13–1657 A(1) (1956): "upon such terms and conditions as the court determines."

[16]*Cal. Pen. Code* § 1203.1 (1958 Supp.).

[17]*E.g.*, Redwill v. Superior Court, 43 Ariz. 68, 78, 29 P.2d 475, 479 (1934): "[The] condition ... must be one which has some reasonable bearing upon the prevention of future crime"; Varela v. Merrill, 51 Ariz. 64, 76, 74 P.2d 569, 574 (1937): "It would be almost impossible to present a case which would justify this court in finding that the trial court had abused its discretion in regard to whether sentence should be suspended or not."

[18]People v. Blankenship, 16 Cal. App. 2d 606, 61 P.2d 352 (1936).

[19]People v. Baum, 251 Mich. 187, 231 N.W. 95 (1930).

[20]People v. Billingsley, 59 Cal. App. 2d 845, 139 P.2d 362 (1943).

[21]*E.g.*, People v. Becker, 349 Mich. 476, 84 N.W.2d 833 (1957); People v. Prell, 299 Ill. App. 130, 19 N.E.2d 637 (1939); State v. Barnett, 110 Vt. 221, 2 A.2d 521 (1939); People v. Good, 287 Mich. 110, 282 N.W. 920 (1938).

fairness and reasonableness, but on the whole they have refused to review conditions imposed by the trial court in terms of constitutional language.[22]

Do not provisions in the federal and in state constitutions offer a possible source of limitations on the substantive content of probation provisions? Three such provisions in the United States Constitution would appear to be applicable: the due process clause in the fifth and in the fourteenth amendments, the prohibition of cruel and unusual punishment in the eight amendment, and the equal protection clause in the fourteenth amendment.

The case law shows little evidence of the courts' readiness to apply these constitutional limitations to probation cases. The one clear exception is the 1957 *Becker* case referred to at the beginning of this paper. In that case, the Michigan Supreme Court (emphasizing the legal distinction between restitution and reparation) held that it was a violation of due process to impose as a condition of probation in a hit-and-run conviction the payment of a sum of money by the defendant to the injured witness, inasmuch as the liability of the defendant for the injuries sustained had not been fixed in a constitutional sense.[23]

Another possible constitutional approach to protect probationers against harsh probation conditions would be through the eighth amendment. It can well be argued that the condition imposed by the California court, requiring sterilization, constitutes the infliction of cruel and unusual punishment. It is uncertain, of course, to what extent the fourteenth amendment prohibits states from inflicting such punishment in the absence of a specific provision to that effect in the state constitution.[24] But even in a federal case the argument has not been successful. The Ninth Circuit Court of Appeals has held that "the conditions of probation are not punitive in character and the question of whether or not the terms are cruel and unusual and thus violative of the Constitution of the United States does not arise for the reason that the Constitution applies only to punishment. These conditions of probation are intended to be an amelioration of the punishment prescribed by law for the given offense."[25] If the court admits that probation is intended to substitute a milder form of retribution for the original punishment, how can it follow that probation must not meet at least the same degree of constitutional limitation against cruel and unusual terms? A reviewer rightly remarks that there is in fact no meaningful distinction from the point of view of a convicted defendant

---

[22]The one clear use of constitutional language may be found in People v. Becker, 349 Mich. at 486, 84 N.W.2d at 838: "[E]ven where imposition of the restitution requirement is held to be proper under the circumstances of the particular case before the court, it can be imposed only as to loss caused by the very offense for which defendant was tried and convicted. As to the other crimes or offenses there has been no fixing of his liability therefore in a constitutional sense."

[23]*Ibid.*

[24]See Note, *Legal Aspects of Probation Revocation*, 59 Colum. L. Rev. 311, 319 n.59 (1959). Some state constitutions, however, contain prohibitions against the infliction of cruel and unusual punishment: Mo. Const. art. I, § 21; Wis. Const. art. I, § 6; Utah Const. art. I, § 9.

[25]Springer v. United States, 148 F.2d 411, 415 (9th Cir. 1945).

between imposition of the condition and imposition of punishment for the crime for which he was convicted. The threat of lengthy imprisonment may virtually force the defendant to accept such a condition.[26]

This argument could be extended even further. One may ask, in view of the large number of first offenders placed on probation, whether fulfilment of the conditions contained in the probation order does not in reality become the punishment to which the convicted defendant is sentenced? Is the reasoning of the Ninth Circuit Court of Appeals really valid? The Supreme Court has pointed out that sterilization "involves one of the basic civil rights of man. Marriage and procreation are fundamental to the very existence and survival of the race. The power to sterilize, if exercised, may have subtle, far-reaching and devastating effects. . . . There is no redemption for the individual whom the law touches. Any experiment which the State conducts is to his irreparable injury. He is forever deprived of a basic liberty."[27] Can it be maintained that a defendant placed on probation has less of a right to be protected against sterilization than the courts might be willing to grant to a defendant facing punishment? In *Trop v. Dulles*, Mr. Chief Justice Warren has interpreted the eighth amendment very broadly: "The Amendment must draw its meaning from the evolving standards of decency that mark the progress of a maturing society."[28] Perhaps this language indicates that "cruel and unusual punishment" has no intelligible outline at all. But if it does have such an outline, "the progress of a maturing society"—which has substituted rehabilitation for imprisonment—requires that the conditions of probation should not be permitted to be any more cruel and unusual than the terms of punishment.

Finally, it may be asked whether the equal protection clause of the fourteenth amendment does not place constitutional limits on probation conditions? The "equal protection" argument is forcefully advanced in a recent Comment on "Probationer's Right to Appeal; Appellant's Right to Probation" in this *Law Review*.[29] The author of that Comment argues convincingly that it is against the equal protection clause to require a defendant to make a choice between probation and appeal. It is irrelevant, in his opinion, that probationers are not incarcerated. They are neither more nor less worthy of protection than prisoners because the court has adjudged them capable of rehabilitation. "The indisputable fact is that to be placed on probation is to be punished. Defendants ought not to be discriminated against on the ground that they have received probation rather than incarceration any more than should defendants who have

---

[26]Note, *Legal Aspects of Probation Revocation*, 59 Colum. L. Rev. 311, 319 (1959).

[27]Skinner v. Oklahoma, 316 U.S. 535, 541 (1942). The Oklahoma sterilization statute was declared unconstitutional under the equal protection clause; but the Court expressly reserved the question of whether the statute violated the cruel and unusual punishment prohibition. *Id.* at 538.

[28]356 U.S. 86, 101 (1957).

[29]28 U. Chi. L. Rev. 751, 760–761 (1961).

been fined rather than incarcerated."[30] This argument applies with equal force to conditions of probation. In the *Skinner* case the state discriminated between thieves (subject to sterilization) and embezzlers (not so subject); in probation cases the discrimination is between defendants amenable to rehabilitation (probationers) and defendants not so amenable (prisoners).

III

Despite the broad discretion of the trial court to grant or to withhold probation and to impose conditions, it is a universal rule that probation, once granted, cannot be revoked except for violation of a condition.[31] But there is a good deal of diversity as to the procedure accorded probationers in case of revocation with regard to the right to receive notice, have a hearing, inspect and present evidence and cross-examine, and be assisted by counsel.

The most crucial and elementary problem of procedure is that of allowing the accused a hearing before revoking his probation. Statutory requirements vary. The Federal Probation Act and the probation statutes of a number of states require that a probationer accused of violating the conditions of his release should be "taken before the court,"[32] or must be given an "opportunity to be heard,"[33] a "summary hearing,"[34] an "opportunity to be fully heard,"[35] or simply that he should be given a "hearing."[36] Other statutes specifically state that a hearing is not required.[37] A third group of statutes, including the Arizona and the California probation laws, are construed as not requiring a hearing,[38]

---

[30]*Id.* at 761.

[31]*Compare* Note, *Legal Aspects of Probation Revocation*, 59 Colum. L. Rev. 311, 314 (1959), *with* cases cited note 24 *supra*.

[32]*E.g.*, 18 U.S.C. § 3653 (1958); Miss. Code Ann. § 4004–4025 (1956) ("brought before the court"); Wash. Rev. Code § 9:95.220 (1951) ("brought before the court"); Wis. Stat. § 57.01 (1959) ("brought before the court").

[33]*E.g.*, N.Y. Code Crim. Proc. § 935; N.Y.C. Crim. Cts. Act § 154.

[34]*E.g.*, Idaho Code Ann. § 20–222 (1949); N.H. Rev. Stat. Ann. § 504.4 (1955); N.J. Stat. Ann. § 2A. 168–4 (1953); Ore. Rev. Stat. § 137.550 (1953); W. Va. Code Ann. § 6291(17) (1961).

[35]*E.g.*, Fla. Stat. Ann. § 948.06 (1944); Ga. Code Ann. § 27–2713 (Supp. 1958).

[36]*E.g.*, Ala. Code tit. 42, § 24 (1961); Colo. Rev. Stat. Ann. § 39–16–9 (1953); Ind. Ann. Stat. § 9–2211 (1956); La. Rev. Stat. § 15:533 (1950); N. C. Gen. Stat. § 15–200 (Supp. 1959); Tenn. Code Ann. § 40–2907 (1955); Tex. Code Crim. Proc. art. 781b(5) (1950).

[37]*E.g.*, Del. Code Ann.tit. 11, § 4321 (1953) ("without any further proceeding"); N.Y.C. Dom. Rel. Ct. Act. § 135 ("without a further hearing").

[38]Ariz. Rev. Stat. § 13–1657 (1956) ("without warrant or other process"). See *Ex parte Johnson*, 53 Ariz. 161, 164, 87 P.2d 107, 108 (1939). Cal. Pen. Code § 1203.2: "At any time during the probationary period . . . the court may in its discretion issue a warrant for the rearrest of any such person and may thereupon revoke and terminate such probation, if the interests of justice so require, and if the court in its judgment, shall have reason to believe from the report of the probation officer, or otherwise, that the person so placed upon probation is violating any of the conditions of his probation, or engaging in criminal practices, or has become abandoned to improper associates or a vicious life," See *In re* Davis, 37 Cal. 2d 872, 874–5, 236 P.2d 579, 581 (1951): in the absence of statutory procedural regulation, "the administration of justice is better

though the California Courts have granted probationers a hearing regularly as a matter of discretion.[39]

In a number of cases probationers have asserted that the lack of certain procedural safeguards, such as the right to an adequate hearing, is violative of the constitutional requirement of due process of Law. The courts are divided on this issue. Most state supreme courts refuse to find a violation of due process on the ground that probation is a privilege not protected by the Constitution. A typical example of this type of judicial reasoning is presented by the Michigan Supreme Court:

> "Respondent has not been deprived of his liberty without due process of law. When he pleaded guilty to the information filed against him, he might have been sentenced at once. It is only by the mercy of the law that he was given probation. If by the violation of the terms of his probation he is called before the court for sentence for the crime of which he had freely pleaded guilty, it cannot be said that he is deprived of his liberty without due process of law.[40]

The United States Supreme Court, in one of the rare cases reaching that tribunal on questions of probation procedure, has held that "while probation is a matter of grace, the probationer is entitled to fair treatment and is not to be made the victim of whim or caprice."[41] Some state courts have gone further and have admitted the probationer's right to due process in the constitutional sense. The New Mexico Supreme Court has held that: "Upon principle it would seem that due process of law would require notice and opportunity to be heard . . . ."[42] The same opinion was expressed by the Utah Supreme Court in a decision which is also worth noting for its reasoning:

> "The purpose of the law permitting the suspension of sentence is clearly reformatory. If those who are to be reformed cannot implicitly rely upon promises or orders contained in the suspension of sentence, then we may well expect the law to fail in its purpose. Reformation can certainly best be accomplished by fair, consistent, and straightforward treatment of the person sought to be reformed. It would therefore seem, both upon authority and principle that when a sentence is suspended during good behavior, without reservations, the person whose sentence is thus suspended has a vested right to rely thereon so long as such condition is complied with. The right to

---

served by permitting ex parte revocation of probation than by absolutely requiring notice and hearing." *Accord, In re* Levi, 39 Cal.2d 41, 244 P.2d 403 (1952), where the court held that there is no constitutional or statutory right to a hearing preceding revocation of probation. If such a hearing is granted, it is not subject to the rules governing criminal trials. In People v. McClean, 130 Cal. App. 2d 439, 279 P.2d 87 (1955), it was held that revocation solely on the basis of the report of a probation officer was valid.

[39]*E.g.,* Wadler v. Justice Court, 144 Cal. App. 2d 739, 301 P.2d 907 (1956).

[40]People v. Dudley, 173 Mich. 389, 397, 138 N.W. 1044, 1047 (1912); *Accord,* Varela v. Merrill, 51 Ariz. 64, 70, 74, P.2d 569, 572 (1937).

[41]Burns v. United States, 287 U.S. 216, 223 (1932). For a discussion of the *Burns* case see Comment, *Probation—Progress Through Legislation,* 3 Wayne L. Rev. 125, 131–32 (1957).

[42]*Ex parte* Lucero, 23 N.M. 433, 438, 168 Pac. 713, 715 (1917); *Accord,* State v. O'Neal, 147 Wash. 169, 172, 265 Pac. 175, 176 (1928).

personal liberty is one of the most sacred and valuable rights of a citizen, and should not be regarded lightly. The right to personal liberty may be as valuable to one con- victed of crime as to one not so convicted, and so long as one complies with the conditions upon which such right is assured by judicial declaration, he may not be deprived of the same. Such right may not be alternatively granted and denied without just cause."[43]

Professor Wechsler recently has argued that the Bill of Rights "leave[s] room for adaptation and adjustment if and when competing values, also having constitutional dimension, enter on the scene."[44] It is suggested that certain aspects of probation have this "constitutional dimension." It constitutes a minimum requirement of fairness—in the sense in which the Supreme Court has applied this standard to pre-trial and trial procedure in order to satisfy the requirements of due process—to allow a probationer accused of probation violation to be heard before revoking the order granting him liberty. If, for instance, the Supreme Court of the United States considers arraignment so critical a stage of criminal procedure that denial of counsel at arraignment must result in reversal of a defendant's conviction,[45] is it not reasonable to argue that the right to counsel and the right to a hearing also are critical and are as worthy of constitutional protection in a revocation of probation pro- ceeding?

The discretionary character of the grant of probation should not deprive its recipient of the standards of procedural protection necessary for a fair deter- mination of his conduct. One has to agree with the conclusions reached in a Note on "Legal Aspects of Probation Revocation" in the *Columbia Law Review* that recent Supreme Court decisions in the area of public employment[46] and in a case involving admission to the bar[47] "cast increasing doubt on the proposition that an interest is unprotected by the due process clause merely because it was granted as a matter of grace or discretion."[48] Though he found no case discussing this line of reasoning, the author of the Note further suggests that probationers may also "claim a constitutional right to procedural safe- guards under the equal protection clause by contending that the differences between factual determinations in a revocation proceeding and those in a trial ... does not reasonably justify the difference between the procedures utilized in each."[49]

---

[43]State v. Zolantakis, 70 Utah 296, 303, 259 Pac. 1044, 1046 (1927).

[44]Wechsler, *Toward Neutral Principles of Constitutional Law*, 73 Harv. L. Rev. 1, 19 (1959).

[45]Hamilton v. Alabama, 368 U.S. 52 (1961). See note 2 *supra*.

[46]Slochower v. Board of Educ., 350 U.S. 551 (1956); Wieman v. Updegraff, 344 U.S. 183 (1952).

[47]Schware v. Board of Bar Examiners, 353 U.S. 232 (1957).

[48]59 Colum. L. Rev. 311, 325 (1959). Weihofen. *Revoking Probation, Parole or Pardon Without a Hearing*, 32 J. Crim. L. & C. 531 (1942), favors a hearing in all these cases as a constitution?! right as well as a matter of good practice. But on parole see White, *Some Legal Aspects of Parole*, 32 J. Crim. L & C. 600 (1942).

[49]59 Colum. L. Rev. at 326.

In the opinion of the present writer the increased use of probation as a modern substitute for traditional forms of legal punishment calls for an extension of constitutional standards to some aspects of probation procedure. The report of a probation officer by itself should never be sufficient cause to revoke a probation order. The accused should always be granted a hearing and have an opportunity to present his side of the case. Explained by the defendant, the alleged probation infraction may appear in an entirely different light. The American Law Institute has found the question of a hearing to be "an area where dangers of abuse are real and the normal procedural protection proper. That a defendant has no right to the suspension or probation does not justify the alteration of his status by methods that must seem and sometimes be unfair."[50] Accordingly, the *Model Penal Code*, Section 301.4 provides: "The Court shall not revoke a suspension of probation or increase the requirements imposed thereby on the defendant except after a hearing upon written notice to the defendant of the grounds on which such action is proposed. The defendant shall have the right to hear and controvert the evidence against him, to offer evidence in his defense and to be represented by counsel."[51]

IV

Finally, it may be asked, what happens when a probation order is revoked? Here, statutes permitting the judge to suspend imposition of sentence normally impower the court to pronounce the sentence which could originally have been imposed.[52] Probation statutes permitting the trial court to suspend the execution of sentence provide in case of revocation either that the original sentence shall become effective,[53] or that the court may impose lesser sentence,[54] or that the court may now impose the punishment which could originally have been imposed.[55]

Where statutes permitting the court to suspend the execution of sentence provide that the judge upon revocation of probation may impose the punishment which could originally have been imposed for the offense committed, the distinction between suspension of the imposition of sentence and suspension of the execution of sentence is artificial. In either case, the defendant whose probation has been revoked may receive the maximum penalty prescribed by law

---

[50] Model Penal Code § 301.4, comment (Tent. Drafts Nos. 2, 1954 & 4, 1955).

[51] *Ibid.*

[52] *E.g.*, Ariz. Rev. Stat. Ann. § 13–1657 (1956); Colo. Rev. Stat. Ann. § 39-16-9 (1953); Ky. Rev. Stat. Ann. § 439.050 (1955).

[53] *E.g.*, Ariz. Rev. Stat. Ann. § 13–1657 (1956); Cal. Pen. Code § 1203.2; Wash. Rev. Code § 9:95.220 (1951).

[54] *E.g.*, 18 U.S.C. 3653 (1958); Conn. Gen. Stat. Rev. § 54–114 (1958).

[55] *E.g.*, Colo. Rev. Stat. Ann. § 39-16-9 (1953); Ind. Ann. Stat. § 9–2211 (1956); N.Y. Pen. Code § 2188; N.Y. Code Crim. Proc. § 470(a), 483(4). See also the Federal Probation Act of 1925, ch. 521, § 725, 43 Stat. 1260.

for the offense of which he was convicted. But in jurisdictions with statutes which provide that in case of the revocation of a probation order suspending the execution of sentence the original sentence shall become effective, or that a lesser sentence may be imposed, the distinction between suspension of the imposition of sentence and suspension of the execution of sentence becomes a matter of practical significance. In such jurisdictions probationers under suspended imposition of sentence face the maximum penalty if their probation is revoked; while defendants on probation under suspended execution of sentence are confronted with only the punishment to which they had been originally sentenced.

The authority to increase a suspended sentence upon revocation and the practice of suspending the imposition of sentence until the time of revocation raise basic questions inherent in the whole probation process. Admittedly, probation is a privilege which in most jurisdictions the defendant may refuse if he prefers the punishment. But, where the court suspends the imposition of sentence, does the defendant know his punishment?[56] Does he really have a choice? Faced with the possible threat of a long, indeterminate sentence, is the defendant not actually forced into accepting probation and all its conditions? Suspension of imposition of sentence results in great uncertainty. Is such uncertainty necessary for the orderly administration of a successful probation system? Could not trial courts make the alternative to probation more specific without jeopardizing the objectives of probation? A person accused of crime has the right to have a specific charge brought against him. Should not a person found guilty and convicted, but also found deserving of probation, have the opportunity of knowing the alternative to his refusal or violation of probation? Would not such knowledge further the rehabilitation of an offender by making him more willing to fulfill the conditions of the court's probation order.

Another consideration enters into this matter. The trial judge, in granting probation, cannot from a realistic point of view rely on future performance alone. He must also, perhaps primarily, consider the defendant's past character, history and record. Probation is granted on the basis of what the judge knows at the time of sentencing. If later the grant of probation has to be rescinded, the penalty for the original offense still ought to be determined by the circumstances known at the time of sentence. It should not be aggravated by the fact that the accused later violates his probation, a matter for which he had no proper trial. Probation should not become a test of how deserving the defendant was of punishment for the original crime. The fact that only undeserving probationers, those who have broken conditions of probation, are affected by the present practice of increasing sentence does not matter. Probation is not intended to be punitive in character. Suspension of sentence bears inherent

---

[56] For examples of the wide range between possible minimum and maximum sentence see Wood & Waite, *op. cit. supra* note 1, at 436–37.

dangers to proper procedural conduct. It would be desirable if the courts would discontinue their practice.[57]

The same argument may be used against statutes permitting the court to set aside the original sentence and to impose the punishment which could originally have been imposed. It is doubtful that the courts will find such procedure in violation of the double jeopardy clause of the Constitution: "Under the probation act an increase in sentence is expressly authorized by the statute . . . and, consequently, it is potentially a part of the original sentence."[58] Therefore, revocation of a suspended sentence and imposition of a higher penalty "did not constitute double jeopardy under the Fifth Amendment to the Constitution."[59] But, again, nothing stands in the way of judicial self-restraint; and it is interesting to note that when the Supreme Court of the United States came to deal with the issue of increasing sentence upon revocation of probation under the Federal Probation Act of 1925, it ruled that the act had not intended to grant this power: "[H]aving exercised its discretion by sentencing an offender to a definite term of imprisonment in advance of probation, a court may not later upon revocation of probation set aside that sentence and increase the term of imprisonment."[60]

To sum up the ideas advanced in this paper: The rigid distinction between the procedural safeguards of a person accused of crime and those of a convicted defendant granted probation is unrealistic. In the interest of the protection of individual rights, which include the rights of persons convicted of a criminal offense, probation procedures should be brought into as much conformity with procedural and substantive safeguards as the purpose and the administration of a sound probation program will permit. Though probation is an act of clemency in the discretion of the trial court, a probationer should not be subjected to conditions violative of the intention if not the letter of due process and the

[57]*But see* the arguments of Mr. Justice Frankfurter, in Roberts v. United States, 320 U.S. 264, 273 (1943) (dissenting opinion).

[58]Remer v. Regan, 104 F.2d 704, 705 (9th Cir. 1939).

[59]Roberts v. United States, 131 F.2d 392, 393 (5th Cir. 1943). Reversing on other grounds, the Supreme Court of the United States in this case reserved the question of double jeopardy. See Roberts v. United States, 320 U.S. 264, 265 (1943).

[60]320 U.S. at 272–73. *But see* Mr. Justice Frankfurter's dissent, *id.* at 273–77; and the discussion of the *Roberts* case in Puttkammer, *The Trial Court's Freedom of Discretion in Sentencing After Revocation of Probation*, 11 U. Chi. L. Rev. 286 (1944). The language of 18 U.S.C. § 3653.4 (1958) is now changed to bring about conformity with the decision in the *Roberts* case: "Thereupon the court may revoke the probation and require him to serve the sentence imposed, or any lesser sentence, and, if imposition of sentence was suspended, may impose any sentence which might originally have been imposed." However, the Model Penal Code § 301.2(2) (Tent. Draft No. 4, 1955), permits the imposition of the originally possible sentence in suspension-of-execution cases under certain circumstances: "when the Court revokes a suspension or probation, it may impose on the defendant any sentence that might have been imposed originally . . . except that the defendant shall not be sentenced to imprisonment unless: (a) he has been convicted of another crime; or (b) his misconduct indicates that his continued liberty involves excessive risk that he will commit another crime; or (c) such disposition is essential to vindicate the authority of the Court or the probation officer and is not unjust to the defendant."

equal protection of the law. Before revocation of his probation, or the imposition of more severe probation conditions, the accused should be entitled, as a matter of right, to a hearing before the trial court. Finally, a judicial effort should be made to reconcile the element of flexibility essential to the probation system with safeguards against a later increase in punishment by making the alternative to probation as predictable as possible.

34

Conditions of Probation

UNITED STATES COURTS

PROBATION FORM No. 7
(February 1964)

Conditions of Probation

UNITED STATES DISTRICT COURT
FOR THE

_____

To _____   Docket No.

Address _____

In accordance with authority conferred by the United States Probation Law, you have been placed on probation this date,   , for a period of   by the Hon.   United States District Judge, sitting in and for this District Court at

CONDITIONS OF PROBATION

It is the order of the Court that you shall comply with the following conditions of probation:

(1) You shall refrain from violation of any law (federal, state, and local). You shall get in touch immediately with your probation officer if arrested or questioned by a law-enforcement officer.

(2) You shall associate only with law-abiding persons and maintain reasonable hours.

(3) You shall work regularly at a lawful occupation and support your legal dependents, if any, to the best of your ability. When out of work you shall notify your probation officer at once. You shall consult him prior to job changes.

(4) You shall not leave the judicial district without permission of the probation officer.

(5) You shall notify your probation officer immediately of any change in your place of residence.

(6) You shall follow the probation officer's instructions and advice.

(7) You shall report to the probation officer as directed.

The special conditions ordered by the Court are as follows:

I understand that the Court may change the conditions of probation, reduce or extend the period of probation, and at any time during the probation period or within the maximum probation period of 5 years permitted by law, may issue a warrant and revoke probation for a violation occurring during the probation period.

I have read or had read to me the above conditions of probation. I fully understand them and I will abide by them.

(Signed)_____   _____

You will report as follows: Probationer   Date

_____   _____

U. S. Probation Officer   Date

35

Conditions of Probation: An Analysis

JUDAH BEST AND PAUL I. BIRZON

INTRODUCTION

Basic to modern penology are the premises that society as a whole profits most from a rehabilitation and reformation of the criminal offender, that correction is most effective when attention is paid to the particular difficulties of the individual offender (an "individualized justice,"[1] so to speak), and that rehabilitation should and must be accomplished, whenever feasible, without resort to the corrupting influence of institutional life. These premises, hardly novel,[2] find their greatest realization today in the procedure known as probation.[3]

"Probation enables the offender to reshape his life in the framework of normal living conditions; it preserves family life and other normal social relationships; it enables the offender to carry out his responsibilities by supporting himself and his family.

SOURCE. *Georgetown Law Journal*, **51**, 1963, pp. 809–836. Copyright 1963, by the Georgetown Law Journal Association.

[1] Probation and Criminal Justice 225 (Glueck ed. 1933). See National Probation and Parole Ass'n Advisory Council of Judges, Guides for Sentencing 5–11 (1957).

[2] The theory of probation evolved from antecedent practices, all intended to lessen or otherwise mitigate the severities of the penal code. In English common law the courts were presumed to have power to suspend sentence for specified purposes and periods. On this basic authority rest the devices which preceded probation. Dressler, Practice and Theory of Probation and Parole 6–7 (1959).

[3] Probation may be defined as a procedure of social investigation and supervisory treatment used by the courts for selected individuals convicted of law violations. During the period of probation the offender lives a comparatively normal life in the community and regulates his conduct under the conditions imposed by the court and subject to the supervision and guidance

Probation avoids the shattering impact of imprisonment on personality; it avoids imprisonment's stimulation of hatred of law-abiding society; it avoids confining the reformable offender with hardened criminals who might have a contaminating effect on him; [and] it avoids the stigma attached to imprisonment. . . ."[4]

One of the most important aspects of probation is the matter of conditions accompanying the grant. Ideally, they should be imposed with a view toward assisting the offender in his rehabilitation. Practically, they may be used to assist the court in its supervision of the probationer. Too often, however, they are used to accomplish results which, while socially desirable in the eyes of some, serve neither of these ends. Take, as an illustration, the following situation. A twenty-three year old male defendant pleads guilty to having had sexual relations with a female minor and makes application for probation. Both he and the girl are suffering from syphilis, but there is no positive evidence to demonstrate that the defendant communicated the disease to the girl. All of this information is before the court at the time of sentencing. The trial court sentences the defendant to a term of imprisonment for five years with execution of the sentence suspended upon the fulfillment of certain conditions, among which is the requirement that the defendant be sterilized.

An unreal situation? This occurred in California in 1936. In affirming the trial court's refusal to modify the condition, the California District Court of Appeals stated that:

"As the trial court very properly observed, it was not so much concerned with curing the disease with which appellant was afflicted as it was with preventing appellant from transmitting the disease to his possible posterity. If reproduction is desirable to the end that the race shall continue, it is equally desirable that the

---

of a probation officer. The National Probation and Parole Ass'n, Probation Handbook 5. The suspended sentence should not be confused with probation. "The latter involves supervision of the convicted offender; the former does not." National Probation and Parole Ass'n, Advisory Council of Judges, op. cit. supra note 1 at 23. In many jurisdictions the courts have the power, either inherently or by statute, to suspend sentence and to release the offender without placing him under the supervision of a probation counselor. "This is sometimes more suitable than probation which it is sometimes incorrectly called." National Probation and Parole Ass'n, Standards for the Practice of Adult Probation 14 (Tent. Draft 1958). Finally, parole may be distinguished from probation in that:

Parole is a form of release granted after a prisoner has served a portion of his sentence in a penal institution; probation, properly applied, is granted an offender without requiring incarceration. Parole is an administrative act of the executive or an executive agency. Probation is a judicial act of the court . . . . 4 U.S. Dep't of Justice, Attorney General's Survey of Release Procedures 1 (1939).

In 1961, in the state of California, 12,566 adult offenders were granted probation. This number comprised 48.3% of those seeking probation. California Bureau of Criminal Statistics, Delinquency and Probation in California (1961).

[4] National Probation and Parole Ass'n Advisory Council of Judges, op. cit. supra note 1, at 16.

race shall be a healthy race and not one whose members are afflicted by a loathsome and debilitating disease."[5]

The defendant (quite properly, we submit) refused probation on the terms offered and went to jail. Yet, since the trial court had initially determined that he was a fit candidate for rehabilitation, it would seem that society as well as the defendant profited little from the five years incarceration.

While this case may present an extreme factual situation which is not likely to be repeated, it is nevertheless representative of the many uses to which probation has been put and of the attitudes which have made them possible. Because the trial courts are under very little restraint as to the conditions which they may impose as concomitants of the probation grant, because all too few procedural safeguards are provided the offender, and because there is a general reluctance on the part of the reviewing courts to inquire into the purpose of conditions already imposed, probation may be used as a vehicle for ends wholly unrelated to the reformation of the offender. Of even greater concern, moreover, is the danger that in permitting such a latitude in imposing conditions, the purpose and effect of probation may be negated.

The function of this article is to examine the proper purpose of the conditions imposed within the probation process. In so doing, we have attempted to categorize and evaluate those types of conditions most commonly imposed upon the would-be probationer. This evaluation of necessity requires an appraisal of the safeguards provided by the legislature and the reviewing courts against the imposition of unreasonable, illegal, or in some instances, unconstitutional conditions. With this end in mind, it is hoped that the weaknesses which presently exist in the probation system will be pointed out and some constructive suggestions for their improvement offered. Prior to embarking upon this evaluation, however, some consideration should be given to certain general concepts of probation along with a brief outline of the probation process itself.

THE PROBATION PROCESS

While certain procedural rights may attach once probation has been granted,[6] it is generally conceded that its initial grant is a matter of privilege to be granted or refused at the discretion of the state. In determining whether

---

[5] People v. Blankenship, 16 Cal. App. 2d 606, 61 P.2d 352, 353 (Dist. Ct. App. 1936).

[6] The requirements of notice and hearing in a proceeding to revoke probation have been incorporated into the statutes of many jurisdictions. See, e.g., N.Y. Code Crim. Proc. § 935 (right to hearing); Ore. Rev. Stat. § 137.550 (Supp. 1961) (summary hearing); cf. State v. Zolantakis, 70 Utah 296, 259 Pac. 1044 (1927) (requirements of hearing and right to cross examination judicially read into statute). Contra, Hyser v. Reed, No. 16716, D.C. Cir., April 11, 1963, p. 50 (Bazelon, J., dissenting). See generally, Note, Legal Aspects of Probation Revocation, 59 Colum. L. Rev. 311 (1959).

probation shall be made available to certain classes of offenders, controlling emphasis has been variously placed by the legislatures upon the nature of the offense,[7] the type of punishment called for by the offense,[8] and the character of the offender.[9] However, in a minority of jurisdictions probation may be extended to all classes of offenders without regard to such qualifications,[10] and the drafters of the Model Penal Code have taken the position that since no legislative classification of offenses can take account of all contingencies, discretion to authorize probation should be vested in the trial court in all cases save where sentence of death or life imprisonment is ultimately prescribed.[11]

While these restrictions on the courts' power exist largely because of a subordination of the community's desire for rehabilitation to its desire for retribution and deterrence,[12] further limitations have been imposed

---

[7] E.g., Pa. Stat. tit. 61, § 331.25 (Supp. 1962) (first degree murder); Colo. Rev. Stat. Ann. § 39–16–3 (1953); Hawaii Rev. Laws § 258–53 (1955); Nev. Rev. Stat. § 176.3001 (1959) (first or second degree murder); Okla. Stat. Ann. tit. 22, § 991 (Supp. 1957) (manslaughter); Cal. Pen. Code § 1203; D.C. Code Ann. § 24–102 (1961); Iowa Code Ann. § 247.20 (Supp. 1962) (arson); Hawaii Rev. Laws § 258–53 (1955); Ill. Ann. Stat. ch. 38, § 785 (Smith-Hurd 1961); Neb. Rev. Stat. § 29–2217 (1956) (rape); D.C. Code Ann. § 24–102 (1961); Idaho Code Ann. § 19–2601 (Supp. 1961); Ind. Ann. Stat. § 9–2209 (1956) (treason); Cal. Pen. Code § 1203; Hawaii Rev. Laws § 258–53 (1955); Nev. Rev. Stat. § 176.300(1) (1959) (kidnapping); Cal. Pen. Code § 1203; Hawaii Rev. Laws § 258–53 (1955); Iowa Code Ann. § 247.20 (Supp. 1962) (robbery); Ind. Stat. Ann. § 9–2209 (1956); P.R. Laws Ann. tit. 34 § 1027 (Supp. 1962) (burglary); Ohio Rev. Code Ann. § 2951.04 (Page 1953) (assault with intent to rape); Cal. Pen. Code § 1203; N.Y. Pen. Laws § 2188; Ore. Rev. Stat. § 166.230 (Supp. 1961) (commission of a felony while armed with a weapon); P.R. Laws Ann. tit. 34 § 1027 (Supp. 1962) (larceny); Tex. Code Crim. Proc. art. 781 d (Supp. 1962); See Nev. Rev. Stat. § 176.300(1) (1959) (offenses against morals).

Certain crimes which are viewed with especial disfavor by a particular jurisdiction have been deemed non-probationable. E.g., Mass. Gen. Laws Ann. ch. 279, § 1 (1959) (influencing voter in connection with employment).

[8] E.g., Ga. Code Ann. § 27–2709 (Supp. 1961); N.Y. Pen. Law § 2188; Wyo. Stat. Ann. § 7–318 (1957) (death); Me. Rev. Stat. Ann. ch. 27–A, § 6 (Supp. 1959); N.C. Gen. Stat. § 15–197 (1951) (life imprisonment); Ala. Code tit. 42, § 19 (1958); Tenn. Code Ann. § 40–2901 (Supp. 1962) (imprisonment for more than ten years).

[9] See, e.g., Okla. Stat. tit. 22, § 991 (Supp. 1957), which authorizes the court to suspend sentence, provided, inter alia, the defendant has "prior thereto previously borne a good reputation." The offender's record of previous convictions is often a specific consideration. E.g., Ill. Ann. Stat. ch. 38, § 785 (Smith-Hurd 1961).

[10] See Ark. Stat. Ann. § 43–2324 (Supp. 1961); Utah Code Ann. § 77–35–17 (1953).

[11] Model Penal Code § 6.02 (3) (c), Comment (Tent. Draft No. 2, 1954); See Standard Probation and Parole Act § 12, comment (1955).

[12] See Model Penal Code § 1.02 (2), comment (Tent. Draft No. 2, 1954) wherein it is stated:

The section is drafted in the view that sentencing and treatment policy should serve the end of criminal prevention. It does not undertake, however, to state a fixed priority among the means to such prevention, i.e., the deterrence of potential criminals and the incapacitation and correction of the individual offender. These are all proper goals to be pursued in social action with respect to the offender, one or another of which may call for the larger emphasis in a particular context or situation.

where it is deemed that a special expertise may be required. In Utah, for example, there can be no probation for a defendant with a "mental abnormality" until the Superintendent of Hospitals certifies that a release is in the best interests of the public, at which point the probation authority may impose conditions to safeguard the public and the defendant.[13] Similarly, in New Mexico, a defendant who has been convicted of alcoholism may, notwithstanding the court's order, be permitted to go on probation "for such time and under such conditions" as a majority of the Commission on Alcoholism shall judge best.[14] The statutes of such jurisdictions, a brave minority, demonstrate an awareness that in certain zones of human behavior, even the most well equipped judge would be at a loss to adequately handle the problems of correction.

The probation process itself may be divided into three consecutive elements: (1) The preparation and presentation of the pre-sentence report which serves to guide the court in its decision, (2) suspension of the offender's sentence for a period under such conditions as the court may determine,[15] together with the retention of the offender within the community rather than in prison,[16] and finally (3) the supervision of the probationer by a carefully

[13]Utah Code Ann. § 77–49–7 (Supp. 1961).

[14]N.M. Stat. Ann. § 46–12–8 (1953); cf. Cal. Pen. Code § 288.1; R.I. Gen. Laws Ann. § 21–28–57 (1957).

[15]The power to suspend sentence may be vested in the trial court distinct from the power to impose probation, e.g., Nev. Rev. Stat. § 176.300 (1959), or as an incident thereof, e.g., Cal. Pen. Code § 1203.1, People v. Sidwell, 27 Cal. 2d 121, 129, 162 P.2d 913, 917 (1945).

In the absence of statutory authorization, the courts may have inherent power to suspend sentence. E.g., State v. Mungioli, 131 N.J.L. 52, 34 A.2d 752 (Sup. Ct. 1943); People ex rel Forsyth v. Court of Sessions, 141 N.Y. 288, 36 N.E. 386 (1894); State v. Pelley, 221 N.C. 487, 20 S.E.2d 850 (1942). Contra, State v. Bigelow, 76 Ariz. 13, 258 P.2d 409 (1953); Pagano v. Bechly, 211 Iowa 1294, 232 N.W. 798 (1930); State v. Blanchard, 156 Me. 30, 159 A.2d 304 (1960); Ex parte Boyd, 73 Okla. Crim. 441, 122 P.2d 162 (1942).

The statutory authority for probation in the federal courts is the Federal Probation Act. 18 U.S.C. § 3651 (1958); cf. Burns v. United States, 287 U.S. 216 (1932); Ex parte United States, 242 U.S. 27 (1916) (no inherent power in the federal courts to suspend sentence in absence of statutory authorization). The statutory authority for probation in the District of Columbia Court of General Sessions is contained in D.C. Code Ann. § 24–102 (1961). As to the applicability of the Federal Probation Act in the District of Columbia see note 155, infra. There appears to be some confusion as to whether the District of Columbia courts have inherent power to suspend sentence. Compare Miller v. United States, 41 App. D.C. 52, cert. denied. 231 U.S. 755 (1913) (inherent authority to suspend imposition of sentence at common law) with Ziegler v. District of Columbia, 71 A.2d 618 (D.C. Munic. App. 1950) (no inherent authority to suspend execution of sentence).

It would seem that where the legislature has provided a procedure for probation, that procedure should be the exclusive method for suspending punishment as a corrective device. See Ex parte Slattery, 163 Cal. 176, 124 Pac. 856 (1912); In the Matter of Grove, 43 Idaho 775, 254 Pac. 519 (1927); People ex rel Boehert v. Barrett, 202 Ill. 287, 67 N.E. 23 (1903). But see Pinkney v. State, 160 Fla. 884, 37 So.2d 157 (1948); People v. Cordell, 309 Mich. 585, 16 N.W.2d 78 (1944); People v. Kaiser, 95 Misc. 681, 159 N.Y. Supp. 322 (Sup. Ct. 1916).

trained probation officer.[17] While this article is primarily concerned with the second element, each of the three plays an important part in determining the success or failure of the probation program.

In determining whether a defendant shall be admitted to probation, the sentencing court is often instructed by the legislature to take inventory of the history and character of the offender, the nature of the offense and any other circumstances under which the offense was committed.[18] With the recognition that such an accounting calls for facts which a judge, unaided, would be inadequately equipped to gather, a decision as to sentencing is commonly delayed until a sizeable body of information concerning the offender has been collected and organized by the probation service of the court.

The results of such an investigation, which may include observation and interviews, as well as physical and mental examinations,[19] are then incorporated into a pre-sentence report which is placed at the disposal of the sentencing judge. In many states, such a pre-sentence report has been made a statutory prerequisite to probation generally,[20] or with respect to certain classes of crimes[21] or offenders.[22] The report's content may be limited to certain specific information, such as the age of the defendant, his occupation

[16]See Standard Probation and Parole Act § 2, comment (1955). The practice nevertheless exists, of granting probation subject to a condition that the probationer spend some time in jail. See, e.g., United States v. Wittameyer, 16 F. Supp. 1000 (D. Nev. 1936); People v. Osslo, 50 Cal. 2d 75, 323 P.2d 397, cert. denied, 357 U.S. 907 (1958); cf. People v. Good, 287 Mich. 110, 282 N.W. 920 (1939).

While other jurisdictions also have statutory authority for the imposition of this condition, California is notable for the frequency of its imposition. In 1961, of 12,566 adult offenders placed upon probation in California, 1766 received straight probation, 2750 received jail alone as a condition of probation, 2676 received jail plus fine or restitution as a condition. In all, 43% of those placed upon probation were required to serve some jail term as a condition of probation. California Bureau of Criminal Statistics, Delinquency and Probation in California (1961).

[17]Probation and Criminal Justice 3 (Glueck ed. 1933); Standard Probation and Parole Act § 2 (a) (1955).

[18]See, e.g., Del. Code Ann. tit. 11, § 4321 (1953); Minn. Stat. Ann. § 610.37 (Supp. 1962); Wis. Stat. § 57.01(1) (1957). See also, Model Penal Code § 7.07(3), comment (Tent. Draft No. 2, 1954); Standard Probation and Parole Act § 11 (1955). Cf., Williams v. New York, 337 U.S. 241, 249 (1948).

[19]See, e.g., Del. Code Ann. tit. 11, § 4343 (1953); N.Y. Pen. Law § 2188.

[20]E.g., Cal. Pen. Code § 1203; Nev. Rev. Stat. § 176.300(2) (1959); P.R. Laws Ann. tit. 34 § 1027 (Supp. 1962).

The report may be mandatory unless the court orders otherwise in some jurisdictions. See e.g., Fed. R. Crim. P. 32(c) (1); Ore. Rev. Stat. § 137.530 (Supp. 1961); S.C. Code § 55–592 (1962).

[21]A pre-sentence report may be made mandatory by statute as to felonies. See Colo. Rev. Stat. Ann. § 39–16–2 (1953); Ohio Rev. Code Ann. § 2951.03 (Page 1953); Model Penal Code § 7.07(1), comment (Tent. Draft No. 2, 1954). Such report may be mandatory as to specific offenses. E.g., Mass. Gen. Laws Ann. ch. 272, § 45 (Supp. 1962) (intoxication).

[22]Conn. Gen. Stat. Rev. § 54–109 (Supp. 1959) (first offenders); Ky. Rev. Stat. § 439.280(1) (Supp. 1962) (felons).

and background,[23] or may include recommendations as to probation[24] or both as. to probation and the imposition of specific conditions.[25]

The next step in the process is the actual grant of probation. The trial court may suspend the imposition, or pronounce sentence and then suspend execution thereof.[26] Thereupon, the offender is released, with the express understanding that he comply with one or a series of conditions enumerated by the sentencing court. The period during which the conditions are to run will often be left to the discretion of the court,[27] but statutory minima[28] and maxima[29] are frequently provided.

Upon the grant, the probationer is placed in the care of the probation officer. Many jurisdictions charge this officer with the duty to keep informed of the probationer's conduct and conditions,[30] and also authorize him to "use all suitable methods to aid and encourage him [the probationer] and to bring about improvement in his conduct and condition."[31] However, such authority is informal at best, and in one jurisdiction the officer has been limited merely to ordering the probationer to report—and even in this instance, the court must first impose such a condition to report.[32]

In addition to the authority given to the probation officer in his capacity as the immediate supervisor of the probationer, the probation department of the state is itself frequently authorized to exercise power concurrent with the court to adopt rules or regulations concerning the probationer's conduct.[33] At

---

[23] See Ill. Ann. Stat. ch. 38 § 786 (Supp. 1962); Neb. Rev. Stat. § 29–2217 (1943).

[24] Colo. Rev. Stat. Ann. § 39–16–3 (1953); Mo. Ann. Stat. § 549.251(2) (Supp. 1962); Vt. Stat. Ann. tit. 28 § 1008 (1959).

[25] Cal. Pen. Code § 1203; W. Va. Code Ann. § 6291(14) (1961).

[26] Virtually every jurisdiction authorizes both procedures by statute. E.g., Federal Probation Act, 18 U.S.C. § 3651 (1958); Cal. Pen. Code § 1203.1; Colo. Rev. Stat. Ann. § 39–16–6 (1953). The Model Penal Code contemplates only suspension of sentence and not the imposition of a sentence and suspension of its execution. The rationale for this approach is "that if a suspension works out badly and sentence is to be imposed, we do not think the nature of the sentence should be pre-determined at the moment of conviction; the causes of the failure of suspension ought to be before the Court before the sentence is determined." Model Penal Code § 6.023(b), comment (Tent. Draft No. 2, 1954).

[27] See, e.g., Colo. Rev. Stat. Ann. § 39–16–6 (1953); Utah Code Ann. § 77–35–17 (1953).

[28] E.g., La. Rev. Stat. § 15:530 (Supp. 1962) (one year); N.J. Rev. Stat. § 2A: 168–1 (1953) (one year); Ore. Rev. Stat. § 137.510 (1) (b) (Supp. 1961) (one year).

[29] E.g., Federal Probation Act, 18 U.S.C. § 3651 (1958) (five years); Ariz. Rev. Stat. Ann. § 13–1657 (1956) (maximum term called for by the offense); Fla. Stat. Ann. § 948.04 (Supp. 1962) (two years beyond the maximum term for which defendant might have been sentenced).

For the argument that utilizing criterion established to determine maximum terms of imprisonment in order to gauge the duration of probation is logically defective, see Model Penal Code § 301.2, comment (Tent. Draft No. 2, 1954).

[30] See, e.g., Conn. Gen. Stat. Rev. § 54–108 (Supp. 1959); Hawaii Rev. Laws § 258–55 (1955).

[31] Ibid; see Standard Probation and Parole Act § 10 (1955).

[32] N.Y. Code Crim. Proc. § 932 (c), People ex rel. Benacquista v. Blanchard, 267 App. Div. 663, 48 N.Y.S.2d 22 (Sup. Ct. 1944); see Standard Probation and Parole Act § 14 (1955).

[33] See, e.g., Kan. Gen. Stat. Ann. § 62–2241 (Supp. 1961); Me. Rev. Stat. Ann. ch. 27–A, § 3 (Supp. 1959); Wis. Stat. Ann § 5702 (1957). In some states responsibility for supervising probation-

least one jurisdiction requires compliance with such rules as a mandatory condition of probation,[34] while another has included such compliance in its enumeration of permissible and suggested conditions.[35] Once again these administrative rules remain subordinate to the authority of the sentencing court, and may exist only insofar as they are "not inconsistent with the conditions imposed by the court."[36]

During the probation period, the conditions imposed may be modified or the offender may be discharged completely. Upon violation of any of the conditions, the court may revoke its order of probation and impose sentence if the imposition thereof has been suspended, or remove the suspension of execution of the sentence previously imposed.[37] Technically, the probationer need not be credited with the period of time spent on probation.[38] If, however, probation has not been revoked and the offender has fulfilled the commitments imposed upon him by the court and society, he is no longer liable to imprisonment for the crime of which he was convicted.[39]

CONDITIONS OF PROBATION

As has been indicated earlier, the trial court must initially determine the nature of the condition to be imposed upon the would-be probationer. In some jurisdictions, statutes require the imposition of certain conditions in all cases where probation is to be granted. These may require that the probationer shall not violate the criminal laws of any state or the federal government,[40] shall not leave the state without the court's consent,[41] shall comply with the rules and regulations prescribed by the court or by the agency design-

---

ers is vested in Parole Boards or a Board of Prison Commissions also empowered to impose conditions. See Iowa Code Ann. §§ 247.20, 247.21 (Supp. 1962); Mont. Rev. Code § 94–9830 (Supp. 1961). "These statutes confuse probation and parole." Model Penal Code § 301.1, comment (Tent. Draft No. 2, 1954).

[34] W. Va. Code Ann. § 6291 (24) (1961).

[35] See Ore. Rev. Stat. § 137.540 (11) (Supp. 1961).

[36] Federal Probation Act, 18 U.S.C. § 3655 (1958). Accord, N.C. Gen. Stat. § 15–205 (1953); Ore. Rev. Stat. § 137.630 (Supp. 1961); Va. Code Ann. § 53–278 (Supp. 1962).

[37] See generally, Note, Legal Aspects of Probation Revocation, 59 Colum. L. Rev. 311 (1959). But see the dissenting opinion of Judge Bazelon in Hyser v. Reed, No. 16716, D.C. Cir., April 11, 1963, p. 50 where he states: "But no specific violation of a condition need be found in order to revoke probation. . . . Probation may be revoked solely on the basis of predictive judgments about likely future behavior."

[38] See La. Rev. Stat. § 15.534 (Supp. 1962).

[39] Under the federal rule revocation proceedings may be brought at any time during the five-year period following the grant for breach of a condition during the probation period. Federal Probation Act, 18 U.S.C. 3651 (1958).

[40] See Ill. Ann. Stat. ch. 38, § 787 (Smith-Hurd Supp. 1962); Mich. Stat. Ann. § 28.1133 (1) (Supp. 1961); W. Va. Code Ann. § 6291(16) (1) (1961).

[41] Ibid.

ated for his supervision,[42] shall report periodically with regard to his where-abouts, conduct and employment,[43] shall post bond with or without sureties for the performance of the conditions imposed,[44] or shall pay costs to the court.[45]

With respect to these conditions, no discretion is lodged in the trial court; they must be incorporated within every order of probation. But this does not prevent the court from imposing conditions in addition to those made manda-tory by statute. Certain typical conditions found authorized but not required by statutes in most states, are, *inter alia*, support of dependents[46] (which generally comprises the largest single category of probationers[47]) the making of restitution to the victim of the crime committed,[48] and initiation of a course of vocational training.[49]

This legislative enumeration is by no means exhaustive of the conditions that can or have been imposed as an incident to a conditional release. In the somewhat less conventional cases conditions have been imposed which run the gamut of every conceivable human relationship; *e.g.*, take care of mother and father,[50] do not make remarks against the sheriff,[51] join the Navy,[52] insure a third party's car against accident and casualty loss,[53] disclose names of associates in crime[54] and shore up an adjacent building.[55] These latter condi-tions result from powers conferred upon the courts through statutes permitting a defendant to be admitted to probation upon such terms and conditions as the

---

[42] W. Va. Code Ann. § 6291 (16) (1961).

[43] See Ill. Ann. Stat. ch. 38, § 787 (Smith-Hurd Supp. 1962); Mich. Stat. Ann. § 28.1133 (Supp. 1961); Vt. Stat. Ann. tit. 28 § 1015 (1959); Mo. Ann. Stat. § 549.100 (1949).

[44] See Ill. Ann. Stat. ch. 38, § 787 (Smith-Hurd Supp. 1962); Mo. Ann. Stat. § 549.150 (1949).

[45] Mo. Ann. Stat. § 549.150 (1949).

[46] See, e.g., Conn. Gen. Stat. Rev. § 53–304 (Supp. 1959); Minn. Stat. Ann. § 617.56 (1947); N.Y. Code Crim. Proc. § 932. Wyoming has repealed a provision which had permitted probation with a condition of support for a defendant convicted of abandonment of his spouse, but has provided that the State Commission on Prison Labor divert the convict's earnings at prison to the use of his wife. Wyo. Stat. Ann. § 20–71 (Supp. 1961). There is still a provision for defendants to be placed upon probation upon conviction of nonsupport of his child. Wyo. Stat. Ann. § 20–74 (1957).

[47] Nonsupport constituted the highest percentage of cases placed on probation in New York State in a recent two-year period, with 16.6% and 16.2% of the respective totals for 1954 and 1955 being found in that category. Filiation proceedings, with 14.5% in 1954 and 14.7% in 1955, constituted the second largest group placed upon probation. Report of the Dep't of Correction of the State of New York 103 (1955–1956).

[48] See, e.g., N.Y. Code Crim. Proc. § 932(j).

[49] Cf. N.J. Rev. Stat. § 2A:168–2 (1953); N.Y. Code Crim. Proc. § 932(f); Ore. Rev. Stat. § 37.540 (6) (Supp. 1961).

[50] Ex parte Pittman, 157 Tex. Crim. 203, 248 S.W.2d 159 (1952).

[51] Morris v. State, 44. Ga. App. 765, 162 S.E. 879 (1932).

[52] People v. Patrick, 118 Cal. 332, 50 Pac. 425 (1897).

[53] City of Rochester v. Newton, 169 Misc. 726, 8 N.Y.S.2d 441 (1938).

[54] United States v. Worcester, 190 F. Supp. 548 (D. Mass. 1961).

[55] People v. Sarnoff, 302 Mich. 266, 4 N.W.2d 544 (1942).

court deems best,[56] proper,[57] or the like.[58] In some jurisdictions there is no preliminary enumeration, and the sole direction given the court is that it should affix terms and conditions as the court in its discretion shall determine,[59] fix,[60] prescribe[61] or see fit to impose.[62]

This then is the authority under which the courts operate. Let us now consider those conditions which commonly result from the exercise of that authority and the circumstances and rationale attending their imposition.

Costs

Frequently the payment of costs is imposed as a condition of probation.[63] Ordinarily the amount of such payment is equivalent to the cost of the judicial proceeding involved, though the measure imposed may be the expenses of the ensuing probation. On occasion the exaction may be gauged by some extrinsic factor, as for instance, the cost of utilizing a private prosecutor.[64]

Like the other pecuniary conditions involving payment to the state rather than to a private party, the rationale for the condition of costs is supposedly the rehabilitation of the defendant. By making the defendant pay, the argument runs, his sense of obligation to society is awakened. This approach to rehabilitation, namely, that the defendant is returned to complete freedom in society only through undergoing some tangible sacrifice, has its counterpart in psychoanalysis, where the sacrifice undergone through payment of substantial fees plays a significant role in treatment. However, the rationale is rarely articulated in the "costs" cases, and it would seem from the enormous range of offenses in which the condition has been imposed that rehabilitation of the offender is a secondary consideration.

[56]E.g., Federal Probation Act, 18 U.S.C. § 3651 (1958); Colo. Rev. Stat. Ann. § 39–16–6 (1953).

[57]E.g., Del. Code Ann. tit. 11, § 4321 (1953); Fla. Stat. Ann. § 948.03 (1941); Md. Ann. Code art. 27, § 639 (1957); Mass. Gen. Laws Ann. ch. 276, § 87 (1959).

[58]E.g., Idaho Code Ann. § 19–2601 (Supp. 1961) (necessary and expedient); Ill. Ann. Stat. ch. 38, § 787(6) (Smith-Hurd Supp. 1962) (necessary for the proper conduct and reform of the defendant); Minn. Stat. Ann. § 610.38 (Supp. 1962) (suitable). Compare the formulation in the Model Penal Code, wherein the defendant may be required "to satisfy any other condition reasonably related to the rehabilitation of the defendant and not unduly restrictive of his liberty or incompatible with his freedom of conscience." Model Penal Code § 301.1(2) (1) (Proposed Official Draft, 1962).

[59]E.g., Ariz. Rev. Stat. Ann. § 13–1657 (1956).

[60] R. I. Gen. Laws Ann. § 12–19–8 (1956).

[61]Vt. Stat. Ann. tit. 28 § 1008 (1959).

[62]Mo. Ann. Stat. § 549.070 (1949).

[63]See, e.g., People v. Marks, 340 Mich. 495, 65 N.W.2d 698 (1954); Ex parte Sethers, 151 Tex Crim. 553, 209 S.W.2d 358 (1948).

[64]State v. Hardin, 183 N.C. 815, 112 S.E. 593 (1922); State v. Weeks, 14 Wis. 2d 186, 10 N.W.2d 889 (1961). See also Comment, Conditions of Probation Imposed upon Wisconsin Felons Costs of Prosecution and Restitution, 1962 Wis. L. Rev. 672. On rare occasion, the trial cour will impose the condition of costs with an eye to the ability of the defendant to discharg the conditions. See State v. Crook, 115 N.C. 529, 20 S.E. 513 (1894).

Costs may be imposed as a condition precedent to probation[65] or they may also be imposed concurrently with probation,[66] or as a condition subsequent to a jail sentence.[67] The condition becomes most inconsistent with the general aims of probation when it is used in the first of these ways, *i.e.*, when its fulfillment is a condition precedent to probation. What generally happens in this circumstance is that the person who has been regarded as otherwise suitable material for probation is denied such opportunity because of a lack of funds. This is a regrettable situation, both because of the likelihood of inequality of opportunity among defendants,[67a] and because the factor of economic status seems irrelevant once the initial determination has been made that the defendant can be reformed. It is more humane, as well as more nearly in keeping with the aims of probation, to either impose costs as a condition concurrent with probation, or arrange a system of installment payment of such costs.

Usually the exact amount of costs is not determined by the trial judge at the time of the pronouncement of the condition. However, on occasion a definite figure[68] or some prescribed fraction of total costs[69] is settled upon. As has been stated previously, such figure bears no relation to the economic situation of the individual defendant. There also appears to be a tendency to utilize costs as a form of punishment. This practice is most prevalent in connection with minor offenses, where typically sentence is suspended solely upon fulfillment of this condition.[70] When used in this manner the condition of costs is indistinguishable from the imposition of a fine. Where the condition imposed is in excess of an amount necessary to reimburse the state, the trial court may well be exceeding its statutory authority.[71]

Fines

The same rationale used to justify the imposition of costs as a condition to probation is applicable to imposition of the condition of fines: it quickens the

[65]E.g., State v. Kelly, 217 Iowa 1305, 253 N.W. 49 (1934); Gray v. Graham, 128 Kan. 434, 278 Pac. 14 (1929); People v. Fisher, 237 Mich. 504, 212 N.W. 70 (1928); Campbell v. State, 287 P.2d 713 (Okla. Crim. 1955).

[66]State ex rel. Vanderheis v. Murphy, 246 Wis. 168, 16 N.W.2d 413 (1944).

[67]Kemp v. Meads, 162 Ga. 55, 132 S.E. 533 (1926).

[67a]It may very well be that the imposition of costs as a condition of probation upon indigent defendants may constitute a denial of equal protection of the law. See Ex parte Banks, 74 Okla. Crim. 1, 6, 122 P.2d 181, 184 (1942) (dictum).

[68]Quality Egg Shippers v. United States, 212 F.2d 417 (8th Cir. 1956) (costs of $852.65); Campbell v. State, 287 P.2d 713 (Okla. Crim. 1955) ($20 costs); State v. Barnett, 110 Vt. 221, 3 A.2d 521 (1939) ($18.40 costs).

[69]Commonwealth v. Keenan, 178 Pa. Super. 461, 116 A.2d 314 (1955) (one half the costs of prosecution).

[70]State v. Edwards, 192 N.C. 321, 135 S.E. 37 (1926).

[71] In determining the validity of an order of probation, it must be measured by the ultimate purposes of the probation statute. See People v. Teasdale, 335 Mich. 1, 55 N.W.2d 149 (1952) commenting upon Mich. Stat. Ann. § 28.1133 (Supp. 1957)).

sense of social responsibility in the offender. A fine, nevertheless, is clearly punitive in character, usually varying in amount with the gravity of the offense for which the defendant has been convicted, and is payment to the state in expiation for the defendant's offense. Sometimes the sum exacted as a fine is diverted for the "use of the county,"[72] or in rare instances, for the use of a private individual.[73] In these circumstances, the money exacted cannot properly be termed a fine, for a primary purpose appears to have been some form of *restitution* rather than punishment of the defendant. What has occurred is that a statutory measure is being utilized as a rough gauge to satisfy other ends of the criminal law.

A distinction must be made between fines which are true conditions, and fines which are in themselves the imposition of a sentence.[74] The former category is included within the scope of this survey because of the apparent inability of the courts to distinguish between the two forms.[75] The importance of the distinction lies in the fact that where the fine is deemed to be a sentence, a court might not be able to imprison the defendant for its violation,[76] whereas it has been held that even the payment of a fine required as a condition of probation does not make the probation order a final sentence which would preclude a subsequent sentence upon violation of other conditions of probation.[77] In addition, attempts to impose a fine in the form of a sentence as a condition precedent to the suspension of some remaining portion of the sentence have been held unauthorized by statute.[78]

It has been held in at least one jurisdiction that probation cannot be imposed concurrently with a sentence.[79] The rationale is that the statute[80] contemplates probation in lieu of and not in addition to sentence. However, occasionally fines are imposed simultaneously as a sentence and as a condition precedent to probation in a conviction involving multiple counts in an indictment. This has occurred most frequently in prosecutions for wilful evasion of income tax.[81]

As in the case of the condition of costs, the payment of a fine has been

---

[72] Commonwealth v. Keenan, 178 Pa. Super. 461, 116 A.2d 314 (1955). This amount may not exceed the fine fixed by law for the offense involved. Pa. Stat. tit. 19, § 1051 (1930).

[73] See Bohannon v. State, 271 P.2d 739 (Okla. Crim. 1954). However, the fine may not be diverted to the use of the trial judge. Tumey v. Ohio, 273 U.S. 510 (1927).

[74] See Standard Probation and Parole Act § 12 (1955).

[75] Generally the amount imposed as a condition cannot exceed the maximum statutory imposition as a sentence. People v. Kuhlman, 86 Cal. App. 2d 566, 195 P.2d 53 (Dist. Ct. App. 1948).

[76] 2 U.S. Dep't of Justice, Attorney General's Survey of Release Procedures 227 (1939)

[77] People v. Fisher, 237 Mich. 504, 212 N.W. 70 (1927).

[78] See Scott v. Griffin, 170 Ga. 368, 153 S.E. 25 (1930) (no authority, by statute or at common law, once sentence has been imposed, to suspend a portion thereof). See also Kemp v. Meads 162 Ga. 55, 132 S.E. 533 (1926).

[79] Frabizzio v. State, 44 Del. 395, 59 A.2d 452 (1948).

[80] Del. Code Ann. tit. 11, § 4321 (1953).

[81] E.g., United States v. Rosner, 161 F. Supp. 234 (S.D.N.Y. 1958).

imposed as a condition precedent to probation,[82] or as a condition concurrent with probation.[83] When a fine is imposed as a condition concurrent with probation, often probation constitutes nothing more than an organized method for the monthly collection of fines, and other than this rather humane method of allowing installment settlement of the fine, differs in no way from the sentence suspended upon condition of payment.

Generally, there is a limit upon the amount of money to be exacted as a fine, whether in the form of sentence or condition. There has been an attempt in some jurisdictions, notably California, to justify amounts in excess of a statutory maximum for fines by characterizing such excess as, say, reparation.[84] However, in view of the necessity for clarity in sentencing such ambiguous conditions cannot be justified.

There are occasions when the inability to meet the payment of a fine imposed as a condition to suspended sentence results in the imposition of a severe jail term, as for example, one day for every two dollars.[85] What has happened in these circumstances is the imposition of a jail term upon the hapless convict of far greater length than would be otherwise allowable as a maximum statutory term.[86] Such use of the probation system by the trial court is a deliberate misconstruction of the ultimate aims of the probation statute as promulgated by the legislature.

Bonds

The posting of bond either for appearance or for assurance that the probationer will faithfully observe the conditions of probation also seems inconsistent with the premise that the erstwhile probationer is worth salvaging. The rationale of individual treatment of the offender can retain very little vitality in the states where a statute requires the posting of bond as a condition of probation.[87] A suggestion has been made that the omnipresent bond is a vestige of an early, unsupervised probation or suspension of sentence.[88] In any

[82] E.g., People v. Kuhlman, 86 Cal. App. 2d 566, 195 P.2d 53 (Dist. Ct. App. 1948); Towns v. State, 25 Ga. App. 419, 103 S.E. 724 (1920); People v. Page, 125 Misc. 538, 211 N.Y. Supp. 401 (Sup. Ct. 1925).

[83] E.g., United States v. Taylor, 305 F.2d 183 (4th Cir. 1962); Springer v. United States, 148 F.2d 411 (9th Cir. 1945); People v. Labarbera, 89 Cal. App. 2d 639, 201 P.2d 584 (Dist. Ct. App. 1949).

[84] See People v. Kuhlman, 86 Cal. App. 2d 566, 195 P.2d 53 (Dist. Ct. App. 1948).

[85] Ex parte McVeity, 98 Cal. App. 723, 277 Pac. 745 (Dist. Ct. App. 1929). See also Lee v. Superior Court, 89 Cal. App. 2d 716, 201 P.2d 882 (Dist. Ct. App. 1949) wherein for a conviction for statutory rape, a sentence of imprisonment for one year would be suspended if defendant accepted the following conditions: (1) Jail for one year, then two years' probation; (2) Fine of $500; (3) No longer see the girl; (4) Steady employment; (5) Report regularly to the Probation Officer. The defendant was placed on probation against his will.

[86] Ex parte McVeity, supra note 85.

[87] See generally 2 U.S. Dep't of Justice, op. cit. supra note 76, at 224–227.

[88] Ibid.

event, the net result of this requirement is that those capable of obtaining bonds most easily are those professional criminals who have a reputation for not bolting.[89]

Occasionally, a bond is imposed as a condition in support cases.[90] No attempt is made to justify such a condition upon the theory of rehabilitation. In this situation, the bond acts only as a guarantee against any default by the husband which can be looked to for payment before additional measures can be taken against him. Only one jurisdiction allows a civil cause of action for recovery against a bond posted as a condition precedent to suspension of sentence in a criminal prosecution. In such a case the prosecuting witness in the previous criminal action enjoys the position of a third party beneficiary of the bond.[91]

Support

The support of dependents remains the one most common condition imposed upon probationers, since even states which had no other adult probation law created a somewhat analogous system with regard to persons convicted of nonsupport.[92] Generally the condition is handled by payment to the probation officer of a monthly installment[93] for remittance to the child, wife or indigent parents.[94] The support of dependents cannot be predicated upon a rehabilitation of the offender, save as compulsory payment may awaken a sense of responsibility. However, this is never seriously raised as the purpose of the condition of support. In effect, the legislature has taken a position that this is the only way remaining to provide for dependents other than by the state itself assuming the burden.[95] This is most apparent in cases where the crime for which the defendant has been convicted does not bear a direct

---

[89]See, e.g., Beeley, The Bail System in Chicago (1927). For a recent discussion of the inequities of the professional bondsman system, see Pannel v. United States, D.C. Cir., No. 17,557, filed May 16, 1963.

[90]State v. Goins, 122 S.C. 192, 115 S.E. 232 (1922).

[91] Meyers v. Barnhardt, 202 N.C. 49, 161 S.E. 715 (1932); see Manley v. Butterfield, 111 F. Supp. 783 (D.D.C. 1953). But see People v. Prell, 209 Ill. App. 130, 19 N.E.2d 637 (1939) (prosecuting witness not entitled to sum posted as recognizance, in part because this would be contrary to the purposes of probation).

[92] 2 U.S. Dep't of Justice, op. cit. supra note 76, at 234.

[93] For description of this procedure, see Towns v. State, 25 Ga. App. 419, 103 S.E. 724 (1920).

[94] Cf. Vt. Stat. 1933, No. 157, § 2876, by which the entire income of probationers convicted of nonsupport went to their dependents under the airy assumption "that the defendant will be sustained and supported by his good conduct alone." 2 U.S. Dep't of Justice, op. cit. supra note 76, at 236. This statute has been modified. Vt. Stat Ann. tit. 15, § 205 (1958). As to support of indigent parents, see Ind. Ann. Stat. § 10–1411 (1956).

[95]It becomes apparent that the effect on the probationer is a secondary consideration. The function of the condition is "not to punish the defendant, but to secure support for the neglected wife." City of New York v. Kriegel, 124 Misc. 67, 72, 207 N.Y. Supp. 646, 650 (Sup. C 1924).

relationship to the condition.[96] If, however, we discard the rehabilitation rationale, and assume that the purpose is nothing more than to provide for dependents, then we remove the conceptual inconsistency. Unfortunately, we are still confronted with a legal inconsistency. In those jurisdictions where fornication or seduction remains a punishable offense, attaching a condition of support to suspension of sentence may well raise a problem of procedural due process, for there has not been a prior adjudication of paternity.[97] In these situations, the courts almost invariably extricate themselves from difficulty by finding authority in the portion of the statutory grant relating to the power of the court to impose such conditions as it deems best, and justifying the condition as being for the public good.[98] The problem seems to be analyzed upon review not in terms of any rights vested in the defendant, nor in terms of the ultimate aims of probation, but rather in terms of the discretion of the trial judge.

There is also confusion as to the duration of the condition. While the sentence of imprisonment for abandonment is relatively short, it has been held that the condition runs during the minority of the child, thus confronting the offender with the prospect of either receiving a twelve-month sentence, or accepting a twenty-year condition.[99] However incongruous this may seem, it can be reconciled since the crime is a constantly recurring one; *i.e.*, were probationer to refuse the condition and accept the sentence, at the end of the year's incarceration, after a reasonable interval during which he refuses to support his offspring, he could be rearrested and charged with a new offense.

There are certain limitations upon judicial imposition of filial or parental obligations. Generally, the condition of support may not be imposed for a longer period of time than that recognized as legal duty. At least one court has

[96]The term relationship is used in the sense of a direct causal relationship between offense and condition. Thus, the imposition of a conditional suspension of sentence for the offense of nonsupport, where the condition is one of support, is an example of a causal relationship, where as a conviction for failure to support an illegitimate child which contains as a condition of probation that the defendant pay the confinement expenses of the mother, Commonwealth v. Gross, 324 Mass. 123, 85 N.E.2d 249 (1949), lacks such causal relationship. Compare In re McClane, 129 Kan. 739, 284 Pac. 365 (1930) (upon conviction for attempt to commit rape, a condition of parole [sic] is imposed that the defendant support wife and child), and State v. Jackson, 226 N.C. 66, 36 S.E.2d 706 (1946) (upon conviction of assault on person other than wife, execution of sentence suspended upon condition that the offender support his wife), with State v. Summers, 375 P.2d 143 (Wash. 1962) (condition in manslaughter case that defendant support own children held illegal).

[97]Swanson v. State, 38 Ga. App. 386, 144 S.E. 49 (1928) (sentence of hard labor on chain gang for fornication suspended upon support of child); State v. Teal, 108 S.C. 455, 95 S.E. 69 (1918) (execution of sentence for seduction suspended upon support of child "alleged by her to be the child of the defendant").

[98]Swanson v. State, supra note 97.

[99]Popham v. Sears, 204 Ga. 759, 51 S.E.2d 845 (1949). Contra, Schultz v. State, 227 Ind. 8, 83 N.E.2d 784 (1949). Some states restrict the length of the probation period in non-support cases. E.g., Ind. Ann. Stat. § 10–1406 (1942) (two years).

held that the probationer is only liable for the bare minimum legal obligation established by statute, and hence any moral responsibility existing beyond this point is legally superfluous, and cannot be imposed by a court of law.[100] Nevertheless, there are occasions when the administration of such conditions fails to respond to the practicalities of changing family situations with the result that the condition is stolidly enforced beyond the point where it is either socially necessary or desirable.[101]

Restitution

Restitution to aggrieved parties for loss or damage caused by the defendant's unlawful act is frequently made a condition of probation, and authority to impose such a condition is granted to the courts either expressly by statute[102] or is sanctioned by practice pursuant to a broad grant of authority relating to the terms and conditions of probation.[103] A distinction will be drawn, for the purposes of the present analysis, between restitution and reparation. Restitution normally consists of reimbursement of that sum of money which the defendant appropriated in the commission of his criminal act. The imposition of such a condition occurs commonly in the area of embezzlement,[104] income tax evasion[105] and larceny.[106] Reparation is generally considered to be synonomous with tort damages; *i.e.*, a sum of money paid to an injured party that is roughly commensurate with special and general damages. The amount of such reparation may be set by the sentencing court,[107] the probation officer[108] or it

---

[100] "[B]ut where the condition has no bearing on either of these two matters, (restraint and reparation) but relates only to a future moral and not legal obligation, we think it is an abuse of the discretion vested in the trial court. . . ." Redewill v. Superior Court, 43 Ariz. 68, 81, 2? P.2d 475, 480 (1934).

[101] Most striking as an illustration of this danger is a North Carolina case wherein sentence upon conviction of abandonment of spouse had been suspended upon condition of support. At a later date the wife obtained a divorce. Probationer attempted to cease payments, but his obligation of support continued despite the change in legal status. State v. Henderson, 207 N.C. 258, 17 S.E. 758 (1934).

[102] Federal Probation Act, 18 U.S.C. § 3651 (1958); Mich. Stat. Ann. § 28.1133 (Supp. 1961); U.S. Dep't of Justice, op. cit. supra note 76, at 231.

[103] Such court shall pass sentence on the accused, if he is convicted, and may then suspend all or part of such sentence and place the person so convicted and sentenced in the care and custody of the state probation officers upon such conditions and for such time as it may prescribe or until further order of the court.

Vt. Stat. Ann. tit. 28, § 1008 (1959). Accord, D.C. Code Ann. § 24–102 (1961), Basile v. United States, 38 A.2d 620 (D.C. Munic. App. 1944).

[104] Karrell v. United States, 181 F.2d 981 (9th Cir.), cert. denied, 340 U.S. 891 (1950).

[105] United States v. Rosner, 161 F. Supp. 234 (S.D.N.Y. 1958).

[106] People v. Funk, 117 Misc. 778, 193 N.Y. Supp. 302 (Erie County Ct. 1921).

[107] E.g., United States v. Berger, 145 F.2d 888 (2d Cir. 1944), cert. denied, 324 U.S. 848 (194? State v. White, 230 N.C. 513, 53 S.E.2d 436 (1949).

[108] People v. Marin, 147 Cal. App. 2d 625, 305 P.2d 659 (Dist. Ct. App. 1957) (condition imposed that the defendant reimburse in the amount of $544 "or in such amounts as Probation Officer shall determine").

may be deferred until a subsequent civil hearing is held on the issue.[109] When the last is the case, the sentencing court may require as a condition of probation that the defendant "should have the financial ability to pay any judgment rendered against him in a civil action for damages."[110]

The rationale articulated for the imposition of the restitution and reparation conditions is the reformative effect the imposition of such a responsibility will have upon the probationer's character. To be clearly consonant with such a purpose, it is necessary that the defendant be closely supervised during the period of the condition's existence. Such supervision of course should not entail harassment, but rather an examination into the financial situation of each defendant in order to work out a system of payment which most effectively accomplishes reimbursement, and yet does not interfere with the defendant's family and other responsibilities.[111] However, it is difficult to tell in some circumstances whether the best interests of the *probationer* are uppermost. Restitution has been utilized so often to achieve its own admittedly desirable goal that the courts fail to articulate any real concern as to reformation and rehabilitation of the probationer.[112]

Most of the statutes limit restitution to the amount alleged and proven to have been appropriated by the defendant;[113] the same limitation confines reparation to the persons proven to have been injured by the act of the defendant.[114] The wisdom of these limitations is best shown by the fact that in those jurisdictions where there is no specific enumeration of permissible conditions, the amount of restitution ordered may well exceed the measure of loss caused.[115]

Occasionally circumstances will arise not covered by the statute, as in convictions for wilful evasion of income tax,[116] when the "appropriation" has not been adjudicated. Generally the condition upon which sentence is suspended in such cases is that the defendant will make an honest effort to come to a settlement of his debt with the Internal Revenue Service. However, with the prospect of criminal sanctions hanging over his head, realistically, it is doubtful whether the probationer will contest such a Service determination

---

[109]Gross v. United States, 228 F.2d 612 (8th Cir. 1956).

[110]People v. D'Elia, 73 Cal. App. 2d 764, 769, 167 P.2d 253, 255 (Dist. Ct. App. 1946).

[111]See Model Penal Code § 301.1, comment (Tent. Draft No. 2, 1954); 2 U.S. Dep't of Justice, op. cit. supra note 76, at 238–39.

[112]There can be no real reformation of a wrongdoer unless there is at least a willingness on his part to right the wrong committed. The effect of such an act upon the individual is of inestimable value, and to a large extent, determines whether there has been any real reformation. People v. Lippner, 219 Cal. 395, 399, 26 P.2d 457, 458 (1933).

[113]See People v. Funk, 117 Misc. 778, 193 N.Y. Supp. 302 (Erie County Ct. 1921). See also People v. Holzapple, 9 Ill. 2d 22, 136 N.E.2d 793 (1956).

[114]See Karrell v. United States, 181 F.2d 981 (9th Cir.), cert. denied, 340 U.S. 891 (1950).

[115]Basile v. United States, 38 A.2d 620, 622 (D.C. Munic. Ct. App. 1944) (dictum).

[116]E.g., Hensley v. United States, 257 F.2d 681 (5th Cir. 1958); United States v. Steiner, 239 F.2d 660 (7th Cir. 1957); United States v. Stoehr, 196, F.2d 276 (3d Cir. 1952).

and utilize normal civil remedies such as a court proceeding in order to protect his property.[117]

Reparation is imposed as a condition of probation most frequently where there has been criminal violation relating to the unlawful operation of an automobile.[118] Ideally, the determination of a specific sum in reparation for injury should be deferred to a subsequent civil action. Without the opportunity which would be afforded by such a hearing, the defendant would not be allowed affirmative defenses which might bar recovery by the aggrieved party.[119] It may be argued that presenting such an opportunity would unduly complicate the probation process, and in fact, be quite irrelevant, since the trial court has already determined that the fulfillment of this condition will have a salutary effect upon the defendant's character.[120] The problem may be reduced to a conflict between aims of the criminal law (probation in particular) and those individual rights the defendant retains in spite of his conviction. Thus, payment and rehabilitation, desirable without relation to a specific context, may yet be in conflict with such safeguards as are contained in the due process and equal protection clauses of the Constitution of the United States.[120a] Much clearer are the objections raised when reparation bears no relation to the crime.[121] In such circumstances the purpose involved is quite plainly to enforce payment through a use of the probation machinery and without regard for the defendant. Such a condition must be presumed invalid not only as having been imposed without statutory authority, and as being against public policy, but also as a violation of substantive due process.

Banishment

Normal probation procedure requires the probationer to remain within the jurisdiction and to keep the probation officer informed at all times of

[117] I have no intention of permitting the probationary power of this court to be used as a club to force the defendant to settle his tax liabilities on terms dictated by the Government. Defendant is entitled to assert any bona fide defenses passed upon by the appropriate civil tribunal.
United States v. Rosner, 161 F. Supp. 234, 238 (S.D.N.Y. 1958). See also United States v Taylor, 305 F.2d 183 (4th Cir. 1962).

[118] E.g., Freeman v. United States, 103 U.S. App. D.C. 15, 254 F.2d 352 (1958); Henry v State, 77 Ga. App. 735, 49 S.E.2d 681 (1948).

[119] See People v. Good, 287 Mich. 110, 282 N.W. 920 (1938).

[120] See Gross v. United States, 228 F. 2d 612 (8th Cir. 1956).

[120a] See Hink, The Application of Constitutional Standards to Probation, 20 U. Chi. L. Rev 483, 490, 491 (1962). Professor Hink's paper is directed mainly to the problem of probation revocation.

[121] "But if we take this definition and apply it to restitution conditions in probation case it is apparent that the restitution must be for loss sustained as a direct consequence of the commission of the particular crime for which the respondent stands convicted...." State v Barnett, 110 Vt. 221, 231–232, 3 A.2d 521, 525 (1939). Accord. People v. Becker, 349 Mich. 476 84 N.W. 2d 833 (1957).

his whereabouts. A condition of probation that the offender leave the state,[122] United States,[123] county,[124] town,[125] village[126] or neighborhood[127] would be inconsistent with such procedure. Nevertheless it has been imposed from time to time by a sentencing court—and quite as readily the condition is struck down as invalid by the reviewing court.

The condition of banishment suffers from the same opprobrium that attaches to the sentence of banishment: It is contrary to public policy to allow one state to foist its undesirables onto sister states. There sometimes appears to be an attempt to justify the imposition of such a condition (especially where the condition consists merely of removal from one nearby village to another) upon the ground that the offender can be rehabilitated only by removing him from an environment which prompted commission of the offense. Granting some merit to this thesis, it seems anachronistic and as a practical matter, unusable today.

Imprisonment

A condition of imprisonment as one of a number of conditions imposed with probation is theoretically inconsistent with the rationale of probation.[128] Probation is based upon the premise that the offender has been found fit to re-enter society, supervised to some degree, but otherwise enjoying the same freedom as anyone else. There is simply no way to reconcile incarceration with this premise. However, there are cases where a condition of imprisonment has been imposed upon the offender as a part of his probation requiring as long or longer a term in prison than the maximum that could be imposed as a sentence.[129] California, in particular, consistently utilizes a period of incarceration as a condition precedent to probation.[130] This is sometimes justified by the interesting assertion that "a taste of punishment" will not harm the probationer.[131] Because the condition of imprisonment is not subject to the statutory and customary limitations of a sentence, the danger of unfairness increases. As has been pointed out above, the condition may impose a longer term than a

[122] Roberts v. Lowry, 160 Ga. 494, 128 S.E. 746 (1925).

[123] People v. Patrick, 118 Cal. 332, 50 Pac. 425 (1897).

[124] Hoggett v. State, 101 Miss. 269, 57 So. 811 (1912); People ex rel Pasco v. Trombly, 173 App. Div. 497, 160 N.Y. Supp. 67 (1916).

[125] Ex parte Pittman, 157 Tex. Crim. 203, 248 S.W.2d 159 (1952).

[126] Shondell v. Bradley, 42 Ohio App. 8, 181 N.E. 559 (1931).

[127] People v. George, 318 Mich. 329, 28 N.W.2d 86 (1947); People v. Smith, 252 Mich. 4, 232 N.W. 397 (1930).

[128] Standard Probation and Parole Act § 2, comment (1955); 2 U.S. Dep't of Justice, Attorney General's Survey of Release Procedures 249–50 (1939). But see, Model Penal Code § 301.1(3) and comment to § 6.02 (Proposed Official Draft 1962).

See, e.g., Ex parte McVeity, 98 Cal. App. 723, 277 Pac. 745 (Dist. Ct. App. 1929).

[130] E.g., People v. Osslo, 50 Cal. 2d 75, 323 P.2d 397, cert. denied, 357 U.S. 907 (1958); People v. Stanley, 162 Cal. App. 2d 416, 327 P.2d 973 (Dist. Ct. App. 1958); People v. Frank, 94 Cal. App. 2d 740, 211 P.2d 350 (Dist. Ct. App. 1949).

[131] Ex parte Glick, 126 Cal. App. 649, 650, 14 P.2d 796, 797 (Dist. Ct. App. 1932).

sentence; in addition, the term of imprisonment imposed as a condition precedent to probation may be harsher than the sentence.[132]

Moreover, since discretion remains vested in the trial judge, he retains the power to modify this condition before it is completely discharged so as to lengthen the period of incarceration.[133] While California, in particular, consistently upholds such mid-term modification,[134] it would seem that such maintenance of control over the offender once he has entered prison should be struck down as an unwarranted extension of the trial court's jurisdiction.

The federal courts commonly impose a sentence simultaneously with probation in the case of convictions based upon multiple counts. This occurs most frequently in the successful prosecution for wilful evasion of income tax. Consequently, it is not at all strange to find offenders who are to serve consecutive or concurrent prison terms on several counts before they embark on probation. This practice has been extended by statute to include even the sentence under one-count indictments. In 1958, section 3651 of the Federal Probation Act was amended to permit confinement of the offender for a period not exceeding six months as a part of the probation grant in cases involving conviction based upon a one-count indictment.[135] Essentially, this change had come about in order to bring the practice with regard to single-count convictions in line with the already existing practice as to multiple-count convictions.[136] With regard to this imprisonment-probation practice, the Administrative Office of the United States Courts has stated that many federal judges "are of the opinion that confinement for a brief period in a suitable jail or treatment institution has a salutary effect upon an offender and is conducive to his rehabilitation on probation to follow."[137] No statistics are available, however, to test this proposition.

JUDICIAL REVIEW OF THE IMPOSITION OF CONDITIONS OF PROBATION

As we have seen, it is an understatement to say that great power has been lodged in the sentencing court.[137a] Administrative in nature, affecting

---

[132]See, e.g., In re Acosta, 65 Cal. App. 2d 63, 149 P.2d 757 (Dist. Ct. App. 1944) (as a condition precedent to probation, one year in jail with no time off for good behavior).

[133]Cf. Wilson v. Carr, 41 F.2d 704 (9th Cir. 1930); In re Hazlett, 137 Cal. App. 734, 31 P.2d 448 (Dist. Ct. App. 1934).

[134]E.g., In re Larsen, 44 Cal. 2d 642, 283 P.2d 1043 (1955); Ex parte Marcus, 11 Cal. App. 2d 359, 53 P.2d 1021 (Dist. Ct. App. 1936); People v. Roberts, 136 Cal. App. 709, 29 P.2d 43 (Dist. Ct. App. 1934).

[135]Federal Probation Act, 18 U.S.C. § 3651 (1958).

[136]See S. Rep. No. 2135, 85th Cong., 2d Sess. (1958).

[137]Id. at 3.

[137a]As one court has recently stated: "In the act of sentencing, the judge approaches the attribute of the Almighty—he sits in judgment of his fellow man." Leach v. United States, D.C. Cir., No. 17,549, April 25, 1963, p. 4.

vast areas of everyday life, the conditions imposed under probation tend to cut across a whole range of possible legal safeguards in order to get a job done. Moreover, although it has been said that the proper exercise of such authority is guaranteed through strict supervision by the appellate courts,[138] unhappily this view has not been borne out in practice. Indeed, it may be said that the reviewing courts are reluctant to overturn any conditions once they have been imposed. Such reluctance is generally based upon one of several grounds: (1) the broad discretion accorded the trial court; (2) the ambiguity in the "reasonable condition" test; and (3) the consent theory.

As to the first of these grounds, a condition of probation generally can be sanctioned by statutory language which authorizes the trial judge to impose as an incident of probation any condition he may deem best.[139] Such conditions may be declared invalid only where the trial court has clearly abused its discretion, and in order for an appellate court to arrive at such a conclusion, it must decide whether the condition imposed is consistent with the ultimate aims of probation. The problem, then, should become one of statutory interpretation, both as to the express and implied purposes of the Probation Act. Rarely, however, does such an analysis take place.

As to the second ground for upholding the trial court's imposition of a condition of probation, the statement that the condition is "reasonable" is a rubric which in practice is seldom subjected to careful analysis.[140] Normally all a reviewing court signifies by this term is that the imposition of the condition is within the discretion of the trial court, or that the condition does not appear to be immoral, impossible to perform, or the like.[141] On occasion the appellate court will inquire into the relationship between the condition and the crime committed by the offender; such relevance then becomes a factor in assaying the reasonableness of the condition.[142] However, since the discretion of the trial court is broad, and conditions imposed normally are not such as would shock the conscience, invariably all manner of conditions are termed reasonable. The case of *State v. Smith*[143] presents a striking instance of the tendency. In a conviction for the larcenous taking of grain, the condition imposed was that

---

[138] See Model Penal Code § 301.1, comment 10 (Tent. Draft No. 2, 1954).

[139] See statutes cited notes 56–62, supra.

[140] See Hink, The Application of Constitutional Standards of Protection to Probation, 29 U. Chi. L. Rev. 483, 488 (1962).

[141] The formulation most often articulated is that the court in its discretion may "attach any condition to the parole [sic] that are [sic] not immoral, illegal, or impossible of performance." State v. Harris, 116 Kan. 387, 389, 226 Pac. 715, 716 (1924). Accord, Davis v. State, 53 Ga. App. 325, 185 S.E. 400 (1936); Pagano v. Bechly, 211 Iowa 1294, 1298, 232 N.W. 798, 799 (1930). See also Note, 71 Yale L.J. 551 (1962).

[142] Relevance may be a significant factor in determining the statutory authorization for the imposition of a condition, see State v. Barnett, 110 Vt. 221, 3 A.2d 521 (1939), or in determining whether such imposition is in violation of a constitutional requirement of procedural due process, see People v. Becker, 349 Mich. 476, 84 N.W.2d 833 (1957).

[143] 233 N.C. 68, 62 S.E.2d 495 (1950).

the defendant shall refrain from driving a car upon the highways. While the condition is *reasonable* enough in the sense that it is not horrendous, the appellate decision does not satisfactorily spell out the especial relevance between the offense and the condition.

In many cases, however, the reasonableness of the condition upon which sentence is suspended is never even at issue. Particularly in the revocation hearing, where the defendant, accused of failure to live up to the condition, is pleading the unreasonableness or illegality of the condition, courts have found it convenient to avoid the issue by resort to a theory of waiver:[144] the defendant has consented to the condition in the trial court and therefore cannot raise the issue of its illegality.[145] Some courts have gone one step beyond, and have analogized the transaction between the defendant and the trial court to a *contract*[146] and at least one court has gone so far as to criticize the defendant for "welching."[147]

Difficulty arises with such reasoning, however, because the analogy is not complete. The law of contract is posited upon the notion of an equality of bargaining position between parties which culminates in a voluntary agreement. However, defendants are not in a position to bargain with a court because virtually any condition is preferable to jail. The nonfederal narcotics cases are perhaps the best instance of the inequality of positions. In these cases the offender is faced with Hobson's choice, for the alternative to accepting probation and its concomitant conditions is to endure the effects of narcotic withdrawal in a county jail.[148] In apparent recognition of the defects in the consent theory, within recent times at least one jurisdiction has held with consistency that acceptance of an unreasonable or illegal condition is no bar to a later objection.[149] It would seem that this holding may even be explained upon the strict contract theory that a person cannot consent to an illegal contract.[150]

Aside from the "contract analogy" the reviewing courts generally hold that there is no necessity to inquire into the consonance of the condition with the aims of probation on the grounds that the defendant is free not to accept the State's offer,[151] and that the offer is being made by the state as a matter

---

[144] E.g., Ex parte McClane, 129 Kan. 739, 284 Pac. 365 (1930); State v. Collins, 247 N.C. 248, 100 S.E.2d 492 (1957).

[145] "Concensus tollit errorem." Hoggett v. State, 101 Miss. 269, 271, 57 So. 811, 812 (1912).

[146] See, e.g., State v. Shephard, 187 N.C. 609, 122 S.E. 467 (1924); Glenn v. State, 168 Tex Crim. 312, 327 S.W.2d 763 (1959).

[147] McGrew v. Commonwealth, 308 Ky. 838, 215 S.W.2d 996 (1948).

[148] See Fisher v. Commonwealth, 312 Ky. 321, 243 S.W.2d 881 (1951) (conviction for drug addiction); McGrew v. Commonwealth, 308 Ky. 838, 215 S.W.2d 996 (1948). See also 42 U.S.C § 259(e) (1958). The Kentucky practice will undoubtedly be sharply curtailed. See Robinson v California, 370 U.S. 660 (1962).

[149] E.g., State v. Cole, 241 N.C. 576, 86 S.E.2d 203 (1955); State v. Smith, 233, N.C. 68, 6 S.E.2d 495 (1950).

[150] See People v. Barrett, 282 Ill. 287, 299, 67 N.E. 23, 28 (1903).

[151] See People v. Osslo, 50 Cal. 2d 75, 323 P.2d 397, cert. denied, 357 U.S. 907 (1958); State v. Teal, 108 S.C. 455, 95 S.E. 69 (1918).

of grace and clemency.[152] It is submitted, however, that this approach taken by the courts to the problem is misleading. The conduct of the defendant is largely irrelevant if the real question is the legality or illegality of a condition.[153] The duty of the reviewing court is to interpret the laws and to ensure that the trial court does not exceed its jurisdiction. Indeed, aside from this strictly statutory consideration the public policy of the state should mark such transactions as invalid regardless of any consent of the parties.[154]

CONCLUSION

On the basis of the above material, it becomes apparent that one of the principle deficiencies in the present use of conditions of probation is need for more definite legislative control over the use of probation by the courts. This control should take the form of a specific enumeration of permissible conditions which the sentencing courts may impose as an incident of probation.

The presence of such a legislative enumeration would act as a guide to the sentencing court, and establish a standard for review as well.[155] At the same

[152]E.g., People v. Blankenship, 16 Cal. App. 2d 606, 61 P.2d 352 (Dist. Ct. App. 1936); State v. Farmer, 39 Wash. 2d 675, 237 P.2d 734 (1951).

[153]See People v. Osslo, 50 Cal. 2d 75, 323 P.2d 397 (dissenting opinion), cert. denied, 357 U.S. 907 (1958), observing that the trial court,

has deprived these three defendants of their means of earning a livelihood since they may not even work as the most menial laborers in their own union and cannot receive remuneration "from *any* union." The terms of probation are wholly out of line with the cases holding that probation is an act of grace and clemency for the purpose of permitting rehabilitation. . . .

Id. at 126, 323 P.2d at 427; see French, Unconstitutional Conditions: An Analysis, 50 Georgetown L.J. 234 (1961); cf. Torcaso v. Watkins, 367 U.S. 488, 495–96 (1961).

Courts commonly require as a condition of probation that the defendant refrain from engaging in a particular occupation. E.g., Stone v. United States, 153 F.2d 331 (9th Cir. 1946) (defendant shall not be employed as a steward on any railroad engaged in interstate commerce); United States v. Greenhaus, 85 F.2d 116 (2d Cir. 1936) (defendant shall engage in no stock or bond sale); People v. Stanley, 162 Cal. App. 2d 416, 327 P.2d 973 (Dist. Ct. App. 1958) (defendant, convicted of conspiring to commit offense of bookmaking, was not to have a telephone in his home or upon any property under his control). The condition that the probationer shall seek a particular type of employment is also imposed on occasion. See Springer v. United States, 148 F.2d 411 (9th Cir. 1945) (defendant to obtain employment with Veterans' Hospital as a ward attendant).

[154]See State v. Barnett, 110 Vt. 222, 232–33, 3 A.2d 521, 526 (1939).

[155]Unfortunately, the District of Columbia has only partial benefit of such legislative directive. The only criterion established for sentencing in the Court of General Sessions is that the trial court may impose probation "upon such terms as it may deem best." D.C. Code Ann. § 24–102 (1961). This vague standard is in sharp contrast with the enumeration of permissible conditions set forth in the Federal Probation Act which governs the grant of probation, inter alia, in the United States District Court for the District of Columbia. 18 U.S.C. § 3651 (1958). However, it would be noted that the Federal Probation Act also empowers the trial court to impose other conditions "as the court deems best." Ibid.

Prior to 1958, the United States District Court for the District of Columbia was specifically excepted from the operation of the Federal Probation Act. Act of June 25, 1948, ch. 645, § 3651, 62 Stat. 842. This exception has been removed and section 102 of the D.C. Code was repealed insofar as it applied to the District Court. Act of June 20, 1958, 72 Stat. 216.

time however, it is recognized, albeit reluctantly, that the fullest realization of the objectives of probation requires the sentencing court to be vested with some discretion to impose other conditions when necessary for reformation of the offender. The problem then becomes one of determining the permissible limits of judicial discretion, and, hence, the validity of the conditions imposed. In this regard it is suggested that the following standards be employed by the reviewing courts.

Is the Condition Validly Authorized by Statute?

Where a jurisdiction already has a legislative enumeration of permissible conditions, there is a ready-made standard by which to judge the validity of the contested condition. In such a jurisdiction, if restitution, for example, is limited by statute to an amount actually lost by an aggrieved party, a condition imposing a greater payment is clearly illegal.

Does the Condition Come Into Conflict With One of the General Aims of Probation?

A condition that the would-be probationer be sterilized cannot be reconciled with the avowedly corrective aims of probation. Granting some leeway to the discretion of the trial judge, there must nevertheless be some discernible relationship between the condition imposed and the reformation of the offender. If such relationship does not exist the condition is unnecessary to the probation process and is therefore invalid. This test is easily enough applied when the conditions imposed are harsh and punitive; in such circumstances one may readily enough discern no reasonable relationship between, say, sterilization and reformation. The difficulty arises where the condition is not itself onerous. Thus, the condition that a probationer not allow people to congregate in her home after the hours of darkness is not in itself a difficult condition to perform—but is it reasonably related to the probationer's reformation?[156]

Does the Condition Conflict With Some Right of the Defendant?

The defendant, despite his conviction, nevertheless retains certain basic personal rights. On occasion, a condition will be imposed which violates such rights. In one such case, the United States Court of Appeals for the Ninth Circuit held invalid as an unwarranted intrusion into the privacy of the person, a condition that the defendant donate a pint of blood to the Red Cross.[157] There is no difficulty in concluding that such a condition is an unwarranted violation of the personal rights of the defendant, and is therefor

---

[156] See State v. Davis, 243 N.C. 754, 92 S.E.2d 177 (1956).
[157] Springer v. United States, 148 F.2d 411 (9th Cir. 1945).

invalid. Much less clear are the conditions which place limitations upon the offender where the activity limited may not be legally protected as a right. For example, in those cases where the sentencing court has imposed as a condition of probation that the defendant shall not engage in a specific course of employment,[157a] what sometimes happens is that a defendant is effectively deprived of the means of securing a livelihood, particularly when through age or lack of training he is unable to adapt to his change of circumstances. In such a case, it is suggested that the condition would be invalid as offending against the individual's basic right to work.

Does the Condition Come into Conflict With a Basic Tenet of Our Society? Is it Fair?

This standard is the most elusive of all:[158] it is clear that a condition offends against our concept of fair play and is therefore invalid where the condition imposed upon a defendant totals up to a harsher punishment than the maximum sentence available pursuant to statute.[159] Similarly, the courts should find invalid the support condition imposed where no prior adjudication of responsibility has been made, or the situation where the trial court imposes a condition that a probationer enter a sanitarium when the record fails to demonstrate evidence of insanity.[160] What has happened in these circumstances is that the sentencing court has performed functions which are normally assigned to other mechanisms of our society. In the support case, the criminal court has undertaken to determine paternity, a function assigned to the civil forum; in the other illustration, the court has functioned without regard to the commitment procedures designed for involuntary treatment of the mentally ill. And in both cases the criminal court has by-passed the safeguards that custom, time and practice have incorporated into these other processes of our society. In these circumstances, quite clearly the conditions imposed are unfair, are invalid, and the imposition is an abuse of judicial discretion.

[157a]See cases cited note 153, supra.
[158]Cf. Hannah v. Larche, 363 U.S. 420, 442 (1960).
[159]Lee v. Superior Court, 89 Cal. App. 2d 716, 201 P.2d 882 (Dist. Ct. App. 1949).
[160]Ex parte Glick, 126 Cal. App. 649, 14 P.2d 796 (Dist. Ct. App. 1932).

36

When Should Probation Be Revoked?

EUGENE C. DICERBO

Just as disparities in sentence have been of concern to judges and probation officers, so are the disparities in the revocation of probation. The criteria for revoking probation are not uniform in district courts throughout the country and, at times, not even among judges in the same district court.

Some judges and probation officers insist that convictions for new offenses should be the only basis for revocation. Others believe that infractions of the conditions of probation other than the commitment of a new offense should also be justification for revocation, particularly where such violations are committed by an indifferent probationer who is unwilling to cooperate with the probation office and the court. And other judges contend that the circumstances of the violation, the general attitude and outlook of the probationer, his adjustment with his family, in the community, and on the job, and his efforts to comply with the conditions should also be considered by the probation officer before recommending revocation and the court before revoking probation.

It is the purpose of this article to focus attention on the question of when and when not to revoke probation and to offer some guidelines which will help the probation officer in making recommendations to the court where there are alleged violations.

I have long been of the opinion that it should not be necessary for the probation officer to bring each probation violator to court. The court should have sufficient confidence in his probation staff to allow it to decide when any

SOURCE. *Federal Probation*, XXX, June 1966, pp. 11–17.

single infraction or series of infractions should be brought to the court's attention.

What, then, are some of the criteria for determining whether to bring a case to court on a revocation hearing and to recommend for or against revocation?

MINOR VIOLATIONS

Let us begin with a discussion of the more or less minor infractions of the conditions of probation. Suppose a probationer, who otherwise has been cooperative, does not keep an appointment or two. Is this sufficient grounds to bring him to the court as a violator? Hardly.

Consider the probationer who on two or three occasions overlooks sending or bringing in his monthly supervision report. Should he be brought to court as a violator? Hardly.

If a young probationer persists in staying out late hours despite the admonition of his parents, does this constitute a valid reason for reporting him as a violator considering the fact that he does not get into trouble? I have had but few cases where a compromise could not be reached—where the parents, the probationer, and probation officer could not arrive at an understanding as to what hours the probationer should maintain.

What is to be done with a probationer who, now and then, receives a traffic ticket for illegal parking, for driving 5 or 10 miles over the speed limit, for failing to come to a complete stop at a stop sign? It is my contention that these infractions seldom fall within the criteria for revoking probation.

What should be done with a probationer who purchases an automobile or motorcycle contrary to the instructions of the probation officer? The probation officer may be concerned about serious consequences that may result if the probationer has a car or motorcycle. Instead of bringing the probationer to court, would it not be better to ask the probationer to sell the vehicle? Should he not comply, then revocation proceedings might be instituted. If liability insurance is the concern, he should be asked either to obtain the insurance or to sell the vehicle.

Should a probationer be brought to court when he, contrary to the instructions of the probation officer, marries? It is doubtful whether any court would revoke probation in such a case. Some courts would even regard this as an unreasonable and unwarranted restriction.

Is a probationer who quits his job without first clearing with his probation officer in violation of probation? Should not the probation officer determine the circumstances for his leaving the job, especially if it was on short notice? Were there interpersonal relationships and problems on the job which made it unpleasant or even unbearable?

What if the probationer refuses to take a job suggested by the probation officer? Should the officer not first learn the probationer's reasons for not doing so? They may be quite valid and understandable.

What if a probationer refuses to attend group counseling sessions? Is this to be considered in violation of his probation? He may have good reasons for not participating in group meetings.

FELONIES AND MISDEMEANORS

We now come to violations which involve convictions for a new felony or misdemeanor.

A probationer is convicted of a minor offense such as "disorderly conduct" or "assault and battery" in a fist fight with no serious injury resulting. Is his probation to be revoked? It is my feeling that the matter should be brought to the court's attention. But in his report the probation officer may recommend that probation not be revoked if the probationer's probation adjustment has been satisfactory.

Take the case of a probationer with no prior criminal record and an excellent probation adjustment who was convicted and committed for a minor offense for which he served a 30-day jail sentence. The offense and the jail sentence did not come to light until some time after his release from jail. Meanwhile, the probationer returned to his place of employment and continued to work regularly. The officer is faced with the decision whether to institute revocation proceedings or notify the court of the offense and recommend that probation continue. True, the welfare of the community takes precedence over the welfare of the individual. But this man posed no threat to society and, moreover, was highly respected by the members of his community. Would society benefit more from additional punishment or more from his rehabilitation which was interrupted by the short period of incarceration?

Let us assume that the same person was committed on a felony conviction and for a longer period. What consideration, if any, should be given to the absence of a prior criminal record and an excellent adjustment up to the time of the new offense? At first glance this might appear to be a clear-cut violation of probation. A closer examination into the facts might reveal a more complex situation because of the presence of mitigating factors and extenuating circumstances. Perhaps the probationer should receive the benefit of the doubt if he manifests redeeming characteristics, if the details of the offense indicate nothing heinous, if he became involved unwittingly, or if the period of incarceration is of such length that there would be little gained by additional confinement.

There is the question whether a conviction is necessary before any court action can be taken in a revocation proceeding. The following case illustrates the question in point.

Amassing a record of nine arrests, all for illicit liquor and all pending in local court during active supervision, a bootlegger was referred to the court for violation of probation because there was continuation of a pattern disclosed in the presentence report. He had no visible means of support and was, in effect, making a mockery of probation. At a hearing before the court he maintained he was being harassed by the local police and that he was innocent of all of the charges. In deferring action the judge elected to wait for a conviction on the alleged offenses. The probation officer fulfilled his obligation by calling the alleged violation to the court's attention.

Cases pending in local and even in federal courts present a problem when the 5-year maximum probation period is soon to terminate. Should the probationer be brought before the court despite the fact that disposition has not been made of the pending case? In view of the possibility of an acquittal, it would seem unfair to declare a probationer a violator. Perhaps the wisest course would be to permit probation to terminate on the assumption that if convicted the probationer will be punished adequately for the new offense. Another possibility is to have a warrant issued and execution deferred until the outcome of the pending case.

REALISTIC CONDITIONS OF PROBATION

The degree to which probation conditions are violated is directly related to the extent to which the conditions are realistic. Unrealistic conditions invite violations. Whether sanctions are to be imposed for violating a condition of probation would depend to a large extent on whether they are reasonable and enforceable. A comprehensive presentence investigation report will assist the court in deciding what special conditions of probation should be imposed in a given case. If the court, for example, contemplates assessing a fine, the presentence report will inform the judge of the financial status of the defendant. Too often a fine or restitution places a burden on the defendant, adding to the financial problems that got him into difficulty in the first instance. Nothing is gained by imposing a fine or restitution that he obviously cannot live up to and which actually cannot be enforced.

Other unrealistic conditions of probation which may be difficult to enforce are regular attendance at church, abstaining completely from alcoholic beverages, association with persons with arrest records, leaving the boundaries proscribed by the court or the probation officer. When such conditions are established, the probationer who does not comply may believe he is getting by with something; or he may have a sense of guilt for circumventing the conditions without disclosing the violation to his probation officer. Neither reaction is good.

Conditions of probation should be established by the court primarily to assist the probationer to become a law-abiding, self-respecting person. Conditions of probation should not be imposed as a punitive device. Nor should rigid compliance be expected in every instance. There should be flexibility in the application of the conditions, depending on the merits of the individual case.

What shall be the position of the probation officer when the court imposes conditions that are unrealistic and almost impossible to enforce? The probation officer is charged with the responsibility of seeing to it that the probationer complies with all conditions. Where he finds the conditions are unreasonable and he is losing control of the situation, he should notify the court that the conditions are difficult to enforce and also offer suggestions for modification of the conditions.

It is important that the probation officer make certain that the probationer fully comprehends each condition of probation and what is expected of him. It is not sufficient merely to have him indicate by his signature on the "Conditions of Probation" form that he understands each condition.

FINES AND RESTITUTION

Where the court orders payment of a fine or restitution at a fixed rate within a prescribed time, should the court be notified when an otherwise cooperative probationer falls behind a payment or two? It would seem that this condition is akin to the requirement that monthly supervision reports be submitted by a certain date each month. The probation office should have the responsibility for determining whether it is necessary to bring a probationer to court when a specified amount is not paid by a certain date.

In evaluating the financial situation of a probationer, the probation officer is confronted with two considerations: Was the probationer in a position to make payment of even nominal amounts, manifesting good faith, or was he unable to make payments because of inadequate earnings, illness, or other valid reason? Deliberate failure to make payments, on the other hand, is tantamount to flouting the order of the court.

Recently, two brothers on probation were brought before the court for failure to make regular payments on a sizeable fine. One was delinquent in the amount of several hundred dollars; the other had failed to meet a deadline date but later paid the fine in full. Expressing the opinion that these men had deliberately defied his order and that there were no mitigating circumstances, the court revoked probation and imposed a prison sentence. In an appeal, the decision of the District Court was upheld by the Circuit Court of Appeals.

By no means academic, these questions are based on actual cases. When they arise, they require the careful examination of every probation officer. They also vividly portray the need for a common denominator for determining what type of action the officer should take when a probationer jeopardizes his status. Careful consideration is especially required where a balance remains as the 5-year maximum period of supervision draws to a close. Although I do not generally subscribe to the policy that a jail sentence should be imposed for nonpayment of fine or restitution, I do believe that the attitude of the probationer and his reasons for failure to comply demand careful scrutiny. The following court decision covers this very point:

"Where one convicted of tax offenses was granted probation on condition that he pay fines within a specified time, bare nonpayment of fines was not conclusive of disobedience of probation terms and did not subject him to imprisonment as of course; his probation was not beyond redemption if in reality he was too poor to pay, not to blame for it, and sincere in his try. . . . Even though accused accepted probation when sentenced, two years later when he defaulted in payment of his fines and his probation was revoked he could deny commensurate fairness of fines."[1]

Judges often have remarked that they do not deem it wise to have their orders ignored or to leave defendants with the impression that the court does not always mean what it says. Therefore, where a balance remains on a fine or restitution the court should be so apprised. If a justification exists, probation may be allowed to terminate with restitution remaining as a moral obligation and the fine either remitted or left as a money judgment to be confessed at some future date if circumstances so warrant.

Where conditions of probation are unfulfilled as the expiration date of probation approaches, the action taken by probation officers may vary. In some districts the court allows the probation officer to determine whether probation should be allowed to terminate without fulfillment of the conditions imposed. In our court, when it appears a condition of probation will not be met, the matter is brought to the court in advance of the expiration date, often with a plan or suggestion for a course of action—for example, extension of the period of probation. In this respect, it would be helpful if each court would let its probation officers know what types of unfulfilled conditions should be brought to its attention.

IS THE VIOLATION DELIBERATE?

When a probationer violates the conditions of his probation, the probation officer must determine whether the violation is deliberate, whether the violation is the result of an unrealistic condition, whether the probationer is the victim of a generally poor social adjustment. We are dealing with persons who are "socially wrong" or "socially sick." We are dealing with patterns of behavior that have been firmly established over many years. Some of these patterns are acceptable to the cultural group of which the probationer is a part, but are not necessarily acceptable to the larger society. For many of our probationers general adjustment to school is not good, school truancy is high, trade training and industrial skills are lacking, there are marital breakdowns, there are poor adjustments to military service, and social and moral values are in conflict with society in general. Life, for them, is filled with maladjustments of one kind or another. In many instances violations of probation may be symptoms of a poor social adjustment, but a poor social adjustment should not necessarily be regarded as a violation of probation.

[1]*U.S.* v. *Taylor*, 4th Cir. 1963, 321 F.2d 339.

In determining whether to recommend revocation, the probation officer must keep in mind the attitude and outlook of the probationer. Certainly a person who is penitent and who has done his best to live up to the conditions of his probation should be placed in a different category than one who is indifferent, or even arrogant, and whose only regret is that he was caught. And it is especially important at this time for the probation officer to help the probationer appreciate the advantages that will accrue when he meets his financial and moral obligations and measures up to the trust the court has placed in him.

The probation officer should avoid setting limits for his probationers based on his own standards of living and moral and social values. The standards of conduct he establishes must not only be realistic, but also meaningful and acceptable to the probationer.

REVOCATION SHOULD SERVE A CONSTRUCTIVE PURPOSE

When it becomes necessary to revoke probation a constructive purpose should be served. A plan should be formulated that is in the best interests of the probationer, his family and the community. Little is gained where the court disposition is for the sake of punishment only.

It may be that the probationer has demonstrated that he is not a law-abiding, responsible person, and even poses a threat to society. He may need the kind of discipline and training he will get in an institution. If employment has been his problem, he may obtain in the institution the kind of training needed to find a job.

Assuming the probationer is not in need of discipline or training and does not impose a threat to the free community, should probation be revoked? This would depend on a number of factors, including his attitude, his home and community adjustment, his adjustment on the job, and the nature of his probation violation. Imprisonment should be imposed only as a last resort.

The argument that commitment for violation of probation serves as a deterrent is not without merit. Several years ago an epidemic of theft and forgery of government checks in the form of income tax refunds spread through a section of our district. Despite the fact that these checks had been issued in rather small amounts, the practice became more than a nuisance because restitution was not made in a majority of the cases. As more and more jail terms were imposed for violation of probation, not only did restitution payments increase in the active probation cases, but thefts also diminished to the point that they were no longer widespread.

Thus far our discussion has centered for the most part around the probationer and the officer. In restitution cases that eventually result in violation of probation, what consideration should be given to the aggrieved party? When a probationer is sentenced to imprisonment for failure to make restitution, the victim suffers the entire loss. If the probationer is not a menace to the community, perhaps a recommendation can be made that probation be allowed to continue if for no other reason than to satisfy the losses suffered by the victim. This problem will be resolved, in part, when we have legislation providing compensation to victims of crime.

There is also the possibility that the probationer believes he is getting away with something and that the court does not mean what it says. What has to be resolved, then, is the question: Does rigid compliance and swift justice make for better probation or a fuller appreciation of probation on the part of the public?

VIOLATION HEARING AND REPORT

It is the general practice of courts to require a violation report in connection with a revocation hearing. In it are presented the facts surrounding the alleged violation. Included in the report should be a summary of the probationer's conduct while on probation, and his general attitude and outlook. The report should indicate whether the violation is incidental or a part of a general pattern. The probationer is required by law to be present at the revocation hearing.[2]

It is not necessary that the violation hearing be conducted as a trial. With respect to specifications of charges or a trial upon charges, it is not formal.[3]

The law further stipulates that "As speedily as possible after arrest the probationer shall be taken before the court for the district having jurisdiction over him.[4]

With the recent decisions of the Supreme Court that a defendant be represented by counsel at every step of due process, it would seem that the probationer's attorney should be present at the hearing. The United States attorney should also be part of the proceeding to make whatever comments or recommendations are indicated.

If, after listening to all parties concerned, the court decides to revoke probation, it might be limited with respect to the sentence it can impose. In the event imposition of sentence was suspended originally, the court is empowered to impose any sentence within the limits prescribed by the penalty provisions of the statute involved.[5]

If a definite sentence was imposed originally and the execution of the sentence was suspended, the court may not exceed the original sentence.[6]

---

[2] 18 U.S.C. 3653. See also *Escoe* v. *Zerbst*, 295 U.S. 490.

[3] *Manning* v. *U.S.* 5th Cir. 1947, 161 F.2d 827, Cert. den. 322 U.S. 792; 68 S.Ct. 102. *Bernal-Zaguetta* v. *U.S.* 9th Cir. 1955, 225 F.2d 64; *U.S.* v. *Hollien*, D.C. Mich. 1952, 105 F. Supp. 987.

[4] 18 U.S.C. 3653

[5] *Scalis* v. *U.S.* 1st Cir. 1932, 62 F.2d 220; *Gillespie* v. *Hunter*, 10th Cir. 1948, 170 F.2d 546; *Roberts* v. *U.S.* 320 U.S. 264, 64 S.Ct. 113.

[6] *Roberts* v. *U.S.* 320 U.S. 264, 64 S.Ct. 113.

There are occasions where a probationer is serving a state or local sentence which continues beyond the expiration date of the period of probation imposed by the United States district court. To allow the probation to terminate or to seek a warrant for violation of probation is a question that, at times, is difficult to decide.

If returning the probationer to court in the distant future will not serve a constructive purpose, perhaps the ends of justice can be met by permitting probation to expire or, better yet, by the court entering an order terminating probation. To impose additional imprisonment after a lengthy period of incarceration is tantamount to adding salt to the wound.

In such cases, careful scrutiny of the presentence report and an evaluation of the probationer's conduct while under supervision can help determine the proper course of action. If a person poses a threat to society, a warrant is in order. The court will then have at the time of the probationer's release a report of his attitude toward authority, his adjustment in prison, and also the presentence report.

What shall be done about the probationer who absconds? After all possible efforts have been made to locate the probationer, a warrant should be requested. In fugitive status a probationer may possibly become involved in other infractions of the law in order to avoid apprehension.

Some years ago we supervised a 35-year-old unmarried male whose background was favorable and whose adjustment was most satisfactory. Suddenly he moved and quit his job to accept another without notifying the probation officer. Members of his family were asked where he lived and where he was employed. They did not know. The family saw him occasionally, reporting that he was well and was working regularly. Each time the probation officer's message was relayed to him, asking that he get in touch with his officer.

Convinced that he had not absconded, the probation officer continued to make inquiries until there came to his attention the name and address of an acquaintance of the probationer who might know his address. In writing to the acquaintance it was explained that unless the probationer was heard from within 10 days, there would be no alternative but to refer the matter to the court for appropriate action. It had been 9 months since the last monthly supervision report had been received. Within a few days all nine reports, properly executed, were received in the mail. When the probationer was interviewed later he explained that he was frightened when he entered into a clandestine relationship with a woman who was separated from her husband. At our insistence the affair was terminated and the probationer successfully completed the balance of his period of supervision.

No doubt this was an extreme case and 9 months was an unreasonably long time. Nevertheless, it illustrates the need for exercising patience and understanding lest the officer fall victim to a hasty and faulty decision.

In general, it is my belief that after all possible leads to locate an absconder have been exhausted, the probation officer has valid reason for petitioning the court for a warrant.

SUMMARY OF GUIDELINES FOR REVOCATION

1. Conditions of probation should be realistic and purposive and geared to help the probationer develop into a law-abiding, self-respecting person. They must be flexible in their application. Each case should be judged on its own merits—on the basis of the problems, needs, and capacity of the individual offender. Unrealistic conditions which cannot be enforced invite violations.

2. The probation officer should ·make certain that the probationer fully understands the limitations placed upon him in the general and special conditions imposed by the court. Merely signing the "Conditions of Probation" form does not mean he has correctly interpreted each condition.

3. Violations of the conditions of probation do not necessarily reflect a poor probation adjustment. The conditions imposed may have been unrealistic. Perhaps too much was expected in requiring some probationers to live up to certain conditions. The customs, feelings, attitudes, habit patterns, and moral and social values of the cultural group of which a probationer is a part should be considered in assessing his noncompliance with the conditions. Probationers differ in their ability to comply or conform. It is entirely possible we are imposing a standard of conduct which is realistic for us but not for the probationer.

4. In offenses where a fine and/or restitution are being considered by the court, the probation officer should explain in detail the defendant's financial obligations and resources in order that the fine or restitution imposed will be commensurate with the defendant's ability to pay. In too many instances an automatic fine or restitution is imposed without knowledge of the financial burden it places on the probationer and his family.

5. While I do not advocate revocation of probation merely for failure to keep appointments, to submit monthly reports, to observe a curfew, to remain within the district, I do believe that a generally unfavorable attitude and deliberate noncompliance with the conditions of probation and the instructions of the probation officer are grounds for revocation.

6. Although I believe that all convictions for new offenses should be brought to the court's attention, it does not follow that probation should be automatically revoked. No violation should result in automatic revocation. It may be more beneficial to society, and also to the probationer and his family, to have him continue on probation than to sentence him to imprisonment.

7. Where a probationer is arrested on a new charge and is held in jail, I do not believe he should be regarded as a violator until he has been convicted. There is always the possibility of an acquittal. And we must keep in mind that in some local jurisdictions considerable time elapses between arrest and trial.

8. Lest the probation officer be guilty of usurping the power of the court, all unfulfilled conditions of probation—for example, not paying a fine or restitution in full by the terminal date—should be brought to the court's attention in advance of the termination date. Recommendations for a course of action should be included in the report.

9. To assist the court at the revocation hearing, the probation officer should prepare a formal report containing details of the alleged violation, factors underlying the violation, the probationer's attitude toward the violation, a summary of his conduct during supervision, and his general attitude and outlook.

10. The probationer should be present at the revocation hearing. It would seem that the United States attorney and also counsel for the probationer should be present. But it must be remembered that the revocation hearing is not a new trial.

11. Where it is necessary to revoke probation, imprisonment should serve a constructive purpose and not be used merely for punishment's sake. In certain cases, particularly where an indifferent probationer deliberately fails to comply with the conditions of probation, it may be necessary to revoke probation so that the public—and other probationers, too—will have a fuller appreciation for probation, and realize that the primary purpose of probation is the protection of the public, that the court means what it says, and that the conditions of probation are not to be flouted.

37
Parole: A Critique of its Legal Foundations

MICHAEL GOTTESMAN AND LEWIS J. HECKER

Over 50,000 inmates will be released this year from institutions throughout the United States to serve the remainder of their sentences in their communities under a form of supervision and regulation known as parole.[1] By the year-end approximately 15,000 of these and other already released parolees will violate their paroles and be returned to institutional life.[2]

Parole, in some form or another, has been in effect in this country for over 100 years.[3] This institution has outgrown its early experimental nature, which contemplated the release of a select group of offenders,[4] to such an extent that by 1961 six out of every ten inmates released from incarceration were released on parole.[5] Every state in the Union maintains some form of parole system as

SOURCE. (Notes and Comments) *New York University Review*, **38**, June 1963, pp. 702–739. Copyright 1963, New York University Law Review. (Editorial Adaptations.)

[1]This projection is based on statistics for the year 1961 when 51,445 parolees were released U.S. Dep't Justice, National Prisoner Statistics No. 30, Prisoners in State and Federal Institutions, 1961 Table 3 (1962) [hereinafter cited as Prisoner Statistics]. The 1961 figure represented a 6.2 percent increase over the preceding year. 1d at 2.

[2]In 1961 the total number of violators returned to prison amounted to 14,822. Prisoner Statistics, Table 3. This represented an increase of 9.1 percent over 1960. Id at 1.

[3]See 4 Att'y Gen. Survey of Release Procedures 7 (1939) [hereinafter cited as Survey].

[4]The early parole movements in this country centered around the release of young adults, aged sixteen to thirty, who had never before committed a felony. Dressler, Practice and Theory of Probation and Parole 55 (1959).

[5]The precise percentage was 59.7 percent. Regionally, the northeastern states released 75.5 percent on parole, the northcentral states 69.3 percent, the western states 80.0 percent, and the

an integral part of its administration of criminal justice.[6] This fact manifests the unanimous legislative conviction that it is more desirable to return the offender to freedom through a period of controlled liberty than abruptly to return him to complete freedom at the termination of his prison sentence. This legislative conviction is based upon the belief that the offender can better achieve successful integration into society as a useful and lawabiding citizen through a method of controlled release.[7]

The judicial response has not been as sanguine. Parole has confused the courts.[8] Faced with the widespread release of potentially dangerous individuals, the courts have searched for a rationale to accommodate society's interest in releasing the convict with the threat the released offender poses to the safety of the community. The search has been fruitful; three distinct theories of parole have been found. They may conveniently be denominated the "grace," "contract-consent," and "custody" theories. The purpose of this Note is to analyze these theories and the results which have flowed from their use, and to examine the safeguards the legislatures and parole authorities have instituted to achieve the dual aims of returning the parolee to freedom and preventing him from threatening public safety.

THE JUDICIAL RESPONSE TO PAROLE

The purpose and the effect of parole are to restore to the convict a measure of his forfeited liberty before the expiration of his maximum prison term. The convict is to be released only if the paroling authorities (commonly called "parole boards") are satisfied that two objectives are reasonably possible of achievement. Restoration of liberty must appear to promise a benefit to the convict and, at the same time, to be compatible with the public safety.[9] No doubt there is a point in time when the parolee is no longer a threat to the community, *i.e.*, when he is fully rehabilitated. Before this point is reached, however, the released convict represents a potential source of danger and, if

---

southern states 38.8 percent. The state releasing the smallest percentage on parole, 13.0 percent, was South Carolina; the highest percentage of releases was found in New Hampshire, 100.0 percent. Prisoner Statistics, Table 3.

[6]See, e.g., Ariz. Rev. Stat. Ann. §§ 31.401 to .461 (1956); Colo. Rev. Stat. Ann. §§ 39-17-1 to -17 (Supp. 1961); Ga. Code Ann. §§ 77-501 to -519 (Supp. 1961); Okla. Stat. Ann. tit., 57 §§ 332 to 350 (Supp. 1962) Vermont does not call its release system parole; prisoners are released under a "conditional pardon." The Governor determines eligibility and the state probation officer exercises supervision. Vt. Stat. Ann. tit. 28 § 904 (1959).

[7]See, e.g., National Conference on Parole, Parole in Principle and Practice 66 (1957); Giardini, The Parole Process 19 (1959). See also Survey 31.

[8]See, e.g., notes 66–74 infra and accompanying text.

[9]See, e.g., Ariz. Rev. Stat. Ann. § 31-412 (1956); Md. Ann. Code art. 41, § 124 (1957); Mich. Stat. Ann. § 28.2303 (1954).

necessary, his newly achieved liberty must be forfeited to the paramount interest of society in protecting itself.[10]

The courts have been acutely aware of the dangerous nature of the parolee, and their unhesitating reaction has been to look toward the safety of the community.[11] Yet they have been sorely troubled by the facts that the parolee, despite his threat, is a man at liberty, and that the concept of liberty is surrounded by constitutional protection. The nub of the parole problem facing the courts is the reconciliation of the public safety with the safeguards of liberty set out by the Fourteenth Amendment.

Whenever the courts are called upon to balance the public safety with the guarantees of the Constitution, a complex problem is raised. In the parole area the courts, almost without exception, have avoided the problem by resorting to the theories of grace,[12] contract—consent[13] and custody.[14] Once the appropriate theory is applied, the constitutional issue is nicely avoided, to the detriment of the parolee and his liberty. Seldom in any area of law has there been more groping for the proper theory and less willingness to recognize that constitutional rights may be protected without impairing the safety of society. Time has hardened the judicial approach, and the parolee with his liberty is often worse off than his fellow convict who has remained behind in prison.

THE THEORY OF GRACE. The grace theory, as developed by the courts, rests upon a dual foundation. First, that the parolee has been convicted and sentenced for crime and thus has been deprived of his liberty in accordance with due process of law.[15] Second, that the state has the uncontrolled option to require those convicted of crime to remain imprisoned for the full length of their sentences.[16] From these two premises springs the conclusion that by providing for an earlier release by parole the state has acted *ex gratia* and has conferred no legally protected right to remain at liberty. Because parole is thus a mere privilege, rather than a right, the board may revoke it at its uncontrolled

---

[10]Thus, statutes provide that if the parolee poses a criminal threat to the community, his parole is to be revoked. See, e.g., Fla. Stat. Ann. § 947.22 (1944); Ind. Ann. Stat. § 13-249 (Supp. 1962).

[11]"[T]he public is entitled to maximum protection in the administration of the parole system. ... Many a vicious crime is committed by parolee, shocking the faith of the public in the efficacy and desirability of parole." People v. Denne, 141 Cal. App. 2d 499, 508, 297 P. 2d 451, 457 (2d Dist 1956). See also In re Varner, 166 Ohio St. 340, 142 N.E.2d 846 (1957); Ex parte Anderson, 191 Ore, 409, 229 P.2d 633 (1951).

[12]See, e.g., Summers v. State, 31 Ala. App. 264, 15 So. 2d 500 (1943); Orme v. Rogers, 32 Ariz. 502, 260 Pac. 199 (1927).

[13]See, e.g., Sellers v. Bridges, 153 Fla. 586, 15 So. 2d 293 (1943); Lee v. Gough, 86 R.I. 23, 133 A.2d 779 (1957).

[14]See, e.g., Mahan v. Buchanan, 310 Ky. 832, 221 S.W.2d 945 (1949); People ex rel. Natoli v. Lewis, 287 N.Y. 478, 41 N.E.2d 62 (1942).

[15]See Fuller v. State, 122 Ala. 32, 26 So. 146 (1899). This idea can also be used to justify the contract theory. See note 41 infra and accompanying text.

[16]See, e.g., In re Varner, 166 Ohio St. 340, 142 N.E.2d 846 (1957). See Bates, On the Uses of Parole Restrictions, 33 J. Crim. L.,C. & P.S. 435, 436 (1943).

discretion, with or without cause, and its actions will be free from judicial scrutiny.[17] But grace does not merely free the authorities from judicial review of their failure to explain the revocation of parole. Its consequences extend much further:

"It is ... clear than the board in its discretion could revoke the original parole agreement with or without a hearing and return relator to its custody with or without cause, notwithstanding the fact that relator's. . .[act] did not constitute a violation of the conditions of his parole."[18]

Despite the fact that the state, as part of the administration of criminal justice, has restored the parolee to liberty in a conscious effort to enable him to conform his conduct to the law, grace means that the board can take him off the streets and send him back behind bars without cause, without notice, without a hearing and without accounting to the courts for its action.[19] In contrast, it is interesting to note than many states have elaborate *pre-release* procedures for determining fitness for parole.[20] Detailed factual data must be assembled, hearings must be held and, if release is denied, there are provisions for follow-up reports, new hearings and new determinations. Further, the courts will inquire into the pre-release procedures, at least to the extent of insuring compliance with the statutory requirements.[21] But once the prisoner is released and picked up as a violator, the court's sympathy is expended, and it assumes that the parolee has violated the trust placed in him and is not worthy of judicial care.[22] Whether or not there may be cause, the very fact

---

[17]State ex rel. McQueen v. Horton, 31 Ala. App. 71, 14 So. 2d 557, aff'd, 244 Ala. 594, 14 So. 2d 561 (1943); Summers v. State, 31 Ala. App. 264, 15 So. 2d 500 (1943). Some statutes also provide for the revocation of parole with or without cause. See, e.g., Neb. Rev. Stat. § 29.2623 (1956).

[18]State ex rel. Bush v. Whittier, 226 Minn. 356, 362, 32 N.W.2d 856, 859 (1948).

[19]Mahan v. Buchanan, 310 Ky. 832, 221 S.W.2d 945 (1949); Vigil v. Hughes, 24 N.M. 640, 175 Pac. 713 (1918). Cf. Ex Parte Edwards, 78 Okla. Crim. 213, 146 P.2d 311 (1944). The non-intervention of the courts in the parole area is analogous to the same doctrine applied to court review of the claims of prisoners. Wright v. Wilkins, 26 Misc. 2d 1090, 210 N.Y.S.2d 309 (Sup: Ct. 1961). See generally Note, 110 U.Pa. L. Rev. 985 (1962).

[20]See, e.g., Ala. Code tit. 42, § 8 (1958); Colo. Rev. Stat. Ann. § 39-17-3(a) (1953); N.Y. Correc. Law § 214; Mo. Ann. Stat. § 549.261 (Supp. 1962); S.C. Code § 55.611.1 to 612 (1952).

[21]See, e.g., Roberts v. Duffy, 167 Cal. 629, 140 Pac. 260 (1914); Bartkowiak v. Hunt, 38 N.Y.S.2d 717 (Sup. Ct. 1942), aff'd per curiam, 266 App. Div. 942, 46 N.Y.S.2d 22 (4th Dep't 1943). The courts will not, however, review the merits of the pre-release determination of the board. Hines v. Parole Board, 293 N.Y. 254, 56 N.E.2d 572 (1944).

[22]"This position [that the absence of notice and hearing violates due process] takes no account of the fact that the person being dealt with is a *convict*, that he has already been ... convicted of crime, and been sentenced to punishment therefor. In respect of that crime and his attitude before the law after conviction of it he is not ... entitled to invoke the organic safeguards which hedge about the citizen's liberty, but he is a felon, at large by the mere grace of the executive."

In re Varner, 166 Ohio St. 340, 344, 142 N.E.2d 846, 849 (1957).

that the parolee is in some difficulty with the board should be sufficient reason for the courts to intervene to protect against an arbitrary forfeiture of liberty. Yet innumerable pleas of parolees that their liberty has been forfeited without the slightest regard to the Constitution have fallen on deaf ears.

There are constitutional doubts about the validity of the grace theory.[23] But even apart from the constitutional questions, we must inquire into the soundness of the theory itself. The foundations of the grace theory are not unimpeachable. In its pristine simplicity, when parole contemplated the release of a select few,[24] the theory of grace may have had some validity. Today, however, the sheer volume of prison traffic has rendered grace an obsolete concept. It is now financially impossible to release only a small group of offenders. At the close of 1961, there were 220,329 prisoners confined in federal and state institutions for adult offenders.[25] The cost of maintaining these prisoners is staggering. No responsible legislature could conceive of keeping convicts imprisoned until the expiration of their maximum terms. State costs in maintaining a convict in an adult institution range from about $500 to over $2500 per year.[26] Parole, in addition to the incalculable savings it effects in human terms, achieves as well a significant pecuniary saving for every state. In North Carolina, for instance, the yearly cost of maintaining a convict in prison is $1188.90, whereas the cost of supervising a parolee is only $149.65. To the cost of maintaining a convict in prison must be added the cost of welfare aid to support his family and the amount of lost tax revenue resulting from keeping the convict economically unproductive.[27] Parole not only releases the prisoner; it returns him to both his family and the tax rolls. For North Carolina parole "represents a net savings of $6,721,809.25."[28] The savings effected by parole in the more populous states is still more striking. In New York the approximate annual cost of maintaining a prisoner is $2300, while parole costs $375 per parolee.[29] To the former figure must again be added the indirect costs of confinement (welfare, lost taxes, etc.). During 1961 New York had 14,610 parolees under supervision.[30]

[23]See notes 50-55 infra and accompanying text.

[24]See note 4 supra.

[25]Prisoner Statistics, Table 1.

[26]The state of Georgia spends $475.00 per annum to maintain a prisoner. Parole costs per parolee in that state are only $39.00. Letter From State Board of Pardons and Parole to Governor E. Vandiver, Jan. 25, 1962, on file in National Council on Crime & Delinquency, New York City.

Michigan estimates that it spends $3,000 per prisoner per year in direct and indirect costs. Parole costs an average of $150 per man per year. National Probation and Parole Ass'n, Costs of Michigan's Corrections Programs 12 (1958) (ms.).

[27]Such indirect savings almost equal the direct savings. Gennert, Effect of Parole on Public Assistance Grants, 5 NPPA Journal 273 (1959).

[28]Board of Paroles, The North Carolina Parole System 3 (1960).

[29]Letter From State of New York, Division of Parole to New York University Law Review, Feb. 8, 1963.

[30]New York State Division of Parole, Facts and Figures of the Division of Parole 21 (1963).

Nor is this the end of the expense. With an increasing crime rate, new facilities must be erected to handle incoming convicts. In 1961 there were 80,073 offenders committed to state institutions, an increase of 6.8 percent over the preceding year.[31] Construction costs are high. A prison requires an outlay of from 12,000–15,000 dollars per inmate unit. For one state, absent a liberal parole program, this would require a capital outlay of $40 million by 1970 to provide space for new confinees.[32] These economic facts have been recognized by parole boards which constantly present them to cost-conscious legislatures in an attempt to broaden the parole base.[33] In view of these figures, it can no longer be said that the state has the uncontrolled option of keeping every prisoner incarcerated for his maximum term. The state's option is illusory, and the courts must accommodate theory to fact and recognize that each year a certain number of convicts must be set at liberty. It will not do at this point to say that the state can, and will, keep convicts in prison notwithstanding the financial burden. This position ignores a fundamental tenet of penology that it is far safer to release men under controlled supervision, than to maintain them in confinement until the expiration of their terms and then abruptly set them free.[34]

In holding that parole is a matter of grace, the courts have misconceived both the purpose and the effect of the indeterminate sentence laws. The indeterminate sentence is an adjunct of parole.[35] Since parole contemplates a period of liberty during which the state can exert supervision, it is desirable to have a convicted person remain under sentence for a long enough period to achieve rehabilitation.[36] There can be no standard formula of the length of time neces-

[31] Prisoner Statistics, Table 1.

[32] National Probation and Parole Ass'n, Costs of Michigan's Corrections Program 1 (1958) (ms.). Commenting on parole, Chief Justice Warren, in the keynote address to the National Conference on Parole, said, "If we had no adjusted release of prisoners, it would be but a few years until we would need many times the number of prisons with many times the capacity of those we have today. I am sure the future of penology is not to be found in any such solutions." National Conference on Parole, Parole in Principle & Practice 29 (1957).

[33] Space does not permit ... for the board to point out to you the many millions of dollars saved over the years by judicious use of the parole ... function, resulting in savings not only in prison operations but millions in welfare outlays, loss of salaries, loss of taxes, and loss of other contributions which productive citizens can make to the economy of the State. ...

Letter from State Board of Pardons and Paroles to Governor E. Vandiver, Jan. 25, 1962, on file in National Council on Crime & Delinquency, New York City.

[34] The memory of the public is short. It feels satisfied when a wrong-doer is sent to prison, and does not wait for the end of the story. It is very comfortable to think of dangerous criminals locked up in prison and a most dramatic and important fact about prison is forgotten—that there are very few men, less than 3 percent who die in prison. The other 97 percent eventually come out and, unless they are under parole supervision, are without any restraining aid to keep them from going into crime.

New York State Division of Parole, Facts and Figures of the Division of Parole 5 (1963).

[35] State ex rel. Neilson v. Hardwood, 183 Tenn. 567, 194 S.W.2d 448 (1946); Ex parte Collins, 51 Mont. 215, 152 Pac. 40 (1915); People v. Adams, 176 N.Y. 351, 68 N.E. 636, aff'd, 192 U.S. 585 (1904).

[36] The merit of the indeterminate sentence is that it was a pioneering idea and that it

sary to rehabilitate a convict. Hence the resort to an indeterminate sentence—a sentence with a stated minimum and maximum. The minimum determines eligibility for parole; the maximum permits a supervisory period. In effect, however, an indeterminate sentence is a definite sentence for the maximum.[37] Only upon the expiration of the maximum term does the parolee have a right to be discharged. The indeterminate sentence tends to be more severe than determinate sentences, since maximums tend to be longer than under determinate sentences.[38] Further, the court loses its sentencing discretion under an indeterminate sentence law and can only impose the statutory minimum and maximum; the former plea of mercy which may have effected a lesser sentence than the maximum is transferred to the parole board, which can now set the prisoner back in society before the expiration of his term.[39] Did the legislature intend that the convict should remain in prison under a longer sentence, until released by an act of grace? If so, then it seems preferable to save the convict from this favor, and to release him earlier under a determinate sentence, on the expiration of which his departure from confinement comes as a matter of right.

It would seem that if the sentence were made longer, so as to permit the convict to be released earlier, then his release would come not as an act of grace, but as part of a statutory scheme designed to mitigate the rigors of the old penitentiary system, whereby each convict remained incarcerated until the expiration of the maximum term.[40]

The foundations of the grace theory are unsound. The theory ignores the fact that it is no longer financially possible not to release convicts on parole. And it ignores the proposition that the public safety will be better served by releasing as many convicts as possible under controlled supervision. Grace is out of harmony with the administration of criminal justice. Moreover, there is no place for it when constitutional arguments are presented to the courts.

THE THEORY OF CONTRACT-CONSENT. The contract-consent theory is an offshoot of grace. Basic to it is the notion, similar to the grace theory, that

---

made people think of imprisonment as a methodical preparation for parole, which is the true test of social readjustment." United Nations, The Indeterminate Sentence 29 (1954). See also Survey 14-25, 125.

[37]See, e.g., United States ex rel. Palmer v. Ragen, 159 F.2d 356 (7th Cir.), cert. denied, 331 U.S. 823 (1947); People v. Washington, 264 N.Y. 335, 191 N.E. 7 (1934).

[38]See United Nations, The Indeterminate Sentence 30 (1958): Bruce, Burgess & Harno, The Workings of the Indeterminate Sentence Law and the Parole System in Illinois 51 (1928). In New York, the indeterminate sentence law has the curious effect of making possible a longer sentence for the first time offender than for the incurable recidivst for the same offense. People v. Thompson, 251 N.Y. 428, 167 N.E. 575 (1929); People v. Tower, 308 N.Y. 123, 123 N.E.2d 805 (1954). See generally Note, 26 Brooklyn L. Rev. 92 (1959); Rubin, The Indeterminate Sentence, Success or Failure, 28 Focus 47 (1949).

[39]Ex parte Pardee, 327 Mich. 13, 41 N.W.2d 466, cert. denied, 339 U.S. 961 (1950); State v. Moore, 21 N.J. Super. 419, 91 A.2d 342 (1952).

[40]See Roberts v. Duffy, 167 Cal. 629, 140 Pac. 260 (1914).

the state has the absolute option of holding the convict in prison until the end of his term.[41] But instead of restoring liberty as an act of grace, the contract-consent theory restores it through the medium of a bargain. The state theoretically surrenders its power to retain the convict and grants him liberty in consideration of the convict's consent to be bound by any conditions the state may impose.[42] It is said that:

"The convict was not forced to accept the parole. He had the option of accepting or rejecting it under the terms and conditions therein imposed. When he did give his written acceptance of the parole with the condition inserted therein that it could be revoked for any cause deemed sufficient by the Governor, he became bound by such terms and may not question the motivating influence behind the revocation. Even for the grossest abuse of this discretionary power . . . the law affords no remedy."[43]

Judicial emphasis falls heavily upon the idea that the convict is free to refuse a parole, and that he cannot be forced to surrender his cell.[44] Notwithstanding judicial adherence to this concept, it is difficult to believe that convicted criminals have a right to reject parole and insist on keeping their cells even though the legislature demands that they be set free.[45] If the state has determined that society will be better protected if convicts are released under supervision, rather than abruptly returned to freedom at the end of their terms, it would be nonsensical to say that convicts could subvert that safety by withholding their consent. Over thirty-five years ago, Mr. Justice Holmes exploded the consent myth:

"When granted it is the determination of the ultimate authority that the public welfare will be better served by inflicting less than what the judgment fixed. . . .Just as the original punishment would be imposed without regard to the prisoner's consent and in the teeth of his will, whether he liked it or not, the public welfare, not his consent, determines what shall be done.[46]"

But courts continue to insulate themselves from any inquiry into the constitutional validity of the conditions and their application by invoking the consent theory.

[41]See notes 15-16 supra.

[42]See, e.g., Lee v. Gough, 86 R.I. 23, 133 A.2d 779 (1957); In re Charizio, 120 Vt. 208, 138 A.2d 430, cert. denied, 356 U.S. 962 (1958). The contract approach has also found legislative acceptance. See R.I. Gen. Laws Ann. § 13-8-16 (1956).

[43]Ex parte Edwards, 78 Okla. Crim. 213, 216, 146 P.2d 311, 314 (1944).

[44]See, e.g., Gulley v. Apple, 213 Ark. 350, 210 S.W.2d 514 (1948); Lilley v. Platt, 17 Conn. Supp. 101 (1950). While there is much judicial language expressing this idea, only one court has ever held that' a parolee has a right to remain in jail. Ex parte Peterson, 14 Cal. 2d 82, 92 P.2d 890 (1939). Here the authorities were going to parole the convict into the hands of the Texas authorities to serve a thirty year sentence in the latter state. Pushing this theory to its logical conclusion, the court held that the convict's consent was a prerequisite to his going on parole.

[45]See Weihofen, Revoking Probation, Parole or Pardon Without a Hearing, 32 J. Crim. L., C. & P.S. 531 (1942).

[46]Biddle v. Perovich, 274 U.S. 480, 486 (1926) (prisoner refused to accept executive pardon).

It is time the courts recognized that parole is not a contract reached through bilateral bargaining. The convict cannot determine the conditions of his release: and his consent cannot effect it.[47] Under the parole system, the convict is released by order of the state alone. It is true that many states require the parolee to read and sign the parole agreement embodying the conditions of release.[48] This is not a contract but merely a means of bringing the conditions home to the parolee.[49] His consent is significant only in determining the wisdom of his release. Failure to sign may indicate that the convict, on release, will not obey the conditions, but it is impossible to say that the state would be powerless to release him if it so wished.

Even if it is assumed that the foundations of grace and contract are sound, it does not follow that a state may deal with parolees in a manner violative of the Constitution. By the doctrine of "unconstitutional conditions" a state may be free to withold certain benefits or privileges, but if it confers them it must deal with those so benefited in a manner consistent with the Constitution.[50] The power to prohibit does not include the power to grant subject to conditions which are unconstitutional. This principle has been applied, for example, to corporations. While the state has the power to prevent a corporation from incorporating within its borders, it cannot require the corporation to agree to forego its constitutional rights as a condition of incorporation.[51] Similarly, an individual may have no right to be employed as an instructor in a

---

[47]Further, the conditions of parole may be changed without the parolee's consent, so long as no additional punishment is imposed. State ex rel. McQueen v. Horton, 31 Ala. App. 71, 14 So. 2d 557, aff'd, 244 Ala. 594, 14 So. 2d 561 (1943); Ex Parte Knaesone 22 Cal. App. 2d 667, 72 P.2d 216 (1937).

[48]See, e.g., N.Y. Correc. Law § 215; N.C. Gen. Stat. § 148–61 (1958).

[49]See People ex rel. Marvin v. McDonnell, 280 App. Div. 367, 113 N.Y.S.2d 585 (1st Dep't 1952).

[50]See generally Hale, Unconstitutional Conditions and Constitutional Rights, 35 Colum. L. Rev. 325 (1935); Merril, Unconstitutional Conditions, 77 U. Pa. L. Rev. 879 (1929); Note, 73 Harv. L. Rev. 1595 (1960).

[51]Terral v. Burke Constr. Co., 257 U.S. 529 (1922). While prior to this decision it was recognized that a waiver by a corporation of its right to transfer cases to the federal courts extracted as a condition of incorporation was invalid, Insurance Co. v. Morse, 87 U.S. (20 Wall.) 445 (1874), in Doyle v. Continental Ins. Co., 94 U.S. 535 (1876), the Supreme Court held that a state could revoke the corporate license if the corporation transferred a case to a federal court in violation of the condition. This decision was overruled by Terral v. Burke Constr. Co., supra. Thus, if the doctrine of unconstitutional conditions is applied to parolees there is no room for the argument that while a condition of parole may be invalid, the parole board can revoke parole for a violation of the condition. Further, the situation of the parolee and the corporation should not be distinguished on the ground that while a parolee has no right to parole, a corporation has a limited right to do business in a state under the commerce clause. In Terral v. Burke Constr. Co., supra, the Court expressly rejected the idea that the corporation's right to transfer a case to a federal court depends "on the character of the business the corporation does, whether state or interstate. . . ." Supra at 532. Rather, the Court based its holding on the principle that "the sovereign power of a State in excluding foreign corporations, as in the exercise of all others of its sovereign powers, is subject to the limitations of the supreme fundamental law." Supra at 532-33.

public school, but once the state hires the individual, it may not require that he waive the exercise of his constitutional rights.[52] The most persuasive analogy, however, to support the proposition that the Constitution applies to a parolee, is the fact that substantive and procedural due process rights attach to the alien who has entered the country although he has no initial right to enter our borders.[53] The positions of the alien and the parolee are not dissimilar. Neither has a right to join the society of free men; only by the permission of the sovereign is either permitted to enter that society.

The Supreme Court has at least recognized that the Constitution applies to aliens, although it has permitted a circumscription of their rights when it supposed that the safety of the nation so demanded.[54] With respect to parolees, however, the Court has held the Constitution to be inapplicable.[55] If aliens are afforded due process of law, it is difficult to see why parolees should not receive like protection. To answer that the parolee has already been convicted pursuant to due process of law and has thus forfeited his liberty begs the question, for that fact goes only to the question of whether the parolee shall initially be given his freedom. Once liberty is restored, and the Constitution is drawn in issue, the past should not control the rights of the parolee any more than it controls the rights of the alien. The very process of parole is a conscious effort to eradicate the past. The courts should not resurrect it in an attempt to control the future. Admittedly the past can be determinative, as it is with aliens, in determining the scope of parolees' Constitutional rights, but it has no bearing whatsoever in deciding whether the Constitution applies in the first instance. The use of these theories should not control the applicability of the guarantees of the Fourteenth Amendment to the parolee's liberty.

THE THEORY OF CUSTODY. We have seen that the purpose and the effect of parole is to place the convict at liberty in the community to serve out his sentence under supervision. While the courts are prepared to accept the rehabilitative purposes of parole, they have been troubled by the "liberty" afforded the parolee. The final theory to be discussed skirts the problem completely by denying that the parolee has any liberty. It says, in effect, that though parole does have the effect of restoring liberty, that

---

[52]See, e.g., Slochower v. Board of Educ., 350 U.S. 551 (1956).

[53]Since an alien obviously brings with him no constitutional rights, Congress may exclude him in the first instance for whatever reason it sees fit. . . . The Bill of Rights is a futile authority for the alien seeking admission for the first time to these shores. But once an alien lawfully enters and resides in this country he becomes invested with the rights guaranteed by the Constitution to all people within our borders. Such rights include those protected . . . by the due process clause of the Fourteenth Amendment.
Bridges v. Wixon, 326 U.S. 135, 161 (1945) (concurring opinion).

[54]See Carlson v. Landon, 342 U.S. 524 (1952); Galvan v. Press, 347 U.S. 522 (1954). See generally, Hesse, The Constitutional Status of the Lawfully Admitted Alien: The Inherent Limits of the Power to Expel, 69 Yale L. J. 262 (1959); Hesse, The Constitutional Status of the Lawfully Admitted Alien: The Pre 1917 cases, 68 Yale L.J. 1578 (1959).

[55]Escoe v. Zerbst, 295 U.S. 490 (1935).

effect will be ignored when the board deems the parolee's liberty a threat to public safety.[56] At the outset, it must be stated that the legislatures have contributed much toward the muddy thought in this area. The parole statutes are conceptually inconsistent. With one clause of the parole act the convict is placed at liberty, and with another he is placed in custody. "[A] prisoner at liberty shall be deemed to be still in the legal custody and under the control of the board" is the constant refrain of state paroling statutes.[57] With this uncertain legislative mandate as their guide the courts have utilized the custody concept to confine the parolee within ever expanding prison walls.[58] And since the "prison walls" surround the parolee at all times, parole rules and regulations become nothing more than prison rules and regulations.[59] The "liberty" or privilege of living in society becomes a reward for proper behavior behind bars, and the parolee is analogized to the prison "trusty":

"[The parolee's] position, though usually more desirable, is in substance similar to that of a prisoner... who, because of good behavior, may, as a so-called 'trusty' be allowed temporarily to leave the confines of the institution, but is obviously, while enjoying that privilege, still within the legal custody and under the control of the head of that institution. It would hardly be contended that such a prisoner would be entitled to any hearing because of a determination... that he was no longer entitled to privileges which he had previously been accorded as a trusty."[60]

The analogy to the "trusty" is specious. While a trusty earns his favored status because of model conduct and good prison work, the parole statutes are emphatic that:

"[N]o parolee shall be released on parole merely as reward for good conduct or efficient performance of duties assigned in prison, but only if the board is of the opinion that there is a reasonable probability that, if such person is released, he will live and remain at liberty without violating the law."[61]

---

[56]See, e.g., Gobin v. Clarke, 94 N.H. 167, 49 A.2d (1946). State ex rel. McQueen v. Horton, 31 Ala. App. 71, 14 So. 2d 557, aff'd, 244 Ala. 594, 14 So. 2d 561 (1943); Commonwealth ex rel. Nerwinski v. Cavell, 186 Pa. Super. 627, 144 A.2d 401 (1958), cert. denied, 359 U.S. 915 (1959).

[57]Del. Code. Ann. tit. 11, § 7710 (1953). See also Ariz. Rev. Stat. Ann. § 31-412 (1956); Ohio Rev. Code. Ann. § 2965.01 to .09. But cf. Colo. Rev. Stat. Ann. §39–18–3 to –4 (Supp. 1961).

[58]"A prisoner released on parole is not a free man.... Parole has simply pushed back the prison walls." People v. Denne, 141 Cal. App. 2d 499, 508, 297 P.2d 451, 456-57 (2nd Dist. 1956). See also People v. Triche, 148 Cal. App. 2d 198, 202, 306 P.2d 616, 618 (1957) (parolee is in a prison without bars).

[59]"Rules and regulations for the conduct of a paroled prisoner are rules and regulations for control of prisoners.... Such rules confer no legal rights." McCoy v. Harris, 108 Utah 407, 413, 160 P.2d 721, 723 (1945).

[60]In re Varner, 166 Ohio St. 340, 345, 142 N.E.2d 846, 850 (1957).

[61]Ala. Code tit. 42 § 7 (1958). The Ohio statute is similarly emphatic that the parolee is to be released only if there is reason to believe he will remain at liberty without violating the law, and that his parole will be consistent with the safety of society. Parole is not a matter of reward in Ohio. Ohio Rev. Code Ann. § 2965.09 (Page Supp. 1962).

Further, the duration of the trusty's stay outside the walls is ordinarily very brief, perhaps a few hours, while parole contemplates a prolonged period of productive life away from the artificial existence of prison society. A trusty derives his sustenance from the prison; the parolee derives his from his independent employment.[62] Notwithstanding these differences, the courts, and, to a large extent, the legislatures, complete the analogy by maintaining that the parolee, like the trusty, becomes an escaped prisoner and a fugitive from justice when he violates a condition of his parole.[63]

The Supreme Court has pushed the custody doctrine to its logical extreme, holding that while parole "is an amelioration of punishment, it is in legal effect imprisonment."[64] Since parole is seen as the equivalent of imprisonment, there can be no possible constitutional objection, under the custody theory, to a parolee's being removed from his home without notice, without hearing, and without cause given.[65]

But the custody approach, since it cannot be reconciled with the idea that the parolee is at liberty, has been inconsistently applied. Few courts, if any, are prepared to adhere to that theory for all parole problems. The result has been to recognize the parolee's liberty for some purposes, and to deny it for others. For instance, if the parolee commits another crime while on parole, the parolee will be found at liberty in order to permit prosecution under the laws of another sovereign.[66] Perhaps the most prevalent judicial denial of custody occurs where a forfeiture of "street time" is imposed on the parolee. Street time is a phrase used by convicts to denote the time spent at liberty while on parole. Many state statutes provide that if a parolee violates a condition of his parole, the street time spent on parole is forfeited, and the parolee will be required to serve out his maximum period, calculated from the date of release on parole.[67] A simple example will demonstrate the effect of these

[62]See People v. Howard, 120 Cal. App. 45, 8 P.2d 176 (1932); People v. Flanigan, 174 N.Y. 356, 66 N.E. 988 (1903).

[63]See, e.g., State ex rel. Stephenson v. Ryan, 235 Minn. 161, 50 N.W.2d 259 (1951); Wears v. Hudspeath, 167 Kan. 191, 205 P.2d 1188 (1949); *Cal. Pen.* Code § 3059; Neb. Rev. Stat. § 29-2628 (1956).

[64]Anderson v. Corrall, 263 U.S. 193, 196 (*1923*).

[65]See Mahan v. Buchanan, 301 Ky. 832, 221 S.W.2d 945 (1949); State ex rel. McQueen v. Horton, 31 Ala. App. 71, 14 So. 2d 557, aff'd, 244 Ala. 594, 14 So. 2d 561 (1943); Vigil v Hughes, 24 N.M. 640, 175 Pac. 713 (1918).

[66]Gilchrist v. Overlade, 233 Ind. 569; 122 N.E.2d 93 (1954).

[67]See, e.g., Colo. Rev. Stat. Ann. § 39–18–2 (Supp. 1961); Okla. Stat. Ann. tit. 57 § 350 (Supp. 1962). In some states the board has discretion as to whether a forfeiture will be required. See Ky. Rev. Stat. § 439.480 (1959). In other states a forfeiture is required only if the parolee commits a substantive criminal offense. See N.J. Rev. Stat. § 30.41-123.24 (Supp. 1960); W. Va. Code § 6291 (26) (1961). In still others the board is given discretion to forfeit street time only if the parolee commits a substantive criminal offense. N.Y. Correc. Law § 219. Statutes in many states provide that there shall be no forfeiture of street time. Ala. Code tit. 42 § 12 (1959); Conn. Gen. Stat. Ann. § 54.128 (1960); Kan. Gen. Stat. Ann. § 62-2252 (Supp. 1957). Nevertheless time from the date of delinquency may still be forfeited. See note 84, infra.

provisions. A convict is sentenced under an indeterminate sentence law to a term of not less than one nor more than twenty years in prison. The minimum ordinarily determines eligibility for parole. If the convict is never paroled, he must be released, absent another substantive offense while in prison, at the expiration of the maximum. But three years after entering prison he is placed on parole. The parole period, absent an earlier discharge, will last seventeen years. The parolee serves fifteen years successfully, but in the nineteenth year of his sentence he violates a condition: he may, for example, take a forbidden drink. If the board so desires he will not only be returned to jail as a violator but may be required to forfeit the fifteen years spent on parole. This means that he will, unless again paroled, serve seventeen more years behind bars, making a total of thirty-five years "in custody" for an offense punishable by a maximum of twenty years. It may rightly be asked how this is possible if all the time spent on parole was legal imprisonment. Certainly, if a convict committed a breach of the internal disciplinary rules of the prison, the warden could not possibly extend his term for fifteen years without performing an unconstitutional act. How then can the parole board accomplish the same thing, when its rules are nothing more than prison rules? The rationale is that *for this purpose*, the parolee is at liberty and not in custody.

"[Parole] simply gives to the convict the chance to earn . . . his release from further imprisonment and his restoration to society. While he is released on parole, subject to certain regulations, nevertheless, he is set free from prison restraint and confinement. . . . He is not serving time in the penitentiary as contemplated by the sentence imposed."[68]

By the simple expedient of finding the parolee at liberty the courts have managed to avoid a dangerous constitutional objection to the delegation of "sentencing authority" to the board.[69] But if the parolee relies on his being at liberty, and demands a hearing, the court may easily avoid the constitutional

[68]Commonwealth ex rel. Meinzer v. Smith, 118 Pa. Super. 250, 254, 180 Atl. 179, 181 (1935). But see Commonwealth ex rel. Banks v. Cain, 345 Pa. 381, 28 A.2d 897 (1942), where the court held parole to be legal imprisonment.

[69]Even apart from its inconsistency with the custody theory, forfeiture of street time can be attacked as an unconstitutional exercise of the judicial power by an administrative agency. The constitutions of the United States and of the several states provide that the judicial power shall be vested in the courts and it is a violation of this mandate for any other branch of government to perform judicial functions such as the imposition of a sentence requiring imprisonment as a criminal penalty. Wong Wing v. United States, 163 U.S. 228 (1896). See also Gellhorn & Byse, Administrative Law 165 (1960). As a forfeiture of street time has the effect of lengthening the term through which the state may exercise control over a convicted individual, in effect it amounts to an imposition of an additional sentence or at least to the lengthening of the original sentence. Both of these functions are within the province of the courts and are excluded from the jurisdiction of the board. People ex rel. Ingenito v. Warden, 267 App. Div. 295, 46 N.Y.S. 2d 72 (4th Dep't 1943); Commonwealth ex rel. Banks v. Cain, 345 Pa. 581, 28 A.2d 897 (1942); Wyback v. Board, 32 Wash. 2d 780, 203 P.2d 1083 (1949). It is thus an improper usurpation of the judicial function for an administrative agency to require a forfeiture of street time and if such is the case it becomes an improper delegation for the legislature to authorize or

problem by finding the parolee really in custody.[70] Facile shifting of concepts from liberty to custody and vice-versa has placed the judiciary and the parolee in a position where neither is quite certain what parole means.

Some courts, in order to maintain a semblance of consistency between custody and the forfeiture of street time, have developed the equally curious theory that parole has the effect of conditionally suspending the running of the sentence while street time is in progress.[71] There is, however, substantial authority for the opposing view that parole cannot suspend the sentence.[72] To maintain that parole suspends the running of the sentence is to ignore the purpose of the parole law, which is to permit the convict to serve out his sentence in the community and to be discharged at its expiration.[73] Further, if the parolee is legally in prison there is no general power vested in the prison authorities to suspend the running of the sentence for an infraction of the rules.[74] In short, the suspension-of-sentence concept, while nothing more than an attempt to rationalize the custody theory, is, in itself, antithetical to that theory.

The final inconsistency in the application of the custody theory arises where a parolee petitions for a writ of habeas corpus. The cases have come to the courts in two postures: where the parolee has had his parole revoked for an alleged violation and where a parolee contests not a revocation of parole but

---

require an administrative agency to forfeit street time for violation of parole. As one would expect the courts have answered this argument by denying its premise; they maintain that forfeiture of street time is not an imposition of an additional sentence because it was within the contemplation of the sentencing court. Kirkpatrick v. Hollowell, 197 Iowa 927, 196 N.W. 91 (1923). Thus, when the court first imposed an indeterminate sentence, it had parole in mind, and because forfeiture provisions are included in the parole statutes, it also contemplated the possibility of a forfeiture of street time. There is one technical defect in this answer. The indeterminate sentence law provides the maximum sentence which a judge may impose. If it is true that in imposing an indeterminate sentence the judge contemplates a forfeiture of street time which will lengthen the sentence, then in effect he is imposing a longer sentence than the maximum allowed under the indeterminate sentence law. Further, although the possible need for requiring a forfeiture of street time might have been contemplated in the original sentence, one would nevertheless expect a judge and not an administrative officer to determine whether the parolee had committed an act justifying setting the forfeiture provision in motion.

[70]Compare Ex parte Anderson, 191 Ore. 409, 229 P.2d 633 (1951); Commonwealth ex rel. Carmelo v. Burke, 168 Pa. Super. 109, 78 A.2d 20 (1951).

[71]Suspension of sentence thus solves the forfeiture of time problem. See Ex parte Walrod 74 Okla. Crim. 134, 124 P.2d 264 (1942); Doyle v. Hampton, 207 Tenn. 399, 340 S.W.2d 89 (1960); Watts v. Skeen, 132 W. Va. 737, 54 S.E.2d 563 (1949).

[72]People ex rel. Rainone v. Murphy, 1 N.Y.2d 367, 135 N.E.2d 567, 153 N.Y.S.2d 21 (1956) Commonwealth ex rel. Banks v. Cain, 345 Pa. 581, 28 A.2d 897 (1942).

[73]See Giardini, The Parole Process 16 (1959).

[74]The prison authorities may cancel the prisoner's good time credits (time deducted from a maximum sentence because of good behavior) but they cannot extend the sentence beyond the maximum imposed by the courts. People v. Garmon, 177 Cal. A. P. 2d 301, 2 Cal. Rptr 60 (3rd Dist. 1960); State v. Williams, 57 Wash 2d 231, 356 P.2d 99 (1960).

rather the validity of the underlying conviction. In the first type of case, the courts have split. One view holds that habeas corpus does not lie.[75] This is consistent with the custody theory. Since parole is merely a shift from one form of imprisonment to another, and since that imprisonment is constantly lawful, there is no proper function for the Great Writ. An opposing view holds that habeas corpus will lie to challenge the legality of the present incarceration, since the revocation of parole deprives the parolee of his liberty.[76] The latter position is, of course, an admission that parole does restore liberty to the parolee.

This situation must be contrasted with the second situation involved in the habeas corpus cases—where the parolee, while still lawfully on parole, seeks to attack the sentence under which he was paroled. Until a recent decision by the Supreme Court a majority of federal courts held that after the prisoner is paroled he is no longer in custody and hence the writ cannot lie.[77] The Court recently held that, while on parole, the parolee is under a sufficient restraint of liberty to support the writ against the parole board.[78] In a careful opinion, Mr. Justice Black did not accept the implications of the custody theory. Rather, the Court relied on the fact that parole "significantly restrains petitioner's liberty to do those things which in this country free

---

[75]See, e.g., Scott v. Callahan, 39 Wash. 2d 801, 289 P.2d 333 (1951); Mahan v. Buchanan, 310 Ky. 832, 221 S.W.2d 945 (1940). Other courts will permit habeas corpus but only to ascertain the identity of the parolee. Lilly v. Piatt, 17 Conn. Supp. 101 (1950).

[76]"[T]he writ of habeas corpus will lie in behalf of any person who has wrongfully been deprived of the liberty which he enjoys under his parole. . . ."
State ex rel. Vadnais v. Stair, 48 N.D. 472, 477, 485 N.W. 301, 303 (1921).

[77]The federal courts refused the application for the writ on two grounds. First, the application was directed at the warden, and since the parolee had been released on parole from the custody of the warden to that of the board, the cause was held moot. United States ex rel. St. John v. Cummings, 233 F.2d 186 (2d Cir. 1956); Adams v. Hyatt, 173 F.2d 896 (3d Cir. 1949) (per curiam); Weber v. Squier, 124 F.2d 618 (9th Cir. 1941), cert denied, 315 U.S. 810 (1942). Second, it was reasoned that a parolee is not in sufficient custody to support the writ. "A prisoner out on parole probably cannot maintain habeas corpus against anyone. No one has his body in custody, or could lawfully arrest him by virtue of his parole status so long as he observes its conditions. A mere moral restraint will not support habeas corpus." Van Meter v. Sanford, 99 F.2d 511 (5th Cir. 1938). Cf. Whiting v. Chew, 273 F.2d 885 (4th Cir. 1960). In Jones v. Cunningham, 294 F.2d 608 (4th Cir. 1961), rev'd, 83 Sup. Ct. 373 (1963), the parolee sought to add the state parole board as respondent, thus raising the constitutional validity of the second reason. The circuit court refused the request on the grounds that the parolee was not in the board's custody. The court held that to attach significance to the state statutory declaration that the parolee is in custody "which at best is highly technical, hypothetical and insubstantial, would prefer empty labels to a realistic appraisal of actualities." 294 F.2d at 612. Chief Judge Sobeloff, concurring, stated that he found it "difficult to explain why the statutory fiction of constructive custody over a parolee may not be availed of to supply the custody . . . [necessary to support the writ]." 294 F.2d at 613. But see United States v. Brilliant, 274 F.2d 618 (2d Cir. 1960); United States v. Bradford, 194 F.2d 197, 200 (2d Cir. 1952).

[78]Jones v. Cunningham, 83 Sup. Ct. 373 (1963).

men are entitled to do. Such restraints are enough to invoke the help of the Great Writ."[79]

The Court's conclusion is a sensible one. It demonstrates that courts need not confine themselves to the narrow concepts of "liberty" and "custody." Parole is a matter of *restraint*, and restraint need not rise to the level of legal imprisonment.[80]

A contrary holding by the Court would enable penal authorities to avoid a challenge of the legality of a conviction by the simple process of releasing the prisoner on parole. While such practices may seem remote, certain other manipulative practices by parole authorities have received judicial condonation. For the better understanding of these manipulative practices, a few general principles derived from the custody theory should be outlined. One is that a parolee who has violated his parole occupies the status of an escaped convict.[81] The rationale is that, since the parolee is in custody, a parole violation is similar to an escape from prison, and operates to end that custody. Since custody has terminated, the time spent outside of custody cannot count towards fullfilment of the sentence. When custody ceases, live time becomes "dead time."[82] Procedurally, the "escape" is completed by a declaration of delinquency by the parole board, which usually dates from the time of the violation.[83] Until the board reasserts actual custody over the escapee, dead time cannot turn back into live time.[84] The time between the declaration of delinquency and rearrest being dead, an opportunity for manipulation is presented.

In the simple case where the delinquency is declared but the board does not act promptly to rearrest because it cannot, for some reason, reduce the

[79]83 Sup. Ct. at 377. Some years earlier the Florida Supreme Court reached the same result on the same grounds. Sellers v. Bridges, 153 Fla. 586, 15 So. 2d 293 (1943).

[80]The Court justified this conclusion on the ground that habeas corpus is not restricted to situations where the petitioner is in actual physical custody. The Court preferred to view the custody of the board as a matter of restraint through regulations rather than through ever-expanding prison walls.

It should be noted, however, that this case will not bind state or federal courts in the situation where the parolee uses the writ to contest the validity of a parole revocation. The holding in Jones that a parolee is entitled to use habeas corpus to contest the validity of the underlying conviction does not contradict the view that a parolee claiming only that the revocation was invalid, has always been in legal custody and therefore not entitled to the writ.

[81]See note 63 supra.

[82]Ex parte Payton, 28 Cal. 2d 194, 169 P.2d 361 (1946); People ex rel. Dote v. Martin, 294 N.Y. 330, 62 N. E.2d 217 (1945).

[83]Matter of Cilento, 276 App. Div. 632, 97 N.Y.S.2d 201 (3d Dep't 1950); Ala. Code tit 42, § 12 (1958).

[84]See, e.g., Overlade v. Wells, 234 Ind. 436, 127 N.E.2d 686 (1955). Graves v. Amrine 154 Kan. 407, 118 P.2d 542 (1941); In re Ginivalli, 336 Mich. 101, 57 N.W.2d 457 (1953); State v. Van Dorn, 43 N.J. Super. 406, 128 A.2d 871 (1957); People ex rel. Dote v. Martin, 294 N.Y 330, 62 N.E.2d 217 (1945). Some states, however, require the parole board to declare a delinquency as soon as possible after they form a belief that a parolee has committed a violation N.Y. Correc. Law § 218.

parolee to actual custody, the courts have uniformly denied the parolee credit for time spent at large after the delinquency.[85] Many courts, however, have failed to distinguish between the situation where the board has the ability to retake the parolee and the situation where the board is powerless to act. The effects of a failure to distinguish can be illustrated by the following example. A parolee was sentenced in Minnesota in 1933 to fifteen to twenty years imprisonment. In 1940 he was paroled. He then left the state in violation of his parole and was arrested for a sexual offense in Texas. In 1947 the Texas authorities notified the Minnesota parole board, "We have your man Lutz here in jail . . . and you can have him upon your arrival here." The board replied: "You have him now, keep him as we don't want him."[86] Texas convicted and sentenced him to the penitentiary. Prior to his release from the Texas prison in 1954, the board has a change of heart and decided it wanted Lutz after all. It picked him up and returned him to a Minnesota prison, there to serve out the remainder of his term. Even though the board had the clear ability to reduce him to custody in 1947, the court held that the parolee could not be credited with any live time.

For the parole board to refuse to act promptly to retake the parolee where it easily could retake him appears to be an abuse of administrative discretion. It empowers the board to toll the running of the parolee's sentence for the duration of his life and to keep over him the constant threat of imprisonment.[87] Further, to allow an alleged violator to remain at large may endanger the public safety.[88] The effects of this practice run counter to the dual aims of

---

[85]See cases cited note 84 supra. The board may not have the ability to reduce the parolee to custody either because it does not know of his whereabouts or because, knowing of his whereabouts, it cannot retake him because he is serving a sentence under the laws of another jurisdiction. If the board does declare a delinquency before the expiration of his sentence, the chronological termination of the sentence prior to apprehension does not deprive the board of jurisdiction over the parolee. People ex rel. Atkins v. Jennings, 248 N.Y. 46, 161 N.E. 326 (1928); Magistro v. Wilson, 253 App. Div. 48, 300 N.Y. Supp. 1216 (3d Dep't 1937).

[86]State ex rel. Lutz v. Rigg, 256 Minn. 241, 242, 98 N.W.2d 243, 244 (1959).

[87]In response to a direct question by the court the Attorney General stated it to be the position and theory of the State that: If a parolee violated the terms of his parole at any time within the term of his original sentence, then the state of Illinois, through its parole officers, could exercise or withold its right to recapture and re-imprison the parolee, and that the State could withhold such action as long as it pleased and exercise it when it pleased within the lifetime of the parolee, regardless . . . of the long-time expiration of the original sentence. And in this position the Attorney General is sustained by the decisions of the Supreme Court of Illinois.

United States ex rel. Howard v. Ragen, 59 F. Supp. 374, 376 (N.D. Ill. 1945). This in effect gives the parole board a power analogous to that possessed by courts under some statutes to evoke the suspension of a sentence even though the period covered by the sentence has expired. State v. Davis, 56 Wash. 2d 729, 355 P.2d 244 (1960).

[88]See People ex rel. Watkins v. Murphy, 3 N.Y.2d 163, 169, 143 N.E.2d 910, 913–14, 164 N.Y.S.2d 719, 725 (dissenting opinion), cert. denied, 355 U.S. 858 (1957). While in the Lutz case the parolee committed a substantive offense and was imprisoned, and the threat he

parole, to rehabilitate the parolee and to protect the public safety. Yet surprisingly few voices have been raised condemning this exercise of administrative discretion. One federal court has held that this practice violates the Fourteenth Amendment,[89] and a single state court has restrained use of this manipulative practice by holding that a board's failure to retake a parolee where it has the clear ability to do so starts live time running.[90]

One further board practice warrants mention, since it is justified in the name of custody. This is the paroling of a convict into the hands of another jurisdiction either to stand trial or to serve a prison term. If a state voluntarily surrenders a convict undergoing a prison term in its institution to another state via *extradition*, there is authority holding that he cannot later be returned to the asylum state through extradition. This is so either because the state, by its act of surrender, has forever waived jurisdiction over the convict, or because the convict is not a fugitive from justice.[91] However, no such difficulty is presented when the parole board *paroles* the prisoner directly into the hands of the demanding state. For this purpose the state, it is held, does not waive legal custody over the parolee. At most there is a temporary waiver of its right to custody in order that another sovereign may exercise jurisdiction over him.[92] This procedure permits a state to accomplish indirectly what is impossible for it to accomplish directly. One court, perhaps sensitive to this, avoided the difficulty by upholding extradition to the paroling state on the ground that the very act of releasing the parolee to the out-of-state authorities constituted him a fugitive from justice.[93]

If the parole board does not lose custody by paroling the parolee to another jurisdiction, one might expect the courts to hold that the time spent in the other jurisdiction is live time. Such has been the case. The reason for this result is,

---

presented to society thus eliminated, this will not occur in all cases. For example, if the parole indicates a lapse into criminal ways through a technical violation, and does not commit a substantive offense, he will not be reduced to custody unless the parole board decides to act.

[89]United States ex rel. Howard v. Ragen, 59 F. Supp. 374 (N.D. Ill. 1945).

[90]In re Colin, 337 Mich. 491, 60 N.W.2d 431 (1953). Compare In re Ginivalli, 336 Mich. 101, 57 N.W.2d 457 (1953). Practices such as these prompted the following dissent: "This court ought to put a stop to the parole authorities of this state playing cat and mouse with these prisoners. When a paroled prisoner commits...a violation of his parole, they ought not be permitted to stand by and refuse to act promptly to rearrest the prisoner...." Overlade v. Wells, 234 Ind. 436, 445–456, 127 N.E.2d 686, 695 (1955) (dissenting opinion).

[91]Matter of Whittington, 34 Cal. App. 344, 167 Pac. 404 (2d Dist. 1917); People ex rel. Barrett v. Bartley, 383 Ill. 437, 50 N.E.2d 517 (1943). Contra, Bartlett v. Lowry, 181 Geo. 526, 182 S.C. 850 (1935); Commonwealth ex rel. Kamans v. Ashe, 114 Pa. Super. 119, 173 Atl. 71 (1934). See generally, Kopelman, Extradition and Rendition: History—Law—Recommendations, 14 B.U.L. Rev. 509, 631 (1934).

[92]Gilchrist v. Overlade, 233 Ind. 569, 122 N.E.2d 93 (1954; State ex rel Lampi v. Tahash, 261 Minn. 310, 112 N.W.2d 357 (1961).

[93]Robinson v. Leypoldt, 74 Nev. 58, 322 P.2d 304 (1958). Cf. Matter of Langley, 325 P. 2d 1094 (Okla. Crim. App. 1958).

however, not loyalty to the custody theory, but a desire to prevent the board from accomplishing a tolling of the sentence.[94]

The confused application of the custody theory reflects the basic illogic of holding that a man can be at liberty while being in custody. A more realistic method of analysis is to view the parolee as an individual at liberty under certain restraints necessary to insure the success of parole. While restraints may temper the exercise of liberty, they are not inconsistent with it so long as they do not rise to the level of legal imprisonment. A careful application of restraints, in the form of parole conditions, can well further the purposes of parole without resort to inconsistent fictions which deny constitutional protections inherent in the concept of liberty.

---

[94]People ex rel. Rainone v. Murphy, 1 N.Y.2d 367, 135 N.E.2d 567, 153 N.Y.S.2d 21 (1956). In this case the parolee violated a federal statute and was picked up by the parole board as a violator. The board turned him over to the federal authorities to stand trial. After a conviction, the federal authorities returned him to the parole board. The parole board subsequently returned him to the federal authorities to begin service of the federal sentence. The parolee spent over three years in the federal jail which the parole board refused to count toward the New York sentence. The New York Court of Appeals held that by a voluntary surrender of custody the board could not effect a tolling of the sentence. The court noted that while surrender to another jurisdiction to stand trial serves the purpose of enabling the trial to take place when the facts are still fresh, surrender for service of sentence served no useful purpose in the administration of justice. Compare Perillo v. Parole Board, 4 N.Y.2d 1013, 152 N.E.2d 540, 177 N.Y.S.2d 523 (1958), affirming 4 App. Div. 2d 355, 165 N.Y.S.2d 139 (3d Dep't 1957), where the parolee was picked up by the federal authorities on a charge of having committed a federal crime. The federal authorities released him on bail and he was arrested by the parole authorities for having violated his parole. The parole authorities turned him over to the federal authorities to stand trial and serve a sentence. The court held that the time spent in federal prison did not count towards fulfillment of the state prison sentence. The court reasoned that as the federal authorities picked him up first, the parole board was compelled to return him to allow the federal authorities to complete prosecution to the point of imprisonment. The Rainone case was distinguished on the ground that there the parole authorities arrested the parolee first and their relinquishment of custody to the federal authorities was a voluntary act. It is interesting to note that the New York courts have maintained this distinction in the situation where the parole authorities declare a parolee delinquent but refuse to pick him up despite their knowledge of his whereabouts and their ability to reduce him to custody. In People ex rel. Grosso v. Additon, 185 Misc. 670, 59 N.Y.S.2d 357 (Sup. Ct. 1945), under these facts it was held that time spent after the declaration of delinquency counted towards fulfillment of the parolee's sentence. But see People ex rel. Watkins v. Murphy, 3 N.Y.2d 163, 143 N.E.2d 910, 164 N.Y.S.2d 719 cert. denied 355 U.S. 858 (1957).

38

A Summary of Parole Rules

NAT R. ARLUKE

In 1956 a summary was published of the conditions of parole then existing in each of the forty-eight states.[1] The general conclusions reached at that time were that in many states the conditions were entirely too numerous to be of much real value, that some of the statements listed as conditions were actually interpretations of policy or were included in the penal statutes of the state, that many of the regulations were unrealistic and unenforceable, and that the basic rules were not uniform throughout the states.

How, if at all, have parole rules changed since 1956?

Currently, as was the case thirteen years ago, no single parole regulation is common to all the states.

In the states that have added regulations, marked increases occur in the categories of motor vehicle registration and license restrictions; narcotics usage; support of delinquents; the purchase and possession of weapons and the use of hunting licenses; limitations on out-of-state, county, or community travel; compulsory agreements to waive extradition; limitations on indebtedness; and approval of marriage and divorce.

Some states—notably California, Colorado, Mississippi, and Missouri—have decreased the number of conditions; most have increased them.

Conditions of parole are authorized by law and, once adopted, should have the full impact of the law. However, in many cases, their impact i[s] greater than that of the law: although a violation of a parole condition i[s] not universally an offense requiring court appearance, trial, conviction, an[d]

SOURCE. Crime and Delinquency, 15, April 1969, pp. 267–274. Reprinted with the permissio[n] of the National Council on Crime and Delinquency. Copyright, 1969, National Council o[n] Crime and Delinquency.

[1]Nat R. Arluke, "A Summary of Parole Rules," *NPPA Journal*, January 1956, pp. 6–1[?]

sentence, the parolee's loss of freedom probably will be much more expeditious than a return resulting from the trial process.

Practically all the rules of parole can be justified in one way or another, including the prohibition of liquor, undesirable associates, and changing employment or living quarters. Yet many arguments can be made in each case indicating the inconsistency and unworkableness of the rules. If they are to serve as positive guides in the development of acceptable behavior patterns, they must be administered in a manner that will finally permit the parolee, on release from parole supervision, to lead the life of a normal citizen.

The rules must be reasonable, practical, and within the intent of the law, and they should not require behavior that is illegal, immoral, or impossible. Redundancies, impracticability of application, multiplicity of regulations, and lack of uniformity are among the serious defects that continue to exist in most states.

The courts have become more concerned with the rights of prisoners, probationers, and parolees. There is every indication that technical violations of parole may have to be considered in an adversary-type hearing on the site of the alleged revocation, with witnesses and attorneys present. The current tendency in some states to increase the number of rules and regulations may be related to the fact that obtaining a revocation will depend on proof in court that the regulations in question have been violated.

Conditions of parole, like those of probation, can be extremely broad because the grant is a privilege; yet, to be effective, they must be tailored to the needs of the parolee. But they must not be disproportionate to his needs and must not impose undue hardships.[2]

Violation of parole conditions—there are about fifty different ones throughout the country—is frequently the basis of the adverse public image of parole systems and correction. The public might better understand and parolees might better comply with the conditions if they were simplified and standardized. Standardization will become increasingly more important as we become an even more mobile nation. There is no adequate reason for us to delay in developing a model code of conduct and requirements applicable on local, state, and federal levels.[3]

Some parole conditions are moralistic, most are impractical, others impinge on human rights, and all reflect obsolete criminological conceptions. On the whole they project a percept of a man who does not exist. Nevertheless, prisoners are required to sign the agreement, obviously with many reservations, before being paroled. The most tangible result is the growing number of violations of the conditions imposed.[4]

[2]Weigard v. Kentucky, 397 S.W.2d 180 (1968), which struck down banishment as a condition of probation.

[3]"A Plea for a Stronger, More Active American Correctional Association," Harry C. Tinsley, *American Journal of Correction*, September-October 1964, pp. 6–10.

[4]Manuel Lopez-Rey, "Release and Provisional Release of Sentenced Prisoners," *British Journal of Criminology*, July 1966, pp. 236–68.

Conditions should be regarded as aids to successful adjustment rather than as punitive restrictions. Today, courts and paroling authorities are retreating from long lists of specific prohibitions and restrictions. At one time, conditions were predominantly couched in negative terms, and many such prohibitions are still in use: the parolee is required to be in at certain hours and is forbidden to touch intoxicating liquor or to frequent places where it is sold, to own a car, to get married, to leave town, and to participate in a variety of similar activities. The current trend is to frame conditions in positive terms: the parolee is expected to support his dependents, is encouraged to work steadily, is expected to live a law-abiding life and to confer with his parole officer on all basic decisions, etc. A long list of prohibitions was, I believe, characteristic of the era when probation and parole officers were generally untrained, the service was new, and the list was deemed capable of controlling behavior. Courts and paroling authorities have since discovered that improved selection of parole officers makes it possible to place more discretion in their hands and that casework services are more effective than mechanical rules.[5]

Conditions of parole should be realistic and flexible. Each case should be judged separately, taking into consideration the problems, needs, and capacity of the individual offender. Conditions that cannot be enforced invite violations.

The parole officer should make certain that his client fully understands the limitations placed upon him by the general and special conditions imposed by the court. Merely signing the "Conditions of Parole" form does not mean he has correctly interpreted each condition.[6]

FREQUENCY OF PAROLE RULES

A comparison of the chart with the results published in 1956 shows the following developments:

1. *Liquor usage.*—Oddly, three states (Florida, Idaho, Michigan) have moved from "allowed but not to excess" to "prohibited." To counter-balance this, three states that had prohibited the use of liquor (Kansas, Louisiana, Mississippi) have discarded this regulation. Missouri, Virginia, and West Virginia previously were the only states with no liquor regulation; West Virginia now prohibits usage. Hawaii and Alaska have both included liquor usage as "prohibited."

2. *Change of employment or living quarters.*—Five states (Arizona, Okla-

⁵Ben S. Meeker, "Probation and Parole Officers at Work," *NPPA Journal*, April 1957, pp. 99–110.

⁶Eugene C. DiCerbo, "When Should Probation Be Revoked?" *Federal Probation*, June 1966, pp. 11–17.

homa, Vermont, West Virginia, and Wyoming) have no regulation in this regard now and did not have any thirteen years ago. One state (Mississippi) has dropped the regulation, while four states (Alabama, California, Montana, and New Mexico) have added it.

3. *Undesirable associations or correspondence.*—Five states (Iowa, Montana, New Mexico, West Virginia, and Wyoming) had no such regulation but have now included it. Virginia did not have it then and has not included it now, while Wisconsin has dropped the rule. One state (South Dakota) has moved from "prohibited" to "must have permission," while two states (Colorado and New Hampshire) have done the opposite.

4. *Filing written reports.*—Six states (Delaware, New Jersey, New York, North Carolina, Rhode Island, and West Virginia) did not require this previously and still do not. Four states (Maryland, Alabama, Colorado, and Utah) that did not require it before do so now, while four others (Indiana, Mississippi, South Dakota, and Wisconsin) so specifying have eliminated it.

5. *Marriage approval.*—Six states (Arizona, Georgia, Louisiana, Mississippi, South Carolina, and Virginia) that did not have this requirement still do not have it. Nine states previously without it have added it, and four states (Delaware, New Hampshire, New Jersey, and New Mexico) have included divorce approval in their regulations. Hawaii and Alaska include this regulation.

6. *Out-of-state travel.*—Six states (Alaska, Arizona, California, Florida, North Dakota, and Virginia) do not mention this regulation; seven states (including Hawaii) have added it; and four states (Louisiana, Mississippi, Tennessee, and Washington) have deleted it.

7. *First arrival report.*—Eleven states (including Hawaii) do not have this condition. Six states (Alaska, Kansas, Montana, Nevada, North Dakota, and Wyoming) that did not have it before have added it, and four states that did have it (Mississippi, Missouri, New Mexico, and Tennessee) have eliminated it.

8. *Motor vehicle registration and license.*—Eight states (including Hawaii) did not and still do not have this regulation. Twelve states that did not have it have now added it. One state (South Carolina) did have it but has deleted it.

9. *Narcotics usage.*—Eleven states have no parole condition specifically restricting the use of narcotics. Ten states have added regulations and five states that restricted usage (Kansas, Louisiana, Mississippi, New York, and Washington) have expunged the rule.

10. *Participation in anti-narcotics program.*—Three states (California, Illinois, and Texas) require in certain cases that the parolee participate in an anti-narcotics program.

11. *Support dependents.*—Twelve states do not mention this condition. Ten states previously without it have since added it. Two states (California and Wisconsin) have withdrawn it.

12. *Possession, sale, or use of weapons*; *obtaining hunting license.*—Seven states did not and still do not specify any regulations. Sixteen (including Alaska

COMPARISON OF

	Federal Parole	Alabama	Alaska	Arizona	Arkansas	California	Colorado	Connecticut	Delaware	Florida	Georgia	Hawaii	Idaho	Illinois	Indiana	Iowa	Kansas	Kentucky	Louisiana
1. Liquor usage	4	2	2	2	2	2	2	2	2	2	2	2	2	2	2	2		2	
2. Change of employment or living quarters	1	1	1		1	1	1	1	1	1	1	1	1	1	1	1	1	1	1
3. Undesirable associations or correspondence	1	2	2	2	2	2	2	2	2	2	2	2	2	2	2	2	2	2	2
4. Filing written reports	3	3	3	3	3	3	3	3		3	3	3	3	3		3	3	3	3
5. Approval of marriage (or of divorce*)		1	1		1	1	1	1	1*	1		1	1	1	1	1	1	1	
6. Out-of-state travel		1			1		1	1	1		1	1	1	1	1	1	1	1	
7. First arrival report	3	3	3		3	3	3	3		3	3		3	3	3	3	3	3	3
8. Motor vehicle registration and license			1		1	1	1	1	1	1			1	1	1	1	1	1	
9. Narcotics usage	2	2			2	2	2	2	1	2	2	2	2	2	2	2		2	
10. Participation in anti-narcotics program						3									3				
11. Support dependents	3	3	3				3	3	3	3	3	3		3			3	3	3
12. Weapons; hunting license	1		1		2	2	2	2	1	1	2	2	2	2	2	1	1	1	
13. Out-of-county or community travel (limited to specific area*)	1				1	1		1						1	1		a	1	1
14. Waiver of extradition		3	3		3	3	3	3	3	3	3	1	3	3		3			
15. Indebtedness		1			1	1		1			1	1					1		
16. Curfew												b		c					
17. Civil rights; suffrage															2				
18. Gambling				2					2										

Maine	Maryland	Massachusetts	Michigan	Minnesota	Mississippi	Missouri	Montana	Nebraska	Nevada	New Hampshire	New Jersey	New Mexico	New York	North Carolina	North Aakota	Ohio	Oklahoma	Oregon	Pennsylvania	Rhode Island	South Carolina	North Carolina	Tennessee	Texas	Utah	Vermont	Virginia	Washington	West Virginia	Wisconsin	Wyoming
2	2	2	2	2			2	2	2	2	4	2	2	2	2	2	2	2	2	2	2	2	2	2	2	2		2	2	2	2
1	1	1	1	1		1	1	1	1	1	1	1	1	1	1	1	1		1	1	1	1	1	1	1	1		1	1		1
2	2	2	1	1	2	2	2	2	2	2	2	2	2	2	2	2	2	2	2	2	2	1	2	2	2	2		2	2		2
3	3	3	3	3		3	3	3	3	3		3			3	3	3	3	3		3		3	3	3	3	3	3			3
1	1	1	1	1		1	1	1	1	1*	1*	1*	1	1	1	1	1	1	1	1	1	1		1	1	1	1	1		1	1
1	1	1	1	1		1	1	1	1	1	1	1	1	1	1		1	1	1	1	1	1	1		1	1	1			1	1
3	3		3	3		3	3	3	3	3		3		3	3	3	3	3	3	3		3			3			3			3
1	1	1	1	1		1	1	1	1	1	1	1	1	1	1	1		1	1	1		1	1	1	1		1	1	1	1	1
2	2	2	2			2		2	2	2	2		2		2	2	2	2	2	2		2	2	2			2				
																								3							
3	3	3	3		3	3	3	3		3	3	3	3	3		3	3	3	3		3		3	3	3	3	3				
1	1	1	1			1	2		1	1	2	2	1		2	2	2	1	1	1	1	2	1	1	2	1	2	2	1	1	1
1			1	1	2*	1		1	1			1	1	1	1	1	1		1	1		1	1	1	1		1	1			
3	3		3	3		3	3	3	3		3	3	3		3	3		3	3	3			3	3		3	3	3	3		
1	1		1	1		1	2	1	1	1			1	1			1			1		1		1		1		1		1	
6		6	6								6					6							6	c		6					
									2			2				2															
									2															2							

COMPARISON OF

	Federal Parole	Alabama	Alaska	Arizona	Arkansas	California	Colorado	Connecticut	Delaware	Florida	Georgia	Hawaii	Idaho	Illinois	Indiana	Iowa	Kansas	Kentucky	Louisiana
19. Airplane (or power boat*) license																1*			
20. Report if arrested	3							3											
21. Treatment for V.D.		3						3											
22. Credit on return as P.V.										5									
23. Criminal registration		3																	
24. Church attendance		7								7									
25. Permit home or job visits (search*)		3			3*	3		3	3				3					3	
26. Comply with law	3	3	3		3	3	3	3	3	3	3		3			3	3	3	3
27. Maintain gainful employment (inform employer of parole*)	3	3	3		3	3		3	3	3	3	3	3				3	3	3
28. Return to county (or state*) of commitment								1					1*						
29. Act as informer	2									2									

Key: 1. Must have permission. 2. Prohibited. 3. Compulsory. 4. Allowed but not to excess. a. 50 miles. b. 11:00 p.m. c. 10:30 p.m.

and Hawaii) that did not mention it now do so. One state (Missouri) has eliminated the rule.

13. *Out-of-county or community travel.*—Sixteen states do not have any restriction in this regard. Nine states that did not have it have added it. Five states (Arkansas, Georgia, Idaho, Iowa, and South Carolina) have deleted it. Kansas has limited travel without approval to a radius of fifty miles, while Mississippi has limited it to "a specified area."

14. *Agree to waive extradition.*—Fourteen states (including Hawaii) do not have this requirement. Seventeen states (including Alaska) that did not have it have now added it. Two states previously having it (Kentucky and Missouri) have withdrawn it.

PAROLE REGULATIONS

Maine	Maryland	Massachusetts	Michigan	Minnesota	Mississippi	Missouri	Montana	Nebraska	Nevada	New Hampshire	New Jersey	New Mexico	New York	North Carolina	North Aakota	Ohio	Oklahoma	Oregon	Pennsylvania	Rhode Island	South Carolina	North Carolina	Tennessee	Texas	Utah	Vermont	Virginia	Washington	West Virginia	Wisconsin	Wyoming
																1*			1												
3												3	3	3	3																
																			3												
												5	5		5				5	5											
													3						3												
								3							7																
3							3				3		3	3*	3*			3		3	3	3				3		3			
3	3	3	3	3	3	3	3	3	3		3	3		3	3	3	3	3	3	3	3	3	3	3	3	3	3	3	3	3	3
		3	3	3		3						3	3	3	3	3		3	3*		3			3	3	3	3	3			
									1*										1*												

5. May receive. 6. Reasonable hour. 7. Advised or recommended.

15. *Indebtedness.*—Twenty-six states do not have any regulation in this regard. Thirteen states have added the condition: no state that had it has eliminated it.

16. *Curfew.*—Forty states do not have any curfew regulations. Three states did have it but deleted it (Colorado, Nevada, and New York). Five states (Illinois, Maine, Michigan, New Hampshire, and North Dakota) have continued the regulation and five states have added it (Hawaii, Minnesota, South Dakota, Tennessee, and Utah).

17. *Civil Rights; Suffrage.*—Forty-two states did not and still do not have any regulations in this area. Four states that had restrictions (Alabama, California, Colorado, and Maine) have removed them. One state (Nevada) has added restrictions.

18. *Gambling.*—Four states (Arizona, Florida, Nebraska, and South Dakota) have a regulation prohibiting gambling. One state (Iowa) that did prohibit it deleted the rule. The rest of the states did not and still do not have any restriction.

19. *Airplane license.*—Of the three states requiring approval, Pennsylvania did so previously; Iowa and Ohio have added it and also require approval for powerboat licenses. Two states (California and Maine) have withdrawn the requirement.

20. *Report if arrested.*—Two states previously having this regulation have kept it (Maine and New Jersey). Colorado, which did have it, has discontinued it, while four states that did not have it (Delaware, New Mexico, New York, and North Carolina) have added it.

21. *Treatment for venereal disease.*—Two states that had this requirement (Florida and Pennsylvania) continue it, while Alabama, which did not have it, has now included it.

22. *May receive credit if returned as a violator.*—Of the four states that permitted credit for the time served on parole, New Jersey still does, while Colorado, New York, and Ohio have eliminated the rule. Five states (Hawaii, New Mexico, North Carolina, Pennsylvania, and Rhode Island) have added it.

23. *Criminal registration.*—Three states (Alabama, New Mexico, and Pennsylvania) require registration.

24. *Church attendance.*—This condition is advised or recommended in Alabama, Florida, and North Carolina; is compulsory in Nebraska; and has been removed in Kansas.

25. *Permit home and job visits by parole officer.*—This condition is a requirement in nineteen states. In three of these states (Colorado, New York, and North Carolina) the condition includes approval for search of the parolee's person or his property.[7]

26. *Comply with the law.*—Forty-three states have a condition specifying that the parolee agrees to comply with the law.

27. *Gainful employment.*—Maintenance of gainful employment is a condition in thirty-one states, including Pennsylvania, where the parolee must inform the employer of his parole status.

28. *Return to county or state of commitment.*—In Colorado, the parolee may not return without permission to the county where he was convicted; in Idaho, Montana, and Oregon, he may be banished from the state.[8]

29. *Act as informer.*—Only in Hawaii is the parolee specifically barred from serving as a police informer.

---

[7]See Alexander Holtzoff, "The Power of Probation and Parole Officers to Search and Seize," *Federal Probation*, December 1967, pp. 3–7.

[8]Brent T. Lynch, "Exile within the United States," *Crime and Delinquency*, January 1965, pp. 22–29.

Conclusion

The license issued to a parolee under England's Criminal Justice Act (1967) says he must do these five things:

1. He shall report to an office indicated.
2. He shall place himself under the supervision of an officer nominated for this purpose.
3. He shall keep in touch with his officer in accordance with the officer's instructions.
4. He shall inform his officer at once if he changes his address or loses his job.
5. He shall be of good behavior and lead an industrious life.

Ideally, the movement in the U.S.A. ought to be in the direction of reducing all our parole rules—at least twenty-nine of them and perhaps as many as fifty—to the five listed above and perhaps eventually to only the fifth, which seems to cover everything. Obviously, no single one of our present proliferation of prohibitions is absolutely necessary. Therefore, closer examination should be made and a reorganization effected that recognizes the relationship between the parole officer and his client as more important than a bank of do's and don't's.

39

Certificate of Parole

UNITED STATES BOARD OF PAROLE

Parole Form H-8
(Rev. Jan. 1967)
(Formerly Parole Form 17)

The United States Board of Parole

Washington, D.C. 20537

___

Certificate of Parole

Know all Men by these Presents:

It having been made to appear to the United States Board of Parole that

...., Register No. ...., a prisoner in

the ....,
is eligible to be PAROLED, and that there is a reasonable probability that he WILL REMAIN AT LIBERTY WITHOUT VIOLATING THE LAWS, and it being the opinion of the said United States Board of Parole that the release of this person is not incompatible with the welfare of society, it is ORDERED by the

said United States Board of Parole that he be PAROLED on ...., 19......,

and that he remain within the limits of ....until

......................................, 19........; or in the event of a committed fine or a committed fine and costs, until the same have been paid or he has been discharged under the provisions of Section 3569, Title 18, U.S. Code, or until other action may be taken by the said United States Board of Parole.

Given under the hands and the seal of the United States Board of Parole

this .... day of ...., nineteen hundred and ....

UNITED STATES BOARD OF PAROLE,

By ....

Parole/Youth Division Executive.

[SEAL]

ADVISER ....

PROBATION OFFICER ....

This CERTIFICATE OF PAROLE will become effective on the date of release shown on the reverse side. If the parolee's continuance on parole becomes incompatible with the welfare of society, or if he fails to comply with any of the conditions listed on the reverse side, he may be retaken on a warrant issued by a Member of the Board of Parole, and reimprisoned pending a hearing to determine if the parole should be revoked.

CONDITIONS OF PAROLE

1. You shall go directly to the district shown on this CERTIFICATE OF PAROLE (unless released to the custody of other authorities). Within three days after your arrival, you shall report to your parole adviser if you have one, and to the United States Probation Officer whose name appears on this Certificate.

2. If you are released to the custody of other authorities, and after your release from physical custody of such authorities, you are unable to report to the United States Probation Officer to whom you are assigned within three days, you shall report instead to the nearest United States Probation Officer.

3. You shall not leave the limits fixed by this CERTIFICATE OF PAROLE without written permission from the probation officer.

4. You shall notify your probation officer immediately of any change in your place of residence.

5. You shall make a complete and truthful written report (on a form provided for that purpose) to your probation officer between the first and third day of each month, and on the final day of parole. You shall also report to your probation officer at other times as he directs.

6. If in any emergency you are unable to get in touch with your parole adviser, or your probation officer or his office, you shall communicate with the United States Board of Parole, Department of Justice, Washington, D.C. 20537.

7. You shall not violate any law. You shall get in touch immediately with your probation officer or his office if you are arrested or questioned by a law-enforcement officer.

8. You shall not enter into any agreement to act as an "informer" or special agent for any law-enforcement agency.

9. You shall work regularly unless excused by your probation officer, and support your legal dependents, if any, to the best of your ability. You shall report immediately to your probation officer any changes in employment.

10. You shall not drink alcoholic beverages to excess. You shall not purchase, possess, use, or administer marihuana or narcotic or other habit-forming or dangerous drugs, unless prescribed or advised by a physician. You shall not frequent places where such drugs are illegally sold, dispensed, used or given away.

11. You shall not associate with persons who have a criminal record unless you have permission of your probation officer. Nor shall you associate with persons engaged in criminal activity.

12. You shall not have firearms (or other dangerous weapons) in your possession without the written permission of your probation officer, following prior approval of the United States Board of Parole.

I have read, or had read to me, the foregoing conditions of parole. I fully understand them and know that if I violate any of them, I may be recommitted. I also understand that special conditions may be added or modifications of any condition may be made by the Board of Parole at any time.

....
(Name)   (Register No.)

WITNESSED ....

....
(Title)   (Date)

UNITED STATES BOARD OF PAROLE:

The above-named person was released on the ....day of ...., 19........,
with a total of...........................days remaining to be served.

....
(Warden or Superintendent)

40

Law and Practice in Probation and Parole Revocation Hearings

RONALD B. SKLAR

The Advisory Committee on Criminal Rules recently proposed a new sub-division (f) to Rule 32 of the Federal Rules of Criminal Procedure:

"Revocation of Probation. The court shall not revoke probation except after a hearing at which the defendant shall be present and apprised of the grounds on which such action is proposed."

This new provision, as the Committee observes in its Note to Rule 32, is intended to replace that portion of 18 U.S.C. §3653 which provides that upon arrest for a suspected violation of probation, a probationer "shall be taken before the court" and his probation revoked, or, as the case may be, modified or continued. The net result of the new amendment, again as observed by the Committee, would be to codify the decision of *Escoe v. Zerbst*,[1] in which the United States Supreme Court construed the statute's direction that the probationer "shall be taken before the court" to require that an informal hearing be held with the probationer present before probation is revoked.[2]

SOURCE: *Journal of Criminal Law, Criminology and Police Sciences*; 55, June 1964, pp. 175–198. Copyright 1964, Northwestern University School of Law; Reprinted by special permission.

[1] 295 U.S. 490 (1935).

[2] The hearing, said the Court, is to be "so fitted in its range to the needs of the occasion as to justify the conclusion that discretion has not been abused by the failure of the inquisitor to carry the probe deeper." *Id.* at 493. In the earlier case of Burns v. United States, 287 U.S. 216, 222, 223 (1932), the Court had said that the question in the case of the revocation of

Although the Committee's proposal, therefore, would add nothing new to the present state of the law regarding the revocation of probation in federal courts, it represents an improvement over state legislation in specifying that a "hearing" must be held. In many states the statutes contain no indication as to whether a hearing is or is not required. Such legislative passivity concerning this important phase of the probation and parole process would be censurable under any circumstances; it is all the more extraordinary today when one considers the emphasis of recent years on the punishment and rehabilitation stage of the criminal law.

It is not a little discouraging to note that in the parole revocation field the number of states lacking legislation concerning the presence or absence of a hearing, as a group, outnumbers all other categories into which the states may be placed. More specifically, 16 jurisdictions have no pertinent legislation,[3] as compared, for instance, with nine jurisdictions which specify that no hearing is required and 14 jurisdictions which specify, without further elaboration, that a "hearing" is required before parole may be formally revoked. Eight jurisdictions in the probation revocation field are guilty of this kind of legislative oversight.

In those jurisdictions, and there are many, where the pertinent statute compels the revoking authority—usually a court in the case of probation, an administrative body in the case of parole—to hold some kind of hearing on the violation charges, the statute may simply require a "hearing," or may direct that the hearing be "summary" or "informal" in nature, or may, instead, specify in more or less detail the nature of the hearing to be held. For the most part, however, the statutes in the area do not elaborate on the scope and depth—the "quality"—of the hearing, but deal instead with the broader question of whether or not hearings are required. Judicial opinions ordinarily concern themselves with the same basic problem, leaving to the revoking authority the task of formulating the procedures before it.

State and federal cases do exist where the court, in working with a statute which simply directs that a hearing be held, has strived to set some ground rules for the hearing, struggling in this endeavor with basic constitutional and policy issues, more often with the former.

When statutes or court decisions make some kind of hearing mandatory, it remains basically within the province of the revoking authority to prescribe the type of hearing to be held. This is particularly the case where the law in the jurisdiction has not proceeded beyond the bare direction that a hearing be held. Moreover, even where the applicable statute or decisional law authorizes revocation without a hearing, it is, of course, still within the power of a trial court or parole board to grant, as a matter of practice, some kind of hearing before taking action on the charges.

---

probation "is not one of formal procedure either with respect to notice or specification of charges or a trial upon charges," but that the probationer is nevertheless "entitled to fair treatment."

[3]Note that in each of these jurisdictions there are statutes which govern the revocation procedure, but they are silent on the hearing question.

THE STATUTES

The statutes throughout the country in the probation and parole revocation field may be grouped, generally speaking, into one of six categories. These will be presented in Tables 1–6.

Table 1 *Statutes Expressly Authorizing Revocation Without a Hearing*

PROBATION

State	Statutes	Comments
Delaware	DEL. CODE ANN. tit. 11, §431 (1953).	Process issued for probationer's arrest "and thereupon without any further proceeding" sentence is imposed. Separate statute for Wilmington Municipal Court, having misdemeanor and city ordinance jurisdiction, categorized below.
Iowa	IOWA CODE ANN. §247.26 (1949).	Probation may be revoked "without notice" to probationer.
Missouri	MO. ANN. STATS. §549.101 (1963 Supp.).	Court "may in its discretion with or without a hearing" revoke probation. This statute, enacted in 1963, seemingly repeals § 549.254 which required an "informal" hearing. See Revisor's Notes to §549.254.
Oklahoma	OKLA. STATS. ANN. tit. 22, §992 (1958).	Probationer arrested and "delivered forthwith" to the place to which originally sentenced.

PAROLE[a]

State	Statutes	Comments
California	CAL. PENAL CODE §3060 (1956).	Revoking authority may "revoke any parole without notice, and . . . order returned to prison" any parolee.

[a]In four of the states listed in this category—Colorado, North Carolina, Oregon, and South Dakota—the statute, while not expressly negating a hearing, sets up an ex parte revocation and commitment procedure. That is, the parolee is taken into custody pursuant to order of the revoking authority and reimprisoned in the institution from which he was paroled, without any appearance before the authority. No provision is made for a hearing after commitment. Since a hearing is not expressly denied, these statutes might have been included among those which are silent on the hearing question. The line of demarcation is uncertain. However, their ex parte language has impelled the writer to include them in the present category. The statute of a fifth state in this group, North Dakota, interestingly enough, provides for a "full hearing" on any parole violation charge. However, following the hearing the board *then* orders the parolee taken into "actual custody," which order is to be executed by a peace officer and the parolee upon apprehension delivered to the warden of the penitentiary for recommitment. It is clear, therefore, that the "hearing" contemplated by the statute is ex parte which, for purposes of this paper, is no hearing at all.

PAROLE[a] (*continued*)

State	Statutes	Comments
Colorado	COLO. REV. STATS. ANN. §39-17-6 (1961 Supp.).	See footnote 4.
New Jersey[b]	N.J. STATS. ANN. §§30:4–123.22, 30:4–123.23 (1963 Supp.).	Prior to revoking parole, the board "*may*, in accordance with its rules, permit [the parolee] an opportunity to appear before the board and show cause why his parole should not be revoked" (emphasis added).
North Carolina	N.C. GEN. STATS. §148–61.1 (1958).	See footnote a. Table 1.
North Dakota	N.D. CENT. CODE. §12–59–15 (1963 Supp.).	See footnote a. Table 1.
Oklahoma	OKLA. STATS. ANN. tit. 57, §346 (1950).	Parolee may be "rearrested and recommitted without any further proceedings."
Oregon	ORE. REV. STATS. §§144.340–144.370 (1961).	See footnote a. Table 1.
Rhode Island	R.I. GEN. LAWS §13–8–18 (1956).	Board "may . . . revoke with or without a hearing."
South Dakota	S.D. CODE §13.5307 (1960).	See footnote a. Table 1. (revocation by Governor).

[b]As indicated in the "comment" column, the board in New Jersey "may" but is not required to hold a hearing. If a hearing is held, however, N. J. STAT ANN. §30:4-123.25 provides that the parolee "shall have the right to consult legal counsel of his own selection" and, if the board consents, may submit a "brief or other legal argument on his behalf to the parole board."

Table 2 *Statutes Which Do Not indicate Whether a Hearing Is or Is Not Required*

PROBATION		
State	Statutes	Comments
Arizona	ARIZ. REV. STATS. §13–1657 (B) (1957)[a].	
Arkansas	ARK. STATS. ANN. §43–2324 (1963 Supp.).	

[a]Arizona's statute is typical. It reads, in part: "The court may, in its discretion, issue a warrant for the re-arrest of any probationer and may thereupon revoke and terminate the probation."

PROBATION (*continued*)

State	Statutes	Comments
California	CAL. PENAL CODE §§1203.2, 1203.3 (1963 Supp.).	
District of Columbia	D.C. CODE §24–104 (1961).	
Massachusetts	MASS. ANN. LAWS ch. 279, §3 (1956).	
Nebraska	NEB. REV. STATS. §29–2219(3) (1956).	
South Dakota	S.D. CODE §34.3708–2 (1960).	
Utah	UTAH CODE ANN. §77–62–37 (1953).	

PAROLE[b]

State	Statutes	Comments
Arkansas	ARK. STATS. ANN. §§43–2802, 43–2808 (1947).	
Connecticut	CONN. GEN. STATS. §54–126 (1960).	See footnote b. Table 2.
Idaho	IDAHO CODE §§20–216, 20–228, 20–231 (1947).	*Cf.* § 20–229.
Illinois	ILL. ANN. STATS. ch. 38, §§123–3 (eff. Jan. 1, 1964), 807 (1962 Supp.).	See footnote b. Table 2.
Iowa	IOWA CODE ANN. §247.9 (1949).	See footnote b. Table 2.
Massachusetts	MASS. ANN. LAWS ch. 127, §149 (1957).	

[b]Several of the statutes in this category, it must be admitted, have an ex parte revocation "flavor." As observed in note 4 *supra*, the line dividing this category from the preceding one is not certain. The statutes considered here, however, are not as detailed as the statutes discussed in note 4, with some few exceptions. The Iowa statute is more or less typical: "All paroled prisoners shall remain, while on parole, in the legal custody of the warden or superintendent and under the control of [the] board, and shall be subject, at any time, to be taken into custody and returned to the institution from which they were paroled." The phrase "subject at any time to be returned to the institution" appears, in substance, in the statutes of Illinois, Minnesota, Nevada, South Carolina, Wisconsin, and Wyoming. The statutes of Connecticut and Nebraska, although not referring to a hearing one way or the other, specify that the parolee may be reimprisoned "for any reason that seems sufficient to said board" (Connecticut) or "with or without cause" (Nebraska).

PAROLE[b] (*continued*)

State	Statutes	Comments
Minnesota	MINN. STATS. ANN. §243.05 (1963 Supp.).	See footnote b. Table 2.
Nebraska	NEB. REV. STATS. §§29–2628, 29–2623 (1956).	See footnote b. Table 2.
Nevada	NEV. REV. STATS. §§213.150, 213.110 (1) (1960).	See footnote b. Table 2.
Ohio	OHIO REV. CODE ANN. §2965.21 (1963 Supp.).	
South Carolina	S.C. CODE §§55–614, 55–616 (1963 Supp.).	See footnote b. Table 2.
Utah	UTAH CODE ANN. §77–62–38 (1953).	
Vermont	VT. STATS. ANN. tit. 28, §904 (1958).	
Virginia	VA. CODE §53–258 53-262 (1958).	
Wisconsin	WIS. STATS. ANN. §57.06(3) (1963 Supp.).	See footnote b. Table 2.
Wyoming	WYO. STATS. §7–326 (1957).	See footnote b. Table 2.

Table 3   *Statutes Which Imply That a Hearing Is to Be Held*

PROBATION[a]

State	Statutes	Comments
United States	18 U.S.C. §3653 (1951).	
Alaska	ALASKA STATS. §33.05.070(b) (1962).	
Delaware	DEL. CODE ANN. tit. 11, §4346 (1953).	Wilmington Municipal Court only. See category I above.
Kentucky	KY. REV. STATS. §439.300(1) (1963).	§439.300(3) provides that probation may be revoked "without a hearing" if the probationer has been convicted of a subsequent crime.
Mississippi	MISS. CODE ANN. §4004–25 (1956).	

[a]These statutes require for the most part that the probationer be "brought before the court" and his probation revoked. The leading case construing such a phrase as a direction that some kind of hearing be held is Escoe v. Zerbst, 295 U.S. 490 (1935).

Probation[a] (continued)

State	Statutes	Comments
Nevada	NEV. REV. STATS. §176.330 (1960).	
Pennsylvania	PA. STATS. ANN. tit. 19, §1084 (1930).	
Rhode Island	R.I. GEN. LAWS §§12–19–9, 12–19–14 (1956).	
Virginia	VA. CODE §53–275 (1958).	
Washington	WASH. REV. CODE §9.95.220 (1961).	
Wisconsin	WIS. STATS. ANN. §§57.03, 57.04 (2). (1957).	
Wyoming	WYO. STATS. §7–321 (1959).	

Parole

None

Table 4   *Statutes Which Expressly Require a Hearing*[a]

Probation

State	Statutes	Comments
Alabama	ALA. CODE tit. 42, §24 (1958).	
Colorado	COLO. REV. STATS. ANN. §39–16-9 (1953).	
Connecticut	CONN. GEN. STATS. ANN. §54–114 (1960).	
Illinois	ILL. ANN. STATS. ch. 38, §117–3 (eff. Jan. 1, 1964).	
Indiana	IND. STATS. ANN. §9–2211 (1956).	
Maryland	Charter & Public Local Laws of Baltimore City §279 (Flack 1947).	The revocation of probation in Maryland is primarily handled on a local level. Only Baltimore is listed here, although hearings are generally required in other cities and counties in Maryland.

[a]Included within this category are statutes which provide that the alleged violator shall have "An opportunity to appear" before or "an opportunity to be heard" by the revoking authority, or which direct the revoking authority to "inquire into" the charges. Such provisions are more prevalent in the parole revocation field.

PROBATION (*continued*)

State	Statutes	Comments
Maine	ME. REV. STATS. ch. 27–A, §8 (1963 Supp.).	
New York	N.Y. CODE CRIM. PROC. §935 (1958).	
North Dakota	N.D. CENT. CODE §§12–53–11, 12–53–15 (1963 Supp.).	
Ohio	OHIO REV. CODE ANN. §§2951. 08, 2951.09 (1958).	
South Carolina	S.C. CODE §§55–595, 55–596 (1962).	
Texas	TEXAS CODE CRIM. PROC. art. 781d, §8 (1962 Supp.).	

PAROLE

State	Statutes	Comments
United States	18 U.S.C. §4207 (1951).	
Alaska	ALASKA STATS. §33.15.220 (1962).	Hearing "without unreasonable delay" and under rules adopted by board.
Arizona	ARIZ. REV. STATS. ANN. §31–417 (1956).	
Hawaii	HAWAII REV. LAWS §83–65 (1961 Supp.).	No hearing required, however, when parole violation charged is conviction of a new crime while out on parole.
Indiana	IND. STATS. ANN. §13–1611 (1963 Supp.).	Hearing is held under rules and regulations adopted by board.
Kansas	KAN. GEN. STATS. §62–2250 (1961).	Hearing is held under rules and regulations adopted by board.
Kentucky	KY. REV. STATS. ANN. §§439. 330(1)(e), 439.430(1), 439.440 (1963).	
Louisiana	LA. REV. STATS. §15:574.9 (1963 Supp.).	Hearing shall be held "at the request of the parolee."
Maine	ME. REV. STATS. ch. 27–A, §15 (1963 Supp.).	
Maryland	MD. ANN. CODE art. 41, §115 (1957).	

PAROLE (*continued*)

State	Statutes	Comments
Mississippi	MISS. CODE ANN. §4004–13 (1956).	
Missouri	MO. ANN. STATS. §549.265 (1963 Supp.).	Hearing is held under rules and regulations adopted by board.
New Hampshire	N.H. REV. STATS. ANN. §607:46 (1955).	
Pennsylvania	PA. STATS. ANN. tit. 61, §331.21a(b) (1963 Supp.).	Hearing only required for "technical" violations. No hearing necessary when violation charged is conviction of a new crime while out on parole.
Texas	TEXAS CODE CRIM. PROC. art. 781d, §22 (1962 Supp.).	Hearing is held under rules and regulations adopted by board.

Table 5   *Statutes which expressly provide that hearing may be "summary" or "informal"*

PROBATION

State	Statutes	Comments
Idaho	IDAHO CODE §20–222 (1947).	
Kansas	KAN. GEN. STATS. §62–2244 (1961).	
Louisiana	LA. REV. STATS. §15:534(c) (1963 Supp.).	
Montana	MONT. REV. CODE §94–9831 (1963 Supp.).	
New Hampshire	N.H. REV. STATS. ANN. §50:4 (1955).	
New Jersey	N.J. STATS. ANN. §2A:168–4 (1953).	
Oregon	ORE. REV. STATS. §137.550(2) (1961).	
Vermont	VT. STATS. ANN. tit. 28, § 1015 (1958).	
West Virginia	W. VA. CODE §6291(17) (1961).	

PAROLE

None

Table 6 *Statutes Which Expressly Guarantee or Dispense With*[a] *Certain Traditional Elements of a Fair Hearing*

PROBATION		
State	Statutes	Comments
Florida	FLA. STATS. ANN. §948.06 (1944).	Probationer entitled to counsel and to be "fully heard." Probationer advised of charges and allowed, in effect, to plead to them, after which probation may be revoked (if charge admitted) or charge may be dismissed or probationer may be held for a hearing.
Georgia	GA. CODE ANN. §27-2713 (1963 Supp.).	Probationer entitled to counsel and to be "fully heard."
Hawaii	HAWAII REV. LAWS §258-56	Probationer is to "appear ... and show cause" why probation should not be revoked, implying, at least, a right to produce evidence.
Michigan	MICH. STATS. ANN. §28.1134 (1954).	"Summary and informal" hearing, with "a written copy of the charges" given to the probation prior to the hearing.
Minnesota	MINN. STATS. ANN §609.14 (1963 Supp.).	"Summary hearing" at which probationer "entitled to be heard and to be represented by counsel."
New Mexico	N.M. STATS. ANN. §40A-29-20 (1963 Supp.).	Alleged violation read to probationer who may admit or deny charges; if he denies them, he is to be "furnished a copy of the petition" to revoke and a hearing is set down no sooner than 5 days or more than 10 days later.
North Carolina	N.C. GEN. STATS. §§15-200, 15-200.1 (1963 Supp.).	Probationer to be informed of the grounds of the intended revocation and, at his request, the court "shall grant a reasonable time for the defendant to prepare his defense."
Tennessee	TENN. CODE §40-2907 (1963 Supp.).	Probationer entitled to counsel and "the right to introduce testimony."

PAROLE		
State	Statutes	Comments
Alabama	ALA. CODE tit. 42, §12 (1958).	Parolee entitled to counsel and may "produce witnesses and explain charges made against him."

[a]Elements of a fair hearing are expressly denied to the alleged violator in the parole revocation field only.

State	Statutes	Comments
Delaware	DEL. CODE ANN. tit. 11, §7714 (1953).	No specific elements guaranteed but extent of hearing indicated by unique provision "in case the Board finds there is reasonable doubt of a violation of parole, ... the prisoner shall be continued on parole. ..."
District of Columbia	D.C. CODE. §24–206 (1961).	Parolee entitled to counsel.
Florida	FLA. STATS. ANN. §947.23 (1) (1963 Supp.).	Parolee entitled to counsel "and a hearing shall be had at which the state and the parolee may introduce such evidence as they may deem necessary and pertinent to the charge of parole violation.
Georgia	GA. CODE ANN. §77–519 (1963 Supp.).	Parolee entitled to introduce evidence; parole "may be revoked without a hearing" if parolee has been convicted of "any crime" while on parole.
Michigan	MICH. STATS. ANN. §28.2310 (1954).	Very detailed provision: parolee entitled to counsel "of his own choice"; "may defend himself, and he shall have the right to produce witnessess and proofs in his favor and to meet the witnesses who are produced against him"; board may subpoena witness for parolee "without whose testimony he cannot safely proceed to hearing." Statute not applicable where parolee has been convicted of a new crime while on parole.
Montana	MONT. REV. CODE §§94–9838, 94–9835 (1963 Supp.).	Parolee entitled to counsel.
New Mexico	N.M. STATS. ANN. §41–17–28 (1963 Supp.).	Parolee not entitled to counsel.
New York	N.Y. CORRECTION LAW §218 (1963 Supp.).	Parolee may "appear personally, but not through counsel or others, ... and explain the charges made against him."
Tennessee	TENN. CODE §40–3619 (1955).	Parolee may "appear personally, but not through counsel or others, ... and explain the charges made against him."
Washington	WASH. REV. CODE §9.95.120 (1961).	Parolee entitled to counsel and may present evidence and witnesses in his own behalf; hearing to be "fair and impartial." No hearing required if parolee convicted of new crime while on parole.
West Virginia	W. VA CODE §6291(26) (1961).	Parolee entitled to counsel at a "prompt summary hearing."

CASES DECIDED UNDER STATUTES WHICH DO NOT REQUIRE A HEARING (CATEGORIES I AND II OF CHARTS)

No Right to Hearing: Probation

The approach utilized by the courts of jurisdictions in which statutes, expressly or by silence, do not require hearings to be held before probation is revoked is typified by the 1942 Oklahoma case of *Ex Parte Boyd*.[4]

Although it was at one time a matter of dispute whether courts possessed the inherent power to suspend the imposition or execution of sentence for a definite period and place the defendant on probation "upon considerations extraneous to the legality of the conviction,"[5] the matter of probation is now completely regulated by statutes. Accordingly, in the *Boyd* case, emphasis was first placed on the Oklahoma statute and the controlling role it plays "in determining the procedure to be followed" in revoking probation.[6] It necessarily followed from this emphasis that cases interpreting statutes containing language different from that of the forum had to be set to one side.[7] The next step, naturally, was to examine the Oklahoma statute to determine just what powers it conferred upon the revoking court. The court, in deciding that a hearing was not required by the statute, noted the absence of any express provision in the statute for notice or a hearing and the presence of a provision authorizing imprisonment "forthwith" upon a finding of probation violation.[8] Having construed the statute to authorize revocation without a hearing, the court was then compelled to grapple with the due process question, that is, whether the revocation of probation without a hearing is consonant with procedural fairness.

As might be expected, the courts throughout the country divide on this question. The *Boyd* court held that revocation of probation without a hearing accords with due process, reasoning:

"While under a suspended sentence, a duly convicted person is not freed from the legal consequences of his guilt. He is merely enjoying a conditional favor, postponing his punishment, which may be withdrawn. When the suspension is revoked the convict is punished for the crime of which he was convicted, and not for violating the terms of his [probation]. The suspension of sentence can never be demanded as a matter of legal right. It is granted at the mere will of the court. When granted, it is not held as a vested right, but as a matter of favor or grace. . . . In exercising [their revocation powers] . . . courts must necessarily have a large discretion. . . . They are not dealing with specific legal rights and are not bound by the standards of legal procedure which usually control judicial proceedings. [Therefore], an order suspending sentence may be revoked without granting the defendant a trial upon the facts."[9]

---

[4]73 Okla. Crim. 441, 122 P.2d 162 (1942).

[5]See *Ex parte* United States, 242 U.S. 27 (1916).

[6]73 Okla. Crim. at 448, 122 P.2d at 166.

[7]*Ibid.*

[8]*Id.* at 459, 122 P.2d at 170.

[9]*Id.* at 452–53, 454, 122 P.2d at 168, quoting from the dissenting opinion in State v. Zolantakis, 70 Utah 296, 259 Pac. 1044 (1927).

This line of reasoning supporting the revocation of probation without a hearing—that probation is a matter of grace conferring only a privilege upon the probationer and not a legal right—is commonly referred to as the "act of grace" or "privilege" theory.

A caveat is often attached to the decisions approving revocation without a hearing, namely that an order revoking probation will be set aside "if it can be shown that the court's action was arbitrary or governed solely by whim or caprice of the judge, without a legal foundation."[10]

The case law in Arizona,[11] California,[12] District of Columbia,[13] Iowa,[14] Missouri,[15] North Dakota,[16] and South Dakota[17] is basically in accordance with the view taken in *Boyd*.[18]

The cases in California and Iowa not only permit revocation without a hearing, but condone ex parte revocation—revocation ordered in the absence of the probationer. At least two of the other jurisdictions listed, Oklahoma and South Dakota, will permit ex parte revocation only if the ex parte demonstration to the trial court clearly establishes a breach of one or more conditions

---

[10] 73 Okla. Crim. at 462–63, 122 P.2d at 172. The *Boyd* decision has been consistently followed in Oklahoma. See Valentine v. State, 365 P.2d 166 (Okla. Crim. 1961); *In re* Luckens, 372 P.2d 635 (Okla. Crim. 1962) ("better practice" is that application by authorities to revoke probation "apprise the accused of the specific grounds" of the violation charged, but failure so to do is not violative of due process; only question for review is whether revocation was "arbitrary and capricious").

[11]Varela v. Merrill, 51 Ariz. 64, 74 P.2d 569 (1937); *Ex parte* Johnson, 53 Ariz. 161, 87 P.2d 107 (1939). Compare McGee v. Arizona Bd. of Pardons and Paroles, 92 Ariz. 317, 376 P.2d 779 (1962) (due process requires notice to the prisoner and an opportunity to be heard on application for commutation of a death sentence).

[12]*In re* Davis, 37 Cal. 2d 872, 236 P.2d 579 (1951); *In re* Levi, 39 Cal. 2d 41, 244 P.2d 403 (1952); *In re* Dearo, 96 Cal. App. 2d 141, 214 P.2d 585 (1950).

[13]Stevens v. District of Columbia, 127 A.2d 147 (D.C. Mun. Ct. App. 1956) (dictum). Cases indicate, however, that the practice in the District of Columbia is to hold a hearing at which counsel is present and evidence is taken. Cooper v. United States, 48 A.2d 771 (D.C. Mun. Ct. App. 1946); Stevens v. District of Columbia, *supra*; United States v. Freeman, 160 F. Supp. 532 (D.D.C. 1957), *aff'd*, 254 F.2d 352 (D.C. Cir. 1958).

[14]Pagano v. Bechley, 211 Iowa 1294, 232 N.W. 798 (1930); Lint v. Bennett, 251 Iowa 1193, 104 N.W.2d 564 (1960).

[15]State v. Brantley, 353 S.W.2d 793 (Mo. 1962), decided under former statute which provided for an "informal" hearing. Court, in dicta, but after careful consideration, adopted the view that notice or a hearing is not required by the constitution.

[16]State v. Uttke, 60 N.D. 377, 234 N.W. 79 (1931); State v. Cowdrey, 73 N.D. 630, 17 N.W.2d 900 (1945) (by implication in both cases; hearings in fact held).

[17]Application of Jerrel, 77 S.D. 487, 93 N.W.2d 614 (1958); State v. Elder, 77 S.D. 540, 95 N.W.2d 592 (1959).

[18]Note that, prior to the enactment of its present hearing statute in 1963, the law in Minnesota was also in line with the *Boyd* case. State v. Chandler, 158 Minn. 447, 197 N.W. 847 (1924); State *ex rel.* Jenks v. Municipal Court, 197 Minn. 141, 266 N.W. 433 (1936); Breeding v. Swenson, 240 Minn. 93, 60 N.W.2d 4 (1953). The same was true in Kansas and Michigan under their earlier statues. *In re* Patterson, 94 Kan. 439, 146 Pac 1009 (1915); People v. Dudley, 173 Mich. 389, 138 N.W. 1044 (1912).

of release.[19] South Dakota goes further, in fact, and requires a "hearing" if the ex parte demonstration is not "sufficient to justify the exercise of the court's discretion."[20]

The Arizona courts will not review the record on appeal to determine whether there has been an abuse of discretion on the part of the trial judge. This, as noted, is contrary to the ordinary practice.[21] If it appears that the probationer in Arizona was allowed an opportunity to make some kind of statement to the court prior to the order revoking probation, which statement was not sufficient to convince the trial court that he had lived up to the conditions of his probation, then it will be "conclusively presumed" that the trial court had sufficient cause to revoke.[22]

The case law in California is worth further attention. As already observed, California permits ex parte revocation. The case establishing this rule, *In re Davis*,[23] advanced the "act of grace" or "privilege" theory to support its position. A later case, *In re Levi*,[24] added as a ground for denying a hearing that a proceeding to revoke probation is not a criminal prosecution.

Nevertheless, the practice in California, as indicated by the case law, is to hold hearings before probation is revoked. The imprint of *Davis* and *Levi* is seen, however, in the nature of the hearing granted. The "informality" of the proceedings is continually stressed in the cases.[25] The court may revoke probation solely on the basis of the probation officer's report.[26] There is no right to present witnesses,[27] even those who are present in the courtroom during the hearing.[28] The probationer may even be denied the right to testify.[29] There is no right to counsel,[30] although the defendant may sometimes be represented by counsel.[31]

There is one curious twist to California law. *In re Davis* and the other cases noted involved instances where sentence was imposed and execution thereof suspended—the ordinary case in California. Where, however, the imposition of sentence is suspended, a hearing must be held before probation may

[19]*Ex parte* Boyd, 73 Okla. Crim. at 459, 122 P.2d at 170–71; Application of Jerrel, 77 S.D. at 492–493, 93 N.W.2d at 617.

[20]Application of Jerrel, *supra* note 26.

[21]*Supra* note 17, and accompanying text.

[22]Varela v. Merrill and *Ex parte* Johnson. *supra* note 18.

[23]*Supra* note 19.

[24]*Supra* note 19.

[25]*In re* Levi, *supra* note 19; *In re* Young, 121 Cal. App. 711, 10 P.2d 154 (1932); *In re* Cook, 67 Cal. App. 2d 20, 153 P.2d 578 (1944); People v. Johns, 173 Cal. App. 2d 38, 343 P.2d 92 (1959); People v. Wimberly, 30 Cal. Rptr. 421 (Dist. Ct. App. 1963).

[26]People v. Root, 192 Cal. App. 2d 158, 13 Cal. Rptr. 209 (1961); People v. Walker, 30 Cal. Rptr. 440 (Dist. Ct. App. 1963).

[27]People v. Hayden, 99 Cal. App. 2d 141, 221 P.2d 221 (1950).

[28]People v. Slater, 152 Cal. App. 2d 814, 313 P.2d 111 (1957).

[29]People v. Natividad 29 Cal. Rptr. 468 (Dist. Ct. App. 1963).

[30]*In re* Levi, *supra* note 19; People v. Wimberly, *supra* note 32.

[31]People v. Walker, *supra* note 33.

be revoked,[32] at which the probationer is entitled to counsel.[33] These rules apply because when judgment is not pronounced and further proceedings are suspended, no judgment is outstanding against the probationer. Upon revocation, the probationer is entitled to a hearing at which judgment is pronounced. This situation is, according to the California courts, unlike the case where sentence is imposed and its execution suspended, since in the latter case revocation simply brings the sentence which was already imposed into effect.[34]

Note, however, that the hearing required in California where the imposition of sentence has been suspended is not the hearing ordinarily contemplated in a probation revocation case. That is, the fact of a violation of probation is not before the court. The probationer is in the same position as he would be if probation had not been granted and he were to be sentenced immediately following conviction. He may show that there is legal cause why judgment shall not be pronounced against him or that he is now insane, or he may show good cause to order a new trial or to grant a motion in arrest of judgment.[35] None of these arguments involves the question whether he violated the terms and conditions of his probation, although, of course, the sentencing court would have discretion to hear and consider argument on this question.

No Right to Hearing: Parole

Parole, it should be noted at the outset, is not the sole form of conditional release from imprisonment. The governor may grant what is called a "conditional pardon." Conditional pardons were more prevalent around the turn of the twentieth century than they are now for the simple reason that parole, as a method of conditional release, was then only in the formative stages.[36] The "conditional pardon" was the only means by which a prisoner could be released subject to a threat of reimprisonment if he failed to conform his conduct to the requirements of society. Full pardon was inapposite. It operated as a remission of guilt, completely freeing the offender from the control of the state.[37] It was an act of mercy,[38] whereas a conditional pardon is rehabilatory in nature,[39] similar in that respect to present-day parole

---

[32]Stephens v. Toomey, 51 Cal. 2d 864, 338 P.2d 182 (1959); *In re* Klein, 197 Cal. App. 2d 58, 17 Cal. Rptr. 71 (1962).

[33]*In re* Levi, *supra* note 19.

[34]Stephens v. Toomey, 51 Cal. 2d at 874, 338 P.2d at 187.

[35]*In re* Levi, *supra* note 19, at 46, 244 P.2d at 405.

[36]See generally 4 Attorney General's Survey of Release Procedures 2–27 (1939).

[37]*Id.* at 2.

[38]See, *e.g.*, *Ex parte* Grossman, 267 U.S. 87, 120–21 (1925); Biddle v. Perovich, 274 U.S. 480 (1927).

[39]See, *e.g.*, Fuller v. State, 122 Ala. 32, 37, 26 So. 146, 147 (1899); *In re* Patterson, 94

systems. While the conditional pardon is slowly becoming extinct, early cases dealing with its revocation, because of its similarity in purpose to parole, form the basis in many jurisdictions for modern parole revocation decisions and are included in the discussion to follow.

A leading decision in the parole revocation field is the Oregon case of *In re Anderson*.[40] The revocation there was ex parte. After construing its statutes "in their context" and deciding that the board was empowered to revoke the prisoner's parole without notice or hearing, the court turned to the constitutional issue. Its decision thereon followed upon a particularly exhaustive analysis of the relevant case law. The court held the ex parte procedure constitutional, relying primarily, through quotations from other cases, on the "act of grace" theory. A special concurring opinion rested squarely on this theory.[41]

The opinion of the court alludes to the familiar doctrine that the parolee, while not entitled to a hearing in the first instance, may challenge the revocation on habeas corpus and is entitled to his release if he can establish that the board acted arbitrarily, capriciously, or in abuse of its statutory powers.[42]

The Ohio case of *In re Varner*,[43] reaching the same conclusion as the *Anderson* case, observed, first, that a legislative intent to grant a hearing should not be recognized "unless it is clearly expressed" in the statutes and not left to conjecture;[44] it then proposed certain "policy reasons" for upholding revocation without notice or hearing. The policy reasons advanced were (1) "potential witnesses justifiably are fearful of testifying publicly against a paroled convict" and, therefore, in order to determine whether the parolee should be returned to prison as a violator "it may be necessary for the commission to rely upon secret investigations"[45] and (2) if parole could not be revoked except after a hearing, "the resulting burdens of administration of the commission and its desire to protect the public would undoubtedly discourage the commission from granting many paroles that it otherwise would grant," thus defeating the purpose of parole.[46] The court concluded on the more familiar note that the parolee had no right to a parole, so "it would seem that he should have no right to contest what may be in substance a revocation of his parole."[47]

Kan. 439, 442, 146 Pac. 1009, 1011 (1915); 4 Attorney General's Survey of Release Procedures 2 (1939).

[40] 191 Ore. 409, 229 P.2d 633 (1951).

[41] *Id.* at 451–52, 229 P.2d at 651.

[42] *Id.* at 430–31, 447, 229 P.2d at 642, 649.

[43] 166 Ohio St. 340, 142 N.E.2d 846 (1957).

[44] *Id.* at 345, 142 N.E.2d at 849.

[45] *Ibid. Accord*, State *ex rel.* McQueen v. Horton, 31 Ala. App. 71, 76, 14 So. 2d 557, 560, aff'd, 244 Ala. 594, 14 So. 2d 561 (1943).

[46] 166 Ohio St. at 345, 142 N.E.2d at 849.

[47] *Id.* at 347, 142 N.E.2d at 851. The order revoking parole, it seems, is non-reviewable n Ohio. *Ibid*; Bussey v. Sacks, 172 Ohio St. 392, 176 N.E.2d 220 (1961).

In Oklahoma[48] and Minnesota,[49] also, the revocation of parole without a hearing is supported by the "act of grace" theory.[50]

Revocation of conditional pardon without a hearing has been held permissible on the ground that the pardon was accepted subject to the condition that it might be summarily revoked without notice or hearing, and that, therefore, the parolee is bound by this condition—denominated the "contract" theory—[51] in Iowa,[52] Minnesota,[53] Massachusetts,[54] Nebraska,[55] Oklahoma,[56] and Vermont.[57]

In Utah, the Supreme Court approved revocation of the prisoner's parole without a hearing on the principle ground that the parolee "is legally in custody the same as the prisoner allowed the liberty of the prison-yard, or of working on the prison farm. The realm in which he serves has been extended."[58]

There is dicta in four California cases that "parole may be validly revoked without notice or hearing."[59]

Right to Hearing: Probation

Of those jurisdictions where the statutes presently do not require that a hearing be held before probation is revoked, the courts of three states have decided that a hearing is mandatory.

[48]*Ex parte* Ridley, 3 Okla. Crim. 350, 106 Pac. 549 (1910); Application of Cooley, 295 P.2d 816 (Okla. Crim. App. 1956).

[49]State *ex rel.* Jaffa v. Crepeau, 150 Minn. 80, 184 N.W. 567 (1921); State *ex rel.* Bush v. Whittier, 226 Minn. 356, 32 N.W.2d 856 (1948).

[50]In Rhode Island, the statute expressly authorizes revocation of parole "with or without a hearing." While no case has dealt with the hearing question, a recent case, considering another phase of the parole process, has emphasized its privilege aspects and the power of the legislature "to attach conditions to the grant of parole and to provide for the administration thereof," an indication that when the hearing question is raised the statute will be upheld State v. Fazzano, 194 A.2d 680, 684 (R.I. 1963).

[51]See Weihofen, *Revoking Probation, Parole or Pardon Without a Hearing*, 32 J. Crim. L. & C. 531 (1942).

[52]Arthur v. Craig, 48 Iowa 264 (1878); State *ex rel.* Davis v. Hunter, 124 Iowa 569, 100 N.W. 510 (1904).

[53]Guy v. Utecht, 216 Minn. 255, 12 N.W.2d 753 (1943); Washburn v. Utecht, 236 Minn. 31, 51 N.W.2d 657 (1952). The court in Guy v. Utecht was careful to point out, however, that revocation without a hearing is permissible only where the conditional pardon contains a reservation that it may be revoked summarily without a hearing or, as is the case with parole (see note 56 *supra*), where statutes authorize revocation without a hearing. Otherwise, the prisoner is entitled to a "judicial inquiry into the alleged breach" of the terms of his conditional pardon. 216 Minn. at 267, 12 N.W.2d at 759, approving the early case of State *ex rel.* O'Conner v. Wolfer, 53 Minn. 135, 54 N.W. 1065 (1893).

[54]Kennedy's Case, 135 Mass. 48 (1883).

[55]Owen v. Smith, 89 Neb. 596, 131 N.W. 914 (1911).

[56]*Ex parte* Rigley, *supra* note 55 (called a "parole" but granted by the Governor).

[57]*In re* Saucier, 122 Vt. 168, 167 A.2d 368 (1961).

[58]McCoy v. Harris, 108 Utah 407, 410, 160 P.2d 721, 722 (1945). The authority of this case was seriously weakened by dicta in Baine v. Beckstead, 10 Utah 2d 4, 347 P.2d 554 (1959), a probation revocation case considered *infra* notes 69 to 72.

[59]*In re* McLain, 55 Cal. 2d 78, 85, 357 P.2d 1080, 1084–85 (1960), *cert. denied*, 368 U.S.

In Utah, the requirement of a hearing is postulated on both constitutional and policy grounds. The conditional liberty of probation, rather than a matter of grace, is viewed in the leading case of *State v. Zolantakis*[60] as a "valuable right" not to be "regarded lightly" and not to be taken from the probationer except after a hearing "according to some well recognized and established rules of judicial procedure." From a policy viewpoint, the court added that reformation—the sole purpose of probation—"can best be accomplished by fair, consistent and straightforward treatment of the person sought to be reformed."[61] At the hearing, the court instructed, the defendant should have the opportunity to plead to or answer "a written pleading setting forth the facts relied upon for . . . revocation", and he should be given the right to be heard and to cross-examine witnesses who testify against him.

The later Utah case of *Baine v. Beckstead*[62] reaffirmed the *Zolantakis* case, but pointed out that the hearing procedures outlined in *Zolantakis* should be limited to cases where a factual dispute exists, where "the circumstances in fairness and justice warrant the granting of a hearing to the defendant."[63] In dicta, the court said that there should be no difference between probation and parole, since both have as their purpose reformation of the individual. Both probationer and parolee "should be able to rely upon the representation that if he measures up to his responsibilities, he will not have his liberty taken from him capriciously nor arbitrarily."[64] The parole revocation case of

---

10 (1961) (term of imprisonment increased and parole, which was to go into effect at a future date, revoked, without affording prisoner a hearing); *In re* Dearo, 96 Cal. App. 2d 141, 144, 214 P.2d 585, 587 (1950) (probation revocation case); *In re* Etie, 27 Cal. 2d 753, 758, 167 P.2d 203, 206 (1946); *In re* Tobin, 130 Cal. App. 371, 375, 20 P.2d 91, 92 (1933). In the last two cases hearings were in fact held to determine whether "good-behavior" credits, which were earned prior to the alleged parole violation, were to be forfeited. This question turned on whether or not parole had been violated. Hearings are customarily held in California when parole is revoked since the forfeiture of "good-behavior" credits is a normal consequence of violating parole and, by statute (Cal. Penal Code §2924 (1963 Supp.)), a hearing, at which the prisoner "shall be present and entitled to be heard and may present evidence and witnesses in his behalf," must be held before "good-behavior" credits may be forfeited. See *In re* Etie and *In re* Tobin, *supra*; *In re* Taylor, 216 Cal. 113, 13 P.2d 906 (1932); *In re* Payton, 28 Cal. 2d 194, 169 P.2d 361 (1946); *In re* Borgfeldt, 75 Cal. App. 2d 83, 170 P.2d 94 (1946). Further complicating California law is the decision that the parole authority may redetermine and increase the sentence of a person out on parole from eight to ten years without affording him notice or a hearing. *In re* Smith, 33 Cal. 2d 797, 205 P.2d 662 (1949). Although such action does not result in reimprisonment and is clearly distinguishable from parole revocation for that reason, the *Smith* case has been cited in California as authority for revoking parole without a hearing. *In re* McLain, *supra*; *In re* Dearo, *supra*.

⁶⁰70 Utah 296, 259 Pac. 1044 (1927).

⁶¹*Id.* at 303, 259 Pac. at 1046, 1047.

⁶²10 Utah 2d 4, 347 P.2d 554 (1959).

⁶³*Id.* at 8, 10–11, 347 P.2d at 557, 559. And see McPhie v. Turner, 10 Utah 2d 237, 351 P.2d 91 (1960), holding that revocation of probation without a hearing on the facts there presented "was a denial of due process of law."

⁶⁴10 Utah 2d at 9, 347 P.2d at 558.

McCoy v. Harris,[65] which sanctioned revocation of parole without a hearing, was distinguished on the ground that no factual dispute existed which required resolution at a hearing.

Revocation of probation without "notice and an opportunity to be heard" was held violative of due process of law by the New Mexico Supreme Court in *Ex parte Lucero,*[66] the court stressing that suspension of sentence "gives to the defendant a valuable right," that of "personal liberty," and by the Washington Supreme Court in *State* v. *O'Neal,*[67] the court quoting extensively from the *Lucero* case. Both cases were decided under statutes which did not require a hearing. The Washington statute presently requires that the probationer be "brought before the court." A 1963 amendment to the New Mexico statute requires that a hearing be held.

In Arkansas, without reliance upon the constitution, it has been held error to deny the probationer the right to testify and call witnesses at the hearing to revoke his probation.[68] Similarly, in Nebraska, without resort to the constitution, the courts have consistently held that the revocation process be instituted either by a "verified information stating specifically the conduct constituting a violation of probationary conditions" or by a motion to revoke probation and order to show cause. The information, however, need not be as precise as is necessary when instituting a formal criminal proceeding.[69] If the probationer pleads not guilty to the information or motion to revoke probation, a hearing is held.[70]

Right to Hearing: Parole

A case of importance is *Fleenor v. Hammond.*[71] decided by the United States Court of Appeals for the Sixth Circuit. A conditional pardon granted by the governor of Kentucky was revoked in that case without notice or hearing on the ground that a power to revoke in such a manner had been reserved by the governor in the pardon.[72] The federal court, bound by the construction placed on the pardon by the state court, framed the question for decision as whether summary revocation of a pardon, without a hearing, impaired petitioner's rights under the Fourteenth Amendment. The court held that it did,

[65]*Supra* note 65.

[66]23 N.M. 433, 168 Pac. 713 (1917), followed in State v Peoples, 69 N.M. 106, 364 P.2d 359 (1961). Both cases apply the universal rule that a defendant is not entitled to a jury trial on the question of revocation, unless he pleads "want of identity of himself and the person originally sentenced."

[67]147 Wash. 169, 265 Pac. 175 (1928), approved in State v. Shannon, 60 Wash. 2d 883, 376 P.2d 646 (1962).

[68]Gerard v. State 363 S.W.2d 916 (Ark. 1963).

[69]See Sellers v. State, 105 Neb. 748, 750, 181 N.W. 862, 863 (1921); Moore v. State, 125 Neb. 565, 251 N.W. 117 (1933); Carr v. State, 152 Neb. 248; 40 N.W.2d 677 (1950); Young v State, 155 Neb. 261, 51 N.W.2d 326 (1952); Phoenix v. State, 162 Neb. 669, 77 N.W.2d 237 (1956).

[70]Moyer v. State, 144 Neb. 673, 14 N.W.2d 220 (1944); Reinmuth v. State, 163 Neb. 724, 80 N.W.2d 874 (1957); Carr v. State, Young v. State, Phoenix v. State, *supra* note 76.

[71]116 F.2d 982 (6th Cir. 1941).

[72]Commonwealth *ex rel.* Meredith v. Hall, 277 Ky. 612, 126 S.W.2d 1056 (1939).

and, in a significant passage, took direct issue with the "act of grace" theory:

"We may grant at once that the *giving* of a pardon is an act of grace; that to it the Governor may attach conditions; that if any condition is broken the Governor may revoke and that his judgment as to the breach is final and conclusive upon the courts. It does not follow, however, from the reservation of a right to revoke, that it may be exercised arbitrarily or upon whim, caprice, or rumor. . . . It is our conclusion that the petitioner's right to his freedom under the terms of the pardon could not be revoked without such hearing as is the generally accepted prerequisite of due process. . . ."[73]

In three states having statutes that do not require a hearing, it can fairly be said that case law exacts a hearing before parole can be revoked. In one of these states, Utah, the requirement of a hearing is to be found in a dictum in *Bain v. Deckstead*, considered in the preceding section. The Illinois Supreme Court, viewing the due process clause as applicable to every proceeding which may deprive a person of his liberty, "whether the process be judicial or administrative or executive in its nature," refused to regard parole as "a mere act of grace and favor by the board of pardons or the warden." Construing the statute then on the books to require that a hearing be held, the court wrote: "As we hold that the relator is entitled to a hearing . . . , the act does not deprive him of his liberty without due process of law. . . ."[74] The present Illinois statute does not contain the clause relied on by the court for its construction of the earlier statute. It would have to follow, however, under the authority of this case, that revocation of parole without a hearing would be declared unconstitutional in Illinois.

The Virginia court in *Hudson* v. *Youell*,[75] observing that its statute failed to specify the procedure for revoking a conditional pardon, decided that a hearing should be held because it was "the established practice at common law and in the American States" to hold such hearings, at least in the absence of any statute or reservation in the pardon authorizing revocation without a hearing.

CASES DECIDED UNDER STATUTES WHICH EXPRESSLY OR IMPLIEDLY REQUIRE A HEARING (CATEGORIES III TO VI OF CHARTS)

Probation

It would be expected that decisions in jurisdictions where hearings are expressly or impliedly required by statute would recognize the right of a probationer to a hearing on the revocation of probation. Such is indeed the

---

[73] 116 F.2d at 986. (Emphasis added.) *Accord,* State *ex rel.* Murray v. Swenson, 196 Md. 222, 76 A.2d 150 (1950), holding that revocation of a conditional pardon without a hearing amounts to deprivation of a valuable right through "arbitrary action."

[74] People *ex rel.* Joyce v. Strassheim, 242 Ill. 359, 366, 367–68, 90 N.E. 118, 120, 121 (1909).

[75] 178 Va. 525, 17 S.E.2d 403 (1941), *modified on other grounds,* 179 Va. 442, 19 S.E.2d 705 (1942).

case; however, the nature and type of hearing required vary with the jurisdiction and, to some extent, the language of the statute.

Two influential decisions are out of the United States Supreme Court, construing the federal statute which requires that the probationer be "taken before the court." In *Burns v. United States*,[76] a unanimous Court, noting that probation is a "privilege and cannot be demanded as a right," formulated certain "principles":

"The question, . . . in the case of the revocation of probation, is not one of formal procedure either with respect to notice or specification of charges or a trial upon charges. The question is simply whether there has been an abuse of discretion and is to be determined in accordance with familiar principles governing the exercise of judicial discretion. That exercise implies conscientious judgment, not arbitary action. . . . While probation is a matter of grace, the probationer is entitled to fair treatment, and is not to be made the victim of whim and caprice."[77]

In *Escoe v. Zerbst*,[78] the Court expanded on what is said in *Burns*, explaining that the hearing, while it need not be formal in nature, must be "so fitted in its range to the needs of the occasion as to justify the conclusion that discretion has not been abused by the failure of the inquisitor to carry the probe deeper." The probationer must be given the opportunity "to explain away" charges which "may have been inspired by rumor or mistake or downright malice. He shall have a chance to say his say before the word of his pursuers is received to his undoing."[79]

Then, in a celebrated dictum, the *Escoe* Court rejected the probationer's contention that a hearing is mandated by the federal Constitution. The lawmakers, the Court observed, could, if they wished, "dispense with notice or a hearing." "Probation or suspension of sentence comes as an act of grace to one convicted of a crime," the Court wrote tersely, "and may be coupled with such conditions in respect of its duration as Congress may impose."[80]

Following the lead thus set by the Supreme Court, state and lower federal court decisions are legion which stress the informality of the hearing granted by their statutes, occasionally adding that the test is one of the exercise of sound judicial discretion, whether the probationer was accorded "fair treatment."[81]

---

[76] 287 U.S. 216 (1932).

[77] *Id*. at 222–23.

[78] 295 U.S. 490 (1935).

[79] *Id*. at 493.

[80] *Id*. at 492–93. State and lower federal courts tend to give this dictum the weight of a holding. See, *e.g.*, Hyser v. Reed, 318 F.2d 225, 238 (D.C. Cir. 1963); United States v. Freeman, 160 F. Supp. 532 (D.D.C. 1957), *aff'd*, 254 F.2d 352 (D.C. Cir. 1958); *In re* Davis, 37 Cal. 2d 872, 236 P.2d 579 (1951), discussed *supra* notes 19, 30; *In re* Anderson, 191 Ore. 409, 434, 438, 447, 229 P.2d 633, 644, 646, 649 (1951), discussed *supra* notes 47–49.

[81] See, *e.g.*, Bennett v. United States, 158 F.2d 412 (8th Cir. 1946); Brown v. United States, 236 F.2d 253 (9th Cir. 1956); United States v. Feller, 17 Alaska 417, 156 F. Supp. 107 (1957);

The courts do not agree, however, as to just how "informal" the hearing is to be. Certain traditional elements of a fair hearing are accorded the probationer by the courts of some jurisdictions,[82] and denied to him by others. A close majority of the cases require that the probationer receive notice prior to the hearing of the particular grounds upon which revocation is sought;[83] it is sufficient, according to other cases, if the notice informs the probationer that he is charged with a violation of his probation, as by an order to show cause—that is, if it simply brings him before the court.[84] A clear majority of the cases hold that the probationer is entitled to introduce evidence and produce witnesses on his own behalf;[85] some few deny him that right.[86] The courts of Michigan require the authorities to produce witnesses if the charges are denied.[87] Revocation based only on a probation report has been reversed in Illinois.[88] The courts in three states explicitly recognize the probationer's right to cross-examine adverse witnesses.[89]

No court has expressly denied the probationer the right to be represented

---

Brill v. State, 159 Fla. 682, 32 So. 2d 607 (1947); *Ex parte* Medley, 73 Idaho 474, 253 P.2d 794 (1953); Ridley v. Commonwealth, 287 S.W.2d 156 (Ky. Ct. App. 1956); Edwardsen v. State, 220 Md. 82, 151 A.2d 132 (1959); Murphy v. Lawhon, 213 Miss. 513, 57 So. 2d 154 (1952); State v. Zachowski, 53 N.J. Super, 431, 147 A.2d 584 (1959); People v. Oskroba, 305 N.Y. 113, 111 N.E.2d 235 (1953); State v. Theisen, 167 Ohio St. 119, 146 N.E.2d 865 (1957); Arney v. State, 195 Tenn. 57, 256 S.W.2d 706 (1953); Stratmon v. State, 333 S.W.2d 135 (Tex. Crim. 1960); Berry v. Commonwealth, 200 Va. 495, 106 S.E.2d 590 (1959); State v. Shannon, 60 Wash. 2d 883, 376 P.2d 646 (1962).

[82]Note that some statutes confer specific rights on the probationer. See category VI of charts. Decisions which merely echo such legislative fiat are not considered here.

[83]Dingler v. State, 101 Ga. App. 312, 113 S.E.2d 496 (1960); People v. Price, 24 Ill. App. 2d 364, 376–377, 164, N.E.2d 528, 533 (1960); Crenshaw v. State, 222 Md. 533, 161 A. 2d 669 (1960); State v. Zachowski, *supra* note 88, at 441, 147 A.2d at 590; People v. Oskroba, *supra* note 88; State v. Gooding, 194 N.C. 271, 139 S.E. 436 (1927). See generally Note, 59 Colum. L. Rev. 311, 326–328 (1959).

[84]Manning v. United States, 161 F.2d 827 (5th Cir. 1947); Ridley v. Commonwealth, *supra* note 88; State v. Theisen, *supra* note, 88; State v. Maes, 127 S.C. 397, 120 S.E. 576 (1923); Berry v. Commonwealth, *supra* note 88 (no advance notice given of any kind). As to the federal rule, however, see Holtzoff, *Duties and Rights of Probationers*, 21 Fed. Prob. 3, 8 (Dec. 1957).

[85]Fiorella v. State, 40 Ala. App. 587, 590, 121 So. 2d 875, 878 (1960); Zerobnick v. City and County of Denver, 139 Colo. 139, 337 P.2d 11 (1959) (must be the "taking of evidence"); Moye v. Futch, 207 Ga. 52, 60 S.E.2d 137 (1950); People v. Enright, 332 Ill. App. 655, 75 N.E.2d 777 (1947); *In re* Bobowski, 313 Mich. 521, 21 N.W.2d 838 (1946); Mason v. Cochran, 209 Miss. 163, 46 So. 2d 106 (1950); State v. Haber, 132 N.J.L. 507, 512, 41 A.2d 326, 329 (1945); People v. Oskroba, *supra* note 88 ("opportunity to attack or deny the charge").

[86] Brozosky v. State, 197 Wis. 446, 222 N.W. 311 (1928); *cf.* Pritchett v. United States, 67 F.2d 244 (4th Cir. 1933) (whether to hear probationer's character witnesses is discretionary with court).

[87]People v. Myers, 306 Mich. 100, 10 N.W.2d 323 (1943); *In re* Bobowski, *supra* note 92; People v. Rudnik, 333 Mich. 216, 52 N.W.2d 671 (1952).

[88]People v. Warren, 314 Ill. App. 198, 40 N.E.2d 845 (1942); People v. Enright, *supra* note 92.

[89]Robinson v. State, 62 Ga. App. 539, 8 S.E.2d 698 (1940); Moye v. Futch, *supra* note 92; People v. Price, *supra* note 90, at 377–79, 164 N.E.2d at 534–35; State v. Zachowski, *supra* note 88, at 441, 147 A.2d at 590.

at the hearing by counsel of his own choosing.[90] However, a split exists on whether there is a right to have counsel appointed by the court. The federal courts hold that no such right exists.[91] New York seems to agree,[92] as does Washington.[93] Illinois, on the other hand, requires assignment of counsel for the indigent probationer.[94] The Maryland Court of Appeals has informed trial courts that they "may" assign counsel to represent the probationer,[95] but it does not appear that a "right" exists in that jurisdiction to have counsel assigned, at least in the absence of extraordinary circumstances.[96]

Parole

Here, again, we deal with cases decided by courts of jurisdictions in which hearings are guaranteed by statute.[97]

The most active court in the country in this area is the District of Columbia Court of Appeals. Under the provisions of the Federal Administrative Procedure Act, the parolee whose parole has been revoked and who has suffered reimprisonment may seek his release by habeas corpus or a declaratory judgment action either from the federal district court sitting in the district

[90]The federal courts permit representation by retained counsel. See Holtzoff, *supra* note 91. In Maryland, however, the Court of Appeals has observed that the revoking court "may, but is not obliged to, advise the defendant of his right to obtain counsel. . . ." Crenshaw v. State, 222 Md. 533, 535, 161 A.2d 669, 671 (1960).

[91]Bennett v. United States, 158 F.2d 412 (8th Cir. 1946); Gillespie v. Hunter, 159 F.2d 410 (10th Cir. 1947); Kelley v. United States, 235 F.2d 44 (4th Cir. 1956); Cupp v. Byington, 179 F. Supp. 669 (S.D. Ind. 1960). *But see* Mason v. United States, 303 F.2d 775 (9th Cir. 1962) ("safe practice" is to see that probationer "is furnished with counsel, if he does not have it, and to give an opportunity for allocution").

[92]People v. Valle, 7 Misc. 2d 125, 127, 164 N.Y.S.2d 67, 70–71 (Ct. Spec. Sess. App. Pt. 1957) (dictum); *cf.* People *ex rel.* Ambrose v. Combs, 33 Misc. 2d 360, 224 N.Y.S.2d 874 (Sup. Ct. 1962).

[93]Jaime v. Rhay. 59, Wash. 2d 58, 365 P.2d 772 (1961).

[94]People v. Burrell, 334 Ill. App. 253, 79 N.E.2d 88 (1948); People v. Price, *supra* note 90, at 373, 164 N.E.2d at 534.

[95]Crenshaw v. State, *supra* note 97, at 535, 161 A.2d at 671.

[96]Edwardsen v. State, 220 Md. 82, 89–90, 151 A.2d 132, 136–37 (1959). One commentator refers to an unreported case in Maryland in which counsel was appointed for a probationer who claimed a mental defect, which claim had some support in the evidence. Mutter, *Probation in the Criminal Court of Baltimore City*, 17 Md. L. Rev. 309, 321 n.61 (1957).

[97]There are many cases from these jurisdictions, however, which approve revocation of a conditional pardon without a hearing if such a power was expressly or impliedly reserved in the pardon. See Fuller v. State, 122 Ala. 32, 26 So. 146 (1890); Muckle v. Clark, 191 Ga. 202, 12 S.E.2d 339 (1940); Woodward v. Murdock, 124 Ind. 439, 24 N.E. 1047 (1890); Boaz v. Amrine, 153 Kan. 614, 113 P.2d 80 (1941); Silvey v. Kaiser, 173 S.W.2d 63 (Mo. 1943); Pope v. Wiggins, 220 Miss. 1, 69 So. 2d 913 (1954); *In re* Davenport, 110 Tex. Crim. 326, 7 S.W.2d 589 (1927); Scott v. Callahan, 39 Wash. 2d 801, 239 P.2d 333 (1951).

Note also that in two jurisdictions, under earlier statutes which did not require a hearing, revocation of a parole without a hearing had been upheld against a claim of unconstitutionality. Johnson v. Walls, 185 Ga. 177, 194 S.E. 380 (1937); *In re* Tabor, 173 Kan. 686, 250 P.2d 793 (1952).

in which he is confined *or* from the District of Columbia district court.[98] Since, as will soon become apparent, the construction of the federal parole revocation statute, which directs that the retaken parolee "shall be given an opportunity to appear before the Board," is notably more liberal in the Court of Appeals for the District of Columbia than in other federal circuits, reimprisoned parolees have sought relief from the courts of the District.

The starting point for our discussion is *Fleming v. Tate*,[99] in which the District of Columbia Court of Appeals construed the statute governing the revocation of parole in the District of Columbia, which is separate and apart from the federal parole revocation statute.[100] The court held in *Fleming* that the parolee was entitled to be represented by counsel of his own choice at the parole revocation hearing.[101] This decision was extended in *Moore v. Reed*[102] to impose upon the board the duty to advise the parolee of his right to retain counsel.

In *Robbins v. Reed*[103] and, later, *Glenn v. Reed*,[104] the holdings in *Fleming* and *Moore* on the right to counsel were explicitly extended to revocations ordered pursuant to the federal parole revocation statute. In *Reed v. Butterworth*,[105] the federal parole board was ordered to allow the parolee to testify in his own behalf, if he elects, and to present voluntary witnesses.

The rights of the parolee, as recognized and enforced by the District of Columbia Court of Appeals, apparently end at this point. For in *Hyser v. Reed*[106] the court, sitting *en banc*, held, over a strong dissent, in a carefully structured opinion that the parolee is not entitled (1) to appointment of counsel, (2) to confront and cross-examine persons who have imparted information against him, (3) to examine reports made by the parole officer and other members of the board's staff, and (4) to the right to compulsory process to secure witnesses.

Notwithstanding the decision in *Hyser*, the federal parolee is better advised to seek his release from the courts of the District of Columbia than from federal courts outside the District. The latter have construed the federal parole revocation statute in a far more niggardly fashion. There is no right to representation by retained counsel.[107] There is no right to produce voluntary

[98] Hurley v. Reed, 288 F.2d 844 (D.C. Cir. 1961).

[99] 156 F.2d 848 (D.C. Cir. 1946).

[100] *Cf.* Cooper v. United States, 48 A.2d 771, 773 (D.C. Mun. Ct. App. 1946).

[101] The District of Columbia statute was amended after *Fleming* to provide for representation of counsel.

[102] 246 F.2d 654 (D.C. Cir. 1957).

[103] 269 F.2d 242 (D.C. Cir. 1959).

[104] 289 F.2d 462 (D.C. Cir. 1961).

[105] 297 F.2d 776 (D.C. Cir. 1961).

[106] 318 F.2d 225 (D.C. Cir. 1963).

[107] Hiatt v. Compagna, 178 F.2d 42 (5th Cir. 1949), *aff'd by equally divided court*, 340 U.S. 880 (1950); Washington v. Hagan, 287 F.2d 332 (3d Cir. 1960); Lopez v. Madigan, 174 F. Supp. 919 (N.D. Cal. 1959); Poole v. Stevens, 190 F. Supp. 938 (E.D. Mich. 1960); Hock v. Hagan, 190 F.

witnesses,[108] although on this point the Court of Appeals for the Second Circuit seems in disagreement.[109] And, of course, there is no right to confrontation and cross-examination.[110]

The courts of Delaware and Maryland have held that the hearings guaranteed by their statutes include the right to representation by counsel of one's own choice,[111] but not the right to have counsel appointed by the board. In New Jersey, where the statute makes the granting of a hearing discretionary with the board, but guarantees counsel of one's own "selection" if a hearing is, in fact, held,[112] it has been decided that there is no right to be advised of one's right to retain counsel, at least where it is not shown "that counsel, if present, could have done more than present to the board the substantive point argued. . . ."[113]

In Delaware, the courts have further held that the parolee must be given the opportunity to call witnesses in his own behalf.[114] The Supreme Court of Florida has ruled that the parolee is entitled to be confronted by and meet the evidence against him. "The Commission," the court wrote, "[has] no right to treat as evidence material not introduced as such or to consider any information outside the record in its disposition of the case."[115] The Supreme Court of Pennsylvania has reached a different conclusion, holding that a hearing at which the parolee was informed that the board had evidence establishing the violation of six different rules of his parole agreement, which evidence was never produced, was adequate within the terms of their statute. "[T]he only person whom the Board is actually required to hear is the parolee," the court explained. "All other information and evidence may be brought to the attention of the Board as a result of a report prepared by its agents or employees."[116]

Supp. 749 (M.D. Pa. 1960); Gibson v. Markley, 205 F. Supp. 742 (S.D. Ind. 1962). However, as to current practice, see notes 128–130 *infra*.

[108] Poole v. Stevens, *supra* note 114; United States *ex rel.* McCreary v. Kenton, 190 F. Supp. 689 (D. Conn. 1960) (but board enjoined "to give fair consideration to what the prisoner [has] to say" and to make "further investigation of sources of information where warranted"); Gibson v. Markley, *supra* note 114. However, as to current practice, see note 131 *infra*.

[109] United States *ex. rel.* Frederick v. Kenton, 308 F.2d 258 (2d Cir. 1962).

[110] Gibson v. Markley, *supra* note 114.

[111] State v. Boggs, 10 Terry (49 Del.) 277, 114 A.2d 663 (Super. Ct. 1955); Warden v. Palumbo, 214 Md. 407, 135 A.2d 439 (1957). Note that several statutes confer on the parolee the right to retain counsel, while some expressly deny him such a right. See category VI of charts. Cases which are simply declarative of statutes granting one or more rights to the parolee (see, *e.g.*, Petition of Vaughan, 125 N.W.2d 251 (Mich. 1963), holding that the parolee was not confronted by adverse witnesses as required by the statute) are not considered in this section.

[112] See note 5 to the charts, *supra*.

[113] Jerabek v. State, 69 N.J. Super, 264, 174 A.2d 248 (1961).

[114] State v. Boggs, *supra* note 118; Lockwood v. Rhodes, 11 Terry (50 Del.) 287, 129 A.2d 549 (Super. Ct. 1957).

[115] Jackson v. Mayo, 73 So.2d 881, 882 (Fla. Sup. Ct. 1954), relying in part, however, on the language of the Florida statute. And *cf.* Senk v. Cochran, 116 So.2d 245 (Fla. Sup. Ct. 1959).

[116] Hendrickson v. Pennsylvania State Bd. of Parole, 409 Pa. 204, 209, 185 A.2d 581 585

The hearing which is held to revoke parole is "informal" and is not governed by judicial rules of procedure, "any more than the application of these rules is necessary in many informal administrative hearings."[117]

THE CURRENT PRACTICE

Hearings, as was observed early in this paper, may be granted in practice although the right to a hearing is denied by statute and case law. In at least two jurisdictions in which the statutes do not require a hearing on the revocation of parole—Colorado and Connecticut—rules and regulations promulgated by the board fill the gap. In Colorado,[118] the parolee upon his return to the institution "shall be informed of the reason for the suspension and of any grounds which have been asserted for revocation of his parole and shall be given an opportunity to be heard in regard thereto." In Connecticut,[119] the rules provide that upon his return to prison the parolee shall be given "reasonable notice of the charges against him . . . [and] an opportunity to appear before the Board at its next regular meeting at the State Prison to admit, deny, or explain the violation charged." These rules and regulations point up the practice, generally prevailing, to hold parole revocation hearings *after* the return of the parolee to the institution from which he was paroled.[120]

The United States Board of Parole, influenced perhaps by the trend of decisions in the District of Columbia[121] or by the fear that its present policy would not be favorably received by the United States Supreme Court,[122] recently issued two memorandums to all federal prisons.[123] The first, dated April 24, 1961, allows the parolee, not less than 30 days prior to the date of

---

(1962). Note that the Pennsylvania statutes specifically authorize the Board when revoking parole to act on reports "submitted to them by their agents and employees. . . ." PA. STATS. ANN. tit. 61, §331.22 (1962 Supp.).

[117]Fleming v. Tate, *supra* note 106, at 849; and see Hiatt v. Compagna, *supra* note 114; State v. Boggs, *supra* note 118; Jackson v. Mayo, *supra* note 122; Hendrickson v. Pennsylvania State Bd. of Parole, *supra* note 123.

[118]Rules and Regulations of the State Board of Parole, adopted December 11, 1958, at page 4 (supplied to the writer by Edward W. Grout, Director of Parole),

[119]Rules and Regulations of the Board of Parole for the State Prison, effective November 5, 1958, at page 11 (supplied to the writer by James J. M'Ilduff, Executive Secretary to the Board).

[120]See parole statutes cited in categories IV and VI of charts; *cf.* Martin v. Warden, 182 F. Supp. 391 (D. Md. 1960), holding that reimprisonment prior to receiving the hearing guaranteed by the Maryland statutes is not violative of the Fourteenth Amendment.

[121]See discussion *supra* notes 105–113. In Reed v. Butterworth, 297 F.2d 776, 778 (D.C. Cir. 1961), the District of Columbia Court of Appeals criticized the parole board's apparent "notion . . . that revocation hearings are mere formalities, and the result a foregone conclusion," which philosophy, the court believed, the board evidenced by denying parolees "fundamental procedural safeguards."

[122]See Note, 57 Nw. U.L. Rev. 737, 743–44 (1963).

[123]Both memorandums were furnished to the writer by James C. Neagles, Staff Director, United States Board of Parole, under letter dated January 10, 1962.

the scheduled hearing, to elect on a suitable form to retain counsel to represent him at the hearing. If counsel makes an unscheduled appearance at the hearing, and the parolee has no objections, counsel will be permitted to attend the proceedings. The board will not furnish counsel for the prisoner unable to retain his own.

Under a memorandum dated November 30, 1961, the parolee may present voluntary witnesses at the hearing. He signifies his desire to exercise this right on a form provided by the prison. If unscheduled witnesses appear at the hearing, and the parolee elects, they will be permitted to appear before the board and testify.[124]

The United States Parole Board has not changed its policy of nonconfrontation. In responding to two questionnaires,[125] James C. Neagles, Staff Director, United States Board of Parole, indicated that neither the parole officer nor persons who may have given information against the parolee appear at the hearing, and this is the case even if the facts of the alleged violation are disputed by the parolee. A written report is submitted to the board by the parole authorities, which report is not shown to the parolee or his counsel. Mr. Neagles offered this reason for the board's present policy of nonconfrontation:

"To present an entire communication from the parole officer to the parolee would tend to damage the public informants who might have contacted the parole officer to give information regarding parole violations. It might cause ultimate repercussions to such persons as wives, other family members and neighbors."[126]

---

[124]The claim has been made that the board has virtually nullified the right to present "voluntary witnesses" by choosing inappropriate places for the hearing and refusing to pay the expenses of witnesses who are willing to appear voluntarily. Note, *supra* note 129, at 745.

[125]Two questionnaires were prepared by the writer in December, 1961, and January, 1962, and were sent to parole boards and probation departments through out the country. Fifty-two questionnaires were sent to parole boards. Thirty-six, or 69 percent were returned. Second questionnaires were sent to 26 of the parole boards which had responded to the first. These were returned by 24, or 92 percent. Sixty-one questionnaires were sent to probation departments. In 19 states which have no centralized probation department, questionnaires were sent to departments in the counties having the greatest population. Fifty-five, or 90 percent were returned. Second questionnaires were sent to 49 probation departments, and 44, or 90 percent were returned. The questionnaires are reproduced and the replies from each jurisdiction are individually charted in the writer's unpublished thesis. The Revocation of Parole and Adult Probation, May 1962 (Northwestern University Law Library), at pages 12–18, 155–223.

[126]Letter to the writer dated January 10, 1962. The same point was made in a letter to the writer dated December 21, 1961, from the Director of Probation and Parole in Maine, John J. Shea. Mr. Shea observed:

"[W]hile a parole violator has certain rights and while the State Board has certain obligations to the violator in terms of substantiating the return to the institution, the State Board also has a concurrent responsibility to outside citizens in the community whose safety and welfare might be jeopardized at a later date through any vengeful act by the violator after his release from the institution. . . . Therefore, the State Board may discuss with the parole violator at time of parole violation hearing only a sufficient number of items to substantiate the fact that the man is in violation of parole."

And see *In re* Varner, 166 Ohio St. 340, 142 N.E.2d 846 (1957), discussed *supra* note 52.

State parole boards, responding to the writer's two questionnaires,[127] indicated that hearings are usually limited to an appearance by the parolee before the board at which time he may explain, admit, or deny the charges.[128] Witnesses against the parolee rarely appear before the board, even if the facts are disputed by the parolee.[129] Instead, the board relies on reports submitted by the parole authorities. The reports generally are kept confidential. The parolee rarely presents evidence or witnesses, although most jurisdictions report that such a right exists.[130] The failure to exercise this right is perhaps explained by the fact that in most cases, according to some of the parole boards responding, the parolee has been convicted of a new crime while on parole or has admitted the charges against him.[131] About half of the jurisdictions reporting indicated that the parolee may retain counsel if he wishes. Significantly, however, several jurisdictions pointed out that counsel, if retained, may present arguments on behalf of the parolee at the board's offices and not at the hearing.[132] Three jurisdictions indicated that the parolee "seldom" retains counsel.[133] No jurisdiction indicated that it would assign counsel for the parolee. Notice of the charges is ordinarily given to the parolee at some time before the hearing, either upon arrest or in an interview by a parole official at the prison. However, in a few jurisdictions, the charges are not made known to the parolee until the actual hearing.[134]

Probation revocation hearings, being held in court, tend to be more judicial or formal in nature than parole revocation hearings.[135] This is not the case in every jurisdiction, however. Louis B. Sharp, Chief, Probation Division, Administrative Office of the United States Courts, commenting on the hearing

---

[127] See note 132 *supra*.

[128] Responses from Iowa, Nevada, South Dakota, and Vermont indicated that hearings are not ordinarily held in these states.

[129] Ohio and Pennsylvania, amplifying answers on the questionnaires, reported that no outsiders are permitted at the hearing, Pennsylvania adding that "We use a format similar to that used in Military Court Martial procedures. . . ." South Carolina and Hawaii indicated, however, that the parole officer will attend the hearing. This is probably the case in other jurisdictions as well.

[130] Louisiana, Maryland, and Virginia reported, however, that the parolee's witnesses will be heard at the board's offices, out of the parolee's presence. Georgia and Utah noted that whether the parolee's witnesses will testify in his presence will depend upon the "nature" or "circumstances" of the case. The writer believes that such may be the rule in many other jurisdictions which signified, without amplification, that the parolee may present his own witnesses.

[131] Louisiana, Ohio, Pennsylvania, Utah, Vermont, and Washington specially reported that cases are rare where the violation charged is not supported by a conviction or admitted by the parolee.

[132] Louisiana, Minnesota, Pennsylvania, and Virginia noted this by way of amplifying their responses to the questionnaires.

[133] Minnesota, Missouri, and Wisconsin.

[134] This appears to be the case in Maryland and Ohio. Notice of the charges in the District of Columbia is given to the parolee prior to the hearing "if represented by counsel." Otherwise, the "specifications are read to [the parolee] at the opening of the hearing."

[135] Note that the statutes in Florida and New Mexico set up a "pleading" procedure somewhat similar to procedure in criminal trials. See category VI of charts.

procedures in the federal courts, reported that the probation officer ordinarily testifies at the hearing and a written report is submitted to the court. The report is not shown to the probationer. Witnesses against the probationer usually do not appear in court, even if the facts are disputed. If witnesses are produced by the probation authorities, the probationer may not cross-examine them as of right, but "may with permission of the court." He may not present evidence or witnesses "as a general rule." Retained counsel is not permitted at the hearing. Counsel will not be assigned. Notice of the charges is "generally" given "at the time of arrest" and "prior to the hearing."

According to responses received from state and county probation departments, the probation officer is often the sole witness against the probationer. Witnesses against the probationer generally are produced if the facts are disputed by the probationer. Factual disputes, however, are not the rule, since in most cases the probationer has admitted the essential charges or the violation is supported by a judgment of conviction.[136] Several jurisdictions emphasized the trial court's power to order witnesses produced if he believes the case demands it.[137] When witnesses do appear, the probationer or his counsel, as a general rule, may cross-examine them.[138] Written reports are submitted to the court in the vast majority of jurisdictions. Roughly one-third of the jurisdictions responding indicated that the report is shown to the probationer or his counsel "on request." Retained counsel may represent the probationer at the hearing, and evidence and witnesses may be produced on his behalf, in almost all of the jurisdictions reporting on their procedures.[139] Again, however, the frequency of cases in which the charges are either admitted or substantiated by a judgment of conviction may, as a practical matter, obviate the need for presenting evidence and witnesses. Slightly better than half the jurisdictions reporting indicated that the court will assign counsel for the indigent probationer who desires counsel. Notice of the charges against him is generally

[136]This point was specially noted in the responses received from the statewide probation departments of Massachusetts, Utah, and Washington and those of Los Angeles and San Diego counties in California. It also appears to be the case in New York. See Note, 59 COLUM. L. REV. 311, 322 (1959). The probation department in Marion County (Indianapolis), Indiana indicated that probation is normally revoked for failure to pay fines or costs, or failure to report to the probation officer, in which case the judge will "rely on the officer's word."

[137]The statewide probation departments in North Carolina and Vermont so indicated, as well as the probation departments of Baltimore City, Maryland, Hennepin (Minneapolis) and Ramsey (St. Paul) counties in Minnesota, Essex County (Newark) in New Jersey, Philadelphia County, Pennsylvania, and Milwaukee County, Wisconsin.

[138]Here, again, the trial court has discretion to determine whether or not cross-examination should be permitted and to what extent. The statewide probation departments of Missouri, Vermont, and Washington and the federal probation department made this point.

[139]A notable exception appears to be the federal courts, as already pointed out.

given to the probationer on or soon after his arrest and is repeated at the hearing.

CONSTITUTIONAL AND POLICY CONSIDERATIONS

The Constitutional Issues

The constitutional issues imbedded in the area have been thoroughly canvassed elsewhere. The pros and cons of whether due process requires a fair hearing before probation or parole may be revoked have been explored in the law reviews,[140] in a recent multi-opinioned decision of the Courts of Appeals for the District of Columbia, sitting *en banc* for the occasion,[141] and by this writer in his unpublished thesis,[142] and need not be further explored here. Suffice it to say that the hardiest of the arguments against the due process claim—perhaps because it twice has been articulated by the United States Supreme Court[143]—is that probation and parole are "privileges" and not "legal rights" and, hence, may be withdrawn in any manner the granting authority chooses. This has been undercut by recent decisions of the Supreme Court in the field of public employment. These decisions stress *harm*—whether the "governmental action seriously injures an individual"[144]—and refuse to allow the frozen terms "privilege" and "right" to be decisive on the issue of procedural fairness.[145] They also point out that substantial interests, even if deno-

---

[140] Weihofen, *Revoking Probation, Parole or Pardon Without a Hearing*, 32 J. Crim. L. & C. 531 (1942); Hink, *Application of Constitutional Standards of Protection to Probation*, 29 U. Chi. L. Rev. 483 (1962); Note, 65 Harv. L. Rev. 309 (1951); Note, 59 Colum. L. Rev. 311 (1959); Note 57 Nw. U.L. Rev. 737 (1963).

[141] Hyser v. Reed, 318 F.2d 225 (D.C. Cir. 1963).

[142] Sklar, The Revocation of Parole and Adult Probation, 226–45, May 1962 (unpublished thesis in Northwestern University Law Library).

[143] Burns v. United States, 287 U.S. 216 (1932); Escoe v. Zerbst, 295 U.S. 490 (1935).

[144] "Certain principles have remained relatively immutable in our jurisprudence. One of these is that where governmental action seriously injures an individual, and the reasonableness of the action depends on fact findings, the evidence used to prove the Government's case must be disclosed to the individual so that he has an opportunity to show that it is untrue." Greene v. McElroy, 360 U.S. 474, 496–97 (1959). See Cafeteria & Restaurant Workers Union v. McElroy, 367 U.S. 886, 895–96 (1961): *cf.* Hannah v. Larche, 363 U.S. 420, 440–44 (1960); Silver v. New York Stock Exchange, 373 U.S. 341, 364–65 nn. 17 & 18 (1963).

[145] Cases *supra* note 151. In Green v.. McElroy, the security clearance of an aeronautical engineer was revoked after a hearing at which he was denied access to much of the evidence against him and had no opportunity to confront or cross-examine adverse witnesses. As a result of the revocation he lost his job with a private manufacturer doing classified government work and was unable afterwards to secure similar employment. The revocation order was reversed by the Court, but on non-constitutional grounds, 360 U.S. at 508. In Cafeteria & Restaurant

minated "privileges," cannot be taken from an individual through arbitrary governmental action.[146] This, it will be recalled, was the position taken by the United States Court of Appeals for the Sixth Circuit in regard to revocation of a conditional pardon without a hearing.[147]

Policy Considerations Against Granting a Full Hearing

Constitutional issues, especially weighty Fourteenth Amendment problems, while demanding and being entitled to careful attention, often retard mature deliberation on policy considerations of great practical import. The question whether hearings should be granted before probation or parole is revoked involves such policy considerations.

Absolute denial of a hearing has been justified on the policy ground that hearings would result in increased burdens of administration on the courts and parole boards and undoubtedly would discourage them from granting proba-

---

Workers Union v. McElroy, the Court held that the revocation of a security clearance permit without notice or a hearing, resulting in the discharge of a short-order cook from a military installation, was not violative of due process. *Restaurant Workers*, it has been said, underscores "the relatively narrow thrust of the Greene holding." Hyser v. Reed, *supra* note 148, at 239. On the contrary, however, the *Restaurant Workers* case underscores and strengthens the true thrust of the holding in Greene v. McElroy, for, as compared to the employment loss suffered by Greene, the employee in *Restaurant Workers* lost only the opportunity to work as a short-order cook "at one isolated and specific military installation." 367 U.S. at 896. See Willner v. Committee on Character & Fitness, 373 U.S. 96, 103 n.2 (1963); Williams v. Zuckert, 371 U.S. 531, 534 (1963) (dissenting opinion of Justice Douglas). Such a loss does not come within the sweep of the phrase "serious injury."

Unfortunately, however, the concept of "privileges" and "rights" lingers on in the opinions. See Jay v. Boyd, 351 U.S. 345 (1956), suspension of deportation being an "act of grace," an application for same may be denied on "confidential information"; note the analogy to probation in the majority opinion (at p. 354) and the treatment of the majority's analogy in Justice Black's dissenting opinion (at pp. 366–67); Willner v. Committee on Character & Fitness, *supra*, at 102, person cannot be excluded from the practice of law without an opportunity to confront and cross-examine those who give information against him—practice of law "is not 'a matter of grace and favor.'" And *cf.* the use of the term "legal rights" in Hannah v. Larche, *supra* note 151, at 441–42.

[146] Wieman v. Updegraff, 344 U.S. 183 (1952); Slochower v. Board of Higher Education, 350 U.S. 551 (1956); Cafeteria & Restaurant Workers Union v. McElroy, *supra* note 151, at 894, 897–98; Cramp v. Board of Public Education, 368 U.S. 278, 288 (1961); *cf.* Fleming v. Nestor, 363 U.S. 603, 611 (1960); Sherbert v. Verner, 374 U.S. 398, 404–05 (1963).

[147] Fleenor v. Hammond, 116 F.2d 982 (6th Cir. 1941), discussed *supra* note 78–80. *Accord*, State *ex rel.* Murray v. Swenson, 196 Md. 222, 76 A.2d 150 (1950), discussed *supra* note 80. The United States Supreme Court has said in this connection: "While probation is a matter of grace, the probationer is entitled to fair treatment, and is not to be made the victim of whim or caprice." Burns v. United States, *supra* note 150, at 223. However, aside from the question whether or not the *Burns* Court was only referring to the probationer's rights under the federal statute (see Escoe v. Zerbst, *supra* note 150, at 492–93), it is probable that when the Court spoke of protecting the probationer against "whim and caprice" it had in mind revocation on patently inadequate grounds and not revocation without a hearing. 287 U.S. at 223–24. Moreover, it seems equally probable that the "public employment" cases, cited *supra*

tions or paroles they otherwise would grant.[148] The same argument has been offered as a basis for severely limiting the scope and extent of a hearing required by statute.[149] There is no evidence that such expectations have materialized in jurisdictions where fuller hearings are mandated.[150] Indeed, knowledge that a hearing is needed before conditional release can be revoked may have the beneficial effect of compelling the granting authority to exercise greater care in selecting worthy candidates for rehabilitation.

A forceful answer to this policy argument is found in an opinion of the Utah Supreme Court:

"It has been suggested that [the necessity of a hearing] may cause the trial courts to deny any stay of execution because of the complications involved even in cases where the public interest requires probation. We see no merit to this contention. It suggests that courts, in order to exercise arbitrary and capricious power, will violate their oath of office and their duty to the public. Why should any honest judge adopt such a policy? The very suggestion shows a lack of confidence in the integrity of our courts, which we do not share."[151]

The next two policy considerations relate to the question of confrontation by adverse witnesses. The United States Parole Board has maintained that "to require [parole officers] to appear at hundreds of revocation hearings annually, convened in many instances at places distant from areas under their supervision, would render it impossible for them to carry on their normal duties."[152]

---

note 153, when they admonish that "privileges" may not be taken away "arbitrarily," are referring more to non-existent or irrational grounds than non-existent procedure. See Cafeteria & Restaurant Workers Union v. McElroy, *supra* note 151, at 897–98. This is not to say, of course, that the position taken in Fleenor v. Hammond, *supra*, has been discredited. Logic, as well as language in the opinions, support it, at least in a case where probation or parole is revoked without an adequate hearing for conduct which is neither admitted nor substantiated by uncontrovertible proof. See notes 173–181 *infra*, and accompanying text.

[148] *In re* Varner, 166 Ohio St. 340, 345, 142 N.E.2d 846, 849 (1957).

[149] Burns v. United States, 287 U.S. 216, 222 (1932).

[150] In fact, it has been observed that Michigan, where the statute grants an unusually full and complete hearing before parole is revoked (see chart VI), "has one of the highest proportions of parole grants." Davies & Hess, *Criminal Law—Insane Persons—Influence of Mental Illness on the Parole Return Process*, 59 Mich. L. Rev. 1101, 1110 n.47 (1961).

[151] McPhie v. Turner, 10 Utah 2d 237, 240, 351 P.2d 91, 93 (1960). A requirement that a violation charged be proved by a degree of proof approaching that demanded in criminal cases justifiably might make courts and parole boards reluctant to grant probation and parole even in deserving cases. Campbell v. Aderhold, 36 F.2d 366, 367 (N.D. Ga. 1929). This, clearly, is a different matter. It is avoided by recognizing in the revoking authority a broad discretion to revoke whenever it is reasonably satisfied that the best interests of the public and the offender are no longer being served by his conditional liberty. Evidence that a new crime has been committed is unnecessary. *E.g.*, Campbell v. Aderhold, *supra*; Hyser v. Reed, 318 F.2d 225, 242 (D.C. Cir. 1963); Swan v. State, 200 Md. 420, 90 A.2d 690 (1952); Sellers v. State, 105 Neb. 748, 181 N.W. 862 (1921). See generally Note, 59 Colum. L. Rev. 311, 332–33 (1959).

[152] Brief for Appellees, p. 47, Neiswenter v. Chappell, 318 F.2d 225 (D.C. Cir. 1963), quoted in Note, 57 Nw. U.L. Rev. 737, 754 (1963). The readier accessibility of courts makes this argument less persuasive in the area of probation revocation.

However, it is probable that the board has exaggerated the burden to the parole officer. Parole officers would be required witnesses only if they had personal knowledge of the facts of the violation charged. They would generally have such knowledge, in turn, only where the charges constitute technical or non-criminal violations of the terms of the parole agreement. Where the charges amount to criminal offenses, and this is frequently the case, the logical witnesses would be police officers and private citizens. Furthermore, the board could alleviate this problem by scheduling the hearings at the place of the parolee's initial confinement rather than at the federal penitentiary to which he was returned.[153] Finally, even if this policy consideration is not without some merit,[154] the problem posed by the board is one faced by all law enforcement agencies, which are thus forced to "provide enough skilled men to allow for the presence of some of their number in court."[155]

The third policy consideration, and one that was verbalized in letters received by the writer from the federal parole board and the Maine board,[156] relates to the danger of reprisal. Requiring adverse witnesses to confront the probationer or parolee or turning the violation report over to him for perusal, it is maintained, may endanger the safety of the informants. Witnesses fearing reprisal may be reluctant to come forward and give information against the violator if they know this information will not remain secret.[157] Such a "danger," of course, exists as well in the trial of a criminal case, but it has never been seriously advanced there. It is clearly outbalanced by greater and more compelling considerations. The question is whether the balance in a revocation hearing should be struck in favor of secrecy. Into this balance must be thrown the danger of misguided, faulty, or biased information. The "faceless informer," who may peddle his rumors, but escape the ordeal of confrontation and cross-examination, is abhorrent to the Anglo-American sense of justice. True, some witnesses, fearing reprisal, may be unwilling to impart information if they know their identity will not be kept secret. However, the reason for this unwillingness, it seems to this writer, is just as, if not more likely to be, attributable to fear that the information they have will not withstand the test of cross-examination, as to fear of reprisal. No public policy is served by encouraging persons to come forward with information of this nature.[158]

[153]The latter is the current practice of the board. See Hyser v. Reed, 318 F.2d 225 (D.C. Cir. 1963).

[154]See Note, *supra* note 158, at 754.

[155]*Ibid.*

[156]See note 133 *supra.*

[157]This point is also made in the cases. See *In re* Varner, *supra* note 155; State *ex rel.* McQueen v. Horton, 31 Ala. App. 71, 76, 14 So. 2d 557, 560, *aff'd*, 244 Ala. 594, 14 So. 2d 561 (1943).

[158]"Faceless informers," it has properly been written, "are often effective if they need not take the stand." Justice Douglas, dissenting in Beard v. Stahr, 370 U.S. 41, 43 (1962). Moreover, if the informer justly needs protection, his identity should be kept secret. At the same time, however, his information should not be used as a means of depriving another of his liberty. If

A fourth policy argument is waged against allowing retained counsel to attend the informal hearings before the parole board. Counsel, it is argued, "would convert the hearing into a legal battle." The issues at a revocation hearing—whether the parolee's conduct demonstrates that he is no longer a good parole risk—are not issues for which counsel is necessary or desirable. "It is difficult for us," one state parole board communicated to the writer, "to visualize how counsel can make a worthwhile contribution . . . at a parole violation hearing."[159] The answer to these contentions was supplied by the Court of Appeals for the District of Columbia:

"The presence of counsel does not mean that he may take over control of the proceeding. The receipt of testimony offered by the prisoner need not be governed by the strict rules of evidence, any more than the application of those rules is necessary in many informal administrative hearings . . . . The participation by counsel in a proceeding such as this need be not greater than is necessary to insure, to the Board as well as to the parolee, that the Board is accurately informed from the parolee's standpoint before it acts, and the permitted presentation of testimony by the parolee need be no greater than is necessary for the same purpose. . . . The presence of counsel is meant as a measure of protection to the prisoner; it should not be permitted to become a measure of embarrassment to the tribunal."[160]

Policy Considerations for Granting a Full Hearing

Policy considerations are not lacking on the side of granting a full and fair hearing. Probation and parole have as their sole purpose rehabilitation of the offender. The conditionally released offender, simply from the fact of release, has been deemed by the granting authority a proper subject for rehabilitation and has been given his liberty on condition that he follow a course of good behavior. He has thereby attained "a favored status." "He should be able to rely upon the representation that if he measures up to his responsibilities, he will not have his liberty taken from him capriciously nor arbitrarily."[161]

Furthermore, the purpose of the revocation hearing itself, one court has observed, "is as much to form a part of the rehabilitation process as to provide a check on the administrative decision, already tentatively made, that the conditions of release were violated."[162] Reformation, in turn, can "certainly

---

secrecy and revocation cannot be accomplished at the same time, revocation should not be ordered. The revoking authority must make a choice; either reveal its information and allow it to be tested fairly, or justify its order of revocation without resort in any way to the information suppressed. To put it another way, the revoking authority must support its disposition of the case on the basis of facts developed at the hearing. Jackson v. Mayo, 73 So. 2d 881 (Fla. Sup. Ct. 1954); cf. Jencks v. United States, 353 U.S. 657, 671–72 (1957).

[159] Letter dated December 21, 1961, from John J. Shea, Director of Probation and Parole in Maine.

[160] Fleming v. Tate, 156 F.2d 848, 849–50 (D.C. Cir. 1946).

[161] Baine v. Bechstead, 10 Utah 2d 4, 9, 347 P.2d 554, 558 (1959).

[162] Hendrickson v. Pennsylvania State Bd. of Parole, 409 Pa. 204, 207, 185 A.2d 581, 584 (1962).

best be accomplished by fair, consistent and straightforward treatment of the person sought to be reformed."[163] Although it would be to some extent engaging in speculation to maintain that the process of rehabilitating conditionally released prisoners is aided by their knowledge that they will receive a hearing should they be charged with violating the conditions of their release, the effect of revocation without a hearing upon *future* attempts at rehabilitation seems clear. A person who feels that he did not receive fair treatment at the hands of the revoking authority more than likely would become a difficult subject for any future reformation. Having made what he might consider an honest attempt to perform the conditions of his release, and having been imprisoned without an opportunity to answer his accusers and fairly to present his version of the facts of the alleged violation to the authorities, it is quite conceivable that he might develop "a feeling that he is [being] picked on or abused by society."[164]

Such considerations "rather argue the advisability of being careful, not only to treat him fairly, but in such manner that he will see the fairness of it."[165]

Several other policy grounds for granting a full hearing were suggested in the Attorney General's 1939 *Survey of Release Procedures*. Written in connection with parole, they apply equally to probation.

"[T]he possibility exists that the parole agent was over-hasty in his action in returning the parolee as a violator. Parole agents are human and it is possible that friction between the agent and parolee may have influenced the agent's judgment. In fairness to the violator, this is a possibility which should be investigated by some higher authority....

"Another reason for holding a hearing is that often the true psychology of the parolee precedent to the commission of the violation is revealed. The trend of the parolee's thought in trying to rationalize his behavior may afford clues to his mental and emotional make-up which will be useful in effecting his future adjustment in society.

"Third, the hearing is an opportunity for the violator to discuss his behavior and to have it analysed by men who, by virtue of the position they occupy, necessarily have an interest in his future behavior. If, through his own statements, a parole violator can be made to see how irrationally he has acted,... a long step toward his ultimate rehabilitation may have been taken."[166]

NECESSITY OF A HEARING WHEN "FACTUAL DISPUTE" EXISTS

When the reasonableness of governmental action which seriously injures an individual "depends on fact findings," the United States Supreme Court has

[163] State v. Zolantakis, 70 Utah 296, 303, 259 Pac. 1044, 1046 (1927). See also, Escoe v. Zerbst, 295 U.S. 490, 493–94 (1935).
[164] Baine v. Beckstead, *supra* note 167, at 9, 347 P.2d at 559.
[165] Ibid.
[166] Attorney General's Survey of Release Procedures 246–247 (1939).

said, the individual is entitled to a hearing at which he may test the truthfulness of the evidence against him and offer his own proof in rebuttal.[167] The presence of a genuine factual dispute when the revocation of probation or parole is sought mandates such a hearing—one that includes reasonable notice of the precise charges, the right to present evidence and witnesses, the right to retain one's own counsel, and the vital elements of confrontation and cross-examination.[168] Such hearings would not unduly hamper the administration of probation and parole. The number of cases in which a dispute as to material facts exists is relatively small.[169]

If the probationer or parolee had admitted the truth of the allegations against him, or if the violation has been proved by a judgment of conviction, there is no genuine or material issue of fact, and a hearing with a full panoply of rights is unnecessary. This point has been recognized time and again in the decisions[170] and is recognized in the statutes of several states.[171] The only question for determination by the revoking authority in such a case is whether the admitted or proved conduct requires the severe sanction of revocation or whether the violator's conditional liberty should nevertheless be continued

---

[167]Greene v. McElroy, 360 U.S. 474, 496–497 (1959); *cf.* Williams v. New York, 337 U.S. 241, 247, 249–250 (1949). See generally 1 Davis, Administrative Law § §7.01, 7.02, 7.04, 7.05 (1958).

[168]The Model Penal Code, § 301.4, recommends that probation not be revoked except after a hearing embracing each of these elements. These elements are traditionally associated with a procedurally fair hearing under due process. *E.g.*, Powell v. Alabama, 287 U.S. 45, 68–70 (1932); Morgan v. United States, 304 U.S. 1, 18 (1938); *In re* Oliver, 333 U.S. 257, 273 (1948). On the question of the right to assigned counsel, see Hyser v. Reed, 318 F.2d 225 (D.C. Cir. 1963); Note, 57 Nw. U.L. Rev. 737, 758–760 (1963), both relating to the right to assigned counsel at the parole revocation proceeding. Neither probation nor parole revocation hearings can properly be termed "criminal prosecutions." *E.g.* Burns v. United States, 287 U.S. 216 (1932); *In re* Levi, 39 Cal. 2d 41, 244 P.2d 403 (1952); People v. Dudley, 173 Mich. 389, 138 N.W. 1044 (1912); Jaime v. Rhay, 59 Wash. 2d 58, 365 P.2d 772 (1961). It would seem to follow that a right to assigned counsel cannot be based either on the Sixth Amendment or the due process clause of the Fourteenth Amendment. However, the United States Supreme Court recently held in Douglas v. California, 372 U.S. 353 (1963), that counsel must be appointed on appeal from a criminal conviction, otherwise the indigent defendant is discriminated against because of his indigency. Thus, in jurisdictions where paid-for counsel is allowed to appear at the revocation hearing, either under statute or case law, a strong argument under the equal protection clause of the Fourteenth Amendment can be made for extending the right to probationers or parolees who are unable to provide their own legal assistance. Hyser v. Reed, *supra*, at 255 (dissenting opinion of Bazelon and Edgerton, JJ.); Note, *supra*, at 758–759.

[169]See notes 138 and 143 *supra*, and accompanying text.

[170]Hearings have been denied or severely restricted in such cases. See Hyser v. Reed, *supra* note 174 (dissenting opinion of Bazelon and Edgerton, JJ.); Whitehead v. United States, 155 F.2d 460 (6th Cir. 1946); Bennett v. United States, 158 F.2d 412 (8th Cir. 1946); Buhler v. Pescor, 63 F. Supp. 632, 639 (W.D. Mo. 1945); Hulse v. Pescor, 17 Alaska 353, 359–360 (1957); People v. Burrell, 334 Ill. App. 253, 79 N.E.2d 88 (1948); *In re* Carpenter, 348 Mich. 408, 83 N.W.2d 326 (1957); State v. Zachowski, 53 N.J. Super. 431, 440, 441, 147 A.2d 584, 589, 590 (1959) (a particularly illuminating opinion); Baine v. Beckstead, 10 Utah 2d 4, 347 P.2d 554 (1959).

[171]In the probation revocation field: Kentucky, see chart III, Florida and New Mexico, see chart VI; in the parole revocation field: Hawaii and Pennsylvania, see chart IV, Georgia, Michigan, and Washington, see chart VI.

with or without modification. This is a policy determination. It may be decided without hearing evidence. The hearing granted need extend no further than affording the violator a chance to explain his conduct.[172] Such a hearing, although limited, would be "appropriate to the nature of the case."[173]

Denial of a procedurally fair hearing in the few cases where genuine factual issues exist is "arbitrary governmental action."[174] None of the policy considerations inveighing against a hearing can justify depriving the probationer or parolee of his conditional liberty on the basis of untested fact findings arguably open to dispute. Only a hearing at which the proof against the alleged violator is introduced in his presence and, in the case of witnesses, subjected to the antiseptic test of cross-examination, and at which countervailing proof may be produced, can fairly be said to satisfy the needs of the situation.[175] Aside from the demands of justice and fairness framed in the Fourteenth Amendment, the orderly and proper administration of our penological system demands no less.

[172]Hyser v. Reed, *supra* note 174, at 247; Bayken v. United States Bd. of Parole, 322 F.2d 430 (D.C. Cir. 1963); Note, 59 Colum. L. Rev. 311, 322–323 (1959).

[173]See Mullane v. Central Hanover Bank & Trust Co., 339 U.S. 306, 313 (1950); Hannah v. Larche, 363 U.S. 420, 440–442 (1960).

[174]Greene v. McElroy, *supra* note 173, at 496–499, 508. "It is not without significance that most of the provisions of the Bill of Rights are procedural. It is procedure that spells much of the difference between rule by law and rule by whim or caprice. Steadfast adherence to strict procedural safeguards is our main assurance that there will be equal justice under law." Justice Douglas, concurring, in Joint Anti-Fascist Refugee Committee v. McGrath, 341 U.S. 123, 179 (1951).

[175]Contrary to expressions in some of the opinions (*e.g., In re* Anderson, 191 Ore. 409, 424, 229 P.2d 633, 640 (1951); McCoy v. Harris, 108 Utah 407, 413, 160 P.2d 721, 723 (1945)), there should not be any distinction drawn between probation and parole insofar as hearing procedures are concerned because one is judicial in nature and the other is an administrative determination. Both have the same purpose—rehabilitation of the offender—and both involve the same factual questions and determinations. See Baine v. Beckstead, 10 Utah 2d 4, 9, 347 P.2d 554, 558 (1959). When an administrative agency makes a binding factual adjudication directly affecting substantial interests of an individual—as does the parole board in revocation matters—"it is imperative that those agencies use the procedures which have traditionally been associated with the judicial process." Hannah v. Larche, 363 U.S. 420. 442 (1960). These procedures embrace "not only the right to present evidence, but also a reasonable opportunity to know the claims of the opposing party and to meet them." Morgan v. United States, 304 U.S. 1, 14–15, 18 (1938); Londoner v. Denver, 210 U.S. 373, 385–86 (1908); Greene v. McElroy, *supra* note 173, at 496–497. The administrative hearing, of course, may be less formal than a judicial proceeding. Londoner v. Denver, *supra*. For example, the atmosphere may be more relaxed. 1 Davis, Administrative Law §8.13 (1958). Technical rules of evidence are more or less inapplicable. 2 *id.* § § 14.01, 14.06.

41

The Power of Probation and Parole Officers to Search and Seize

ALEXANDER HOLTZOFF

In an article published in the December 1957 issue of FEDERAL PROBATION, this writer had occasion to consider "Duties and Rights of Probationers." The purpose of the present discussion is to examine more intensively one aspect of control, namely, to what extent probation officers and parole officers may search and examine the person of a probationer or parolee for the purpose of determining whether he carries a firearm, or some contraband article such as narcotics, or for the purpose of determining whether he has been taking narcotics by examining him for needle marks; and second, whether a probation or parole officer may conduct a search of the place where the probationer or parolee lives or works, and seize any contraband article.

LEGAL STATUS OF PAROLEES AND PROBATIONERS

At the outset it is necessary to analyze the status of probationers and parolees. They fall into four distinct groups from a legal standpoint—two categories of parolees and two classes of probationers.

SOURCE: *Federal Probation*, XXXI, December 1967, pp. 3–7.

Parolees

The first category of parolees consists of defendants who had served a part of a prison sentence and were paroled by the Board of Parole. Such parolees are governed by 18 U.S.C. 4202, which reads as follows:

"A Federal prisoner, other than a juvenile delinquent or a committed youth offender, wherever confined and serving a definite term or terms of over one hundred and eighty days, whose record shows that he has observed the rules of the institution in which he is confined may be released on parole after serving one-third of such term or terms or after serving fifteen years of life sentence or of a sentence of over forty-five years."

Those offenders who have been paroled under the terms of the Federal Youth Corrections Act and juvenile offenders who have been paroled under the Federal Juvenile Delinquency Act, may be included in this group.

The second group of parolees—generally known as persons on mandatory release—consists of those who have served a term of imprisonment and were released as a result of commutation for good conduct prior to the expiration of their maximum term. Releases of this type are governed by 18 U.S.C. 4164, which reads, in part, as follows:

"A prisoner having served his term or terms less good-time deductions shall, upon release, be deemed as if released on parole until the expiration of the maximum term or terms for which he was sentenced less one hundred and eighty days."

Apparently the deduction of 180 days is purely for administrative convenience in order that neither the Board nor probation officers should be burdened with supervision of released prisoners the balance of whose sentence is less than 180 days.

As concerns the extent of supervision and control over the two types of parolees, there is no difference between them. Parole and probation officers have the same authority over members of each of these two groups.

Probationers

Probationers also may be divided into two groups. The pertinent statutory provision is found in the first paragraph of 18 U.S.C. 3651, and reads as follows:

"Upon entering a judgment of conviction of any offense not punishable by death or life imprisonment, any court having jurisdiction to try offenses against the United States when satisfied that the ends of justice and the best interest of the public as well as the defendant will be served thereby, may suspend the imposition or execution of sentence and place the defendant on probation for such period and upon such terms and conditions as the court deems best."

The first class of probationers consists of those defendants who are sentenced to imprisonment but the *execution* of whose sentence is suspended and who are placed on probation. The second category comprizes defendants who have been convicted but the *imposition* of sentence has been suspended and the defendants have been placed on probation. As a practical matter, it is customary to deal with the two types of probationers as though they were equivalent from the standpoint of duties and obligations of probationers and supervision and control by probation officers. Actually the legal status of these two types of defendants is different. Those who belong to the first group are under sentence of imprisonment but have been enlarged from actual custody in a penal institution. Those in the second group are not under sentence. It may possibly be argued with some degree of cogency that members of the second group are not even in constructive custody and that, therefore, probation officers have less control over them than is the case with the members of the first group. The author is not aware of any reported federal decisions making this distinction, but it is a matter that may well be considered in connection with the subject matter of this article.

Dealing first with parolees, a person who is confined in a penal institution pursuant to sentence loses some of his constitutional rights. Obviously he loses the right of freedom of movement. He loses some of his rights of freedom of speech, in that his communication with the outside world may be limited and censored. On the other hand, he retains some of his constitutional rights. Primarily the prohibition of cruel and unusual punishment contained in the Eighth Amendment applies to him. He is entitled to the ministrations of his religion under the First Amendment with the limitation that the size, times, and places of religious gatherings within prisons may be limited and regulated, and inflamatory sermons affecting the morale and discipline of the inmates may be excluded.

THE FOURTH AMENDMENT: ITS APPLICATION

The subject matter of this article deals with the Fourth Amendment, insofar as it relates to search and seizure. Within prison walls the Fourth Amendment does not apply. Prison officials may search the prisoner and his cell at any time and seize any articles that are contraband under prison rules. Whether the privilege against self-incrimination under the Fifth Amendment applies to an inmate of a penal institution during his incarceration, is a question that is outside of the scope of this article.

The next question to be considered is whether the provisions of the Fourth Amendment relating to search and seizure become operative as to the defendant from the moment he is released on parole, and also whether they are applicable to the sentenced defendant if the execution of his sentence has been suspended and he has been placed on probation.

A parolee, or a probationer, who has been sentenced but the execution of whose sentence has been suspended, is in legal effect in custody although the nature of the custody does not require him to remain within prison walls. He is not a free man, however. Thus in *Taylor* v. *United States Marshal*, 352 F. 2d 232, 235, Judge Phillips speaking for the Tenth Circuit, stated that, "While parole is an amelioration of punishment, it is in legal effect imprisonment, . . ."

Judge Parker speaking for the Fourth Circuit, in *United States* v. *Dillard*, 102 F. 2d 94, 96, stated:

"The status of the prisoner while under conditional release was that of a prisoner on parole . . . . While this was an amelioration of punishment, it was imprisonment in legal effect."

It is reasonable to assume that as a matter of self-protection the probation officer should have the right to search a probationer or a parolee for a concealed weapon. As a practical matter, it is doubtful whether any probationer or parolee would resist a search of his person for narcotics, or an examination of parts of his body, say his arms, to determine whether they bear any evidence of his having recently administered narcotics to himself. There appear to be no reported federal cases on the question whether articles obtained by such a search of the person would be admissible in evidence in a criminal prosecution against the person from whom they were seized, and the point cannot be determined without an authoritative judicial decision in a case when it actually arises, or without legislation.

The next step relates to the right and power of a probation or parole officer to make a search of the premises in which the person under supervision lives or is employed. The Fourth Amendment permits such a search be made if it is reasonable. Court decisions hold it to be reasonable if it is incidental to, and substantially simultaneous with an arrest made in the premises that are being searched. It would seem to follow that if a probation officer is arresting a probationer or parolee on a charge of violating the conditions of his probation or parole, and the arrest is made inside premises that are under the control of the probationer or parolee, the probation officer may make a search for contraband articles in so much of the premises as are under the control of his person under supervision. For instance, if the probationer or parolee occupies a room in a rooming house and the probation officer makes his arrest there, he may search the room and seize contraband articles if any are found. On the other hand, the search may not extend to parts of the premises that are not occupied by, or are not under the control of, the person who is being arrested. Such are the rules that apply to arrests generally and there would appear to be no reason why they should not govern arrests made by probation or parole officers.

Federal probation and parole officers are not vested with the *general* power of arrest. Such an authority could be conferred upon them by statute. Their authority to make arrests is limited to cases comprising violations of conditions of parole or probation. It must be borne in mind, however, that any citizen has a right to make arrests under certain circumstances, and probation officers have the same power as is the case with other citizens. A citizen's authority to make arrests, however, varies from state to state, and the federal courts in determining the validity of an arrest and of a search and seizure made incidental thereto, take cognizance of the state laws. It may prove desirable to request legislation from Congress to confer upon probation and parole officers authority to make arrests for violations of laws of the United States, similar to that possessed by law enforcement officers, such as members of the Federal Bureau of Investigation, Federal Bureau of Narcotics, and the Secret Service. If probation and parole officers had such authority, their power to make searches and seizures would be broadened equally, since they would have authority to make arrests in circumstances under which they do not possess such authority at the present time, and if they had lawful authority to make arrests they would likewise be empowered to make searches and seizures incidental thereto.

A more important and difficult question arises in connection with the question whether a probation or parole officer may conduct a search of premises not incidental to any arrest in order to determine whether the person whom he is supervising is violating the law, or the conditions of his release, or has possession of contraband articles. For example, suppose the probation officer has a strong suspicion based on reliable information that the defendant is engaged in a clandestine traffic in narcotics, but is not sufficiently sure to make an arrest on a charge of violating probation. May he invade the defendant's home and conduct a search in order to determine whether the defendant is hiding narcotics? In a case of any other person than a probationer or a parolee such a course would not be permissible. It would be a clear violation of the Fourth Amendment.

SOME COURT DECISIONS

Does the Fourth Amendment extend to a probationer or parolee? There is a paucity of federal decisions on this question. In *Martin* v. *United States*, 183 F. 2d 436, 439, the Court of Appeals for the Fourth Circuit in an opinion by Judge Soper expressed the view that the Fourth Amendment applies to probationers and, therefore, parolees, but that the test of reasonableness of a search and seizure is different as to probationers and parolees than it is as to other persons. The court upheld the validity of a search of a probationer's automobile conducted under circumstances which probably would have rendered the search invalid if it involved a person who was not technically in custody.

No other circuit appears to have passed upon this question and consequently this author expresses no opinion in the matter. None can be reached without an authoritative decision in each circuit, or by the Supreme Court. Several states, however, have had occasion to pass upon this question and it is of interest to examine some of the state cases on the subject.

In New York there is an interesting and significant decision by the Supreme Court, which in New York is a trial court of original jurisdiction, in *People* v. *Langella*, 214 N.Y.S. 2d 802, decided 4 years ago. That case involved an arrest of a parole violator by a parole officer followed by a search of the parolee's automobile in which a firearm was found. The parolee was then prosecuted for unlawful possession of the weapon and moved to suppress the Government's evidence on the ground that it had been obtained by illegal search and seizure. The court sustained the validity of the search. The district attorney argued that the search was valid as an incident of a lawful arrest. From our standpoint the decision is important because the judge upheld the validity of the search on a different ground. He said (p. 805):

"I prefer to rest this decision on the broader ground that applicable and controlling law expressing and implementing a sound public policy subordinates the parolee's rights to the reasonable exercise of the parole board's powers of supervision and investigation."

"I hold that, on the facts developed by the proof in this case, the action taken by the parole officer was legally justified and that the defendant cannot, consequently, sustain his claim that the search and seizure were unreasonable. Within the spirit and intendment of the law, it seems plain that the test of reasonableness is not necessarily the same, when applied to a parolee, as when applied to a person whose rights are not similarly circumscribed and there is hardly any doubt that, within the constitutional framework, the parolee's rights may be and are properly conditioned and limited."

The California courts have had occasion to pass upon the question we are discussing and by a series of controlling decisions the rule has been established in that state that the Fourth Amendment does not apply to probationers and parolees and that a probation or a parole officer may search the probationer's or parolee's person as well as his home, and seize any contraband articles that may be found. These cases are of sufficient importance to justify a detailed analysis.

The landmark and leading opinion is one by the District Court of Appeal, Second District, which comprises Los Angeles, in *People* v. *Denne*, 297 P. 2d 451. The District Court of Appeal is an intermediate appellate court and its decisions have authoritative weight. After serving a part of a sentence of imprisonment, the defendant had been released on parole. Two parole officers, receiving information that he was trafficking in narcotics, obtained access to the defendant's apartment in his absence. They induced the building manager to climb through a window and then open the front door of the apartment for the officers. No one else was present on the premises. The parole officers made a search of the apartment and found a package of marihuana. They then went to the defendant's place of employment and arrested him. He was tried on a charge of unlawful possession of marihuana. At the trial the court overruled an objection to the admission of the marihuana in evidence based on the ground that it was illegally seized pursuant to an unconstitutional search. The court did not pass upon the question whether the Fourth Amendment applies to a probationer or parolee and, if so, to what extent. It upheld the validity of the search on the ground that it was not unreasonable for a parole officer to make a search such as was conducted in that case. I the course of its opinion, the court made the following significant remarks (pp. 456–458):

"A prisoner on parole is not free from legal restraint by the penal authorities, . . . but 'is constructively a prisoner of the state in the legal custody and under the control of the state board of prison directors".

"Having reasonable cause to believe defendant had breached his conditions of parole by associating with a felon engaged in the narcotics traffic, the propriety of the search by the parole officers of their prisoner's quarters cannot be gainsaid.

"By accepting the privilege of parole a prisoner consents to the broad supervisory and visitatorial powers which his parole officer must exercise over his person and property until the term of his sentence shall have expired or been terminated."

In *People* v. *Triche*, 306 P. 2d 616, also a decision of the District Court of Appeal of California, this time for the First District, which comprises Alameda County, a parole officer went to the parolee's apartment and did not find him at home. At his request the landlady gave him admission to the apartment. He searched the apartment in the defendant's absence and found several bundles of heroin. The validity of the search was upheld on the authority of the *Denne* case, *supra*. The courts said at p. 618:

"It was there held that the granting of parole does not change the status of a parolee as a prisoner. He is in penal custody in a prison without bars, subject to the rules and regulations for the conduct of paroled convicts to be enforced by the parole officer. For the protection of the community as to whose security the parolee constitutes a calculated risk, the parole officer exercises an ubiquitous supervision over him, including broad visitatorial powers. Having constructive custody of his prisoner at all times, there is nothing unreasonable in a parole officer's search of the prisoner's premises where he has reasonable cause to believe that the parole has been breached. It is unnecessary for a parole officer to apply for a warrant to arrest a parolee, who is already his prisoner and who is at all times in custodia legis. In the case before us there was reasonable cause to believe that Triche had breached his parole and the search of the premises where he admittedly lived and acted in violation of his parole was under the above rule no invasion of his constitutional right to be free from unreasonable searches or seizures."

In *People* v. *Robarge*, 312 P. 2d 70, also a decision of the District Court of Appeal of California for the Second District, a parole officer accompanied by a policeman searched a motel room registered to a parolee. They made the search because the parolee had failed to notify the parole authorities of a change of address. At the time of the search the parolee was not in his room. At the request of the officers the owner of the motel unlocked the door and permitted them to enter. The officers found some marihuana in the room and the parolee was arrested and prosecuted for its possession. The court held that the search was valid and admitted the marihuana in evidence at a subsequent criminal trial in which the parolee was charged with its possession. The court made the following comments in the course of its opinion (p. 72):

"Having constructive custody of his prisoner at all times, there is nothing unreasonable in a parole officer's search of the prisoner's premises where, as here, he has reasonable cause to believe the parole has been breached."

In *People* v. *Contreras*, 315 P. 2d 916, a decision of the District Court of Appeal for the Third District, which comprises Sacramento County, the validity of a similar search was sustained and the Court made the following observations (p. 919):

"The only difference in his status from that of other prisoners is that he is permitted to remain outside the prison walls, although he is still in custody. In the *Denne* case the court further held that the place of residence of a parolee may be entered and searched by prison officials or parole officers in the same manner as the search of a prisoner's cell and under the circumstances it cannot be said that the search of the defendant's apartment by the parole officer was an unreasonable one."

The same court rendered a significant opinion on the status of prisoners and parolees in *People* v. *Hernandez*, 40 Cal. Rptr. 100, which also sustained a similar search of the premises occupied by a parolee. The court stated (pp. 103, 104):

"Inmates of state prisons do not have the usual array of federal and state constitutional rights guaranteed to nonincarcerated citizens. . . . Prison authorities may subject inmates to intense surveillance and search unimpeded by Fourth Amendment barriers. . . . Although a parolee is not a prison inmate in the physical sense, he is constructively a prisoner under legal custody of the State Department of Corrections and may be returned to the prison walls without notice and hearing."

"For the purpose of maintaining the restraints and social safeguards accompanying the parolee's status, the authorities may subject him, his home and his effects to such constant or occasional inspection and search as may seem advisable to them. Neither the Fourth Amendment nor the parallel guaranty in article I, section 19, of the California Constitution block that scrutiny. He may not assert these guaranties against the correctional authorities who supervise him on parole."

The same doctrine was reaffirmed by the District Court of Appeal for the Fifth District in *People* v. *Gastelum*, 46 Cal. Rptr. 743.

CONCLUSION

As previously indicated in this discussion, so far as the federal courts are concerned, the question is open and does not appear to have been decided in any reported case. If it is deemed desirable that federal probation officers be clothed with authority to search a parolee's person, or his place of abode and seize any contraband articles that may be found, without being subject to the restraints of the Fourth Amendment, there are two possible courses to pursue. One is to await decisions of test cases in the federal courts in order that the law may be definitively determined. There are two possible objections to this procedure. The first is that it may take several years before the law can be settled; and, second, that there is always a possibility of different circuits reaching different results. This is particularly true in criminal cases. For example, the District of Columbia Circuit and the Second Circuit are in radical disagreement over the manner in which the rule of the Mallory case should be applied and administered.[1] Consequently, even if some test cases are decided we cannot be reasonably sure of uniformity.

The second course is to make the right to conduct a search and seizure, such as has been described in this article, an express condition of parole or probation, as the case may be, which the defendant knowingly accepts. Constitutional rights may be waived and if a court should hold that the Fourth Amendment is applicable in these instances, the rights could be waived in this manner. Presumably it would take the action of the Parole Board to impose such a condition of parole, and the action of various district courts to exact such a condition in cases of probation.

As has already been indicated, the legal status of a person put on probation after the suspension of imposition of sentence, is drastically different from that of a person on whom sentence has been imposed but the execution of the sentence suspended. Probationers of the first type are *not* prisoners whose custody has been enlarged, and it may well be that the control of probation officers over them may not be as extensive as that over probationers of the second type. The courts do not seem to have considered this difference as far as this writer is aware, but have treated all probationers alike. Possibly it may be well for a judge who is placing a defendant on probation to consider in which of the two classes the probationer should be placed and frame the disposition of the case accordingly, being guided to some extent by how much control over the probationer the court desires to grant to the probation officer.

[1]See *United States* v. *Mihalopoulos*, 228 F. Supp. 994.

42

Interstate Supervision of Parole and Probation

RALPH C. BRENDES

Only two juridical documents have formal and practical application throughout all of our fifty states—the Constitution of the United States and the Interstate Compact for the Supervision of Parolees and Probationers.

Unlike the Constitution, little has been written on the Compact; the *Handbook on Interstate Crime Control*, published by the Council of State Governments, which serves as Secretariat to the Parole and Probation Compact Administrators' Association, is the only published source of information on the Compact. This paper will analyze the present operation of the Compact and discuss problems likely to arise in the future.

The states have collaborated in this form of crime control for two reasons: (1) the ever increasing mobility of the American citizen, which frequently results in his conviction away from his home state, although it is in his home state that rehabilitation is more likely to occur because of the positive influences of family and friends; (2) the need to eliminate "sundown probation"—a procedure whereby a criminal sentence would be suspended if the offender left the state by sundown. To improve protection of communities, each state found it mutually advantageous to supervise its resident probationers and parolees who had been convicted in other states. This combination of humanitarianism and local self-interest to avoid unregulated and uncontrolled

SOURCE. *Crime and Delinquency*, 14, July 1968, pp. 253–260. Reprinted with the permission of the National Council on Crime and Delinquency. Copyright, 1968, National Council on Crime and Delinquency.

interstate movement of unsupervised probationers and parolees led to the drafting of the Interstate Compact for the Supervision of Parolees and Probationers.

The beginning of the Compact can be traced to the Crime Control Consent Act of 1934,[1] which permitted two or more states to enter into agreements of mutual assistance in the prevention of crime. The operative section of the Act reads:

> The consent of Congress is hereby given to any two or more states to enter into agreements or compacts for cooperative effort and mutual assistance in the prevention of crime and in the enforcement of their respective criminal laws and policies, and to establish such agencies, joint or otherwise, as they may deem desirable for making effective such agreements and compacts.[2]

A national conference called by the United States Attorney General in 1934 to discuss implementation of the Act resulted in establishment of the Interstate Commission on Crime. Representatives of the states and the federal government met in Trenton, N.J., to draft uniform laws designed to improve law enforcement practices and eliminate the infirmities of multijurisdictional authority. The Commission drafted the Compact, which almost immediately was signed by twenty-five states; today, all fifty states, as well as Puerto Rico and the Virgin Islands, are signatories, agreeing to serve as every other state's agent in the supervision of parolees and probationers.

GENERAL PROVISIONS

The Compact provides that (1) any state (receiving state) will supervise a parolee or probationer from any other state (sending state) if he is a resident of the receiving state and has employment there; (2) the receiving state will supervise the sending state's parolee by the same standards used for its own parolees; (3) the sending state may revoke parole or probation in any case and retake the parolee or probationer at its discretion and with a minimum of formality.

---

[1] Public Law 293, 73rd Congress, 2nd Session; Title 4, U.S.C. 111.

[2] Such consent may not have been required. Article 1, Section 10, of the Constitution says that "No state shall, without the consent of Congress, . . . enter into any agreement or compact with another state . . ."; however, under the doctrine of *Virginia v. Tennessee*, 148 U.S. 503 (1893), such compacts as are discussed in this article may be valid without Congressional consent. In that case the two states had agreed to the exact location of their boundary lines. Virginia later attacked the agreement, requesting the Supreme Court to declare it null and void since it was entered into without the consent of Congress. The Court held that this was not the type of agreement that the clause was intended to cover and that the terms "compact" and "agreement," as used in the Constitution, "were directed to the formation of any combination tending to the increase of political power in the states which may encroach upon or interfere with the just supremacy of the United States." If a compact did not do this, Congressional approval was not necessary.

To be classified a resident of the receiving state, the parolee or probationer ust have been an inhabitant of that state for more than a year before he went to the sending state and must have resided within the sending state for less than six months immediately preceding the commission of the crime for which he was convicted. If he fulfills those conditions of residence, the receiving state must accept him, provided his family resides in the state and he is able to find employment there. In all cases the receiving state is given the opportunity, before the parolee or probationer is sent there, to investigate his home and his prospective employment. If he lacks the residence or employment qualifications, he may nevertheless be sent from one state to another if the receiving state consents.[3]

Actual state use of the Compact is impressive. On June 30, 1967, about 10,500 parolees and about 11,000 probationers were under Compact supervision [4]

States working under the Compact are not bound by any strict rules; they adapt the general terms of the Compact to the specifics of each case.

The Compact has never had an unfavorable court decision. Most courts have construed the Compact liberally. While there has never been a ruling by the United States Supreme Court on the Compact, denials of *certiorari* may indicate the Court's endorsement of the Compact.[5]

Constitutional attacks on the Compact were resolved favorably in *Ex parte Tenner*.[6] After endorsing the principles of the rehabilitative ideal and stressing the importance of interstate cooperation in this regard, the California court said that provision by a state for the compulsory return of parole or probation violators was not unconstitutional. The states were not to be restricted to extradition, the sole method provided in the Constitution. The Compact method does not conflict with or render ineffectual the federal extradition laws, which are always available to a state. The violator still has a right to complain by means of habeas corpus if the authorities do not comply with the law, but he has no right to choose the method a state uses in returning him.

ADMINISTRATORS' ASSOCIATION

Formed in 1946, the Parole and Probation Compact Administrators' Association meets annually to discuss questions of policy and Compact

---

[3]Copies of the Compact are available from the Council of State Governments, 36 West 44 St., New York City, as are copies of all Compact materials referred to in this paper. Résumés of some of the major cases dealing with the Compact are printed in the *Handbook on Interstate Crime Control* (Chicago: Council of State Governments, 1966).

[4]Council of State Governments. "The Interstate Movement of Parolees and Probationers under the Parole and Probation Compact," Annual Report, July 1, 1966, to June 30, 1967 (New York: Council of State Governments).

[5]*Handbook, op. cit. supra* note 3. p. 74.

[6]20 Cal. 2d 670, 128 P.2d 388 (1942), *cert. denied*, 314 U.S. 585, 317 U.S. 597 (1942).

interpretations and develop necessary administrative regulations. The annual meetings, affording opportunities to solve many operating problems by personal contact among administrators, are a significant factor in the successful operation of the Compact.

Some accomplishments of the Association include establishment of regular statistical reporting, development of the *Parole and Probation Compact Administrator's Manual*, outlining of standard administrative procedures under the Compact,[7] sponsorship of the *Handbook on Interstate Crime Control*, and development of certain new agreements relating to control of interstate crime.

PROBLEMS SOLVED

Progress Reports

The Compact's regulations call for quarterly progress reports on each case. Many states, however, have changed their own reporting systems to require less frequent reports, maintaining that they need to hear about their men more often only if some problem arises concerning an individual case, and therefore have suggested that this be the procedure under the Compact also. Consequently, an annual meeting of the Administrators decided that any two or more administrators could agree among themselves to send reports less frequently.

Residence and Employment

A second problem arose in the early days of the Compact, when many states required strict adherence to the residence or job requirements. Today, most states will take any man who presents evidence of bona fide residence in their jurisdiction and some likelihood of employment. Many states will even take a man if he fulfills only one of the two requirements. At the same time, most states will not send a man under terms they would not accept themselves. If they have any doubts in the matter, they may ask the receiving state to investigate before they send a man. If a probationer or parolee does not have the necessary residence or employment qualifications, the transfer decision rests with the administrator of the proposed receiving state.

Can a state refuse to supervise a probationer or parolee who fulfills the residence and employment requirements but is considered a poor risk? Though a receiving state may indicate its reluctance to accept such a person, it must undertake supervision if the sending state authorizes transfer. Very few states will force a man on another state, however, even though they have the legal

---

[7]Copies of the forms used as well as other material relating to the Compact's operation are described in the *Parole and Probation Compact Administrator's Manual*, available on loan from the Council of State Governments, New York City.

power to do so under the Compact. In any instance where the sending state and the receiving state cannot agree upon the facts of residence and employment, they refer the matter to the Association's Council.

In a few cases, states which consistently refused probationers were persuaded by the Association that they could not do this.[8] The incidence of states refusing reception of parolees or probationers even in borderline cases is rare.

Apprehension of Violators

A third problem often discussed at Association annual meetings is the apprehension of technical violators by one state for another state. There was some question whether a state which permitted its officers to arrest its own violators without a warrant could allow them to arrest its out-of-state violators without a warrant if that other state required a warrant, and vice versa. The Compact provides that "the same standard of supervision as applies in the receiving state in the supervision of its own parolees shall apply to out-of-state parolees sent there,"[9] and the *Manual* reports: "The policy adopted by many states holds that the power to arrest is inherent in the power to supervise since power to supervise is useless without power to apprehend."[10]

Informal Arrangements

A fourth problem involves parolees or probationers who are not sent to what would have been a receiving state under the Compact but who nevertheless move there. Sometimes, without any instructions to do so, they report to an official of the second state, who has no prior knowledge of the case. In such instances, the second state usually requires the supervisee to sign a waiver of extradition.

If one state wishes another to retake a violator who never was under the terms of the Compact, it may do so only if he has waived extradition as a condition of being granted parole or probation:

Since he (the local parolee) has waived extradition on good consideration—*i.e.,* the grant of parole—he personally is barred from objecting to any failure to use

---

[8] In 1961, Oklahoma decided it would no longer supervise out-of-state probationers. The annual meeting discussing the problem pointed out that a state could go to court to force another state to abide by the Compact, but decided that more subtle means of persuasion should be attempted. A resolution sent to the governor and other Oklahoma officials set forth the facts and requested them to take steps to alleviate the situation. Oklahoma complied with the Association's resolution.

A somewhat similar problem arose in Arizona, where the Compact administrator said that his office lacked the facilities to administer probation cases properly. The Association decided, therefore, to distribute to every Compact administrator a list of Arizona's county probation officers so that he could deal with them directly.

[9] *Handbook, op. cit. supra* note 3, p. 12.

[10] *Manual, op. cit. supra* note 7, ch. 2. Sec. 408.4.

formal extradition. . . . He is not paroled under the Compact. Hence, the Compact itself would not apply. On the other hand, since his. . .waiver bars his rights to object to being retaken anywhere by any proper officer of the paroling state, . . . only the authorities of the state where he is arrested, or the authorities of the state which has paroled him, . . . can object to his arrest and return in that manner. Such arrest and return, while not under the Compact, would nevertheless seem practically to be effective, unless the state where he was arrested desired to make trouble for the state which had paroled him.[11]

UNSOLVED PROBLEMS

Several Compact problems have arisen which may require more than action by the administrators at their annual meeting for resolution. These involve detainers, return of violators, and local officer cooperation.

Detainers

A prisoner who has committed crimes in various jurisdictions before being apprehended will often have a number of detainers placed against him. Until these are resolved, it is difficult for the prisoner and his supervisor to make intelligent decisions concerning his future. To alleviate this problem, the Agreement on Detainers has been promulgated by the Association of Administrators and the Council of State Governments.

The Agreement on Detainers [says the Council] makes the clearing of detainers possible at the instance of a prisoner. It gives him no greater opportunity to escape just convictions, but it does provide a way for him to test the substantiality of detainers placed against him and to secure final judgment on any indictments, informations, or complaints outstanding against him in the other jurisdiction. The result is to permit the prisoner to secure a greater degree of knowledge of his own future and to make it possible for the prison authorities to provide better plans and programs for his treatment.

Basically, the Agreement provides that a prisoner may, in writing, petition the prosecuting officer for a final disposition of the indictment, information, or complaint which forms the basis of the detainer. In most cases, the prisoner is entitled to a reply, within 180 days after the request, which either initiates a trial or drops the charges. In this way, the prisoner is able to have a clearer view of his future and prison officials have a better chance to bring about his rehabilitation, because definite plans can be made for his eventual release, free from the fear that a trial after his release will result in continued imprisonment.

Drafted in 1957, the Agreement has been passed by twenty states.[12] The

[11]*Id.*, Sec. 501.6.
[12]California, Connecticut, Hawaii, Iowa, Maryland, Massachusetts, Michigan, Minnesota, Montana, Nebraska, New Hampshire, New Jersey, New York, North Carolina, Pennsylvania, Rhode Island, South Carolina, Utah, Vermont, and Washington.

intention was to observe its operation in a few states before encouraging uniform ratification, because this Agreement is more complex than the Compact and an experimental period seemed advisable. Experience under the Agreement has been so successful that the Council of State Governments and the Administrators' Association are now actively soliciting all states to join. The Association of Attorneys General has passed a resolution endorsing the Detainer Agreement and urging its enactment.

Returning Violators

Another problem which could not be solved by the administrators themselves involves the return of violators, totaling more than 250 probationers and 1,500 parolees annually. Often a supervisee has only a short period left to serve, so there is some question that it is worth the sending state's time and money to retake him; yet, if he is not retaken, some of the strength and leverage of the rehabilitative system is lost. Two plans—the Agreement for the Joint Return of Violators and the Out-of-State Incarceration Amendment—have been worked out by the Council and the Association; a third plan, calling for the posting of a cash bond before the supervisee leaves the state, is being used by Maryland and some other states.

Essentially, the plan for the joint return of violators requires only legislation permitting the deputization of out-of-state agents. Some type of clearinghouse system would be used to notify each state when other states intended to transfer violators to or through its state. The state then would deputize the agents of another state to enable them to transfer its violators in their custody at the same time as they took their own. For example, New York might want to bring back a violator from California at the same time that Illinois would want to bring back a violator from New York, and California one from Illinois. The New York agent could be deputized by California and Illinois, and thus one man would do the job of three, saving the states time and money. This plan has not been well received because (1) if a state cannot incarcerate a violator from another state for more than a very short period (and most states cannot or do not), the statistical probability of the above circumstances is not high; (2) communication by a clearing house or any other plan has not been established. In practice, few state administrators feel that the return of violators is a significant enough problem to warrant such a proposal; also, the increased speed and lower costs of transportation may eliminate the need for such arrangements.

The Out-of-State Incarceration Amendment to the Compact is also used infrequently. It provides that the receiving state may put a violator in its own prison to serve the remainder of his term. The sending state would then reimburse the receiving state for the expense involved, thereby saving the expense of bringing the violator back to its own prison. The amendment is applicable only if both states have ratified it. Only eight states have done so, and three of them—New York, New Jersey, and Connecticut—are geographically juxtaposed, so that it is easier to return violators rather than incarcerate them out-of-state. A true test of the agreement has not yet occurred.

The plan independently developed by the Maryland authorities requires a parolee or probationer to post bond sufficient to cover the cost of his return. A number of Maryland's neighbors have adopted this idea and it has apparently worked very well. Because the sending state does not have an obligation under the contract to send a supervisee out of the state, attaching conditions to such action is not illegal. The argument can be made that this bond requirement violates the *spirit* of the Compact by imposing a financial obstacle to placing the supervisee in the best possible rehabilitative location. The social-policy consideration may outweigh financial considerations. Maryland's approach to the financial problem has been to permit the supervisee to send payments back to the state on the installment plan. Furthermore, there is no bond-posting requirement if the parolee or probationer is sent to a nearby state. Authorities in Maryland are pleased with the system. Last year, the total cost to the state for returning violators was under $500.

Local Cooperation

Few major problems have arisen since the inception of the Compact. Some of them can be traced to the administrative policies of the state. While parole is everywhere a statewide operation, probation is not. Some states have county-based probation programs without state-wide coordination or supervision. Other probation programs may be locally run with an advisor or coordinating central agency. Often this high degree of local autonomy causes problems of cooperation between states under the Compact.

Some difficulty results from local officials and judges' ignorance of the Compact. To alleviate this, the Administrators' Association has published a brochure, detailing the advantages and operations of the Compact, which many states have distributed to local officials and judges with a good deal of success. Some states have gone even further in persuading the local probation authorities to operate under the Compact. Minnesota, for example, has enlisted the assistance of the state's Judicial Conference in preparing some of the forms to be used, and the Compact administrator addresses the judges twice a year, stressing the importance of following Compact procedure. A Pennsylvania court has ruled that when a probationer or parolee is sent out of the state without the use of Compact procedure, the state loses jurisdiction over him. This decision may help to persuade more people to operate within the Compact, even where judges have been reluctant to do so in the past.

Recent decisions providing the parolee or probationer with greater rights in the determination of an alleged parole violation may create administrative problems. The leading case on this subject is *Hyser v. Reed*,[13] in which the court held that federal parolees charged with parole violation were entitled

[13] 318 F.2d 225 (1963).

to an informal preliminary interview, before being transferred to prison, at a point as near as possible to the place where the alleged violation occurred and as promptly as possible after the arrest. The court refused to hold, however, that due process required the hearing to have the trappings of a trial such as appointment of counsel to indigents, confrontation of witnesses, cross-examination, discovery, and compulsory process. Nevertheless, if state courts follow the lead of this case and preliminary hearings become necessary in cases of parole violation, some changes will become necessary in Compact operation. The Compact will have to be amended to enable states to hold a violator in their jails and to conduct hearings for the sending states. The trend is not yet entirely clear, however, and it may be that procedural changes will suffice. There is a great resistance to changing or amending the Compact in any way. Since it is, aside from the Constitution, the only document accepted in all fifty states, there is a fear that amendment, which would need approval by all states to be effective, might jeopardize the smooth operation of the Compact.

The Compact has been very successful so far and gives every indication of continued success. Effective means of operation have been devised to carry out its administration, and equally effective methods have been provided to enable necessary adaptations to be made should future conditions necessitate them. Annual meetings, increased sophistication of parole and probation authorities, more knowledgeable judges in this area, and an effective Secretariat—these are just a few of the factors that have brought about the Compact's success.

RESEARCH AND PREDICTION

This section emphasizes the general aspects, problems, and potentials for research and prediction rather than specific or programmatic products or reports about research and prediction. This theoretical and philosophical emphasis complements the growing awareness of the need for additional research and further evaluation of actuarial devices in improving and evaluating correctional performance. The first three selections, by Professor Daniel Glaser, researcher Robert Fosen and Professor Jay Campbell, and Professor Jerome Rabow, are generally directed toward conceptualization of the difficulties and the promise of systematic examination of corrections.

The lead article on prediction by Hermann Mannheim and one of the editors emphasizes simplicity, efficiency, repeatability, and validity as essential requirements of prediction. Professor Lloyd Ohlin's important 1951 contribution to prediction, reported in *Selection for Parole*, is described because of its historical significance, operational aspects, and methodology. Professor Ohlin's approach to prediction may be compared or contrasted with "new" prediction methods outlined by one of the editors and University of Toronto Professor P. Macnaughton-Smith.

An excellent survey on parole prediction by Victor H. Evjen, Editor of *Federal Probation* and Assistant Chief of the Federal Probation system is followed by Professor Norman S. Hayner's article on the attitude of parole boards toward the use of prediction devices.

A specific research report on a time study of Federal probation and parole officers by Chief United States Probation Officer Albert Wahl and Professor Glaser is of value in this anthology. The report describes how the officer utilizes his time, the limits on job performance by time, and the difficulty of complying with arbitrary standards relating to workloads.

The section closes with an important contribution by sociologist-researchers Robert Martinson, Gene Kassebaum, and David Ward. Their analysis of parole research (also applicable to probation) finds it deficient in three areas: a narrow focus of prediction on success or failure, emphasis on the parolee to the exclusion of the parole agent as decision-maker, and an absence of study on the social organization of the parole agency.

43

Correctional Research: An Elusive Paradise

DANIEL GLASER

The history of correctional research resembles the history of religion. There have been successive periods of discontent, new cults promising simple solutions, and social movements institutionalizing the new approaches in judicial or correctional practice. But discontent recurs, and new movements continually emerge.

SCIENCE AS SALVATION

Commitment to a penal policy has almost always rested purely on faith in its efficacy, or on a selfish interest in it, rather than on empirical evidence proving that it achieves its professed purposes. Yet proponents of each way of treating criminals, whether it be capital punishment or solitary confinement, hard labor or nondirective counseling, have all asserted that their method succeeds, either in changing criminals or in deterring others from becoming criminals. The literature proposing penal standards, from Old Testament injunctions to Beccaria's essay, from Bentham's "felicific calculus" to the latest pronouncements of prison psychiatrists, is replete with empirical claims. But this literature is almost uniformly deficient in scientifically adequate evidence

SOURCE. *The Journal of Research in Crime and Delinquency*, 2, January 1965, pp. 1–11. Reprinted with the permission of the National Council on Crime and Delinquency. Copyright 1965 by the National Council on Crime and Delinquency.

on the validity of these claims. Successful experience is illustrated or implied for each treatment method, but there is no proof that the cases cited are typical of those to whom the treatment would be directed if a correctional system adopted it; often there is not even adequate evidence that the reformation of cited cases occurred *because of* a particular treatment rather than *despite* it. Indeed, usually the only evidences of change in the criminals are favorable impressions gained by the reporter rather than actual statistics on posttreatment criminality.

With the rise of science in the nineteenth and twentieth centuries, proposals for penal reform at times shifted from specific prescriptions for changing criminals, to demands for institutionalizing scientific research as a guide for penal practice. Research was to be the new Utopia to inspire reform movements, and sometimes it was described in moving exhortations, for it had to compete with other proposals, each generally supported by exaggerated claims. Thus Enrico Ferri, in his *Criminal Sociology*, which had its first Italian edition in 1884, asserted:

"The naturalistic philosophy from the year 1850, impelled by the new data furnished by the experimental sciences, from astronomy to . . . sociology, has completely dissipated the moral and intellectual mists left by the Middle Ages. . . . We enter, with the natural study of crime . . . upon a road that the jurists have not yet attempted, and whose difficulties we recognize without fear, because combat was always a condition of victory."[1]

And in 1903, Aschaffenburg, in Germany, insisted:

"The system of criminal law . . . must . . . bow to the advance of science . . . Only the natural scientific method . . . can smooth the way that leads to a knowledge of crime and of criminals. Not until then will a sure foundation be laid for the proud structure of legal security."[2]

Professor Ernest W. Burgess, dean of applied sociology, represented the University of Chicago in 1927 on an inter-university commission to evaluate the Illinois sentencing and parole system. Law school professors, representing Northwestern and the University of Illinois, raised legal and administrative questions, but Burgess addressed the behavior prediction problem inherent in sentencing and parole decisions. As this was a scientific matter, he systematically tabulated data on the correlates of parole outcome for 3,000 cases. In this pioneer parole prediction study he proposed that the state regularly improve his prediction tables:

"An expectancy rate should be as useful in parole administration as similar rates have proved to be in insurance. . . . Our prisons and reformatories should become

---

[1] E. Ferri, *Criminal Sociology* (Boston, Little, Brown, 1917), pp. 566–567.
[2] G. Aschaffenburg, *Crime and its Repression* (Boston, Little, Brown, 1913), pp. 321–322.

laboratories of research and understanding into the causes of the baffling problem of the making and unmaking of criminal careers."[3]

The ideal of resolving the crime problem by relying on science found its most vociferous salesman in Sheldon Glueck, who glowingly set forth the prospect for science in the sentencing process by this conjecture:

"Suppose . . . that a judge had before him separate prognostic tables based on fines, on imprisonment in a penitentiary, on imprisonment in a reformatory, on probation, or even more discriminately on results obtained by different probation officers. And suppose that the judge, on consultation of the prognostic tables, found that Prisoner X according to past experience with other prisoners who in certain pertinent particulars resembled X, had, say nine out of ten chances of continuing in crime if sent to a prison, seven out of ten if sent to a reformatory, five out of ten if placed on probation, and only two out of ten if placed on probation, under Supervisor Y. Clearly, the judge . . . [by] using objectified and organized experience . . . based on hundreds of similar cases . . . would greatly improve his exercise of discretion in imposing sentence."[4]

ABANDONED UTOPIAS

From time to time in the past few decades, research offices have been established in correctional agencies and assigned the task of procuring facts for the guidance of correctional decisions. Like other Utopian colonies, these offices either disappeared quickly or survived only by a metamorphosis in their goals and practices, through which they ceased to be a force for change. The research movement, however, is still with us, and there are signs that it may have a continuing impact on correction. A survey of its recent history can provide source material for new exhortations to mobilize research on the effective handling of criminals. It may also stimulate research on the integration of research with practice.

In the early 1930's Professor Burgess launched an epoch of sociological prediction research (not only in criminology, but also in marriage and other fields). He persuaded the state of Illinois to establish in each of its three major prisons an office manned by civil-service employees entitled "sociologistactuaries." The assignments of this new kind of correctional official were first, to advise the parole board of the violation probability predicted by the Burgess tables for each parole applicant, and second, to conduct research to improve the prediction tables. This, ideally, would create a cumulatively increasing contribution of science to correctional decision-making.

[3]A. A. Bruce, E. W. Burgess, and A. J. Harno, *The Workings of the Indeterminate-Sentence Law and the Parole System in Illinois* (Springfield, Ill., Department of Public Safety, 1928), pp. 248–249.

[4]S. and E. Glueck, *After-Conduct of Discharged Offenders* (London, Macmillan, 1946), pp. 68–69.

The three sociologist-actuary offices, now in operation for over thirty years, have been manned by two to four sociologists at all times. These research personnel have served some useful functions, but their contribution to the scientific guidance of policy has been far short of that which Burgess envisioned. Why was this dream unfulfilled? Does its history have lessons for applied research elsewhere?

Illinois had a part-time parole board consisting predominantly of lawyers who were politically appointed, were generally oriented toward reaching their decisions in a minimum of time, and frequently responded precipitously to badgering by the press. They seemed to want to retry each case, so as to assess what would be just punishment. Probably their major social function was the latent one of somewhat equalizing the impact of disparate sentencing policies among the many judges sending men to prison. Some parole board members indicated that in their decisions they took into account the predictions submitted by the sociologist-actuaries, but few understood the derivation of the prediction tables, or their potentialities and limitations.

Over the years the Illinois parole boards solicited longer and longer narrative summaries for each case from the sociologist-actuaries. During the 1940's and 1950's preparation of these reports, based on interviews with the inmates, became almost the sole task of these presumed research personnel. Any improvement of the prediction tables occurred primarily because some sociologist-actuary was interested in parole prediction research for thesis purposes. When he received his higher degree, he moved to the academic world. What happened, essentially, was that the correctional researchers were coöpted to serve the primarily legal and political interests of the parole board, in exchange for which they received job security. As long as the narrative reports seemed to be prepared competently and were ready when the parole board members came to the prison to conduct their hurried hearings, the work of the sociologist-actuaries was approved by those who controlled their salaries. Any actuaries who were concerned with research interacted in a different social and cultural world from all except one or two of the many parole board members who they served in this thirty-year period; there was little communication between these two worlds.[5]

Simultaneously with the employment of actuaries in Illinois, many other state correctional administrations established research positions in their central offices. These were concerned primarily with the compilation of statistics to monitor the effectiveness of the correctional system. Actually, few of these offices compiled the kinds of longitudinal statistics on criminal careers which are needed for an evaluation; some isolated California work was the most

---

[5]The few years when sociologist Joseph Lohman headed the parole board provided the major exception to this pattern, but his term was too brief to affect drastically the total validity of these generalizations.

notable exception.[6] I have heard reports of other evaluative studies conducted by such offices but suppressed from publication by administrators who considered the findings unflattering or feared that they would be misunderstood. At any rate, these researchers soon were assigned the task of counting the volume of business conducted by the correctional system, as a means of justifying budgets. This so-called "research" mainly produced tables for annual reports which indicated prisoners on hand at the beginning and end of fiscal periods, or received and released during these periods. Again we see the coöptation of researchers by administrators trying to equate correctional research with simple head-counting.

THE NEWEST JERUSALEMS

A resurgence of research enterprise in correctional agencies has occurred in the past decade. The British Parliament, in the 1948 Criminal Justice Bill, instructed the Home Office to conduct research on the effectiveness of judicial and penal policies. This directive was finally followed in the 1950's by sponsorship of the Mannheim and Wilkins analysis of prediction possibilities in the Borstal youth prisons.[7] A Research Unit was then established in the Home Office with Leslie Wilkins as a senior researcher. By 1959 they could report about 80 research projects under way, all either conducted or facilitated by the Home Office.[8]

In 1957 the Budget Committee of the California legislature, faced with immense increases in correctional costs, insisted that research offices be established in the Department of Corrections and the Youth Authority to assess the effectiveness of treatment expenditures. In an annual correctional budget of approximately 100 million dollars, this state now spends approximately half a million per year for research.[9] Although small as a percentage, the amount far exceeds correctional research expenditures by any other state or national government. In addition, California has encouraged and facilitated much correctional research financed by private foundations or federal research agencies.

In the late 1950's a group of top federal prison officials and outside persons solicited foundation funds to finance university research in the federal correctional system. This resulted in the 1958–63 University of Illinois study

[6]State of California, *California Male Prisoners Released on Parole, 1946–49* (Sacramento, California Board of Corrections, 1953).

[7]H. Mannheim and L. T. Wilkins, *Prediction Methods in Relation to Borstal Training* (London, Her Majesty's Stationery Office, 1955).

[8]British Home Office, *Penal Practice in a Changing Society* (London, Her Majesty's Stationery Office, 1959).

[9]Estimate by R. A. McGee, Administrator, California Youth and Adult Correction Agency, in a discussion at the Working Conference on Probation, National Institute of Mental Health. Bethesda, Md., July 8, 1964.

of federal penal programs, financed by the Ford Foundation.[10] While this was in progress, offices which had previously compiled only routine "head-count" statistics in the U.S. Bureau of Prisons, and in Wisconsin, Minnesota, and other state correctional systems, were expanded. They now performed some types of research which could test the effectiveness of correctional practices, or they engaged others to conduct such research.

It is interesting that so much of the initiative for this expansion of correctional research came from outside the correctional administrations. In Britain and California, legislative bodies were the prime movers; elsewhere, prominent citizens and public foundations, both outside the government, provided leadership in what ostensibly were government undertakings. What "cultural base" had Western society reached, which resulted in these recent nearly simultaneous and largely independent expansions of correctional research? Clearly there must have been a conjunction of reduced public interest in punishment, continued public concern with the crime problem, and widespread skepticism about the claims of competing treatment approaches. Such skepticism, obviously, was a potential source of conflict between the researchers and the administrators in correctional agencies.

TERRORS AND TEMPTATIONS

Are the new research establishments any more successful than the older ones at achieving the goal of scientifically guided correctional practice? Do they have any more influence on the treatment of criminals than did the sociologist-actuaries, or the correctional "head-count" statisticians?

To some extent, the developments which vitiated older endeavors have recurred in the new research efforts. One or more researchers in almost every one of the half-dozen correctional systems which conduct the most extensive evaluative research have, at one time or another in recent years, informed me of the suppression of their research reports. In some state correctional systems it is quite evident that research units have been largely coöpted into service of the *status quo*, for they have abandoned longitudinal evaluative statistics compilation in favor of "head counts" only.

The reasons for this are quite obvious. Correctional officials procure financial appropriations for their agency by convincing the legislature that their programs protect society, either by incapacitating criminals or by changing them into noncriminals. When research confirms these claims, the officials are happy to promulgate the findings. Frequently, however, research has indicated that added appropriations to make treatment more effective, by reducing caseloads, hiring more psychiatrists, etc., have made no difference in posttreatment criminality or may even have increased it. Time-study analysis of the average

---

[10]Reported in D. Glaser, *The Effectiveness of a Prison and Parole System* (Indianapolis, Bobbs-Merrill, 1964).

hours per week which presumed treatment personnel actually spend in what might be considered treatment activity almost invariably yields a figure which the public would find surprisingly low. These are types of research findings which agency heads are reluctant to release.

There have been two styles of research suppression in correctional agencies. One style not only prohibits release of the report, but cancels further research as dangerous to the agency's "public image," or as the British express it, "embarrassing to the Minister." The real problem usually is that some officials, just above the researchers in a staff hierarchy, feel threatened by negative findings; the Minister or his American equivalent never hears of the research.

A more constructive style of research suppression involves the insistence of higher officials that there be further research before any results are released. This may simply be an enlargement of the sample, often to cover a more recent time period, on the usually spurious assumption that the treatment services studied have been getting better all the time. Frequently it is a reanalysis, perhaps requiring additional data, to permit cross-tabulations, perhaps leading to inferences as to the conditions under which the treatment studied is ineffective and the conditions under which it is effective. Reanalysis of this sort often indicates, roughly speaking, that special treatment services succeed in reducing failure rates appreciably only for "middle risk" cases; the least criminal cases have a low failure rate with or without special services; the highly criminal or unstable cases often fool and exploit treatment personnel or get unrealistic expectations from special training, so their long-run failure rates are higher following some of the special measures than after traditional programs.[11]

In some projects, reanalysis of research has involved an alteration of the criterion by which a program is evaluated. For example, cases given special treatment often compare much more favorably with cases not receiving this treatment if the two groups are evaluated by "total *time* reconfined" during a given period after release, rather than by "*per cent of cases* reconfined."[12] The reason is that special programs often reduce the *speed* with which released offenders get into further difficulty with the law more markedly than they reduce the proportion who eventually get into difficulty.

Occasionally the release of research results is deferred long enough for the officials involved to realize that any results can be interpreted favorably if the program is given multiple goals, such as "treatment" and "control." Under these circumstances, a more rapid return of cases to incarceration is credited to "control," but a less rapid return would have been credited to

[11]*Cf.* J. Havel and E. Sulka, *Special Intensive Parole Unit, Phase Three (SIPU 3)*, Research Report No. 3 (Sacramento, California Department of Corrections, March 1962).

[12]*Cf.* S. Adams, "The PICO Project," *The Sociology of Punishment and Correction*, N. B. Johnston, *et al.*, eds. (New York, Wiley, 1962), pp. 213–224; and B. M. Johnson, *Parole Performance of the First Year's Releases, Parole Research Project: Evaluation of Reduced Caseloads*, Research Report No. 27 (Sacramento, California Youth Authority, Jan. 31, 1962).

"treatment." This "heads I win" and "tails you lose" arrangement achieves the gambler's dream, for the state does have this dual objective, although ideally it would achieve control by successful treatment.[13]

Some research reports from correctional agencies are not suppressed, but might as well be, for few officials—or even researchers—can understand them. Most notable among such reports are those which describe the use of various types of multiple correlation or multiple association statistical analysis of case data in administrative records to find guides for correctional operations. These reports are submitted to correctional officials who do not understand the statistical terminology and who feel no urgency to learn to understand it since the researchers share with the operations officials the impression that this statistical analysis has little or no practical value at present. Thus, these researchers operate in a separate world, inadequately linked either with the university social system, which seems to be their reference group, or with the leaders of the correctional system, which they are presumed to serve.

It is statistical maxim, in most behavioral science problems, that with strong data you can use weak methods; the strong methods (e.g., factor analysis) are useful primarily to squeeze a suggestion of relationship out of weak data. Strong relationships can be demonstrated adequately with simple tables of percentages. Perhaps the high intelligence and dedicated effort invested in research into statistical methods would be more fruitful to the correctional system if they were employed not so much in seeking new methods of analysis for old types of data (that can be left to mathematical statisticians in the universities, who can be hired as consultants), but preferably in obtaining new types of data, derived from closer study and greater involvement in correctional operations. Furthermore, greater confidence in the reliability of correctional research results generally is gained by obtaining a redundancy of data, by procuring similar findings independently from several correctional situations, and by having several alternative indices of the key variables, than by mere statistical tests which assume the absence of bias in sampling or measurement.

PROGRESS FROM PITFALLS

In the long run, I believe, the paradise lost is most likely to be regained by controlled experiments. In the past two decades we have had many evangelical movements, from Cambridge-Somerville to SIPU and beyond, vainly preaching salvation by experimentation. The earlier sects repeatedly assembled the faithful to await miracles—and then disappointed them. Many of the sins we have been ascribing to correctional research grew out of frustration from experimentation. Yet negative or inconclusive results are but trials by which

---

[13]*Cf.* W. R. Burkhardt and A. Sathmary, *Narcotic Treatment-Control Project, Phases I and II.* Research Report No. 19 (Sacramento, California Department of Corrections, May 1963).

these pilgrims to the shrines of science are tested. They still may progress toward grace if they recognize past sins and seek salvation through new research design.

The value of experiments, when comparing two ways of handling offenders, is that they reduce the prospect of statistically uncontrolled variables accounting for the findings obtained. As an extreme example, consider a comparison of prison and probation. The higher rate of return to crime following imprisonment may not mean that prison is a more criminalizing experience than release on probation would be, but that most offenders receiving imprisonment are more criminalized when sentenced than are most who receive probation. Even if we compare only prison and probation cases that are matched by every index considered relevant (number of previous arrests, age, employment record, marital status, and so forth), it is possible that within each category of classification by these variables the judges have differentially selected worse risk cases for prison and better risk cases for probation, employing some subjective indices or weights not taken into account by the researchers' categories. Sometimes researchers have reason for inferring that such judicial perspicacity does not prevail, an inference suggested by the superiority of statistical to case study prediction.[14] Nevertheless, judges and top correctional officials are not readily convinced by such indirect evidence. Only when they are willing to have an appreciable number of treatment decisions made by purely random selection can we sharply increase everyone's confidence that differences in the subsequent behavior of offenders are due to differences dependent on the correctional treatment to which they were assigned, rather than due to selection variables. But even this is not an easy path to knowledge.

The history of medicine is marked not only by major progress through experimentation, but also great resistance to such experimentation. People refuse to be in a control group if they know this means they are denied a treatment which they presume is helpful, or they refuse to be in an experimental group receiving a treatment whose worth still is unestablished. There are also confounding variables which render experimental results inconclusive. For example, the "placebo effect"—which sociologists know as the "Hawthorne effect"—arises from the fact that the special attention given any group just by their being studied can alter their lives in a more influential way than the treatment being investigated.

These familiar difficulties of medical research recur in correctional research, but often only the physician has checks against them. For example, medical researchers use the double-blind technique of randomly mixing medication with placebos, so that even the persons administering the drugs do not know which is which. In correctional research (as in such medical fields as psychiatry, surgery, and physical therapy), treatments cannot be readily masked. Furthermore, if several programs are provided at one location, both

---

[14]*Cf.* H. G. Gough, "Clinical versus Statistical Prediction in Psychology," *Psychology in the Making*, L. J. Postman, ed. (New York, Knopf, 1962), ch. 9.

staff and subjects may have strong feelings about alleged reasons for differential treatment of control and experimental cases, and these feelings may have an impact on treatment results. If two programs are operated at different locations, there may be many other uncontrolled situational variables. Experimentation can nevertheless go on, but the prospect that confounding factors affect the results makes the repetition of experiments in many places highly desirable.

In addition to these parallels to problems in medical research, special research problems arise from the extent to which correctional treatment still is administered in a tradition of punishment and adjudication, and frequently in a setting of public hysteria over the crime problem, the latter leading to occasional searches for correctional whipping boys. All these influences have impinged upon the conduct of some experiments. Such problems, and some of their implications as well as solutions, may be illustrated by comparing three widely heralded correctional experiments with counseling centers for youthful offenders: the Highfields Project, the Provo Experiment, and the Sacramento-Stockton Community Treatment Program. These were initiated sequentially, and the design of the second and third was based upon the experience of the preceding project.

Highfields

The Highfields Project, while an innovation, was not truly an experiment, for it had no control group selected by the same process as the treatment group. However, after Highfields had been in operation for some time the postrelease behavior of its wards was compared to that of a number of offenders from the same counties, matched by age, offense, prior delinquent record, and other variables, who had been committed to the state training school at Annandale. While the Highfields cases had a somewhat better postrelease record than the Annandale youth, serious questions still could be raised about these findings. Was the judicial selection for Highfields such as to give it cases with better prospects for avoiding future criminality than those of ostensibly similar youth sent to Annandale? After all, Highfields youth were placed on probation by the court, with the stipulation that they go to Highfields for four months. Some of them may have been comparable to cases whom the judge would otherwise have placed on probation in the community, rather than comparable to Annandale cases. Even if one assumes that there were no distorting influences on judicial selection, one can question whether the Highfields youths had better records because the program was different there, or because they were not confined with older and more advanced offenders, as were the youth sent to Annandale.[15]

---

[15]In the research directed by Weeks, in which the data were analyzed independently by several persons, Highfields boys were compared with boys who were received at Annandale at about the same time and who met the Highfields admission criteria with respect to age, lack of prior instit-

Provo

The Provo Project modified the Highfields design in three major respects. In the first place, instead of being sent to reside at a small institution devoted to "guided group interaction," the Provo youth resided at home and were required to report daily to the counseling center. Second, the group counseling technique was somewhat altered by an increase in self-government in the group, including powers to discipline their members and even to recommend to the project director that a youth be briefly committed to jail. Third—and most notable for this discussion—the judge, after deciding that a case warranted serious state intervention, was to draw from an envelope a random number which would determine whether the youth would be released on probation with traditional supervision, would be released on probation with the requirement that he participate in the counseling center, or would be sent to the state reformatory.[16] The difficulty with executing this research design was foreshadowed when I described it to a professor of criminal law. He said that he wished he had as a client some youth sent to the reformatory under this program, since he considered it a violation of the right to due process. Regardless of the possible legal rebuttal to this charge, the research design is not being followed with respect to commitment to the reformatory; the experiment now is primarily a comparison of probation with and without a special counseling program.

Sacramento-Stockton

The Community Treatment Program, operated in Sacramento and Stockton by the California Youth Authority, has benefited by studying the Provo experience. It starts with youth whom courts of these two cities commit to institutionalization under the Youth Authority. The Authority's paroling board immediately screens out those youth whom it considers too emotionally unstable or dangerous for immediate release (so far only 26 percent of the boys

---

utional commitments, and lack of psychosis or feeble-mindedness. See H. A. Weeks, ed., *Youthful Offenders at Highfields* (Ann Arbor, University of Michigan Press, 1958). In the research conducted separately by Highfields staff, an effort was made to control for judicial selection by comparing Highfields cases with boys sent to Annandale in the years just preceding the opening of Highfields, with the two groups matched by the same variables as those used by Weeks, except that a few boys in each group who made a very poor institutional adjustment were eliminated. See L. W. McCorkle, A. Elias, and F. L. Bixby, *The Highfields Story* (New York, Holt, 1958). If Highfields received both boys whom the judges would otherwise have sent to Annandale and boys whom the judges might have placed on probation in the community had Highfields not existed, absence of the latter in the staff's control group of pre-Highfields commitments to Annandale may also impose judicial selection bias. For a highly critical review of Highfields research, see C. C. Sherwood and W. S. Walker, "Some Unanswered Questions about Highfields," *American Journal of Correction*, May-June 1959, pp. 8–9, 25–27.

[16]*Cf.* L. T. Empey and J. Rabow, "Experiment in Delinquency Rehabilitation," *American Sociological Review*, October 1961, pp. 679–696.

and 7 percent of the girls). The remainder is then divided randomly. About half are sent to the court-authorized regular institution program, in which the average stay of youth from these cities in past years has been eight months; and half are paroled immediately, with the special requirement that they attend community treatment centers.

The experimentally released youth in the Sacramento-Stockton program receive intensive supervision by parole agents who have caseloads varying from as little as eight to a maximum of about thirty. (The Authority's average with regular parolees is about seventy cases per officer.). The community treatment center conducts a guided group interaction program much like those at Highfields and Provo, in addition to providing individual and group psychotherapy, tutoring, and other special assistance to the delinquents and their families. Most distinctively, this program attempts to offer a different style of supervision for each classification type, using both social and personality, diagnostic variables. Thus, it has primarily supportive relationships for the highly immature, who are viewed as largely unsocialized in any adult role; it has firm, though fair, supervision for youth socialized into delinquent subcultures and manipulative toward officials; it has an open and interpretative approach to those viewed as mature and conventionally socialized but delinquent because of neuroses or situational problems. Still another distinctive feature of this program is that the parole agents may confine a youth for from one to thirty days in a local youth detention facility, without returning him to the Youth Authority as a parole violator.[17]

From the standpoint of the evolution of research design, the Community Treatment Program is notable for its accommodation of the conflicting pressures which impinged on prior experimentation in correction. Because the law does not permit incarceration of anyone who does not, by the court's judgment, merit so extreme a denial of liberty (even if it is called "treatment"), this experiment—to compare a program in the community with commitment in traditional institutions—starts with persons adjudicated for incarceration. Because the public insists upon punishment for notorious offenders and blames the parole board if serious new offenses are committed by parolees, this research starts with a pool of cases committed to institutions but screened by the parole board to eliminate those whom it is not willing to risk immediately in the community. (This, of course, imposes the research burden of identification of these types of cases denied eligibility for the experiment. Fortunately this group has been relatively small.) Finally, the parole agents can swiftly impose brief arrest on a non-cooperative youth instead of waiting for him to commit infractions sufficiently serious to warrant his return to longer-term incarceration. This breaks down traditional barriers, and the sense of working at cross-purposes, between

[17]M. Q. Warren, T. B. Palmer, and J. K. Turner, *Community Treatment Project*, CTP Research Report No. 5 (Sacramento, California Youth Authority, February 1964); H. G Stark, "A Substitute for Institutionalization of Serious Delinquents: A California Youth Authority Experiment," *Crime and Delinquency*, July 1963, pp. 242–248.

correctional and law-enforcement agencies; it integrates rehabilitation and control, the dual aspects of protecting society from known criminals.

The project has had its difficulties. One law enforcement leader was vociferous about the release of a little so-and-so just after there had been so much trouble catching him. However, this same official now has joined others in loudly praising the program, for it appears to have had impressively successful results. Not only has the percentage of new offenses been smaller for those treated in the community than for the members of the control group (paroled after regular institution commitments), but also, among those who committed new offenses, the community-treated new offenders were apprehended more quickly, and more often by the parole agent than by the police. Finally, the community treatment program, despite all its special services and small caseloads, costs less per man-month than commitment to an institution.

CONCLUSION

The recurrent criminological dream of a correctional system directed through research has not been a prophetic one, since researchers have been either coöpted by administrators or oriented to a monastic world divorced from practice. Yet progress toward this dream of scientific correction has been made, particularly in the past decade and particularly through experimentation.

Experimentation has its pitfalls which often lead to abandonment of the research faith. On the other hand, even when blessings follow experimentation, there is a need for caution. For example, the success of the Sacramento-Stockton project was cited, but would the same type of community treatment program work as well in a large city slum as it has in cities with relatively less severe and less concentrated delinquency? This points up the need for redundancy in the correctional research ritual, and for meeting negative results by new designs.

The discontent which generated the cult of research in correction probably will always be with us. As Durkheim pointed out, even in a society where everyone was what today would be considered saintly, some people would have still higher or different standards of behavior and would be offended by others.[18] Indeed, we have reason to believe that despite some increases in the causes of crime with increased urbanization, there has been a net decrease in the behavior traditionally called criminal[19]; "crime waves" may express not increased violence but only an increase in the intensity of society's reactions to violence.

Most social movements are sustained by the belief of their followers that

---

[18]E. Durkheim, *The Rules of Sociological Method* (Glencoe, Ill., Free Press, 1950), pp. 67–69.

[19]*Cf*. H. A. Bloch and G. Geis, *Man, Crime and Society* (New York, Random House, 1962), p. 259.

their cause is right, and that what is right will ultimately prevail. The movement for research in correction is no exception to this rule. In the judicial and correctional areas, so many decisions radically affecting the lives of others are made by vague subjective impressions, untested rules of thumb, and non-rational prejudices, that almost any strengthening of the empirical basis for decision policies inspires the faithful.

Faith in the progressive growth of what Ohlin has called the "routinization of correctional change"[20] also is justified by empirical study of societal trends. For correctional change to occur not just by crisis reaction, but by planned development on the basis of research, would be part of what Moore has called "the institutionalization of rationality."[21] This is a trend in almost all parts of any society undergoing modernization, although it grows most slowly in the more tradition-ridden and subjectively guided components of these societies, such as the agencies of criminal law interpretation.

[20]L. E. Ohlin, "The Routinization of Correctional Change," *Journal of Criminal Law and Criminology*, November-December 1954, pp. 400–11.

[21]W. E. Moore, *Social Change* (Englewood Cliffs, N. J., Prentice-Hall, 1963), p. 95.

44

Common Sense and
Correctional Science

ROBERT H. FOSEN AND JAY CAMPBELL JR.

We seem to be getting accustomed to the fact that delinquency and crime are the natural and predictable outgrowths of a carelessly urbanized society. Accelerating crime figures have become commonplace.[1] Now it takes a Watts riot (or perhaps the youngster next door) to remind us of our need to do something about the rising costs of the alienation and ineffective socialization which lead to delinquency and crime.

We also seem to be getting comfortable with our achievements. We can take pride in the modern prison by reflecting on the demise of punitive revenge and the "con boss" system. The educational programs available to many offenders compare favorably with those of our public school systems. In higher education, studies are under way, through assistance from the Ford Foundation, to determine the feasibility of developing a prison college that would operate side-by-side with San Quentin.

Probation-in-lieu-of-imprisonment incentives to counties, community

Source. *The Journal of Research in Crime and Delinquency*, **3**, July 1966, pp. 73–81. Reprinted with the permission of the National Council on Crime and Delinquency. Copyright 1966, National Council on Crime and Delinquency.

[1] U.S. Department of Justice, Federal Bureau of Investigation, *Uniform Crime Reports*, Washington, D. C.: U. S. Department of Justice, March 8, 1966 (1965 Preliminary Annual Release). Of little surprise to anyone, the FBI's *Uniform Crime Reports* indicate a nation-wide rise of 5 percent in the crime index for calendar year 1965 over 1964. Suburban communities lead other areas of the nation in reporting an increase of 8 percent.

correctional centers, halfway houses, prerelease centers, and reduction of parole caseloads, though not uniformly accepted throughout the country, nevertheless are answers to the demand to "do something now." Recent amendments to criminal law, permitting such innovations as civil commitment for narcotics addicts and work furlough during prison terms, buttress belief in the progressive growth of criminal justice.

Since public protection and restoration of the offender to trouble-free community living represent at least the manifest goals of most correctional systems, there is generally uniform agreement on the objectives implied and the actions taken in producing these changes in correctional programing. Decisions to maintain existing practices or to wrestle with innovation are based on assumptions which require only that present or contemplated policy reflect a common-sense compatibility with these general goals. There can be no argument with the goals. And to challenge the need for innovation would be obviously absurd.

"COMMON SENSE"

The point of challenge must be directed at our assumptions, and specifically at our apparent willingness to live with them interminably. One such assumption is: *Common sense is sufficient as a means of advancing and defending correctional policies and practices.*

Common sense is *not* enough. In medicine, bloodletting was once accepted as a common-sense cure for many ills—ranging from high fever to incorrigibility. In the history of penology, it was at one time common sense to attempt redirection of behavior through the "silent system" and corporal punishment. It is presently common sense to assume that psychiatry has knowledge everyone needs and no one has—including psychiatrists. Is this common sense good sense? It may or it may not be. But we *are* living comfortably with the assumption that it is.

Common sense by itself not only is insufficient but also can be dangerous. Some relatively high-prestige forms of treatment may be detrimental to some offenders. Research carried out through the U.S. Navy Retraining Command at Camp Elliott, Calif.,[2] reveals interesting differences in the postrelease adjustment of military prisoners exposed to intense and professionally directed living-group treatment while confined. Assignment to treatment followed classification of each offender as either "high" or "low" in maturity.[3] One

[2]This particular Retraining Command function has since been relocated within naval districts. See J. D. Grant and Marguerite Q. Grant, "A Group Dynamics Approach to the Treatment of Nonconformists in the Navy," *Annals of the American Academy of Political and Social Science,* March 1959, pp. 126–35.

[3]C. E. Sullivan, Marguerite Q. Grant, and J. D. Grant, "The Development of Interpersonal Maturity: Applications to Delinquency," *Psychiatry,* November 1957, pp. 20, 373–85.

of the most striking (and statistically significant) findings of this study was that psychodynamic, living-group treatment apparently produced decidedly different results with the high-maturity as contrasted to the low-maturity offenders. Follow-up of adjustment six months after release from confinement indicated a restoration-to-duty success rate of 70 percent for the high-maturity men and 41 percent for the low-maturity men. A challenging difference— especially when we consider that the average success rate for *all* high- and low-maturity offenders (including those supervised under treatment teams of custody-oriented staff predicted to be least effective) was a remarkable 62 percent! It may be common sense to assume that if a little psychology is a good thing, more psychology will be better—or that offenders have similar treatment needs. But this study strongly suggests that different offenders have different treatment needs, that some forms of treatment may be detrimental to some offenders, and that to assume otherwise may not be good sense.

A similar result was obtained in Phase I of the PICO (Pilot Intensive Counseling Organization) Project at the Deuel Vocational Institution in 1955–60.[4] In this setting, youthful offenders were judged by clinical staff as either "amenable" or "nonamenable" to a treatment program consisting of individual counseling sessions and periodic group therapy. Random assignment of these two types of offenders to experimental (treatment) and control (no treatment) subgroups permitted observation of postrelease behavior over four parolee classifications (amenable-experimental, nonamenable-experimental, amenable-control, and nonamenable-control). One view of community adjustment, calling for comparisons on percentage of postrelease time spent in *return to custody*, presented some unexpected results—especially thirty-three months after release from confinement.[5] At this point, the average time spent in reconfinement for the amenable-experimental youths was 2.06 months—the best performance among the four groups. However, the average reconfinement time for the nonamenable experimental subjects was 5.50 months—the poorest performance among the four groups. Again, a significant and provocative outcome—particularly when we discover that the average reconfinement time for all PICO Phase I offenders (including the amenable and nonamenable control subjects who received *no* treatment) was only 4.29 months! Parallel to the Camp Elliott research, the PICO study suggests a serious need to plan and devise *kinds* of treatment for *kinds* of offenders. And there is little hope that common-sense assumptions will do this for us.

Common-sense correctional programing has had its day. And quite a day at that! Under its guidance, the so-called new penology abandoned indifferent and self-righteous confinement of the offender, and efforts to restore the offender to crime-free and responsible community life replaced the philosophy

---

[4] A California Department of Corrections facility for youthful offenders located at Tracy.

[5] S. Adams, "Interaction between Individual Interview Therapy and Treatment Amenability in Older Youth Authority Wards," *Board of Corrections Monograph No. 2* (Sacramento: Board of Corrections, July 1961), pp. 27–44.

of control and punishment. The new penology, or the deepening of humanitarianism, reflected good common sense and it produced and carried the prison
reforms of the twentieth century. There are now few major prisons which do not
offer some opportunity for individual growth and development. Therapies are
in abundance. The word-therapies (individual and group) of the psychiatrist,
psychologist, sociologist, and social worker are pressed forward with increasing determination. The teaching-therapies pursued by academic and
vocational education are backed by an expanding list of still others—work-
therapies, religious-therapies, recreation-therapies, occupational-therapies,
and now inside and outside community-therapies.

A preliminary analysis of survey results indicates that only a few correctional agencies in the country are currently attempting serious evaluation of
any programing. Of the forty-eight responding agencies (forty- six states, the
federal government, and the District of Columbia), nineteen report some kind
of research operation. Approximately $1,300,000, or roughly one-third of 1
percent of the total annual budget in U.S. adult correction (over $400,000,000),
is invested in self-study through these organizations. Over one-half of this
small research investment is spent in California and New York.

We spend over three hundred times as much on running our business as we
do on evaluating our product. Yet, there is some basis for optimism. Three-
quarters of the agencies report a definite interest in either initiating or expanding self-study within their jurisdictions.

AN EMERGING MODEL FOR CORRECTIONAL SCIENCE

It is now time to bring correctional science to the aid of common sense.
Two critically important and interrelated problems face us. First, we must
unravel the right kinds of programs for the right kinds of offenders. This is
another way of saying that the new penology never gave us client-specific treatments. It simply said that all offenders ought to have opportunities to make
gains across-the-board—in such areas as individual treatment, education, and
vocational training. Present evidence indicates little, if any, improvement in
recidivism rates when offenders are in this way assumed to be the same and are
given the same treatment. We are undoubtedly getting here what might be
called masking effects. That is, the gains in treatment by some offenders are
concealed by an understandable lack of response by others. As illustrated by
the Elliott and PICO studies, lack of response may all too often be coupled
with detrimental impact in producing the masking effect we see as "no
measurable difference following treatment."

Second, we must address directly the question of who should come to
prison in the first place. Progress has not kept pace with the problem beyond
the point of agreeing that there are some people in prison who probably
shouldn't be. Finding out who these people are, how many of them are currently
incarcerated and will be in the future, and what program alternatives to in-

carceration would be effective is a difficult and unavoidable challenge. We have to get started now. And we can get started with the reasonably safe assumption that the resocialization value of the institution has been over-estimated. Also, it may be true that public interests in protection, restoration of the offender, and cost will be best served through management of some offenders in the community.

Pioneering work in this area is under way in the California Community Treatment Project.[6] Jointly sponsored by the California Department of the Youth Authority and NIMH, this action-research program provides for random assignment of male and female juvenile offenders to experimental and control programing. After brief reception-guidance center confinement, juveniles in the experimental group are returned immediately to the community, while those in the control group are assigned to traditional confinement and management. Treatment in the community is *not* the same for all of the youngsters in the experimental group—and this is the chief significance of the project. Through tailoring relatively standardized treatment techniques (such as supportive counseling, analytic psychotherapy, guided group interaction, and the like) to the widely different and measured maturity levels of the juveniles treated in the community, a major break-through is apparently being achieved.

Fifteen months from date of release to this community-based intervention, the experimental group juveniles (combined as one group) have produced a recidivism rate of 35 percent. The control group exposed to essentially similar counseling and therapeutic techniques—but in the traditional institutional setting and undifferentiated with regard to specific maturity level or client type—have demonstrated a recidivism rate of 47 percent after fifteen months.[7]

Again, the significance (statistical and otherwise) of this study lies in the strong implication that treatment is effective *when* treatment is adapted to clients—in this instance, *within* the community as an experimental alternative to incarceration.

The point here and earlier is not that our common sense has failed us; it is rather the absolute necessity of combining the power of good judgment derived from correctional experience with the power of science. Why? Because only science can separate what we *hope* from what *is* the case; what *seemed* helpful from what *was* helpful; and perhaps what can *never* be from what *can* be. The need is for objective facts that lie beyond the sum total of past experience.

Readiness to build correctional science is more complex than simple fusion of need and money. Like all measuring instruments, science has life and func-tions independent of the desires of the consumer. The readings do not always

---

[6]Marguerite Q. Warren, "The Community Treatment Project: An Integration of Theories of Causation and Correctional Practice" (paper read at the Annual Conference of the Illinois Academy of Criminology, Chicago, May 14, 1965).

[7]Marguerite Q. Warren, Project Director, California Community Treatment Project (personal communication, April 13, 1966).

tell us what we want to hear—the thermometer tells us we are sick, the stethoscope tells us we are dying. Correctional science, therefore, must be based on a flexibility of mind that permits one to look for the facts.

Science in our field must grow from basic counting and description, but the available narrative records of correctional agencies require serious appraisal. They have consumed enormous amounts of time for preparation, and, as they accumulate, their collective volume alone infringes on needed storage space. More important, the utility of voluminous records is increasingly questioned, even for individual case decisions and casework supervision. These records have been compiled as aids to decision—but experience indicates that they are unwieldy and the retrieval of information from them is excessively time-consuming, even if we could grant their objectivity and completeness.

Nineteenth century habits of recording experience with clients, efforts to deal with clients, and assumed results must give way to modern methods. As opposed to the interminable chronicles of quasi-relevant historical facts and guesses, the critical focus must be on what we do to whom, and why, and with what consequences.

Contemporary data-processing techniques promise not only to reduce the time of recording this more useful information, but to make the information accessible for management decisions as well as for research. Admittedly, the phasing-in period of automation is time consuming, initially frustrating, and expensive. Ultimately, however, it will permit access to accumulated experience and will free personnel to plan and develop treatment relationships with their clients.

Modern access to information will facilitate the development of actuarial prediction equations. These prediction devices permit the formulation of baseline estimates of performance, in essence, "the known efficiency" of agency operations. While admittedly crude, such devices have more than held their own when compared with professional clinical judgments.[8] There is little reason to believe that they cannot be improved as more standardized and objective information is made available. As an aid toward the development of release criteria, and as a means of identifying treatment impact, they permit a practical exploratory evolution toward more sophisticated studies in which variables, such as exposure to a specific program, can be manipulated and tested with some scientific precision.

Armed with better access to the correctional experience of clients and some prediction capability, research can make visible the processes and results of progressing correctional activity. Constant measurement of additional delinquency, rearrest, parole violation, or commitment of new felonies is funda-

---

[8]D. Gottfredson, "Comparing and Combining Subjective and Objective Parole Predictions," *Research Newsletter* (Vacaville: California Medical Facility, September-December 1961); H. Gough, "Clinical v. Statistical Prediction in Psychology," *Psychology in the Making*, L. Postman, ed. (New York: Knopf, 1962); P. Meehl, *Clinical v. Statistical Prediction* (Minneapolis: University of Minnesota Press, 1954).

mental. Combined with measures of recidivism, answers to what we do, to whom, and why permit attainment of correlational research and progress in scientific management. Eventually, guessing about recidivism and its relationship to programing will become obsolete.

Correlational research is, in effect, clue-hunting among measures of what we do with our clients and the outcomes we observe. More meaningful and useful inquiries will develop into experimental designs in which relationships between kinds of offenders, kinds of staff, and kinds of treatment are examined. Within this framework, the number of experimental variations possible is unlimited, and the selection of research strategy is dependent on existing information, clues, and creativity. For example, an experimental design could be developed in which offenders of a known recidivism class are randomly assigned to experimental and control treatment programs. The high recidivism rate of the alcoholic bad-check writer is an illustration of the type of offender to be studied by this methodology. Variations between traditional institutional treatment and treatment in the community are long overdue for this and many other identifiable offender groups. Numerous other experimental designs are possible. They represent not only the most precise scientific approach, but portend advancement in correctional policy and practice.

SCIENTIFIC MANAGEMENT: AN EVOLVING IMPERATIVE

Democratic social and legal institutions have brought about limited compliance with the law among the majority of our citizens. Has this compliance come about through a positive absorption of these institutions into the society or has it resulted from punitive sanctions? The fact remains that the overwhelming majority of the population does not test our correctional apparatus. The negative side of the ledger, however, does indicate shortcomings in our traditional methods of social control and corrective treatment. Criminogenic influences become apparent, but unspecified, as we measure increases in crimes reported to police, increases in numbers of convicted offenders, and increases in the incidence of recidivism.

Such problems of correctional systems are frequently eclipsed by the more "worth-while" and redeemable plights presented by the physically handicapped, the mentally ill, and the needy. The rationale for this, if any is stated, is that the adult prisoner deserves what he gets. Progress made by correctional agencies in the journey from outright barbarism to at least reasonable care and custody usually results from crises—such as riots, brutality, and corruption—rather than from serious study.

To the extent that the law and the courts specify length of confinement—in effect, the kind of intervention—the correctional apparatus is limited in its choice of alternatives. Whatever intervention is attempted *must* be applied within the custodial setting specified by the courts or the code. A nation-wide survey indicates that sentencing is stipulated by the law in about 20 percent of forty-eight reporting jurisdictions, and left to wide judicial discretion in about 66 percent of the reporting agencies. Mandatory definite sentences for most offenses are delineated by law in over 20 percent of the jurisdictions. Over one-third report that the institution of confinement is specified by the courts. Correctional systems, therefore, and their developmental needs must be viewed in a broad perspective—preferably in a broad context of social control, but at least within the context of the administration of criminal justice.[9]

In efforts to discern capacities for correctional research, evidence accumulates that precious little choice is left to administrators of adult correctional institutions as to alternate dispositional interventions. In all jurisdictions, it is mainly within the custodial setting that the administrator must attempt to apply those hopeful, but rarely tested, techniques of rehabilitation.

The control of crime through the manipulation of the known offender, while admittedly only one facet of the solution to the crime problem, is at least tangible and definite action susceptible to scientific investigation. Over 215,000 adult felons are confined in the United States. Over one-third of them are incarcerated in California, New York, Texas, and the federal system. The cost of confining them is more than $400 million per year. Over half of the total expenditure is in California, New York, Michigan, and the federal system.

For a nation whose technology promises to place a man on the moon by the 1970's it seems ludicrous that we have our head in the sand when it comes to applying scientific techniques to the solution of the problems presented by thousands of confined offenders. Current knowledge of correctional effectiveness falls short of accurately estimating the number of these offenders who will commit new crimes. More embarrassing is the void of information on which correctional interventions, if any, have been effective in meeting rehabilitative objectives. Less than half of the reporting jurisdictions indicate even a minimal attempt to determine an overall recidivism rate within their domains. For the most part, comparative statistics are simply unavailable. It is difficult to achieve even a primitive understanding of jurisdictional legal definitions of crime, let alone any evidence for the treatments which may be effective for some offenders. Complexities in the management of massive, confined populations underscore the need to adopt those technical management tools so effectively utilized by private industry. Information from those jurisdictions which report a serious research effort illuminate, for the most part, the fact that we are running blind. Although most of our efforts are expended in compiling voluminous records and making decisions, little is done to systematically relate those activities to the offenders or to evaluate the impact of decisions and programs on their future adjustment.

Both the researcher and the administrator predicate their planning and action on the facts of the past as a clue to the future. The success of the adminis-

---

[9]J. Campbell, "A Strict Accountability Approach to Criminal Responsibility," *Federal Probation*, December 1965, pp. 33–36.

trator is determined, to a large degree, on how accurately he has been able to study his past experience and apply this understanding to the current decisions which face him. With perhaps more precision, and probably less hurry, the researcher compiles his data, applies the analytic techniques of science, and makes his interpretations or formulates his hypotheses. Both are increasingly faced with complexities of operation in which, without the tools of science, the problem cannot even be comprehended, to say nothing about making effective decisions to do something about it.

The essential facts needed for effective administration are often the same as those needed by the behavioral scientist to conduct his investigations. The methods the scientist uses to ascertain the reliability and validity of his information can assist the administrator to separate the extraneous from the relevant. The rules governing the growth of science—essentially, clear thinking and rigorous investigation—can guide the administrator toward the general policies needed for scientific management. Wilkins[10] points out that research can give the administrator immediate help with decision problems while at the same time enabling the scientist to evolve the generalized theoretical formulations needed to satisfy the tenets of science. A workable compatibility is essential in which the manager can be given immediate information for current decisions as the scientist evolves more applicable universalities of human behavior.

The action needs of the correctional administrator and the increasing financial and human costs of his action constitute a mandate for scientific management. Complacency by either manager or researcher contrasts sharply with increasingly serious responsibilities. Human needs overshadow organizational and academic concerns, and the case for more effectiveness is written in human despair.

BLUEPRINT FOR A MERGER

The idea of developing correctional systems to include the functions of social research laboratories may be difficult to sell. Answers to the questions of effective institutional and community programing cannot be expected to simply tumble forth following acceleration of research activity. As evidenced by the studies reviewed previously, significant gains *can* be expected from scientific management—but we must be prepared for the frustrations that will parallel achievement.

First, answers have an irritating tendency to raise new questions. Even if we learn more about effective programing, we find ourselves directly confronted with the following questions:

1. How can we improve staff training to match *more* efficiently the resocialization needs of different clients?

---

[10]H. Mannheim and L. T. Wilkins, *Prediction Methods in Relation to Borstal Training* (London: Her Majesty's Stationery Office, 1955), p. 223.

2. How do community forces, such as shifting employment patterns, increasing industrial automation, law enforcement practices, and public opinion, act upon our attempts to retain the probationer or parolee in the community?

3. What does increased treatment impact in institutional and community programing tell us about causes of delinquency and crime? Are we getting feedback to the etiology of deviance[11] from efforts to correct deviance?

4. What role should modern correctional systems play in public efforts to check the rising incidence of serious nonconformity?

Second, moving into scientific management involves more than friendly cooperation. Correctional researchers and correctional operators have to develop teamwork—a concept easily stated but not easily implemented. Scientific management forces us to ask who has to do what to make it possible.[12]

Operations staff can do the following:

1. Develop program objectives *with* research staff if evaluation is to be carried out. Research cannot assess action in the absence of knowing its intended target.

2. State the operations or models through which the objectives are to be achieved and share the plan with research staff.

3. Work with researchers in stating program and research schedules as a single package. This forms an action partnership.

4. Be realistic about program continuity. With it, research is possible; without it, research must be postponed in favor of different approaches to evaluation.

5. Call on researchers to explain methods and findings and to assist in implementation of results. Researchers need identity *with* action as much as operations staff need research *for* action.

6. Contribute to the staff time and energy needed to do the job. This is imperative. Institution and community research require that operations staff work "on the other end." For example, until we keep better records of what we are doing, *whatever* it is we are doing will escape evaluation. Operations staff are essential in the task of developing and maintaining relevant records—the raw materials of scientific management.

Research staff can do the following:

1. Join the team whose responsibility it is to run and manage an entire operation, not just a social research laboratory. This means that some questions research must answer may be uninteresting—but nonetheless necessary in running the system.

2. Be explicit about what they have to offer and be prepared for such questions as: "It's interesting, but how will it help?" "Why will it take so long?" "What do you want me to do?" "Does this have the support of top administration?" These are legitimate questions. Researchers must be ready with the answers.

3. Acknowledge that the process of stating and clarifying questions for research is a joint venture. These questions range from comparatively straight-forward ones

[11] R. H. Fosen and Marguerite Q. Grant, "Variations among Offenders in Perception of Norms: Implications for the Theory of Differential Opportunity Systems" (paper read at 56th Annual Meeting of the American Sociological Association, St. Louis, 1961).

[12] R. H. Fosen, "Who Has the Ball Now?" *Correctional Review,* September-October 1964, pp. 4–7.

about population numbers and movement to those about group process and response to treatment. Since no one group of us has all the knowledge needed to state these questions, our best bet is to do it together.

4. Keep operations staff (particularly administrators) informed of how it's going and what it means. Resistance and loss of valuable time and action are the products of "surprise" research findings.

EPILOGUE

It is the evolution of functionally accurate typologies, through the joint efforts of research and operations personnel, that will have the greatest impact on correctional practices and on the field of applied criminology in the next few decades. By delineating specifically the methods and procedures which may be usefully applied to one kind of criminal behavior, while recognizing their limited applicability to others, we will be able to formulate interventional strategies directly related to correctional objectives. More effective treatment of deviance may generate better understanding of the causes of deviance. We expect that the development of behavioral theory and correctional policy will make parallel gains through the behavioral sciences. By encouraging correctional science along the applied continuum, we may expect our growth to be reasonably parallel to the advances made in medicine. This does not contradict the need for theoretical development. It merely indicates that theories must be generated with sufficient clarity and delimitation of scope to permit some kind of empirical reference and test. Theory must be evolved from experience rather than solely through contemplation from a safe distance.

45
Research and Rehabilitation: The Conflict of Scientific and Treatment Roles in Corrections

JEROME RABOW

The contribution any rehabilitation program can make to a field of knowledge is determined not by impressionistic evidence that can be gathered in favor of the program but by scientifically adequate evidence that places the program within the context of a sound research design. By this means a program can be evaluated rigorously in comparison with other treatment approaches. Nevertheless, the urgent need for sound research in corrections has, as yet, not been met on any wide scale by social scientists. As Ohlin has pointed out "the creation of a realistic design for evaluative research would unquestionably do more to speed the development of a science of penology than any other single contribution."[1]

Although some factors, such as the difficulties involved in setting up cont-

SOURCE. *The Journal of Research in Crime and Delinquency*, **1**, January 1964, pp. 67–79. Reprinted with the permission of the National Council on Crime and Delinquency. Copyright 1964, National Council on Crime and Delinquency.

[1] Lloyd E. Ohlin, *Sociology and the Field of Corrections*, New York: Russell Sage Foundation, 1956, p. 52.

rolled experiments in correctional facilities, are discussed in the literature,[2] some of the main reasons for the paucity of sound research are unarticulated. One important aspect of this lack of articulation is not intrinsic to the difficulties associated with setting up and describing well designed programs, but is inherent in an ideological gulf separating those persons responsible for treatment from those responsible for treatment evaluation.

This gulf, which has been described as an "age old split,"[3] has created many difficulties in corrections. In certain instances, historical arguments between professionals in the behavioral sciences have proved to be important for scientific advancement; members of opposing groups were willing or pressured to reexamine and revise concepts, assumptions and premises, and occasionally procedures. The arguments between treatment and research groups in corrections have not, as yet proved especially fruitful.

While both groups agree that knowledge about treatment is important, in practice, their disagreements seem to belie their common orientation. Perhaps this is because the disagreements are inherent in the present division of labor with respect to treatment. The treatment group focuses on *practical* problems of a "here and now" nature, while researchers are more concerned with the abstract problems of setting up research so that there might be some *ultimate* evaluation.

The resulting differences between the two have been akin to political debates in which the debaters tend not only to utilize different facts to support their points of view, but disagree with the interpretation of the facts which they have in common. Thus, typically, the clinician says, "Recidivism is not a good criterion of success because it overlooks those who are 'better adjusted' and whose offenses, therefore, are 'less serious'."[4] The researcher counters with, "You may be right, but what empirical evidence do you have that the success rate might not have been just as high for those who received no treatment whatsoever or perhaps received a different kind of treatment?"

This paper will focus on some of the sources of conflict between scientific and treatment personnel as well as the dysfunctions created by those conflicts for the field of corrections. Specifically the researcher-evaluator role and the

---

[2]Joseph Zubin, "Design for the Evaluation of Therapy," *Psychiatric Treatment*, Baltimore: The Williams and Wilkins Co., 1953, XXXI, pp. 10–15; Eli A. Rubinstein and Morris B. Parloff, eds., *Research in Psychotherapy*, Washington, D.C.: American Psychological Association, 1959; Elizabeth Herzog, "Some Guide Lines for Evaluative Research," Washington, D.C.: U.S. Department of Health, Education, and Welfare, 1959, pp. 64–71.

[3]Benjamin Kotkov, Chapter 19, "Research," in *The Fields of Group Psychotherapy*, ed. by S. R. Slavson, New York: International Universities Press, Inc., pp. 316–317. Kotkov describes experimental contributions without emphasizing the dysfunctions of the division. Paul E. Meehl in *Clinical v. Statistical Prediction*, presents a precise but detailed examination of the more general conflict existing between clinicians and actuarialists, University of Minnesota Press, Minneapolis, 1959.

[4]Donald R. Cressey, "The Nature and Effectiveness of Correctional Techniques," *Law and Contemporary Problems*, Vol. 23 (Autumn, 1958), pp. 754–771.

clinician-therapeutic role are under examination. It should however, become clear to the reader that the description of the problems described in this particular case study and the suggested solutions have a much broader application to the difficulties generated by contact of the practitioner, be he teacher, social worker or administrator, with the researcher. The obvious similarities to other areas will be ignored and the focus will be upon the conflicts as they manifest themselves in the corrections field.

HISTORICAL PERSPECTIVE FOR THE SEPARATION

This ideological separation between clinician and researcher is part of the age old split between men of socially planned action and men whose lives are devoted to the abstract problem of cultivating and formulating knowledge.[5] The men of action have undertaken rehabilitation, educational training and settlement house work, all with the very practical problems of having to do something. Traditionally their idea has been that the effectiveness of the methods they used could be based upon common sense and testimony as to their efficacy.

This kind of humanitarian approach is obvious in many American correctional practices today. Any techniques which make the offender's life more comfortable or his surroundings more home-like are embraced and considered helpful. They are considered beneficial because they seek both to reduce deprivations resulting from impoverishment or incarceration and to produce the warm emotional environment of which many offenders were supposedly deprived in earlier years.

But, in addition to humanistic values, such treatment approaches also include many middle class values,[6] some residues of a punishment philosophy and an admixture of Freudian Psychology and social science information. From a researcher's point of view, this amalgam is an evaluative nightmare. The *potpourri* of humanistic and middle class values which form the foundations for many practices, because they have been viewed as absolutes, have not been subjected to evaluation. In a similar way many clinical practices are viewed as an art in which any evaluation must be intuitive and subjective[7] rather than empirical and objective.

[5] Robert K. Merton, *Social Theory and Social Structure*, Glencoe: The Free Press, 1957, p. 209.

[6] Donald R. Cressey, "Limitations on Organization of Treatment in the Modern Prison," *Theoretical Studies in Social Organization of the Prison*, New York: Social Science Research Council (March, 1960), pp, 92–93.

[7] Reik contends that most insights and understanding in psychoanalysis spring from the therapist's and the patient's unconscious. Any attempts to categorize treatment in a "systematic, orderly, consistent" manner will result in drivel. Theodor Reik, *Listening With the Third Ear*, New York: Grove Press, Inc., 1948, pp. 440–441.

As a consequence, treatment practices are accepted *a priori* and the men who hold them tend to proceed with unbounded faith in what they are doing, apparently feeling that any problems are due to a failure to apply what is known rather than to evaluate that which is in progress. They are more concerned with pointing out the need for "professional treatment" than in defining the precise way in which such treatment is applied or is successful in changing people.

On the other hand, the traditional position of the evaluator might best be compared to that of an "unattached intellectual"[8]—an individual who has little commitment to the system he is examining: economic, emotional, or otherwise.

The researcher can continue to be adamant in abiding by his suggestions and findings since he is not intimately involved in translating them into action. Consequently he often fails to recognize the multifarious problems which must be borne by administrators and clinicians who are responsible for treatment.[9]

The traditional arguments and counter-arguments by both treaters and researchers have been latently functional in that they have served as ideologies which have given each group a sense of identity, meaning, and purpose. But the manifest functions for which each group supposedly exists, i.e., to improve and apply treatment successfully, has been lost in the effort of each to maintain its own vested interest. Any possibilities for treatment to be viewed as a dynamic and creative phenomenon has been stifled because latent functions have become ascendant. But just as the question of federal aid to education may not be *effectively* resolved by the clash between vested interests, the question of improved treatment likewise may not be effectively resolved on the merits of latent arguments designed to protect existing patterns.

Instead, the dysfunctions of these latent positions must be demonstrated, any virtues residing in them must be brought out, and new alternatives explored which might make possible an inventive approach to treatment. The remainder of the paper is devoted to this task.

SOME BASIC QUESTIONS AND A RESEARCH MODEL

Scientifically selected treatment and control groups are imperative for any realistic evaluation of treatment. Yet, only rarely have such groups been systematically compared. But to add complexity to an already difficult problem, it should be noted that a comparison of groups, whether on the basis of recidivism rates, personality tests, or other characteristics, is only one dimension

---

[8]Merton, *op, cit.*, p. 211.
[9]*Ibid.*, pp. 218–219.

of evaluation. In the absence of supporting information, significant statistical differences among groups do not necessarily justify attributing these differences to one treatment method or the other. In many cases differences might not be a direct function of treatment, but due to the effect of other variables which the statistical comparison does not reveal.

Before differences can be attributed to the utilization of a particular treatment approach, evaluation would have to be seen as occurring in a series of stages in which answers to several important questions were available. The following are possible stages.

Stage I is concerned with the population of offenders from which treatment and control groups will be selected. Answers for such questions as the following are needed:

1. How is the population of offenders from which groups will be selected defined with respect to age, record of offenses, geographical location, or any social or personality characteristics thought to be important?
2. How is selection carried out in order to eliminate bias—by random means or some matching process?
3. When, and by whom, is selection carried out? What are the mechanics?
4. What steps are taken to demonstrate the lack of bias in selection?

Stage II is concerned with the treatment process and the need to understand what is involved in it:

1. What is the theory of causation upon which treatment is proceeding?
2. What is the intervention strategy utilized in treatment by which the causation variables will be modified?
3. Can a logical relationship between causation variables and intervention strategy be demonstrated?
4. Can it be demonstrated that the treater is fulfilling role requirements specified by the intervention strategy?
5. Assuming that treatment role requirements are being fulfilled, can it be demonstrated that variables cited in the theory of causation are being modified?
6. How shall any change in variables be measured?

Stage III involves the actual comparisons of groups subsequent to treatment and is concerned with such questions as:

1. What are the goals of treatment; that is, how shall success be defined—in terms of recidivism, attitudinal change, new social relationships, personality modification?
2. How is measurement of these characteristics carried out?
3. Over what period of time are comparisons to continue?
4. How is cooperation of subjects obtained?

Other Variables

In addition to the variables in each of these stages, there are others—race, class, marital status, job status, etc.—which can also affect treatment results. Because these variables are not a direct function of treatment, efforts must be taken to control them or they can result in misleading and unexplained differences.

Figure I sums up graphically the stages just described. It might be viewed as a research model highlighting the need for a systematic integration of research and treatment.

The necessity of having information for each stage of evaluation becomes manifest when one considers a few of the ways in which it can affect the statistical comparisons. Suppose, for example, a statistical comparison of treatment and control groups reveals no differences among them. Without further knowledge it is difficult to assess such findings. But if a careful analysis of Stage II (causation theory and intervention techniques) indicates that the causation variables thought most important were successfully altered, then it is possible that methods for selecting the groups were biased (Stage I) or that treatment has been concentrated on the wrong variables. In either case, one has better information on where to search for answers.

On the other hand, if the statistical comparison of groups revealed that there were significant differences in favor of the treatment group, and that causation variables were successfully altered, then it would be more reasonable to assume that causation and intervention theory had an important effect on rehabilitation—providing, of course, that other important variables such as race, marital status, etc., were controlled.

Finally, in a more complex way, suppose the analysis revealed that, although significant statistical differences occurred between groups, important causation variables were not actually altered. In attempting to discover what had caused the differences, one would have to investigate several problems: Was there bias in the method of selecting treatment and control groups (Stage I)? Is causation theory correct (Stage II)? Was the comparison carried out over a long enough period of time (Stage III)? Were outside variables sufficiently controlled?

Since answers to these questions form the foundation for knowledge about treatment programs, any examinations of the arguments between clinician and researcher should be analyzed in the light of them. In this way it might be possible to pinpoint present difficulties. It should be kept in mind, however, that this paper is not concerned with all of the difficulties which inhibit effective treatment and evaluation. It focuses instead upon the manner in which the bifurcation of treatment and research roles permits treatment to proceed without scientific validation.

DYSFUNCTIONS PERPETUATED BY THE TREATMENT GROUP

The Dearth of Research on Treatment Techniques

Most professionals in corrections, or otherwise, seem to feel that some evaluation of treatment methods is warranted, although, as Goode points

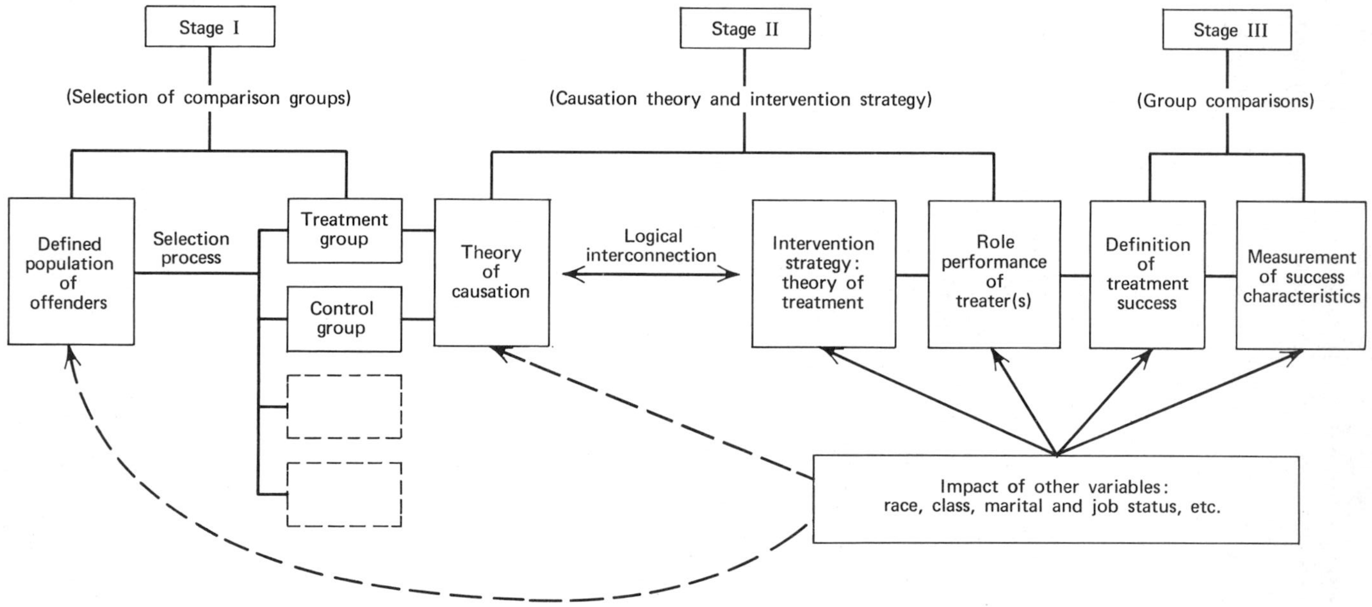
Stage I
(Selection of comparison groups)
Stage II
(Causation theory and intervention strategy)
Stage III
(Group comparisons)
Defined population of offenders
Selection process
Treatment group
Control group
Theory of causation
Logical interconnection
Intervention strategy: theory of treatment
Role performance of treater(s)
Definition of treatment success
Measurement of success characteristics
Impact of other variables: race, class, marital and job status, etc.

Figure 1

out, the few evaluations of such techniques as psychotherapy that have been made do not meet "minimum canons of research design."[10] But most clinicians are either unwilling or unaware of the need to subject themselves and their techniques to the various stages of evaluation by which statistical comparisons can be made meaningful.

One of the greatest obstructions is the tendency for existing treatment theories and methods to be accepted virtually on an *a priori* basis. For example, many people have assumed that since "the effectiveness of psychotherapy has long since been established,"[11] it can be applied effectively to the treatment of criminals. Yet, *neither* assumption is empirically validated.[12]

The psychotherapist's role has seldom, if ever, been examined since many clinicians feel that research on it is superfluous. In their opinion all of the necessary rules of conduct in therapy are known.[13] Yet, most descriptions of the clinical role are derived from different schools of thought and are generalized rather than specific in nature.[14] Thus, the assumption that all therapists follow a recognized and shared treatment role is highly questionable and merits examination.

If the treatment role remains unarticulated and unevaluated, results such as

[10]William J. Goode, "The Profession: Reports and Opinions," *American Sociological Review*, 25 (Dec., 1960), p. 912.

[11]Rubinstein and Parloff, *op. cit.*, p. 278. These authors do not assume the effectiveness of psychotherapy but mention those who do.

[12]Hans J. Eysenck, "The Effects of Psychotherapy: An Evaluation," *Journal of Consulting Psychology*, 16 (1952), pp, 319–324; Karl R. Schuessler and Donald R. Cressey, "Personality Characteristics of Criminals," *The American Journal of Sociology*, 55 (March, 1950), pp. 476–484; LaMay Adamson and H. Warren Dunham, "Clinical Treatment of Male Delinquents: A Case Study in Effort and Result," *American Sociological Review*, 21 (June, 1956), p. 320. Davidson goes so far as to suggest that the "psychiatric" approach does not work with delinquents. Henry A. Davidson, "The Semantics of Delinquency," *The Welfare Reporter*, New Jersey State Department of Institutes and Agencies, XI (July, 1960), p. 135.

[13]Hans-Lukas Tueber and Edwin Powers, "Evaluating Therapy in a Delinquency Prevention Program." *Psychiatric Treatment*, Baltimore: The Williams and Wilkins Co., XXXI (1953). p. 145.

[14]Gisela Konopka, "The Role of the Social Group Worker in the Psychiatric Setting," *American Journal of Orthopsychiatry*, 22 (1952), pp. 176–185; Rudolf Kaldeck, "Group Psychotherapy by Nurses and Attendants," *Diseases of the Nervous System*, 1950–1951, 12 (February, 1951), pp. 138–142; Margaret Hagan and Marion Kenworthy, "The Use of Psychodrama as A Training Device for Professional Group Workers in the Field of Human Relations," *Group Psychotherapy*, IV (April–August, 1951–1952), pp. 23–40; Henrietta T. Glatzer and Helen E. Durkin, "The Role of the Therapist in Group Relations Therapy," *The Nervous Child*, 4 (April, 1945), pp. 243–251; S. H. Foulkes and E. J. Anthony, *Group Psychotherapy: The Psycho-Analytic Approach*, Penguin Books (1957); Rudolph Ekstein and Robert S. Wallerstein, *The Teaching and Learning of Psychotherapy*, New York: Basic Books, Inc., 1958, *passim*; Robert G. Hinkley and Lydia Hermann, *Group Treatment in Psychotherapy: A Report of Experience*, Minneapolis: University of Minnesota Press (1951), *passim*. One recent exception is a publication by Henry L. Lennard and Arnold Bernstein, *The Anatomy of Psychotherapy*, New York: Columbia University Press, 1960, *passim*.

those obtained in the Cambridge-Sommerville Study will continue to occur.[15] In that project, statistical comparisons revealed that the number of offenses for the treatment group was greater than those for the control group, while counselors felt that therapy was effective with two-thirds of the treatment group. This discrepancy highlights the importance of having information on the treatment procedure (Stage II). Counselors in that study had the opportunity before they began treatment to define the "helping" role, to indicate their goals, and how they expected to achieve these goals. However, because they failed to do so, it is impossible to know what led to the results obtained: whether they were due to the theory of treatment utilized, the failure of counselors to fulfill roles derived from treatment theory, or to other variables. Thus, treatment, as the independent variable, cannot be taken for granted. It must be subjected to scrutiny.

Likewise, the way in which personality disorders might relate to criminality have not been empirically demonstrated.[16] Yet, treatment methods based upon the idea of their importance have flourished. Until it can be shown that there is a clear relationship between any transformed personality characteristic and a lower recidivism rate, the theory must be subject to question. At present we have neither the evidence to accept or reject it.

The Treatment Potpourri

Another treatment problem contributing to research difficulties lies in the extent to which correctional facilities, as part of their general treatment programs, include a great variety of treatment practices. Each of these practices might be viewed as a separate treatment technique and evaluated as such. Yet, the entire host of procedures is also often considered as a single entity for which evaluation is asked. For example, Gersten describes how interview group therapy, directive and nondirective therapy, handicrafts, films, and psycho-drama were employed in a single treatment program. Although the program was judged successful by several criteria, it is difficult, if not impossible, to tell which specific techniques of the program contributed to its success.[17]

Before legitimate examination can be made of any total treatment program, steps must be taken by which to assess the merits of specific treatment practices in the total picture. Obviously this is a difficult task, but there are at least two

[15]Tueber and Powers, "Evaluating Therapy in a Delinquency Prevention Program," *op, cit.*, pp. 138–146. See also Edwin Powers and Helen Witmer, *An Experiment in the Prevention of Delinquency: The Cambridge-Somerville Youth Study*, New York: Columbia University Press (1951).

[16]Schuessler and Cressey, *op. cit.*; see also Henry D. McKay, "Differential Association and Crime Prevention: Problems of Utilization," paper read at the annual meetings of the American Sociological Society, Chicago, September 2–5, 1959.

[17] Charles Gersten, "An Experimental Evaluation of Group Therapy for Juvenile Delinquents," *International Journal of Group Psychotherapy*, I (1951), pp. 18–33, pp. 318–331.

principles whose adoption might maximize a solution to the conundrum of relative effectiveness.

First, treatment personnel might pay greater attention to the need for establishing logical integration among the treatment techniques they utilized. The ideal would be to devise a treatment program around specific and logically integrated theories of causation and intervention. Only those techniques shown to have relevance would be included. A *potpourri* of unrelated activities could, and probably would, set up conflicting goals. For example, if one theorized that delinquency is primarily a peer group phenomenon, he might then want to test this theory by concentrating on techniques designed to change peer relationships. Attempts on his part to utilize individualized as well as group techniques, each of which is derivable from different intervention theories, could easily destroy his efforts to make a systematic evaluation of his causation and treatment theories.

The second principle would involve the integration into any program, means by which specific segments of that total program could be examined and evaluated with respect to their contribution to successful rehabilitation. Later evaluation of the total program as a single entity might then have greater meaning. The corollary, and ideal result, would be the development of a self-correcting system capable of discarding those techniques which are inadequate and promoting those which are of value.

Professional Canonization

Treatment personnel who have the practical problem of dealing daily with inmates cannot be expected, any more than the general medical practitioner, to create many new and revolutionary approaches to treatment. Nevertheless, the efforts of some schools of treatment to maintain their vested interests go beyond the necessity to train treatment personnel. Their efforts are dysfunctional for a scientific penology because they place an undue emphasis on the canonization of new inductees at the expense of determining the validity of their own treatment methods.

Current training procedures seldom emphasize skepticism and creativity as an approach to treatment, but instead concentrate upon the steps necessary for certification. Concern over the latent function of maintaining professional stature and prestige tends to outweigh the manifest need for improved treatment techniques. As a consequence, the treater role is circumscribed with a whole series of prerequisites which can be obtained only under the observation and supervision of those already canonized.[18]

It is difficult to take exception to the idea that treatment personnel should

---

[18]These prerequisites emphasize personality charactersitics as well as training. In some schools, personality requirements include: the therapist's ability to deal effectively with his own anxieties; to be comfortable with certain types of emotional behavior; (Morris B. Parloff, "Some Factors Affecting the Quality of Therapeutic Relationships," in *Group Psychotherapy*, ed.

be well trained. But all too often the techniques, and the process of learning them, become ends in themselves. The resulting effect on the trainee is to provide him with an efficient set of blinders—blinders which enable him to misperceive or ignore programs whose rehabilitative efforts do not include techniques consistent with the standards which he has been taught to accept.

The Anxiety of Evaluation

The canonization of treatment personnel, and the institutionalization of treatment techniques, introduce problems of evaluation which are unrelated to the tremendous methodological difficulties involved. Besides clinicians, administrators and board members concentrate more upon lending credence to already accepted methods than to an objective, unbiased appraisal of the techniques used. This approach again is analogous to the debater who seeks mainly for evidence to support his previously accepted proposition rather than to the scientist who refrains from making any conclusion until he examines both sides of a question. The debater presents only those data which support his viewpoint and discards the remainder. The scientist must draw his conclusion from the total mass of data.

Because many people are committed to *particular* treatment approaches, any objective evaluation is viewed with anxiety. As a result, the evidence presented in favor of a program by treaters is usually anecdotal in which striking examples of success are illustrated, but in which failures are rarely mentioned, or, if mentioned, are explained with a series of complex rationalizations. Thus, we may hear: "The technique is effective enough, but it is not designed for this particular individual (failure)," or, "This study doesn't really invalidate our approach. It just points up the need for a much longer experimental study," or, "Our program may be a statistical failure, but how can you judge a program by its failures! If one man was saved from a life of crime, then I consider it worthwhile."[19]

By hiding behind such rationalizations those responsible for treatment are seldom required to define their goals or to attempt to relate them systematically to their intervention techniques. Consequently, treatment may often pursue ends which may not be directly associated with lawbreaking, e.g.,

---

by William F. Hill, Utah State Hospital, Provo, 1961, pp. 179–187) and to have come from a background with a wide variety of personal experiences. (S. R. Slavson, "Qualifications in Training of Group Therapists," *Mental Hygiene*, XXXI (1947), pp. 386–391; Gisela Konopka, "Group Therapy; Knowledge and Skills of the Group Therapist," *American Journal of Ortho-Psychiatry*, XIX (1949), pp. 56–60.) Training includes observation, practiced application, supervision and often stresses individual therapy for the candidate. Aichhorn stressed the latter point in 1925. August Aichhorn *Wayward Youth*, New York: The Viking Press (1935), p. 9.

[19]Cressey, "The Nature and Effectiveness of Correctional Techniques," *op. cit.*

personality adjustment, educational achievements, or the learning of handicraft or athletic skills. Perhaps this is what occurred in the Cambridge-Sommerville Study when the treatment group seemed to benefit in ways unrelated to lawbreaking. The recidivism rates of offenders were not appreciably changed, but certain qualitative adjustment differences occurred.

If greater efforts were expended in the direction of carefully defining treatment goals and in attempting to show how they relate to lawbreaking, research might then be able to indicate: (1) whether important goals were actually realized; and (2) whether, if they were realized, they helped to lower the recidivism rate. But, again, a systematic articulation and examination of goals depends upon the extent to which treatment is a function of logically integrated causation and intervention strategy. A conglomeration of unrelated activities is functional in maintaining vested interests because there is something in it for everyone. But it also makes a careful definition of goals difficult and effective evaluation impossible.

DYSFUNCTIONS PERPETUATED BY THE RESEARCHER

Research personnel have also perpetuated dysfunctions with regard to effective treatment evaluation. The following are some of the more important ways in which they have done this.

The Emphasis on "Pure" Research

It has become traditional among many social scientists to question the scientific objectivity of any individual who becomes involved in an action program.[20] This tradition is not without some validity. William Grahams Sumner pointed out, early in the development of American sociology, the difficulty of discussing and criticizing any social system of which one is an intimate part.[21]

But this tradition is dysfunctional for scientific penology in at least three ways: (1) It does not take into account advancements in such fields as Anthropology, Psychology, and Sociology, which give the modern social scientist considerable insight into social-psychological mechanisms and the relativity of any approach to treatment, (2) It separates the researcher from

---

[20] See the discussion of Max Weber by Harry E. Barnes and Howard Becker, *Social Thought From Lore to Science*, New York; D. C. Heath & Co., 1938, II, pp. 896–898; and Donald R. Cressey, "Changing Criminals: The Application of the Theory of Differential Association," *The American Journal of Sociology*, 61 (July, 1955), p. 116, who says ". . . Sociology is essentially a research discipline . . ." For opinions to the contrary see Robert S. Lynd, *Knowledge For What*, Princeton University Press, 1939; and Edward A. Shils, "Social Inquiry and the Autonomy of the Individual," in *The Human Meaning of the Social Sciences*, ed. by Daniel Lerner, New York: Meridian Books, Inc., 1959.

[21] William G. Sumner, *Folkways*, Boston, 1907, pp. 97–98.

intimate contact with the subjects of his study, and, while he may have contributed to an understanding of the causes for delinquency, he is dependent upon the intuitive interpretations of the clinician for information regarding both the usefulness of his theory and its application in the treatment process, (3) It removes him from the process of planning and evaluating the early stages of any research project—that is, he is seldom involved in helping to integrate logically the intervention strategy with the theory of causation, with helping to define and examine the treatment role, and with defining treatment goals in such a way that they can be evaluated. Thus, he usually enters the picture late in the process in an attempt to evaluate a program that he knows relatively little about. His principal recourse is to make a statistical comparison of groups or to do post-mortem interviews with treaters and subjects. However, as suggested above, such techniques may be notoriously inadequate.[22]

In the absence of specific information about the treatment process, the researcher is incapable of determining the errors or strengths in the intervention strategy or errors or strengths in the way the strategy is applied. Consider the following example from the author's own experience.

An offender, two months after release from the Provo Experiment in Delinquency Rehabilitation,[23] burglarized a home with his younger brother and stole $380. Yet, at the time of his release there was little question in anyone's mind that this boy would be a success. The therapist in charge of the boy's daily therapy group, as a part of the research evaluation, predicted that the boy would be a success. Likewise, the interviewer who gave him his release interview was impressed with his acuity and perceptiveness. He was able to verbalize well about the treatment system: The stages of development through which his group had gone, the importance of his own ability to help other boys and be helped in return, the changes in his friendship and familial relationships, and his feelings about himself. After he had gotten into trouble, however, a careful look at the treatment process was in order. Fortunately, some data were available.

The following is one example of the types of information that were revealed. One of the basic assumptions for treatment in the program was never utilized as a part of the boy's treatment experience. This assumption involved anxiety and suggested that because most habitual delinquents are affectively and ideologicaly dedicated to the delinquent system, they must be made anxious about the ultimate utility of that system for them. Several things revealed, however, that this boy had never really been made uncomfortable in his entire stay in the program. It seemed likely that he had never been forced by a feeling

---

[22]See also Tueber, *op. cit.*, p. 141, who discusses the weaknesses of interviewing with delinquents.

[23]Lamar T. Empey and Jerome Rabow, "The Provo Experiment in Delinquency Rehabilitation," *American Sociological Review*, 26 (Oct., 1961), pp. 679–696.

of necessity to examine himself deeply or to evaluate realistically the implications of continued delinquent behavior. In summary, it appeared that the role of the therapist had not been adequately filled.

Such a finding does not, by itself, constitute a complete answer as to why the boy failed. It does suggest, however, at least two important things: (1) that so long as the therapist does not perform consistently with the theory of intervention, treatment technique designed to test that theory will not be adequately examined; and (2) that if the program had relied solely on the therapist's subjective interpretation or upon the researcher's statistical analysis this and other factors contributing to an understanding of the boy's failure would have remained undetected. An emphasis on "pure" research at the expense of an intimate surveillance of the treatment process leaves too many unanswerable questions.

Inadequate Knowledge of Treatment for Predictive Purposes

The greater portion of research in penology has concentrated upon "objective" variables—work reports, length of stay, job prospectus, etc.—as a means of measuring success or failure on parole. In terms of the ideological conflict between researcher and treater, this concentration is the counterpart of the treater's resistance to a rigorous evaluation of the treatment process *per se*. Although "objective" variables are important because of their impact on the offender, they can be seen, when viewed in terms of the theoretical scheme mentioned earlier, as variables which *impinge* upon treatment but are not always a function of it. Therefore, predictions based upon them do not include any information on, or evaluation of, the very variables—i.e., those which *are* a direct function of some treatment technique, which, according to the treater, are most important in changing people. Consequently, most predictions are based on a segment of variables which affect the offender, not upon a total configuration.[24]

Any prediction based upon the results of a particular treatment process can only follow a systematic articulation and understanding of that treatment process. But the researcher seems to have accepted the clinician's premise that therapy, like true art, consists of the "concealment of all of the signs and efforts of the art."[25]

Treatment, the clinician asserts, is an ongoing process: It is a dynamic and subjective experience for everyone involved. How, therefore, can it be systematically codified and articulated? Furthermore, the relationship between

---

[24]The importance of having descriptive information on particular types of populations has been cited recently by Paul Meehl and Edward Rosen. See "Antecedent Probability and the Efficiency of Psychometric Signs, Pattern or Cutting Scores," *Psychological Bulletin*, 1958, pp. 199–211.

[25]Merton, *op. cit.*, p. 14.

counselor and counselee is a subtle but indispensable variable which is of value in and of itself. These delicate but important variables, he maintains, cannot be evaluated except intuitively. Consequently, any predictions based upon them must likewise be intuitive.

Apparently, it has been functional for the researcher to accept this point of view. But, as a result, he and the clinician have ended up using two different frames of reference in evaluating treatment. The researcher uses statistical data and "objective" variables which are not always shown to have a clear connection with the treatment process. And the clinician has utilized subjective interpretations based upon his feelings for what has occurred in therapy. By contrast, there are research findings in the behavioral sciences which suggest that if treatment techniques, *per se*, were productively analyzed, predictions could be based on them *and* "objective" variables as well. The two would constitute a larger body of empirical data from which to make predictions. For example, in addition to controlling such "objective" variables as marital status, job outlook, length of stay, etc., the total treatment setting might be examined as a social system in which participants develop and are guided by a shared set of values, norms, status-roles, and sanctions; the types of treatment interaction thought most productive could be defined and the actual behavior during treatment sessions analyzed to see whether interaction conforms to these standards; or "stimulated recall"[26] might be conducted on subjects following treatment sessions as a means of understanding their reactions—whether, for example, they are actually experiencing treatment in the way the treater thinks they are experiencing it.

Many things might be done, but so long as the researcher prefers to examine variables traditionally defined as "objective," and leaves predictions based upon the treatment process to the subjective interpretations of the therapist, his behavior will be dysfunctional for the development of a scientific penology.

SUMMARY AND CONCLUSION

The foregoing analysis suggests that a successful bridging of the ideological gulf between researcher and treater might contribute significantly to the development of a scientific penology. It is recognized, of course, that efforts to eliminate this gulf in ongoing penal systems will not be simple. In those systems where punitive methods are still in practice, research poses as much a threat to those in control as it does to the clinician in treatment-centered systems. However, since the primary purpose of this paper has been to point out the dysfunctions which are perpetuated by the gulf, it would be hoped that future

[26]Eugene L. Gaier, "When They're Not Talking," *Adult Leadership*, I, No. 10 (March, 1953), pp. 28–29; Eugene L. Gaier, "Memory Under Conditions of Stimulated Recall," *The Journal of General Psychology*, 50 (1954), pp. 147–153; B. S. Bloom, "The Thought Process of Students in Discussion," in *Accent On Teaching*, ed. by Sidney J. Flinch, Harper and Bros., 1954, Chap. 1.

analyses could be devoted to defining, in detail, steps by which a new research-treatment role might be implemented in both types of systems.

A summary of that which has been emphasized in this paper would seem to include two important points:

Research Model

An effective analysis of any treatment system requires an integration of research and treatment efforts. At the very onset this would require a union of researcher and treater on theoretical matters. It would seem impossible to conduct effective evaluation unless the researcher participated intimately with the treater in defining goals in terms of a logical integration of causation theory, intervention strategy, and treatment roles. Therefore, cooperation between these two parties would permit the treater to enter into the problems associated with Stages I and III of the Research Model (the selection and comparison of treatment and control groups) and would permit entry of the researcher into problems associated with Stage II (the actual treatment process). The researcher could help to operationalize treatment techniques and goals, and the treater could illustrate some of the complexities of the treatment process.

Statistical findings on the success or failure of any program (Stage III) could best be understood if data were available by which to establish whether the causation theory or the actual treatment techniques used (Stage II) were responsible for any differences that were found, or whether one must look to other variables impinging upon treatment for explanations. Such differences could be due to variables which are not a direct function of treatment. If this is the case they must be discovered.

Communication and the Avoidance of Anxiety

The second point in bridging the gulf between treater and researcher has to do with the importance of maintaining treater-researcher communication and responsibility regarding research findings.

The goal would be two-fold: (1) to approach current techniques with a disciplined skepticism—that is, any treatment technique would be viewed as an hypothesis to be examined rather than a method based upon absolute knowledge; and (2) to give both parties a greater stake in the development of new knowledge about treatment techniques rather than in the perpetuation of traditional vested interests.

A new and shared vested interest, based upon a desire for new knowledge, would help to reduce anxiety on the treater's part over any results which discredit his technique. Instead of threatening him with economic and prestige problems as though his practices were of an all-or-none variety, he, along with the researcher, would be called upon to revise techniques or develop new ones.

This, of course, would not eliminate anxiety, only modify it. Now, however, both could be more concerned with the dimension of discovery; that is, with the problem of knowing what is really happening to inmates as a result of treatment practices rather than with the maintenance of power in the correctional structure. The latter type of anxiety could only be reduced by a scientific approach to the understanding and improvement of rehabilitative techniques.

The field of corrections is now at a stage where the humanitarian concern for the welfare of prisoners by professionals needs to be at least partially supplanted by a disciplined, scientific orientation. The alternatives open to society and those working with offenders are limited. What can be done with hard-core offenders except to: destroy them, incarcerate them permanently, or rehabilitate them? The tendency among most people has been toward the latter alternative. However, so long as the vested interests of research and treatment personnel continue to pursue divergent goals, it will be difficult to establish a scientific penology by which reliable answers can be discovered. On the other hand, the welding of research and treatment roles might constitute one step towards a comprehensive understanding of, and fruitful approach to, the problems involved.

The exclusive focus on the field of corrections in this paper is a function of the author's experience in that area. I suspect, however, that the problems described above occur in such diversified fields as education, social work, administration and governmental planning. The prerequisites of organizational maintenance seem to necessitate these conflicts and problems. The solution would seem to be not only to call for the development of closer, working relationships, but to institutionalize the training and organization of individuals who can work effectively within both organizational contexts.

46

The Requirements of Prediction

HERMANN MANNHEIM AND LESLIE T. WILKINS

Prediction tables seem to us to have four basic requirements, simplicity, efficiency, repeatability or reliability, and validity. We shall examine the implications of each.

SIMPLICITY IN OPERATION

The final prediction tables must be easy of application to any case, no matter how unique the situation envisaged. No technical skills other than ability to do simple multiplication, addition and subtraction should be required. This does not mean that the techniques used in obtaining the simple end result should also be simple. If the techniques of deriving a prediction table were to be such that all could understand each step, a severe restriction on efficiency would be imposed. But, if a complex system is used in deriving the simple end result, the methods must be capable of explanation in principle, so that every reader can follow the limitations of the essential mathematical concepts. Confidence in the results of the prediction tables should derive both from the argument and from demonstrations by example. The user must have confidence in the tool he is using and this confidence should not be built only on a blind faith in the integrity and competence of the compiler of the system.

SOURCE. *Prediction Methods in Relation to Borstal Training*. London: Her Majesty's Stationary Office, 1955, pp. 137–142. (Editorial adaptations.)

We shall attempt to fulfill our own precepts by giving the basic data in two forms, one by argument and the other by showing the mathematical model in some detail. We thus hope to convince those unfamiliar with the algebra and the geometric models of the reasonableness of the result. We shall reduce the end result to "rule of thumb" procedures.

Simplicity of procedure in this respect we have interpreted to mean the following restrictions. The tables must be applicable in a *general form* to any case. Instructions as to procedure and any tabular matter necessary must be reduced to one schedule, to occupy, say, only one sheet of quarto paper. No reference to external tables (other than this one sheet) nor memory of numerical facts must be required.[1]

Some data must, therefore, be "thrown away" because its use, even at the final stages of application would involve references which would be regarded by some users as complex. The chance of error in calculation must be reduced to a minimum and time taken to make the calculations should be very short.

We must also have regard to the quality and quantity of data likely to be available in the worst cases. Our dependence on the data must be conditioned by and be in terms of its reliability.

EFFICIENCY

Our second requirement is efficiency. The term efficiency as we use it here has a special technical meaning. In simple and not quite accurate terms, this means that the maximum use must be made of the information we have. This requirement, if taken fully into account, opposes our requirement of simplicity by reason of the type of data we are using.[2] We must therefore find a compromise and require the maximum use to be made of data which does not involve the introduction of complex final tables. The main loss of efficiency in previous criminological prediction has been due to the failure to identify and exclude those parts of factors which "overlapped" each other and thus contributed nothing to the prediction. All overlapping is inefficient, but inefficiency may be found in other methods than in those which involve overlap. We shall, for example, reach an apparently better but less efficient result if we extract too much information from too many factors. This is due to the fact that for each additional factor "degrees of freedom" are being used up. If we had, say twelve cases, and five or six factors each considered at two levels (yes or no, above or below average, etc.) we could in general specify or "predict" every case of these twelve accurately, but such prediction although

---

[1]This latter restriction is important in one technical point: it means that data may not be "transformed" (logarithm or sine transformations for example are ruled out), since such requirements would need reference to other tables and extra skills in using them. This is an unfortunate restriction when we consider the skewness, for example, of the distribution of the number of crimes committed by young offenders.

[2]With "skewed" distributions we shall not reach maximum efficiency without transformation.

appearing to be perfect would be wholly meaningless. This is due to the fact that we regard (for purposes of prediction) the sample of Borstal boys in 1946–1947 to be a sample in time as well as a sample of one in three in the year selected. Associated with each factor there is a chance variation, or more correctly, a sampling error or variance. If our number of factors and the levels at which we consider them becomes large in comparison with the number of cases we should be using too much of this chance or error variation in determining our prediction, and the equation although specifying the group on which it was based could not be expected to predict any other cases unless (which we know to be most improbable) the factors were invariant.

An *efficient* prediction table is thus one which achieves its purpose with the *smallest* number of factors which contribute significantly (i.e. above chance variations) to the specification. In this case efficiency and operational simplicity work in the same direction.

We have remarked elsewhere that in "500 Criminal Careers" the Gluecks obtained a prediction value indicated by their coefficients of contingency of 0.42 using one factor alone, whilst when they used six factors (including this one) the value of the prediction rose only to 0.45—a difference of 0.03 which was an insignificant gain. This was due to the use of inefficient statistical methods where the term "inefficient" is used in its technical sense as indicated above.

This does not mean that the Gluecks' system will not work—it does—but rather that a system could be devised which would (with their problems and their data) work better. Reiss has contributed a useful practical demonstration of the effect of using few and several factors by comparing the results obtained for many types of prediction equation. Reiss's contribution makes clear by practical evidence the correctness of the theory we have discussed.[3]

It is clear that most of the loss of information which the result in "500 Criminal Careers" indicates is due to overlapping of factors and to the consequent double-counting of some elements. The Gluecks later recognized this, but their remedy was to reject factors which overlapped rather than to identify the unique parts of each factor and to utilize this information to full efficiency. The individual contributions of each factor in this study were far lower than the individual contributions found in "500 Criminal Careers" (our

Table 1 *Pre-reformatory and Pre-Borstal Factors. Factors Arranged in Order of Individual Prediction Value*

	1	2	3	4	5	6	Total
500 Criminal careers	0.42	0.33	0.29	0.29	0.27	0.26	0.45
Current study	0.23	0.21	0.21	0.19	0.17	0.16	0.45

[3] Reiss's finding although derived laboriously by empirical methods could have been very shortly and precisely obtained by algebra.

highest coefficient of contingency was 0.23 whilst the Gluecks' "work habits" was by itself 0.42). But by combining in an efficient manner a small number of such factors we derive an overall prediction precision equal to that of "500 Criminal Careers". To illustrate the loss due to overlapping and inefficient statistical methods we might compare the individual contribution of each component factor to prediction and the combined score as found in "500 Criminal Careers" and in this study.

It will be seen that there was considerably less information in each component item in the present study, but that the system of building the equations leads to the addition of the effective parts of each relatively small contribution with the end result no worse than that achieved by other statistical systems where one component contained about four times the information.[4]

It may be asked why the amount of information in each component was lower in the current study than in the earlier similar work in the U.S.A. This question, although somewhat irrelevant to the argument, ought perhaps to be answered here. There are two main reasons. The most important is doubtless the fact that Borstal boys are very much more alike than the parolees of the earlier study. Borstal entrants are a highly selected group with respect to age, type of criminal career, past punishment record, physical standard and intellectual level. We were attempting to discriminate between lads who were very much alike—perhaps far more alike than those in the U.S.A. parolees study. The second reason may lie in the nature of the data. In the earlier study special questionnaire and other data were available whilst in the present study only administrative records were utilized.

REPEATABILITY OR "RELIABILITY"

The third requirement is that of repeatability. In some respects this requirement follows from our requirement of simplicity, in that the degree of simplicity specified as necessary in prediction barred any but elementary skills. No variation in the prediction derived should arise when computed by different persons of average intelligence nor should any different result occur when the computation is carried out by quite inexperienced personnel. Any special skills which derive from experience of dealing with offenders should be exercised independently of the prediction equations, and not be needed in deriving the basic data for use in the prediction. We have discussed the problem of subjective judgment and shown that even two highly experienced persons such as Governors and Housemasters of Borstal Institutions do not agree in their assessments of the chances of success of their cases. Such classes of judgment are not therefore repeatable. Where differences occur between subjective judgments it is safe only to use that portion of the judgment about which agreement can be secured and to regard the remainder as individual variation—

---

[4] Squares of these coefficients are rough indications of the amount of information.

or in statistical terms "error". The techniques we have used give only such weights to subjective judgments as can be estimated to be common ground for agreement.

VALIDITY

Fourthly we require the tables to be useful and valid. Exact prediction of the future behavior of any individual is impossible, but the system of prediction derived from experience tables has got to prove that it can carry out the task of differentiating the likely successes from the likely failures with reasonable validity. What level of validity should be regarded as reasonable constitutes a major problem. In vocational guidance and educational selection the future of an individual is at stake as much as in criminological prediction. In these former fields statistical prediction tables (under a different name but using precisely similar techniques as employed here) have been accepted for many years. This is perhaps due mainly to the fact that when groups of individuals to whom the test procedures have been applied were compared with those selected by any other procedure, there was on balance an advantage in the statistical methods. This gain over the subjective procedures was often slight, but it was considered sufficient to show that standardized tests (prediction tables) did on average a better job than the procedures normally used before their introduction. In vocational selection quite often the newer test procedures are linked with the older system of selection board and individual interview.

People seem, however, to be more inclined to accept the judgment of other people than to trust numerical procedures which appear abstract and impersonal. It seems that if this prejudice is to be overcome we require the experience table procedures to be *more accurate* than other systems of making assessments. It would apparently be insufficient to show that the two systems were equally good. The statistical procedures might be cheaper to operate, but they would not be so acceptable. The degree of precision or validity of criminological prediction is thus best judged by relative standards and not in absolute terms.

In this study it seems that the statistical procedures were at least three times as efficient as the subjective judgments of Governors of the Institutions, and more accurate than a psychologist's prognosis.

So far we have used the term "prediction" rather loosely, and now that the general concept is established we might perhaps be more precise and show how the criminological use of this term differs from others. It is noteworthy that Ohlin to whose work in this field we have referred earlier, prefers the term "experience tables" to "prediction tables". In any case it will be clear that "prediction tables" are in fact experience tables—there is no difference in their content but only in their use. Their use for prediction tacitly assumes that the experience of the past is a guide to the future. This, indeed is the basis also for subjective human judgment and we are more inclined to accept a judgment that is supported by extensive and intensive experience than one based on limited experience. The philosophy underlying the use of "experience" as "prediction" is thus commonly accepted. There is, however, one important difference which only very recent statistical theory is beginning to take into account. The experience of living persons changes with time and the Borstal and other criminal populations also change with time. Thus subjective judgments are based on dynamic experience, whilst the statistical model we have used in this study gives a static experience table. It becomes clear, therefore, that the experience tables, if they are to be valid as prediction tables will need revision. Good results will only be achieved whilst the experience on which they are based remains representative of the population to which they are applied. There are now available rigorous and highly efficient statistical methods for dealing with such dynamic situations, and a note will be given later showing how these might be applied in criminological prediction problems. In the meantime, let us attempt to assess how serious the effect of using a static model *without* revision is likely to be, if no major changes of policy cause a discrete break in the natural pattern of changes with time.

Since 1938 the proportion of "successes" after Borstal training has not been subject to wide variation. This does not suggest anything about the future likely proportion of successes. Nevertheless, let us suppose that in a future year the "failures" were to drop to 35 percent, this might be due to two things, (a) the proportion with undesirable characteristics had decreased (i.e. the equation would make allowance for the change), or (b) the success rate had risen for all or some groups of "risk". For example, at the time of this study we know that "Group A" had a 7:1 chance of success; in the future hypothesized case we might experience the higher overall success rate, (a) because the proportion of people with experience fitting them for "Group A" was larger and those whose experience resulted in their being classed as D was smaller, or (b) because the success rate for experience group A had itself increased. If the latter case were true the prediction based on experience tables (and most likely also that based subjectively on experience) would deteriorate, whilst in the former case no significant deterioration in the prediction from experience tables would result. Of course, such changes need not be independent, and both might occur together. Compensatory changes might also take place within the groups, so that a deterioration of prediction could take place without significant change in the overall success/failure rate.

In view of the fact that the experiences we found to be prognostic of success have, in general, been found by others over many years in many different countries, there seems to be good ground for expecting prediction based on these factors to hold for a period long enough to be administratively useful. It does not appear that much is lost because this study is based on static experience so long as the need for revision is always considered.

Strictly, then, our prediction tables do not predict—they tell us only what other factors help us to "specify" success or failure in this sample and what weight we should attach to each factor in order to maximize the efficiency of the specification. We cannot therefore state exactly the validity of the present system, but only the degree of its precision in specification.[5] We know, however, from other work that good specification provides good prediction, and the best prediction is obtained from the best specification.

[5] This remains true after a "validation study." A "validation" merely provides an estimate of the validity at other points in time. The validation study helps to suggest the *level* of confidence we may place in the prediction, but it is not a "proof" of the predictive value of the tables when applied to periods of time other than those used in the original study and the validation study.

47
Predicting Parole Behavior

LLOYD E. OHLIN

SELECTION OF PREDICTIVE FACTORS

In order to predict parole outcome we need reliable information which will help to separate the offenders with a high probability of success on parole from those with a high probability of failure. Some facts about parolees will point strongly in the direction of a successful outcome and others toward failure. The facts which reflect most clearly the actual influences at work in the parole situation will also provide the sharpest separation of the two outcome groups. The difficulty, however, is that we do not know exactly what the influences or causes of violation are.

In the physical sciences it has often proved possible to control the factors at work in a situation and to determine their effect in causing a given event. Through the accumulation of such knowledge, prediction has achieved a high degree of accuracy. In the social sciences, however, control of factors is very difficult to establish. The situation is usually a highly complex one in which the interaction of many uncontrolled factors operates to produce a particular event. This is the problem that confronts us in studying behavior on parole.

LAYING THE GROUNDWORK. For many years criminologists have sought to isolate the conditions and influences associated with criminal behavior. In the course of their study a fund of knowledge has been gained about the relations between personality, social and cultural experiences, and crime. These experiences are now regarded as responsible for the way in which the criminal, as contrasted with the conventional person, views himself, the social world, and his place and relation to that world. The prediction worker must seek objective measures of these special definitions of self and the social world

SOURCE. *Selection for Parole,* New York: Russell Sage Foundation, 1951, pp. 47–52, 53–67, 124–129. (Editorial adaptations.) Copyright 1951, Russell Sage Foundation.

held by the offender as a basis for prediction. The most useful prediction factors have generally been secured when the search has been closely guided by the theories and results of previous criminological research, which has featured the part played by early family experiences, contacts with delinquent associates, and repeated handling by correctional agencies.

It must be remembered, however, that parole prediction is concerned with a special kind of criminal activity, the violation of parole. Parolees are returned to prison not only for new acts of crime but also for technical violations of the parole agreements. In this connection the search for good predictive factors can profit greatly by making use of the observations and insights gained by parole agents in their routine contact with parolees. This knowledge relates directly to the special stresses and strains experienced by the parolee as he tries to make a satisfactory community adjustment. Thus in addition to selecting factors which reflect the theoretical and factual results of research on all types of criminal behavior, it is necessary to choose factors that relate to particular experiences in the parole situation.

The search for good predictive factors therefore must be continuous. As our theories of crime become more precise, as research knowledge accumulates, and as understanding of the influences at work in the parole situation increases, new factors may emerge which will improve the accuracy of predictions. The greatest increases in predictive accuracy will undoubtedly depend on securing better factors rather than on refining the techniques and methods of prediction work.

The Best Predictive Items

Once the factors have been chosen, a series of subclasses, or items, should be set up on each factor so as to give the best possible separation between parole successes and failures. Each of these subclasses should then be defined objectively in order to rule out bias and prejudice in classifying the cases. As an illustration let us take the factor *family interest*. Parole workers have often observed the controlling and supporting effect of close family ties. Theoretical and research results have emphasized the important role of the parolee's family in easing the transition between prison life and life in the outside community. Close family relationships help the parolee feel that he is wanted and that society accepts him. His adjustment is made easier because he finds a clearly defined place for himself and a conventional role to play. The effect is to direct his activity along conventional lines and to offset feelings of being rejected, different, or set apart—as though he, an ex-convict, were on one side of an impassable barrier and the conventional person on the other. These beneficial effects are greatest in instances where the family has maintained an active interest and given much-needed support and encouragement to the offender during his imprisonment.

The extent of family interest in the imprisoned offender has been found to be a good index of the effect of close family ties in the parole situation, and bears a significant relation to parole outcome. The prediction table now being used in Illinois breaks this factor down into five subclasses as follows: very active, active, sustained, passive, none. Parolees are classified according to objective criteria, namely, the number of letters and visits received in prison. For example, those classified as having *very active* family interest receive five or more letters each month from relatives, and each visit from the family is arbitrarily considered the equivalent of two letters. The classification *none* is given to offenders receiving no letters or visits from relatives. No restrictions are placed by prison officials on the number of letters received but visits are limited to one every two weeks except under special circumstances.

The next step in the selection of prediction items is to secure a violation rate for each of the subclasses, which is obtained by dividing the number of violators by the total number of persons in each subclass. Violation rates give the first clue as to the relative value of each item in separating the failures from the successes. In the current Illinois prediction table the subclasses of the factor *family interest* show the following range in violation rates:

	Percent
Very active	5
Active	24
Sustained	31
Passive	33
None	40

For the 4,941 parolees on whom this table was based, the violation rate was 28 percent. Persons classified as having a *very active* family interest violated less frequently than the group as a whole, while those classified in the category *none* violated more frequently.

By applying a series of tests the value of the subclasses as selection items can be more accurately determined. These tests involve the standard statistical measures of significance, association, reliability, and stability. The object of the tests is to make sure that the violation rate of the subclass is not just a chance variation from the average rate but that it shows a significant difference; that it varies sufficiently from the average violation rate to show a high association with parole outcome; that the classification of parolees into a subclass can be made repeatedly, and hence reliably, with only slight error; and that the favorable or unfavorable character of the subclass, as shown by the violation rate, remains consistently the same over several time periods, indicating marked stability. In applying these tests to the family interest factor it was discovered that the subclass *very active* could be confidently accepted as a favorable item and *none* as an unfavorable item. The other three subclasses, *active, sustained*, and *passive*, did not meet these tests and therefore did not distinguish between parole successes and failures well enough to be counted in the final scoring procedure.

All the factors on which data are gathered must be treated in the same manner. The final result yields a set of favorable and unfavorable subclasses of factors which can be used to classify the probable successes and failures on parole. The statistical tests and measures permit the use of the subclasses which are most significantly, reliably, and consistently related to outcome of parole and thereby ensure the maximum possible degree of confidence in the final predictions or selections.

Information covering 27 factors has been secured on parolees from the Joliet-Stateville and Menard Divisions of the Illinois State Penitentiary System back to 1925.

Of the 27 factors 12 have been retained for use in the current Illinois prediction table. These 12 factors and the subclasses for each are listed in Table 1. In the remaining 15 factors there were no subclasses or items which

Table 1 *Rating of Prediction Items, Joliet-Stateville and Menard Divisions, Illinois State Penitentiary System*[a]

	Rating of Items		
Prediction factors and Items	Favor- able	Neu- tral	Un- favor- able
1. *Type of Offense*			
Homicide and assault	1		
Robbery		0	
Burglary			x
Larceny and stolen property		0	
Forgery and fraud		0	
Sex offenses	1		
Miscellaneous		0	

[a]The definitions for the subcategories of each of the 12 factors are as follows:

I. TYPE OF OFFENSE

Enter the official charge for which the offender is committed. When the offender has been committed on more than one offense, enter all the offenses but score the case only on that offense which is regarded as the most serious. Generally that offense will be considered the most serious which carries the longest statutory limit as a maximum. If two different offenses carry the same statutory maximum, the one that appears to indicate the most advanced type of criminal behavior should be selected for scoring.

II. SENTENCE

Enter the sentence given the offender and in parentheses the number of concurrent or consecutive indictments for which he was committed. In the event of multiple offenses and sentences, score that sentence which corresponds to the offense scored on the first factor.

III. TYPE OF OFFENDER

1. *First:* An offender who has no more serious record than arrests or fines for misdemeanors.
2. *Technical first:* An offender who has had no convictions for felonies, but may have been committed to jail, detention home, state farm, probation, workhouse, or supervision for misdemeanors.
3. *Occasional:* A person who has no more than one previous conviction for a felony, or who has been repeatedly convicted for misdemeanors.
4. *Juvenile recidivist:* A youthful offender who has had more than one period under supervision, probation, or commitment to juvenile institutions for a felonious offense.

5. *Recidivist:* An offender who has had more than one previous conviction for a felony, except where the classification *habitual* applies.

6. *Habitual:* An offender who has been repeatedly convicted for felonies.

It is to be understood that this classification applies at the time of the parole under consideration and refers to offenses prior to the present offense, with the following exception. If a man serves time for a new crime committed while on his first parole and is thereafter returned as a parole violator, include conviction for the intervening offense when classifying him at the time of his second parole, even though he is being paroled on his original offense.

IV. HOME STATUS

The classifications on this factor pertain to the dominant character of the offender's early home life.

1. *Superior home:* A home in which there was no serious economic problem, no apparent domestic discord; and there was some evidence of religious and moral training. The parents in such cases will have been conventional, law-abiding persons, frequently active in church, social, or civic affairs.

2. *Average home:* This is a residual category between superior and inferior. It may also be used in the case where one parent dies and the remaining parent remarries, creating thereby a home unmarred by family discord or poverty but one which is not superior in character.

3. *Inferior home:* A home in which there was a pattern of poverty, family strife, abuse of the children, drunkenness, delinquency, etc.

4. *Broken home:* A home disrupted by separation, desertion, divorce, or death of a parent prior to the offender's sixteenth year. This classification also applies if it appears that the offender left home before sixteen years of age because it was a broken home, or the parents remarried and the remarriage was unhappy.

5. *Left home:* This category should be used where the offender left home of his own accord prior to sixteen years of age, unless the broken home classification applies.

6. *Institution:* This category should be used where the offender was placed in an institution, such as an orphanage, and institutional treatment represented an important part of his early life as compared to home contacts.

V. FAMILY INTEREST

1. *Very active:* Inmate receives five or more letters a month from relatives.

2. *Active:* Inmate receives two to five letters a month from relatives.

3. *Sustained:* Inmate receives fewer than two letters a month, but more than one every three months.

4. *Passive:* Inmate receives letters only at rare intervals.

5. *None:* Inmate receives no letters from relatives.

The number of visits is also taken into consideration in the above classifications. One visit is arbitrarily set as the equivalent of two letters.

VI. SOCIAL TYPE

The classification should reflect the way in which the offender was, or would be, regarded by conventional society.

1. *Erring citizen:* An older man who has apparently been entrusted with responsibility; a substantial and reliable citizen, but one who erred on this occasion.

2. *Marginally delinquent:* A borderline classification between an erring citizen and a socially inadequate person.

3. *Socially inadequate:* An offender who has failed to establish a place for himself in conventional society, by virtue of mental deficiency, irresponsibility, or an unstable personality. He does not exhibit steadiness in his work history or responsibility in his family relationships.

4. *"Farmer":* A rural-type person who generally leads a normal social life but becomes easily involved in situations that lead to trouble.

5. *Ne'er-do-well:* An irresponsible person who seldom seeks work, lives by the easiest way possible, and is considered to have a bad reputation in the community as a thief, gambler, drunkard, etc.
6. *Floater:* A man who drifts about the country, rides freights, lives in jungles, gets tagged for vagrancy, and frequently commits minor crimes en route.
7. *Socially maladjusted:* A person who cannot adjust himself to conventional society by virtue of strong criminal orientation or serious personality disturbances.
8. *Drunkard:* An offender who continually loses his job because of drinking, frequents saloons constantly, and works only to keep drinking. Generally he has a reputation for being an alcoholic and his crime is related to his drinking.
9. *Drug addict:* A person who has acquired the habit of using narcotics and whose crimes are generally related to this habit.
10. *Sex deviant:* A man who engages in recognized deviant sex behavior as a common practice.

VII. WORK RECORD

This classification is a combination of (1) the proportion of a man's working life that he has been employed, and (2) the frequency with which he has changed jobs. "Working life" is here used to indicate the period of a man's life that he has been free to work; in most cases this will be the portion of his life since he finished his schooling.
1. *Regular:* A person who has worked steadily all of his working life at one or only a few jobs.
2. *Irregular:* A man who does not hold a job for any length of time, but shows fairly continuous employment. He must have held a job for one year or more in a working life of five years or more, or for six months or more in a working life of less than five years.
3. *Casual:* A man who cannot hold a job for more than a few months at a time, and who is generally discharged or quits because of his indifferent attitude toward work in general.
4. *None:* A person who has never worked at a legitimate pursuit.
5. *Student:* A person whose previous work history consists principally of school attendance, except for summer or after-school work.

VIII. COMMUNITY

This factor refers to the type of community in which the offender resided prior to the offense.
1. *Urban:* The offender resided in a city or town of more than 2,500 population.
2. *Rural:* The offender lived on a farm or in the open country.
3. *Transient:* The offender had no established residence and had been continually on the move.
4. *Armed service:* The offender resided in an Army camp or other armed service installation.
5. *Institution:* The offender resided in an institution.

IX. PAROLE JOB

This factor should be classified on the basis of the offender's knowledge of his parole job possibilities at the time of the sociologist's interview, prior to the parole board hearing. The following definitions will serve as a guide:
1. *Adequate:* The offender has made definite contacts for a favorable job consistent with his previous work history, intelligence, and social type.
2. *Inadequate:* The offender has made only tentative parole job contacts, or has made arrangements for a job of an unfavorable nature inconsistent with his previous work history, intelligence, and social type.
3. *None:* The offender has made no contacts for a particular job.

X. NUMBER OF ASSOCIATES

Enter on this factor the number of persons associated with the offender on the offense for which he is serving time. Where there are several different charges, enter the largest number of associates indicated.

XI. PERSONALITY RATING

The classifications on this factor are based on the report of the mental health office of the institution. The classifications given should be scored according to the following categories, whichever is most appropriate:

1. *Normal* (no gross defects)
2. *Inadequate*
3. *Unstable*
4. *Egocentric*
5. *Some gross defect or serious personality deviation*
6. *No record*

XII. PSYCHIATRIC PROGNOSIS

Record the classification on this factor as provided by the mental health office of the institution. Where no information is available, use the classification *no record*.

[1]The subclass *sex deviant* contained too few cases to permit a reliable violation rate to be calculated.

Table 1 (*continued*)

Prediction factors and Items	Rating of Items		
	Favor- able	Neu- tral	Un- favor- able
2. *Sentence*			
All definite sentences	1		
All other sentences		0	
3. *Type of offender*			
First	1		
Technical first		0	
Occasional		0	
Juvenile recidivist		0	
Recidivist			x
Habitual			x
4. *Home status*			
Superior	1		
Average		0	
Inferior		0	
Broken		0	
Institution		0	
Left home		0	
5. *Family interest*			
Very active	1		
Active		0	
Sustained		0	
Passive		0	
None			x
6. *Social type*			
Erring citizen	1		
Marginally delinquent	1		

Prediction factors and Items	Rating of Items		
	Favorable	Neutral	Unfavorable
"Farmer"	1		
Socially inadequate	1		
Ne'er-do-well		0	
Floater			x
Socially maladjusted			x
Drunkard			x
Drug addict			x
Sex deviant		0	
7. *Work record*			
Regular	1		
Irregular		0	
Casual		0	
Student		0	
None		0	
8. *Community*			
Urban		0	
Rural		0	
Transient			x
9. *Parole job*			x
Adequate		0	
Inadequate			x
None		0	
10. *Number of associates*			
None		()	
One or two		0	
Three and over	1		
11. *Personality*			
Normal (no gross defects)	1		
Inadequate		0	
Unstable		0	
Egocentric		0	
Gross personality defects		0	
No record		0	
12. *Psychiatric prognosis*			
Favorable	1		
Problematic		0	
Doubtful		0	
Guarded		0	
Unfavorable		0	
No record		0	

met the rather statistical tests used as a basis for retaining a factor. Each subclass in Table I has been marked with *1, 0,* or *x* to indicate whether it was rated as a favorable, neutral, or unfavorable predictive item. A subclass was considered neutral if it failed to measure up to the statistical standards necessary for making effective distinctions between parole successes and failures.

It can be seen from this table that the factor *social type* proved to be one of the most useful factors for prediction purposes. Eight of its ten subclasses met the statistical tests well enough to be counted in the final scoring procedure. The subclass *ne'er-do-well* failed to meet these tests, and *sex deviant* included too few cases to permit any confidence in the results. When a sample of cases on this factor was restudied a year after the first classification, there was 83 percent agreement between the two classifications. This percentage of agreement was the lowest for any of the 12 factors and reflects the presence of a subjective element in the judgment of the investigator. Notwithstanding this fact, the percentage of agreement was quite high, and the marked ability of the subclasses to make distinctions between successes and failures offset the tendency to unreliability.

In general, this factor is designed to reflect the way the offender was, or would be, regarded by conventional society. It is assumed that people guide their actions in large part by the conceptions they have of themselves. These conceptions, in turn, reflect how they are regarded and treated by others. Consequently the way an offender is regarded by conventional society will have both a direct and an indirect effect on the course which his behavior is likely to take. The following violation rates for the subclasses[1] of the factor *social type* give support to this observation:

	Percent
Erring citizen	0
Marginally delinquent	3
"Farmer"	13
Socially inadequate	18
Ne'er-do-well	34
Floater	39
Socially maladjusted	41
Drunkard	44
Drug addict	48

The highest violation rate found among the subclasses of the 12 factors was for the item *inadequate* under the factor *parole job*. The violation rate for those persons classified as having an inadequate parole job prospect was 65 percent. Parolees are so classified if at the time of the pre-parole interview it was apparent that they had only a very vague notion of parole job possibilities, or if they had made arrangements for a parole job that was inconsistent with their previous work history, ability, and social type. Although considerable subjectivity in judgment also entered into this classification, there was 90 percent agreement between the first and second attempts to classify a sample of cases on this factor.

The Illinois experience in choosing factors on which to gather information, in defining subclasses, in classifying cases with regard to these subclasses, and in selecting the best predictive items offers some interesting results. The factors and subclasses which most clearly reflect the theoretical insights derived from research and practice furnish the best items. It is preferable to base the final prediction table only on those subclasses whose violation rates vary markedly from the average violation rate in either a favorable or an unfavorable direction, provided they also meet strict statistical standards of inclusion. Subclassifications of a factor involving some judgment on the part of the interviewer or investigator often furnish excellent predictive items, provided they are theoretically oriented to important influences in the parole situation and the basis of the judgment is fairly clearly defined.

The careful selection of predictive items is the most important step in creating a prediction table. The value of such a table for parole selection varies directly with the ability of the prediction worker to secure factors which reflect the important differences in the life experiences of parole failures as opposed to parole successes. It would be possible to predict parole outcomes perfectly if a factor could be found in which all the failures on parole fell into one subclass and all the successes on parole fell into still another. However, since human behavior does not permit accurate classification in such simple terms, it is unlikely that such a "magic key" to prediction will be found. The best that we can do is to seek those factors which separate the failures from the successes most clearly, and use the combined knowledge gained thereby as a basis for prediction.

THE EXPERIENCE TABLE

After the relevant predictive items have been selected in the manner described in the preceding chapter, creating a table of experience from which predictions can be made is the final step. The term *experience table* is more accurate than *prediction table*, which is commonly used, since the table is simply a device for summing up the experience acquired with past parole failures and successes. It can be used to predict probable success or failure on parole and the specific rates of violation for certain groups of parole applicants. It can also provide additional knowledge of value to a parole authority in the selection process.

SCORING METHODS. In the course of the prediction research carried on in Illinois, a great deal of experimentation was conducted with different methods of scoring in order to combine the information provided by the various factors. It was discovered that when only the subclasses of each factor which vary most from the average violation rate are counted, highly complicated scoring and weighting procedures add little to the value of the final table. In fact, a simple combination of widely deviant favorable and unfavorable items gives more useful and stable results than can be secured by complicated weighting systems. With the types of factors currently available for use in prediction work, the simple subtraction of the unfavorable from the favorable items in each case offers good results.

As shown in Table 1 the method of item selection now used in Illinois divides the subclasses of each factor into three groups: favorable, unfavorable, and neutral. The basis of this grouping, it will be recalled, is the degree to which the subclasses meet the statistical tests of a good predictive item, and whether the violation rate of the subclass is above or below the average violation rate. The method of scoring follows quite naturally from this grouping of subclasses. Each case is scored separately. Each parolee is given one favorable point for every favorable subclass in which he falls, one unfavorable point for every unfavorable subclass, and zero for every neutral subclass. A final score is obtained by subtracting the number of unfavorable points from the number of favorable points. For example, a parolee might fall in a favorable subclass on two of the 12 factors, in an unfavorable subclass on six of the factors, and in a neutral subclass on the remaining four factors. By subtracting unfavorable from favorable points, the final score would be -4, indicating that the parolee fell in four more unfavorable subclasses than he did in favorable ones. The neutral subclasses just drop out of the scoring picture since they have no predictive value.

Computing the Experience Table

The experience table can be constructed after all the cases have been scored. One column lists the score groups and three columns list percentages, as illustrated by the current Illinois experience table shown in Table 2. The second column gives the violation rate for each score group, and is computed by dividing the number of violators by the total number of persons in the group. These violation rates give the percentage of persons who have violated parole within each score group and serve to indicate the violation rate that can be expected for similar score groups in the future. Only 3 percent of the persons having from 5 to 10 *favorable* points violated parole, while 75 percent having 5 and 6 *unfavorable* points were violators. This represents a range in violation rates of 72 percent from the most favorable score group to the most unfavorable.

These violation rates are often referred to as *expectancy* rates because they are used to anticipate the violation rates for future groups of parolees making like scores. Similarly, the score groups are often called *risk* groups since the violation rates associated with each group indicate the risk of violation incurred in paroling from the different score groups.

The third column represents the percentage of minor violators in each

Table 2   *Experience Table for 4,941 Parolees, Joliet-Stateville and Menard Divisions, Illinois State Penitentiary System, Paroled 1940–1945*

Score Group	Violation Rates Violators per 100 Cases in Each Score Group		
	Total Violators	Minor Violators	Major Violators
5 to 10	3	2	1
4	7	5	2
3	10	7	3
2	18	10	8
1	19	10	9
0	29	16	13
−1	40	25	15
−2	46	27	19
−3 and −4	56	34	22
−5 and −6	75	62	13

score group. The term *minor violators* refers to the parolees for whom a warrant was issued because they seriously violated the rules and regulations of parole supervision contained in the parole agreement, or they persistently flaunted the conditions set up to control their conduct.

The fourth column lists the percentage of persons in each score group who committed major violations. The term *major violators* applies to cases in which a warrant was issued because the parolee committed a new crime.

The rates for minor violators in Table 2 are higher than the rates for major violators in each of the score groups, but this has not generally been the case. In experience tables constructed in Illinois for cases paroled in the 1920's and early 1930's, the rates for major violators were higher than the rates for minor violators in the unfavorable score groups. The consistently higher rates of minor violations, as opposed to major violations, in recent years reflect a tendency on the part of the parole authorities to be more concerned about serious or repeated infractions of the parole agreements as such. This may represent an increasing awareness that persistent violation of the parole rules is closely associated with a decreasing interest on the part of the parolee in making a conventional adjustment. It accompanies a return to criminal activity in some cases, and in others a gradual drift in that direction. To the extent that the parole authorities continue to recognize repeated breaking of the parole rules as a danger signal, the rates of minor violation will continue to exceed the rates for major violation in all the score groups. In fact, the relation between these two types of rates may be used as an index of increasingly close parole supervision. Where the rates of minor violation are considerably higher than the rates of major violation in the most unfavorable score groups, the conclusion may safely be drawn that close supervisory attention is being given to those parolees who need it most. Thus the rates of minor and major violation can provide the parole board with an estimate of the degree of reliance which can be placed on parole supervision to prevent further criminal acts among different groups of offenders.

It is often difficult to present a clear picture of the total effect resulting from a series of statistical operations. In parole prediction work the various steps taken to prepare an experience table involve the use of statistics to select the best predictive items, to score cases, and to compute the experience table. A brief review of these techniques in nonstatistical terms may serve to give a clearer understanding of the final result.

In preparing an experience table the prediction worker starts first with a sample of paroled cases. In each instance the outcome of parole is known and background information should be available. Hence each case may be classified on a number of different factors which are regarded as being related to the outcome of parole. In the second step, by a series of statistical tests, those subclasses of the various factors which are most closely related to success and failure on parole are selected. In the third step the number of unfavorable subclasses in which a case falls is subtracted from the number of favorable subclasses and a score is assigned to each case. The score indicates whether the case had more or fewer favorable than unfavorable factors, or an equal number of each. In the fourth and final step all the men with the same score are recognized as belonging to the same score group and a violation rate is obtained for each group showing the percentage of persons who violated parole. This violation rate can then be used to indicate the expected rate of violation among future parolees who may obtain a like score.

In the Illinois study we started with a large group of 4,941 paroled cases for whom the violation rate was 28 percent. In the final experience table we had broken this large group up into ten smaller groups with violation rates ranging from 3 to 75 percent. The effect of using favorable subclasses, closely related to success on parole, was to pull those cases most likely to succeed out of the total group, and classify them into smaller groups, where the low violation rates of these cases would show up. Similarly, by using unfavorable subclasses closely related to failure on parole, we were able to classify these potential failures into smaller groups, in which their high violation rate would be apparent. Some cases fell into favorable subclasses on certain factors and unfavorable subclasses on others. In order to give a single score to those cases, it was necessary to subtract the favorable and unfavorable score points in each instance. Sometimes the favorable and unfavorable points tended to cancel each other. However, since we were counting only the extreme subclasses highly related either to success or failure, it was unlikely that a parolee would fall in a very favorable subclass on one factor and in a very unfavorable subclass on another.

The nature of the experience table becomes more understandable if we regard it as a set of scores which concentrate as many of the potential successes as possible among the favorable score groups and as many as possible of the potential failures among the unfavorable score groups. The resulting distribution of scores and violation rates gives a clearer picture than one can get otherwise of the probable adjustment of parole applicants on parole.

Routine Adjustment of the Experience Table

It is becoming increasingly clear that routine readjustment of an experience table is required if the table is to retain its usefulness. The experience table reflects the parole conditions which existed for a sample of parolees in a certain period. However, as time goes on changes occur in the extent of pre-release preparation in the institution, in the policies practiced by the parole board, and in the efficiency and helpfulness of parole supervision. Widespread changes also occur in the parole situation in the community, as dramatically revealed by the effects of war and economic depressions on the employment possibilities for parolees. Since these changes lead to altered problems and experiences for parolees, the rates and types of violation expected on the basis of past parole conditions no longer apply. Some method is obviously required to keep the experience table abreast of such changes.

In Illinois the tendency has been to deal with this problem by making new studies and computing new tables. The experience table shown as Table II, for example, was recently put into use. It is based only on cases paroled from 1940 to 1945. The 4,941 cases used for the computation were regarded as a large enough sample to give reliable violation rates and at the same time to keep the parole experience as close as possible to current parole conditions. The average Illinois parole period is three years, though many parolees continue on parole up to five years. In order to allow sufficient time for all the paroled cases to terminate their parole, paroles after December 31, 1944 were not included in the table. Well over half of the cases were still on parole during the post-war period.

The research study which produced this table, however, involved considerable experimentation with different prediction methods. Information on 17,097 cases, paroled over a twenty-year period from 1925 to 1945, was placed on punched cards for tabulating purposes. Different methods of factor selection, scoring, and computing of experience tables were tried out. In each instance the tables were tested on cases paroled in a later time period in order to observe how well the results would stand up.

A very important result of this research has been the observation of a steady decline in average parole violation rates over the years studied. The rates have varied from a high of 57 percent in 1926 to a low of 26 percent in 1943. Quite obviously this steady decline in rates has a critical effect on the rates of violation which are predicted. For example, the average violation rates during the period from 1925 through 1935 was 44 percent, while the average violation rate for the period 1936 through 1944 dropped to 29 percent.

Predictions based on the experience acquired in the earlier period would over-estimate the violation rates in the later period. Of importance, however, is the fact that the total decrease in the over-all violation rate from the first to the second period was spread quite uniformly over the different score groups. In other words, nearly all the probabilities upon which the predictions are based decreased in like proportion.

In the course of this analysis a method was developed for routinely adjusting the experience table on an annual basis. This method makes it possible to keep the experience table adjusted with only a lag of one year behind the cases currently being paroled. Tables corrected in this fashion reflect more accurately than the kind of tables generally used any changes which might occur in the conditions of parole. The violation rates of such tables correspond more closely to the violation rates actually incurred by parolees. They also permit the parole board to be more quickly informed of the effect of its parole decisions.

The basis for this method of routine adjustment of experience tables lies in using the number of violations occurring in the first year of the parole period to estimate the number of violations that will occur throughout the total parole period. Several trials of this method disclosed that the total-parole-period violation rates for the various score groups could be estimated with an average error of only 2 percent. Chance alone could easily account for the small difference between the estimated and the actual violation rates. An average error of only 2 percent in the violation rates of the experience table is of little importance as compared with the increased confidence the parole board can place in the readjusted rates, since these rates reflect a more accurate picture of the situation which currently paroled cases face on their release. A system for regularly recording information about paroled cases on punched cards is now being instituted in Illinois, with a view to making an annual readjustment of the Illinois experience table in accordance with the methods described above.

A Master Experience Table

There is a growing interest in a number of states in the kind of information which experience tables provide as an aid to parole selection. Some considera-tion, therefore, should be given to the possibility of adapting the Illinois parole prediction methods and results for use in other jurisdictions. The desirability of having a master experience table which would be generally applicable in a large number of states is apparent. It does not appear, however, that such a table can be composed at the present time.

The possibility of such a master experience table was given extended and careful consideration in the course of research for *The Attorney General's Survey of Release Procedures*. The survey revealed much variation among the different states in the composition of the prison populations, the extent of preparation of the offenders for release, the amount of information available on each parolee, the policies of parole selection and supervision, the length of the parole periods, the methods of calculating violation rates, and the general conditions faced by the paroled offender in the community. In view of these differences the survey concluded that no general experience table could be composed which would be applicable in all states.

It is interesting to note, however, that a comparison of the results obtained in Illinois with the results of the Attorney General's survey showed a close correspondence in the relation of the various factors to outcome of parole for those states where the necessary information was available. This suggests that the Illinois prediction items and experience table may be directly applicable in those few states which are quite similar to Illinois in regard to the conditions listed above. The Illinois table might be accepted as a first approximation, and gradually adapted to local conditions by methods of routine readjustment as paroled cases accumulate. However, this approach, in setting up a prediction system, is not strongly recommended since there is no way of knowing in advance just how closely the Illinois results will correspond to the parole results in other states, and to what extent the established violation rates will actually reflect local conditions.

A more acceptable approach to setting up a prediction system, which would make maximum use of the items, techniques, and procedures developed in Illinois and afford reliable results, would involve an initial study of paroled cases in order to secure local violation rates for the various prediction items and score groups. This could be done without great difficulty by using the parole board records of previously paroled cases. Information could be gathered on factors which reflected special features of the local parole conditions, in addition to the prediction factors now used in Illinois. Its methods of item selection, scoring, and computing of the experience table could then be applied directly to these data. Its methods of routine application and readjustment could be used to build up the sample of paroled cases and to keep the table constantly adjusted to changes in the conditions of parole. Information on new factors could be gathered regularly during the course of pre-parole interviews and added to the current prediction factors as they proved their value for prediction and selection. An experience table so prepared could be relied upon to reflect the actual parole conditions and the reactions of different types of paroled offenders to these conditions.

It is quite likely that the parole board records in some states will not contain sufficient information of predictive value. The alternative, in such a situation, would be to obtain the necessary information through interviews with offenders who are granted a parole until enough data have been secured. It is estimated that the predictive items and methods used in Illinois would require at least 1,000 cases to give reasonably reliable results. In states where the annual number of paroles is small the problem is somewhat complicated, since time would have to be allowed for the sample of cases to accumulate and for the outcome of the paroles to become determined. Once the basic data have been completely gathered, however, the remainder of the task could be accomplished quite rapidly in accordance with the procedures described.

48

New Prediction and Classification Methods in Criminology*

LESLIE T. WILKINS AND P. MACNAUGHTON-SMITH

This paper describes and gives examples of the application of some recently developed analytical techniques to criminological data. It is thought that in some circumstances these techniques will prove to be more powerful and more soundly based than those used previously. The emphasis is on basic principles and on applications rather than on technical methods for which the reader is referred to original sources.

Prediction studies aim to relate the probability of some future event to information already known. Without defining our terms too closely, we can in criminology divide this given information into two classes; input information (e.g. past history, psychological and sociological characteristics) and treatment information (relating to disposal, sentence, therapy, etc.). In any one study, either or both of these types of information may be considered in relation to some particular outcome. The accuracy of the probability-estimates obtained for this outcome will then depend on the amount of relevant information available, and on the ability of the mathematical techniques to express the relationship between the relevant information and the outcome

*The views expressed in the paper are the personal ones of the authors and do not necessarily coincide with those of the Home Office.

SOURCE. *The Journal of Research in Crime and Delinquency,* **1**, January 1964, pp. 19–32. Reprinted with the permission of the National Council on Crime and Delinquency. Copyright 1964, National Council on Crime and Delinquency.

probabilities (and to exclude irrelevant information). It will also depend on how far the knowledge of the outcomes for a sample can validly be used to predict for a larger and less defined population.

Both of the techniques described in this paper result in the division of the sample of individuals into groups, each with its own outcome-probability or prediction equation. Thus the methods may in some circumstances be found more appropriate than multiple regression equations which assume a homogenous population. The resulting divisions into groups may sometimes have interesting implications in typological research. A further point of interest is that as the groups are relatively homogenous, within-group measures of treatment-outcome interactions may be possible. However, these last two points await further development, and in the present paper we restrict ourselves almost entirely to the question of prediction equations.

With any prediction method, if the amount of relevant information known for all members of the group is unduly restricted, the estimation will lack power, since really distinct individuals will be lumped together if the information which should distinguish them is lacking. This is very often the case, especially in studies such as the present one, when offenders sent to different types of treatment are being considered. For such people, different sets of information are normally collected.

In the particular research reported in this paper the new methods of analysis were applied to two groups, one consisting of young prisoners and the other of borstal trainees. Apart from their subsequent convictions only 13 items of information could be found common to both groups. This analysis is therefore not expected to be very powerful, and its interest is in development of techniques, not in results obtained. It is known that some items of information available in respect of only one of the two samples would have been very valuable if they had been available for both. It is emphasized that because of the limited information-set considered, none of the results may be regarded as proving or disproving any particular point, other than of a methodological nature.

TECHNIQUES IN COMMON USE AND THEIR LIMITATIONS

Before the present study is discussed, the background to the new methods and their relationship to methods of prediction used in earlier studies must be considered in some detail.

The problem of using available information to estimate future outcome has been approached in many ways. The earliest analytical methods used in setting up prediction tables are now generally agreed to be intolerably crude and inadequate. Such early methods examined only the direct relationship between each item of information and the outcome (zero-order correlations) and based predictions tables on rough measures of these relationships. Burgess, for example (2) merely added or subtracted one point of score for any item of information found to be positively or negatively correlated with outcome. E. and S. Glueck (3) gave a weight proportional to the percentage success in a constrained sample to items significantly associated with outcome. These methods have been discredited by many writers and are only mentioned for their historical importance.

Even when the need is accepted for some method soundly based on probability theory, and therefore making use of more than zero-order correlations, several approaches remain. Every method of analysis implies some structural relationship between information and outcome, or in mathematical language, different models imply different sets of assumptions. Ordinary multiple regression, for example, is in some fields in very common use, so much so that the underlying assumptions are often ignored or forgotten; but in fact it assumes among other things that the predictive factors are additive and linear. It is important that the inevitable existence of a set of assumptions, explicit or implied, is appreciated if different approaches to the problem of building prediction tables are to be understood.

Thus the assumptions behind multiple regression technique make it highly suitable for discovering and measuring main effects associated with single factors, and it can easily handle a few specified interactions between factors in the case of a homogeneous population; but where there is a large number of unspecified but possibly important interactions and heterogeneities, multiple regression will be at a disadvantage.

Now many theorists considered that such interactions would be important in criminology, especially interactions between "inputs" and "treatments". This widespread belief was first confirmed experimentally in a study of methods of treatment at a Naval Retraining Establishment by the United States Office of Naval Research (4).

This study relied on a random input of delinquents to three training groups. A large number of measurements and assessments were made for each case. Among these was one of "social maturity", and offenders were classified as tending to be of high or low grading on this scale. Follow-up revealed that the results for the three treatments were very similar. Those for the two grades differed to some extent, but the result of importance to our present study was the presence of an interaction between the treatment type and the maturity level. The summarized results were:

Table 1 *Percent Successful after Different Types of Treatment*

Social Maturity	Type of treatment		
	Type 1	Type 2	Type 3
High	70	72	61
Low	41	55	60
Total	59	65	61

Thus some of the treatments appeared to interact significantly with the social maturity of the offender. These results suggest that to ask whether a particular form of treatment is effective or not may not always be meaningful; in some cases questions may only be asked about the effectiveness of types of treatment for different types of offender. This implies that unless we can specify the interacting variables in advance, some less limited analytical technique than multiple regression will be desirable.

THE NEW TECHNIQUES

Association Analysis

The requirement is to produce prediction equations from data containing unspecified interactions and heterogeneities. By a heterogeneity we mean in this context a sub-group of the population for whom an appropriate prediction equation is significantly different (at some convenient significance level) from that appropriate to the rest of the population.[1] In a homogeneous population the success-probabilities of the individuals may vary widely but they can all be related reasonably closely to the input and treatment information by the same equation.

Association analysis, the first of the two methods described in this paper, was originally devised by Williams and Lambert (7) to deal with heterogeneity in botanical field data. Their problem was to make an objective classification of plots of land according to the plant communities found on them. The method, which uses an electronic computer, was not at this stage concerned with prediction, but with sorting the plots of land into groups so as to maximise the similarities within these groups and the contrasts between them, in terms of the plant communities found on the plots.

It was felt that the same technique could be applied to classifying individuals according to their possession (or lack) of groups of attributes. Such classifications would be basically descriptive rather than predictive. They could, however, be used predictively if the contrasting homogeneous groups of individuals isolated by the method could be shown to have significantly different outcome-probabilities. This was a reasonable hope, assuming that the information originally collected was relevant to the outcome. A possible further refinement might be to apply traditional prediction methods such as multiple linear regression within each homogeneous group, but this was not done in the present study, and the implications of such a course have not been fully considered.

We shall not here recapitulate the details of the method, but a few observations are necessary. The method of subdivision is hierarchical; that is, at each stage we proceed by dividing some group into two sub-groups, consisting

---

[1]The term heterogeneity is also applied in statistics to systematic differences in the scatter of observations about the predicted value; but when the observed values are restricted to two, representing success or failure, the scatter will be a known function of the success-probability.

respectively of those members of the original group who possess or lack some attribute which is found to be strongly associated within the group with the possession or lack of other attributes. The main assumptions are firstly that this hierarchical approach, treating each group in complete isolation from all other groups, is appropriate; and secondly certain mathematical assumptions about the best method of determining the most appropriate attribute for splitting at each stage, and about the decision when to terminate the process.

The method may be compared with the more conventional component analysis; this latter could be used on similar sets of data if a rather different set of assumptions held. Like association analysis, it could be used to classify the data according to the possession or lack of attributes, but each defining attribute would be assumed to be important for *all* the individuals, instead of merely for those in some particular groups. Thus in our situation where we are assuming a high degree of unspecified interaction and heterogeneity, association analysis was thought to offer a hope of overcoming a limitation of the older methods.

Predictive Attribute Analysis

Since the basic aim of Association Analysis is descriptive, one of the present authors devised a similar method with a specifically predictive aim (5). This method, Predictive Attribute Analysis, resembles Association Analysis in that both proceed by successive "hierarchical" divisions of the individuals into groups defined by the possession or lack of a specified attribute; but in Predictive Attribute Analysis the attribute chosen is that most strongly associated with the "outcome" attribute. Thus the method will provide a more accurate prediction than association analysis, but the attributes on which this prediction is based are not necessarily those which indicate the greatest *general* differences between the individuals. Thus the prediction may sometimes be less "meaningful" and less widely applicable than the rather less precise prediction obtained from an association analysis.

Just as Association Analysis may be compared with Component Analysis, so Predictive Attribute Analysis can be compared with multiple regression. When the assumptions of multiple regression are abandoned, we no longer know where to look to find our best predictors, or the relationship between them and the outcome. The purpose of Predictive Attribute Analysis is to provide an "order of search" over this wider, less predetermined field of possible equations.

AN APPLICATION OF THE NEW TECHNIQUES: YOUNG PRISONERS AND BORSTAL DETAINEES

The data on which these methods were tried referred to samples of young male offenders sentenced to prison or borstal. The interest in this particular application arose as follows:

Table 2 *Attributes Used in the Present Analyses*

	Number of Offenders	
Attribute	Prisoners (433 in Sample)	Borstal (504 in Sample)
Input		
1. Younger (i.e. under 19)	55	338
2. Urban	397	432
3. Below average detention (Borstal or less than six months sentence (Prison) [a]	20	313
4. Breaking involved	181	not known[b]
5. Violent offenders	100	26
6. Two or more previous convictions	334	384
7. Past record of drunkenness	17	24
8. Previously fined	147	141
9. Previously on probation	157	170
10. Previously at approved school	210	196
11. Unskilled occupation	242	242
12. Held no job for more than nine months	135	151
13. No stable home	316	307
Treatment		
14. Prison	433	—
Borstal	—	504
Outcome		
15. Reconvicted within three years of discharge	300	233

[a]These two items, although combined to form one attribute in the analysis, are not really satisfactory for this purpose. In any case they are half-way between an input variable (showing the nature of the offender or his offence) and a treatment variable.

[b]Among the Borstal detainees the records of "breaking" were very unreliable, so that to make the analysis possible all these offenders were arbitrarily scored as "non-breakers". This means that possessors of this attribute are defined as "Young prisoners who are known breakers" and those who lack it as "non-breaking prisoners, or Borstal detainees". This attribute sounds extremely arbitrary, but it was found to be usefully associated with other attributes and so was allowed to remain in the analysis. It was felt to be more important to have a set of figures which would illustrate the possibilities of the new analytical methods than to reduce the illustrative value by rejecting all "impure" information.

In 1955 Mannheim and Wilkins (6) produced an equation predicting the probability that an offender sent to a borstal would be reconvicted within three years of discharge. This probability was expressed as a linear function of seven variables, although for simplicity six of these were treated as attributes.

In 1959 Benson (1) applied this equation to data relating to a sample of young prisoners, and found a good fit between observed and predicted outcome probabilities, although the prediction equation was not designed to predict for that population. His conclusion that "so far as results are concerned there is little or no difference between Borstal and imprisonment" was felt to require more detailed investigation, as did the whole question of distinguishing the effects of "input" and "treatment". As mentioned earlier, the present study does not claim to be such an investigation; convenient techniques for a powerful analysis of input and treatment effects on outcome still await development, and our object now is simply to report a trial application of techniques which represent some advance in this direction. The sample used consisted of 937 cases from Benson's (1) study and from the "validation study" carried out by Mannheim and Wilkins (6). Each offender had been followed-up for three years from the date of discharge. In addition to "outcome" (whether reconvicted or not within the follow-up period)[2] and "treatment" (prison or borstal) information was available for only 13 "input" variables, which were all reduced to attribute form (i.e. yes or no answers) to fit the methods of analysis being tried. A list of these attributes is given in Table 2.

It appears that the main distinction between the two samples was age; although both treatments cover the same age range there was a strong tendency for the courts to send older offenders to prison rather than to borstal training. It is less likely that the violent offender would go to borstal. Neither of these factors had any weight in the borstal prediction formula of Mannheim and Wilkins (6), indeed in terms of the items included in their table there was little difference between the groups. The items and differences are:

Items Used in Mannheim Wilkins Formula	Numbers in Present Study	
	Prisoners	Borstal
Urban[a]	397	432
Previously fined	147	141
Previously on probation	157	170
Previously at approved school [a]	210	196
Previous record of drunkenness	17	24
Held no job for more than nine months	135	151
Have no stable home[a]	316	307
Total numbers in sample	433	504

There is a higher proportion (significant at 5 percent level) of prisoners than of Borstal boys possessing the attributes marked[a], although the differences are not great.

[2]Trivial reconvictions were excluded, the criterion used being that specified by Mannheim and Wilkins (6) that simple fines were ignored.

THE ASSOCIATION ANALYSIS

The association analysis was carried out using the input attributes but not the treatment or outcome. In other words, we begin by grouping the offenders in terms of the information available about them and their offences.

The sample was found to divide into the ten sub-groups listed below; (see Table 3) the quoted percentages of failures refer to the prison and borstal samples taken together. The process of splitting by which these groups were reached is shown in Figure 1.

It is not known to what extent the importance of "known breaking" as a defining attribute arises from its strong spurious association with a prison sentence, or to what extent it represents a real and important attribute of the offender himself.

Ranking the above groups in order of the percentage reconvicted we have—

Group	Percent Reconvicted	Number in Group
9	24.7	77
5	37.6	117
10	38.0	108
2	42.1	19
4	53.8	145
6	58.2	98
8	60.0	15
7	76.6	184
1	78.9	162
3	83.3	12
		937

The efficiency of this as a method of prediction can only be discussed if the purpose of the prediction is known; for some purposes the aim is to reduce as far as possible the size of a so-called "unpredicted" group (really those for whom the predicted probability is fairly near 50 percent). For other purposes the object would to be to minimise the number of "wrong" predictions (i.e. predictions of over 50 percent failure probability for individuals who in fact succeed, and vice versa). The terms "unpredicted group" and "wrong prediction" belong more to the theory of decision functions than to our present probability estimates. A more appropriate measure of efficiency is the contingency coefficient ϕ. For a classificatory type of prediction this serves the same purpose as the correlation coefficient in a regression equation; ϕ^2 measures the proportion of the original variance that has been accounted for by the prediction. In our present case $\phi = .38$.

We must note that since the predicted figures are probabilities and the observed figures are outcomes, ϕ would only equal 1 if we could predict with

Table 3   *Sample of Young Offenders Classified by the Method of Association Analysis*

Group	Number	Characteristics	Percent Reconvicted
1	162	Two or more previous convictions, known 'breaker'	78.9
2	19	Known breaker, less than two previous convictions	42.1
3	12	Two or more previous convictions Younger Drunkenness record Not known breaker	83.3
4	145	Two or more previous convictions Younger No drunkenness recorded Previous Approved School Not known breaker	53.8
5	117	Two or more previous convictions Younger No drunkenness recorded Not previously at Approved School Not known breaker	37.6
6	98	Two or more previous convictions Older Short sentence or detention Not known breaker	58.2
7	184	Two or more previous convictions Older Short sentence or detention Not known breaker	76.6
8	15	Less than two previous convictions Short sentence or detention Unstable job record Not known breaker	60.0
9	77	Less than two previous convictions Shorter sentence or detention Good job record Not known breaker	24.7
10	108	Less than two previous convictions Longer sentence or detention Not known breaker	38.0

See Table 2, note b for interpretation of "known breaker."

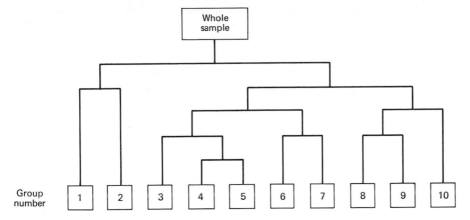

(See table 3)

Figure 1 Sample of offenders classified by Method of Association Analysis (for interpretation of groups, see Table 3).

complete certainty. So long as the outcome depends appreciably on factors independent of those included in our information set (which obviously cannot include any circumstances arising after discharge) ϕ cannot assume a very high value, and the value of .38 obtained from our present very small information set is regarded as highly encouraging.

The ϕ obtained here cannot be compared with the results obtained by Mannheim and Wilkins (6); for reasons which they discuss they used different coefficients of association. In any case a very much larger information set was available to them.

Unfortunately in this study it is known that offenders guilty of breaking and entry ('breakers') were not adequately identified for the borstal sample, and this is a major weakness of the analysis, but it is a weakness that can very simply be put right in later studies. Bearing this limitation in mind, it is possible to examine the success and failure rates for the groups found by the analysis separately for borstal training and imprisonment. The relevant data are given in Table 4.

It is found that in general there was no significant difference in outcome for the different treatments, but one group comes very near to showing a significant difference in favour of borstal training.

This is group 7 where in borstal training 13 out of 35 cases were not reconvicted within three years, whereas of 149 sent to prison only 30 were not reconvicted from a total of 149 cases. This result could occur by chance about once in eighteen times. ($\chi^2 = 3.67$). Similar effects in other groups would be hard to detect. The very arbitrary "known breaking" attribute became very important in the analysis, and partly as a result of this there is a tendency for the bulk of offenders in any group to be assigned to the same treatment. This greatly increases the difficulty of separating and measuring the effects of input and treatment on outcome.

Table 4 *Reconviction-Rates for Each Group of Prisoners and Borstal Detainees*

	Borstal Detainees		Young Prisoners	
Group	Number in Group	Percent Reconvicted	Number in Group	Percent Reconvicted
1	0	—	162	77.8
2	0	—	19	42.1
3	12	83.3	0	—
4	136	51.5	9	88.9
5	115	36.5	2	100.0
6	86	58.1	12	58.3
7	35	62.9	149	79.9
8	14	64.3	1	0.0
9	72	22.2	5	60.0
10	34	41.2	74	36.5
Total	504	46.1	433	69.3

Although the result in group 7 is promising and interesting it is no more than an indication of what may be possible given reliable data.

ANALYSIS OF ATTRIBUTES

Williams and Lambert (8) devised an extension of their method, an "inverse" technique which groups the attributes instead of the individuals. So far in this paper we have identified the groups of individuals, not by listing their names but by defining the group. However, in forming the inverse groups of attributes it is more convenient to list in full the attributes in each of the groups in which they cluster. This analysis is based on 76 individuals only, because of the limited size of the computor's "memory".

This inverse technique showed promising results. Three groups were identified where the offenders tend to have (or lack) the attributes in the "cluster" given below.

Group 'A' Urban
        2 or more previous convictions
        Previously at Approved School
        No stable home
Group 'B' Younger
        Previously on probation
        Held no job for more than nine months

Group 'C' Breaking known to be involved
      (See Table 2 note b)
      Violence involved
      Drunkenness involved
      Previously fined.

The fact that the analysis produces these sub-divisions is interesting. Many people have proposed typologies of offenders based on their observations in clinical and social situations, and it is often claimed that such typologies provide a better guide to the optimum method of treatment than test scores or other similar methods of allocation. Since the analysis derived from the computor provides the sub-divisions shown above, it is interesting to compare these with some typologies which have been proposed. Similarities between our sub-divisions and some of these suggested typologies can easily be imagined. Thus the first group of characteristics look very much like those possessed by the 'professional' type, or at least the group with the worst prognosis. It seems clear that if the list of 13 items were presented for subjective expert assessment, those items picked out as characteristic of the 'professional' type would be very similar to those in group A in the present objective analysis. It would appear that if more and better data could be fed into the analysis, better and more meaningful typologies might be obtained by this technique.

Table 5 *Young Offenders.*[a] *(Prisoners and Borstal Detainees) Classified by Probability of Prison Sentence (Method of Predictive Attribute Analysis)*

Group Number	Description	Number	Number Sent to Prison	Percent Sent to Prison
1.	Younger, guilty of violence, not more than 2 previous convictions, not previously on probation	11	11	100
2.	Older, guilty of violence	91	87	96
3.	Older, not guilty of violence, has been to approved school	106	62	58
4.	Older, not guilty of violence, has not been to approved school	190	72	38
5.	Younger, guilty of violence, not having 2 or more previous convictions, has been on probation	4	1	25
6.	Younger, not guilty of violence	334	18	5
7.	Younger, guilty of violence, has 2 or more previous convictions	20	1	5
	Total	756	252	33

[a]Known "breakers" omitted. (See Table 2, note b).

PREDICTIVE ATTRIBUTE ANALYSIS

As one object of the present study was to consider similarities and differences between Borstal detainees and young prisoners, it was decided in trying out the method of Predictive Attribute Analysis to attempt not only to predict success or failure after *release* but first to predict which sentence would be imposed in each case. Our interest is in the general relationship between input, treatment and reconviction. Technically it is legitimate to regard any variable as an "outcome" and so to "predict" it from any other set of variables. Thus it is permissible to regard the sentence passed as an "outcome" depending on the other information available. In this analysis attributes 3 and 15 (length of sentence and ultimate reconviction) were not used, so as to make the prediction depend entirely on information available immediately before sentence.

In our sample, none of the 181 people recorded as guilty of offences involving breaking were found among those sent to Borstal. This is due to an error in data-collection about breaking (see Table 2, note b). Among those not listed as guilty of breaking the analysis distinguished 7 levels of probability of prison. The seven groups are listed in Table 5; their logical relationship may be more clearly seen in Figure 2.

In general these groups are what one would expect to find if the decision were made entirely on age, present offence, number of previous convictions and type of previous disposal, and if factors concerned with home, work and so on were ignored. There is one rather strange feature. Of the younger offenders guilty of violence, those who had a long record of convictions rarely went to

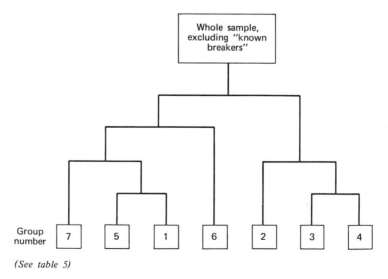

(See table 5)

Figure 2   Stages of treatment evaluation.

prison; those with no long record who had been on probation were more likely to go to prison; and those who had no long record and had not been on probation all went to prison. There may be a chance explanation (in terms of the individual magistrates' severity) or some rational explanation in terms of information outside our present set, but the figures are at first sight rather puzzling. For this prediction (for non-breakers only) $\phi = .67$.

Having considered which people go to prison or Borstal, we now return to our original problem of predicting their reconviction probability on leaving. Analyses were carried out for the Borstal boys, the prisoners, and for both groups together. The analysis for the Borstal boys is given in Table 6.

In interpreting this analysis we must remember that an attribute found in a "bad" group is not necessarily a "bad" attribute. Each group is obtained by successive splitting from larger groups, and this splitting will sometimes be by "good" attributes for a group whose final position is "bad", or vice versa. What we can say is that each individual belongs to a group defined by a cluster of attributes, each of which has at some stage been found to be relevant to the reconviction probability of the individual concerned. Each attribute has been marked with a + (good) or a − (bad) to show whether its association with reconviction was negative or positive for the particular sub-group in which it was found to be the best discriminator. This does not imply that the association was in the same direction (or even that it was present at all) in other parts of the sample.

The only puzzling feature is the bad effect associated with a skilled or semi-skilled job. The failure to sub-divide the large third and fourth groups must be due to the inadequacy of the available information. This is analogous to the situation found by Mannheim and Wilkins (6); after various factors (in their case mainly concerned with past criminal history) had been used to separate high and low success rates, a large central group was left, with some indication that it might be better analyzed in terms of more personal factors. The classification of the information into "criminal" and "personal" is not important; the point is that after any analysis a large centre group may be found requiring a further set of information to split it.

The comparable analysis for young prisoners alone is given in Table 7.

Again an attribute concerning work (length of longest job) has an unexpected association. Apart from this the main impression is of the greater homogeneity of the young prisoners (in terms of the information available).

The two samples were pooled and analysed together. In this case it is interesting to see that in some but not all cases the sentence appears as a predictor of outcome. The analysis is given in Table 8.

Apart from features already noticed in the earlier analyses, one very striking factor appears. We have already in Table 7 seen that for certain young prisoners (those with 2 or more previous convictions who have been at an approved school), having held a job for more than 9 months is a bad prognostic sign. We now find a group of offenders (those who have not been to approved school, have more than six months prison sentence or Borstal training and have less than two previous convictions) for whom having held a job for

Table 6   *Borstal Detainees, Classified by Probability of Subsequent Reconviction*

Description		Number in Group	Number Reconvicted	Percent Reconvicted
Has record of drunkenness	—			
Has not been to approved school	+	9	9	100
Has a skilled[a] occupation	—			
Older	—			
Has been to approved school	—	44	35	80
Younger	+			
Has been to approved school	—	152	83	55
2 or more previous convictions	—			
No record of drunkenness	+			
Has not been to approved school	+	94	50	53
Has a skilled[a] occupation	—			
Longer period of detention	—			
Has not 2 or more previous convictions	+			
Has no record of drunkenness	+	17	9	53
Has not been to approved school	+			
Has a skilled[a] occupation	—			
Has not been to approved school	+			
Has an unskilled occupation	+	153	40	26
Short period of detention	+			
Has not 2 or more previous convictions	+			
Has no record of drunkenness	+	35	7	20
Has not been to approved school	+			
Has a skilled[a] occupation	—			
Total		504	233	46

[a]or semi-skilled. $\phi = .38$.

N.B. Although the method makes no use of the signs of the associations, it is convenient to indicate "locally good" and "locally bad" attributes by a + or − respectively.

more than nine months is a good prognostic sign. Here is a case of an interaction of the sort discussed above sufficiently strong to make the same factor operate in opposite direction for different groups. Obviously such an effect would not be discovered by ordinary multiple regression techniques. It is not claimed that the present technique is particularly elegant or powerful in discovering such interactions, but whereas they would obviously reduce the accuracy of a multiple regression very seriously, a predictive attribute analysis is not weakened by their presence.

Table 7 *Young Prisoners, Classified by Probability of Subsequent Reconviction*

Description		Number in Group	Number Reconvicted	Percent Reconvicted
2 or more previous convictions	—			
Has been to approved school	—	125	113	90
Has held a job for more than 9 months	—			
2 or more previous convictions	—			
Has been to approved school	—	83	65	78
Has held no job for more than 9 months	+			
2 or more previous convictions	—	126	84	67
Has not been to approved school	+			
Less than 2 previous convictions	+	99	38	38

$\phi = .41$

It can be seen from the asterisked groups in Table 8 that for offenders who have not been to approved school, have more than six months' sentence or detention, and have two or more previous convictions, the sentence to prison or borstal is the most important remaining predictive factor. It is not known whether this is because the different treatments affect outcome differently or because the sentencing decision is associated with other factors; further analytical techniques need to be developed to decide this sort of point; but

Table 8 *Young Prisoners and Borstal Detainees Combined, Classified by Probability of Subsequent Reconviction*

Description		Number in Group	Number Reconvicted	Percent Reconvicted
Has not been to approved school	+			
Less than 6 months sentence	+	9	8	89
Past record of drunkenness	—			
Has been to approved school	—	233	198	85
Older	—			
Has not been to approved school	+			
More than 6 months sentence	—	121	83	69*
2 or more previous convictions	—			
Sentenced to prison	—			

Table 8 (*continued*) *Young Prisoners and Borstal Detainees Combined, Classified by Probability of Subsequent Reconviction*

Description		Number in Group	Number Reconvicted	Percent Reconvicted
Has not been to approved school	+			
More than 6 months sentence	−			
Less than 2 previous convictions	+	19	12	63
Held no job for more than 9 months	−			
Has not been to approved school	+			
More than 6 months sentence	−			
2 or more previous convictions	−	35	22	63*
Sentenced to Borstal	+			
Skilled or semi-skilled occupation	−			
Has been to approved school	−	173	99	57
Younger	+			
Has not been to approved school	+			
Less than 6 months sentence	+			
No past record of drunkenness	+	64	32	50
Skilled or semi-skilled occupation	−			
2 or more previous convictions	−			
Has not been to approved school	+			
More than 6 months sentence	−			
2 or more previous convictions	−	34	12	35*
Sentenced to Borstal	+			
Unskilled occupation	+			
Has not been to approved school	+			
More than 6 months sentence	−			
Less than 2 previous convictions	+	104	35	34
Held a job for more than 9 months	+			
Has not been to approved school	+			
Less than 6 months sentence	+			
No previous record of drunkenness	+	107	24	22
Unskilled occupation	+			
Has not been to approved school	+			
Less than 6 months sentence	+			
No previous record of drunkenness	+	38	8	21
Skilled or semi-skilled occupation	−			
Less than 2 previous convictions	+			

$\phi = .45$

*These three groups are pooled and reanalysed without using the sentencing decision in Table 9.

Table 9 *Re-analysis of Three Groups from Table 8*

Description		Number in Group	Number Reconvicted	Percent Reconvicted
Has not been to approved school	+			
More than 6 months sentence	–	168	109	65
2 or more previous convictions	–			
Urban	–			
Has not been to approved school	+			
More than 6 months sentence	–	22	8	36
2 or more previous convictions	–			
Not urban	+			

The effect of not using the sentencing information is to reduce ϕ from .45 to .43.

this group was reanalysed without using the sentencing decision, without any significant loss of precision. The result of this process is that the three asterisked groups are removed from Table 8 and replaced by the following two groups. It will be noted that when any variable is suppressed, other variables of lower predictive value may emerge as "best predictors" (e.g. "Urban"), and yet other variables (e.g. occupation) may drop out.

Within the other (non-asterisked) groups of Table 8 we know that there is no significant association (at 5 percent level) of greater success with either sentence; it is however possible that some of the differences *between* groups are partly due to their different proportions of prisoners and borstal boys rather than to the factors named in the analysis. Again, the answer to this question depends on further development of analytical techniques.

CONCLUSIONS

The two techniques described represent an attempt to produce predictions in circumstances where interactions and heterogeneities might be expected to reduce the power of multiple regression methods. When applied to a very unsatisfactory set of data they produced promising results. The methods proceed by dividing the offenders into groups, and this procedure has interesting implications for the study of typology. The methods give a pointer to the existence of treatment-offender interactions, but are in need of refinement and development in this direction.

The methods are, therefore, worth thorough testing on good data relating to offenders in the expectation that they will—

(a) improve upon regression-based prediction tables in terms of power and efficiency.

(b) provide meaningful typology of offenders.

(c) provide a means for legitimate comparisons of treatment effects upon different types of offenders.

REFERENCES

1. Benson, Sir George, "Prediction Methods and Young Prisoners" Brit. J. Del. IX 3 (1959).
2. Bruce, Burgess and Harno, "The Working of the Indeterminate Sentence Law and the Parole System in Illinois" (1928).
3. Glueck, S. and E. T., "500 Criminal Careers," 1930, New York, Alfred A. Knopf.
4. Grant, J. D. and M. Q., "A Group dynamics approach to the treatment of noncomformists in the Navy," Ann. Amer. Acad. Polit. and Soc. Sci. 1958, *322*, 126–135.
5. Macnaughton-Smith, "The Classification of Individuals by the Possession of Attributes Associated with a Criterion." Biometrics, 19 (2): 364–366, June, 1963.
6. Mannheim and Wilkins, "Prediction Methods in Relation to Borstal Training," 1955, London, Her Majesty's Stationery Office.
7. Williams and Lambert, "Multivariate Methods in Plant Ecology; II. The Use of an Electronic Digital Computer for Association Analysis," J. Ecol. 48, 689–710, 1960.
8. Williams and Lambert, "Multivariate Methods in Plant Ecology; III. Inverse Association Analysis," J. Ecol. 49, 717–729, 1961.

49

Current Thinking on Parole Prediction Tables

VICTOR H. EVJEN

In the past quarter-century, tests have been developed to measure intelligence, special abilities, emotional states, and social attitudes; to discover the personal and situational elements associated with successful performance of an activity—i.e., which factors are significantly relevant to success or failure; to predict success in school, work, marriage, and military service; and to identify predelinquent children.

The predictive method has also been developed for parole selection. Its actuarial instruments—referred to as prediction scales, prediction statistics, expectancy tables, and experience tables—are not a recent innovation. As long ago as 1928 Professor Ernest W. Burgess, of the University of Chicago, wrote: "The practical value of an expectancy table should be as useful in parole administration as similar rates have proved to be in insurance."

Noting the growth in knowledge of factors related to parole success and failure, Burgess held that it was possible to predict parole behavior. The paroling authority would do its job more effectively, he maintained, if it had available a reliable indication of the probabilities of violation on parole for different classes of offenders.

Sociologist-actuaries believe today that the probable outcome of parole can be predicted by experience tables. Those working closely with such tables

SOURCE. *Crime and Delinquency*, **8**, July 1962, pp. 215–224. Reprinted with the permission of the National Council on Crime and Delinquency. Copyright 1962, National Council on Crime and Delinquency.

assert that research has steadily improved their accuracy in predicting parole outcome.

Prediction tables are developed by systematic study of factors closely identified with parole success and failure. Each inmate is scored on the basis of this series of factors, and predictions are made on the basis of the score. To learn how prediction tables are developed, tested, and applied in parole selection, read Ohlin's *Selection for Parole.*[1] It should be in the library of every parole board member, penal administrator, and correctional worker.

The goal in parole prediction, according to Ohlin, is "to increase the number of paroles granted to offenders who are likely to succeed on parole and correspondingly to reduce the number granted to those who are likely to fail." "As this is accomplished," he continues, "violations will not adversely affect the parole possibilities of future applicants."[2] Parole prediction methods determine the chances a person has of making a successful or unsuccessful adjustment after release from a penal institution. They are not designed to give the optimum time for release or to portend responsiveness to supervision.

BOARDS' USE OF PREDICTION TABLES

To learn the extent to which paroling authorities use prediction statistics in parole selection, I sent a form letter, in August, 1961, to the parole boards of the fifty states and several other jurisdictions. The letter asked these two questions:

1. Have prediction statistics (schedules, ratings, etc.) ever been used by your Board in the selection of parolees?
2. Does your paroling authority use prediction devices at the present time? If so, please indicate briefly the manner in which they are used.

Of the forty-eight states responding, forty-four indicated they had never used prediction statistics in parole selection and are not now using them.

The U.S. Board of Parole, the New York City Parole Commission, and the paroling authorities of Puerto Rico, Canada, the U.S. Army, and the District of Columbia also answered "No" to each question.

Illinois has had nearly thirty years of experience with prediction tables. And it is the only state in which a routine system of parole prediction has been established. Since 1933 a sociologist-actuary at each of the major penal institutions has been conducting research in parole prediction and selection and has prepared for the parole board a routine prediction report on each inmate appearing for a parole hearing. He computes the prisoner's statistical chances of making a successful adjustment on parole. The final sentence in the report reads "This inmate is in a class in which——percent may be expected

[1] Lloyd E. Ohlin, *Selection for Parole* (New York: Russell Sage Foundation, 1951).
[2] *Ibid.*, p. 39.

to violate the parole agreement." Together with sociological, psychiatric, and psychological reports, and interviews by the Board, the probability score is used as an aid in selecting prisoners for parole. The Joliet-Stateville and Menard branches of the Illinois State Penitentiary have one prediction table; the Pontiac branch for "younger improvable offenders" has another. The women's institution at Dwight has none. The tables used at Joliet were originally developed by Burgess (1928) and modified by Ohlin (1951 and 1954). The table now used at Pontiac was developed by Daniel Glaser (1954).

In Ohio a parole prediction index has been developed under the direction of Dr. John Pruski, member of the Pardon and Parole Commission, from a constellation of variables obtained from responses on the Minnesota Multiphasic Personality Inventory (MMPI). Inmate testing under this system began in September, 1961.

In California the Youth Authority and the Department of Corrections have begun an extensive program of establishing "base expectancy" scores, which will be used in parole selection when they become standardized and perfected.

In Colorado the Parole Board, according to Edward W. Grout, Executive Director of the State Department of Parole, is now developing prediction statistics.

In Minnesota, the St. Cloud Reformatory experimented with the Ohlin Prediction Report in the fifties[3]; prediction tables are not used in the state at present.

EXPERTS' COMMENTS ON PREDICTION

Last July I wrote to fifty leaders in criminology, penal and correctional administration, and parole, asking each to give in about 200 words his opinion about prediction devices and their place in parole selection. My purpose, the letter explained, was merely to present a poll of reactions to prediction statistics.

Replies were received from 44 persons: 24 criminologists and sociologists (to whom I have assigned the symbol "C"); 11 parole board members ("PB"); 8 prison administrators ("P"); and 1 probation administrator ("PR"). Nine of the respondents are authors of criminology texts.

Of the 44 who replied, 33 (75 percent) believe in the potential value of prediction tables (C-16; PB-9; P-7; PR-1); 11 question the value of prediction statistics (C-8; PB-2; P-1). Their thoughts on parole prediction statistics are summarized below: the complete text of the remarks of 35 respondents is in the Appendix. Though the survey was somewhat limited and the summary is necessarily brief, I hope they will help to pave the way for a renewed, continuous, systematic study of prediction statistics and their place in selection.

These are the general comments offered:

[3] See the article in this issue, pp. 276–281, by Alfred J. Barron.

Supporting Arguments

Prediction tables may be used as a useful guide to check one's own thinking (C-15; PB-8; P-3). They are an aid to judgment—not a substitute for judgment. As Professor Sheldon Glueck states in his reply:

"It needs to be emphasized, because it is too often overlooked by critics, that the creators of prediction devices do not urge that such tables be applied in any mechanical, routine fashion; they are adjuncts to both the individual case history and individual experience of the parole board member. . . ."

Fred Finsley, chairman of the California Adult Authority, writes:

"The mechanical predictive tables can sort out and place into categories an abundance of objective data which, if used in conjunction with skilled interviewing, can bring about much better results than either the subjective interview or the prediction table alone. The combined use of both methods can bring us much nearer to a scientific approach to sound parole release procedures."

Prediction tables give consideration to factors which the board may overlook (C-2; P-1). It is very difficult to keep in mind all relevant factors in a case. Apportioning weights to each factor cannot be done satisfactorily without statistical techniques. Some factors are unduly overemphasized and others underemphasized. Board members have a tendency to base predictions on one factor to the exclusion of others. On this point, Professor Thorsten Sellin says:

"Experience has shown that the risk of recidivism depends on many factors in the life history of prisoners. Neither intuition nor "common sense" can evaluate these factors adequately; they can be disclosed by research that seeks to correlate them with the degree of adjustment on parole. It is such research that has led to the development of actuarial, experience, or "prediction" tables of which those in use in Illinois furnish an example."

Experience as a board member is not enough (C-1). J. Douglas Grant, a research psychologist, puts it this way:

"The whole correctional field must start being systematic about observing its experience. The days when programs can be defended on the expertise of eighteen years' experience alone are rapidly being eliminated. We will hear more of such statements as, "When you say you have eighteen years' experience, you mean you have had one year's experience eighteen times." Researchers and the public, if not correctional managers, are rapidly becoming aware that experience without systematic study and feedback may only mean that the same errors are repeated for many, many years."

Individualization—the careful study of each case—depends on hunches (C-1). Board members, at times, will make decisions on hunches without realizing or admitting they are based on hunches.

Prediction tables help to show board members where they erred in judgment (C-1; PB-1). A systematic effort to test the judgments of parole board members not only will help to determine wherein their decisions are correct, but also will lead to improvement in prediction tables.

Prediction scores may serve as a guide to the intensiveness of supervision (C-1). Those with a high probability of success will not need as intensive supervision as those who do not have high scores.

Some Questions and Doubts

The prediction score is for groups and may not fit the specific prisoner about whom a decision must be made (C-6; PB-1; PR-1). Actuarial predictions apply to groups—not to prisoner X. They do not tell what will happen to a specific prisoner. The violation rate is for a particular class and its application to a prisoner falling in this class may be erroneous.

Experience tables are not universally applicable (C-2). Tables cannot be applied to different kinds of populations at different points in time. As Burgess and Sellin suggest in the Introduction to Ohlin's *Selection for Parole*:

"It is highly desirable to try out in other states the items of background, personality, and prison behavior found to be significant in Illinois. Do these items have general applicability or are they limited to Illinois and perhaps to adjoining states?"[4]

Experience tables have to be revised and tested periodically to meet changing conditions and circumstances (P-1; C-2). Factors which are highly predictive at one time may not be at another. As Burgess and Sellin point out, research must be conducted to determine whether predictive items "retain their efficiency through time" and whether "economic and social changes in our society decrease or render null and void the predictive value of items earlier found to have predictive significance."

"It is becoming increasingly clear," says Ohlin, "that routine readjustment of an experience table is required if the table is to retain its usefulness. The experience table reflects the parole conditions which existed for a sample of parolees in a certain period."[5] Changes in parole board policies and in the nature and extent of prerelease preparation and parole supervision, and such major social and economic changes as a depression or a war, of course, affect the tables and make it necessary to adjust them. It is my understanding that at one time in Illinois, new experience tables were computed annually.

"Every few years," says Glueck, "prediction tables should be renovated by a systematic checkup on their actual effectiveness because both correctional facilities and community aid to parolees undergo change with time."

The problem is to develop a system for keeping abreast of these changes.

---

[4]Ohlin, *op. cit.*, p. 17. Ohlin states (p. 65): "The desirability of having a master experience table which would be generally applicable in a large number of states is apparent. It does not appear, however, that such a table can be composed at the present time."

[5]Ohlin, *op. cit.*, p. 62.

The information from which the tables are developed is limited (C-2). Prediction tables cannot be sounder than the information on which they are based. What goes into the computation will determine the reliability of the scores. The value, significance, and reliability of data in presentence investigation reports, classification summaries at institutions, and parole reports depend to a large extent on the qualifications of the probation, prison, and parole officers who supply these data. Their reports often lack objectivity and completeness. As one sociologist has remarked: "Opinions, hearsay, and haphazardly recorded judgments still constitute the bulk of many parole files."

Some good risks are overlooked and some poor risks are granted parole (C-1). Failures occur in the groups with higher scores and some parolees succeed even though they are in the lower-score groups. Some with high predictive scores may be highly dangerous to themselves and the community.

Some persons argue, says Glueck, that prediction tables should not be used because they predict correctly in only 80 to 90 percent of the cases and therefore subject the remainder to the hazard of false prognosis. Such an argument, he emphasizes, overlooks the greater hazard they are subjected to by the hunch method of parole selection.

Prediction scales consider only past and present factors (C-3; PB-1; P-1). They do not take into account unforeseen situations and circumstances which contribute to either success or failure. They cannot take into consideration the special stresses and strains experienced by the parolee in his attempts to make a satisfactory parole adjustment.

"An unexpected, severe, and prolonged increase in unemployment in the area to which a parolee is released," Austin H. MacCormick reminds us, "may outweigh a half-dozen favorable factors."

Several others pointed out that there is little use in predicting future conduct in terms of present attitudes.

Prediction tables do not sufficiently consider the seriousness of the offense and the likelihood that the prospective parolee will repeat the offense (C-1). Certain offenders, such as forgers and counterfeiters, have high recidivism rates.

Despite the prediction score, the parole board cannot ignore the feelings of the community (PB-2). The board, particularly where it is the target of criticism, must be sensitive to public attitudes; it must take account of the public reaction toward certain crimes; it must consider not only the readiness of the prisoner for parole, but also the willingness of the community to accept him as a parolee. The nature of the crime, for example, may preclude parole even though the perpetrator scores high on the prediction table.

In some jurisdictions the grant or denial of parole may be decided by the influence exerted on the board by prominent persons in the community.

The tables overlook subjective elements not easily measured (PR-1; PB-2; C-2; P-1). A person's behavior is a complex of intangibles—his attitudes and feelings, his sense of values, his concept of self—which do not lend themselves to computation. Prediction tables, in general, do not take into account the dynamic interplay of the many elements of an inmate's circumstances, relationships, and situations. Statistical prediction in its present stage of development, say Burgess and Sellin, deals with the external rather than the subjective aspects of behavior. Intensive study is needed, they assert, to probe into the prisoner's subjective life.[6]

Walter M. Wallack, a warden of long experience, declares:

"From what I know about the method of deriving prediction formulae, I have no confidence in their reliability as an instrument for determining whether an individual should be paroled. There are too many intangibles involved. Some of the factors . . . cannot be reduced to objectivity."

Only clinical insight can interpret and predict (C-6; PB-1). "Formulae based on statistical correlations are no substitute for clinical insight," says Howard B. Gill. Individual consideration is required. There is no substitute for the careful study of each case.

Frederick Hoefer, formerly a parole board member, writes that "prediction devices should never be used as a mechanical substitute for individual case study. This is particularly true when we make a decision granting or denying parole." Hoefer continues:

"A strong warning is in order against any attempt to substitute arithmetic for judgment when making a decision concerning a human life. Individual case study by trained professional workers is the only possible basis [for such decisions]. . . . The case analyst, after completing his study and evaluation of the case, could use a prediction table as a control device to check his own thinking and to see if he has overlooked an important element in the case."

Russell G. Oswald says:

"Aside from the obvious limitations of a strictly actuarial approach in the profession of rehabilitating persons, there are always other considerations which demand that the paroling authority rely on its own evaluation of each individual. Among the other considerations are the nature of the crime, the adequacy of the parole program, the kind of parole supervision available, and, finally and most importantly, the conviction of professional parole practitioners that the parole of any person is a matter requiring individual consideration."

We are dealing with personalities, not digits (C-1). Professor Negley K. Teeters says:

"Another serious limitation of mechanical parole techniques is that the parole petitioner is a person, not a mere digit, and this presents a hazard of losing sight of him as a living personality. Prediction charts nullify that indefinable, yet precious quality some parole officers may have which we call insight, a quality that must be accepted in any human interaction."

Sociologist J. P. Shalloo puts it this way:

"We might even suggest computers or electronic historicometers in conjunction

[6]*Ibid.*, p. 15.

with futurometers and we could all sit back and let the vibrations take over to warn and predict. Sounds fantastic? Well, the whole mechanical trend is just that. Prisoners were once numbers. Now they may become holes in a card, and so will their relatives!''

There are too many individual differences for human conduct to be predicted with a high degree of accuracy (P-1; C-1). Significant experiences and influences in both the prison and the free community and the different ways in which different personalities respond to them make it difficult to predict how successful a person may be on parole. Supporting this position, Wallack states that "No two conduct patterns are ever developed in exactly the same way. Heredity and environmental pressures always result in a unique outcome in the development of individual human conduct."

Judgment of the paroling authority is more reliable than a mathematical probability (P-1; PB-1; C-1). Wallack asserts that the total experience and common-sense judgment of paroling officials is more reliable than any formula based on mathematical probability. "This is not to say," he states, "that sometime in the future it will not be possible to find some significant assistance in forming a judgment as to whether or not to parole by means of one of these newfangled, terrifically expensive 'thinking machines.'" He believes "it will always be necessary for one or more human beings to dominate in the judgment as to what might be expected in the conduct of any member of the human race."

Commenting on the judgment of parole board members, Ohlin makes the following observation:

"An examination of the factors in the parole decision leads to the conclusion that no single device which social scientists may contrive can adequately supplant the mature and considered judgment of the parole board members. This judgment is on sounder ground when sociological, psychological, and psychiatric knowledge of the offender is fully used. No one of these single sources of information, however, is in a position to encompass all the implications of a case for the individual and society."[7]

Prediction tables do not account for the impact of prison life on the parolee and for differences in the effectiveness of supervision under different parole agents (C-5; P-1; PB-1). Uneven supervision prevails. The skills, insight, and knowledge of the parole agent and the adequacy of the overall parole program may determine to a large extent whether a person makes good on parole.

A career prison administrator writes: "Are we to assume that what happens to a man in the institution and the type of supervision he receives on parole has nothing to do with whether he succeeds or fails?" Any intelligent selection procedure, he emphasizes, takes these factors into account.

The tables rely on a single criterion of success—namely, recidivism (C-3). As

[7]*Ibid.*, p. 69.

a yardstick for measuring parole failure, the parole violation warrant is clear and objective, but, as several pointed out, it is also unreliable.

Parole violation warrants are issued for a variety of reasons—alleged commission of a crime, drifting back to associations with known criminals, rebellious behavior, mental deviations, and a host of others. The parolee might even be returned to prison for correction of a physical defect which cannot be cared for in the local community.

Some violation warrants are issued for technical infractions and others for convictions on new offenses. Some of these new offenses are misdemeanors of no serious consequence—offenses for which a large proportion of so-called "law-abiding" citizens are brought to court.

In some instances warrants are issued on the first violation without regard to the relative seriousness of the violation. Some parole officers request a parole warrant at the drop of a hat. Others consider technical infractions relatively unimportant. There are those who play ostrich to hold down their violation rates!

Board members and parole officers alike have biases against certain offenses and personality types; their blind spots are reflected in their action on parole violations.

Some boards may have other criteria—such as a continued pattern of criminality or a reasonably good social adjustment—for determining parole outcome. But there is, in general, a lack of agreement as to what constitutes adjustment. As Ohlin emphasizes, prediction systems based on different measures of success would not predict the same event. The important problem in parole prediction, he points out, is to decide which measure of success would prove most practicable for regular use in a correctional system.

A parole board may have reason to believe a person may commit the same offense if paroled, but it cannot tell to what extent a parolee may be involved in technical infractions of his parole conditions. Violation warrants are frequently issued for these infractions. In most jurisdictions these infractions are counted as violations in the same manner as warrants issued charging a new offense.

On this question, Gill writes:

"Although recidivism is the most obvious measure of success in prison work, because it is subject to so many intervening variables it is also the most unreliable. Nevertheless, in order to produce a quick and easy method of insuring popular approval in parole selection, base expectancy analyses have been developed which classify offenders according to risk of recidivism. Thus the vagaries of parole supervision rather than change in criminal tendencies based on individual treatment determine parole selection."

Parole boards would tend to rely solely on the prediction tables (C-2). One criminologist expresses concern as to "whether prediction tables might not give parole agencies a false sense of proficiency and security, discouraging the use of case studies and causing officials to lose sight of the prisoner as a living and changing personality." As has already been pointed out, those who are responsible for developing actuarial tables would be the first to say that the grant or denial of parole cannot be made entirely on the basis of the probability score.

Prediction instruments are too technical (C-2). One respondent says most parole boards show a negative attitude toward prognostic tables, which, they say, are too technical. It is human nature to want to avoid what is difficult to understand. Exposure to an area of knowledge beyond our field of competence makes us uncomfortable.

One author of a criminology text believes that the reluctance of parole agencies to employ prediction tables is caused by "the confusing categories and technical language used in them and the distaste of the average official for statistics of any kind."

Statisticians and sociologist-actuaries do, at times, speak in language not fully understood by those in other disciplines. What they do in composing and testing prediction statistics does involve some heavy arithmetic. But actually the tables in Ohlin's *Selection for Parole* are not complex.

A public relations program is needed to overcome the indifference of parole boards and correctional workers toward prediction tables.

Tables should be developed to enable the paroling authority to determine the optimum time for release instead of merely predicting success or failure on parole (C-4; PB-1; P-1). As already pointed out, present tables do not show when a person is ready for release or whether he should be held for a longer time. Professor Herbert A. Bloch says:

> "Predictive devices . . . should be based upon the determination of factors pertaining to the optimum time for release and measurable criteria indicating responsiveness to treatment, rather than upon attempts to formulate criteria which may portend potential success or failure during the parole period."

Boards do not want to be bound by tables. Boards frequently want to reward prisoners who have taken advantage of the opportunities offered in prison. They believe parole is not a right but something that must be earned. They carefully study the inmate's record of achievement in prison, his efforts toward self-improvement, his changes in attitude, cooperation with the staff, relationships with fellow inmates, and any attitude of remorse he may have displayed. But, as one correctional worker points out, the incentive to gain freedom is so strong that prisoners go out of their way to behave well in institutions.

On the practical level, classification as a poor parole risk is stigmatic. Persons who are scored as potentially poor risks are at a disadvantage in their efforts not only to achieve parole, but also to make good on parole.

Legal restrictions in some instances preclude the use of prediction statistics in parole selection. As Professor Norman S. Hayner points out in his informative article, "Why Do Parole Boards Lag in the Use of Prediction Scores?"[8] intelli-

[8]*Pacific Sociological Review*, Fall, 1958.

gent parole selection often is made impossible because of legal or traditional restrictions. Among the legal impediments are the mandatory sentence, the requirement that a fixed portion of the sentence be served before a person is eligible for parole, and setting the minimum and maximum sentences so close together that few prisoners receive the benefit of parole supervision. These impediments, Hayner suggests, can be modified or removed. "Without changes in such laws or traditions," he declares, "a scientific aid like a prediction table is practically useless."

The results do not justify the costs (C-1; P-1). Computation of experience tables is a long, laborious, and expensive task. The question to be considered, one respondent says, is: How can we obtain maximum results for a particular job at a minimum cost?

There is general resistance to the actuarial approach. The cause of this resistance is more than merely a lack of familiarity with prediction statistics. It may be the ever present cultural lag in the social sciences, particularly in criminology and in the correctional field as a whole; it may be opposition to the introduction of rigid experimental and quantitative techniques into the social science field. Or it may be, as Michael Hakeem points out, the absence of any startling or dramatic demonstration of predictive capacity in the actuarial approach. When such a demonstration is made, he asserts, prediction will be used.

More research is needed. A large number of those who replied express the need for more research in prediction statistics. Several indicate the need to determine the extent to which the case study method or clinical study may determine success or failure on parole. Clinical studies, one suggests, can help to determine the prisoner's attitudes and motivations, and the personality problems which may obstruct his reformation. Another says it may be true that each case is a unique research study. "But," he adds, "we can't get away with just saying so. We have to start doing research to prove it .... Those advocating such an approach are obligated to find out how effective they can be."

50

Why Do Parole Boards Lag in the Use of Prediction Scores?

NORMAN S. HAYNER

Thirty years ago Ernest W. Burgess said: "The practical value of an expectancy rate should be as useful in parole administration as similar rates have proved to be in insurance."[1] Since that time many scholars in the behavioral sciences have been trying to predict the success or failure of prisoners released on parole.[2] Some have provided experience tables suited to specific jurisdictions. But so far, the actual use of predictive instruments as an aid in parole hearings has been quite limited. Why is this?

During the five years 1951–1956, the writer, as a member of a parole board, interviewed more than six thousand candidates for parole.[3] In addition he attended about twenty-five correctional conferences. This experience provided

SOURCE. *Pacific Sociological Review*, **1**, Fall 1958, pp. 73–76. Copyright 1958, by the Pacific Sociological Society.

[1] "Factors Determining Success or Failure on Parole," in *The Workings of the Indeterminate Sentence Law and the Parole System in Illinois*, Springfield: Illinois State Board of Parole, 1928, p. 248.

[2] Lloyd E. Ohlin, *Selection for Parole: A Manual of Parole Prediction*, New York: Russell Sage Foundation, 1951, selected bibliography, pp. 131–135.

[3] In the last two years of the period served on the board the data available on any case up for consideration became increasingly satisfactory and the law was modified so as to make minimum sentences flexible. While studying a file in preparation for the interview it was helpful for the sociologist to know that certain items had been found to be significantly predictive of success or failure. The chances of failure, he knew, for example, were greater

insights into the reactions of parole board members, most of whom show slight interest in prognostic tables.[4] Sociologists themselves have criticized the techniques used in prediction studies and have lamented the absence of an adequate theoretical framework that would give significance to the statistical manipulations.[5] Little attention has been given by social scientists, however, to the attitudes of judges or parole personnel who might logically be expected to make use of such devices as scientific aids to practical decisions. It is the purpose of this paper to present certain hunches about the thinking of parole board members on criteria for parole selection and specifically on the use of prediction instruments.

Attitudes which help to explain the lag by parole boards in the use of prediction tables may be summarized roughly under five heads: (1) sensitivity to public opinion, (2) desire to encourage constructive use of prison time, (3) firm belief in the uniqueness of each case, (4) frustration of intelligent selection for parole because of legal or traditional restrictions, and (5) reactions to the prediction devices themselves.

SENSITIVITY TO PUBLIC OPINION

Although politically appointed, most parole board members are men of integrity and good judgment, with little knowledge, however, of sociology, psychology or psychiatry. They are convinced that if a parole program is to survive attention must be given to public reactions toward certain crimes. They are aware that it is important to get the reactions of the total community and not just individual and group pressures on the board.[6] The way a crime

---

for a parolee whose history showed any of the following characteristics: serving time for forgery or burglary with a prior record for the same or similar offenses, had no letters or visits from relatives while in prison, by age fifteen had left his growing-up home for six months or more to be "on his own," was a chronic alcoholic or drug addict. Associated with success were such traits as: first offender, murderer without a prior commitment, regular employment before incarceration, more than five letters and/or visits per month from relatives, constructive use of prison time. Such items as these provided clues to a better understanding of specific cases.

[4] When he was chairman of the Illinois Parole and Pardon Board under Governor Adlai Stevenson, Joseph D. Lohman used the prediction scores prepared by actuarial sociologists as a check on the judgments of board members. But when he reported this method at correctional conferences, the reactions were largely negative. The present board in Illinois makes little use of these scores.

It is encouraging, however, that a 1957 study found that 10 of 97 federal probation offices use prediction tables to assist in arriving at recommendations for or against probation. See "Presentence Investigation Practices in the Federal Courts: A Study Conducted by the Federal Probation Training Center, Chicago, Illinois," p. 15.

[5] See Marshall B. Clinard's discussion of "Prediction of Recidivism" in *Review of Sociology*, New York: John Wiley and Sons, 1957, pp. 485–488.

[6] See the writer's article on "Sentencing by an Administrative Board" in the Summer 1958 issue of *Law and Contemporary Problems* for examples of individual and group pressures on a parole board.

is reported in the newspapers rarely throws light on causation and frequently errs in factual content, but the extent and nature of the reporting is nevertheless significant.

Although, in general, property offenders—especially forgers—are more likely to violate their paroles than murderers,[7] from a public relations standpoint the questions raised when considering killers for release are more serious. The high percentage of success for homicide cases is not accepted generally as an adequate criterion for parole selection. Murder shocks the public conscience and there is understandably a strong hesitation about accepting a killer back into the community. This point can perhaps be made clearer by reviewing the circumstances involved in the release of a certain murderer whom we shall call Harry Nelson. This man would present a highly favorable score on any prognostic table, but our experience with him illustrates dramatically the importance of considering readiness of the community to accept the parolee.

Harry, age 43, had been found guilty in 1949 of killing his wife with a shotgun. Although he still stoutly maintained that the killing was accidental, he had pled guilty to second degree murder. Harry is a high-school graduate, recognized as a writer. His adjustment to the penitentiary had been outstanding. There were no infractions on his record. He had worked for about four years on the prison paper and at the time of the hearing was its editor. He had recently inherited a tract of land valued at $30,000. It was the feeling of the institution staff that the chances for a favorable adjustment on parole were good. The board decided to cut his sentence of twelve years actual time by five years and set a parole date for four months away.

Shortly after this decision became known the chairman received a long-distance telephone call from the sentencing judge, a man of exceptional ability. The judge followed this with a detailed written statement. The murder plus incarceration had left four children without parents, he said. A military officer and his wife had requested the privilege of raising the children and after a trial period of one year had adopted them. This couple, neighbors of the judge, had been successful in this venture. "I have never seen a better balanced or adjusted family than these people have grown to be," he observed. Naturally no one in that area wanted anything to happen that would spoil this relationship. On our next trip to the penitentiary we talked again with Harry, pointed out that in 1950 he had signed away any legal relationship between himself and the children, and indicated that it would be a condition of his parole that he would not visit the county in which his children were located and that he would make no contact with them. He agreed to this condition and for two years has been serving a satisfactory parole in another state.

---

[7] A follow-up study of 8,954 California male prisoners released on their first parole 1946–1949 showed that, by 1953, 51 percent had been declared violators, 20 percent having been convicted of a new felony. Parolees originally committed for forgery had a violation rate of 64 percent (30 percent new felonies); those committed for burglary, 57 percent (26 percent new felonies); but those committed for homicide had the lowest rate, 17 percent (2.5 percent new felonies). Ronald H. Beattie, *California Male Prisoners Released on Parole, 1946–1949: A Study of the Parole Experience of this Group as of January 1, 1953*, Sacramento: The Director of Corrections and the Adult Authority, 1953, p. 19. This low violation rate for murderers is confirmed by other studies. See Lloyd Ohlin, *op. cit.*, p. 52.

USE OF PRISON TIME

The interest of parole boards in encouraging constructive use of prison time weakens further their confidence in prediction tables. As progress is made in correctional administration, increasing opportunities for self-improvement are available to inmates. Boards want to facilitate the work of prison staffs by rewarding prisoners like Harry Nelson who take advantage of their opportunities. The majority of prognostic instruments give little weight to institutional factors. The common objection by inmates in Illinois that "most actuarial parole predictions are fixed when they enter the prison and cannot be altered by their efforts while confined,"[8] is shared by many staff members.

In a better than average prison system such as that developed in Washington since 1954, resident parole officers prepare progress reports at intervals. Keeping in mind the crime, the criminal record and the personality, boards carefully review reports like these. When there has been from the beginning a better than average work and conduct record, or when a clear-cut change for the better in attitude and behavior has occurred, the action in regard to parole is likely to be favorable. At the same session a man with a very poor work and conduct record or a change of attitude for the worse may have his parole denied. Parole administrators have the conviction that parole is not a right but must be earned.

UNIQUENESS OF CASES

Closely related to this interest in a man's prison record is a third attitude working against statistical predictions—a conviction that each case is unique. Although parole board members may act on the basis of hunches about uniformities in prisoner backgrounds,[9] they hesitate to admit the hunches. The idea is strongly entrenched that there is no substitute for careful study of the individual case.

In April of 1956 the National Conference on Parole divided its many experts into twelve workshops. One of these, under the chairmanship of Walter C. Reckless, dealt with "Criteria for Parole Selection." It came to the conclusion that "The use of prediction instruments should not override the importance of the individual factors in each situation."[10] In spite of the interest of its chairman in prediction, the emphasis in the report of the Reckless workshop

[8] From a mimeographed "Report on Pontiac Parole Prediction Study" by Daniel Glaser, sociologist-actuary, Illinois State Penitentiary, August 10, 1953.

[9] The writer is directing a study of approximately 1,700 consecutive sentence cases to test the validity of parole board hunches about the association of certain trait clusters with five offender types.

[10] National Conference on Parole, *Parole in Principle and Practice: A Manual and Report*, New York: National Probation and Parole Association, 1957, p. 112.

was on analysis of the factors contributing to individual readiness for release. These factors were then classified into four groups: personal history, offense committed, institutional adjustment, and personality changes and growth. The report added that there should be consideration of the readiness of the community to receive the parolee.

LEGAL OR TRADITIONAL RESTRICTIONS

Boards wish to parole a man when the evidence suggests that he will be able to avoid serious trouble on the outside. Intelligent selection for parole is often made impossible, however, by legal or traditional restrictions. Minimum and maximum sentences have been set so close to each other on such a large number of Illinois cases that only about half of the prisoners receive the benefit of parole supervision. Many states have deadly weapon statutes that make certain sentences mandatory and prohibit parole until a fixed proportion of that sentence has been served. In the State of Washington, the mandatory sentence for crimes in which a deadly weapon was used is five years if there is no prior felony and seven and a half years if there is a prior felony. Parole may not be granted until two-thirds of this time is served. The Federal Narcotic Control Act of 1956 specifies mandatory terms of not less than ten years for many narcotics and marihuana offenses and bars most persons convicted under it from either probation or parole. In the State of Washington, prior to 1955, a tradition of "automatic parole" at the end of two-thirds of the minimum sentence frequently prevented intelligent selection for release. In situations such as these the hands of parole board members are tied. Without changes in such laws or traditions, a scientific aid like a prediction table is practically useless.

REACTIONS TO PREDICTION DEVICES

Finally there are negative reactions to certain aspects of the prediction devices themselves. Some of the old-timers in the field of correction, shocked by the high percentages of failure reported by the Gluecks in their *Five Hundred Criminal Careers* (1930) rebelled against such studies. Many parole administrators of today know, however, that the tables do not show what happens if parole is denied. They are aware that the prediction score, which is for a group of individuals, may not fit the specific prisoner about whom a decision must be made. They realize that in the careers of criminal offenders there are probably significant influences—role played in the prison community, for example—which are not included among the more or less static factors on which available prognostic instruments are based. Parole personnel in Illinois, a jurisdiction having twenty-seven years of experience with parole prediction, know that highly favorable or highly unfavorable scores may serve as green or red lights in parole decisions, but that most scores fall into middle classifications.[11] The latter have less value.

Parole administrators may realize also that separate experience tables have to be worked out by competent statisticians for each legal jurisdiction and for such categories as boy delinquents or women offenders. In fact, the additional expense needed to provide satisfactory prognostic tables and to keep them satisfactory might be so great as to raise the question in the minds of parole personnel whether it would be wiser to cut down the high caseload by adding parole officers rather than hiring an actuarial sociologist.

No matter how much improvement may be made in the theoretical basis or the statistical sharpness of parole prediction, many administrators continue to display the skepticism reflected in the statement by Lloyd Ohlin that "no single device which social scientists may contrive can adequately supplant the mature and considered judgment of the parole board members." [12]

CONCLUSION

From the point of view of sociologists, including the writer, prediction scores can and should be used as scientific aids in making parole decisions. But the hesitancy by parole boards to utilize the results of this type of research may operate both to discourage further inquiry and to deny the opportunity of testing and refining prediction tables that would come from systematic use. What then are the prospects, in view of the attitudes described, for more extended use of parole prediction measures?

Each of these five limiting attitudes suggest certain possibilities for both sociologists and parole administrators.

[11]Experience with a prediction table that had been requested in the State of Washington was mentioned as follows in the *Tenth Biennial Report of the Board of Prison Terms and Paroles*, Olympia, 1954, pp. 11–12.

"In February, 1954, a new scientific aid was first made available to the board. Financed by grants from the University of Washington Research Committee and directed by Dr. Clarence Schrag, follow-up studies were made of 1,200 parolees from the two correctional institutions. A tentative prediction table has been worked out for the reformatory. Thirty out of some forty factors were found to have a significant relationship to success or failure on parole. The scores range from a low of −14 to a high of 17. All of the reformatory parolees who received scores of −11 to −14 (24 out of 688 cases) eventually failed on parole, whereas none of the parolees with scores of 13 to 17 (15 cases) were failures. Most cases, of course, fall into middle classifications."

Dr. Schrag is continuing these studies and will publish his findings. Stanton Wheeler's master's thesis in sociology, "Evaluation of Parole Prediction Techniques" (1956) and Donald Garrity's doctoral thesis, "The Effects of Length of Incarceration upon Parole Adjustment and Estimation of Optimum Sentence: Washington State Correctional Institutions" (1956) are available as unpublished manuscripts. See also Garrity's divided article, "Statistics for Administrative and Policy Decisions," in *California Youth Authority Quarterly*, Fall, 1957, and Winter, 1958.

[12]Lloyd Ohlin, *op. cit.*, p. 69.

1. Public opinion is indeed one of the realities of parole board work, but an honest and continuing program of public relations in a given jurisdiction can change the social climate of that area and make the use of prediction tables and other scientific devices more acceptable.[13]

2. The sociologist can himself remove some of the negative reactions of parole boards by including as items in prediction scores additional aspects of prison experience such as the number and nature of changes in job and cell assignments and the number and quality of letters written by prospective parolees to friends and relatives. By relating prediction tables to prison adjustments one of the major sources of skepticism can be reduced.

3. Despite the pre-occupation of parole boards with the unique features of each case, there is evidence of a shift in emphasis in the correctional field from a primary concern with the individual offender to the constructive use of groups. This trend toward "guided group interaction" may be increasingly recognized by parole boards and thus weaken the extreme emphasis on individual case analysis. Any weakening of this emphasis would make statistical analysis more acceptable.

4. Legal and traditional restrictions of the kind described can and should be modified. Without the kind of changes indicated, intelligent selection for parole, including the use of any scientific aid, is impossible.

5. Finally, and probably most important, sociologists can improve the technique of parole prediction in a manner to more adequately meet the needs of parole boards. This can be done both by developing a more satisfactory theoretical basis and by refining the methods of measurement. Efforts in this direction could well remove much of the opposition to prediction tables.

[13]See Norman S. Hayner, "Washington State Achievements in Parole and Probation Services," *Journal of Criminal Law, Criminology and Police Science*, 47 (March–April, 1957), pp. 703–704.

51

Pilot Time Study of the Federal Probation Officer's Job

ALBERT WAHL AND DANIEL GLASER

How does the federal probation officer utilize his work day? What proportion of time is spent in counseling and in presentence investigations? What amount of time does he give to paper work and dictation? How much time does he engage in travel?

An approach to answering these and other questions has been made in a pilot study of 31 probation officers in 15 judicial districts who, in the fall of 1961, kept a minute-by-minute log of all their activity for a 3-week period.

Initiated by the Federal Probation Officers Association, the study was conducted by the United States probation office at San Francisco with planning, tabulation, and evaluation assistance from the University of Illinois Ford Foundation Research Program in the Federal Correctional System, and the Administrative Office of the United States Courts.

The purpose of the study was to give an accurate basis for establishing the amount of time required by a probation officer to perform his various major functions (presentence investigation, preparole investigation, probation and parole supervision) and his major tasks (interviewing and counseling, case recording and other paper work, and travel). On the basis of this information, budget requests for adequate staff can be justified. Data obtained also can

SOURCE. *Federal Probation*, XXVII, September 1963, pp. 20–25.

be used to test the validity of existing workload formulas. Finally, the entire manner in which the job is being done can be reviewed.

PROCEDURES FOLLOWED IN THE STUDY

The Federal Probation System is, of course, nationwide. Officers serve every type of area—densely populated urban to sparsely populated rural. In an effort to get a representative cross-section of workers, one large and one small office was chosen by lot from each of the six regions, previously established by the Administrative Office for administrative purposes.

In the large offices, three officers were selected by lot, one with a predominantly urban, one with a predominantly suburban, and one with a predominantly rural caseload. In the small offices, one officer with an urban and one with a rural caseload were chosen, again by lot. In two districts, where officers had few suburban or rural cases, officers from adjacent districts were substituted. In addition, two urban officers were included from another large district in a densely populated northeastern region.

No supervisory personnel were included; thus the reports of one officer, who was a supervisor and inadvertently included, were deleted from the study, bringing the total participants to 31. Four women officers from metropolitan areas were also asked to participate. Their reports were not included in the study, but were used for comparison with the male officers.

Prior to starting the study, "dry runs" were made by volunteers in several offices. The forms for activity recording were repeatedly tested and revised. The final version had one line for logging each activity, with a separate line used also for each case. Most of the entries consisted only of checks in the appropriate squares. The time for each activity was recorded separately in multiples of 6 minutes, or, to put it another way, in hours or tenths of an hour. The forms also provided for the tabulation of the nature, location, and purpose of each activity, and the type of case involved.

The federal probation officer works for many masters! Although appointed by district court judges, whom he serves as probation officer, he also acts as a parole officer for the U.S. Board of Parole and the Departments of the Army and Air Force, and does social service work for the Bureau of Prisons. How he allocates his time among these is of considerable interest.

During the reporting period, a total of 3,332 man hours were logged by the officers. This article presents some of the highlights of the study.

TIME SPENT WITH DIFFERENT TYPES OF CASES

Probation officers almost invariably say that most of their time is spent on presentence investigation and reporting. As Table 1 shows, however, the probation officers spend 33.7 percent of their time on presentence work. A

Table 1   Allocation of Probation Officer's Time to Different Types of Cases

Type of Case	Percent of Total Time	Time in Terms of Hours (Based on a 168-Hour Month)	Average Work-Load[a]	Average Hours per Case over a Month's Period	Ratio of One Presentence Investigation Time to Time for Other Types of Casework per Month	Percentage Distribution of Time Designated as for a Specific Case
Total	100.0	168.0 hrs.	—	—	—	100.0
Presentence	33.7	56.6	4.0	14.1	1.0	41.3
Probation[b]	29.4	49.4	52.8	0.9	12.8	36.0
Work not for a specific case	18.4	30.9	—	—	—	—
Parole[b]	11.6	19.5	13.0	1.5	8.8	14.2
Prisoner	3.4	5.7	1.0	5.7	2.5	4.1
Mandatory release[b]	2.3	3.9	4.0	1.0	14.1	2.8
Postsentence	1.1	1.8	—	—	—	1.4
Military parole[b]	0.2	0.3	0.2	1.5	9.4	0.3
All supervision cases	43.5	73.1	70.0	1.0	12.8	53.3

[a]Presentence and prisoner workload figures refer to investigations completed per month by the average probation officer during the fiscal year 1962. Other figures refer to men under supervision as of June 30, 1962. Hours, therefore, are for *completion* of one presentence or preparole investigation, and for *1 month's supervision service* for the other cases. They accordingly cannot reasonably be added. Figures are from the *Annual Report of the Director of the Administrative Office of the United States Courts, 1962.*

[b]These are the types of cases included in the bottom line as "all supervision cases."

further examination by regions showed at most only a 10 percent variation. Because of local differences in intake during the study period, this difference could be anticipated in a study which covered only 14 work days. Because of the deadlines which go along with presentence court dates, the attendant pressure tends to distort the volume in the officers' minds.

Similarly, we have heard officers complain about the amount of time demanded by prerelease planning for prisoners. Again, deadlines come into the picture—results are magnified. Table 1 shows that only 3.4 percent of work time was devoted to prisoner activity. Add an additional 1.1 percent for the post-sentence counseling and the entire total for prisoner activity is 4.5 percent. Postsentence counseling (a recently developed service which is growing in use) is a special type of counseling for men who have been sentenced and are awaiting transfer to prison.

Next to the presentence investigation the greatest allocation of time to specific cases is for probation supervision. This amounted to 29.4 percent. Parole supervision (11.6) and mandatory release supervision (2.3) total 13.9 percent. Only a fraction (0.2 percent) was devoted to military parolees from disciplinary barracks. This was to be expected since there were only 114 military parolees for the entire United States.

In terms of supervision, then, the federal probation officer spends 31.9 percent, or almost one-third of his supervision time, on cases under the jurisdiction of the U.S. Board of Parole. These constitute 24.3 percent, or slightly less than one-quarter of his caseload. Prorating the time which cannot be attributed to a particular case, the probation officer spends 77.3 percent of his working hours on probation responsibilities and 22.5 on matters relating to prisoners and parolees, exclusive of the relatively small number of military parolees. This corresponds to the parole and mandatory release caseload percentage of 24.3.

A substantial portion of the logged time could not be charged to a specific case. Totaling 18.4 percent, it covered such activities as opening and reading mail, reading monthly reports, making out travel logs (and the time-study log), miscellaneous administrative duties, staff meetings, professional reading and inservice training, community relations, and, of course, coffee breaks. Travel which cannot be allocated to a specific case, such as driving to another city for a term of court, also comes into this category.

Translated to hours, based on a 168-hour month, the probation officers spend 56.6 hours monthly on presentence work, 5.7 on all prison activity, and 73.1 on supervision. The average for a probation case is 0.9 hours per month, 1.6 for a parole case, and 1.0 for a mandatory release case. For all supervision cases, the time available for each case is slightly more than 1 hour monthly; this includes counseling, travel, dictation, and community contacts. More comment on this will be made later.

TIME SPENT IN OFFICE, COURT, AND FIELD BY TYPE OF CASE

Experienced probation officers say the only way to get field supervision done is to stay away from the office. Table 2 bears out the validity of that statement.

While the officer, percentage wise, spends 30.8 percent of his office time on presentence work and 39.5 percent on supervision, he also gives 26.0 percent of his time to activities which cannot be charged to a specific case. As previously stated, this covers everything from reading mail, to professional development, community relations, and coffee breaks. Very important is the fact that he spends 57.5 percent of his time in the office. In the field, supervision activities are increased to 50.9 percent, presentence work to 36.1 percent, and pre-release work 4.6; "other" work drops to 6.7 percent. In other words, an additional 19.3 percent of the available time is devoted to cases.

In court, as can be expected, more than half of the time spent is in connection with presentence work, either at intake or at time of judgment, with a smaller amount spent on probation revocation hearings. Of the total court time—which represents 3.2 of all time—73 percent is spent on probation matters if the presentence report is considered strictly a probation activity.

Finally, 23.5 percent of the officer's time in court is devoted to nonproductive waiting. This results in $1\frac{1}{4}$ hours per month, not a great amount in itself, but if extended over the entire system of 522 officers, reaches a total of 653 hours, or almost 4 months time for one officer.

Table 3 shows that the large offices, usually located in metropolitan areas, spend more time in the field than their smaller counterparts. This is contrary to expectation since obviously more of the larger office cases reside nearby than

Table 2 *Percent of Time Spent in Office, Court, and Field, According to Type of Case*

Type of Case	Place Where Work Was Performed		
	Office	Court	Field
All cases	100.0	100.0	100.0
Presentence	30.8	55.4	36.1
Probation	26.3	17.6	34.7
Work not for a specific case	26.0	23.5	6.7
Parole	10.0	3.0	14.5
Mandatory release	2.9	—	1.6
Prisoner	2.7	0.5	4.6
Postsentence	0.9	—	1.6
Military parole	0.3	—	0.1

Table 3   *Percent of Time Spent in Office, Court, and Field, by Probation Officer in Large and Small Offices*

Place of Work	All Offices	Large Office	Small Office
Total	100.0	100.0	100.0
Office	57.5	54.9	62.5
Field	39.3	41.9	34.3
Court	3.2	3.2	3.2

is the case with the smaller offices with large rural areas. One explanation is that the larger offices have more administrative personnel (chiefs, deputy chiefs, and supervisors), thus relieving the line officers of many administrative burdens.

COMMUNICATING TIME BY TYPE OF CONTACT

That probation and parole at the federal level is largely a one-to-one relationship is demonstrated by Table 4. Here the probation officer spends 48.2 percent of his communicating time directly with the subject of the case, whether it be probationer, parolee, or a person on mandatory release. An additional 12.6 percent is spent with relatives of the case. Thus, the primary group receives 60.8 percent of direct communication time.

Also noteworthy is the 12.9 percent spent on time communicating with the judges. This, of course, includes the presentence report and its preparation.

Table 4   *Percent of Time Spent in Communication, by Type of Contact*

Type of Contact	Percent of Total Time
All contacts	100.0
Case	48.2
Judge	12.9
Relative	12.6
Law-enforcement agent	9.0
Other probation officers	5.7
Supervisor	4.2
Employer	2.9
Institution	2.3
Attorney	2.2

TIME SPENT IN VARIOUS TYPES OF WORK

If the premise is that the probation officer's primary job is to work with people, Table 5 gives some challenging data. The officers logged 21.2 percent of their time in counseling. If the 6.9 percent attributed to "initial interview" is added to this, the total comes to 28.1 percent. Paper work (report writing, case review, and administrative tasks) on the other hand totals 37.2 percent. Thus, probation officers spend more time planning and telling about what they have done than they do in performing the basic job. This is an area that should be given additional study, but it is not the purpose of this article, nor of the time study itself, to provide these answers. It merely shows what is prevailing practice.

Table 5   *Percent of Federal Officers' Time Spent at Different Types of Work, According to Major Types of Case*

Type of Work Performed	Type of case worked with				
	Pre-sentence	Proba-tion Super-vision	Parole, Mandatory Release, and Military Parole Super-vision	All Other Work Activity	Total Work Time
Total	100.0	100.0	100.0	100.0	100.0
Counseling	3.0	47.1	40.2	3.1	21.2
Administrative	4.2	3.5	2.3	55.7	15.5
Report writing	22.8	12.3	11.9	4.5	14.0
Giving information	12.3	10.2	15.0	7.0	10.9
Case review	12.8	6.6	4.8	3.5	7.7
Initial interview	15.0	2.2	5.9	1.5	6.9
Home investigation	4.0	5.8	6.2	4.4	4.9
Job investigation	3.6	4.0	6.0	2.4	3.8
Other	22.3	8.3	7.7	17.9	15.1
Percent of total time by type of case worked with	33.7	29.4	14.1	22.8	100.0
Number of cases worked with in average month[a]	4.0	53.0	17.2	—	—

[a]This compares presentence investigations *completed* during an average month in 1962, with number of men under probation, parole, or mandatory release supervision as of a given date in 1962. Figures are from the *Annual Report of the Director of the Administrative Office of the United States Courts, 1962.*

Job investigation and home investigation, which may be equally important in the successful end-adjustment of the probationer or parolee, occupied 3.8 and 4.9 percent of the time, respectively, or a total of 8.7 percent. This is less time than was devoted to giving information to other interested parties such as police, employers, social work agencies, and families. It came to 10.9 percent. Again some reevaluation is indicated.

During the planning of the study a category for "getting information"— which would have covered such activities as interviewing neighbors, co-workers, credit associations, and so forth—unfortunately was omitted. The returned logs indicated that much of this was recorded under "other." This accounts for the 15.1 percent of the total time in Table 5. It also explains the 22.3 percent under "presentence" and the sharp drop in "supervision" time spent on other.

As could be anticipated, counseling was the dominant activity in both "probation" and "other supervision," but it still occupied less than 50 percent of the officer's time. This confirms that the probation officer, while a counselor, is many other things too. He is an investigator and has a definite role in home and job placements and in dealing with other aspects of community environment. And, of course, he must keep records!

TIME SPENT IN TYPES OF ACTION AND LOCATION OF ACTION

The interview is the principal tool of the probation officer, according to an old adage of the profession. The pilot study shows on Table 6 that the federal officers spent 39.8 percent of their time in personal interview and an additional 5.7 percent on the telephone for a total of 45.5 percent of their time in conversation with or about their cases. But it also showed that 33.1 percent of their time was spent directly on paper work. In other words, 1 hour in three is spent dictating or reading. An additional 15.7 percent is spent traveling and 2.3 percent goes to "thumb twiddling" while waiting.

In terms of hours per month, the probation officer spends 76 hours talking to people, including cases, relatives, judges, attorneys, law-enforcement officers, fellow workers, supervisors, and so on. He spends 56 hours a month at his desk dictating and reading, 26 hours in travel, 4 hours waiting, 5 hours in miscellaneous activities, and less than one hour at coffee breaks. Of course, coffee breaks during which cases were discussed were charged to another category.

In the office, paper work took 54.2 percent of the time, while personal interviews accounted for 30.7 percent, and time spent on the telephone 9.5 percent. Waiting time was reduced to a minimal 0.4 percent. In court, waiting took 34.1 percent of the time and 51.1 percent was spent presenting cases.

In the field, interviewing was the dominant activity involving 52.2 percent of the time. Telephone became a slightly used adjunct at 0.6 percent. Travel

Table 6 Percent of Time Spent in Various Types of Action of Probation Officer and Where Action Took Place

Type of Action	Percent of Total Time	Office	Court	Field
Total	100.0	100.0	100.0	100.0
Personal interview	39.8	30.7	51.1	52.2
Paper work	33.1	54.2	3.2	4.5
Travel	15.7	1.0	2.4	38.3
Telephone	5.7	9.5	—	0.6
Other	3.0	3.6	8.5	1.6
Waiting	2.3	0.4	34.1	2.3
Nonworking action	0.4	0.5	0.7	0.3

occupied 38.3 percent of the officer's time when away from the office, indicating that about two-fifths of the officer's time is spent behind the wheel of an automobile when away from the office.

THE DISTAFF SIDE

We reported that four female officers participated in the study. They were not included in the totals since their inclusion would have destroyed the lot selection method. All the women came from metropolitan areas.

Despite the old saw that women talk too much, comparison of their time showed no material difference in this regard from their male counterparts. Women spent 45 percent of their time in personal interviews and 8 percent on the telephone; the corresponding figures for men were 40 percent and 6 percent. Such small variations are not material in a study of this duration—and basically their approach time-wise was consistent with that of the men. The largest difference between male and famale officers in allocation of time was that men spent 16 percent of their working hours in travel, while women only traveled 9 percent of their work time, or little more than half the male proportion.

CONCLUSION

This study points up several things. First, there are definite limitations on the probation officer's time. In the office he must spend more than half of his time (54.2 percent) on paper work. In the field almost two-fifths of his time (38.3 percent) is spent in travel and in court one-third (34.1 percent) of the time he "just waits." Any programing must take these items into account. While further study may be indicated, at the present time these factors exist. The idea that the probation officer can use all his working time for investigation, or counseling, or job or home placement is a fallacy. The hidden, (perhaps on the surface) nonproductive activities are part and parcel of his job and must be taken into account when budget estimates are presented or when consideration is given to what kind of a probation service is needed or, more important, wanted.

Second, formulas for probation work are based on the ideal. Thus, the formula that one presentence equals four supervision cases contemplates perfect conditions. This study reflects the prevailing situation and shows how far the federal service is from the ideal. Based on today's practice, one presentence takes as much time as 12.8 supervision cases. More study is indicated, however, before establishing a new formula. But such a study would have to be done under ideal circumstances.

Finally, it should be stressed that this was only a pilot study. Its sample was limited in size and was deliberately selected to include a minimum of each major type of officer and caseload in which we were interested, rather than a number of each type in proportion to the frequency of that type in the total service. This, of course, precludes concluding that our figures precisely state the nationwide use of time by federal probation officers. Nevertheless, the relatively small variation in the overall pattern of our findings by region, size of office, and type of caseload strongly suggests that the general implications of the findings presented here are valid for all of the service.

A future study involving twice the number of officers, covering a period of 1 month and weighed for type of officer and type of caseload, is desirable. A category, "getting information," should be added. To insure more accurate logging, each participating officer should make a trial run for 1 week—at least 1 month prior to the study—in order to check his logging of time and to help him be fully acquainted with logging procedures.

52

A Critique of Research in Parole[1]

ROBERT M. MARTINSON, GENE G. KASSEBAUM,
AND DAVID A. WARD

While crime rates in general are normally regarded as among the most unreliable statistics in the social record, parole violation rates seem to be both more reliable and less ambiguous. For a given system of parole, anything important which happens to a parolee while under supervision must be recorded so that the parole system can continuously account for every one of its charges. Except for probationers, no similar system of mandatory record-keeping exists for other categories of persons with respect to criminal behavior.

The ready availability of the parole disposition—an administrative action taken by the parole division in relation to the parolee—as a criterion of post-prison behavior, has permitted actuarial studies to concentrate on predicting the future parole disposition of a given parolee from the voluminous tracings of his past criminal career found in records kept by interested agencies. The aim of an experience table is to maximize the predictive efficiency of this body of records on the assumption that the parole category, into which past groups of parolees with certain characteristics have been placed, is the best indication available of how similar groups will do.

SOURCE. *Federal Probation*, XXVIII, September 1964, pp. 34–38.

[1] A version of this paper was delivered at the meetings of the Pacific Sociological Association, San Diego, California, March 1964. This is one of a series of reports of the California Study of Correctional Effectiveness of the School of Public Health at the University of California, Los Angeles. This project is supported by a grant from the National Institute of Mental Health (OM-89). The conclusions are not necessarily endorsed by either the California Department of Corrections or N.I.M.H.

The parole population is normally dychotomized into "success" and "failure" categories by arbitrarily choosing one disposition—e.g., return to prison—as the criterion. But different criteria may be constructed by combining categories of reported difficulties while on parole. Success on parole is the usual and reasonable variable used to measure the efficacy of prison treatment programs, and conversely, prediction of recidivism has been the overriding concern in studies of parole. That is to say, studies of parole have taken administrative ends as problems.

EVALUATION RESEARCH AND PAROLE CRITERIA

The evaluation of prison programs aimed at changing behavior must ask the question: Do formal parole dispositions reflect only parolee behavior or are there other sources of the variance of parole violation rates stemming from the parole decision itself?

The difficulties in interpreting parole data might be reduced by expanding research in at least two basic areas: (1) the study of the parole division as a social organization; and (2) the study of the parolee in relation to the parole division. The former would focus on decision-making by the parole agent, the relations of the parole division to other law-enforcement agencies, and the influence of political and public pressures on the division. The latter would seek to determine characteristic experience of parolees, the consequences of reduced civil liberty, special conditions imposed by the parole contract, and the significance of the status of the parolee when interacting with non-parolees in the community.

Inferences from the rates of parole violation about the criminal behavior of free citizens are difficult when so little is known about the implications of the parolee status and the many specific regulations, conditions of surveillance, and possibilities of reimprisonment by administrator rather than court action to which he is subject.

PAROLE AS A SYSTEM

There have been few systematic sociological studies of parole.[2] This is clearly reflected in the sections dealing with parole in most textbooks in criminology. Most of these chapters reiterate the principles of parole as they are enunciated by parole boards and departments of correction. Lists of the

---

[2] An exception to this statement is a recent article by Skolnick who develops a theoretical approach to the understanding of parole. The theory focuses on prison roles, convict expectations concerning parole life, and the tolerance of the parole situation for prison norms. See Jerome Skolnick, "Toward a Developmental Theory of Parole," *American Sociological Review*, 25:4 (August 1960), pp. 542–49.

regulations parolees must abide by and a review of the classic studies of parole prediction follow.

One reason for the dearth of information is that parole has been examined chiefly as a source of data on the outcome of treatment or prison experience. This has been an area in correctional research useful for obtaining information or verifying propositions about other areas, especially the prison community. The principal focus of correctional research has been on prisons, due to the century-long social criticism of prison conditions by reformers, and the ready availability of inmates and their records. However, as more is known about the prison and interest grows to include the impact of prison experience on the behavior of released prisoners, there seems to be a growing interest in other aspects of parole. There is now an interest in the decision-making process of parole boards. Moreover, treatment programs are no longer confined to prison, but are also being introduced into parole.[3] The criticism of the principle of parole has been abated somewhat as the argument of the reduced costs of crime control through parole methods has permeated legislative and public opinion. In addition, the proportion of inmates released to the community on parole has steadily increased in almost all jurisdictions throughout the Nation.

Approximately 60 percent of the prisoners released from state penal institutions are released under some form of parole supervision.[4] From a sociological perspective, parole must be understood as a specialized form of modern bureaucracy—a network of trained agents, each supervising a caseload of specially designated men in the community. From this view, the parole experiment as a type of operations research can also be seen as the modus operandi by which a bureaucracy goes about introducing new methods, as well as an indication of the manner in which it typically interacts with its charges.

From an administrative perspective the question may be posed: What can we learn about parole as a social system that will enable us to clarify the meaning of formal administrative measures, e.g., the sociological meaning of failure rates based on "parolee at large," "parole violator at large," "parolee returned to prison to finish his original term," and "parolee returned to prison with a new felony conviction"?

---

[3] The Social Agency Effectiveness Study under the direction of Don Gottfredson is studying decision making of the Adult Authority of California. For instances of evaluations of parole treatment outcome see Research Reports Nos. 1–5, Special Intensive Parole Unit, Research Division, California Department of Corrections.

[4] Studies of parole followup have only recently carefully taken into account the fact that in some jurisdictions those on parole represent the better risks in the prison population. See, for example, "A Followup Study of Minnesota State Reformatory Inmates," *Journal of Criminal Law, Criminology, and Police Science*, January-February, 1953, 43:622–636; and Daniel Glaser. *The Effectiveness of a Correctional System.* Bobbs Merrill Publishing Company, Indianapolis, Indiana (in press). This consideration does not apply to those states such as Washington, Ohio, Pennsylvania, and California where 90 percent of those released from prison leave under parole supervision.

Parole systems differ profoundly in different states and most attempts to develop a typology of parole systems have leaned heavily on the social welfare kind of variable, such as "type of parole supervision," which assumes the parole agent-parolee interpersonal relationship to be of crucial importance but which often leaves the relationship empty of social content since so little is known about the status of parolee.

An organizational approach would regard the parole agent-parolee relationship as perhaps changeable, but only within limits set in a much larger canvas. The parole agent has discretion within the complex limits set by operations manuals, by district office supervision, and by career concerns. The parolee follows a career hemmed in by special deprivations of civil liberty, special parole conditions, and perhaps a special fate in a program determined by a distant randomization technique. The agent and his charge interact in a series of meetings, conversations, phone calls, and interviews. This relationship may be quite different than those found in prison where inmates are in close physical proximity and hence "organized" by the prison system itself. In parole an effort is made to keep parolees apart by regulations prohibiting association, except for such legitimate gatherings as group counseling sessions and Nalline tests. Hence, generalization from the kind of interaction that characterizes staff and inmates in prison may not apply to parole agents and parolees.[5]

Parole violation rates might be viewed as being built up from the accumulation of a series of decisions made by individual agents, as a result of their contacts (or lack of contacts) with their charges. It is interesting to note that dispositions generally tend to convey negative information about the parolee, although some are more fateful than others. (It is not crucial that the final "legal" decision to revoke parole is in the hands of the agent or another agency, so long as the agent's recommendation carries enough weight.) The moving force in precipitating the making of decisions might be presumed to be parolee behavior (or misbehavior), but since the parolee is seldom directly "present" to his agent, his behavior must be inferred by the agent from what we might call danger signs. These signs are clues to misbehavior rather than evidence presentable before a court. The great mass of these signs are either pieces of information constantly present to the parole agent in the form of records of the parolee's criminal career or messages about the parolee from a great variety of outside sources including the police, the parolee's employer, kin, criminal or noncriminal associates, welfare agencies, and so forth. The "absence" of a parolee may be regarded as an extremely important sign and an extended absence will normally result in the disposition "parolee at large," especially

---

[5]Consideration of the role of the parole officer given by Lloyd E. Ohlin, Herman Piven, and Donnell M. Pappenfort, "Major Dilemmas of the Social Worker in Probation and Parole," *National Probation and Parole Association Journal*, 2:211–225, July 1956; and Donald R. Cressey, "Professional Correctional Work and Professional Work in Corrections," *National Probation and Parole Association Journal*, 5:1–15, January 1959.

if no other signs have accumulated pointing to a new disposition, "parole violator at large."

We have gone into some detail about decision-making in the parole system simply to indicate that there is one set of phenomena we might call signs and quite another set called dispositions and that the relationship between these two sets of phenomena becomes problematic the moment we cease to see parole rates as simple reflections of differences in parolee behavior.

Setting the limits within which parole agents carry on the complex tasks of translating signs into dispositions are the formal rules in the parole agent's manual which offer guides to this process; supervisory conferences during which signs may be discussed, ignored, hidden, created, and where informal pressures may be generated to translate them into one or another form of disposition; and, of course, higher meetings during which overall decision-making can be discussed.

On a macroscopic level, we might view the parole violation rate as a response of the parole division as an organization to significant outside social influences and explore the manner in which it varies with variation in (1) the size of the prison population; (2) political pressures in the state defining parolees (or types of parolees) as more or less "dangerous"; (3) administrative directives affecting the discretion of parole agents in dealing with offenses; and (4) policies of law-enforcement and other significant agencies affecting parole agent operations.

Outside influences may directly impinge on the parole agent or be mediated through higher supervision. In either case, parole agent decision-making may be regarded as a major intervening process.

BEYOND THE "PAROLE EXPERIMENT"

The widespread social acceptance of parole has led to the development of a new branch of operations research which we shall call the "parole experiment." Many departments of correction are concerned with examining the efficiency of their own operations. This is reflected in the wide variety of research programs conducted by the department itself or by outside investigators which deliberately introduce changes in parole conditions for selected categories of parolees with the aim of observing the results. This practice is now widespread in California where currently the following parole studies include:

1. Early release of selected numbers of "high risk" parolees.
2. Experimental reductions in the size of parole agent caseloads.
3. Measuring the increased "efficiency" of parole supervision when agents and parolees are matched according to psychological traits.
4. Measuring the effects of the introduction of Nalline testing on narcotic offenders placed in "experimental" and "control" groups.
5. Controlled introduction of such new techniques as group counseling, parole outpatient clinics, and the Los Angeles "Halfway House" for narcotic offenders.

If the results of these experiments are adjudged "positive" by administrators, the innovation can become part of normal departmental operations. The design of each experiment is arranged in collaboration with the Research Division. Special field units are often set up to carry through the design and collect the data. The Research Department, through its followup section, has regularized the collection, coding, and IBM card storage of followup data on arrests, convictions, and parole dispositions.

Normally, operations research proceeds on a clear and commonly accepted definition of "efficiency" acceptable to administrators and capable of measurement through statistical techniques. In the case of the parole division, no such clearcut definition seems to be in sight.

It is illustrative of the difficulties of interpreting the results of parole experiments to examine figures published by a study of the effects of a parole program for narcotics users.[6] This program assessed the effects of the use of Nalline, a morphine antagonistic drug which detects recent opiate use by inducing pupilary dilation a few minutes after subcutaneous injection. It is not clear how the study could have avoided supporting the use of Nalline. If the recidivism rate were *lower* for the treatment group than the control group, one would say that the fear of detection by Nalline deterred men from using drugs, or at least markedly reduced drug use. On the other hand, if the treatment group had *higher* recidivism rates, the figures can be said to show that Nalline is an effective detection device resulting in the reconfinement of a larger number of drug addicts. This second alternative was indeed the finding. In either case, the program could have been found to be worth using.

Moreover, men in the sample were subject to special "short-term reconfinement" at a segregated unit at California Institution for Men at Chino. In tables of outcome, "short-term reconfinement" is listed as nonrecidivism. However, if "short-term reconfinement" is added to jail sentences and prison returns, the figures show *lower* recidivism among the control group. This parole experiment seems to show that when the parole division increases surveillance, it detects more illegal behavior.

The point here is not to question the wisdom of classifying 90 days of "short-term reconfinement" at Chino as "nonrecidivism," and 90 days or 2 years in jail or prison elsewhere as "recidivism," but rather to point out that data on parole followup may reflect factors other than the rising or falling in the prevalence of some illegal behavior.

CONCLUSIONS

We have examined the literature dealing with parole and found it to be open to criticism on three points: (1) parole has been studied largely from the narrow

[6]Narcotic Treatment-Control Project—Phases I and II: A Synopsis of Research Report No. 19, Research Division, Department of Corrections, State of California, May 1963.

focus of prediction of parole success or failure; (2) parole outcome has been regarded implicitly as simply the function of parole behavior to the neglect of the parole agent as decision maker; and (3) the parole division has not been studied as a complex social organization. We have suggested that recidivism rates cannot be understood without taking into account the civil status of the parolee and the varieties and basis of parole decisions to which he is subject.

Among a number of possible classifications of parole decision one might divide dispositions into (1) those which directly affect the flow of persons into and out of the parole system, and (2) those dispositions which assign degrees of confidence to persons who remain within the system. In the California system "return to prison to finish term" is an example of the first type. The second type may have quite fateful consequences to the parolee, but it does not automatically remove him from the jurisdiction of the parole system. Examples of this decision might be a report that a parolee has missed a Nalline test without prior approval, that he failed to send in a monthly report, that he is AWOL from the halfway house, that he failed to appear at a therapy session, or that he evinced symptoms of mental instability. An organizational analysis might attempt to discover the frequency with which such interim designations eventuate in dispositions of the first type which effect membership in the parole system.

The above distinction warns us against ordering dissimilar criteria into a scale which is presumed to measure degrees of something called "parole adjustment." Even more important, it points toward a sociological study of the function of formal and informal administrative dispositions.

In this approach, *the parole violation rate as measured by various combinations of parole dispositions is taken as problematic, as something to be explained rather than as an "outcome" variable in a prediction equation.* Until such clarification and specification is accomplished, evaluation studies will have to supplement information provided by such rates with whatever additional evidence can be obtained of the behavior of parolees within the complex of social conditions imposed by parole. The exploration of such conditions is a major and pressing task of future correctional research.

PERSONNEL

This brief closing section is concerned with probation and parole personnel. Although the anthology has demonstrated the many complexities of probation and parole—types of offenders, problems of supervision, changing legal concerns, social organization of agencies, and the like—the men and women who are working in the field themselves constitute a most important element in the totality of the correctional process. The section commences with standards for probation and parole officers and parole board members and includes education, experience, and personal qualifications. An article by Professor Gilbert Geis and researcher Elvin Cavanagh focuses on recruitment and retention policies of correctional agencies, and deals with some of the underlying issues involved in recruitment and retention, provides background information concerning methods used by agencies for these purposes, and examines attitudes among agencies toward such personnel matters.

Researcher Edward M. Taylor and Professor Alexander W. McEachern explore the needs and direction of probation (and indirectly, parole) training. Professor T. C. Esselstyn's article on the social system of correctional workers is an important contribution as one of the first examinations of the influence of the social system on correctional worker behavior. The section, and the anthology, terminate with the Code of Ethics subscribed to by the United States Probation and Parole Officer.

53

Standards for Probation Officers

AMERICAN CORRECTIONAL ASSOCIATION

STANDARDS

The selection of personnel by a civil service or merit system, without regard to race, religion or political affiliation is basic in developing acceptable personnel standards. Effective pre-sentence investigation and supervision of probationers requires a high degree of knowledge and skill. The standards for recruitment of personnel should include:

For Probation Officers

A. Education and Experience
  (1) Preferable-completion of two years graduate study in an accredited school of social work or comparable studies in criminology, psychology, sociology and other related fields of social science.
  (2) Minimum-graduation from an accredited college or university with a major in the social or behavioral sciences and one of the following: one year of graduate study in social work or a related field such as guidance or counselling; or one year of full-time paid social work experience under professional supervision and direction in a recognized social agency.

SOURCE. *Manual of Correctional Standards*, American Correctional Association, Washington, D.C., 1966, pp. 103–105. Library of Congress Catalog card number: 66–17761. Copyright, 1966 by the American Correctional Association.

(3) Trainee-graduation from an accredited college or university with a major in the social or behavioral sciences. (Trainees should be hired only if the department has for such employees a special program of appropriate training under the supervision and direction of qualified staff.)

B. Personal Qualities

Emotional maturity, integrity, ability to establish constructive interpersonal relationships; a recognition of the dignity and value of the individual; genuine interest in helping people; intellectual ability; mature judgment; warmth; wide experience and a continuing interest in professional development.

For Supervisory Personnel

A. Preferred Education and Experience
   (1) Completion of two years graduate study in an accredited school of social work or comparable studies in criminology, psychology, sociology and other related fields of social science, preferably with supervised field work and courses in correction.
   (2) Three years of paid full-time supervised experience in an agency maintaining acceptable standards.

B. Personal Qualities
   (1) Same as for probation officers.
   (2) Ability to teach, to develop social work skills in the authoritative setting, and to interpret agency policies and procedures to staff.
   (3) Demonstrated administrative and organizational abilities.
   (4) Ability to speak and write effectively.
   (5) Demonstrated ability to establish and maintain effective working relationship with individuals and groups.

For Director or Chief Probation Officer

A. Preferred Education and Experience.
   An advanced degree in the behavioral sciences, or a master's degree in social work, and a minimum of three years successful supervisory experience in a recognized agency maintaining acceptable standards.

B. Personal Qualities
   The demonstrated ability to plan, organize and direct; the talent for participation in community activities; the knowledge and ability to work with related agencies, the governing bodies and the public; the ability to interpret programs of the agency to the public. An understanding of the social work processes broad and thorough enough to enable him to provide a setting in which staff can function with maximum effectiveness. The capacity to work well with judiciary and other agencies and to provide leadership that inspires and maintains good staff morale. The courage to make decisions even though such action may be unpopular.

PERSONNEL PRACTICES

Good personnel practices are reflected in the quality of workers selected and their opportunity to work with a high degree of morale. Appointment of all probation personnel should be based on merit examinations open to all who meet the minimum qualifications without regard to residence. Examination content should be related to the knowledge and skills required for effective performance, not content that can and should be learned on the job.

A probationary period of employment—preferably one year, but not less than six months, should be provided to enable the agency to evaluate the new workers' competence and aptitude. Tenure should not be subject to change of political office or political influence. Provision should be made for permanent tenure dependent upon satisfactory performance of duties. A review procedure should be available for the appeal of disciplinary action or removal from service.

Salaries should be adequate and provide for minimum and maximum levels which will help to recruit and retain qualified personnel. Salaries should be higher generally than those paid by other social work agencies in the community, because of the requirements of the probation job.

Staff should be reimbursed by the department for necessary expenses incurred in the performance of official duties. These expenses should be paid on a scale compatible with the allowances in comparable governmental or private agencies.

Provisions for vacations, sick leave, and other benefits are necessary and should be compatible with the best practices of governmental or social agencies in the community. To further maintain and retain a qualified staff, educational leave with pay should be available to selected employees who desire to improve their professional competence.

Probation officers are professional persons and are entitled to adequate and efficient working space. Professional personnel should have individual offices. Adequate waiting room space should be provided for clientele and this space should be readily accessible to staff. Modern office equipment and recording devices should be available.

54

A Qualified Parole Staff

AMERICAN CORRECTIONAL ASSOCIATION

A major cause of weakness in parole systems is the inadequacy, both in number and training, of parole staff. The best efforts of the correctional institutions and parole boards are doomed to failure if there are insufficient or incompetent parole officers. Parole boards cannot release on parole all who could benefit by parole supervision if there are too few or inadequately trained staff members. Parole without supervision is parole in name only.

The staff of the parole department or bureau may consist of as many as six categories of personnel, depending on the size of the agency: these would include administrative, supervisory, field, institutional, and specialized parole officers and an adequate clerical force. A staff should include, as a minimum, a chief parole officer or director, enough institutional and field parole officers to carry on the work of investigation and supervision of parolees with workable caseloads. There should be at least one senior officer at the supervisory level for every six parole officers responsible for the supervision and day-to-day training of staff. In the larger parole agencies, additional officers at the administrative level will be needed to direct the work of district offices or divisional operations. Specialists will be required for employment placement, for full-time training and personnel direction, and for statistics and research.

SOURCE. *Manual of Correctional Standards*, American Correctional Association, Washington, D.C., 1966, pp. 120–122. Library of Congress Catalog card number: 66–17761. Copyright, 1966 by the American Correctional Association.

Appointment and Tenure

The parole staff from top to bottom should be under civil service, should be appointed from lists of eligibles established by competitive examinations (qualifying examinations should be held for personnel already in service when civil service provisions go into effect), and should have security of tenure as long as their performance of duty and their conduct are satisfactory. The director should be appointed by the parole board or top department head, and the staff should be appointed by the director, with approval of his superiors. Experience has shown beyond question that the tenure and career of service offered under a merit system can attract and retain a higher calibre of personnel than can be recruited without a merit system. With parole staff, as with the parole board, it is most important that they refrain from partisan political activity. Here again, the merit system of appointment reduces to the minimum the possibilities of staff being subject to political or other partisan pressures in return for job protection or advancement.

Tenure should be permanent except in cases of malfeasance or unsatisfactory performance of professional duties. Impartial hearings should be held on appeal of disciplinary action or removal from service. There should be adequate provisions for disability, retirement with pension, and for vacations and sick leave.

Qualifications

The parole staff should be selected on the basis of the highest professional and technical standards possible. Agencies which recruit parole officers at below college training are narrowing the base of personnel from which they will want to promote future staff specialists and administrative personnel.

The following minimum standards are based on the position that criminal behavior is symptomatic of serious disturbances in the personal and social relationships of offenders; that parolees are selected for their need of the control and treatment afforded by parole supervision and their capacity to profit by this supervision; that the parole staff should be capable of carrying on the treatment program started in the institution and that the supervision of parolees calls for a high degree of professional understanding and practical skill.

EDUCATION   Preference should be given to the completion of graduate study in an accredited school of criminology, social work, psychology, law, sociology, and other fields of social science. The minimum requirement should be graduation from an accredited college or university with a major in the social and behavioral sciences.

EXPERIENCE   A person employed as a parole officer with the minimum of college graduation should, in addition, be required to have at least one year of full-time paid experience under professional supervision in a correctional agency or in a recognized social agency. Where a department has an organized trainee program with professional supervision and training on-the-job, the minimum requirement of one year of prior experience should be waived. One year of graduate work in social work or corrections, or in a related field as indicated above, should be accepted in lieu of the required experience. Related experience should not be substituted for education less than a college degree.

PERSONAL QUALITIES   Despite his training and experience, if the officer does not possess emotional maturity and stability, an interest in helping people, a belief in their capacity for change, and ability to establish effective inter-personal relationships, he will not be a successful parole officer. He should be a person of integrity, able to work co-operatively with other people, interested in improving himself professionally, and possess the qualities of good judgment, tolerance, initiative, and tact.

SALARIES   The salaries will, to a large extent, determine the quality of personnel the agency will be able to recruit and retain. While they should con-form to those salaries paid professional staff in related public agencies requir-ing training in such professions as education, social work and law, they should not adhere to salary scales which have lagged behind acceptable standards. The salary range should provide for regular increases based on merit and perform-ance evaluation and the maximum of the range for parole officers should overlap with the range of salary paid for supervisory staff. It should not be economically necessary for the officer who is an excellent caseworker to advance to a supervisor or administrative position where he could not excel. If a department does not adopt high professional standards for personnel training and performance, it cannot justify requests for high professional salary ranges.

Training

Agencies which recruit parole officers who meet bare minimum stan-dards of college graduation without graduate work should assume the obliga-tion of seeing that they obtain an intensive course of training before they are assigned to carry a full workload. The work of the parole officer is the applica-tion of professional knowledge and techniques taught in graduate schools of social work, or comparable study in corrections, criminology, psychology, sociology and other fields of social science. Whenever possible, the parole agency should, in co-operation with the state's graduate schools, develop a training program incorporating educational leave with stipends and field-work placements in the parole agency for personnel receiving graduate training. Where this is not possible, the agency should develop its own trainee program with professional consultation from the university, state department of educa-tion, and national service agencies in the correctional field. To delay the establishment of such training programs and to require instead that new parole personnel have one or two years of prior casework experience in a related agency will continue to place the parole agencies at a disadvantage in recruit-ing. The related agencies which give the one or two years of first experience can be expected to do everything possible to retain the more capable personnel.

In every parole agency, staff training and development should be considered as a major responsibility by the administration. In small agencies, the function should be carried out by the director or deputy director, and by a full-time training officer in the larger departments. In addition to the trainee program for new recruits, the department should offer a continuous program of staff development through regular casework supervision and consultation related to individual case situations, regular staff meetings for discussions of case problems and participation in development of working policies and procedures, attendance and participation in institutes and professional conferences, a manual setting forth departmental policy procedures, rules and regulations, periodic personnel evaluations, opportunity for participation in community organization and leadership activities, and through the maintenance of an up-to-date professional library.

55

A Qualified Parole Board

AMERICAN CORRECTIONAL ASSOCIATION

APPOINTMENTS. Members of the parole board should be appointed in the manner that will best assure the appointment of qualified persons and continuity through the re-appointment of those whose performances warrant it. Appointments may be made by a governor, by a panel of high government officials, or by a board of corrections where such exists. By any method, the appointments should be made on the basis of published minimum standards to assure excellence in selection. A recommended method of assuring selection from among qualified applicants is the use of the merit or civil service procedure. Members should serve staggered terms to insure a relatively stable parole policy, but also provide for opportunity for new philosophy, knowledge, and administration where the need is evident. Tenure should be sufficiently long to insure independent judgment without undue concern for re-appointment.

SIZE AND COMPOSITION. Whenever possible, the board members should serve full time, and the board should be composed of a minimum of three members. In order to secure sufficient time for hearings and all the other related work, some states will require as many as seven or more board members with provisions for them to function in panels under policies established by the board as a whole. The institutional population, number and location of institutions, and scope of the board's duties will determine the size required. Workload and time studies should be made periodically to see that there are sufficient board members to give the time and attention required to parole matters, and in the

SOURCE. *Manual of Correctional Standards*, American Correctional Association, Washington, D.C., 1966, pp. 117–120. Library of Congress Catalogue Card number: 66–17761. Copyright, 1966 by the American Correctional Association.

case of a part-time board, to determine when full-time members are required.

In states in which the parole board workload does not justify a full time board, the above methods of appointment are recommended for part-time board members to assure continuity and appointment of qualified persons. State officials, such as the governor, attorney general, and secretary of state, should not serve as board members. Experience has shown that they have neither the time nor primary interest to devote to parole work and they are most likely to be sensitive to political influences and other pressures that will make it difficult to be objective in their decisions.

Some states have had experience with boards composed of a full-time chairman and part-time board members, in which organization the chairman may serve as the parole executive or may be the commissioner of institutions or corrections. While this form of board might well be considered as a transitional step between a part-time and a full-time board, it is not recommended because of some inherent weaknesses. Unless the full-time chairman is unusually skillful in involving the part-time members in all decision making of the board, there is real danger that it will become a "one-man board." Where the board serves as the policy-making and administrative board for parole services, the board should appoint a parole executive to direct the services. It is administratively unsound for the parole executive to serve as a member of the board, under whose policies and direction he serves.

The parole board should bear the full responsibility for all parole decisions and should not serve merely as a hearing-and-advisory board with the parole decisions made by one person such as the governor, director of corrections, or other state administrative officer.

QUALIFICATIONS AND SALARY. A parole board member must have important personal attributes, as well as education and experience.

(1) *Personality:* He must be of such integrity, intelligence, and good judgment as to command respect and public confidence. Because of the importance of his quasi-judicial functions, he must possess the equivalent personal qualifications of a high judicial officer. He must be forthright, courageous, and independent. He should be appointed without reference to creed, color, or political affiliation.

(2) *Education:* A board member should have an educational background broad enough to provide him with a knowledge of those professions most closely related to parole administration. Specifically, academic training, which has qualified the board member for professional practice in a field such as criminology, education, psychiatry, psychology, law, social work and sociology, is desirable. It is essential that he have the capacity and desire to round out his knowledge, as effective performance is dependent upon an understanding of legal processes, the dynamics of human behavior, and cultural conditions contributing to crime.

(3) *Experience:* He must have an intimate knowledge of common situations and problems confronting offenders. This might be obtained from a variety of fields, such as probation, parole, the judiciary, law, social work, a correctional institution, a delinquency prevention agency.

(4) *Other:* He should not be an officer of a political party or seek or hold elective office while a member of the board.

SALARIES. The salaries of parole board members should be comparable to those paid to judges of the courts of general criminal jurisdiction. The *per diem* rate and expenses paid part-time board members should be equally as high to attract persons of stature and training.

FUNCTIONS. The functions of the parole board should include regular case reviews to fix the time of parole eligibility; granting and revoking of paroles; discharging from parole when supervision is no longer needed; establishing rules and policies on all matters relating to the work of the board; determining conditions of parole; interpreting parole to the public; and promoting sound parole legislation and services. Another principal function of the board may be to serve as the policy-making and administrative board for the parole staff and services. The direction of staff and services should be delegated to an executive officer, subject to broad policies. Where the parole board also has administrative responsibility for adult probation services, policies for the administration of probation should be worked out with the advice of the courts preferably through a representative committee of judges.

A parole board may appoint parole-hearing examiners to conduct parole and revocation hearings and to make recommendations to the board on the basis of the hearing and a study of the prisoner's file. The board should make the ultimate decision, however, and the hearing examiner should not be authorized to vote on a case. Through the use of hearing examiners, it is possible for a board to remain small enough in size to permit it to perform its primary functions despite a large hearing caseload which may occur. In this manner, the board may retain the function of decision making while delegating to qualified staff the function of information gathering.

56

Recruitment and Retention of Correctional Personnel

GILBERT GEIS AND ELVIN CAVANAGH

Qualified manpower is not, at the moment, a readily divisible commodity that can be apportioned reasonably among diverse social enterprises. A manpower increase in one endeavor will usually occur at the expense of a cognate undertaking. For instance, if trained social workers are to be drawn, by diverse methods, more toward correction than they are at present, they will presumably be withdrawn from other activities which they have been staffing. Psychiatric personnel, perennially in short supply, if channeled into correction, will be diverted of necessity from various mental health assignments which also enter a claim on such talent.[1]

There is, of course, no preordained formula which insists that recruitment and training must proceed at the present pace and that personnel must be drawn from the same pool. In addition, there is always the possibility of rationalizing jobs so that limited personnel can be used more efficiently, but such rearrangements, either in recruitment or in operations, require considerably more force and considerably more patience than most planning blueprints provide. Predictive statements are made hazardous by vested interests of established professionals, social definitions of different kinds of work,[2] and unanticipated

SOURCE. *Crime and Delinquency*, **12**, July 1966, pp. 232–239. Reprinted with the permission of the National Council on Crime and Delinquency. Copyright 1966, National Council on Crime and Delinquency.

[1]See George W. Albee, *Mental Health Manpower Trends* (New York: Basic Books, 1959).

[2]See the provocative volume by Arthur Pearl and Frank Reissman, *New Careers for the Poor*

competitive pressures, plus innumerable exigencies of a society undergoing inordinately rapid change. These factors make it essential that personnel plans include ideas both on the rearrangement of current situations and on the evolution and revolution of future conditions.[3]

At present, correctional work, which deals with the redemption of persons who are usually viewed as "voluntaristically" wayward, possesses few qualities likely to place it among the more preeminent, and therefore the more attractive vocational endeavors of our society. The definition of most kinds of work tends to take on something of the coloration of the clientele, and correction is concerned with déclassé individuals, persons already removed from the social mainstream.

In contrast to correction, the practice of medicine, dealing with the "involuntary" ill, is accorded and has arrogated to itself by diverse tactics a high degree of social esteem. This esteem probably derives from, among other factors, the perceived efficacy of the work, its entrepreneurial nature, and, most particularly, its potential value for all citizens, especially at times of sharp personal crisis and need. It is quite probable that the major resolution of manpower problems in correction lies not in enlargement of financial rewards and corollary benefits, the subject of so much intramural attention, and not in increased educational requirements, but in an altered definition of the importance of the work to the society[4] and particularly the importance of correctional clients. It may be true, for instance, that devices aimed at restoring the civil rights of convicted felons—including the right of prison inmates to vote[5]—

(New York: Free Press, 1965), but note also Jack L. Roach's critical appraisal of the book in *American Sociological Review*, February 1966, pp. 111–112. See also U.S. Department of Labor, Manpower Administration, *Mobility and Worker Adaptation to Economic Change in the United States*, Bulletin No. 1, July 1963.

[3]See Henry David, *Manpower Policies for a Democratic Society* (New York: Columbia University Press, 1965), especially pp. 92–115; and U.S. Department of Labor, *Manpower Report of the President and a Report on Manpower Requirements, Resources, Utilization and Training*, Govt. Printing Office, March 1963. In regard to correction see U.S. Senate, Subcommittee on Employment and Manpower, Committee on Labor and Public Welfare, 89th Cong., 1st Sess., "Correctional Rehabilitation Act of 1965," *Hearings* (1965); U.S. House of Representatives, Special Subcommittee on Education, Committee on Education and Labor, 89th Cong., 1st Sess., "Correctional Rehabilitation Act of 1965," *Hearings* (1965); and Charles S. Prigmore, "Corrections Blueprint for National Action on Manpower and Training," *Federal Probation*, September 1964, pp. 25–30.

[4]See Richard Jessor, "A Behavioral Science View of the Correctional Officer," *Federal Probation*, March 1963, pp. 6–10; Milton G. Rector, "Current Status of Correctional Manpower," in *Pacific Coast Institute on Correctional Manpower and Training* (Boulder: WICHE, May 1965), pp. 1–5; Richard B. Heim, "Prison Personnel: A Review of the Literature," *American Journal of Correction*, January–February 1966, pp. 14–20.

[5]This idea has been advocated by Hans Mattick, associate director, Center for Studies in Criminal Justice, University of Chicago. Among other things, it would provide a deeper involvement in the realities of extramural life for inmates and would force office seekers to respond more knowledgeably and benevolently to the needs of their new constituents.

would be a considerably more efficient recruitment procedure than the incessant jockeying for more mundane competitive advantage among various kinds of services attempting to recruit from a similar and limited personnel pool.

Jobs may, of course, be either upgraded or downgraded in terms of their recruitment goals. In the latter instance, they can be redefined as accessible to a wider range of candidates, persons possessing traits more generally distributed in the society. It would seem essential for correction to determine clearly and quickly whether this is the path it cares to travel. The airlines, for instance, which required at first that their stewardesses be attractive and have a college degree and then found after a while that they could not recruit the number they needed if they insisted on this set of qualifications, downgraded eligibility to "neatness" and a high school diploma. It is questionable whether growing public familiarity with air travel (and the increased number of middle- and lower-class passengers) or the new eligibility requirements contributed to the emerging redefinition of the stewardess job as something less glamorous and more plebeian than it initially was. It is not unlikely, however, that airline service and etiquette remain as adequate as they ever were. In the same vein, correction will have to determine whether it can perform as adequate or more adequate a job using persons with less formal preparation but perhaps with equivalent or superior skills.

Downgrading personnel, however, entails certain risks, some of them rather subtle, including further vulnerability to redefinition of jobs and consequent public slights.

In terms of vocational upgrading, it is probably the possession of skills that are not easy to duplicate and which are brought to bear upon tasks viewed by the public as vital that gives any vocation a particularly high social standing. It is not doubted that the abilities of a brain surgeon or those of a nuclear physicist are not obtainable without intensive training and considerable talent. Correctional endeavors, on the other hand, tend to be viewed as the common-sense application (and, unfortunately, they are probably as often as not regarded as a misapplication) of techniques either possessed by or readily available to most persons of reasonable ability. Sometimes, in fact, it is presumed that the absence of special training provides an individual with an uncontaminated innocence that is preferable to the abilities of a person with special training in correctional work.

In these terms, barriers to entry into correctional work are likely to be seen as arbitrary attempts to impose status by controlling supply and demand. Though they may achieve their purpose to a certain extent, they fail to attend to the basic relationship between the vocational task and the social definition attached to it. It is this relationship which is of consummate importance for the resolution of issues of recruitment and retention of correctional personnel.

CURRENT PERSONNEL PRACTICES

Much of the foregoing is rather speculative, and the relationship between variables is an exceedingly intricate affair.[6] Alterations in the age structure of the nation, changes in economic conditions, upheavals or relaxations of tensions in international relationships, the further introduction of automation processes[7]—any and all of these can have an extraordinary impact upon the correctional manpower situation. It is vital that such items be taken into account to as great an extent as possible, though their basic influence on future conditions must inevitably remain something of an enigma.

It would appear important, therefore, in any assessment of recruitment and retention in correction, to obtain some indication of the present operation of correctional enterprises. To this end, questionnaire inquiries were directed to the thirty state correctional agencies responsible for the largest offender populations and to the thirty probation departments serving the largest metropolitan areas in the United States. The inventory covered a range of informational items and more general personnel issues and provided an opportunity for commentary on any cognate matters that might seem important to the respondent. About 40 percent of the questionnaires were returned, a somewhat low figure considering the tendency of bureaucracies to reply routinely to their mail as a matter of public relations.

Perhaps the flat and rather uninspired nature of the responses was their most marked feature. The almost universal emphasis upon a desperate necessity to increase wages and fringe benefits of employees would seem to indicate that economic determinism dies hard and inventive ingenuity is difficult to evoke. At the same time, reasonably close reading of the responses, once the clichés are put aside, provides material that can be both challenging and disturbing to ingrained manners of thinking about correctional manpower. A respondent from one of the southern states, for instance, quarreled with what he perceived to be the basic thrust of the questionnaire. For him, retention of personnel for more than a short time—a year or two—was patently undesirable. A correctional employee who remained longer than two years in his job with the prison system was regarded by this administrator as lacking either the drive or the ability to move on to more attractive fields, and these shortcomings would be likely to detract from his performance in correctional work.

Views such as this were rather unusual, however, particularly from large agencies, which felt that they offered lifetime career opportunities with reason-

---

[6]An excellent theoretical statement is Peter M. Blau *et al.*, "Occupation Choice: A Conceptual Framework," *Industrial and Labor Relations Review*, July 1965, pp. 531–543. See also Gilbert Geis, "Liberal Education and Social Welfare: Educational Choices and Their Consequences," *Journal of Education for Social Work*, Spring 1965, pp. 26–32.

[7]For a comprehensive bibliography on this question see Mary R. Heslet, "Automation and Its Impact: Selected References," in U.S. Senate, Subcommittee on Employment and Manpower, Committee on Labor and Public Education, 88th Cong., 2nd Sess., "Nation's Manpower Revolution," *Hearings* (1964), pp. 3494–3500.

able promotional ranges and increasingly challenging opportunities. The basic tendency of the respondents, whether from large or small organizations, was to view their agency as a self-contained employment structure, intent upon keeping or gaining ascendancy over competitors in manpower matters. This personnel ethnocentricity is, of course, neither surprising nor necessarily untoward, but it indicates the need for correctional manpower problems to be viewed ultimately in terms much broader than those of the correctional field itself and to be placed sensitively and sensibly in a perspective which involves careful consideration of various strategic and ideological matters. (For example, how much of our limited social resources should be channeled for help of the so-called "undeserving poor," such as criminal offenders, in contrast to the "deserving poor," such as the aged and the ill?)

Recruitment procedures reported by various agencies tended to follow rather traditional and expected lines. Advertising, some direct solicitation in colleges and universities, and the mechanisms of civil service recruitment were often utilized. A large number of responses showed an underlying edginess about the failure of civil service departments to appreciate what were viewed as the special needs and the special problems of the correctional field. Perhaps the most interesting note in responses on recruitment procedures was the reiteration that word-of-mouth and "grapevine" recruitment sources usually proved far more productive than more formal approaches. There was also some complaint by respondents that social work graduates often had already optioned their future to sources which had provided them with scholarships for their advanced training, though only a few of the agencies went so far as to take this lesson to heart and suggest that correction might duplicate such tactics.

There was very little introspection or vocational soul-searching when it came to an inventory of traits desired in prospective employees, despite the fact that correction has persistently been accused by academic writers of inattention to the precise enunciation of goals and indifference to the determination of the relationship between these goals and traits needed in employees to advance them.[8] Respondents placed some stress on adequate probationary periods for new workers, but were virtually unanimous on the qualities needed for good job performance. These could be found, respondents regularly indicated, in "educated and emotionally stable people capable of using mature judgment." Interest in other people was also stressed as an important vocational virtue for correctional workers. The respondents also seemed to have a special nervousness regarding prospective employees who might have criminal records, and much emphasis was placed upon adequate screening of such persons. "We like somone whose personal life can bear social scrutiny," one administrator noted, proceeding along the same line but carrying this point somewhat further than his fellows.

[8]See Don C. Gibbons, *Changing the Law-breaker* (Englewood Cliffs, N.J.: Prentice-Hall, 1965).

The only respondent to stray from the rather stereotyped pattern of these answers touched upon the possible incongruity between his agency's requirements and requirements for successful job performance:

"We generalize and say we want warm, empathetic, understanding, intelligent college graduates who can function in an authoritarian role with hostile, aggressive delinquents. . . . But the stated qualities and the job setting often appear to be mutually exclusive. The warm, responsive type of person may not be able to work effectively in an authoritarian, controlling setting. Also, how do you know when you have been successful? Is the practitioner supposed to be a junior-grade psychiatrist . . . or is he supposed to engage primarily in acts of surveillance to assure compliance with court orders, or is he supposed to be something in-between or something completely different? . . . We cannot really answer the question concerning the kind of person we need to do the job—*what* job?"

There was a rather even division among the responding agencies concerning their present satisfaction or dissatisfaction with matters of personnel recruitment and retention. Discontent tended to be focused on the value of screening devices used by civil service departments to discriminate among applicants and, of course, on salary scales—the universal complaint. Reference letters were criticized as providing wholly inadequate information regarding potential employees; it was suggested that telephone calls tend to yield much better information. The head of one agency added a personal lament that it was self-defeating to undertake elaborate hiring procedures when the jobs being sought were themselves not that attractive.

In regard to tactics for retaining personnel once they are on the job, the agreed approach was that the best method is to build the individual into the system so securely that it would be either financially or emotionally impossible for him to depart. Pension plans scaled to length of service, with sharply increasing benefits toward the later years on the job, were often advocated. Increasing the opportunity for decision-making and expanding the realms for the exercise of power were also seen as rather obvious ways to bind employees more tightly into the agency. Only one respondent provided a cynical reaction to the question of personnel retention, which he apparently regarded as too pretentious an issue in terms of the reality of his agency. "Only two things," he wrote, "serve to keep a correctional worker at his job here—his dedication or his lack of marketability elsewhere." Again, it does not seem unreasonable to point out the patent lack of ingenuity or inventiveness in the answers. Restricted by formal regulations and hampered by the feelings and the scrutiny of the political system and the public, the agency heads seem to add to this heavy burden a rather passive and unimaginative set of procedures and ideas for retaining their manpower.

---

[9] An interesting attempt to indicate "what the job is" on an international scale is United Nations, *The Recruitment, Training and Status of Personnel for Adult Penal and Correctional Institutions*, Report by the Secretariat, March 3, 1955 (A/CONF.6/C.1/L.2).

AGENCY PERSONNEL SURVEYED

The brief questionnaire assessment of personnel matters in correctional agencies and probation departments throughout the country provided information about the procedures and beliefs operative at the present time. An exploratory study, of some personnel issues in a metropolitan probation department may throw some light on how the workers react to different policies and conditions and may provide some insight into how a department can discover and improve upon sore points in personnel matters.[10]

The study involved the dispatch of questionnaires to 163 persons who had entered the probation department during 1959 and 1960—five years before. For purposes of analysis the respondents were divided into three categories: those coming to the rank of probation officer through prior service as counselors in the agency, those entering the department as probation trainees, and those recruited directly into probation from other social service agencies.

The responses to the mail survey indicated, among other things, that the trainees were more likely to be aware of the kind of work they were entering when they accepted their appointments than were members of the other two groups. It also discovered that employees who, once on the job, continue with their education and secure graduate degrees tend, to a much greater degree than other workers, to leave the department.

There was also overwhelming agreement on the satisfaction derived from working directly with probationers. In response to an inquiry asking for suggestions for improvement of departmental personnel policy, few unexpected items emerged. Most remarks centered in the need for smaller caseloads, less paper work, increased promotional opportunities, higher pay, more fringe benefits, horizontal promotions between institutions and field offices, and the need to gain recognition as "professional workers." The study also demonstrated, contrary to prevailing opinion in the department, that trainees have a higher turnover rate than persons coming to probation officer positions from the counselor ranks. The study report pointed out, in addition, that its own value had been handicapped considerably because of inadequate department personnel records, particularly in regard to conditions which had changed during the course of the person's period of employment, such as his marital status and his educational achievements. It also found that the evaluation reports on personnel were totally inadequate for any rating purposes or any approach that might provide better insight into the caliber of persons leaving the department. In regard to such evaluations, the study noted, "platitudes were the rule, rather than the exception." Finally, the study stressed the importance that might be attached to in-depth interviews with officers terminating employment, to discover, from persons usually with less reason that others to gloss

[10] Gwen Moore, Charles Hamson, and Roger Hull, "A Study of Individuals Who Became Deputy Probation Officers during the Years 1959–1960," graduate seminar paper, California State College, Los Angeles, February 1966.

over the dissatisfactions with the agency, what had led them to seek other opportunities.

The utility of such an investigation for any department is readily apparent. The study seems to suggest, for instance, a need for more effective pre-job orientation for personnel other than trainees in order to acquaint them better with the job they will face. It brings into question the value for the department, in terms of its own personnel situation, of encouraging advanced education.[11] It indicates strongly that the enthusiasm for their work found among employees might be exploited for recruitment purposes, either through the use of probation officers to transmit their feelings directly to potential employees in recruitment drives or through the publication of testimonials from such men, published in brochure form and circulated to potential sources of manpower. There also appeared to be a need for more intensive study of career patterns in the department, particularly among its trainees. The necessity to maintain more adequate personnel records was obvious. Such suggestions, emerging from a small pilot study, indicate the possibilities inherent in more comprehensive and continuous scrutiny of personnel matters in any correctional agency.

SUMMARY AND CONCLUSIONS

Personnel issues in correction may be examined by concentrating upon various elements of the question, "Who does what to whom for what purpose and with what result?" To the extent that any of the items in the question shift, the remainder will probably also undergo alteration. In addition, many of the problems involved in recruitment and retention of correctional personnel are intimately tied to corollary problems concerning the nature of the society at any given moment and the extent and nature of crime and its control.

This paper has attempted to indicate briefly a few of the underlying issues associated with questions of correctional manpower, and it has presented the results of two small research probes which provide information on facts and problems involved in agency procedures and those indicated by correctional workers themselves. Both reports suggest the potentialities of more intensive and sophisticated empirical studies.

In conclusion, we again assert the basic theme of the paper, which insists that the definition of correctional work in the larger society would appear to be the most important ingredient in policies concerning correctional manpower. More than two centuries ago, those astute foreign commentators on the American scene, Gustave de Beaumont and Alexis de Tocqueville, sounded a note that continues to ring true. The two men had visited several new American penitentiaries and they compared these with the older, benighted establishments for felons. Their observations included the following personnel note:

[11]See generally Julian Roebuck and Paul Zelhart, "The Problem of Educating the Correctional Practitioner," *Journal of Criminal Law, Criminology and Police Science*, March 1965, pp. 45–53.

"As soon as the penitentiary system was adopted in the United States, the personnel changed in nature. For jailor of a prison, vulgar people only could be found; the most distinguished persons offered themselves to administer a penitentiary where a moral direction exists.[12]"

It may be difficult for us, endowed with hindsight, to appreciate the quality or the benevolence of persons entering correction at the time De Beaumont and De Tocqueville were writing on the "moral direction" of their efforts. But the superiority of such persons to their predecessors remains unquestioned, and the lessons implicit in their recruitment are equally irrefutable. As a job comes to be defined as important in terms of those values regarded highly by the society, to that extent will it be treated well by the society, and to that same extent will its personnel situation be enhanced.

[12]Gustave de Beaumont and Alexis de Tocqueville, *On the Penitentiary System in the United States* (Carbondale: Southern Illinois University Press, 1964), p. 63.

57

Needs and Directions in Probation Training

EDWARD M. TAYLOR AND ALEXANDER W. McEACHERN

The purpose of this article is to discuss the need for nationwide research and training programs for probation and to make some tentative suggestions about the form and content of such programs. There often seem to be two points of view with respect to the shortcomings in the field of probation: One decries the lack of knowledge; the other decries the lack of training. Massive programs are mounted to attack one or another of the problems implicit in these points of view, even though nearly everyone recognizes that at their most divergent they are merely facets of one single problem. The objective of this article is to display these points of view explicitly as facets of a single problem, and to suggest ways in which this problem might be attacked.[1]

Considering the magnitude of crime and delinquency in this country, and the immense resources of time, money, and talent which must be devoted to solving or merely containing these problems, it is apparent that we are past the point where good intentions, intuition, trial and error, charismatic wizardry, or merely habit and tradition can remain the major determinants of policy and practice in the field of probation. The alternative is obvious: research and training. That almost everyone who has anything to say on the subject has been saying so far the past 50 years does not make it less true, but it does suggest that in the field of probation the obstacles to innovation are particularly ponderous.

SOURCE. *Federal Probation*, XXX, March 1966, pp. 18–24.

[1]The preparation of this paper was supported in part by Public Health Service Grant (M H–06597–03) from the National Institute of Mental Health.

THE ROLE OF RESEARCH

Not the least of these obstacles is the fact that research is presently not a standard tool of probation departments and, to the extent that it is not, there is correspondingly little awareness of its possibilities, of the role it could and should play in determining policy. In most departments, research, when it is thought of at all, is considered little more than an exotic intrusion rather than as the normal and necessary basis for forming decisions. The immense variation in philosophy and procedure from one juvenile court to another and from one probation department to another both reflects and creates an indifference toward communication and the possibility that one way of doing things might be better than another.

To a certain extent some of these variations may be more apparent than real: Different methods of reporting may disguise basically similar situations. And to the extent that local variations in procedures and philosophy are a reflection of specific needs and problems, such variations may all be to the good. But whatever the cause, such variation prolongs and frustrates attempts at comparative research, and inevitably limits the degree to which results would be applicable to the work of other agencies. As a result, we are left with a great many fundamental, yet unanswered questions.

How effective is probation? Even so elementary a question as this cannot adequately be answered for the simple reason that there is no way of discovering what probation is attempting to do. There are many well-phrased statements of basic principles and ultimate goals. At the other extreme are the specific instructions for office routine. But in between there are few descriptions of probation work which would enable us to judge whether particular workers or departments are effective at accomplishing whatever it is they wish to accomplish with specific individuals.

This point is worth considering in some detail, for it should be obvious that records which permit an accurate evaluation neither of what an agency does nor of how effectively it does it, represent an administrative shortcoming that would be tolerated in few other circumstances. We shall continue to witness the present complacent toleration so long as it is considered either impossible or unnecessary to compare the procedures of one probation department with those of another. Certain records are kept, of course, and certain comparisons are made. But they do not do what they are supposed to do. They do not define or describe the actual work of probation.

DISCOVERING THE PROBLEMS OF PROBATION

Year after year probation departments faithfully forward to state and federal agencies an account of the "problems" they dealt with during the year. And year after year these are described as so many cases of petty theft and so many of burglary, of so many incorrigibles and so many runaways. For all this tells us about the problems of delinquency, we might nearly as well report the color of their eyes or the number of their teeth. Juveniles are not convicted of crimes in our courts nor are they given specific punishments for having committed a crime. In short, to say that a youngster perpetrated a petty theft, tells us nothing about the problems with which the probation officer will actually be concerned. The only meaningful description would be one which related what the youngster is doing or has done to what the probation officer can or will do about it. Since this has never been done, and we consequently have no real definition of the problems of delinquency, it is at present impossible to make any meaningful generalizations about what probation is attempting to do. Fortunately, the actual working of probation is far in advance of anything that can be gathered from the way in which that work is reported.

Probation officers do not try to "solve" the problem of burglary or assault. They work with whatever causes led to the burglary or assault. The real problems of the probation officer are such things as the boy with an IQ of 60, or whose father beats him, or who has a compulsion to start fires, or who has a reputation to maintain with a gang. And these, of course, may only be manifestations of even more subtle problems.

But of all this, of the actual problems which are related to what the officer says or does in a given case, nothing is known except by the officer himself and perhaps his supervisor. The information may be buried in the files of each case, but the herculean task of extracting it from those files for any meaningful purpose of comparison would be enough to convince anyone, as so many probation workers are convinced, that research is "impractical."

In order to map out an intelligent strategy against the problems of delinquency, we must first have reliable information which describes delinquency in terms of what is done about it rather than, as at present, simply in terms of a list of acts which the community would like to prohibit. Until we can devise more sophisticated systems of describing the various types of offenses and offenders, we cannot plan for the effective utilization of the resources that are available. At present an individual probation officer may do an excellent job of defining the problems in a given case and of employing sound and effective techniques from his own experience and training in dealing with those problems. Departments as well may have developed efficient techniques for handling the various types of cases, but if a case has not been accurately described in the first place, there is really no way of knowing why a particular course of action was taken, of comparing it with similar cases, or of learning from it in order to contribute to a general advancement in the field. So long as delinquency is described neither accurately nor in terms of what is done about it, it remains impossible to evaluate the success of probation services in regard to any particular type of delinquency.

The point of all this is that hardly the first steps have been taken to organize the work and the descriptions of that work in such a way that one can understand what probation does and attempt to improve it on the basis of that understanding. This primitive condition exists in almost every area of the mental health field, in almost every social control or treatment agency.

THE NEED FOR TRAINING

The situation in regard to training is somewhat better since there is at least a traditional acceptance of the fact that a little time lost in training is made up later in increased efficiency. But even here, if we discount the merely procedural matters of office routine which *must* be explained, most probation departments find it extremely difficult to provide the training they know should be made available. Once again there are many reasons why this is so, but in association with the need for more extensive research, the immediate need for allied training programs may be considered a consequence of three primary factors:

1. Professional competence is essential to any meaningful purpose probation might serve.
2. No preservice professional training programs are presently available.
3. None but the largest metropolitan areas have the facilities, personnel, and budgets to carry out effective inservice training programs.

Probation is the primary answer of our society to the problems of juvenile delinquency. How completely this is true usually comes as somewhat of a shock to the layman. Of the 61,775 boys referred to the probation departments of California for the first time in 1963, 42.2 percent were dismissed at intake (a *response* to the problem, but not, perhaps, an *answer*); 3.4 percent were referred to some other agency; 11.9 percent were placed under informal supervision by the probation departments; and the remaining 42.5 percent had petitions filed for hearings in juvenile courts. Of the boys who appeared in court, 82.4 percent were placed on probation. Only 3.3 percent were either remanded to adult court or committed directly to the California Youth Authority. The rest, 14.3 percent, were dismissed, this time by the court.[2]

Police, of course, "counsel and release" a great many youngsters, particularly first offenders, without referring them to probation at all. The content and effect of such police contacts are matters of extreme importance, but at the moment we know so little about them that they should perhaps be considered in the category of the counseling and releasing of parents, teachers, neighbors, and others—a real, but not formal or official response of the society to the problems of delinquency. Of those 61,775 boys referred to probation for the first time during the year, only 678 were sent to be "locked up" in some way by the Youth Authority. And the Youth Authority itself estimates that

---

[2]*Delinquency and Probation in California 1963*, Bureau of Criminal Statistics, State of California Department of Justice, 1964.

40 percent of the commitments it receives could and should have been handled by probation.[3]

These figures are not meant to suggest that only these 678 boys were removed from the community during the year—many who were initially placed on probation were eventually returned to court for commitment to the Youth Authority and many boys placed on probation were sent to county-operated "camps" and other facilities—but they do suggest the importance of probation as the primary resource in the treatment of delinquents. And the reason we stress the importance of probation is to suggest how crucial are the qualities and competence of the probation officer. It should be apparent that the profound changes in the philosophy, practice, and procedures in the treatment of juveniles by our courts demand, for their successful implementation, probation officers with knowledge, attitudes, and skills of a type which can be assured on a large scale only by professional training.

IMPORTANCE OF PROFESSIONAL COMPETENCE

The largest probation department in the United States sums up its philosophy in three principles:

1. The circumstances which bring minors to the attention of the probation officer frequently are but symptoms of deeper problems for which there may be neither a single cause nor a single treatment.

2. Probation services constitute a program of diagnosis, evaluation, and treatment of the particular needs of individual minors, rooted in the belief that, with the proper help, people can change.

3. Juvenile probation services to individual minors are in the best interest and welfare of the community as a whole.[4]

It should be obvious that the third of these principles is questionable unless probation officers possess the ability to deal with the "deeper problems" and to perform the "diagnosis, evaluation, and treatment of the particular needs of individual minors" at a very high level of competence. The point we are making is not simply that probation officers need more training. Anyone does. The real point is this: Either probation officers have reached a certain threshold level of professional competence, or the entire philosophy of probation service requires reinterpretation.

When we realize that the very purpose of our juvenile courts depends on the professional competence of the probation officer, we are in a position to appreciate the severe limitations under which most departments must attempt to implement the philosophy of probation. Lack of preservice professional training schools means that few men and women enter the profession with a proper balance of training in the various disciplines and skills which are necessary for probation work. It may well mean that fewer college students decide on a career

---

[3]*Probation Supervision and Training,* California Youth Authority, 1964.
[4]*Juvenile Manual.* Los Angeles County Probation Department.

in corrections in time to plan their studies accordingly. The fact that probation departments are forced to recruit from various disciplines necessarily limits the level of sophistication to which their own training programs can be directed. Obviously, no single probation department can or ever will be able to "teach" sociology, social work, psychology, criminology, public administration, or whatever the field in which a particular applicant may be deficient. It may even be difficult to recognize the deficiency since even a "course" or two in college taken by someone who was not at the time planning for a career in corrections will tell very little about what he knows that is applicable to probation work. Underlying all this is the lack of a clear image of what probation is or what the probation officer does. If probation is to fulfill its function it must be able to attract capable young men and women early in their academic career and to a great extent this will depend on its ability to improve and make known its professional stature.

ADMINISTRATIVE LIMITATIONS

Probation departments are, with few exceptions, organized and administered at the local city or county level. This means that policies, budgets, facilities, salaries, practices, and even philosophy, may vary considerably from place to place. It also means that the majority of the probation departments will be too small to possess the facilities or personnel to carry out adequate programs of inservice training when the people it must hire have not had prior professional training. Even when the smaller department does invest heavily in time and money training its officers, it is often only to lose them a year or so later to a larger department with the advantages of better pay, a metropolitan location, more facilities, and a greater opportunity for advancement. The existence of many relatively small departments under the direction of local boards of supervisors, or their equivalent, and even judges who may be unaware of, or out of sympathy with, many of the aims and possibilities of probation service inhibits the development of professional stature for probation officers and makes it difficult for them to standardize their work along the most effective and efficient lines. It also makes it difficult for officers to study what is happening elsewhere and local variations in practices and recording techniques make it difficult to make meaningful comparisons even if the opportunity were available. Even in those few places where state aid might be available to help remedy deficiencies in training, it is frequently rejected for fear it would, at the very least, usurp local control over the standards and qualifications of officers.

USING OUTSIDE RESOURCES

The fact is, for the reasons we have discussed and others as well, there is no way that probation can overcome the obstacles it faces in establishing comprehensive research and training programs. There is more professionalism now than there was in the past and there will be more in the future than there is now, but with their own resources alone, it is doubtful that local probation departments will be capable of keeping pace with the magnitude and complexity of the problems they face. We may expect the development of a number of graduate programs in the field of corrections within the next 5 or 10 years and these will be of immense help in respect both to research and training, but even after the many years it will take before such programs create a real effect on the day-to-day work of the profession they will provide only a partial solution to the problem. The well-trained novice is a good beginning, but only a beginning.

INTRODUCING RESEARCH FINDINGS

In the years ahead it will become increasingly important that means be found to introduce social and behavioral science research directly into the working operations and training activities of almost all social service or treatment organizations. As research becomes an ongoing function within the profession, so must inservice training. A certain amount of this research will, like the research of industry, be of interest primarily to administrators and planners who will establish policies based upon it. But a great deal more must be relayed directly to the practitioner since in one way or another most of these agencies rely on the one-to-one relationship of people working with other people and such a relationship cannot be continuously and effectively manipulated by administrative fiat alone. Unlike the factory worker who can be told to sink two rivets rather than one without having to understand the mechanics of stress which led the engineers to make such a decision, the worker in social agencies cannot be expected to change his way of doing things without a clear explanation and reasonable proof that he should. No one envisages the day when dealing with people can be reduced to a rigid science, but as the trial and error method of individual experience becomes increasingly supplemented with adequate research based upon the collective experience of larger numbers of workers, the problems of introducing the findings of this research effectively into a working organization with habits and traditions of its own, will become a crucial issue.

Even today, an immense amount of research has been carried out under the auspices of the Federal Government, private foundations and even individual probation departments and the findings of this research might have a profound effect on a national scale if it could reach the caseload-level professional workers in a form that would be meaningful to them. The few very large departments, some of the departments organized at the state level, and some of the statewide professional organizations either do or could accept the responsibility of trying to create an effect at the working level with this research, but for the vast majority of departments it is practically impossible.

Researchers seldom have the necessary knowledge and experience in a given field, such as probation, to convert their findings into specific suggestions for altering practice in that field and few administrators or workers have either the time or training that would enable them adequately to examine and evaluate the relevant findings with sufficient assurance to justify any change in their present way of doing things. Closing the gap between research and practice will demand cooperation from both sides. Probation departments and the various state and professional organizations should be working much harder toward the achievement of more sophisticated and standardized reporting methods. When this is achieved, the cost of research in terms both of time and money will be greatly reduced, but, more importantly, because standardized reporting methods will permit broader investigation at less expense, the findings of research will have applicability to greater numbers of departments. Increased applicability greatly reduces the difficulty of evaluation and interpretation for individual administrators. Researchers can be more specific in their recommendations since they will not have to hedge them about with so many qualifications about the meaning and reliability of the records of the particular agency with which they worked. Administrators, in turn, can feel more confident that the findings are relevant to their own situation and can place more reliance on the recommendations of state and professional organizations.

Today, however, the picture is considerably more bleak. As we have noted, few probation departments are in a position to make use of what research is available. Even if an administrator could discover and evaluate for himself, or have suggested to him by some other agency or group, research findings with practical implications for the work of his department, he would still face the problem of communicating those findings in an effective fashion to his staff. With certain types of material, this would mean the creation of a special training program. Here again only a handful of departments are capable of instituting such programs.

A NATIONWIDE PROGRAM

Considering the difficulties encountered by medium- and small-sized departments, one possible solution might be the creation of a major training program designed for nationwide distribution. The form of the program should be such that individual departments could profit from it without having to bring in lecturers or academicians to explain and interpret the material. The core of the material, particularly the documentation, would have to be presented in booklet form for private study, but the complete program should include films, film strips, tapes, or other forms of material more suitable for group presentation and for arousing group interest without the aid of a specially trained leader. What is also needed, and preferably at the same time, is adequate research into the problems of producing organizational change. Since there will be an increasing need for such training programs in almost all social treatment or control agencies, now is the time to learn something about it.

Since objections to nationwide programs, particularly if supported by the Federal Government, center on the dangers inherent in forced conformity and usurpation of local control, it would be highly desirable that such training programs be confined, as much as possible, to the presentation of factual and documented material. The goal of selecting, evaluating, and interpreting research findings relevant to probation work would satisfy this condition of objectivity in a national program and would provide a valuable service which most departments cannot supply for themselves.

LEARNING FROM OTHERS

The results of failure to institute such programs are painfully obvious. Perhaps the most painful has been the lack of communication between departments and a consequent inability to profit from what others have learned. No single department has the resources to launch a great number of programs and few have the resources to "experiment" at all. It is extremely important, therefore, that each department be well informed of what others have attempted and how well it worked.

Just to take one example, for almost thirty years the Boston Juvenile Court has been working with a program called the "Citizenship Training Group."[5] Certain boys between the ages of 12 and 17 are required, as a condition of probation, to attend this program 2 hours a day, 5 days a week, for 12 weeks. The program is privately supported and receives no city or state financial aid. On the basis of a 10-year study, it is claimed that 72.6 percent of the boys who passed through the program were successfully rehabilitated. Any program which can survive for 30 years, costs the taxpayer nothing, and succeeds with 72.6 percent of its cases cannot, to paraphrase the late W. C. Fields, be all bad. And yet only four or five other departments have attempted to copy the program. Why so few? It might be that the program will only work in Boston. It might be that the other cities could not find private support and the program might not work with public support. It might be that the program succeeds only because of the talent of its director or the particular juvenile court judge. It might be that the 72.6 success figure does not mean what it appears to mean. It might be that other cities have or are planning programs which they believe will be even more successful. It might be any number of things, but by far the most likely explanation is simply that other departments do not know enough about the program to feel confident in attempting to duplicate it. The Boston probation department cannot afford to send people around the Nation proselytizing for its program and the other departments about the Nation cannot

[5]Louis G. Maglio. "The Citizenship Training Program of the Boston Juvenile Court." *Juvenile Court Judges Journal*, December 1956.

afford to send people to Boston to study what happens there. The same lack of communication which leaves effective programs uncopied makes possible the continued replication of demonstrably ineffective programs.

LEARNING FROM NATURAL EXPERIMENTS

Special programs, however, represent only a small part of the information which should be communicated between probation departments. Because of the legal framework within which they operate, it is difficult for courts or probation departments to experiment in their treatment of criminals or delinquents. Each court or probation department evolves what it believes to be the best methods for treating various kinds of offenders and then attempts to apply these methods as impartially as possible. But while few individual courts or probation departments are willing, or feel they have the authority deliberately to alter their treatment on an arbitrary or experimental basis, the fact is that different courts and probation departments do have very different ways of doing things and careful comparison of these differences might in some cases yield substantially the same information as controlled experimentation within a single court or department.[6]

It can be demonstrated with distressing ease that people who commit similar offenses are given different treatment in different places. Some probation departments dismiss over 60 percent of their cases at intake. Other departments seldom dismiss any case without referring it to the courts.[7] Does this mean that the department which has dismissed over half its cases has failed in its responsibilities to the community or does it mean that the department which passes all its problems on to the court is wasting time, energy, and money on cases that do not require it? Similar questions may be raised in regard to a great many practices which exhibit marked variation from one jurisdiction to another. Some courts demand that minors always be represented by counsel, others do not. Some courts refer a great many delinquents to state correctional institutions, others rely almost exclusively on their own probation services. Some police departments maintain specially trained juvenile officers and attempt to deal with as many of their problems as they can on their own. They

---

[6] A study of this nature has been undertaken by the authors in which background information was collected on all referrals to eight Southern California probation departments during a 2-month period. Records were kept of the disposition of these cases and of any re-referral during a 1-year period. A record was also kept of each contact by a probation officer with any of these youngsters. An attempt will be made to evaluate the relative effectiveness of different dispositions and treatment in the various departments of youngsters with similar backgrounds and offenses. This study is supported by the Public Health Service (Grant number M H–06597).

[7] Of the two California probation departments which received the largest number of referrals during 1963, one department dismissed 68.8 percent of the boys referral at intake, while the other department dismissed only 9.6 percent at intake. (*Delinquency and Probation in California 1963*, Bureau of Criminal Statistics, State of California Department of Justice, 1964.)

tend to view the courts and probation as a last resort for the most serious cases. Other police departments want to have as little as possible to do with juvenile matters and refer almost every case immediately to probation departments. With the best of intentions, some judges or probation departments may feel that youngsters with certain family problems or from certain socio-economic or ethnic backgrounds are better off in state correctional schools than returned to their environment and so, in effect, discriminate against them on grounds unconnected with any offense they may have committed.

These and a great many other variations in practice from one place to another deserve attention, for the seriousness of the problem and justice alike require that we standardize our treatment of offenders in line with the most efficient and effective methods possible. Research on the comparative effectiveness of various police, court, and probation practices would, in addition to evaluations of special programs, constitute a useful area of subject-matter for a national training program. The individual probation department is seldom in a position adequately to evaluate its own procedures, much less go out to study what others are doing. This is particularly true of the smaller departments whose problems are likely to be somewhat different from those of the larger departments where such little research as there is, has usually been undertaken.

A national training program that could provide small- and medium-sized probation departments with documentation to justify changes in their own procedures and to substantiate their attempts to influence the attitudes and practices of local agencies and individuals with whom they share a joint responsibility for dealing with crime and delinquency, would be an immense help and, in fact, perhaps the only effective means of resolving many local deadlocks over questions of practice and philosophy.

GENERAL NEED FOR LARGE-SCALE PROGRAMS

There are several major developments in our society today which serve to increase the significance and necessity of large-scale training programs based on research and designed for the professional already at work in social treatment and control agencies. Technical advancement and a greater use of automation in industry have created both the need, and in some ways the possibility for satisfying the need, for a much broader range of social welfare and treatment programs than have been attempted in our past. Each year witnesses the launching of vast new programs or the steady enlargement of those already in existence. The profound political, economic, and cultural effects of these programs on the life of the Nation cannot be underestimated. The scope of this movement and, more immediately to the point of this discussion, the magnitude of social problems such as crime and delinquency, make it absolutely essential that we know what we are doing. An increasing number of people who in the past have been or would have been trained to work with tools, must be trained or retrained to work with people. The fact that so much remains to be learned in this area means that even those who have received such training must constantly be brought up to date as we acquire the knowledge we need. The field of corrections, and it is, of course, not the only offender in this respect, has failed to provide itself with the continuous, ongoing programs of research and training which are desperately needed now and will be even more desperately needed in the near future. When we contrast the planning, research, control, and development that precede an attempt to launch a rocket to the moon with our preparations for launching a war on crime, poverty, or ignorance, we can see why we sometimes hit the moon, but seldom defeat crime, poverty, or ignorance. Sloppy engineering will suffice for an oxcart, but not a missile, and the vagaries of "common sense" may do for handling most of the problems within a given family, but not for the social problems of a nation of a couple hundred million people. Our research into a major social problem and our training of the people who are to handle it, must be on the scale of the problem itself.

58

The Social System
of Correctional Workers*

T. C. ESSELSTYN

In the past twenty-five years much has been written about the soicial system developed among prisoners and its effects upon inmates and staff. Less has appeared in the literature concerning the social systems of juvenile offenders in institutions. This gap, however, is being closed by studies such as those of Weber, Breed, Fisher, and Polsky.[1] In general, the literature on social systems analyzes the interaction of the offender, adult or juvenile, with other offenders and the way this interaction influences beliefs and values- behavior, and the achievement of correctional goals.

No comparable studies seem to have been made of the social systems existing among correctional workers, about which practically nothing is known. It is as though everyone believed that the processes of social interaction and of emerging social systems do not occur among correctional workers or that, if they do, they have no significance for the correctional field.

SOURCE. *Crime and Delinquency*, **12**, April 1966, pp. 117–124. Reprinted with the permission of the National Council on Crime and Delinquency, Copvright 1966, National Council on Crime and Delinquency.

*Revised version of a paper presented before the Second Annual Institute, California Probation, Parole, and Correctional Association, Lompoc, Calif., Feb. 26, 1964.

[1]George Weber, "Conflict between Professional and Nonprofessional Personnel in Institutional Delinquency Treatment," *Journal of Criminal Law, Criminology, and Police Science*, May–June 1957, pp. 26–43; Allen Breed, "Inmate Subculture," *California Youth Authority Quarterly*, Spring 1963, pp. 3–16; Sethard Fisher, "Social Organization in a Correctional Residence," *Pacific Sociological Review*, Fall 1961, pp. 87–93; and Howard Polsky, *Cottage Six* (New York: Russell Sage Foundation, 1962).

The present paper which challenges that point of view, is a report on a small pilot study of how correctional workers interact and indicates the significance of this interaction.

METHOD

The study did not follow the canons of scientific method. We guessed that correctional workers did interact socially with each other outside working hours, but beyond this, no hypothesis was made. The study sought to discover these social patterns, not to test or validate any theories.

The sample examined, numbering thirty-one workers, while large enough for exploratory purposes, was not large enough to support final conclusions. Moreover, the sample was deliberately biased; none of the established techniques designed to ensure a truly representative selection was employed. We knew in advance that those included in the study did interact with one another to some extent. What we wanted to find out was: how often, how deeply, and with what effects?

The study was concerned exclusively with the frequency of *off-duty* contacts between correctional workers and with the content and meaning of these meetings. It was not concerned with contacts *during the working day* or with off-duty contacts with people in other fields.

The term "correctional worker" is used here to include probation officers (county and federal), parole agents (almost exclusively of the Youth Authority), correctional counselors, and five senior correctional supervisors who had previously served in the other capacities. The data for the study were collected by a questionnaire with the usual guarantees of anonymity, although none of the items touched on sensitive subjects. Thirty-four questionnaires were mailed out; thirty-one were returned. The three which were not returned were not followed up and we do not know which workers did not respond or why they did not. The workers were located throughout California. Distributions and returns were made in November and December, 1962.

FINDINGS

For many decades, commuting to and from the job site has been standard practice in California for all groups of the civilian labor force, even for resident farm workers. Twelve of the thirty-one workers in our sample reported that they commute to and from the job site with other correctional workers, thus creating a setting for some form of interaction or social bond outside of working hours. Table 1 shows something about the duration of that interaction. If we take the midpoints of the two traveling intervals for these twelve workers, the range is from fifteen to forty-five minutes once a day. When this time is multiplied by two (since the table shows commuting time in one direction only), it

Table 1 *If You Commute with Other CW's, How Long Does the Trip Take One Way?*

(a) 5 to 30 minutes	10
(b) 30 to 60 minutes	2

is clear that these workers are in mutual interaction on this occasion alone for sustained periods every day.

The lunch period provides another occasion when workers of all classes get together. Twenty-six, all but five of the sample, eat lunch with one another. The questionnaire did not inquire what they talk about or do in addition to eating their lunch, but we know enough about this noonday ritual to believe that it is another rich setting for conversation, interaction, and the weaving of social bonds.

Do correctional workers socialize with each other at other times of the

Table 2 *During the Past Six Months Have You (Check All Applicable)*

(a) visited a cw at his home?	26
(b) had a cw visit you at your home?	25
(c) taken a vacation with a cw?	1
(d) spent an afternoon or evening "on the town" with a cw?	22

day or night? Where, if at all, does this take place? How long does it last? How frequently does it occur? When it occurs, does the conversation ever become shop talk? Such considerations underlay the items summarized in Tables 2, 3, and 4. (Only those who replied affirmatively—twenty-eight—are included.)

The simple counts shown in these three tables support the following statements with respect to the modal correctional worker of the sample:

He visits his co-workers; they visit him; and now and then, they go off for a big night together. These social contacts last anywhere from an hour to half a day or night or even more, and on average occupy from two to three hours in a

Table 3 *If you checked "yes" in any of the blanks in No. 2 above, estimate the number of after-duty hours (not lunch, not commuting) which you spent in the company of cw's in any typical week during the past six months.*

(a) Less than one hour	6
(b) 1 to 2 hours	9
(c) 2 to 4 hours	7
(d) More than 4 hours	6

Table 4 *In any interval checked in No. 3 above, estimate the proportion of that time devoted to conversation about correction in any phase.*

(a) None	2
(b) Less than 5%	2
(c) 5 to 10%	2
(d) 10 to 20%	7
(e) More than 20%	15

typical week. This is not, then, momentary socializing. It occurs frequently, is widespread throughout the sample, and lasts a long while. When it happens, the conversation almost invariably turns to some phase of correction, often for as long as 20 percent or more of any interval given over to informal social contact.

What is the ideational and, by inference, the behavioral consequence of these off-duty contacts with fellow workers? Do they have any appreciable effect of which the correctional worker is conscious? It was expected that there would be an overwhelming proportion of affirmative replies. The replies, however, as shown in Table 5, fall short of expectations. It may be that the fourth choice, indicating greater influence from reports and departmental directives, was not well worded and frightened too many into checking that particular response for fear of what the respondent's supervisor might say if he knew. However, it is still impressive that about nine of the thirty-one said they have been greatly influenced by these off-duty contacts with fellow correctional workers and that seven others felt that the influence upon them from this source has been at least mild.

Table 5 *With which of the following statements do you agree most closely? (Check one only.)*

My ideas about correction	
(a) have been greatly influenced by my off-duty contacts with cw's.	9
(b) have been mildly influenced by my off-duty contacts with cw's.	7
(c) have been influenced more by clients than by off-duty contacts with cw's.	5
(d) have been influenced more by such sources as scientific reports and departmental directives than either by clients or by off-duty contacts with cw's.	10

Table 6   *Where, if at all, have you felt the influence of off-duty contacts with cw's?(Check all applicable.)*

(a) No appreciable influence	5
(b) My morale, job-satisfaction, sense of belonging.	19
(c) Exchange of news about department or agency.	17
(d) Clarify difficult or conflicting policy issues.	11
(e) Clarify procedures	7
(f) Interpretation of statutes.	3
(g) Behavioral science or research findings.	12
(h) Other. [a]	9

[a]Discuss ethics and principles, home improvements projects, feed-back, philosophy of correction, feelings of other cw's, difficult cases, decision-making.

When the respondents were given an opportunity to specify the effect of off-duty contact with other correctional workers (Table 6), it became quite clear that these informal social experiences were highly valued. The modal correctional worker said this:

Off-the-job contacts with fellow workers make me feel I belong to something important. I learn what is going on in the department in this way. I also learn some things I could not learn in any other way about human behavior and about current research findings. The contacts help clear up my confusion about policy matters or at least let me express my confusions to someone else. They help me in other ways too, but chiefly in the area I have mentioned.

Five members of the sample report that off-duty contacts have had no appreciable influence upon them. It will be recalled that five respondents reported that they never ate lunch with their job mates. Since anonymity was assured throughout, there is no way to tell whether these are the same five.

CONCLUSIONS

While there are many indications that the style of on- and off-duty life of these correctional workers is the same as that of correctional colleagues in other metropolitan regions of California, one cannot be certain. Obviously, it is doubtful whether the kinds of interaction and socialization which have been reported here exist in the sparsely settled "cow counties," about whose correctional problems and efforts to meet them almost nothing is known.[2]

[2]William T. Adams, *A Regional Program to Combat Juvenile Delinquency* (Boulder, Colo.: Western Interstate Commission for Higher Education, December 1962) pp. 20 ff.

Further, it is doubtful whether the comity which exists among correctional workers of all ranks in California can be found in those states where rivalries, dissension, and mistrust are the order of the day.

Thus only limited conclusions are warranted. However, there seems to be enough information to relate this study to inquiries into other job areas, and to guide future students exploring this field.

Relation to Other Studies

1. This report confirms the view that the occupational group has become highly important in mid-twentieth century life. In this group the adult worker experiences his most significant social contacts, acquires and reinforces his sense of personal worth, derives assurance of secure status and dignity, and experiences other rewards of many kinds. Although the data of this report are too sparse to illustrate these views with finality, the evidence is more than suggestive. Associations on the job persist off the job. The life routine, even the life prospect, of the correctional worker is controlled by affiliation with the occupational group, even when he is not working.

2. Management studies by specialists in administration, studies of factory systems by sociologists and psychologists, and studies of job satisfactions by all three of these disciplines testify to the ways in which the worker fights against namelessness and struggles for identity and integrity. Our study suggests that the correctional worker is akin to workers in all other fields in this regard. Therefore many of the lessons which have been so painfully learned in these fields have evident application to the correctional services.[3]

Suggestions for Future Study

The study provides the basis for firmer guesses about correctional workers' relationships to one another both on and off the job and, thus, about correctional workers as a group.

1. For example, after-hours associations with fellow employees may both reflect and reinforce the practitioner's concept of himself as a correctional worker. It seems reasonable to infer that associational patterns which are set up on the job by correctional workers and continued off the job are maintained because of important elements of self-involvement and self-growth and that those who drop out of the field may well do so because of failure to develop this concept of self.

There is the related issue of the correctional worker who sees himself as such, but as being not of the same kind as his fellow-workers. He may, in fact, regard them with disdain, refuse to associate with them informally, and derive

[3] For example, Alvin Gouldner, "Organizational Analysis," *Sociology Today,* Robert K. Merton, Leonard Broom, and Leonard S. Cottrell, Jr., eds. (New York: Basic Books, 1959), ch. 18.

his role-models from outside his agency or department—for example, from the police or from the confraternity of graduate social workers. This type of worker was not examined in the present study but he is not unusual.

2. Interaction proceeds by various means, but primarily through language. The technical language of correction enters into the way and the circumstances in which correctional workers interact with each other. It is highly specialized and largely unintelligible to outsiders; its use promotes unity among those who understand it. What, for example, is a 602, a 1050 E, or two priors plead and proven? The exceedingly complex technical language of correction includes rich mixtures from the law, medicine, and the social and behavioral sciences. It includes terms from prison argot and jive, underworld, and street-corner slang. A word count of the language employed by correctional workers in communicating with one another even off the job would show a heavy reliance upon this specialized vocabulary. It serves the same functions as do all secret languages—fencing out the stranger, speeding the transmission of ideas, and, above all, strengthening one's bond to the system of which it is a part, confirming one's life purpose, and, in the friendly responses which it evokes, reinforcing one's sense of self-worth.

Correctional humor is as technical as correctional jargon and must be savored in context. Like all humor it serves to relieve tension, express aggression, convey ideas, and unify. The following, culled from *The Progress Report*, once released quarterly by the U.S. Bureau of Prisons, are typical examples of humor in correctional circles. They serve all the functions mentioned and illustrate indirectly some of the folk beliefs which can be found within correction as a distinct system.

He had mumps in childhood, gonorrhea in 1954, treated with penicillin and struck by lightning in 1955.

Medical History—Subject gave a history of swollen joints, frequent headaches, chest pains, pounding heart, liver and gall bladder trouble, jaundice, kidney stone, and lameness. Later on the same page appears the diagnosis: Essentially a healthy white male with defective vision.

Subject would be willing to learn a trade but he does not want to be a banker or a moonshiner, because he could never accumulate enough money to lend or whisky to sell.

3. While not evident in the data here presented, the mildest familiarity with the social life of correctional workers shows that gossip about the development of correction in any one area is transmitted throughout correctional ranks of a similar level. Within California, all probation chiefs and their first line assistants are known throughout the state. If one resigns, retires, or dies, the news travels fast; within hours the names of the new applicants for the vacancy are known for a thousand miles—and yet incredibly few letters on the subject will have been exchanged. The situation is similar for correctional counselors and parole agents who will know exactly who holds which rank on which civil service list.

4. The heavy references in Tables 5 and 6 to research in the behavioral sciences and related matters give rise to another guess; i.e., that correctional workers are interested in two opposite aspects of their social relations—change and stability. Item *d* in Table 5 and item *g* in Table 6 suggest that correctional workers are intimately concerned with what is new and with what works better, but they may not necessarily want to adopt the innovation. They may search for information about an innovation in order to sabotage it if its adoption will occasion major changes in the system of social relations to which they have become accustomed. Thus correctional workers may display an interest in the new and the novel and at the same time be very selective about any innovation which threatens the stability of their social system. For these reasons, the recorded replies to items 5*d* and 6*g* must be read with caution.

CONTRIBUTIONS TO CORRECTIONAL THEORY

We do not yet have a well-articulated theory of correction, notwithstanding the monumental underpinnings which have been provided by certain contemporary scholars and outstanding correctional administrators.[4] This pilot study provides material which must eventually be considered in constructing an overall theory of correction if it is possible to formulate such a theory.

First, it is quite clear from the data that the kinds of contacts examined in the study do tie correctional workers into a social system. All of the components for a social system are present: association, a specialized language, channels for communication and interaction, recognized goals, shared values, accepted methods, a network of statuses and roles, and adjustment to change. Beyond the data reported further components may be found: tests for the admission of new members and provision for their orientation and discipline, ways of cleansing the group of dangerous ideas, and appointed and functional leadership.

Whether these factors establish correctional work as a distinct profession is open to argument, but the case for claiming that a social system of correctional workers exists in the setting studied is remarkably complete. It is as much a product of the correctional experience as are social systems among offenders. Like these systems, it serves to strengthen self-concepts and to provide the rationalizations needed for continued affiliation with this system and commitment, in this case, to the goals of correction.

Second, the effects of that social system may go beyond the worker and

---

[4]Paul W. Tappan, *Crime, Justice, and Correction* (New York: McGraw-Hill, 1960), ch. 10; Edwin H. Sutherland and Donald R. Cressey, *Principles of Criminology* (Philadelphia: Lippincott, 6th ed., 1960), ch. 15 and 16; Clarence Schrag, "Some Foundations for a Theory of Corrections," *The Prison*, Donald R. Cressey, ed. (New York: Holt, Rinehart, and Winston, 1961), ch. 8. See also *Manual of Correctional Standards* (New York: American Correctional Association, 1959), ch. 1.

may affect the correctional process itself, over which persons involved in the system have a kind of hidden monopoly. They are in almost complete charge of what happens to all offenders at any stage of the correctional process after arrest and trial. This point is offered as an evident consequence of this kind of social system, which is both a product and an instrument of social control.

Third, the social system of correctional workers may have an effect on recidivism. This effect could not be documented from the present study, but the suggestion of its existence is very strong from analogous social systems. For example, to a teacher the most important judgment is the judgment of other teachers, not pupils; to a nurse or to a doctor the most important judgment is that of other nurses or other doctors, not patients; and the reputation of a priest is that which he has among the hierarchy of priests, not among penitents.

The same ways of establishing and enhancing one's reputation are probably operative among correctional workers. A correctional worker's reputation stems primarily from the way he relates to other correctional workers and only secondarily from the way he relates to offenders. Consequently, there are severe limitations on what correctional workers can do to influence the lives of offenders—limitations which are built into the system and which transcend the personal desires or individual capabilities of a member of that system. He must, in many important senses of the term, be a good "organization man." Offenders know this, and the more discerning of them comment upon it quite cynically. They realize that if their affairs were to receive primary attention from the members of this system, it would occasion vast strain in the correctional worker's maintenance of his role among his colleagues and cause sweeping changes in relationships among correctional workers. Since such change is manifestly improbable, the effect is to relegate to the offender a lesser amount of the intellectual, emotional, and social energies of the correctional worker than is usually conceded. The offender's criminality receives less attention than is popularly believed or than official ideologies declare.[5]

Correctional theorists and personnel should accept the possibility that much that happens in correction occurs primarily to meet the needs of correctional workers and only secondarily to meet the needs of offenders. Relations with clients are formal, imposed, and not free. Relations with fellow-workers are both formal and informal, largely unimposed, and wholly free. In all likelihood, the interests of clients will be safeguarded and most effectively served if the sense of worth among correctional workers is enhanced. This study suggests that the social system of correctional workers provides a powerful means to that end.

---

[5] Experienced correctional workers are quite vocal on this point: "We never stand up to the judge. . . . If an outsider comes around here to ask about a case our first reaction is to close ranks against him—not to ask him what he wants and how we can help him. . . . Actually, we're scared. We've become so secure inside our system, we are really insecure out of it. . . . We're interested in the offender, yes. But only as an afterthought. What really matters is: how do I get along with the rest of the staff. We've lost the spark."

The practical application of this general idea, if it is valid, would be to add criteria to those which already exist for recruitment and training and to foster constant staff and management concern with job satisfaction and with projects to make the correctional worker happier, not necessarily more efficient. He will be more efficient if he is happier and if he likes himself and his co-workers more. Correctional administrators should be prepared to see the worker reach equality with the client as a main center of interest if further inquiry into the associational patterns in correction supports such a change.

Prison is a collective experience, influencing the thought and behavior of prisoners; correctional work also is a collective experience, influencing, even determining, the thought and behavior of its practitioners. The achievement of correctional goals awaits a careful analysis of how correctional workers interrelate.[6]

[6]While this suggestion is not wholly new, such articulations of it as have appeared to date stem chiefly from institutional experience. The implication of the present study is that the social system of correctional workers is not confined to institutional staff but includes probation and parole personnel as well as other types of correctional specialists. The theoretical possibility of subsystems in this general locus is not examined at the present time.

59

Code of Ethics

FEDERAL PROBATION OFFICERS' ASSOCIATION

Code Of Ethics
Federal Probation Officers' Association

As a Federal Probation Officer, I am dedicated to rendering professional service to the courts, the parole authorities, and the community at large in effecting the social adjustment of the offender.

I will conduct my personal life with decorum, will neither accept nor grant favors in connection with my office, and will put loyalty to moral principles above personal consideration.

I will uphold the law with dignity and with complete awareness of the prestige and stature of the judicial system of which I am a part. I will be ever cognizant of my responsibility to the community which I serve.

I will strive to be objective in the performance of my duties; respect the inalienable rights of all persons; appreciate the inherent worth of the individual, and hold inviolate those confidences which can be reposed in me.

I will cooperate with my fellow workers and related agencies and will continually attempt to improve my professional standards through the seeking of knowledge and understanding.

I recognize my office as a symbol of public faith and I accept it as a public trust to be held as long as I am true to the ethics of the Federal Probation Service. I will constantly strive to achieve these objectives and ideals, dedicating myself to my chosen profession.

September 12, 1960

SOURCE. Federal Probation, Officers' Association, September 12, 1960.